A Sourcebook for Genealogical Research

A Sourcebook for Genealogical Research

Resources Alphabetically by Type and Location

FOSTER STOCKWELL

McFarland & Company, Inc., Publishers

Jefferson, North Carolina, and London

LIBRARY OF CONGRESS CATALOGUING-IN-PUBLICATION DATA

Stockwell, Foster.
A sourcebook for genealogical research : resources alphabetically
by type and location / Foster Stockwell.
p.   cm.
Includes bibliographical references and index.

ISBN 0-7864-1782-X (softcover : 50# alkaline paper) ∞

1. Genealogy.   2. United States—Genealogy—Handbooks,
manuals, etc.   I. Title.
CS9.S76   2004
929'.1'072073—dc22   2004005759

British Library cataloguing data are available

Cover photography: ©2004 Photospin; ©1996 EclectiCollections

Manufactured in the United States of America

McFarland & Company, Inc., Publishers
Box 611, Jefferson, North Carolina 28640
www.mcfarlandpub.com

To my son, Norman,
who many years ago sparked my interest in genealogy,
and to his wife, Melanie,
and daughter, Marian

TABLE OF CONTENTS

PREFACE

"It is indeed a desirable thing to be well descended, but the glory belongs to our ancestors." — Plutarch, *Of the Training of Children*

"I don't know who my grandfather was; I am much more concerned to know what his grandson will be." — Abraham Lincoln

Over the years numerous books have been published about resources for genealogists, but finding the needed information in some of them requires a laborious search through lengthy chapters that have been arranged under relatively obscure headings. I have designed this book in an accessible and useable form, with its 271 easy-to-find headings listed alphabetically and cross-referenced so that all researchers can quickly find the information they might be seeking. It is a resource for both professional and amateur genealogists who may be looking for data regarding materials that are available to further their investigations in family history.

Each of the 50 states received its own entry, as is the case for the provinces of Canada. Other countries are listed under their appropriate headings, and there are separate entries on all aspects of genealogical research and family history compilation. The book lists at the end more than 700 addresses from all over the world for the locations listed in the text so that the researcher may contact any one of these to obtain specific information about particular births, marriages, deaths, or other events in order to complete a family tree. Not included are the addresses for the thousands of county record offices, although the locations of all the county seats are listed. To obtain information from these county seats one only need address a request to the county secretaries. However, if one requires an exact county seat address, it can be found in Elizabeth Bentley's *County Courthouse Book*, listed as one of the sources under the heading "Books."

Various titles listed throughout this volume will provide additional information to aid the researcher. Only a few Websites have been listed because their URLs so often change. However, there is information on how to find them on the World Wide Web and how to locate any other materials of interest that the Internet may contain.

Genealogy is the third most popular hobby in America, after stamp and coin collecting. I hope that, in having and using the information this sourcebook contains, both the hobbyist and the experienced researcher will be rewarded with many hours of enjoyment and worthwhile data about their family histories. And as every experienced researcher knows, the location and correct identification of vital records is the key to all genealogical research. Those new to genealogy might best turn to the entry "Genealogy for Beginners."

THE SOURCEBOOK

A

Abbreviations *see* **Word Abbreviations**

Adoption Records, which are almost impossible to obtain, are of particular interest to the genealogists who are compiling medical records for the purpose of following the history of hereditary diseases. For other genealogists, all that needs to be known is whether or not a child was adopted. The birth mother's actual name is usually unimportant in the creation of the family history. Estimates indicate that there are presently about two million adopted children under the age of 18 in the United States, half of them having been adopted by relatives.

Most state laws prohibit adoption agencies from revealing the identity of the natural parents to the adoptive parents. The records in each state are sealed immediately after the adoption is finalized and they can only be inspected with the court's approval. However, recent laws have acknowledged that adopted children may wish to discover their natural parents, and they are thus permitted the information when they reach adulthood.

State laws vary considerably in how this information can be obtained, which parties are allowed access to the information, and the type(s) of information that will be released. Most states allow an adoptee to petition the court to receive identifying information. Only Alabama, Alaska, Kansas, Oregon, and Tennessee routinely provide an uncertified copy of the original unaltered birth certificate to adopted adults. Some states allow restricted access to birth certificates (subject to the birth parent's veto, or restricted to adoptions completed before or after a specified date).

Usually the fact that a child was adopted is a matter of common knowledge within the family, and sometimes family records will list this fact. The researcher compiling a family history needs only indicate that fact on the family chart, followed, when possible, with the specific date of the adoption. As for medical information, it is often possible to obtain permission to access non-identifying adoption data from the records, such as descriptive social and medical information, without any details that could be used to identify positively the names of the parties to the adoption. A few states restrict non-identifying information to the adoptee's medical history.

Although the records are scant, note should be made of the fact that in Colonial America homeless and neglected children probably arrived alone from England and elsewhere as indentured servants to serve in that capacity until they reached adulthood. Orphan asylums did not open in the United States until the early 1800s. They were run by religious groups such as the Catholics and Jews. Illegitimate children were often placed in such orphanages. Orphans were also not always children without parents. Sometimes they were children with one parent who could not support them. *See also* **Orphan Train System**.

Adventist Records in the field of genealogy are relatively sparse, perhaps because the focus of these several Protestant denominations is directed toward the visible, personal Second Coming of Christ rather than on the past activities of family members. The history of this church goes back to an American Baptist preacher, William Miller, who proclaimed that the Second Coming would occur on a specific date in 1844. The failure of this prediction resulted in many members leaving the movement that Miller initiated. A second predicted date also came to nothing and, as a result, the movement split into several groups, the largest of which is the Seventh-day Adventists, who have about two million members throughout the world. Their members accept the Bible as the sole religious authority and hold worship services only on Saturdays. Believing that the body is the temple of the Holy Spirit, Seventh-day Adventists put great stress on health and avoid eating meat and using opiates and stimulants. They maintain more than 360 hospitals and clinics around the world. Smaller Adventist denominations include the Advent Christian Church, and the Church of God of the Abrahamic Faith.

The Seventh-day Adventists have their headquarters and Andrews University at Berrien Springs, Michigan. The university library maintains an obituary index that includes nearly 200,000 citations to obituaries of people who have appeared in a wide range of Seventh-day Adventist periodicals going back to 1849. The library is also the home for the Adventist Heritage Center, which maintains the leading documentary collection for the study of the denomination, its predecessors and related groups, from the Millerite movement of the mid-nineteenth century to the present. Those wishing to conduct genealogical research on Adventist records are advised to contact the individual Adventist churches as well as the Adventist Heritage Center. The library will provide items from the obituary index; these items can also be downloaded from the library's Website.

Africa *see* **African Genealogy**

African-American Records can be particularly difficult to find because of their relative absence, especially before 1865. However, there has been increasing interest in this subject since the publication of Arthur Haley's book, *Roots*. Haley stumbled upon the names of his maternal great-grandparents while going through some post–Civil War records at the National Archives in Washington, D.C. This started him on an extensive search for his ancestral roots. His researches in the libraries of many countries took him 12 years. Finally, traveling into the heart of Africa, he found the village of Juffure, the home of Kunta Kinte, the person he decided must be his first traceable ancestor. Although most professional genealogists are skeptical of Haley's research methods and conclusions, the book is a vivid history of the slave and free black heritage of many Americans, and it has been an inspiration to a whole generation of budding genealogists.

Any search for African-American family histories probably best begins with the 1880 United States Census database. More than 6.5 million African-American names are recorded there. This was the first census to include former slaves as well as free blacks, and the second to record African-Americans as individuals rather than property. In earlier U.S. census listings it is more than likely to find just the person's first name or the word "slave" on the rolls for any of the African-Americans that are listed, particularly in the rolls of the Southern states.

The U. S. government did compile two population records, for 1850 and 1860, consisting only of slaves and their owners. These are known as the slave schedules and can be viewed on microfilm at the various National Archives and Records Administration sites. But these slave schedules do not contain much genealogical information. The slave owners or their agents are listed by their full names, but the slaves are listed only by sex and age. Nevertheless, it may be possible to derive information about some individuals from these lists through careful analysis and comparison with the population censuses of 1870 and 1880. The slave schedules were compiled for Alabama, Arkansas (1860 only), Delaware, District of Columbia, Florida, Georgia, Kentucky, Louisiana, Maryland, Mississippi, Missouri, North Carolina, New Jersey, South Carolina, Tennessee, Texas, Virginia, and the Indian lands west of Arkansas (1860 only). These slave schedules are a critical source of information on African-American families, and can also be used to document relationships among white families. For example, if an executor was responsible for slaves as part of an estate, the testator or owners may be named, thus helping a researcher establish relationships among the white slave owners.

There are also some registers of free blacks that were required by various states at times before the Civil War. Surviving records of these can be found in some county courthouses, state libraries, and state archives. The Maryland Archives, for example, has the Prince George's County Certificates of Freedom, 1806–1852. Other such registers can be found in the Indiana State Library, Georgia Archives, Georgia Historical Society, North Carolina Archives, South Carolina Archives, University of Missouri Library at Columbia, Virginia State Library, Virginia Historical Society, and the National Archives in Washington, D.C. The information in these registers varies, but may include manumission records, affidavits that testified to some person's free status, registrations of free persons as they moved into a new county, and evidence of a free status from wills and deeds. Some of these records have been published in book form and can be found in various genealogical libraries. Various states took state and school censuses between the years that the federal population ones were compiled, and these state censuses sometimes contain information that can locate a household in a particular place at a given time. State archives and historical societies probably have copies of these state archives, and local school offices should have copies of the school censuses. (*See also* **African Genealogy** for information about the African-Americans who emigrated to Liberia in the early 1800s.)

A careful study of the 1830 U.S. population census records by the historian Carter G. Woodson has shown that at the time there were 3,815 free blacks in 20 states, two territories, and the District of Columbia. These were most numerous in Louisiana (966), Virginia (951), Maryland (654), and South Carolina (484). Some of the free blacks owned slaves themselves, and at least two of these black slave owners were listed with white wives. It is also known that in later years many Native Americans owned slaves and fathered children with African slave women.

In addition there were smaller numbers of "Free People of Color" who lived within some of the Indian nations and married persons from those same nations. More than 20,000 slaves and former slaves were adopted into these nations before the end of the 19th century. As a result, many African-Americans have both African and Indian ancestry. Within the Cherokee, Choctaw, Chickasaw, Creek, and Seminole Nations, genealogists can find thousands of records documenting the history of these blacks living among the Indian population.

The Treaty of 1866 abolished slavery in the Indian Territory and resulted in the adoption of the former slaves into four of the five nations. Several census counts were taken between 1866 and 1907, specifically of the African-American people in the Indian Territory. These census records are available at the National Archives. Although some of the Indian nations have now chosen to ignore this critical treaty and to deny that they once adopted these blacks into their tribes, the facts cannot be disputed and stand as an official connection between the Oklahoma Indian nations and their African brothers.

There are some Southern church records that contain information about the antebellum blacks. For example, the records of the Presbyterian Church at Bolivar, Tennessee, show membership and baptism for such persons. One entry has a "servant," E. G. Coleman, who was baptized there in 1858 and the next year her four sons, named Moses, Lewis, Joe, and Thomas, were also baptized. Courthouse records of deeds and bills of sale also identify slaves, sometimes providing information that is helpful in further searching. The same is true of county will books and probate records that contain slave information. And marriage records, particularly in the South immediately following the Civil War, reveal the names of the freed men and women who were wed. The brides and grooms in these cases are often identified as being black by abbreviations such as *col'd* or *col* (colored) and *fmc* or *fwc* (free man of color and free woman of color).

During the Civil War, African–Americans served in significant numbers in the

United States armed forces. In 1863 the 29th U.S. Colored Infantry, the regiment with the largest number of African–Americans, began enrolling men at Quincy, Illinois. Its most noteworthy action was at the Battle of the Crater near Petersburg, Virginia, on July 30, 1864. This unit was mustered out of service on November 6, 1865, at Brownsville, Texas. The muster records for the 29th U.S. Colored Infantry are included among the records at the various National Archives locations of all those who participated on the side of the North during the Civil War. Each soldier's entry includes his name, rank, regiment number, company letter, age, residence, date, and place where mustered in; name of the mustering officer; the date and place of mustering out; remarks concerning transfers, promotions, and special duty; and indication of injury or death. In the Spanish–American War (1898–1899), the 8th Infantry was composed entirely of African–Americans. It served in Cuba and was mustered out of service on April 3, 1899, at Chicago. Relevant records can be found in the various National Archives centers.

Another source of information comes in the many graveyards that were erected specifically for African-Americans. Before the Civil War it was often the practice throughout the South, as evidenced by countless cemeteries, for whites and blacks to be buried in the same grounds. Harsh as slavery was, some white masters apparently felt a paternal instinct toward their slaves, even in death. After the Civil War it became the practice to establish separate cemeteries, segregated by race. One such cemetery, at Alexandria, Virginia, was known as the Freedman's Cemetery. It occupied land formally owned by a pro-Confederate man that had been taken away from him by the federal troops who occupied Alexandria during the Civil War. Many of the former slaves of Alexandria were buried there. And, at first, black Union soldiers who died in Alexandria were also buried at Freedmen's Cemetery. But the African-American troops in the town's hospitals finally demanded that they be accorded the honor of interment in a "Soldiers' Cemetery." About 75 deceased black veterans were

then removed from the Freedmen's Cemetery, in January 1865, and taken to the Alexandria National Cemetery.

At the war's end, responsibility for the Freedmen's Cemetery was transferred to the new Bureau of Refugees, Freedmen, and Abandoned Lands. But Congress curtailed nearly all the Freedmen Bureau's functions at the end of 1868 and the cemetery, with its more than 1,700 burials, was closed. The land's former owner, attorney Francis Smith, then reclaimed it. For eight decades, it remained largely undisturbed, but the wood grave markers quickly rotted away. In 1917, the Smith family conveyed the property to the Catholic Diocese of Richmond, which maintained its own cemetery across the street. The land was rezoned in 1946 and a gas station, and then an office building, were erected on the site. In spite of these changes, and the construction of Interstate Route 95 to the South, hundreds of unidentified graves probably remain there.

Lists of these cemeteries for African-Americans can be found in some genealogical libraries and on Websites. Where grave markers are still standing and can be read, the researcher can usually find birth and death dates.

Newspapers are often good sources for marriage and death information, and in the case of African-American history the white newspapers published before the Civil War contain numerous notices of slave sales and runaway slaves. For the latter the owner often included information about the slave's appearance, age, and talents. Some African-American newspapers did exist before the Civil War, but most of them were established afterwards. Charles Blockson's book *Black American Records and Research*, (1983), and Walter Daniel's *Black Journals of the United States* (1982), both contain extensive lists of the many African-American newspapers. The researcher would also be wise to consult the *Negro Year Book* that was published annually from 1912 to 1952 by the Tuskegee Institute. All these works can be found in the larger genealogical libraries.

The Works Progress Administration (WPA) conducted many interviews in the

1930s with former slaves in order to record their individual histories. Some of these interviewees may represent family lines that a researcher might be studying, but most will not. Yet the information they contain is a valuable heritage of the period of slavery in the United States and is therefore well worth reading. The collection, known as the *Slave Narratives*, were published in 1941 and reprinted in 1972. If a particular library does not have copies, they probably can be obtained through interlibrary loan.

Finally, the Library of Congress in Washington, D.C., has published a resource guide for the study of African-American history and culture, titled *African-American Mosaic*. This guide covers the library's collections of nearly 500 years of black experience in the Western hemisphere, and surveys the variety of African-Americans' books, periodicals, prints, photographs, music, film, and recorded sound. Along with this, the library in 1998 mounted a major exhibition and cultural program that examined the impact of African-American history and tradition on the formation of the American national identity. The exhibition was divided into four areas— Colonization, Abolition, Migration, and the WPA — and the exhibition had the same title as the library's resource guide, that is, *The African-American Mosaic. See also* **Census, United States; Freedmen's Bureau.**

FOR FURTHER INFORMATION SEE:
• Byers, Paula K., ed. *African American Genealogical Sourcebook*. Detroit: Gale Research, 1995.
• Streets, David H. *Slave Genealogy: A Research Guide with Case Studies*. Bowie, MD: Heritage Books, 1986.

African Genealogy, or the pursuit thereof, is mostly limited to persons in the Republic of South Africa, although there are royal genealogies of various ruling dynasties in countries such as Botswana, Burundi, Ethiopia, and Egypt, many of which are based solely on oral tradition. The European families who lived in the various colonies of Africa before these became independent nations may preserve records of their African connections, but these persons are no longer doing their

research on the African continent. Most of the newly-established nations have yet to conduct official censuses or to set up vital records departments. There have been censuses in Egypt, the first of which was conducted in 1897 under British suzerainty. Algeria did not conduct its first census until 1966 after achieving independence from France.

There are extensive genealogical records related to the colonization of the Republic of Liberia, which became a free nation in 1847 after American blacks (most of them former slaves) settled there throughout the 1800s. Promotion of this "back to Africa" movement was conducted by the American Colonization Society in the United States. It was, however, vigorously opposed by the abolitionists. A list of the immigrants who arrived in Monrovia, the city later to become the capital of Liberia, in March 1826, April 1835, and September 1843 was compiled by the Colonization Society. It provides a record of the names of those who emigrated, their ages, whether they were born free or slave, the state in the United States from which they departed, and where they located after their arrival in Liberia. Some of these entries also list the extent of education of the individuals and the date and cause of death for those who did not survive before these records were compiled. Furthermore, there were censuses conducted in 1843 in the towns of Caldwell, New Georgia, and Monrovia. The emigration list and census records were printed in the *Congressional Record* of the second session of the 28th U.S. Congress, and can be obtained from the National Archives and Records Administration in Washington, D.C. They can also be found on some Websites. These records today are probably of more interest to American genealogists than to citizens of Liberia because they form a vital part of African-American history.

Tracing South African roots for the whites living in what is now the Republic of South Africa is relatively easy, considering that the first European settlement of the Cape Colony took place in 1652 and records exist from that time to the present. (South Africa consisted initially only of the Cape Colony.)

These earliest records can be found in what later became known as the Cape Province. The other provinces in South Africa were, until recently, Natal, Orange Free State, and Transvaal, and most records from these provinces have been kept within the provinces. Following the 1994 elections, these four provinces were expanded to include nine new ones, and the relevant records are now in the process of being moved to archives within each of these new provinces. Due to the long history of apartheid and other restrictions, genealogical information for the non-white citizens of the Union of South Africa is almost nonexistent.

Initially the settlement at the Cape Colony was small and centered on the present city of Cape Town. With the pressure of farming and the desire of many of the earliest employees of the Dutch East India Company to remain at that location, the settlement gradually expanded and grew ever outwards. Information on all the earliest settler families and their descendants was compiled and published before 1895 in three volumes as the *Geslacht Register der oude Kaapsche Familiën* (Genealogical Register of the old Cape Families). This publication provided a general survey of the entire white population of the Cape Colony from its very beginning until the end of The Netherlands administration in 1806, and in some instances even much later. Those covered in its pages are primarily of Afrikaner origin, in other words persons of Dutch, German, French, and Scandinavian descent to the exclusion of English families. Over the intervening years this work was corrected and added to by several investigators and then republished in two volumes as the *Genealogies of old South African Families*, edited by Dr. C. Pama.

A new body of work covering South African genealogy is now being prepared, initially under the auspices of the Human Sciences Research Council and now under the direction of the Genealogical Institute of South Africa (GISA) at Stellenbosch, near Cape Town. It is intended to become a seven volume set; the first four volumes, which have already been completed, cover the families with surnames running from A to K.

These records now include English surnames, though not all of them, along with the Afrikaner ones.

Vital statistics registration for all white families in South Africa started in 1900. Such records are kept at the Department of the Interior in Pretoria. There are also archive repositories in Cape Town, Bloemfontein, Durban, and Pietermaritzburg that have various genealogical documents, some of them on microfilm. In addition, the National Archives at Pretoria houses the archives of central government departments and the Transvaal Archives Repository. Researchers can get access to marriage and death records older than 20 years from the relevant Archives Repositories, although the issuing of certificates can only be done by the Department of Home Affairs and the records cannot be photocopied. The National Archives has a well stocked library with many books of a genealogical and historical nature.

Records for the Dutch Reformed Church in South Africa extend almost from the founding of the settlement at the Cape. These records are centralized in a few church archives, which makes their access much easier. The baptismal records generally give the full name and surname of a child, the birthdate and baptism date, the names of both parents, and the names of witnesses. Marriage records may contain the occupations of both parties as well as their names and that of their parents. However, the death records vary greatly according to the minister of the church involved.

Agriculture Schedules *see* **Census, United States**

Ahnentafel *see* **Pedigree Charts**

Air Force Records *see* **Military Records**

Alabama Records mostly contain information about the European immigrants and their descendants who began to settle in this area after 1798. A few of them also relate to slaves brought to the New World from Africa and Native American Indians of the Cherokee, Creek, Choctaw, and Chickasaw tribes who had lived there for many centuries before any Europeans came. At first, the land was designated to be a part of the Mississippi Territory following the Indian cessions in north Alabama in 1798. But after the end of the Creek War in 1814, and a large increase in the number of immigrants, the area was redesignated as the Alabama Territory in 1817. It became the 22nd state on December 14, 1819. The earliest counties—Baldwin, Clarke, Madison, Mobile, Monroe, Montgomery, and Washington—were all formed from the Mississippi Territory.

The area immediately around Mobile was settled somewhat earlier. Founded in 1702 by French explorers, Mobile served as the capital of French Louisiana for 16 years. In 1763, Mobile and the Gulf region of Florida became a British colony. Control of this colony then changed hands several times between 1780 and the War of 1812.

The first U.S. census to enumerate residents of the state of Alabama was completed in 1830. When researching Alabama census data, one needs to be aware of the various ways in which the county boundaries have changed and how even the names of some counties have been replaced. For example, in 1832, 10 counties were formed from land ceded by the Creek Indians. These counties were Benton, Barbour, Chambers, Coosa, Macon, Randolph, Russell, Sumter, Talledega, and Tallapoosa. Then in 1858, Benton County was renamed Calhoun County; and in 1866, Cleburne County was created from portions of Calhoun, Randolph, and Talladega Counties. One can find some of the same persons in the 1850 census living in Benton County, in the 1860 census living in Calhoun County, and in the 1870 census living in Cleburne County, none of whom had moved from their first address.

There are also early census records for the French settlements near Mobile, as well as incomplete territorial and state census records for 1816, 1818, 1820, 1831, 1850, 1855, and 1866. These can be found in many Alabama libraries and also at the Alabama State Archives in Montgomery. The state census for 1820 covers the counties of Baldwin, Conecuh, Dallas, Franklin, Limestone, St. Clair, Shelby, and Wilcox. The one for 1850 covers all counties; but the one for 1855 covers only the counties of Autauga, Baldwin, Blount, Coffee, Franklin, Henry, Lowndes, Macon, Mobile, Pickens, Tallapoosa, and Tuscaloosa. The 1866 state census includes all the counties. There was also a special census taken of Confederate veterans in 1907 that has been indexed and published. It is found in the Alabama State Archives and in many Alabama libraries.

Alabama law did not require the recording of birth or death certificates until 1908. The statewide recording of marriages began in 1936, and divorce records date from 1950. Prior to that, such events were recorded only at the county level. Not all of the county records are complete. Each county had vital events that were never recorded, as well as records that have become lost or damaged. Many courthouses have also burned and their records were thus lost.

Most of the birth records list sex, race, and place and date of birth for the individuals, but without any children's names. The names of parents and the physician or midwife attending the event, however, are sometimes listed. Although the Alabama Board of Health can supply birth certificates from 1908 on, birth records less than 125 years old will not be issued to anyone except members of the immediate family or without permission of the next of kin. There will, of course, be a small fee for this service. The same is true for death records less than 25 years old. Most of these death records list the name of the individual, place of death, age at death, and attending physician. Some include the place of burial and cause of death.

In the case of marriage records, most counties listed these from the time that the county was established, while very few births or deaths were noted for the same period. The marriage records include the names of the husband and wife, the presiding official at the marriage, and the signatures of the two people who posted the marriage bond. Divorce records list only the date of divorce and the names of the parties and officials involved. They were kept with the general or circuit court records.

Some counties separated all their vital records into different books by race. The designations placed on the binders to these volumes are "White," "Black," and "Colored." In 1996 a statewide computer system was established that provides access to all Alabama vital records. Applicants can walk into any county health department in the state and purchase a copy of any Alabama vital record that can be released to the public, regardless of where the event occurred. These county offices, however, are not prepared to handle requests by mail, so all calls and mail should be directed to the state office.

The Alabama Department of Archives and History in Montgomery has indexes to all the state records and many of the county records that have been microfilmed, but original certificates must be obtained from the Alabama Center for Health Statistics, also located in Montgomery. A list of available vital records for Alabama, published in 1942 by the Work Projects Administration, can be found in many of the larger libraries. This *Guide to Public Vital Statistics Records in Alabama* comes in two volumes: *Preliminary Edition* and *Church Archives*. Further information can be found in the archives of the Birmingham and Mobile public libraries and at the Samford University Library in Birmingham.

Researchers seeking information from county records can locate them at the following County seats: (Autauga County) Prattville, (Baldwin County) Bay Minette, (Barbour County) Clayton, (Bibb County) Centreville, (Blount County) Oneonta, (Bullock County) Union Springs, (Butler County) Greenville, (Calhoun County) Anniston, (Chambers County) Lafayette, (Cherokee County) Centre, (Chilton County) Clanton, (Choctaw County) Butler, (Clarke County) Grove Hill, (Clay County) Ashland, (Cleburne County) Heflin, (Coffee County) Elba, (Colbert County) Tuscumbia, (Conecuh County) Evergreen, (Coosa County) Rockford, (Covington County) Andalusia, (Crenshaw County) Luverne, (Cullman County) Cullman, (Dale County) Ozark, (Dallas County) Selma, (Decatur County) Woodville, (DeKalb County) Fort Payne, (Elmore County) Wetumpka, (Escambia County) Brewton, (Etowah County) Gadsden, (Fayette County) Fayette, and (Franklin County) Russellville, (Geneva County) Geneva, (Greene County) Eutaw, (Hale County) Greensboro, (Henry County) Abbeville, (Houston County) Dothan, (Jackson County) Scottsboro, (Jefferson County) Birmingham, (Lamar County) Vernon, (Lauderdale County) Florence, (Lawrence County) Moulton, (Lee County) Opelika, (Limestone County) Athens, (Lowndes County) Hayneville, (Macon County) Tuskegee, (Madison County) Huntsville, (Marengo County) Linden, (Marion County) Hamilton, (Marshall County) Guntersville, (Mobile County) Mobile, (Monroe County) Monroeville, (Montgomery County) Montgomery, (Morgan County) Decatur, (Perry County) Marion, (Pickens County) Carrollton, (Pike County) Troy, (Randolph County) Wedowee, (Russell County) Phenix City, (St. Clair County) Ashville, (Shelby County) Columbiana, (Sumter County) Livingston, (Talladega County) Talladega, (Tallapoosa County) Dadeville, (Tuscaloosa County) Tuscaloosa, (Walker County) Jasper, (Washington County) Chatom, (Wilcox County) Camden, and (Winston County) Double Springs.

FOR FURTHER INFORMATION SEE:
- Banfield, Marilyn Davis. *Researching in Alabama: A Genealogical Guide.* Easley, SC: Southern Historical Press, 1987.
- Elliott, Wendy L. *Research in Alabama.* Bountiful, UT: American Genealogical Lending Library, 1987.

Alaska Records provide information about the people in the largest state geographically and the smallest in population. Almost a third of Alaska lies north of the Arctic Circle. The state's name comes from an Aleut word meaning great land. When the first Europeans arrived in the Alaska region, three groups of natives—Eskimos, Aleuts, and Indians—were living there. The Eskimos were settled near the coast in the far north and west. The Aleuts, closely related to the Eskimos, lived on the Aleutian Islands and the Alaskan Peninsula. The largest Indian groups, the Tlingit and the Haida, lived near the coast in the southeast. Tsimshain Indians also lived there, while Athabaskan Indians lived in the interior.

The Russians established the first European settlement in Alaska on Kodiak Island in 1784. They made slaves of the Aleuts, whom the Russians employed to catch sea otters and other animals, and they treated the Indians quite harshly. In 1867 the United States purchased the territory from the Russians and a few American companies began to build canneries along the coast to harvest salmon. Then in 1880 Joe Juneau discovered gold in the Silverbow Basin of the Yukon. This prompted thousands of would-be miners to migrate to the territory hoping to strike it rich, and aroused nationwide interest in the territory. However it was not until 1958 that Congress finally voted to make Alaska the 49th state.

The genealogical records of Alaska contain not only information on the settlers who came there from the other states, but also remnants of the early Russian community that remained and the native Eskimos, Aleuts, and Indians. Furthermore, some researchers have shown a great interest in identifying the names of those who participated in the Alaskan Gold Rush. The first U.S. census of the territory was conducted in 1880, although there were some earlier attempts when Alaska was still designated as a district. These include an 1870 census of the town of Sitka that has the names and ages of family members, as well as their birthplaces and occupations. An 1881 Sitka census records names, ages, nationality, and occupations for all the non–Indian family members, as well as the names for the heads of families of the Indian village nearby. Other local area records collected after 1880 give names and in some cases birth, marriage, and death dates. These are records for Eskimo families at Cape Smyth, Point Barrow (1885); several resident censuses for St. George Island (1890–1907); and records for St. Paul Island (1890–1895). In 1970 the U.S. Census reported that the state of Alaska had a population of 302,173 persons. The figure had by then increased 34 percent over the 1960 figure.

Under Alaskan law, all vital statistics records are strictly confidential until a specified time has elapsed. Then they can become public. Birth records become public one hundred years after the event; and death, marriage, and divorce records become public 50 years after the event. The Alaska Bureau of Vital Statistics, located in Juneau, is responsible for managing and maintaining all the vital records in the state. Certified copies can be obtained from the bureau for a small fee.

All Alaska court records from 1884 to 1959 are found at the Alaska State Archives in Juneau or at the National Archives Pacific Alaska Region in Anchorage. Some are in manuscript collections. Most of the records from 1959 to the present remain in the offices of the clerks of court in each judicial district. From time to time the older records are transferred to the Alaska State Archives.

The Alaska Archives and Records Management office in Juneau, and the Alaska State Library and its adjoining Alaska Historical Library and Museum, also located in Juneau, have various territorial court records and extensive materials related to the native Eskimo, Aleut, and Indian populations. A useful booklet published in 1997 by the National Archives Pacific Alaska Region (updated in April 2001) is titled *How to Find Your Gold Rush Relative: Sources on the Klondike and Alaska Gold Rushes (1896–1914)*.

FOR FURTHER INFORMATION SEE:
- Bradbury, Connie Malcolm, and David Albert Hales. *Alaska Sources: A Guide to Historical Records and Information Resources.* North Salt Lake City, UT: Heritage Quest, 2001.
- Ulibarri, George S. *Documenting Alaskan History: Guide to Federal Archives Relating to Alaska.* Fairbanks, AL: University of Alaska Press, 1982.

Albanian Records *see* **Eastern European Genealogy**

Alberta Records are centralized at the Provincial Archives in Edmonton, Canada. The repository for the province's documentary heritage is there, and this is where the government records, manuscripts, photographs, tape recordings, maps, and moving images are available to the public for research, reference, and display. This westernmost Prairie Province of Canada did not achieve provincial status until 1905, but since that time it has grown rapidly in population and wealth. Before the first Europeans arrived as fur traders in 1754, the area was populated by Blackfoot, Blood, Piegan, Cree, and a few other North American Indian tribes.

Among the records that can be found in the archives are the vital records (births, marriages, deaths) for the residents of Alberta. These date from 1898, although there are some births recorded as early as 1853 and deaths as early as 1893. Before 1898 there was no civil registration of births, marriages, and deaths in the province. These birth records usually contain the name, sex, parents' names (or father and informant), father's profession, date and place of birth, and date of registration or date and place of baptism. The earlier births and deaths that can be found in the archives were registered much later. It is advisable for any researcher outside of Edmonton to write or phone the archives before visiting to determine whether or not it has the particular information that is being sought. The Alberta Archives has an *Index to the Registration of Births, Marriages and Deaths, 1870 to 1905*, that was prepared by the Edmonton Branch of the Alberta Genealogical Society.

The marriage registrations include the date and place of marriage, religion of the bride and groom, groom's name, age, address, birthplace, status (bachelor or widower), profession, and parents' names, as well as the bride's name, age, address, birthplace, status (spinster or widow), and parents' names. There are also some divorce records, which include the names of the two parties concerned. As to the death records, these may include the name, death date, sex, age, profession, birthplace, cause of death, and religion of the deceased.

Another source for baptism and marriage records in Alberta is various church archives. The Anglican Church of Canada Diocese in Edmonton maintains such records for Edmonton during the years of 1889–1989, Athabasca for 1874–1989, and Mackenzie River for 1859–1942. The United Church of Canada headquarters in Toronto has records for the Alberta and Northwest Conference from 1853–1990, as well as the records of the three denominations that united to form this church in 1925: Presbyterian (1887–1925), Methodist (1863–1925), and Congregational (1910–1912). The Lutheran Church, Alberta Synod, has records dating from 1898, and the Unitarian Church of Edmonton has them dating from 1912, while the Alberta Synod of the Presbyterian Church in Edmonton has records only beginning in 1950. The Roman Catholic records in this province cover five religious orders and one parish. They can be found at the Provincial Archives.

All the wills and probate records are in the courts of the judicial districts where they were probated (Edmonton for the Northern District of Alberta and Calgary for the Southern District). Although Alberta has 27 counties, none of them are record-keeping jurisdictions. It is worth noting that in Alberta a child receives only that which is given in the parents' will. In the event that a child is left out of the will, that child is essentially disowned. All divorce records are maintained by the Provincial Supreme Court in Edmonton, while the provincial the land grants, as well as deeds and other local land records, are also in the custody of the land registries in Edmonton and Calgary.

The homestead records for Alberta, 1885–1930, are available at the Provincial Archives in Edmonton. These contain information about the individuals who obtained land under the Dominion Lands Act of 1873. They do not cover any private sales or the rental of land. These files may provide genealogical information such as the applicant's age, marital status, number of children, place of birth, and employment.

The Alberta Legislature Library in Edmonton has a nearly complete collection of newspaper weeklies starting from 1905, as well as microfilm copies of the major dailies and weeklies from various communities across the province. Local government records in the various towns and two districts of Alberta may contain tax and assessment rolls, as well as school attendance records. *See also* **Census, Canadian.**

Algeria *see* **African Genealogy**

American Indians *see* **Native American Records**

Amish Records *see* **Mennonite Records**

Ancestor Tables *see* **Pedigree Charts**

Ancestral File *see* **Mormon Records**

Ancient Greek and Roman Genealogy arose because of a general desire to explain the origin of the early tribes, their relation to each other, the intermingling of populations, and the cities they erected. The "sons" of a "father" often stand merely for branches of a family as it existed at some particular time, and the genealogical lists that originated at different periods reveal serious discrepancies.

In every one of the numerous states into which ancient Greece was divided there were aristocratic families whose genealogies reached back to prehistoric times and whose first ancestors were heroes of divine descent from whom they derived their names. The Corinthian family of Bacchiadae, for example, traced their genealogy back to the god Heracles, but took their name from Bacchis, a younger ancestor. It is somewhat doubtful whether pedigrees such as these were seriously put forward by those who claimed them. Certainly none of these were supported by any concrete evidence. In any case the public registers of births, adoptions, and so forth do not appear to have been preserved with enough care to make it possible for the ancient Greeks to verify any particular pedigree.

Roman patricians could usually trace their families back to an illustrious ancestor rather than a god. The rigid exclusiveness with which each family preserved these heredities is illustrated by the fact that toward the end of the republic only about 50 patrician families remained. But even in these, although the historical identity of each family could be guaranteed, the personal genealogy of the individuals claiming such descent could not be verified because of the well-recognized practice of frequent adoptions for which no records were kept.

The leading patrician families carefully drew up genealogical tables and often painted them on the walls of their entrance halls. In later times even many plebian families began

to preserve small wooden shrines that contained wax portrait masks of those family members who had attained important public positions. Under these images it was the practice to inscribe the relationship of one mask to another by means of connecting lines. Writing around A.D. 70, the Roman author Pliny bemoans the fact that many of these plebian attempts at genealogy were forged and that the masks of fictitious ancestors probably stood in some of these shrines. *See also* **Census, Ancient**.

Anglican Records *see* **Episcopalian Records**

Apprentice Records *see* **Indenture and Apprenticeship Records**

Arab Genealogy *see* **Islamic Genealogy**

Argentine Genealogy has many advocates and there are flourishing societies devoted to such an interest. However, it is not always easy to obtain genealogical information from this part of the world. By law, civil registration in Argentina began in 1886, as it did in the province of Buenos Aires, but it did not start in all the other provinces at that time. The last one to institute civil registration was the province of Corrientes in 1901. Today birth and marriages certificates can be obtained from the Civil Registry Office (Registro Civil) of the municipality of the rural district in which the birth or marriage took place.

According to the regulations, separate books of births, marriages, deaths, recognition of children by their father, and adoptions were to be kept in each municipal district, while duplicate copies were to be sent to the Archivo General de Tribunales in the federal district that contains the city of Buenos Aires or to the judicial or provincial archives in the provinces. These books can be consulted by any interested party, with no restrictions.

There were national censuses taken in Argentina in 1869, 1895, and 1914, and there were also censuses for the city of Buenos Aires in 1855 and 1881. All of these except for the one for 1914 are available at the National Archives (Archivo General de la Nación) in

Buenos Aires. The 1914 census has not yet been released by the government. Furthermore, there were many censuses taken of various provinces and local areas. These are censuses all kept at the various provincial archives. The 1869 census includes the names, sexes, ages, nationalities, places of birth, occupations, level of literacy, and whether or not a family's children were legitimate. The 1895 census includes these items and also whether or not the individuals listed owned property, how many years they were married, and the physical status of any orphans.

The legal records for wills and other notarial items for the federal district from 1584 to 1883 are preserved in the National Archives. Those after 1883 in the federal district are in the Archivo de Actuaciones in Buenos Aires or in the offices of local notaries. All other such records are in the notarial archives of each province and local notary's offices.

The parish registers of the Catholic churches in Argentina contain much data of use to genealogists; some of these registers have been filmed by the Genealogical Society of Utah. The oldest ones date from the early 1600s. However, many of the earlier records have been destroyed or have otherwise disappeared. In Buenos Aires the first Episcopalian Church was established in 1831, the first Presbyterian Church in 1838, the first Lutheran Church in 1847, and the first Methodist Church in 1870. All these denominations in Argentina have records of their members that may be useful.

An institute for research, the Instituto Argentino de Ciencias Genealogicas, has some genealogical material, but only does historical research. Institute staff will, however, refer interested persons to genealogical experts who can do investigations on a fee basis. Researchers should also consult the many-volumed *Encyclopedia Heraldica y Genealogica: Hispano-Americana* that can be found at the National Library in Buenos Aires. It gives the histories of a number of Argentine families, as well as those in Spain and other Latin American countries.

Arizona Records are available but limited in number, in part because this state was not admitted into the Union until February 14, 1912. It then became the 48th state. At one time considered an almost worthless desert, Arizona has since become a prosperous state. Vast irrigation systems have transformed the desert into rich farmland. Rich mineral resources have been located and are being mined, and the state is growing rapidly in manufacturing. Arizona ranks sixth in state size, with 113,642 square miles of land, and 20th in population, with an estimated 5,130,632 residents in 2000. Its state capital is at Phoenix; and its name comes from a Spanish interpretation of the Aztec Indian word, "Aleh-zon," meaning "little spring place."

The first U.S. census was conducted in the territory of Arizona in 1870. Prior to that, in 1850 and 1860, its population was enumerated as Arizona County in the state of New Mexico. All the U.S. censuses can be found at the various National Archives locations. There are also incomplete Arizona territorial censuses for the years 1864, 1866, 1867, 1869, 1871, 1872, and 1873, located at the Department of Libraries, Archives, and Public Records in Phoenix. The state's vital records for births, deaths, and marriages are maintained in the Office of Vital Records, a division of the Arizona Department of Health Services in Phoenix. They have the records from July 1909 and abstracts of records filed in Arizona counties before then. By law, access to these records is limited to information about persons born more than 75 years ago and about persons who died more than 50 years ago. There is a small charge for providing copies of such records.

Marriage records are also maintained by the clerks of the superior courts in each county, as are the divorce records. From 1891 to 1912 the clerks of the probate courts issued all marriage licenses. The earliest divorce records were granted by the territorial legislature and have been published as part of the territorial statutes.

The Arizona Department of Libraries, Archives, and Public Records maintains microfilm records of births from the 1890s through 1925 and death records from the 1890s through 1950. Here one may also find some cemetery records, church records, newspapers, military records, immigration and naturalization records, tax records, school records, and voter registrations, as well as some family records in letters and Bibles, all places where evidence of vital events may be found. Other state archives are at the Arizona State University Library in Tempe and the Arizona Historical Society Research Library in Tucson.

Researchers seeking information from county records can locate them at the following County seats: (Apache County) St. Johns, (Cochise County) Bisbee, (Coconino County) Flagstaff, (Gila County) Globe, (Graham County) Safford, (Greenlee County) Clifton, (La Paz County) Parker, (Maricopa County) Phoenix, (Mohave County) Kingman, (Navajo County) Holbrook, (Pima County) Tucson, (Pinal County) Florence, (Santa Cruz County) Nogales, (Yavapai County) Prescott, and (Yuma County) Yuma.

FOR FURTHER INFORMATION SEE:
- *A Historical and Biographical Record of the Territory of Arizona.* Chicago: McFarland and Poole, 1896.
- Spiros, Joyce V. Hawley. *Genealogical Guide to Arizona and Nevada.* Gallup, NM: Verlene Publishing, 1983.

Arkansas Records mainly deal with the farm families who arrived there from the eastern seaboard states, but there is also some information about the descendants of early French settlers, English-speaking immigrants from Europe, and the original Indian inhabitants. The state got its name from an Indian word that means "downstream people." Until the first European explorers arrived, the area was inhabited by the Quapaw Indian tribe, who lived on the lower Arkansas River near the Mississippi; as well as by Osage Indians, who roamed the Ozark region; and Caddo Indians, who lived along the streams of the southwest. After 1790 Cherokees, Choctaws, and a few Shawnee and Delaware Indians also came into Arkansas. The first European explorers to arrive were members of a company of Spaniards led by Hernando de Soto in 1541–1542. But the first permanent European settlement was founded in 1686 by the French-

man Henri de Tonty at Arkansas Post on the Arkansas River, south of present-day De-Witt. The French explorers Jacques Marquette and Louis Joliet had already explored the Mississippi to the mouth of the Arkansas in 1673, and Sieur de La Salle had named the land for the King of France in 1682.

The United States acquired Arkansas in 1803 as part of the Louisiana Purchase. It was designated, in 1812, as a section of the Missouri Territory and was separated from this in 1819 as the Arkansas Territory, which included the Indian lands in Oklahoma. Arkansas Post was the capital of the Arkansas Territory until 1821 when the capital was moved to the new town of Little Rock, the capital ever since except for the short period of 1863–1865 when the Confederate state government was located at Washington in Hempstead County. On June 15, 1836, Arkansas was admitted to the Union as the 25th state.

The first U.S. census in Arkansas was conducted in 1830, and there have never been any census enumerations conducted by the state itself. All the national censuses of this state can be seen at the various National Archives locations. The 1830 census has been indexed; this index can be found in many genealogical libraries. Recording of births and deaths by the Division of Vital Records, a part of the Arkansas Department of Health in Little Rock, began on February 1, 1914. There were no marriage records listed until January 1917 and no divorce records until 1921. The Division of Vital Records does have a few birth records dated prior to 1914 as well as a limited number of death records from the same period. These are original copies of the certificates of birth and death that occurred in the cities of Little Rock and Fort Smith in 1881 and after. The Vital Records Division, however, has no early marriage or divorce records. Copies of individual records may be obtained by mail or in person, for a small fee, from the Division of Vital Records at Little Rock.

The Arkansas History Commission in Little Rock, the official state archives, has an index of deaths occurring in Arkansas from 1914 through 1949. This, however, is only an alphabetical listing of the deaths. The commission does not have actual copies of the death records. It does have sheriffs' censuses for several counties in 1829 and for Arkansas county in 1823. Persons interested in Arkansas history can engage in research at the History Commission, but the staff does not undertake research requests from the public, whether delivered in person, through the mail, or by telephone. The research room is open for use from Monday through Saturday, except on state holidays.

Many of the 75 counties in Arkansas have genealogical societies and county libraries that are willing to help the researcher, and all of them have county offices that can be contacted. One should be aware that over time a good number of these counties have been created out of the division of other counties, and some have changed their names and boundary lines. It is wise, then, for researchers to determine the exact geographic name in use at the time for which they may be seeking information. Furthermore, the University of Arkansas at Fayetteville has some good genealogical materials about the state, and one should also look at the records in the Arkansas State Library at Little Rock.

Researchers seeking information from county records can locate them at the following County seats: (Arkansas County) De Witt and Stuttgart, (Ashley County) Hamburg, (Baxter County) Mountain Home, (Benton County) Bentonville, (Boone County) Harrison, (Bradley County) Warren, (Calhoun County) Hampton, (Carroll County) Berryville and Eureka Springs, (Chicot County) Lake Village, (Clark County) Arkadelphia, (Clay County) Piggott and Corning, (Cleburne County) Heber Springs, (Cleveland County) Rison, (Columbia County) Magnolia, (Conway County) Morrilton, (Craighead County) Lake City and Jonesboro, (Crawford County) Van Buren, (Crittenden County) Marion, (Cross County) Wynne, (Dallas County) Fordyce, (Desha County) Arkansas City, (Drew County) Monticello, (Faulkner County) Conway, (Franklin County) Charleston and Ozark, (Fulton County) Salem, (Garland County)

Hot Springs National Park, (Grant County) Sheridan, (Greene County) Paragould, (Hempstead County) Hope, (Hot Spring County) Malvern, (Howard County) Nashville, (Independence County) Batesville, and (Izard County) Melbourne.

Also at (Jackson County) Newport, (Jefferson County) Pine Bluff, (Johnson County) Clarksville, (Lafayette County) Lewisville, (Lawrence County) Walnut Ridge, (Lee County) Marianna, (Lincoln County) Star City, (Little River County) Ashdown, (Logan County) Booneville and Paris, (Lonoke County) Lonoke. (Madison County) Huntsville, (Marion County) Yellville, (Miller County) Texarkana, (Mississippi County) Blytheville and Osceola, (Monroe County) Clarendon, (Montgomery County) Mount Ida, (Nevada County) Prescott, (Newton County) Jasper, (Ouachita County) Camden, (Perry County) Perryville, (Phillips County) Helena, (Pike County) Murfreesboro, (Poinsett County) Harrisburg, (Polk County) Mena, (Pope County) Russellville, (Prairie County) Des Arc and De Valls Bluff, (Pulaski County) Little Rock, (Randolph County) Pocahontas, (St. Francis County) Forrest City, (Saline County) Benton, (Scott County) Waldron, (Searcy County) Marshall, (Sebastian County) Greenwood and Fort Smith, (Sevier County) De Queen, (Sharp County) Ash Flat, (Stone County) Mountain View, (Union County) El Dorado, (Van Buren County) Clinton, (Washington County) Fayetteville, (White County) Searcy, (Woodruff County) Augusta, and (Yell County) Dardanelle and Danville.

FOR FURTHER INFORMATION SEE:
- Clark, Georgia H., and R. Bruce Parham, comps. *Arkansas County and Local Histories: A Bibliography*. Fayetteville, AR: n.p., 1976.
- Wagoner, Claudia. *Arkansas Researchers' Handbook*. Fayetteville, AR: Research Plus, 1986.

Army Records *see* **Military Records**

Asian Genealogy *see* **Chinese Genealogy; Indian Genealogy; Japanese Genealogy; Korean Genealogy**

Assemblies of God Records can be obtained from the individual churches, many of which have attached graveyards where birth and death dates can often be found on the memorial stones. Various genealogists have copied the records from some of these graveyards, such as the one on the Spokane Indian Reservation in Stevens County, Washington, and the one in Houston County, Alabama, and they have conveniently placed them on Websites for others to view.

The denomination is the largest Pentacostal body in the world, claiming more than 8,600 churches and 1,100,000 members. It grew out of a revival movement in the early 1900s and was first organized at Hot Springs, Arkansas, in 1914. Although the Assemblies of God headquarters is located in Springfield, Missouri, that body does not provide access to its archives for genealogical purposes. All such data is maintained by local churches, each of which directs its own local affairs. These local churches meet every two years as a general council.

The history of the Assemblies of God and a few genealogical records can be found at the Flower Pentecostal Heritage Center in Springfield, Missouri. It was formed to collect, preserve, and provide access to materials pertinent to the denomination. The Heritage Center issues a quarterly publication called *Assemblies of God Heritage. See also* **Pentecostal Records.**

Atlases *see* Maps

Australian Genealogy begins in 1788 when the first 11 ships from England, with a cargo of convicts, arrived at Port Jackson to set up a settlement at Sydney. The continent had been claimed for England only a few years earlier by Captain James Cook. The English, denied by the American Revolution from sending any further convicts to the American colonies, began to use Australia as their prison colony. During the following 80 years that Australia served as a penal colony, England sent about 168,000 convicts there, many of them women. The first free settlers arrived in 1793. Although these free settlers protested against the transport of more convicts to Australia, the practice did not finally end until 1868.

Australia has an indigenous population of aborigine tribesmen, who prefer to be known as Koori, since the term "aborigine" was foisted on them by white settlers. When the Europeans first arrived they found that there were about 250 indigenous languages being spoken in Australia. The word "Koori" (coorie, kory, kuri, kooli, koole) comes from some of these languages in the southeast part of Australia (New South Wales and Victoria) and means "person" or "people." Other terms that have the same meaning are preferred by some of the indigenous people in other regions: Murri over most of south and central Queensland, Bama in north Queensland, Nunga in southern South Australia, Nyoongah around Perth, Mulba in the Pilbara region, Wongi in the Kalgoorlie region, Yamitji in the Murchison River region, Yolngu in Arnhem Land, Anangu in central Australia, and Yuin on the south coast of New South Wales. All of the indigenous people have tribal histories that include lengthy genealogies, but these are orally transmitted and filled with much mythology. They are not generally considered to be a part of Australia's genealogical record by the non-indigenous population.

Many records for the Europeans who entered Australia as either free settlers or convicts are stored in the Australian Archives at Canberra. These records include lists of convicts who arrived from England and Ireland. Some of these lists have been posted on Websites. The first population counts of Australia were known as musters and were conducted as early as 1788. They were called musters because they involved all members of the various communities who gathered at a specified time and location to be counted. Such musters were important as a means of matching food and other supplies to the number of people needing them.

Many of the muster lists, which include the names of individuals, still exist and can be viewed at various repositories. Those from New South Wales can be found in the Norfolk Island Mitchell Library at Sydney, the National Library of Australia at Canberra, and the New South Wales State Archives at Sydney. The Mitchell Library and the New South Wales State Archives also have some of the muster lists from Tasmania. Those for Western Australia are at the Swan River Battye Library and the State Archives of Western Australia, both located in Perth. Those for Victoria can be found at the La Trobe University Library in Melbourne, the Public Record Office in Victoria, the State Library in Victoria, the Mitchell Library, and New South Wales State Archives. Those for the Northern Territory are in the National Archives at Canberra. Those for Queensland and South Australia have all been destroyed.

It was not until 1828 that the first census was taken in the colony of New South Wales. After that, each of the Australian colonies conducted its own census up to 1886. A census conference held in Sydney in 1900 arranged for a census of the whole continent to be held on 31 March 1901. But minor differences in the interpretation of the definitions arose among the states and the responses to the census questions were not tabulated in all cases. Thus, to provide greater coordination, the Census and Statistics Act was enacted in 1905. It stipulated that "the census shall be taken in the year 1911, and in every tenth year thereafter." This has been done regularly ever since, except for the year 1931, when the economic depression made it impossible. However, genealogists should know that every census taken since the establishment of the Commonwealth in 1901 has been destroyed, as an officially mandated policy, after the statistical information was extracted.

The registration of births, deaths, and marriages in Australia was initially the responsibility of the colonies and later of the states and territories. What records are available can be located in the state and territory archives. For example, the Victoria State Archives at South Melbourne has indexes of births in that state from 1853 to 1913, marriages from 1853 to 1930, deaths from 1853 to 1985, as well as some earlier deaths that go back to 1837. The Western Australia Records Office is located at Perth, the Tasmania Archives Office is at Hobart, the Queensland State Archives is at Runcorn, the Northern Territory Archives Service is at Darwin, the New South Wales Archival Authority is at

Sydney, and the Australian Capitol Territory Archives is at Canberra.

Two other helpful resources for Australian genealogy are wills and the post office directories. The New South Wales Supreme Court Index, which can be located in the archives at Sydney has an index, available on microfiche, that lists wills and thus gives the place of residence and date of death for a variety of individuals. The post office directories, first published in 1806, are helpful in tracking family migrations from Sydney and other towns in Australia. Such records are particularly useful because of the virtual nonexistence of census records. The Mitchell Library, the State Library of New South Wales, and the La Trobe University Library all have good collections of post office directories.

Austrian Genealogy research tends to be rather difficult for several reasons. It has a somewhat negative connotation because it is often associated with the misuse of genealogical data during the Nazi era (1938–1945) and because many Austrians consider it to be old fashioned, just a pastime for nobility and would-be aristocrats. Furthermore Austrian data privacy laws are quite strict; lookups are difficult, and they frequently require valid powers of attorney, proof of descent, etc.

Austrian genealogy requires a good knowledge of that country's history. From 1438 to 1806 the Archduchy of Austria was the most important state in the Holy Roman Empire. On the dissolution of the Archduchy, the Habsburgs assumed and held the title of Emperors of Austria until 1918, when they were overthrown and Austria became a republic. During the period of Habsburg rule, Hungary became a part of Austria and researchers should remember that the Austro-Hungarian Empire of the late 19th century included many areas that are now separate countries. People who find an immigrant ancestor listed in the U.S. census as being "born in Austria" may soon discover that they should continue their research in Poland, the Ukraine, Romania, the Czech Republic, or Slovenia because the birth place is now in one of these countries. By 1938, Hitler had made Austria a part of Germany, and from

1945 until 1955 it was under Allied occupation. Austria again became an independent nation in 1955.

As in many of the West European countries the impetus for record keeping began with the Council of Trent (1545–1563). However, the oldest parish register in Austria with recorded baptisms dates back to 1457. All registrations of births, marriages, and deaths until 1938 were recorded in the Catholic and Protestant churches. Only after that did registration become a civil matter. These civil marriage records date from August 1938 and the births and deaths from January 1939.

Through much of its history the Austrian government has had little toleration for religious bodies other than the Catholic Church, and so to find most of the vital records a researcher must consult the Austrian Official Calendar. Austrian embassies and consulates can offer help on this. For Protestant records one should consult the High Church Council in Vienna — the governing body of the Protestant denominations. The civil records are kept mainly in the Archives of Austria (Statistisches Zentralamt) in Vienna.

The preservation of wills has remained, since 1900, with the law courts. Before that date they are to be found in the archives of the particular cities. The census was taken in 1869, 1880, 1890, 1900 and 1910, but the source documentation (the enumeration sheets) was destroyed in the Palace of Justice fire of 1927. All that remains is the statistical information about number of inhabitants and houses per village.

A registry of births, marriages, and deaths has been preserved since 1938, but this information, which is at the Archives in Vienna, is restricted, according to the Austrian data privacy laws, to direct descendants only. One library that can provide genealogical information is the Austrian National Library (Österr. Nationalbibliothek). Here one can find Lehmann's *Wiener Wohnunhgsanzeiger*, an alphabetical listing of all the heads of households in Vienna from 1859 onwards.

B

Baltic Region Genealogy involves the ancestry of persons in the independent republics of Estonia, Latvia, and Lithuania on the eastern coast of the Baltic Sea. Until each of these states became independent in 1918, Latvia had been ruled in turn by the Germans, Poles, Swedes, and from 1721 by the Russians. The Estonians were ruled by German nobles until they came under Russian control in 1721. Lithuania once was a grand duchy until it united with Poland in 1385. All three, after their brief period of independence, were incorporated into the Union of Soviet Socialist Republics (USSR) in 1940 during World War II, and then were occupied by Germany in 1941. Recaptured by the USSR in 1944, they remained part of Russia up to 1991 when they again achieved independence.

In the case of Estonia, the government passed a law in 1918 under which the registration of births, marriages, and deaths was to be transferred from the parish clergy to the local administration. It is unclear whether this law ever was actually applied, but in 1925 a new law superseded it that required the civil registration of such vital statistics. However, no central record office was established to maintain these records and many may have been destroyed. Copies of some are in the National Library of Estonia in Tallinn. There is an Estonian Biographical Center in Tartu that is run by a professional genealogist and which offers help in searching for ancestors for a fee. This body will also do any kind of archival research into village history, real estate history, and research on Estonian organizations. If one seeks information about a specific person from the Estonian Historical Archives in Tartu, it is important to know the name, date, and place of birth, and religious congregation of the one being sought. If one is able to visit Estonia in person, one can go to this archive to engage in research without having to pay a fee.

Latvia began the civil registration of birth, marriage, and death records at local offices in 1919, but all these records were eventually taken to Russia. There were also state archives, which were the repositories for wills and other documents of public interest. Some of these records may now be in the Latvian National Library in Riga.

Lithuania, after its independence in 1918, continued the practice of having the clergy, who were given the position of state officials, keep all the vital records. Copies of these registers and many of the older registers were then sent to the central archives in Kaunas. The wills were kept in the law courts that proved them. It has been said that the key to locating Lithuanian ancestors depends on knowing the exact ancestral town where they lived, which can be difficult because of the various occupations of Lithuania over the centuries. Some towns that once were in Lithuania are no longer there, and some towns with large Lithuanian populations may have always been part of Poland or Germany. Researchers often find that they get the most out of the Lithuanian Historical Archives in Vilnius if they can provide the personnel there with whatever information a researcher already possesses. Through responding to requests for genealogical information, the archives have been able to raise desperately needed funds. But all this can take a great deal of time. The National Library of Lithuania in Vilnius may also have genealogical records of some interest.

Baptist Records of church affairs have traditionally been kept by each individual church. Baptists have, however, historically practiced "believer's baptism" rather than the "infant baptism" that takes place in most other denominations. Thus people are not baptized under the Baptist understanding until they are mature enough to profess their faith. Thus finding the record of a baptism in Baptist church minutes only reveals the person's name and date of baptism. It cannot serve to document a date of birth or even help to determine an approximate age for the person in

question. Baptist churches have also traditionally not kept marriage records, although some ministers do have private logs of the marriages they perform. Where such notes have been preserved, they are never indexed by the names of those who were married and they can probably be accessed only through the name of the minister.

The earliest Baptist leaders were John Smyth and Thomas Helwys, English separatists of the Congregational persuasion. They founded the first Baptist church, in 1609, on Dutch soil and at the city of Amsterdam. Helwys later split with Smyth over doctrinal matters and returned to England to found another Baptist church, in 1611, near London.

It was in America that the Baptists experienced their greatest growth. The first Baptist church in the United States was founded in 1639 at Providence, Rhode Island, by Roger Williams, an English Puritan clergyman. At about the same time John Clarke established a Baptist congregation at Newport, Rhode Island. The denomination grew rapidly during the Great Awakening in the 18th century. Like most other Protestant denominations, the Baptists split over the issue of slavery, leading to the formation of the Southern Baptist Convention in 1845. In 1907 the Northern Baptists formed the Northern Baptist Convention (now the American Baptist Churches in the USA). There are also two African-American Baptist groups—the National Baptist Convention of America and the National Baptist Convention, U.S.A., Inc. In Canada there is the Baptist Federation of Canada. Most of these organizations are now linked through the Baptist World Alliance.

Several libraries have extensive records of the Baptist churches, materials that have been deposited by various churches that have either disbanded or become a part of larger congregations. The Southern Baptist Historical Library and Archives in Nashville, Tennessee, holds many such records, as does the Samford University Library at Birmingham, Alabama. The American Baptist Archives Center in Valley Forge, Pennsylvania, and the Samuel Colgate Historical Library in Rochester, New York, maintain extensive records of the Northern Baptist movement. Both exist to document the life and history of the Baptists; they do not intentionally collect genealogical data. But historical data concerns people, and people are, of course, the subject of genealogical studies. Therefore some of the holdings do inevitably have genealogical value.

If the person being sought participated in a local Baptist church, it is highly unlikely that any information can be found about that person in any of these libraries. At best, the only information that might be forthcoming would be the fact that the person once belonged to a given Baptist church at a given time. If, however, the subject was a Baptist minister (particularly in the North) from the mid-19th century or later, or if the subject served as a missionary for the American Baptist Missionary Union (later, the American Baptist Foreign Mission Society), the American Baptist Home Mission Society, or the American Baptist Publication Society, there is a better chance that the library will be able to locate an obituary.

The Canadian Baptist Archives are at the McMaster Divinity College in Hamilton, Ontario, while the Angus Library of Regents Park College in Oxford is the most comprehensive library and archive of Baptist resources in England. It does not include registers of births, deaths, or marriages, but it does include a small selection of local church minute books and information regarding the whereabouts of a few others.

In England a Family Records Center in London has registers and indices of births, marriages, and deaths from 1837. Baptist registers prior to 1837 are listed in Breed's book, a copy of which is also at the Family Records Center, as is an index of obituaries for the majority of ministers in England serving churches affiliated with the Baptist Union. A number of Baptist ministers belong to or have belonged to the Strict and Particular Baptists, a body not allied with the other Baptists of Britain. This group has its headquarters in Dunstable, Bedford County. Information about the Baptists in Wales can be obtained from the Baptist Union in Swansea, and Baptists in Ireland from the Baptist Union in Belfast.

Beginning Genealogy *see* **Genealogy for Beginners**

Belgian Genealogy requires extensive knowledge of French and Flemish because this is a bilingual country and access to the records is obtained only after a determination of which language is being used in each of the eight provinces. The research process is also somewhat hindered by the fact that Belgium has been the scene of much fighting over the years that has resulted in the destruction of some of the records by the armies of the great powers, and the removal of other records to France and Austria.

This country is one of the most densely populated in the world, and it has been ruled at various times by Spain, Austria, France, and The Netherlands. It gained its independence in 1830, but suffered great destruction during both World Wars I and II. Despite these difficulties some lines of Belgian ancestry can still be traced back into the Middle Ages.

Before Napoleon invaded and occupied Belgium in 1795, parish registers were kept only by Catholic priests. The French introduced civil registration in 1795, and since then, at 10-year periods, each township has made a record of the vital data for all its inhabitants. These records are kept in large registers with one page per household. Any change from the previous period of registry is inscribed with the date and location in the case of deaths, marriages, and births. People moving into a township are also registered with the date they moved and their previous address. The old parish registers, those originally kept by the priests, are now preserved either in the provincial archives or in the township archives.

The provincial archives are located in the cities of Antwerp, Arlon, Bruges, Ghent, Hasselt, Liège, Mons, and Namur. If one writes to a municipality for information, it is wise to write in the official language of that municipality. Most of the employees of the municipalities are able to read English, so they may answer the letters written to them in English, but the answers will come back either in Flemish or French, and sometimes in

German. Vital records in Belgium are protected by the Privacy Act of 1955, making them unavailable until they are at least one hundred years old.

The national, or general, archives are located in Brussels. Wills dated before the French Revolution are usually kept in the provincial archives. The Royal Library in Brussels also has some genealogical materials.

One unusual and useful fund of information is that of the records of a government official named Mr. Venesoen, who was in charge of questioning all Belgian emigrants upon their departure from the port of Antwerp from about 1892 to 1910. Most of these records have been preserved, though only a few years are yet accessible. They can be found at the provincial archives in Antwerp. The records give the name, age, place of origin, occupation, and destination in another country for each individual.

Biblical Genealogy, which is found in a number of books of the Old Testament, begins with "the generations of heaven and earth," and then, by a process of elimination, passes from Adam and Eve down to Jacob and his sons (the tribes), and finally to the subdivisions of each tribe. By this process every Israelite male could allegedly trace his ancestry back to Jacob, the common father of the whole nation. Such a genealogical process, however, is full of improbabilities. It demands that every tribe and every clan must have been a homogeneous group that preserved its unity for several centuries from the very earliest times. It also ignores the fact that most of the record had to be passed down by word of mouth because writing methods only developed in the last segment of this history, and everyone is aware of the fallacies that can arise in verbal transmission. And finally it is obvious that many of the Biblical names are nothing more than personifications of nations, tribes, towns, and so forth, which are grouped together to convey some idea of the bond by which they were believed to be connected.

The Biblical genealogies, too, are often inconsistent among themselves. They show,

for example, that the population of southern Judah, so far from being "Israelite," was half Edomite, and several of the clans in this district bear names that indicate their original affinity to Midian or Edom. Moreover, it is known that there was a free intermixture of races, and many cities had Canaanite (i.e. pre–Israelite) populations that must have been gradually absorbed by the Israelites.

The desire to prove the continuity of the race, enforced by the experience of the exile, gave the impetus to the Israelites' genealogical zeal, and many of the extant lists proceed from this age when the true historical succession of names was simply a memory of the past. This applies with special force to the lists in Chronicles that present finished schemes of the Levitical divisions next to earlier attempts at creating a consistent genealogy.

Much of the genealogical data is intricate, and it is difficult to explain the division of sons among the four wives of Jacob as found in Genesis 34 and elsewhere. These are the sons of Leah, who were Reuben, Simeon, Levi, Judah (south Palestine), Issachar, and Zebulun (in the north); of Leah's maid Zilpah, who are Gad, and Asher (east and north Palestine); of Rachel, who are Joseph, Manasseh, Ephraim (central Palestine) and Benjamin; and the sons of Rachel's maid, Bilhah, who are Dan and Naphtali. It was not until the Deuteronomic reformation (about 639–609 B.C.) that the spirit of religious exclusiveness that marks later Judaism became prominent. It is under this influence that the writings began to emphasize the importance of maintaining the purity of Israelite blood.

In the time of Josephus (A.D. 37?–100?) every priest was supposed to be able to prove his descent, and perhaps from the time of Ezra (458 or 397 B.C.) downwards lists were carefully kept. But when Anna is called an Asherite (Luke 2:36), or Paul a Benjamite (Romans 11:1), family tradition was probably the sole support to the claim. The genealogies of Jesus in two of the gospels are intended to prove that he was a son of David. But for the book of Matthew, he is traced back to Abraham, the father of the Jews, while in Luke he, as the second Adam, is traced back to the first man. These two lists are hopelessly inconsistent, not just because one of them follows the line of Mary, but because they represent independent attempts to establish an ancestral record for Jesus.

Studies of Biblical genealogies have a long history and can be found in many theological tomes, Bible concordances, and reader's guides to Biblical literature. But, as a source of material for professional genealogists, these records have proved to be relatively useless.

Biographical Dictionaries, which generally contain particulars about well-known or successful people and sometimes the not-so-famous, can provide helpful genealogical information about a person's birth, family, occupation, education, achievements, and residence. They provide only brief, basic facts, yet in doing so can point the researcher in the direction of more comprehensive sources. And they are easy to use because they are usually one-volume works arranged alphabetically by last names. Some, however, such as *Who's Who in Education*, are multi-volume sets. One can find such dictionaries in most library reference sections where there are also encyclopedias and other types of dictionaries. Some of the best-known biographical dictionaries include *Appleton's Cyclopedia of American Biography* (1887) and the *Dictionary of American Biography* (1928). Over 95 different examples of these types of dictionaries are listed in *The Biography and Genealogy Master Index*, published in 1975.

One popular volume is the *Merriam Webster's Biographical Dictionary*, first printed in 1943; it includes data on famous people from all countries and all times, but no living individuals. Many other biographical dictionaries are equally helpful. For persons recently deceased it may be better to consult the *Reader's Guide*, the obituaries in the *World Almanac* of the year following his or her death, or *Facts on File* of the same year as the person's death.

Volumes beginning with the words "who's who" are usually considered to be biographical dictionaries. They cover many fields, including American law, American women, American education, emerging leaders in America, entertainment, American nursing, finance and industry, science and engineering, religion, and various regions of America — the South and Southwest, East, Midwest, and the West.

Since the development of the Internet, anyone with computer access can go online to find much of the same information that is in most of these dictionaries without having to go to a library. The Arts and Entertainment Network's Biography.com, for example, supplies brief biographies for more than 25,000 individuals. Many of their entries are drawn from the *Cambridge Dictionary of American Biography* (1995). Saur's World Biographical Index, which can be read in either English or German, delivers access to more than 2.5 million biographies of persons in America and the rest of the world. Galenet.com makes this service available in its Literary Index, which includes 130,000 biographical profiles of authors from its printed series, *Contemporary Authors* and *Dictionary of Literary Biography*. Such Websites often restrict access to individuals or institutions subscribing to them for a fee.

The above Websites can yield the basic facts, but for essays and life histories beyond birth and death dates, searchers will usually need to turn to other subscription services, including the Wilson Biographies Plus Illustrated site and the Cambridge Biographical Encyclopedia and Oxford's American National Biography sites. It is likely that the future will bring many more subscription service sites to the World Wide Web. *See also* **Who's Who**.

Birth Records provide nodal points in the compiling of any genealogy. Where they are proven, they clearly document the existence of the persons named. Their details can be obtained from civil registrations, church records, parish registers, family Bibles, newspaper notices, death certificates, headstones, marriage certificates, ship records, and even the birth certificates of siblings. Official birth certificates contain information probably furnished by the parents but not always filed by them. This is one reason why a researcher can find a father's or mother's name given in several different ways on the birth records of his or her several children.

With a verified date and place of birth, as it appears on a civil birth certificate, the researcher can use this data as a clue to persons in the previous generation (father, uncle, etc.) as well as the names of siblings and cousins. Such a record also provides a benchmark from which to find the marriage record, list of children, and death date for the named individual.

To obtain a facsimile copy of any birth certificate in the United States, one must write or go to the vital statistics office in the state or area where the birth occurred. The small fees for this service vary according to the location. One should remember that county offices have limited personnel and genealogical queries are done as a service that is outside of the realm of responsibility for the vital statistics officials. They are often swamped with paperwork, so it may take some time before the information can be located and relayed.

In making requests for such official birth certificates, one should ask for no more than two names at once and should provide a self-addressed stamped envelope for the reply. The requestor should also provide as much of the following information as possible: full name of person (last name in caps): sex of that person; date of birth; place of birth (city or town, county, state, and name of the hospital, if known); mother's maiden name; father's name; relationship to the requestor; purpose for which the record is needed; requestor's name and address; requestor's driver's license number and state (some counties require this); and the requestor's signature. If an exact date is unknown, one should specify the span of years to be searched and be prepared to pay extra for searches through several years. It is helpful also to include all the names that may have been used by the said individual, including nicknames, alternate spellings, etc.

As one might imagine, access to birth records is somewhat more difficult to obtain than it usually is for death or marriage records. This is because birth records are sometimes used fraudulently by others, and because birth records may contain confidential information, such as illegitimacy, about individuals. *See also* **Vital Records.**

Bolivian Genealogy, like that in most other South American countries, has devoted followers. There is also one Bolivian historical and genealogical institution, the Instituto Boliviano de Genealogía in La Paz. Civil registration of births, marriages, and deaths, however, did not begin in this country until the middle of 1940. As early as 1898 some marriages were being performed by the notaries public, and after 1910 the government passed a law that required all marriages to be performed by them. Prior to that, the marriages had been conducted only in churches and copies of the parish registers for such events were used for legal purposes.

A bill passed by the government in 1945 required all persons in Bolivia, regardless of age, to be registered with the civil authorities. The information that was collected is quite complete and probably the best in any civil registry in Latin America. It is stored in the general archive of civil registration in La Paz. Each state also has its own archives.

Most of the Bolivian census records are no longer in that country, but can be found in foreign repositories, such as those of Argentina, Chile, Paraguay, Peru, and even Spain. The largest collection of Bolivian census records is at the National Archives in Buenos Aires, Argentina. There is, however, a National Archives of Bolivia in La Paz, and in the same building is the National Library, both of which have some genealogical records.

The parish registers of the Roman Catholic Church have been maintained since the founding of Bolivia, though most of the earlier ones have been destroyed or have disappeared. These can be found at the individual parishes. The diocesan archives in La Paz, however, contain some records of the old padrones, or masters, that have good genealogical information. These archives also contain some local census records.

The Archivo y Biblioteca Nacional in Sucre has the records of the four notaries that functioned in that city in its earliest days. Most of the later records are in the offices of the various other notaries. These types of documents are of little value in Bolivia as far as the majority Indian population is concerned because they seldom, if ever, use such services.

Books on genealogy and family history number in the thousands and range from simple how-to books such as *Collecting Dead Relatives* all the way to specialist manuals such as *Bullinger's Postal and Shippers Guide for the United States and Canada*, far too many to list here. But some of the most useful ones are the following:

African American Genealogical Research: How to Trace Your Family History, by Harry Bradshaw Matthews. Baldwin, NY: Matthews Heritage Services, 1992 — a guide to African-American genealogy.

The American Genealogical-Biographical Index, 181 volumes, edited by Fremont J. Rider. Middletown, CT: Godfrey Memorial Library, 1942–1952, and 1952–present, an alphabetical listing of individual names found in several hundred family histories, newspapers and magazines, and the 1790 federal census.

Ancestral Trails: The Complete Guide to British Genealogy and Family History, by Mark D. Heber. Baltimore: Genealogical Publishing Company, 1997 — a well-researched guide to British genealogical research.

Biography and Genealogy Master Index, by Mirana C. Herbert and Barbara McNeil. Detroit: Gale Research Company, 1980–; tool for locating information and references to more than eight million notable people.

Complete Idiot's Guide to Genealogy, by Christine Rose and Kay Ingalls. Fort Smith, AR: Alpha Books, 1997 — a fully comprehensive book for beginners in genealogy.

County Courthouse Book, by Elizabeth Petty Bentley. Baltimore: Genealogical Publishing Company, 1995 — describes the court system in each state and gives addresses and whom to contact in the various courthouses.

Discovering Your Immigrant & Ethnic Ancestors, by Saron DeBartolo Carmack. Cincinnati: Betterway Books, 2000 — a sourcebook for those in the United States who have various ethnic backgrounds.

Encyclopedia of American Family Names, by H. Amanda Robb and Andrew Chesler. New York: Harper Collins Publishers, 1995 — lists some 5,000 surnames and the genealogies that have been published by the families.

Finding Our Fathers: A Guidebook in Jewish Genealogy, by Dan Rottenberg. Baltimore: Genealogical Publishing Co., 1986 — a guide to Jewish heritage, including a listing of some 8,000 Jewish family names with clues where to find further information.

Genealogical Researching in the National Archives of the United States, 3rd edition, by Anne Bruner Eales and Robert M. Kvasnicka. Washington, D.C.: National Archives, 2000 — a listing of the records that can be located at the National Archives in Washington, D.C., and at the various National Archive Centers.

Genealogist Companion and Sourcebook, by Emily Croom. Cincinnati: Betterway Books, 1994 — a how-to genealogy book with a good list of source materials.

The Genealogist's Address Book, by Elizabeth Petty Bentley. Baltimore: Genealogical Publishing Company, 1991— a list of the addresses of national and state archives libraries and genealogical societies, as well as ethnic and religious organization research centers.

The Genealogist's Encyclopedia, by L.G. Pine (former editor of *Burke's Peerage*). New York: Weybrights and Talley, 1969 — mainly concerns British genealogical research as well as a history of genealogy in Europe, with sections on heraldry and the clan system.

Genealogy, the Internet and Your Genealogy Computer Program, by Karen Clifford. Baltimore: Genealogical Publishing Company, 2001— basic principles of genealogy as related to computers; includes many charts and forms that can be downloaded from Websites.

Genealogy Online, by Elizabeth Powell Crowe. New York: McGraw-Hill, 2000 — deals with ways to use the computer and the Internet in doing genealogical research.

Guide to Genealogical Research in the National Archives, by the National Archives and Records Service. Washington, D.C.: National Archives, 1983 — a listing of documents available in Washington and other National Archives centers in the U.S.

The Handybook for Genealogists: United States of America. Draper, UT: Everton Publishers, 2002 — a listing of documents available state by state, and county by county.

International Vital Records Handbook, by Thomas Jay Kemp. Baltimore: Genealogical Publishing Company — useful addresses for vital records information overseas.

The Library of Congress: A Guide to Genealogical and Historic Research, by James C. Neagles. Salt Lake City: Ancestry, 1990 — a review of materials available at the Library of Congress.

Native American Genealogical Sourcebook, by Paula K. Byers. Detroit: Gale Research Inc., 1995 — a guide to Native American genealogy.

Printed Sources: A Guide to Published Genealogical Records, by Kory Meyerink. Salt Lake City: Ancestry, 1998 — a comprehensive listing of printed materials.

The Researcher's Guide to American Genealogy, by Val D. Greenwood. Baltimore: Genealogical Publishing Company, 1973 — an extensive listing of genealogical records and their use.

Searching for Your Ancestors, by Gilbert H. Doane and James B. Bell. Minneapolis: University of Minnesota Press, 1908 — an excellent guide to genealogical research that includes data on a number of other countries as well as the United States.

The Source: A Guidebook of American Genealogy, by Loretto Dennis Szucs and Sandra Hargreaves Luebking. Salt Lake City: Ancestry, 1997 — a well-researched listing of genealogical sources, primarily in the United States.

Virtual Roots: A Guide to Genealogy and Local History on the World Wide Web, by Thomas Jay Kemp. Wilmington, DE: Scholarly Resources Inc., 1997 — a listing of Websites throughout the world where genealogical data can be found.

See also books listed elsewhere under state and other entries.

Boolean Searching *see* **Computer Search Engines**

Bosnia and Herzegovinia *see* **Eastern European Genealogy**

Bounty Land Warrants were authorized by the Continental Congress early in the American Revolution and later by Congress at the beginning of the War of 1812, during the Indian wars, and at the beginning of the Mexican War. These were certificates for free public land, authorized as an incentive to persuade men to volunteer for armed service. The bounties provided during the American Revolution were for $50, 50 acres of land, and a new suit of clothes. At the time there was little money to pay the troops, and this was a logical alternative. In addition to the promises of the Continental Congress, various states also provided bounty land to the veterans, reserving tracts in their western territories to make good on these pledges. Connecticut, for example, reserved a section of land in northeastern Ohio that is known as the Western Reserve. The lands that Congress provided during the War of 1812 were situated in special districts of Arkansas, Illinois, and Missouri.

Many of the veterans sold their warrants for scrip certificates because, until 1830, these warrants could only be used to obtain land within the Ohio Military District where they did not wish to live. With scrip the veterans could purchase land anywhere in the public domain. The records of these surrendered warrants, which are now kept at the National Archives in Washington, D.C., give the warrantee's name as well as the names of any heirs who might be filing a claim on behalf of the warrantee and the heir's relationship to that warrantee, as well as their places of residence and the date the warrant was surrendered. Unfortunately many of the records filed prior to 1800 were destroyed in a fire that occurred at the War Department, but lists identifying 14,737 of the applicants whose papers were thus destroyed are viewable at the National Archives. All the remaining bounty land warrant applications for those who claimed land based on their Revolutionary War service have been interfiled with the pension applications at the National Archives.

In an act of Congress passed in 1855, bounty lands were provided for every soldier (or their heirs) who had served for at least 14 days in any of the previous wars, including the American Revolution. This act was unique because the bounty lands were a reward to all soldiers who had served and were not inducements for enlistment. The amount of land provided in each of these bounty warrants was 160 acres.

The kind of information included in the bounty-land applications made after 1855 was usually the name of the warrantee, age, residence, rank, unit of the army or navy, and period of military service. If the applicant happened to be an heir, the record contains the date and place of death of the veteran and the relationship of the applicant to that veteran.

Besides the records of the bounty land warrants issued by Congress, the National Archives has an indexed volume of the warrants issued during the American Revolution by the state of Virginia, entitled the *Virginia Military Warrants, Continental Line.* Virginia provided the great bulk of fighting men in the Revolution, and the first bounty lands designated as such by that state were to be located among the Mississippi, Ohio, and the Green Rivers in what is now Kentucky. However, that area did not provide enough land, and so the Virginia Military Tract was established in what is now the state of Ohio. Continental Army soldiers from Virginia were the only ones allowed to settle in that Ohio area, while other Virginia soldiers were allowed to settle on the lands in Kentucky.

For nearly a century the business of bounty lands was a large enterprise in the United States. There were firms established solely for the purpose of handling bounty land warrants for applicants. These could be assigned to others, but the original applicant was required to apply for the warrant before an assignment could take place. Since many soldiers claimed a portion of bounty land, but promptly sold it once the warrant was issued, one should not conclude that the individual moved to that location unless other records support such an hypothesis.

The National Archives also holds the records of Canadian Refugee Warrants and Canadian Volunteer Warrants. These documents cover Canadians who were "refugees" from Canada and assisted in the American efforts during the Revolution or served during the War of 1812. Of the two types of Canadian warrants, the Volunteer Warrants generally provide more genealogical information.

There were no bounty land warrants issued for service in the Civil War, but veterans of this conflict were given special consideration in the Homestead legislation of 1862. *See also* **Homestead Act.**

Brazilian Genealogy records can be found in abundance at the National Archives (Arquivo Nacional) in Rio de Janeiro. These archives are well organized and Brazilian authorities have published many reports about the holdings in their various collections. In Brazil there are 3,700 municipalities, each with a civil registry office (Registro Civil) where the birth, death, or marriage records are maintained. Duplicate copies are sent to the judicial and state archives in the various states. The law requiring the registration of births and deaths throughout the country was passed in 1850, but the government has accepted marriages in the Catholic Church from as early as 1827.

Brazil has a rich and proud heritage, and it is not difficult for most Brazilians to do research on their ancestry. However, few Brazilians can trace their lines back into the colonial period of the early 1800s and before, or further back into the countries of their family origins—Portugal, Germany, Italy, Russia, and Japan. Yet there are many genealogical and biographical publications in Brazil's archives and libraries. Such sources include state libraries and archives; civil, military, and church repositories; genealogical, heraldic, and historical institutes; as well as private collections. Another important place to find family history records is the National Museum of History in Rio de Janeiro.

The National Archives has a collection of legislative and judicial records that includes an index of the names (more than 40,000 individuals) found in these documents that relate to wills, orphans, divorces, property matters, etc. The archives also has an extensive collection of immigration records listed on cards that fill some 30 drawers. These records give detailed information about the immigrants, mainly Portuguese.

Census enumerations in Brazil have primarily been conducted only for their statistical value, and were generally destroyed once this data was compiled. Some local censuses have been preserved and can be found in regional archives. There were a few ecclesiastical censuses that are located in diocesan archives.

One of the most interesting collections of Catholic records is that compiled by the Colégio Basileiro de Genealogia in Rio de Janeiro. This is a collection of parish records of some 160,000 marriages, as well as births, deaths, and information about children between 1616 and 1900. Brazil has been relatively tolerant of religions other than Catholicism, and one can find communities of Protestants, Jews, Eastern Orthodox Catholics, Buddhists, Shintoists, Moslems, Marionites, and even various religious cults imported from Africa that thrive among the Black communities of the Rio and Bahia areas. However, many of these religious groups keep only scanty records. To locate them, one must contact the individual religious centers.

Brazil's Catholic churches contain many tombs of famous Brazilians. In a crypt within the cathedral of Rio de Janeiro lies Pedro Albares Cabral, the discoverer of Brazil, and at the convent of Santa Antonio, also in Rio de Janeiro, there are tombs of some of the members of the royal family. The cemeteries attached to the many coastal area churches established during the colonial period may provide good information for the genealogist. Non-Catholic cemeteries in Brazil can also be important sources of data for the researcher.

The first notarial records in Brazil date from 1549. These and all the others adjudi-cated since can be found in the public archives (arquivas públicos) throughout the cities and states of Brazil. No inventories or published catalogs exist for these records, although some do have card indexes.

Many prominent Brazilian families have produced family histories that include genealogical information, biographies, photographs, and other useful information. These histories usually cover several generations of a family. A number of them have been published and can be found in various libraries in Brazil. A listing of them can be found in the 10-volume *Índices Genealógicos Brasileiros* (Indexes of Brazilian Genealogies) by Salvador de Moya, published by the Instituto Genealógico Brasileiro in São Paulo. This book can be located in many of the large libraries in Brazil. Unpublished family histories are held by private individuals in Brazil. They pertain mostly to descendants of prominent families and Brazilian nobility. Such materials are generally inaccessible for research unless one can establish contact with the appropriate individuals.

Brethren Records can be found in a number of denominational libraries and churches in Pennsylvania, Ohio, and various farm communities in other states. This Protestant religious denomination, known officially as the Church of the Brethren, developed from the Pietistic-Anabaptist movement in Germany of the 1600s and 1700s. The members were persecuted by the state church in Germany because they rejected its emphasis on ritual, refused to take oaths, and refused to fight in wars. They also believe that the baptismal ceremony requires a believer to be dipped three times, each time at the mention of a part of the Trinity according to the baptismal formula found in Matthew 28:19. Thus the members are also known as Dunkers or Dunkards (from German *tunken*, "to dip"). They emigrated to the United States between 1719 and 1740, settling first in Pennsylvania.

There are now about 1,000 Brethren churches in the United States. Besides supporting an active missionary movement, the denomination now supports a number of colleges, notably Ashland College, at Ashland,

Ohio. There are also some smaller offshoot denominations such as the Seventh Day Baptists, the National Fellowship of Brethren Churches, and the Plymouth Brethren.

Beyond the local churches, Brethren records can be found at the Brethren Historical Library and Archives in Elgin, Illinois (the official repository for the denomination); the United Brethren Historical Center in Huntington, Indiana; and the Alexander Mack-Memorial Library in Bridgewater, Virginia. There is also a three-volume, 2,126 page encyclopedia of Brethren history and practices that was compiled in 1983–1984. A fourth volume is in preparation. It contains more than 230 articles on family history, with extensive listings, indexes, biographies, illustrations, and brief histories of local churches. Brethren members with an interest in family history have their own genealogical society, the Fellowship of Brethren Genealogists, that publishes a quarterly journal, *Brethren Roots*.

Britain see **English Genealogy; Irish Genealogy; Scottish Genealogy; Welsh Genealogy.**

British Columbia Records of births, marriages, and deaths have been registered with the provincial government ever since 1872, and there are even some marriage and baptismal records that go back as far as 1859. But as with most provincial registration beginnings, records from the early years are notoriously incomplete. This province is Canada's third largest, and Britain established a colony here on Vancouver Island in 1849. At that time much of the area was populated by the Athabaskan, Haida, Kwakiutl, Nootka, and Tsimshian Indian tribes. Gold strikes near the Frasier River in the late 1850s brought hordes of prospectors into British Columbia, but most of them left after the gold ran out. Today more than half of the residents live in the Vancouver-Victoria region in the southwest corner of the province.

The British Columbia Vital Statistics Agency in Victoria has recently published a 124-page guide to assist family history researchers in their quest for genealogical materials. Titled *Genealogical Resources for British Columbians*, this guide can be purchased from the agency for a modest fee, or it can be viewed at most public, college, and university libraries in the province. This agency has records of the births, marriages, and deaths in British Columbia. The law prohibits access to these birth registrations if they are less than one hundred years old. The viewable marriage registrations are available about those married 75 years ago or earlier, and the viewable death registrations are available about those who died 20 years ago or earlier.

The Vital Statistics Agency is also where one may find the adoption records. These records, however, can only be obtained by the birth parents after the adopted person has reached 19 years of age or by adopted persons who are 19 years of age or older. A guide published by the agency outlines the steps needed to file an "Application for Service Pertaining to an Adopted Person or Birth Parent Form."

In Victoria is also the British Columbia Archives, where there is an index of the vital records that are located at the Vital Statistics Agency, as well as index of data relating to the deaths of 3,423 British Columbians who died overseas in World War II. The official certificates can be found at the Vital Statistics Agency. The Archives has eight volumes of pre-confederation marriage records. These are the marriages that took place in the two colonies of British Columbia and Vancouver Island from 1859 to 1872 (the two were united in 1866) prior to the entry of British Columbia into the Confederation of Canada. The volumes contain certified copies of marriage certificates, or returns of marriages, that were submitted by the clergy of various denominations.

Other records at the British Columbia Archives that should be of interest to genealogical researchers include the wills probated in the province between 1861 and 1981, as well as the probate case files and other probate records for persons who died with or without a will. There is furthermore a collection of coroner's inquests from 1859 to 1967 and coroner's inquiries from 1859 to 1970. There is also a large collection of newspapers on microfilm, although the major 20th-century Vancouver papers are not available here. They can be accessed at most university and public libraries in the province. Another source of genealogical information in the city of Victoria is the Victoria City Archives.

At all the above sites one can find information regarding persons who entered British Columbia by sea from ships' passenger lists and newspaper sailing reports. These lists are catalogued from 1856 to 1858 (the period of the gold rush) and from 1908 to 1918.

In the city of Vancouver the researcher can find some of the above data and other documents of genealogical interest at the Vancouver City Archives, as well as at the Archives Association of British Columbia and the Vancouver Public Library. Vancouver is also the site of the Provincial Supreme Court that has jurisdiction over all divorces granted in the province. This body maintains those records. Divorces in all of the Canadian provinces are granted only infrequently and then only for a restricted list of reasons.

Land and various other records can be found in the court houses at Kamloops (Yale County), Nelson (Kootenay County), New Westminster (Westminster County), Prince George (Cariboo County), Prince Rupert (Prince Rupert County), Vancouver (Vancouver County), and Victoria (Victoria County). There are other counties in British Columbia but they are not record-keeping jurisdictions. *See also* **Census, Canadian.**

British Genealogy *see* **English Genealogy**

Browser *see* **Computer Genealogy Files**

Bulgarian Records *see* **Eastern European Genealogy**

Burial Records *see* **Cemeteries**

Burke's Peerage is the name commonly given to a book that contains the names of all the peers and baronets of Great Britain. It is also the name of a publishing company that now specializes in books on ancestry, aristocracy, history, and volumes on the aristocracy and imperial and royal families of the world. The original book was titled *Genealogical and Heraldic Dictionary of the Peerage and Baronetage of the United Kingdom.* It has been updated and republished every year since the first 1826 edition designed by the Irishman John Burke.

Besides publishing books, the company locates and researches titles that may be acquired for its clients. These titles are mainly English, Scottish, French, and Irish. The Scottish titles must be approved and recognized by the Queen's representative, the Lord Lyon, in Scotland. The English titles are registered at the College of Arms in London, and the French titles have their coats of arms registered with the Heraldry Society of France (Conseil Francais d'héradique). All American presidents since George Washington have been researched by Burke's Peerage and are included in the company's *Burke's Presidential Families of the USA.* The company representatives have designed coats of arms for President George W. Bush, former President William Clinton and his vice president, Albert Gore, as well as for South African President Nelson Mandela.

Business Clubs *see* **Societies and Fraternal Organizations**

C

Calendar Variations *see* **Date Variations**

California Records begin with the Spanish exploration of San Diego Bay in 1542, but they do not have much genealogical interest until about the time of the California gold rush in 1849. The territory became a state in 1850, and 1850 was also the year of the first national census that was taken there. Prior to the arrival of the first Europeans in California, many Indian tribes lived in the most fertile parts of the territory. Then in 1769 the area began to be colonized by Spaniards, who made it a province of Mexico in 1822. Several forts for fur-trading purposes were also established by Russians along the ocean coast. It was not until 1848, following the Mexican War, that California became a part of the United States.

A special California census was conducted in 1852, the only one undertaken just by the state. An indexed copy is in the California State Library at Sacramento. Some special local censuses were later done for statistical reasons, but they do not provide access by name, nor were they done for the entire state. The national censuses of California, taken every 10 years from 1850 on, can be seen at the various National Archives locations. Also in the State Library is a copy of the 1890 California Great Register of Voters Index, a three-volume set. This statewide alphabetically-arranged index of all the registered male voters at that time is particularly useful since the records for the 1890 census in California were destroyed by a fire at the Commerce Department in Washington, D.C. The voter's registration, however, is limited in genealogical usefulness since it only lists names and gives no information about ages or family members. The State Library also has microfilm listings of registered voters that cover 1866 to 1898 and 1900 to 1944. The listings from 1946 to date are on file in the various county registrars of voters offices.

Hubert H. Bancroft's *California Pioneer Register and Index, 1542–1848, Including Inhabitants of California, 1769–1800, and List of Pioneers* (Baltimore: Regional Pub. Co., 1964) can be found in many libraries, both in California and elsewhere; it includes an extensive list of pioneers and early settlers in the state. The *Guide to Public Vital Statistics Records in California* (two vols.) covers birth and death records. Both volumes were published in 1941 by the Work Projects Administration and are available in several libraries of the state. Many later personages of note can be found in the biographical dictionaries *Who's Who in the West* and *Who's Who in California*.

Many California libraries contain printed or microfilmed editions of county histories, most of which have biographical indexes. Some libraries have Parker J. Carlyle's *An Index*

to the Biographies in 19th Century California County Histories, published in 1979. This book can also be obtained from the California State Library through an interlibrary loan. San Francisco newspaper indexes at the State Library contain approximately three million entries about California people, places, subjects, and events. *The San Francisco Chronicle* index covers the years 1950 to 1985, and the *San Francisco Call* index goes back to 1894.

Birth and death records since 1905 are stored at the Office of Vital Records in Sacramento, where copies can be obtained for a modest fee, while marriage records prior to July 1, 1905, are available from the county recorders and the health departments in many of the larger cities. The vital records for California are also scattered through a series of collected newspaper accounts and gravestone listings that can be found in the State Library as well as in several other genealogical libraries in California. There are, for example, listings of vital records from 1854 to 1874 in the San Francisco newspapers *Daily Alta California*, *Golden Era*, *San Francisco Bulletin*, and *Wide West*. There are also separate listings of birth records from San Francisco in 1900, 1901, 1904, 1905, and half of 1906. There are birth, marriage, and death records from the *Los Angeles Daily Times* from 1881 to 1886, as well as from the Sacramento Union from 1859 to 1886.

Marriage records for Sonoma County from 1843 to 1889, Stanislaus County from 1854 to 1906, and Los Angeles County from 1877 to 1885 and 1888 are also in the State Library, with indexes on microfiche for 1949 to 1959, 1960 to 1965, 1970 to 1979, 1980 to 1985, and 1986, one set for brides and one for grooms. Divorces and guardianships are granted by the various county superior courts, which preserved these records.

The cemetery records that have been compiled and which give the death dates are in 18 volumes, and include some found in the counties of Alpine, Amador, Butte, Calaveras, Colusa, Contra Costa, El Dorado, Fresno, Glenn, Humboldt, Inyo, Lassen, Los Angeles, Marin, Merced, Mono, Napa, Placer, Plumas, Riverside, San Diego, San Francisco, San Joaquin, San Mateo, Santa Barbara, Santa

Cruz, Sierra, Siskiyou, Solano, Stanislaus, Tehama, Tulare, and Yuba, as well as the cities of Kernville, Livermore, Lompoc, Redwood City, and Sacramento.

California wills are filed in the superior courts of the various counties. There are listings of early California wills in the State Library for Butte, Kern, Los Angeles, Placer, San Diego, Santa Clara, Shasta, Solano, Tehama, Trinity, and Yuba Counties. The library also has a California death index (1905–1995) and California bride and groom indexes (1949–1986). The official certificates are obtainable from the Health Data and Statistics Branch of the California Department of Health Services in Sacramento. Records for matters of law can be found in the various county superior courts, while the land records are maintained by the county recorders.

Researchers into the genealogical records of California may also consult the California State Archives in Sacramento, which has some census records for major California cities from 1897 to 1938; the State Genealogical Society in San Francisco, and the University of California at Berkeley, which has an extensive collection of historical and genealogical materials.

Researchers seeking information from county records can locate them at the following County seats: (Alameda County) Oakland, (Alpine County) Markleeville, (Amador County) Jackson, (Butte County) Oroville, (Calaveras County) San Andreas, (Colusa County) Colusa, (Contra Costa County) Martinez, (Del Norte County) Crescent City, (El Dorado County) Placerville, (Fresno County) Fresno, (Glenn County) Willows, (Humboldt County) Eureka, (Imperial County) El Centro, (Inyo County) Independence, (Kern County) Bakersfield, (Kings County) Hanford, (Lake County) Lakeport, (Lassen County) Susanville, (Los Angeles County) Los Angeles, (Madera County) Madera, (Marin County) San Rafael, (Mariposa County) Mariposa, (Mendocino County) Ukiah, (Merced County) Merced, (Modoc County) Alturas, (Mono County) Bridgeport, and (Monterey County) Salinas.

Also at (Napa County) Napa, (Nevada County) Nevada City, (Orange County) Santa Ana, (Placer County) Auburn, (Plumas County) Quincy, (Riverside County) Riverside, (Sacramento County) Sacramento, (San Benito County) Hollister, (San Bernardino County) San Bernardino, (San Diego County) San Diego, (San Francisco County) San Francisco, (San Joaquin County) Stockton, (San Luis Obispo County) San Luis Obispo, (San Mateo County) Redwood City, (Santa Barbara County) Santa Barbara, (Santa Clara County) San Jose, (Santa Cruz County) Santa Cruz, (Shasta County) Redding, (Sierra County) Downieville, (Siskiyou County) Yreka, (Solano County) Fairfield, (Sonoma County) Santa Rosa, (Stanislaus County) Modesto, (Sutter County) Yuba City, (Tehama County) Red Bluff, (Trinity County) Weaverville, (Tulare County) Visalia, (Tuolumne County) Sonora, (Ventura County) Ventura, (Yolo County) Woodland, and (Yuba County) Marysville.

For FURTHER INFORMATION SEE:
- Nicklas, Laurie. *The California Locator: A Directory of Public Records for Locating People Dead or Alive in California.* Modesto, CA: Laurie Nicklas, 1994.
- Pompey, Sherman L. *Genealogical Records of California.* Fresno, CA: Sherman L. Pompey, 1968.

Canadian Genealogy *see* under names of individual provinces.

Cartographic Records *see* **Maps**

Catalogs, Library *see* **Online Library Catalogs**

Catholic Records *see* **Roman Catholic Records**

CDs *see* **Compact Disks**

Cemeteries with tombstone inscriptions provide a wide variety of genealogical information, and in some cases they may offer the only way to determine the name of a female family member. Prior to the 1850 census, such a person would have been recorded in the census just as "female 5–10 years of age." Of course, thousands of people have been buried in unmarked graves, and in spite of laws to protect cemeteries, many of the graves have been bulldozed to make way for highways, parking lots, and office buildings. Existing cemeteries fall into five categories: 1) church-yard cemeteries where members are buried on the church grounds; 2) church-owned ceme-teries not adjacent to a church building; 3) government cemeteries owned by a town, county, state, or national government; 4) pri-vately-owned cemeteries operated as business enterprises; and 5) a family cemetery often located in a small corner of the family farm or estate.

Where tombstones are standing, they may be inscribed with such terse informa-tion as "Our Baby" or "Little Ned, age 4." One for five-year-old Milly Gaylord reads "Soon ripe; soon rotten. Soon dead, but not forgotten." Fortunately there are also many stones that give the first and last years of a person's life: "Adam Smith, 1865–1922." But the best information is gained from tomb-stones that give the person's full name with the day, month, and year of birth and the same for the year of death. Examples in a cemetery in Madison County, Idaho, read "James Eckersell, Aug. 5, 1839–Mar. 6, 1917," and "Melissa Henry Smith, born July 11, 1827, Wood Co., Virginia, died June 15, 1896."

One of the most informative tomb-stones is the one erected for Nathaniel Ward in Salem, Massachusetts. It reads,

> In this grave are deposited the remains of Nathaniel Ward, A.M., late librarian of Harvard College, whom a penetrating genius, improved by an extensive acquaintance with the liberal arts and sciences, rendered superior to most, his native good sense and literary accomplish-ments attracted universal notice, while his amiable disposition and social virtues, espe-cially his singular frankness and undissembled benevolence, gained him the esteem and love of all. He was a dutiful son and affectionate brother, a faithful friend and agreeable com-panion. A sincere piety towards God crowned his other virtues and promised a life eminently useful. But a blasted hope in the vigor of youth, amidst happy prospects, cut off by a raging fever, he breathed forth his soul.

The above is followed by the full dates of Ward's birth and death.

If the location of a graveyard is difficult to find or unknown, one can consult county and local histories, church registers, chambers of commerce, city hall personnel, newspaper obituaries, and anyone who might know or know whom to ask. Maps of most localities from the U.S. Government Geological Survey have sufficient detail to pinpoint even tiny graveyards. Some funeral directors are more than willing to help find information about individuals for whom they have performed pre-burial duties. Some funeral homes have records that go back more than 100 years. There are also repositories with indexes of cemeter-ies, such as those maintained by local chapters of the Daughters of the American Revolu-tion (DAR). These women have undertaken extensive projects in the copying of grave-stone inscriptions from many thousands of cemeteries. The Works Progress Adminis-tration (WPA) undertook similar tasks dur-ing the Great Depression of the 1930s, but not so extensively. Various genealogical so-cieties have also made such gravestone record transcriptions one of their missions.

Sextons' and caretakers' records for a well-kept graveyard may often contain more information than does a gravestone, so it is wise for the researcher to investigate these. If the inscription on a particular stone is too eroded to read, it can usually be made more legible by rubbing over it with chalk or soap-stone. Family members are often buried in groups so that the discovery of a grave site for one may lead to information about oth-ers. *See also* **Gravestones.**

Census, Ancient, representations have been found by archaeologists on Babylonian clay tablet fragments dating back to 3800 B.C. The purpose of these records was apparently to estimate forthcoming tax revenues. The Chi-nese, Egyptians, Greeks, and Hebrews are also known to have conducted censuses. It is recorded in the New Testament book of Luke, for example, that Joseph, the father of Jesus, traveled with his family to Nazareth in order to be enrolled in the census that had been ordered by Caesar Augustus.

The first census enumerations to be con-ducted at regular intervals were those de-signed by the Romans. They were lists of per-sons and property that could be used for taxation and the enforcement of military service requirements. In fact, the term "census" comes from the Latin word "censere," which means to tax. The Roman censuses were conducted every five years under the authority of local censors, who were also in charge of maintaining public morals.

After William the Conqueror took over England in 1066, he ordered that the land be taken from the English nobility and large landowners so that it could be divided among his own followers. Because William wanted to know how much land he now owned and how it was peopled, in 1085 he ordered that a survey be completed. It was finished the next year. This census, now known as the Domesday Book, was the first conducted in England, and its records have been preserved as the primary document of early English names. Many persons today claim that their family history goes all the way back to William the Conqueror because their family surname appears somewhere in the Domesday Book, not because they have complete records to verify the fact.

During the 1400s and 1500s various European cities began to count their populations. Nuremberg, Germany, did so in 1449. But it was not until the 17th century that any European nation attempted to conduct an accurate count of the entire population. Sweden was one of the first countries to do so. The government then required all the churches to keep continuous records of births, deaths, and marriages within their parish boundaries. Belgium, Finland, the Netherlands, and Scandanavia still maintain this practice.

In North America the first true census was taken in 1666 by a French official named Jean Baptiste Talon. It was a census of the colony of New France (now the province of Quebec in Canada). The United States began to take censuses every 10 years from 1790 on as one of the requirements of the Constitution. It was deemed a necessity for a democratic government to do this, and the U.S. census was the first one in which the tabulated information was made available to the public shortly after the figures had been gathered. *See also* **Census, United States; Domesday Book.**

Census, British, covers the population counts of four countries—England, Scotland, Wales, and Northern Ireland—united under one government. Northern Ireland was separated from the rest of Ireland in 1921, when that nation became two countries. The larger part then declared itself the Irish Free State in 1949.

The British census was introduced to help the government understand its population and better utilize that population in times of war. The first census was conducted in 1801 following the passage of the Census Act of 1800. The enumeration showed that in England and Wales, the population was nearly nine million while in Scotland the figure was a little over 1,600,000. (Ireland was not included until 1821, when her population was over 6,800,000.) The British census has been taken in the first year of the decade ever since (with the exception of 1941, when Britain was at war).

The administration of the early census returns 1801 to 1831 was the responsibility of the clergy and the Overseers of the Poor. Most of these early returns have been destroyed, although a few have been preserved in some isolated instances. The census returns for 1841 were the first to be kept, under the administration of the Registrar General. Besides obtaining the names and occupations of persons, the 1841 census asked if persons filling out the forms were born in the places where they were then living. The 1851 census was the first to ask where they were born. The census records of 1841, 1851, and 1861 are preserved in the Public Record Office in Kew, near London, where they can be consulted by any inquirer. This office also has indexes to the census records.

The census information is released by the Public Record Office only after a hundred years, however; the public was given access to the 1891 census returns in 1992 and to the 1901 returns in 2001. Both of these censuses provide the following information: name and surname, address, number of rooms occupied if less than five, where born, age on last birthday, marital status, relationship to head of family, profession or occupation, whether an employer or employed or neither, whether deaf or mute or blind or mentally deficient; and in Monmouthshire, Wales, what language spoken, whether English, Welsh, or both. (The 1931 census was destroyed by fire during World War II, and will never be available.)

The census records for England and Wales can be found at the Family Records Center in London. Those for Scotland are obtainable from the Register General in Edinburgh. The district libraries normally have microfilm copies of the returns for their own areas. It is wise, before making a trip to a library or record office, to check the exact whereabouts of specific census returns in order to avoid a wasted visit. Some libraries may have a limited number of microfilm viewers, so reserving one may be necessary. *See also* **Census, Irish.**

Census, Canadian, has been taken countrywide for most provinces every 10 years since 1851. The names of individuals have been followed by their ages, sex, country or province of birth, religion, racial or ethnic origin, occupation, marital status, and education. There were some earlier censuses conducted in individual provinces at various times from 1666 to 1849, but few of these are complete and they list only the heads of households. Portions of the 1851 census also have not survived. The 1901 census returns include the date of birth for each individual, year of immigration, and address or location of any land farmed.

Newfoundland did not become a province of Canada until 1949, so it was not included in the Canadian census returns of 1851 to 1901. However, separate censuses were taken there in 1921, 1935, and 1945. These records are in the custody of the Provincial Archives of Newfoundland and Labrador at St. John's, Newfoundland. The National Archives of Canada, in Ottawa, also holds microfilm copies of these returns.

The census returns acquired after 1901 (including those for Newfoundland after 1949) are closed under the Statistics Act, which contains strict confidentiality provisions that protect the information. The census records of 1901, however, have been microfilmed and are in the custody of Statistics Canada in Ottawa rather than the National Archives of Canada.

Provincial censuses taken before 1851 include those taken for Acadia, the former French province comprising most of what is now Nova Scotia. Every person there was enumerated in 1671, 1686, 1693, 1698, 1701, and 1714, while in 1703, 1707, and 1739 only the heads of households were listed. In Manitoba, censuses showing heads of families were taken in 1832, 1834, 1835, 1840, 1843, 1846, and 1849. For Newfoundland, at the time a French possession, two censuses enumerating all persons were taken in 1691 and 1693. A Newfoundland census listing that contains only the names of heads of families was completed in 1704.

Researchers can study the unindexed microfilm census returns in person at the National Archives of Canada, but workers there will not undertake any searches in response to individual requests. The microfilm copies can also be obtained for viewing in other cities through inter-institutional loan arrangements. Many libraries in Canada have microfilm copies of some or most of the census records.

In order to undertake a search of the census records, one must know the approximate locality, since the arrangement of these returns is by township or parish within each county. A provincial gazetteer, available in most libraries, is useful for finding the names of the townships or parishes within which a village is situated. There are two published listings of the census holdings that identify which of the reels holds the records for each township or parish of a particular year. These volumes are the *Catalogue of Census Returns on Microfilm, 1666–1891* and the *Catalogue of Census Returns on Microfilm, 1901.* Many libraries have copies of these two catalogues.

Fortunately indexes for some of the census returns have been compiled to make searching through them much easier. The index for the 1871 census of Ontario was compiled by the Ontario Genealogical Society and the National Archives of Canada; the index for the 1891 census of Saskatchewan was compiled by the Saskatchewan Genealogical Society; the index for the 1891 census of Prince Edward Island was compiled by the Public Archives and Records Office and the Prince Edward Island Genealogical Society; the index for the 1901 census of Alberta was compiled by the Alberta Genealogical Society, Edmonton Branch; and the index for the 1881 census of all Canada is part of the Latter Day Saints Family History Library. The latter is available on a compact disc, and can be accessed through the Internet.

Canadian census returns use abbreviations that may need explanation. Those in the "Religion" column are B.C. = Bible Church; C. (of) E. = Church of England; C. (of) S. = Church of Scotland; E.M.C. = Episcopal Methodist Church; F.C. = Free Church (Presbyterian); M.E.C. = Methodist Episcopal Church; P.C.L.P. = Presbyterian-Canada and Lower Provinces; P.F.C. = Presbyterian Free Church; R.P. = Reformed Presbyterian; U.P. = United Presbyterian; and W.M. = Wesleyan Methodist.

In the "Country or Province of Birth" column, the abbreviations are B.C. = Bas-Canada (Lower Canada, Quebec) and British Columbia in 1881 and 1891 returns; C.B. = Columbie-Britannique; C.E. = Canada East (Canada-Est, Quebec); C.W. = Canada West (Canada-Ouest, Ontario); H.C. = Haut-Canada (Upper Canada, Ontario); I.P. = Île-du-Prince-Edouard; L.C. = Lower Canada (Bas-Canada, Quebec); Man. = Manitoba; N.B. = New Brunswick; N.B. = (uncommon usage — North Britain, i.e. Scotland); N.E. = Nouvelle-Écosse; N.O. = Territoires du Nord-Ouest; N.S. = Nova Scotia; N.W. = Northwest Territories; N.W.T. = Northwest Territories; O = Ontario; Ont. = Ontario; P.E.I. = Prince Edward Island; Que. = Quebec; Q = Quebec (the Q sometimes look like an L); and U.C. = Upper Canada (Haut-Canada, Ontario).

Furthermore in the 1851 census, the abbreviation F indicates that the individual was born of Canadian parents. In the 1891 census, residential dwellings were described using letters and numbers (S2/6 indicates a stone house, two stories, six rooms, and W ½ indicates a wooden house, one story, two rooms); under "relationship to the head of the household" D = domestic and L = lodger; and

under "marital status" W = widow, Wr = widower, and x = married. In the 1901 census there are the following abbreviations in the "race" column: w = white (Caucasian), r = red (Native), b = black (African), and y = yellow (Asian); in the "racial/tribal origin" column, the use of "breed" and "half-breed" indicated a person of mixed Native and other background as noted in the following: fb = French breed, eb = English breed, sb = Scottish breed, ib = Irish breed, ob = other breed Cree, and fb = Cree and French breed.

In the case of Native people's names, the enumerators have had difficulty in rendering them into English, so that various individuals may be referred to with different spellings in the different censuses. A Native person may also be identified by a Native name in the 1881 census, by a Christian name in the 1891 census, and by taking his or her father's Christian name as a surname in the 1901 census.

One other Canadian census that deserves mention is the 1877 Indian Reserve Commission (IRC) census taken to support the findings of the federal-provincial commission inquiring into the reserve lands of British Columbia. The IRC was attempting to assign Indian reserves in British Columbia based on the land requirements of the Indian people living in various communities. The taking of this census met strong resistance from the Native population in the Okanagan area, and the results are therefore somewhat underestimated.

Census, Irish, was largely destroyed in a 1922 fire that demolished the Custom House and also burned many wills (the indexes exist) and about a third of the Anglican records. The census had been taken at regular 10-year intervals from 1821 to 1911, but the records of 1821 to 1851 were caught in the fire, and the census records for 1861 and 1871 were deliberately destroyed on government orders. The 1881 and 1891 census returns were pulped because of the paper shortages during World War I. Only the 1901 and 1911 returns of the pre–Independence Irish censuses remain intact. They escaped the fire because they were stored in the General Register Office located in Charlemont House, the present day Municipal Gallery of Art in Dublin.

Although the destruction of the census records was devastating, particularly to genealogists, there are still a number of resources that can aid one in the search for Irish ancestors. These resources include the Old Age Pensioner's Claims (1841–51) on film at the Genealogical Society in Belfast. They also include the Tithe Applotment (apportionment) Books (1823–1838), parish by parish, also on film at the Genealogical Society. There is an index to these records at both the Public Record Office in Belfast and the National Library in Dublin. Then there is Griffith's Valuation (1848–1864), a government survey of all privately held lands and buildings that was taken to determine the amount of tax that each person should pay toward support of the poor and destitute. These records exist for all of Ireland and for the most part are available at the Genealogical Society. An index by surname, parish, and county can be seen at the National Library of Ireland in Dublin. School records (c. 1850–1920) include the names of pupils, their ages, religion, occupation of parents, residence of family, and name of the school. Most of these records are indexed and are at the Public Record Offices in both Dublin and Belfast. The Genealogical Society has microfilmed many of those that are available from Northern Ireland.

There were some earlier religious censuses for certain places that were taken in the 18th century (c.1740–1766) and a complete one in 1813. However, these vary in details. Some of them include the names of the heads of household with their religious preferences, parish by parish; others just give statistics. Some of these returns are available for dioceses such as Ardagh, Armagh, Clogher, Cloyne, Connor, Cork, Derry, Dromore, Down, Elphin, Ferns, Kildare, Kilmore, Ossory, Raphoe, and Ross.

There are also several sources from which genealogical information can be derived that predate the compiling of census records, including lists of large landlords of England and Scotland who were granted land in the northern Irish counties of Cavan, Donegal, and Fer-

managh by King James I of England. The records are preserved as the Historical Manuscripts Commission Report, 4, (Hastings Mss.). There are also the 1630 lists of large landlords in Ulster, and the names of the able-bodied men that they might assemble to fight if the need arose. The lists are arranged by county, and by district within the county. The Armagh County Museum copy is available at the National Library of Ireland. The 1641 Books of Survey and Distribution record land ownership before the Cromwellian and Williamite confiscations, c.1641 and after c.1666. Those for the counties of Clare, Galway, Mayo, and Roscommon are available at the National Library. Even more comprehensive than the Books of Survey and Distribution are the records of land ownership in 1640, compiled between 1655 and 1667. These survived for 12 counties: Cork, Derry, Donegal, Dublin, Kildare, Kilkenny, Limerick, Meath, Tipperary, Tyrone, Waterford, and Wexford. The records have been published by the Irish Manuscripts Commission.

Finally there is the 1659 Pender's Census, edited and published in 1939 by Seamus Pender. It was, however, compiled by Sir William Petty, the founder of the science of statistics, and it records the names of all persons with title to land, the total numbers of English and Irish living in each townland, and the principal Irish names in each barony. All but five counties— Cavan, Galway, Mayo, Tyrone, and Wicklow — are included. The census records from this survey are available at the National Archives in Dublin.

The 1901 census gives the names of inhabitants, religion, age, sex, occupation, marital status, birthplace (country, county, or city), and information on house and property, including the name of the lease holder, as does the 1911 census, which also gives the number of years a person had been married, the total number of children born alive, and the number of children still living. Both the 1901 and 1911 censuses were undertaken under legislation that made no provision for the confidentiality of the information gathered. They were made available as public records in 1961, and are the most frequently used records at the National Archives in Dublin.

The first census following the formation of the Irish State was undertaken in 1926. This was followed by censuses in 1936 and 1946, and commencing with 1951, censuses have been undertaken at five-year intervals. The census planned for 1976, however, was cancelled at a late stage as a government economy measure. The need for up-to-date population figures resulted in a census being specially undertaken in 1979 with a restricted number of questions. This was followed in 1981 by a full census. The most recent census was carried out in 1996. The intention to conduct a 2001 census was postponed until 2002 due to the foot-and-mouth disease outbreak among cattle at that time. None of these censuses have been made public because it is now the law that they will only become available 100 years after the year in which they were enumerated.

Census, United States, is a survey taken every 10 years by the national government that records the size of the population and such information as the name, age, employment, income, race, and sex of each person in the country. There is probably no other single group of records that contain more information about the persons and families who have lived in the United States since 1790 when the first U.S. census was taken. The records of each census up through 1930 are now available for use by researchers. In order to protect the individuals enumerated, the U.S. Census Bureau keeps its records confidential for 72 years from the actual census date so that those conducted after 1930 are not yet available.

The taking of a census is one of the requirements specified by the Constitution in Article 1, Section 1, which states: "The actual Enumeration shall be made within three Years after the first Meeting of the Congress of the United States, and within every subsequent Term of ten Years, in such Manner as they shall by Law direct...." The first census, indeed, did exactly what it was designed to do. It counted the population, at least all those over 16 years of age by sex. But it did one more thing—it listed the names of all the heads of households. The same thing was done every 10 years until the 1850 census. But starting in 1850, the census contains name lists for all the members of each household.

During a population census, the bureau tries to contact each household in the United States. For this it uses two methods of questioning. In an enumerator census, which was the only type used up to 1960, interviewers go from door to door asking questions and recording the answers. In a self-enumerated census, the bureau mails census forms to businesses, households, or other survey groups. Individuals then fill out the forms and return them to the bureau. This is the method used by the bureau in recent years.

No printed forms were provided for taking the first four censuses, so there is little uniformity in the early schedules, although the data they contain was prescribed in the various census acts. Furthermore, the records on these census lists are handwritten by persons of varying penmanship and spelling skills. In examining them one often faces the problem of trying to determine what name is recorded on the page.

The counting process for the 1790 census began on August 2, 1790, and lasted about 18 months. Fewer than four million persons then lived in the United States, but they were scattered throughout a largely undeveloped country. Enumerators on horseback had to ride through the countryside to count most of the population. Many people refused to cooperate because they did not know why the government needed information about them. Even today there are still a few persons who hide from the census takers or refuse to mail in their self-enumeration forms because they fear that the government is trying to take away their freedom, or because they wish to avoid a military draft and taxes.

The results of the 1790 census were published by the federal government in the early 1900s and have since been republished privately. They fill a single 56-page volume and include records for Connecticut, Maine, Maryland, Massachusetts, New Hampshire, New York, North Carolina, and Vermont. Unfortunately the records for the remaining states at that time—Delaware, Georgia, Kentucky, New Jersey, Tennessee, and Virginia—

were burned during the War of 1812. The government has not published other census listings, but many privately published lists are available from libraries and other sources. Although the lists vary considerably in format and geographic scope, they frequently save researchers from fruitless searches and help locate a specific entry in the actual records.

There are census indexes for every state up to and including 1850, as well as for some up to and including 1880. Copies of these indexes can be found in many of the larger genealogical libraries, and some have also been put on CD-ROM disks. Beginners in the field of genealogy often make the mistake of accepting the information found in one of these indexes as being sufficient, without going to the census records themselves to extract all the other information that may be there. They forget that these indexes are only finding tools. One should remember that there are occasionally false entries created by census takers who added bogus names to increase the population count for political reasons. This happened frequently in some of the frontier areas seeking statehood status. For example, seven counties in Minnesota's 1857 territorial census had many fake names added to the census list, and in the 1880 Utah census many households gave the census takers false information to disguise polygamy.

The National Archives and Records Administration in Washington, D.C., and its various regional centers have the 1790 to 1870 records, as well as microfilm copies of the 1880 to 1930 records, which can be viewed at these centers or purchased directly from the National Archives. Practically all of the 1890 census schedules were destroyed by fire in 1921. The remaining entries are for small segments of the populations of Perry County, Alabama; the District of Columbia; Columbus, Georgia; Mound Township, Illinois; Rockford, Minnesota; Jersey City, New Jersey; Eastchester and Brookhaven Township, New York; Cleveland and Gaston Counties, North Carolina; Cincinnati and Wayne Township, Ohio; Jefferson Township, South Dakota; and Ellis, Hood, Kaufman, Rusk, and Trinity Counties, Texas.

During the 1930s and under the auspices of the Works Progress Administration (WPA) the names and other pertinent information about persons in the 1880, 1900, and 1920 censuses were copied onto file cards, alphabetized, and arranged by state according to the Soundex system. Searching for particular names in the microfilm copies of these Soundexed records is a relatively easy task. The Soundex process was also started for the 1930 census, but the WPA was disbanded before the alphabetization process could be completed. Thus only 10 states in the 1930 census were Soundexed: Alabama, Arkansas, Florida, Georgia, Louisiana, Mississippi, North Carolina, South Carolina, Tennessee, and Virginia. For the other states, one must know an exact geographical location in order to find individuals on the 1930 microfilm records.

The type of information gathered in each of the censuses can be somewhat different, and a listing of the categories used from 1790 through 1880 is as follows:

1790 — Names of heads of families; number of males in household under 16 years of age; number of males 16 and over; number of females (no age breakdown); number of free persons not members of household; number of slaves; and place of residence.

1800 — Names of heads of families; number of persons by age categories: 0–10, 10–15, 16–25, 26–44, all older; number of free persons not members of household (except for Indians who are not taxed); number of slaves; and place of residence.

1810 — Names of heads of families; number of persons by age categories: 0–10, 10–15, 16–25, 26–44, all older; number of males ages 16–18; number of free persons not members of household (except for Indians who are not taxed); number of slaves; and place of residence.

1820 — Names of heads of families; number of persons by age categories: 0–10, 10–15, 16–25, 26–44, all older; number of males ages 16–18; number of free persons listed in the age categories of under 14, 14–25, 26–44, 45 and over who are not members of household (except for Indians who are not taxed); number of slaves listed in the age categories by sex of under 14, 14–25, 26–44, 45 and over; number of foreigners not naturalized; place of residence; number of persons engaged in agriculture; number of persons engaged in commerce; and number of persons engaged in manufacturing.

1830 — Names of heads of families; number of males and females (separately) in 5-year age groups under 20 years of age; number of males and females (separately) in 10-year age groups for ages 20–99; number of males and females (separately) 100 years of age and over; number of free persons with those of color listed by sex in the age categories of under 10, 10–23, 24–35, 36–54, 55–99 and 100 or over who are not members of household; number of slaves listed in the age categories by sex of under 10, 10–23, 24–35, 36–54, 55–99 and 100 or over; number of foreigners not naturalized; number of deaf and mute enumerated separately with whites in the age groups of under 14, 14–24, and 25 and over (those of color not divided by age); number of blind (whites and those of color enumerated separately); place of residence; and total number of persons in household.

1840 — Names of heads of families; number of males and females (separately) in 5-year age groups under 20 years of age; number of males and females (separately) in 10-year age groups for ages 20–99; number of males and females (separately) 100 years of age and over; number of free persons with those of color listed by sex in the age categories of under 10, 10–23, 24–35, 36–54, 55–99 and 100 or over who are not members of household; number of slaves listed in the age categories by sex of under 10, 10–23, 24–35, 36–54, 55–99 and 100 or over; number of deaf and mute enumerated separately with whites in the age groups of under 14, 14–24, and 25 and over (those of color not divided by age); number of blind (whites and those of color enumerated separately); number of insane or "idiots" (those in public or private charge listed separately); number of persons engaged in agriculture; number of persons engaged in commerce; number of persons engaged in manufacturing and trades; number of persons engaged in mining; number of persons engaged in ocean navigation; number of engineers and persons employed in learned professions; names and ages of pensioners for Revolutionary or military service; number of persons over 21 years of age who cannot read or write; and total number of persons in household.

1850 — Name of every person in household; age of every person listed; sex of every person listed; color of every person listed (white, black, mulatto); professions for all males over 15; value of real estate owned by person; place of birth of each person; if person was married within previous year; if person attended school within previous year; if person over 20 cannot read or write; if person is deaf and mute, blind, insane, or "idiotic"; and if person was a pauper or a convict.

1860 — Name of every person in household; age of every person listed; sex of every person listed; color of every person listed (white, black, mulatto); professions for all persons over 15 (both male and female); value of real estate owned by person; value of personal estate owned by person; place of birth of each person; if person was married within previous year; if person attended school within previous year; if person over 20 cannot read or write; if person is deaf and mute, blind, insane, or "idiotic"; and if person was a pauper or a convict.

1870 — Name of every person in household; age of every person listed; sex of every person listed; color of every person listed (white, black, mulatto, Chinese, Indian); professions for all persons regardless of age or sex; value of real estate owned by person; value of personal estate owned by person; place of birth of each person; if person was married within previous year (specific month given); if person attended school within previous year; if person over 20 cannot read or write (separate columns for reading and writing); if person is deaf and mute, blind, insane, or "idiotic"; month of person's birth if within previous year; if person's father or mother was of foreign birth; and if person over 21 was a U.S. citizen; if male citizen's right to vote is denied or abridged for various reasons.

1880 — Name of every person in household; street addresses given in cities; age of every person listed; sex of every person listed;

color of every person listed (white, black, mulatto, Chinese, Indian); professions for all persons regardless of age or sex; place of birth of each person; place of birth of each person's father and mother (separately); if person was married within previous year; if person attended school within previous year; if person over 20 cannot read or write (separate columns for reading and writing); if person is deaf and mute, blind, insane, or "idiotic" (separate column for item); month of person's birth if within previous year; relationship of each person to head of family; civil condition (single, married, widowed, divorced); number of months a person was unemployed during the previous year; sickness or temporary disability of person on date of enumerator's visit; and whether a person was maimed, crippled, bedridden, or otherwise disabled.

After the United States annexed Hawaii and acquired several other possessions in 1898, as a result of the Spanish-American War, those areas were added to the regular U.S. census taken every 10 years. The 1900 and 1910 records of the territories of Hawaii, Alaska, Arizona, New Mexico, and the Oklahoma Indian territory (statehood in 1907), which were not yet states were all Soundexed. Puerto Rico, however, for which a census was conducted in 1910, is not Soundexed. The territories and possessions covered by the census and Soundex system for 1920 include the Virgin Islands, Guam, American Samoa, Puerto Rico, Panama Canal Zone, Alaska, and Hawaii.

There were also some special censuses taken at various times to meet particular needs. For example, in 1885 the federal government offered to help pay for a special census for any state that wanted to have one at that time before the taking of the next regular U.S. census. The entities that accepted this offer were Colorado, the Dakotas (still one territory at the time), Florida, Nebraska, and the New Mexico Territory. These censuses were much like the 1880 U.S. enumerations, with agriculture, industry, and mortality schedules included as well. The results are available at the National Archives in Washington, D.C.

Other special census listings that can be found at the National Archives include one for the Minnesota Territory completed in 1857, four for the Arizona Territory taken in 1864, 1866, 1867 (three counties), and 1869 (one county), and a 1907 one for Seminole County in Oklahoma that is not yet available for viewing. There is also a special census of Indians that was completed in 1880.

Besides these population schedules, the Census Bureau compiled censuses of manufacturers in 1820 and 1832, as well as censuses of those in agriculture, those in industry, and mortality schedules from 1850 to 1880. The first type is of limited use to the genealogist, but the others list the names of the persons involved, and in the case of the mortality schedules, the ages, sex, race, free or slave status, marital status, birthplace, month of death, occupation, cause of death, and number of days a person was ill. In the matter of the slaves listed, no surnames are given and the slave owner's name is not specified. *See also* **Native American Records; Soundex System.**

Central American Genealogy includes family records for the republics of Costa Rica, El Salvador, Guatemala, Honduras, Nicaragua, and Panama. In all these countries there are national archives, but little so far has been done with them regarding research into genealogy, and some of them are in disarray, with many files missing. Those who might wish to consult these records must seek special government permission and have a working knowledge of Spanish.

Costa Rica has centralized and computerized its vital records. Civil registration began here in 1888 and the records for all the provinces are relatively complete. There is also an index that is kept in file drawers at the central repository, as well as bound copies of the records. By 1970 there were 2,323 volumes of births, 414 volumes of marriages, and 854 volumes of deaths. A special register is also maintained of persons who have reached an advanced age. The national archives of Costa Rica are located in the city of San José. Costa Rica's surviving parish registers (many have been destroyed) are maintained by the Curia in San José, which has one of the best ecclesiastical archives in Latin America.

The national archives of El Salvador were destroyed by fire in 1889, though approximately 100,000 documents were recovered, many badly burned or water-stained. However, most of these items were administrative records of little genealogical value. A new national archives center was finally opened in 1962 in the city of San Salvador. The notarial archives are also located in San Salvador, at the Ministerio del Interior.

Guatemala's national archives records are in Guatemala City. The archives center was established in 1846 and it is relatively well organized. Most of the Guatemala records relating to deaths, births, and marriages remain in the municipalities, though copies of some have been sent to the national archives. The oldest parish registers date back to 1577 and are preserved in the various Roman Catholic parishes throughout the country.

Civil registration in Honduras began in 1881; the records are in the national archives at Tegucigalpa. The records here cover births, marriages, deaths, divorces, orphans, recognition of illegitimacy, and emancipation cases. The archives also have earlier parish birth records for the city of Tegucigalpa that date back to 1842. There are also some parish records for other parts of the country in the city's museum.

Civil registration began in Nicaragua in 1879, and books were kept in the various municipalities of births, marriages, deaths, divorces, and adoptions. Copies of some of these records were gathered at the national archives at Managua. After the 1972 earthquake, the civil registry in Managua began to microfilm its collection and to prepare indexes of all the material. The 1931 earthquake had completely destroyed the archbishop's archive and all the parish records that had been stored there.

Panama did not begin keeping civil records until 1904, after it seceded from Columbia, with the backing of the United States. The Panamanians then set up a national archives located in Panama City in 1912, though as yet this has few records of genealogical interest. The most extensive collec-tion of genealogical records for this area relates to the U.S. residents of the Panama Canal Zone, a strip of land across the country that was controlled by the U.S. government from 1903 to 1999 and through which the Army Corps of Engineers constructed the Panama Canal. The marriage records from this zone are located at the National Archives in Washington, D.C. Requests for any of them must be made by mail to the National Archives and, if records requested are found, the requestor will be informed of the cost to provide copies. The birth and death records are maintained by the Vital Records Section of Passport Services at the Department of State in Washington, D.C. Again there is a small fee for copies of any of these birth or death records.

Chilean Genealogy is favored by one of the best National Archives in Latin-America, situated in the heart of Santiago. It has a collection of most of the colonial and earlier republic records gathered in one repository. There is also an outstanding genealogical society in this city, the Instituto Chileno de Investigaciones Genealógicas, and copies of all the births, marriages, and deaths since 1900 are located at the Central Office of Civil Registration in Santiago. Unfortunately part of this central repository was destroyed by fire in 1946, and the records for the years 1910 to 1940 were lost. To find the originals, one must go to one of the more than 520 municipal offices throughout the country that hold such records.

Civil registration was established by law in 1885, but it was not fully developed until 1900. Another source for such vital records is the parishes of the Roman Catholic Church. These records are in a fairly good state of preservation, although some of the parishes have been destroyed by earthquakes, floods, and fires. Chile has an abundance of Protestant and other religious groups, and some of them maintain records of births, marriages, and deaths that can be found in the offices of their local congregations.

Throughout the country the land records and various notarial records are kept in the Officianos del Notario y Conservador de Bienes Raices in each city. Those compiled before 1875 and some as late as 1923 can be found at the National Archives.

Chile's public cemeteries, which date back to the start of civil registration in 1885, are maintained in each municipality. These cities all have cemetery record offices that contain books with the following information: names of the deceased, dates of burial, location of the burial, relationship of the deceased to the person paying for the burial, and date for the purchase of the burial site. The cemetery in Santiago, founded in 1821, occupies a large area on Recoleta Street. The cemeteries in the cities of Arica and Puerto Montt, at the north and south ends of Chile's main populated area, were founded in 1885. In looking through the grave records, one is likely to find many names other than those of Hispanics, such as Asians, Jews, and Europeans from Germany, Ireland, and Italy. The information on their tombstones can be extremely valuable and may be the only extant record of their origins. Records of German immigration can be found at the Museum of German Immigration (Biblioteca y Archivo Histórico de la Inmigración Alemaná) in Santiago.

Chinese Genealogy has a long history and includes some of the oldest records in the world, as well as some of the most distinguished. No other nation can boast complete family genealogies that extend unbroken sometimes for many centuries. The family named Kung, for example, which was founded by Confucius about 480 B.C., boasts data on every male member from that date up to today. The Kung genealogies fill several library buildings at the ancestral home in Qufu in Shandong province. More than just genealogical records, these archives contain histories of the political activities of various family members, records of acquired degrees and titles, descriptions of the temple and family residence along with inventory lists, property management records, and lists pertaining to leases, finances, and legal proceedings. It is a vast collection of material covering more than 2,000 years, and Chinese historians today often consult these archives in compiling works on the nation's many historical periods.

Ancestry is part of the essence of being Chinese, and its rules are governed by a strict Confucian code. It is the role of family elders to preserve and pass on the family's historical documents in order to continue the legacy of a traditional Chinese family. However, not all of the genealogical records are complete for each family. Through the passage of time, some family records have been altered, lost, or destroyed.

Yet every Chinese family — including peasant families, as soon as they lift themselves out of illiteracy — keeps a genealogy record. In each generation, the same ideogram in a two-ideogram combination makes up an individual's personal name. This is a form of coding that enables the families to know immediately to which generation a family member belongs. Extended families sometimes number up to 700 to 800 individuals in just two or three generations. Chinese names are recorded with the surname first and the given name, or names, following this. Researchers looking into Chinese genealogy may often be confronted with several given names for one individual. These may include a milk name (name given in infancy), school name, marriage name, professional name, and others.

The Chinese word for genealogy, as well as for a family tree or genealogical tree, is Jiapu. It covers the record of a family clan's history and lineage, documenting the origins of the surname, the migration patterns of the clan, the family lineage, the ancestral biography, and even details about various localities where the clan has resided. Family genealogies have been found by archaeological researchers in China that date to as early as the Shang Dynasty (17th to 11th centuries B.C.) when they were inscribed on turtle shells, cow bones, and bronze vessels. Even prior to the invention of writing, such genealogical information was recorded in China by tying knots on ropes. Objects including miniature arrows, shoes, cradles, bronze coins, and the kneecaps of goats and pigs were tied to the knots to indicate the number of generations, number of members (male and female), etc., in a single family. Before the development of writing, this information was verbally passed on to the later generations.

A Jaipu usually begins with a progenitor who first settled in a particular place and started his family there. Its final entries are those appended by members of the contemporary generation. Between these two points are the data accounting for all the primogenitor's sons and male descendents, listed in columns from right to left. The primogenitor's first-born son and subsequent first-born grandsons are listed vertically downwards in the right column, while the brothers of the first-born are listed laterally to the left. Descriptions of each generation are confined in relatively narrow, horizontal divisions on the same form. These descriptions contain information such as the ancestor's name and aliases, date of birth and death, and official rank. The proceeding generations are recorded in a similar manner.

A Jiapu usually does not have prominent records of any of the women in the family, because in Chinese families greater emphasis is placed on the sons who will carry on the family name. When daughters marry, they are considered to be a part of their husband's family, and although their names are mentioned in both their family and in-laws' Jiapus, the significance of such names is usually marginalized.

In recent years the perception of the objectives of Chinese genealogical research have changed. Researchers are now studying Chinese genealogies as supplements to other research areas such as social economic history, geographical history, history of law, population history, religion and culture, history of overseas Chinese, inheritance practices, and biographies of historical figures. These studies have completely dispelled the myth that Chinese genealogical research is but a mere hobby for amateur genealogists.

Although most Jiapu are preserved by the families that created them, many can also be found in Chinese libraries. The largest collection of them is in the Shanghai Library, which boasts the genealogical records of some 12,000 families filling 90,000 volumes. The earliest of these collections in that library dates back to the Song Dynasty in the 10th century. There are also records of the families of famous Chinese individuals such as

Lu Xun, a well-loved author, and Dr. Sun Yat Sen, the revolutionary founder of modern China. The Shanghai Library has set up a research center that restores the deteriorating Jiapu and studies their origins. Each year, it receives more than 10,000 visitors seeking their family roots.

There is now also a Website dedicated to preserving Jiapu records. According to Steve Simpson, the CEO of the Chinese-language, Singapore-based company know as Cybersia, there are 500 people sitting in front of computer monitors all day long inputting the genealogical information into this site. The company has made an alliance with the Shanghai Library to obtain all its information for Cybersia, and has developed a unique patent-pending methodology of backward data tracing to manage the Chinese data. The company hopes eventually to be in contact with the 70 million-plus people of Chinese descent living outside of China and scattered around the globe.

"The phenomenal growth of the Chinese Internet market has given us a critical mass of users to whom the world's first online Chinese genealogy service can now be offered," says Simpson. "Our goal is to reestablish contacts with the far-flung family members separated by years, decades, or even centuries of immigration."

Two books that may be helpful for anyone searching for Chinese ancestors are *China Connection: Finding Ancestral Roots for Chinese in America*, by Jennie W. Chooey Low (San Mateo, CA: Asian American Books, 1994) and *In Search of Your Chinese Roots: Genealogical Research on Chinese Surnames*, by Shequ-yueh J. Chao (Baltimore: Genealogical Publishing Co., 2000).

Christian Science Records in the field of genealogy are relatively scarce. The church, which stresses spiritual healing, was founded in the United States by Mary Baker Eddy in the 1800s, and the central institution of Christian Science is the First Church of Christ Scientist Church in Boston. Although the denomination has some 3,000 churches around the world, at least two thirds of them are in the United States. They have no clergy and their services are conducted by members elected to serve as readers. The First Church in Boston has a history library, but it provides little in the way of vital statistics information. Possibly the designated readers at the individual churches will provide information about their members or direct the researcher to other members of the congregation who would be willing to do so. Despite the denomination's seeming lack of interest in the genealogy and family history of its members, the organization's world-famous daily newspaper, *The Christian Science Monitor*, has sometimes featured special articles about genealogy and the work of genealogists.

Church of Jesus Christ of Latter-Day Saints *see* Mormon Records

Church of the Brethren Records *see* Brethren Records

Church Records can sometimes be of great help in finding birth, baptism, confirmation, marriage, and death and burial dates. Furthermore, the membership lists, officer lists, Sunday school records, and the minutes of meetings can provide special details about some of the church members. In cases where pertinent civil records have been destroyed in a courthouse fire or flood, church records may be the only way to fill in the needed information. Of course, churches also suffer fires and some close down so that many records of this sort have been lost. The records from churches, however, are among the most under-used in genealogical research. Part of the reason for this is the number of denominations. There are hundreds of different ones, each with its own set of individual churches. So finding the required records can be a daunting task.

This is often a matter of detective work, especially if a church has gone out of existence or combined with another. The first step is to check local and county histories to establish the religious history of the community. The researcher can also try to identify the church from other sources such as relatives, family Bibles, newspaper articles, obituaries, wedding announcements, funeral home files, let-

ters, scrapbooks, the traditions of older relatives, members of the community in which the family lived, or the county marriage and death records. Some of these same sources may provide clues as to the denomination, if that is also unknown. If the denomination still exists in a town, the current church is a likely source of manuscript records. It is quite common, however, for churches to deposit their early records with a local or state historical society or with a denominational agency.

Denominations periodically publish histories of their congregations, and learning about that history will help one to understand migration routes, schisms and splits within the denomination, and the reasons that their churches keep particular types of records. Most local congregations also publish church directories of the phone numbers and addresses of members, as well as their own local histories. Furthermore, old county histories usually give short descriptions of the local churches within that county. Most local churches keep a set of their church bulletins or newsletters. These can be full of genealogical information, as are the diocesan or regional church newspapers.

Local public libraries may have some of these church records and histories, while denominational repositories probably have the personal papers and journals of ministers and church leaders that have been deposited there by their families. The church's institutions, such as a church school, church college, nursing home, orphanage, or hospital, will likely keep records and possibly produce yearbooks, newsletters, or magazines. Even if the institution no longer exists, the records may be stored somewhere. For example, Otterbein Homes, west of Lebanon, Ohio, was once a Shaker Village, then a United Brethren Home for Children and the Elderly, and is now a retirement community supported by the United Methodist Church. At Otterbein there is an archives office and a museum with information dating from the time of the Shakers, the United Brethren Home, and, of course, the present United Methodist facility. For more information, see the entries for the specific religious denominations.

Citizenship *see* **Naturalization and Citizenship Records**

City Directories have been produced in the United States since the 1780s — in New York City, Philadelphia, and Charleston. Their original purpose was to identify commercial enterprises, but soon other persons were listed without any occupation being specified. Genealogists use city directories and sometimes telephone directories in three important ways. First, by knowing the address of a family in or near a census year one can locate their names in the census. Second, they can give clues as to the death or removal of family members. If a person has appeared in the directory for a number of years and then is no longer listed, it may mean he or she died. That points to an approximate year in which to start searching for the death certificate. Third, city directories can be quite useful in tracking the locations and migrations of individuals.

Some early directories only list the names of prominent citizens in a district, and then only the male head of the household. Sometimes, however, those directories list single women and widows in their own right. However, city directories that list every family by name and address often prove most useful in genealogical studies. Such directories are also likely to include businesses and professions that may be linked to specific individuals. If a directory has a reverse listing by street address (called a householder's index) this may prove to be quite useful in that it will allow the researcher to identify neighbors, some of whom may even be married daughters living near their parents.

Information listed in a city directory may contain occupational data that is more accurate than that found in census records. In addition, if the information in the directory was incorrect one year, the person involved had an opportunity to have it corrected in the next year's edition. With census records, what was listed could not be corrected until the next census in 10 years.

In older city directories, the listings for non-white persons were often put in a separate section. This reflects the societal segregation of the times, but it can be useful to researchers, making it easier to differentiate between persons with the same name in the community who were of different races. Unfortunately, the attention paid to the inclusion of non-white citizens was never as thorough as it should or could have been.

Every large library has a collection of city directories from various years as well as old telephone books for the general area in which the library is located. Chambers of commerce can sometimes also be of help locating out of print directories. Some city directories are now being put on CD-ROM disks. One such set of disks is concentrated on the years surrounding the 1890 federal census, which was almost totally destroyed by fire in 1921. *See also* **Telephone Directories.**

Clan Tartans are of interest to genealogists because they are related to specific families, although knowledge of them has little to do with the tracing of ancestry. Originally a distinction of rank or position, the use of these checkered garments dates back to ancient times. The Irish, the Britons, the Caledonians of Scotland, and the Celts in Europe all wore them. They are cited in Scottish literature as early as the 1200s, and at that time were associated with districts rather than families. Later they were used to identify the chief family, or clan, of an area. The Gaelic word *clann* means children, and the central idea of clanship is kinship. It is estimated that there are now over 2,800 different tartan designs.

At one time tartans were not identified by the weave but by the number of colors in that weave. When only one color was used, it depicted a servant; two indicated a farmer of rank; three, an officer of rank; five, a chieftain; six, a poet; and seven, the chief himself. The colors that were used included yellows, blues, whites, greens, browns, reds, black, and purple. Some say that a keen eye can identify the colors with particular islands of Scotland.

Generally the size or scale of pattern is unimportant. What matters is the proportion of the different colors, that is, the relative width of the lines and stripes that make up the whole. The broader bands of color, called the under check, are usually decorated or embellished with narrower lines of color called the over check. The largest group of tartans that can be recognized today use a three-color design based on the Black Watch tartan that is used by military units. Recognizing all the subtle aspects in tartan design requires some training and involves the location of two unique intersection points within the pattern called pivots.

Although most tartans can be traced to specific clans, where no clan tartan exists, families have sometimes developed their own special family tartans. The Canadian provinces also have shown pride in their Scottish and Highland connections by adopting tartans of their own. Corporate tartans, unrelated to any clan or family, have in recent years become popular, with an institution or company adopting a tartan design for uniforms and merchandising. Disputes as to their use and production rely on copyright laws, design acts, and in rare cases trademark laws.

Cluster Genealogy, which some call "extended-family genealogy," is a term used by researchers to designate the study of whole families rather than single genealogical lines. The process involves widening one's search to include not only a direct line of ancestors, but also the sisters, brothers, aunts, uncles, cousins, children, and neighbors in each generation. This can sometimes be a great aid to finding more information about members of a single line than would otherwise be likely.

The study of a cluster of relatives may also eventually confirm the accuracy of whatever information has been found in the documents that have been examined about a few members of a single line. In researching a cluster, one tries to use as many primary and secondary sources as possible.

Coast Guard Records are stored at the National Archives in Washington, D.C. The Coast Guard is the nation's oldest continuous sea-going force, having been established by the U.S. Congress as the Revenue Cutter Service in 1790. It did not, however, take on the name "United States Coast Guard" until 1915. In 1939 the Lighthouse Service of the Department of Commerce was transferred to the Coast Guard.

On file at the National Archives are incomplete records of the officers of the Revenue Cutter Service from 1792 to 1914 and muster rolls of seamen from 1833 to 1914. The National Archives also has the personnel records of the Lighthouse Service. None of these records has ever been indexed, so the researcher must know the name of the vessel or lighthouse facility on which a man served in order to find the appropriate record. Otherwise the genealogist must hunt through roll after roll of microfilm in order to find the desired information.

Coats of Arms *see* **Heraldry**

College of Arms was founded by King Richard III of England in 1484 as the Herald's College. It is the body that decides who is entitled to display a particular coat of arms, and what that coat of arms shall consist of. All of its 13 officers of the college, which is located in London, must be members of the Royal household. Although there has never been an act of Parliament regulating this body, one officer of the college has stated recently that "Entitlement to Arms is created by Letters Patent of Arms, the Arms being granted, under Warrant from the Earl Marshall, to an individual and his descendants in the male line, according to the Laws of Arms." The statement is based on a number of legal decisions that have been made by the British courts over the years.

The College of Arms, of course, has no jurisdiction in the United States. However, since 1962, several American corporations have obtained heraldic designs (divisals) from the college. The ones created for cities and states have been awarded only with the consent of the state governor. For example, the town of Manteo, North Carolina, was awarded a coat of arms designated as *Argent on a Cross Gules six Lozenges conjoined palewise of the field in dexter chief a Roebuck statant also Gules.* This is a variation of the arms granted in the 16th century to the city of Raleigh, which once stood on the site where Manteo is now located.

The college building in London contains a magnificent collection of heraldic and genealogical books, records, and documents. Unfortunately these are not available to the public, although an officer in waiting is on duty to receive inquiries and to respond to correspondence. The principal responsibilities of the officers of the college are to participate in ceremonial duties on behalf of the Crown. *See also* **Heraldry.**

Colombian Genealogy does not have as avid a group of researchers as do most of the other South American countries. Civil registration here did not begin until 1936, and it did not really become widespread until some years later. Prior to that, the registration of births, marriages, and deaths was done by the notaries public in the cities where they existed and by the officer of statistics in the places where there were no notaries. In some cases the mayor's (Alcalde's) office took care of such matters. At a notarial office in Bogotá there are 11 books of births, marriages, and deaths for the years between 1854 and 1887 that are not indexed and include the records for some of the surrounding areas as well as for persons in the city.

Colombia was one of three countries that formed after the collapse of Simón Bolívar's Republic of Great Columbia in 1832, the other two being Ecuador and Venezuela. At first it was known as the Republic of New Grenada, but following civil strife and confusion, a constitution that was adopted in 1886 restored the name Colombia to the country.

The National Archives (Archivo Nacional de Colombia), which is part of the National Library, has the records of a series of censuses of various cities, the earliest of which was conducted in Espiritu Santo in 1586 and the last in San Sebastián de Madrid in 1776. A royal census was conducted in 1777 at the municipal level. The results of this census were then sent to the respective provincial capitals. Some censuses were conducted in various cities starting in 1778. The National Archives also has a good collection of records from colonial times, as well as other genealogical items of interest.

One of the best places to find vital records information in Colombia is in the parish records of the many Roman Catholic churches. These records, in most cases, have been well kept and are available for public view. However, the researcher must have written permission to see them from the vicar-general of the diocese in which the parish is found. Some of these parish registers date back to the latter part of the 16th century. The Catholic church was the only authorized keeper of cemeteries in Colombia until the 20th century, and many of these cemeteries were abandoned once they ran out of space. When located, the gravestones may yield good genealogical data. Some civil cemeteries have been developed in recent years, as well as Protestant and other religious ones.

Colorado Records of births and deaths were not officially registered in the state until the year 1908. Prior to that only a very few counties, notably Denver, registered some. Colorado had few settlers until the 1850s. Then, in 1858, prospectors found gold along Cherry Creek, near the site of present-day Denver. Gold hunters rushed in by the thousands. The rush reached its peak by the end of 1859, by which time about 50,000 persons had come into the area. Creating a stable government for this body of newcomers became a major problem. The Indians claimed that the land there had been given to them by various treaties, but the miners ignored those claims. They set up what they called the Jefferson Territory, which the U.S. Congress refused to recognize. In 1861 Congress created the Colorado Territory and then, in 1876, made this the 38th state.

The first federal census was conducted in the Colorado area in 1860. This did not include Arapahoe County, which was listed in the Kansas Territory census of the same year, nor did it include the northeast Colorado towns, which were included with Nebraska. Some parts of south central Colorado were put into the New Mexico Territory census. However, the next census, the 1870 Colorado Territory census, included all of these parts that had been misplaced in 1860.

A special Colorado census in 1885 was completed in conjunction with the federal government. That year the U.S. Congress had agreed to provide funds to any state or territory that wished to have a census prepared between the regular 10-year periods of the national census. Colorado was one of the five states and territories that took up this offer. Unlike the regular 10-year census enumerations, this one was never Soundexed. However, a separate alphabetical listing was created for half of the 40 Colorado counties that existed at the time. It includes the names along with ages, race, gender, nativity, and marital status, but this listing does not refer to a sheet and page number in the census, so it is sometimes difficult for researchers to cross reference the names. Yet the alphabetical extraction, of course, is quicker to search than the actual census. The 1885 Colorado census is stored at both the National Archives and the Colorado State Archives in Denver.

Another special group of Colorado censuses is the annual Native American/Indian Census Rolls of 1885–1944. The tribes represented in these records that can be found at the Colorado State Archives are the Cheyenne, Arapahoe, Sioux, Crow, Ute, Kiowa, Comanche, Apache, Caddo, Wichita, Navajo, Hopi, Nez Pierce, Shoshoni, Shebits, Kaibab, Utah, Ouray, and Paiute. These census records were submitted by the reservations' agents. Before 1930 they provide information on a person's name, date of birth, gender, and relationship to the head of the family. After 1930, they provided information on an individual's degree of Indian blood, marital status, ward status, and place of residence, as well as miscellaneous commentaries.

Birth and death records in Colorado, copies of which can be obtained for a small fee, are not open to the public until 100 years after the occurrence, although there is no such stipulation for marriage records. The Colorado Vital Records Office, a division of the Colorado Department of Public Health and Environment in Denver, has an index to these that covers the years from 1900 to 1939, and 1975 to the present. This marriage index is also available at the Denver Public Library and the Colorado State Archives. The 1975-to-present index includes either the groom's or bride's name(s). The index for 1900 to 1939 is listed only by the groom's name. One can obtain a copy of any marriage license from the county clerk's office in the county where the marriage took place, if that is known. The district courts in the various counties have the power to grant divorces, but there is a state-wide filing of the divorce records. These records are kept in the state's Vital Records Office; there is an index of the divorces granted, except for the years 1940 to 1967. Probate records and wills are also in the county clerk's offices except for those in Denver, where there is a separate probate court. Guardianship records are kept by the district courts in the counties of a child's residence, except again for those in Denver where the juvenile court has jurisdiction.

During the 1930s, the Work Projects Administration compiled a *Guide to Vital Statistics Records in Colorado* in two volumes. The first covers the public archives and the second covers the church archives. These books can be found in the Denver Public Library as well as in many genealogical libraries around the United States.

The district courts in the counties of Colorado have jurisdiction over legal and equitable actions, and that is where the records are kept. Land records are in the hands of the county recorder, while registered wills are in the hands of the district court in each county except for the city of Denver, which has a probate court. The naturalization records are usually separated from other court cases and do not have case numbers.

Researchers seeking information from county records can locate them at the following county seats: (Adams County) Brighton, (Alamosa County) Alamosa, (Arapahoe County) Littleton, (Archuleta County) Pagosa Springs, (Baca County) Springfield, (Bent County) Las Animas, (Boulder County) Boulder, (Broomfield County) Broomfield, (Chaffee County) Salida, (Cheyenne County) Cheyenne Wells, (Clear Creek County) Georgetown, (Conejos County) Conejos, (Costilla County) San Luis, (Crowley County) Ordway, (Custer County) Westcliffe, (Delta County) Delta, (Denver County) Denver,

(Dolores County) Dove Creek, (Douglas County) Castle Rock, (Eagle County) Eagle, (El Paso County) Colorado Springs, (Elbert County) Kiowa, (Fremont County) Canon City, (Garfield County) Glenwood Springs, (Gilpin County) Central City, (Grand County) Hot Sulphur Springs, (Gunnison County) Gunnison, (Hinsdale County) Lake City, (Huerfano County) Walsenburg, (Jackson County) Walden, and (Jefferson County) Golden.

Also at (Kiowa County) Eads, (Kit Carson County) Burlington, (La Plata County) Durango, (Lake County) Leadville, (Larimer County) Fort Collins, (Las Animas County) Trinidad, (Lincoln County) Hugo, (Logan County) Sterling, (Mesa County) Grand Junction, (Mineral County) Creede, (Moffat County) Craig, (Montezuma County) Cortez, (Montrose County) Montrose, (Morgan County) Fort Morgan, (Otero County) La-Junta, (Ouray County) Ouray, (Park County) Fairplay, (Phillips County) Holyoke, (Pitkin County) Aspen, (Prowers County) Lamar, (Pueblo County) Pueblo, (Rio Blanco County) Meeker, (Rio Grande County) Del Norte, (Routt County) Steamboat Springs, (Saguache County) Saguache, (San Juan County) Silverton, (San Miguel County) Telluride, (Sedgwick County) Julesburg, (Summit County) Breckenridge, (Teller County) Cripple Creek, (Washington County) Akron, (Weld County) Greeley, and (Yuma County) Wray.

FOR FURTHER INFORMATION SEE:
- Clint, Florence R. *Colorado Area Key, A Comprehensive Study of Genealogical Records Sources of CO, Including Maps and a Brief General History*. Fountain Valley, CA: Edin Press, 1968.
- *Colorado Families: A Territorial Heritage*. Denver, CO: Colorado Genealogical Society, 1981.

Compact Disks (CD-ROMs) are being used to distribute large quantities of genealogical data because one, thin CD can contain the texts of several books. The disks can be accessed by any computer with a CD drive. The types of materials found on these disks include maps, newspapers, journals, city directories, serials, periodicals, telephone directories, registers of voters, U.S. histories, county histories, census records, and indexes to genealogical records. Most of the CDs are available for purchase, but their cost may be prohibitive to some researchers. One can also find some of them available for use in public, university, and genealogical libraries.

Professional genealogists may wish to purchase many disks that contain all the various U.S. census listings starting in 1790, but it doesn't make much sense for the average researcher to purchase such disks when looking for only one or two names in a single county in one or two census years. The same names can be found for free by looking through the microfilm collections at the various National Archives sites. The same census disks possibly might also be rented from one of the genealogical libraries.

Compact disk records are not limited to American resources. There are also large collections for foreign materials relating to genealogy on various CDs. Marthe Arends's *Genealogy on CD-ROM* (Baltimore, 1999) lists many of the CDs that are available and indicates where they can be purchased.

Computer Chat Programs are Internet channels that allow persons from more than 60 countries around the world to communicate in real time by typing messages into the computer that others can read and to which they can respond. Such a multi-user chat system is properly called an IRC, or "Internet Relay Chat" system. Various Internet servers provide the "chat rooms" that allow users to connect to the IRC. Such chat rooms are usually dedicated to specific topics of conversation.

Messages sent by way of a chat program may be public, where everyone on a channel can see what is typed, or private, i.e., messages between only two people who may or may not be using the same channel. There is no restriction on the number of people who can participate in any given discussion, or on the number of channels that can be formed on an IRC. However, the IRC is not a game, and users need to treat the others they contact through a chat room with the same courtesy they would use in talking face-to-face with another person or in talking on the telephone.

Several larger and smaller IRC networks exist. The largest one, called EFnet (Eris Free net), usually serves over 15,000 users at any given moment. Smaller ones, like Undernet (10,000) and Dalnet (5,000), are less populated but often offer more stability and convenience. Computer users who wish to participate in a chat room must first install an IRC client on their own computers. Such a client program can be downloaded from an FTP (File Transfer Protocol) site through a Web browser and can then be installed on the computer relatively easily.

There are a number of chat rooms devoted to conversations about genealogy. Among them: the Acadian-Cajun Chat Room; the AnancyWeb Genealogy Chat Room; the Australian Genealogy Forum Chat Room; the Canadian Genealogy Links and Chat; the Chat with Dear Myrtle room that is a genealogical advice and discussion center; the Genealogy & Native Americans Communities Chat Center; the Genealogy Chat Room; the Genealogy Online Chat Room; the Irish-Genealogy Live Chat, and the Jewish Genealogy Links Chat Room. There are also chat rooms devoted to specific U.S. counties and to specific family names. A list of most of the best chat rooms can be found at the Cyndi's List Website.

The first time anyone runs an IRC program, one must fill in some personal information, such as one's Internet address, the name of the IRC server with which one wishes to connect, password, real name, email address, and the nickname one wishes to use when chatting. These options are usually found under the File/Setup directions at the time of installation. One is free to choose any nickname up to nine characters in length. It is not unusual to find two people using the same nickname on a chat program, so the first-time user may be asked to switch to another nickname in order to avoid confusion.

As soon as the IRC program is operating on one's computer, it is best to type "/help" in order to get as much information about the program and its commands as possible.

All IRC commands start with a "/" and most of the commands are just one word. Typing "/names," for example, will result in a list of all the nicknames being used by others on that program. The most widely understood language on an IRC is English. However, since each IRC is used in many different countries, English is by no means the only language one may find there. Also many researchers use smileys as well as chat-room jargon. :-) is a smiley face. Tilt your head to the left to see it. Likewise, :-(is a frown, ;-) is a wink, :~~(is crying, while :-P is someone sticking his tongue out. :-P~~ is drooling, etc. There are hundreds of these faces. Some of the jargon in use includes: brb, which means be right back; np, (no problem); bbiaf, (be back in a flash); rotfl, (rolling on the floor laughing); and wb, (welcome back). As for courtesy, typing in all caps, LIKE THIS, is considered "shouting" and should be avoided. Likewise, one should not repeat oneself or otherwise "flood" the channel with many lines of text all at once. Stepping over the bounds of courtesy may result in being kicked off the channel by the chat program operator. *See also* **Computer Genealogy Files; Genealogical Websites.**

Computer Genealogy Files, of which there are many thousands, can be downloaded to one's own computer at no cost from various Internet, or World Wide Web, sites. These files often arrive in ZIP form so that they have to be decompressed before they can be viewed or copied. ZIP is the popular data compression system that saves space and allows for the transfer of files online much more rapidly. ZIP files are easily recognizable because each ends with a .ZIP extension; they can be decompressed with one of the several ZIP AND UNZIP programs that can also be downloaded from the Web. Sometimes the ZIP file will be a self-extracting one ending with an .EXE extension. One can then decompress the file simply by activating it.

In the past the Internet was much more difficult to use than it is today. For each function (or "Internet service"), one needed to be familiar with a different program and a different set of arcane commands. When one mastered these, it wasn't hard to use the Internet; however, switching from one program to another was always clumsy.

To download a file, one used an FTP, or File Transfer Protocol. To search for a desired file, one could use a search program called Ardjie. To run a computer on the Internet by remote control, one used Telnet. To look at documents on a system, say a university's information system, one might use a menu-based display program called a Gopher. And to search all the Gophers for a specific document, one might use a program called Veronica, but to search for just one Gopher one might use a program called Jughead.

Eventually a Swiss research group, CERN, decided to try to pull all these different services into one interface, with a single protocol. At first, their new program, known as a browser, was only text-based, just as was the entire Internet at that time. But very soon graphic interfaces were added, making the browsers much easier to use. The set of interlinked documents from around the world eventually became known as the World Wide Web (WWW).

Thus for most computer users the word "Internet" and the words "World Wide Web" are synonymous, and can be thought of as a computer-based system to link information from all over the world. Of course all communications between computers take place only when they are using the same protocol, or set of operations, for the data being transferred. At the very least, any computer communications protocol must include the following: the rate of transmission (in bauds or bits per second), whether transmission is to be synchronous or asynchronous, and whether data is to be transmitted in half-duplex or full-duplex mode. In addition, protocols can include sophisticated techniques for detecting and recovering from transmission errors and for encoding and decoding data. When one installs a modem and a browser on a computer, these segments of the protocol are usually installed automatically, and if they are not, the browser service agent can provide instructions by telephone to the computer user so that the correct adjustments can be implemented by the computer user.

The FTP system is still available for individual use, as are the other programs listed above, but data transfer is much more conveniently handled by one of the several browsers that have been developed by such companies as MSN, AOL, Earthlink, AT&T, and others. Most FTP servers require the user to log on to the server in order to transfer files. In contrast, a Hyper Text Transfer Protocol, or HTTP, is the protocol used to transfer files from a Web server to a browser. Unlike FTP, where entire files are transferred from one device to another and copied into the computer memory, HTTP only transfers the contents of a Web page into a browser so that it can be viewed. When genealogy and other files are listed on the page as available for downloading, there will be a place on the page that, if clicked, will begin the downloading process. Many computer genealogy programs will translate one's genealogy data into the HTML format, so that it can be posted and sent out on the World Wide Web.

One other term used in the sending of data back and forth from one computer to another is TCP/IP or Transfer Control Protocol/Internet Protocol. This is the suite of communications protocols used to connect hosts on the Internet. TCP/IP is built into the computer operating system and is used by the Internet, making it the de facto standard for transmitting data over computer networks. Even network operating systems that have their own protocols, such as Netware, also support TCP/IP. *See also* **Computer Programs for Genealogy; World Wide Web.**

Computer News Servers *see* **Genealogical Mailing Lists and Newsgroups**

Computer Programs for Genealogy can be especially useful for preparing charts, both ascendant and descendant, and for keeping genealogical data in an organized way. They are not essential for the purpose of entering genealogical data into a computer, and some professionals prefer using common word processing and flat database programs, believing these to be equally adequate and somewhat faster. But only the specially designed computer programs can produce attractive charts with inserted photographs of family members.

There are dozens of such computer programs that have been designed to contain one's family history. Most are continually being improved, with new features added frequently. The latest version of any computer genealogy program is likely to have some of the features that emulate the best in others. Which program one selects largely depends on availability, price, and personal choice. Fortunately, most of these genealogy programs can provide a demonstration copy for the purchaser to experiment with in order to determine its desirability. Any purchaser needs to consider the following in making such a choice:

First, how user-friendly is the program? In other words, can one use the program intuitively without having to constantly consult the manual or help screen? Are the program operations easy to find and clearly defined? Is the entered data saved automatically when one exits the program, or at least does the program prompt a user to save the last work session when exiting?

Second, how compatible is a program in relation to one's own and other computers? Genealogy programs are designed for specific operating systems, and a Macintosh version will not work on a Windows 95, Windows XP, OS/2, Amiga, or Linux platform. The program needs to be compatible with the processor, operating system, available memory, and available disk storage. But the program should also be able to interchange data with other genealogy programs on other computers, as well as to transfer data from one program to another program within a single computer. The standard format for such interchanging, found on most commercially available genealogy programs, is called GEDCOM (GEnealogical Data COMunications Format). Any purchaser would be wise to be certain that any selected program is GEDCOM compliant.

Third, what is the capacity of the program? As genealogical data is entered into a computer file, its size grows and takes up ever greater amounts of disk space. Particular genealogical programs sometimes have capacity limits that were placed there when the programs were originally designed. Some

of these limitations are an inability to handle more than one separate family file, a maximum number of entries (records) allowed in a family file, and a maximum number of characters allowed for surnames, given names, and place names. Discovering that the capacity is too limited after a program has been installed on a home computer can be quite irritating. All genealogy programs also provide a minimum standard set of fields for each data record. As a rule these are fields for date and place of birth, date and place of marriage, and date and place of death, but they may also provide additional standard fields, such as those for baptism, confirmation, burial date and place, marriage status, divorce date, and immigration or emigration place and date. The most sophisticated programs include user-defined fields that can be customized to hold information relevant to a particular culture or religious group. There also may be special fields to denote the reliability or certainty of the data, as well as special flags to denote special conditions, such as those used in genetic research to indicate all known individuals who have suffered from a particular ailment or were born with red hair.

Fourth, how flexible is the program? A user may want to customize a program to fit individual requirements, and some of the computer programs make this easy. Others don't. Included is the ability to split data into two separate files so that a part of it may be given to others working on the same family records or to merge another's file into the existing program records. The most advanced programs allow one to do this with ease. The flexibility factor should also probably include the ability to check the integrity of one's data file and correct any errors found.

Fifth, how stable is the program? Before purchasing any software program one should investigate the manufacturer's support policies. Is there on-line service or an 800 number one can call to get questions answered and to obtain fixes for any program bugs that may develop? Some manufacturers will make free bug fixes available if needed when complaints are registered with their service representatives.

Sixth, what kind of printouts does it

produce? These are commonly family group sheets (wife, husband, children), descendants charts (listing of all direct descendants from a single individual), ancestor or pedigree charts (list of direct ancestors of a single individual working back in time through all generations), register reports (list of all the information known about an individual and his or her descendants in narrative form), and other useful charts, such as the results of a statistical analysis on the compiled data, birthday calendars, and mailing labels. The most flexible programs will export the reports in a format suitable for one's favorite word processor, which allows the user to add special family histories, notes, and other information to the record.

Seventh, at what speed does the program accept user input? Some programs help speed up data entry by automatically filling in default data such as the surnames of children, or they provide a menu of place names previously entered that can be edited if necessary. Most programs also provide "shortcut" keys to move between screens or to perform various other operations.

Eighth, what is the program's ability to handle other languages? This can be important if the names entered use any unique characters, such as the Spanish ñ, á, é, í, ó, ú and ü.

Some of the most popular genealogical programs for the computer are Ancestral Quest (Windows platform), Family Origins Deluxe (Windows), Family Tree Maker (Windows), Family Trees Quick & Easy (Windows), Gene (Macintosh platform), Genelines (Windows), Generations Family Tree Plus (Windows), Legacy Family Tree (Windows), LifeLines (Unix platform), MacFamilyTree (Macintosh), Reunion: The Family Tree Software (Macintosh), and The Master Genealogist (Windows).

There is also the Personal Ancestral File (PAF) program designed for MS/DOS, Windows, or Macintosh platforms by the Church of Jesus Christ of Latter-day Saints. Its entries are called PAF files, and there are a number of freeware and shareware programs that can be obtained from the Family History Department Website to enhance the program. According to the designers, records for some 35.6 million different names of genealogical interest are now available for users of this program.

Furthermore, there are many programs for foreign language users such as Cumberland Family Tree (Spanish), Aldfaer — Gratis (Dutch), Anarkiv (Swedish), DoroTree (Hebrew), Dynas-Tree (German), Genealogia (Italian), Généatique pour Windows (French), Winkwast en Genkwa (The Netherlands), and a number of programs that handle multiple languages. *See also* **Family History Library; Genealogical Text Formats for Computers.**

Computer Search Engines have become a necessary and highly useful means of finding genealogical information on the Internet. In fact many people are unaware of how easy it is to gather a substantial amount of genealogical data without cost through the World Wide Web. Just as it is physically impossible for any researcher to examine all the books in a library, it is impossible to hyperlink to all the documents on the Web. Almost anything one might be looking for can be found there, and each day more and more people are adding information to Websites by contributing cemetery data, transcribing census records, posting obituaries, and uploading surname files to assist others in their family history research. But with the many available search engines, each working somewhat differently from the others and accessing different Websites, it can be something of a challenge to find exactly the information for which one might be looking.

Search engines are quite different from the subject directories that organize library books and mail-order catalogs. Search engines rely on computer programs called spiders or robots to crawl over the Web and log the relevant words on each Web page. When accessed, the search engine scans its database of more than a billion documents and returns a list of links to any Websites containing the word or words specified. Because such Web databases are very large, search engines can often return thousands of results. So without search strategies or techniques, finding what one desires is daunting.

Some of the leading computer search engines are Google, AllTheWeb, AltaVista, Vivisimo, Copernic, Ez2www, Kartoo, Surf-Wax, Daypop, Yahoo, mySimon, Teoma, Es-potting, MSN, Scirus, Dogpile, Excite, Hot-Bot, InfoSeek, Lycos, AskJeeves, and Internet Archive. Google (http://www.google.com/) has the largest database at 1.5 billion pages and is quite adept at returning relevant results. It uses mathematical formulas to rank each Web page based on the number of "important" pages that link to it. When a search is conducted, Google determines the Web-sites that meet one's search criteria and then produces a list starting with the most popular pages at the top. AllTheWeb (http://www.alltheWeb.com/) uses a database of 625 million pages, slightly larger than that used by AltaVista (AltaVista http://www.altavista.com/), and it allows both fast and advanced searching, much as AltaVista does. Fast searching displays a maximum of 10 results at a time, while advanced searching displays 100 or more at once. If one clicks on the title of any desired document in that list, the entire document will appear on the screen ready for reading (or saving to disk).

A search engine's ability to understand what the researcher may desire is quite limited. It will obediently look for occurrences of the input keywords all over the Web, but it can't understand what the keywords mean. To a search engine, a keyword is just a string of characters. It doesn't know the difference between cancer, the crab, and cancer, the disease. And, of course, it doesn't care. The researcher must supply the brains; the search engine will supply the raw computing power.

Successful searching on the Web involves two key steps. First, the researcher must have a clear understanding of how to prepare for the search. One must identify the main concepts in the subject being sought and determine any synonyms, alternate spellings, or variant word forms for it that might be used. Second, one needs to know how to use the various search tools available on the Internet. Because each search engine works a little differently from the others, one is wise to view the instructions that each search engine provides before beginning its use.

It is also wise to become somewhat conversant with the Boolean terms of logic that are used by some of the search engines for seeking data, at least those terms that deal with AND, OR, and NOT. Connecting search terms (or keywords) with **AND** tells the search engine to retrieve Web pages containing all the keywords. For example, the keywords Puerto Rico and births will return a list of all the pages that contain both the words Puerto and Rico and the word births. It will not return a list of pages with just one or the other of these words. Thus, AND helps to narrow the search results because it limits the results to only the pages where all the keywords appear.

Linking search terms with **OR** tells the search engine to retrieve Web pages containing any and all of the keywords. Thus Puerto Rico or births will return a list of pages that contain one or both of these keywords. To narrow results as much as possible, one can combine OR statements with AND statements, putting each Boolean form in parentheses like this: (Puerto Rico or San Juan) and (Jose or Miguel) and births. This will locate any pages with information about the birth of either Jose or Miguel in the leading city of Puerto Rico or elsewhere in Puerto Rico.

The Boolean logic phrase **AND NOT** tells the search engine to retrieve Web pages containing one keyword but not the other. In many search engines, the plus and minus symbols can be used as alternatives to the formal Boolean AND and AND NOT. The plus sign (+) is the equivalent of AND, and the minus sign (-) is the equivalent of AND NOT. In such a use there should be no space between the plus or minus sign and the keyword, as in (Puerto Rico+births).

Surrounding a group of words with quotes will tell the search engine to only retrieve documents in which those words appear side-by-side. This is a search technique that can significantly narrow the number of search results, and it should be used as often as possible. For example, "John F. Kennedy" will produce pages only about this former president and not all the pages with the word John and all the pages with the word Kennedy, as well as possibly all the pages with capital Fs. Again, such phrase searching can be combined with other search words as in +"John F. Kennedy" +"White House."

Most search engines interpret lower case letters as either upper or lower case. Thus, if one wants both upper and lower case occurrences returned, one should type all the keywords in all lower case letters. However, if one wishes to limit the results to initial capital letters (e.g., "George Washington") or all upper case letters, one should type the keywords that way. A few of the search engines support what are called wildcard features. These allow variations in spelling or word forms. The asterisk (*) symbol will tell the search engine to return alternate spellings for a word at the point where the asterisk appears. For example, capital* returns Web pages with capital, capitals, capitalize, and capitalization.

Some search engines, AltaVista for one, can translate Website pages into English from French, German, Italian, Spanish, and Portuguese (and vice versa). In these pages, after the search results appear, one can click the translate button at the top or bottom of the screen to get the results.

Finally a researcher can take advantage of the option that many search engine sites are now offering: one can "query by example," or "find similar sites," to the ones that come up on the initial hit list. Essentially what the researcher is doing here is telling the search engine, "yes, this looks promising, give me more like this one."

Those who become adept at using the various search engines will add the most interesting sites to their "favorites" list. There are two reasons for this: They don't want to become bogged down in the midst of a search by having to spend time combing through each newly-discovered site, and they want to save a "roadmap" of where they've been and what sites they've already encountered.

Making use of the vast resources that the Internet provides can guide one through even the most daunting of research projects. Even though one may not find endless information online, one can always use the references that are found to narrow down the number of books and documents one will need to examine off-line. The wise use of the

Internet will significantly shorten one's research time. *See also* **Genealogical Mailing Lists and Newsgroups.**

Computer Websites *see* **Genealogical Websites**

Computerized Genealogy *see* **Genealogy Done by Computers**

Congregational Church Records *see* **United Church of Christ Records**

Connecticut Records of births, marriages, and deaths up to 1850 were collected and published under the direction of Lucius Barbour, the state examiner of public records from 1911 to 1934. These volumes can be found in many genealogical libraries, sometimes on microfilm, as well as at the Connecticut State Library in Hartford. Known as the Barbour Collection, they encompass 14,333 typed pages of vital statistics from 137 towns. The records were transcribed by a number of individuals under the direction of Barbour, and they were collected from towns, churches, and cemeteries throughout the state. Only a few towns, such as Scotland and Mansfield, are not listed in the Barbour collection, but these have since been covered by other investigators. Also of great use to genealogists are the town histories that have been published and can now be found in many genealogical libraries. There is one for almost every city, town, and village in the state, and each contains quite a bit of genealogical information, particularly about the early inhabitants.

Connecticut's first English settlers came from Massachusetts in 1633. They established their base at Windsor and within a few years the towns of Hartford and Wethersfield had been founded. A book about these first colonists, written by Royal R. Hinman in 1846, is titled *A Catalogue of the Names of the First Puritan Setters in the Colony of Connecticut; with the Time of Their Arrival in the Colony, and Their Standing in Society*. It was reprinted in 1968 in Baltimore and can be found in the Connecticut State Library as well as in a number of genealogical libraries throughout the country.

The original vital records for most Connecticut towns from their inception to the present are in the custody of the town clerks. However, birth records less than one hundred years old are only open to certain parties, including the individual in question, his or her guardian or legal representative, or a member of a genealogical society incorporated or authorized to do business or conduct affairs in Connecticut. The other vital records from 1897 to the present were formerly available at the Connecticut Department of Public Health, Vital Records Section, in Hartford, but these records have now been closed to the public for an indefinite period in preparation for microfilming. One must contact the registrar of vital statistics of the town or city in which the birth, death, or marriage occurred in order to obtain a certificate of record. Some statewide indexes to the 20th century vital records are available at the Vital Records office.

One other set of published records also exists. This is the Charles R. Hale collection of the burial records of military veterans. This collection is the legacy of a dedicated and persistent individual who initially began, in 1916, to chart the Connecticut graves of veterans of the Civil War in one Hartford graveyard and then continued to locate other veterans' graves all over Hartford County. Hale was eventually designated the state military necrologist, and in 1934 his plan to study all the Connecticut veterans' graves from the original settling of the colony to 1934 became a project endorsed by the Works Progress Administration. Altogether 80 people were employed by Hale for this research in 2,269 Connecticut cemeteries. The Hale Collection includes the record of Connecticut cemetery inscriptions; a collection of newspaper marriage and death notices, ca. 1750–1865; a collection of newspaper abstract volumes, and a veterans' death index.

The only Connecticut state census that lists individuals was taken from 1669 to 1670, and it lists only heads of households. The other state censuses were statistical in nature. This heads of household census is now part of the Wyllys papers in the State Historical Society in Hartford, and it is indexed.

The probate courts handle wills and guardianship matters in the state, and Connecticut's 169 large and small towns are divided into 118 probate districts. However, all the original county and early district probate files that have been preserved are now at the Connecticut State Library, where there is also a complete index of these files starting from 1641. Land records can be located in the various towns, although copies are usually sent to the county recorder. The district courts in the various counties have jurisdiction in civil court actions. Divorce decrees, since June 1947, can be verified through requests to the local courts that issued them.

FOR FURTHER INFORMATION SEE:
- Giles, Barbara S. *Connecticut Genealogical Resources: Including Selected Bibliographies.* Seattle: Ficke Genealogical Foundation, 1991.
- Kemp, Thomas J. *Connecticut Researcher's Handbook.* Detroit: Gale Research, 1981.

Coroner and Mortician Records can sometimes provide quite useful genealogical information. Although the coroner's records are usually stored in the city archives or in the county coroner's office, the records of morticians can be located at the various funeral homes.

One should not think that coroners only process murder victims. They are called to investigate deaths that occur under a number of circumstances, such as accidents, suicides, the sudden death of a person in apparent good health, deaths of persons unattended by licensed physicians, deaths occurring under suspicious or unusual circumstances, poisoning or adverse reactions to drugs or alcohol, a disease constituting a threat to public health, a death during medical or therapeutic procedures, deaths in any prison or penal institution or while the deceased were in police custody, a subject dead on arrival at the hospital, and unclaimed bodies.

As with most records, the contents and condition of an individual's inquest file vary greatly from county to county, and sometimes even from year to year. However, most inquest files do contain sworn statements by family members and friends of the deceased, as well as by any other witnesses present when the body was discovered. The records may also include the address, age, sex, marital status, race, and birthplace of the deceased. The most extensive coroner's records even include the length of residence in the United States, length of residence in the city, occupation, employer, past occupation, wages or salary due, amount of life insurance and to whom it is payable, value of personal and real estate property, level of education, number of dependents, and questions regarding the decedent's physical and mental health at the time of death.

The records kept by funeral directors are just as reliable as those kept by the county vital record's office and they usually contain much more information about the deceased. For example, they often give the names of the insurance companies with which the deceased had contracts. Insurance companies, of course, have extensive genealogical data in their records. However, insurance records are private and available only at the discretion of company officials. The same is true for funeral directors' records. Fortunately, most funeral directors are more willing to help the genealogical researcher than are insurance company officials.

Some funeral directors' records go back more than a hundred years. When they deal with persons who died at an advanced age, the records may bridge two or three generations at a time. As with the county's vital records, those of the funeral directors give names, dates, and places of death. They usually also contain the names of relatives and other data that will not be found in the vital records. But the vital records may give the name of the specific funeral home that handled the deceased when that is not otherwise known, so that the researcher can then approach the designated funeral director.

A mortuary is only required to retain the records covered by state law. These are primarily the records that account for the disposition of the remains and a death certificate. Mortuaries are not required to keep such other items as a list of relatives and funeral attendees. But many funeral directors do maintain such extensive records and, if willing, will let the genealogical researcher examine these private records.

One other set of data surrounding the deaths of individuals are the body transit permits. These are required by local governments in many states for all bodies arriving in their jurisdiction from elsewhere. The purpose is to stem the spread of communicable diseases. In New York City the records of bodies in transit covering the years from 1859 to 1894 have been microfilmed and are available at the Municipal Archives of the City of New York. Some body transit records are also available in a number of other states and cities. The permits may be interfiled with death records in the location where the burial took place. *See also* **Insurance Records.**

Correspondence is as essential to genealogical research as it is to the business world or to maintaining contact with friends in other cities. All investigations into family history inevitably result in some letter writing, unless a researcher has unlimited funds with which to travel to each and every resource destination. For this reason good correspondence techniques are an asset in obtaining information from others.

Writing good letters is never easy. Some people waste a great deal of time and effort at the task with limited results. They would profit by following a few simple rules of good letter writing:

First, never ask for too many things in a single letter, and make each request easy to answer. If one knows something about the records held at a certain public repository, one is in a better position to judge what a reasonable request for such information might be. If additional information is needed, this can be sought in follow-up letter. One should never write to an archive center or relative asking for "everything you have" about so and so. If one wants answers, be concise and ask specific questions. Furthermore, sending forms such as pedigree charts to a recipient, unless these have been specifically requested, may only cause confusion. It is better when writing to relatives to put any family data in a tabular form with a statement such as "This information is all I have on the family. Can you add anything or make corrections?" And, of course, never send such family data to public officials.

Second, always enclose a self-addressed, stamped envelope. Be sure a letter is addressed properly so that it reaches the correct place. The story has been often told of a lady who wrote to President Abraham Lincoln asking for some advice and his signature so that she could have it as a memento. His reply was: "When asking strangers for a favor, it is customary to send postage. There's your advice and here's my signature. A. Lincoln." Most genealogists make a copy of each letter they send for their record files.

Third, express thanks for any help rendered. Usually there is no legal obligation to answer letters requesting information or to give help to those who request assistance. Such help is a favor that should be recognized by gratitude, particularly since one may need to go to these sources sometime later for more help. At the same time, there is no need to apologize when making a request. Often one must send a small payment for services rendered by state and county records officials, so it is wise to tell the recipient that you will be quite willing to provide whatever fee is expected.

When writing for copies of vital records certificates, be as brief as possible. This is a matter of practicality. Busy public officials don't have time to read long and involved letters. In fact, if a letter appears to require more than what might be reasonable time to read the contents, it will likely be put aside for a while so that the official can turn to more important tasks. In requests for birth records, one should include the names of the parents and a date as close as possible to when the event took place. In requests for death records, one should state all one might know about the exact happening and its date.

Just as it is essential for one to keep records of all the sources that have been investigated as one works on a genealogical history, so it is wise to keep a correspondence calendar of all the letters written. At the least this record should include the date a request is made, the subject of that request, the resulting information, and a record of the fees charged by the respondent. Of course, it is also wise to make a duplicate copy of every letter, note, or form that one sends so that it can be referred to when necessary.

Finally, for those who despise the task of writing letters, there is the *International Vital Records Handbook*, published by the Baltimore Genealogical Publishing Company, that provides sample letters that may be photocopied and used to request vital records from any state. Some computer Websites, such as genealogy.com, will provide form letters in English as well as other languages that can be used.

Costa Rica *see* **Central American Genealogy**

County Histories, much like published family histories, reflect a wide variety of research abilities in terms of quality and reliability. Because many of them include biographical sketches of individuals or families, they can be important to genealogical research. These volumes often give good historical background on the local area as well as containing brief histories of the towns, churches, schools, and fraternal organizations in the county. Most of them include information about the first settlers, first officers, and first institutions as well. They usually describe the geography, terrain, and water courses in the county and their effect on the county's settlement and population.

Many of these county histories were published in the 1880s by companies that specialized in such works. A large number of them can be found in any genealogical library, as well as some more general libraries. For some states there are histories for every county, as is the case of New York and Iowa, and for a few states there are also a surprising number of town histories. Furthermore, there are some regional histories, such as the *History of Western Maryland* (1882).

A helpful guide for locating county histories is the *Consolidated Bibliography of County Histories in Fifty States in 1961*, compiled by Clarence S. Peterson (1963). Also useful is *A Bibliography of American County Histories* by F. William Filby (1985). Both of these volumes were published in Baltimore.

Court Records of genealogical interest are of many kinds and for the most part can be found in the repositories of the various county courts. They can generally be divided into four types: 1) vital records—births, marriages, and deaths; 2) records dealing with matters of property; 3) civil and criminal records—land deeds, wills and probate actions, divorce proceedings, tax records, orphan and guardianship decisions, commitment papers, and others; and 4) administrative records—minutes of county commissioners, etc. With some justifiable exceptions, all court records are open to public use.

Both the statutes in question and the judgments rendered can suggest the prevailing understanding of law and morality and areas of conflict in families and communities. Many surviving court records are spare, listing only the plaintiff, the defendant, and the disposition of the case. Where fuller records (depositions, for example) exist, they can provide insight into individual events both ordinary and extraordinary. In most states the court records of one type or another go back to the founding of the state. But because each state sets up its own court system, researchers must find out the particular names and jurisdictions of the courts in the specific states where they are seeking information. The older records, of course, will likely be stored in hard-to-get-to locations because they are no longer needed for current cases. Sometimes the record custodian may not even know where they have been placed and an extensive search for them will be required.

The records and files of some court cases are voluminous, but there are likely to be digests of them to give the researcher clues as to what sections may be worth investigating further. Some court docket and minute books have been microfilmed or abstracted for publication, and sometimes the court clerks have created consolidated indexes of the estate documents, with separate books for wills, administration, bonds, and other records.

One can find court minutes, court order books, inventory books, bond books, account books, settlement books, estate packets, and more in the probate office. In the civil records office there will be papers involving small and large claims: citations, debts, attachments, levies, summons, divorces, notices re-

quired to be published in the newspaper, and depositions, just to name a few.

Although researching court records can be tedious and time consuming, it often provides quite-useful genealogical information. The complaint of a plaintiff (the portion at the beginning of a case file where the cause is explained, also sometimes called the petition, declaration, or statement of claim), the plea of the defendant (or answer to the complaint), and the decree (final judgment) usually have genealogical details found nowhere else. For example, one's ancestors' court appearances will reveal why a couple might have divorced, why they might have sought water rights, or why their land might have been threatened with foreclosure. These are happenings that no vital records lists or family Bibles will reveal.

In extracting court records, one must be sure to record the complete citations so that all the pertinent information will be available. Witnesses or those who gave bond for certain transactions, for example, may turn out to have been relatives of the person whose name appears on the record docket.

Croatia *see* **Eastern European Genealogy**

Cuban Genealogy has a large following among those who have emigrated to the United States and some other countries, but no one knows how much interest there may be in this subject within the island nation itself. The country was supervised from 1535 to 1821 by the viceroyalty of New Spain (now Mexico), except for a brief interlude in 1762 and 1763 when the British were in control. Then it came under the direct control of Spain until 1899, when it became an economic and political protectorate of the United States. In 1959 Fidel Castro led a revolution that overthrew the government of dictator Fulgencio Batista. This event soon resulted in strained relations between the United States and Cuban governments that continues to this day.

The first registration of births, marriages, and deaths, whether conducted by religious or civil authorities, began in Cuba in 1899. After 1918, the performance of a civil marriage was made mandatory, whether accompanied by a religious ceremony or not.

The records of these events are held in the civil registries of the towns in which they occurred. There are also some parish registers that are in the hands of local parish priests. The legal actions of notaries are held in the archives of the notarial districts, some of them dating back to the 18th century. A national archives, the Archivo National Compostela y San Isidro, in Havana, has genealogical and historical materials such as census returns, land petitions, and military records.

It is against the law in Cuba to send official documents to the United States, so the only way the researcher can obtain documents from the civil registers or the national archives is to go to Cuba, a difficult task considering that the U.S. government enforces a general ban on travel to Cuba by American citizens. One must pay a small fee to obtain copies of any documents from these archives.

Two biographical and genealogical works that may be of help to the researcher in Cuban genealogy are the seven-volume *Diccionario Biográfico Cubano* by Francisco Calcagno, first published in 1878. A facsimile edition was published in 1996 by Editorial Cubana, Inc. in Miami. The other work is the nine-volume *Historia de Familias Cubanas*, by Francisco Xavier de Santa Cruz y Mallen, Count of Jaruco. The first six volumes were published in Havana and the last three in the U.S. by Ediciones Universal in Miami, Florida.

Czechoslovakian Records *see* **Eastern European Genealogy**

D

Danish Genealogy had its beginnings in 1645 when the clergy were directed to keep parish registers. Some of these registers were initiated much earlier; the earliest one extant is the parish register of Hjordkær, near Aabenraa, that dates from 1573. Until 1814 only one copy of each of these parish registers was maintained, so rectory fires eventually destroyed some of them. But in 1814 an ordinance was issued that required all parish registers be kept in duplicate form and that none of them were to be held under the parish roof overnight. After that, no more register records were lost. In addition to the registration of births, marriages, and deaths, the parish registers contain lists of people who moved into and away from a parish, indicating where they came from and where they moved.

Starting in 1831, it became the rule that each duplicate copy of these parish registers be sent to the provincial archives 30 years after its recording. The records were then made available to public view after 50 years. These registers are now stored at four provincial sites, namely Copenhagen (those embracing Zealand, Lolland-Falster, Bornholm, and the former Danish colonies), Aabenraa (South Jutland), Viborg (North Jutland), and Odense (Funen). This practice of keeping parish registers was discontinued for the most part after 1875, and from that time until the introduction of the national register in 1923 there is little that a researcher can find to indicate the migration patterns of the population.

The provincial archives hold records for both ecclesiastical and temporal matters, and it is compulsory for the state administration to give copies of its records to the provincial archives. The municipal administrations also have the right to do so. Most market towns since the municipal reform of 1970 have increasing numbers of records from the rural districts.

The earliest census lists date from 1787, 1801, 1834 and 1840. From 1845 onwards, the census records give the place of birth of every individual, and thereafter a census was taken every five or 10 years. The latest census returns that are available to public view are those of 1916.

Another group of records that can be found in the provincial archives is those of the probate courts. These records contain detailed information about the assets of the deceased, as well as the names of all their heirs and often their places of residence. Until about 1800, there was a confusing multitude of probate jurisdictions held by the prefect, manorial landlord, rural dean, or the recorder of a town. But since then all of these authorities have surrendered their records to the provincial archives, and one can now find them in the archives search room. Probate records later than 1919 are still in the custody of local judges. The protocols of the trade licenses that were granted often contain information about the origins of new traders and craftsmen, and in the fire insurance valuations one can still find descriptions of the houses.

Two difficulties face a researcher in dealing with Danish genealogical data. Until about 1900 the common handwriting in Denmark was the so-called Danish Script (Gothic Script), in which all documents were written. Because many rectors and others had their own personal form of handwriting that sometimes is difficult to read, the deciphering of Danish Script records is often just a matter of guesswork.

The other difficulty comes from the fact that the large majority of the Danish rural population did not have a permanent family name until sometime after 1850. The sons were given their fathers' Christian names with a "-sen" added as their surnames, and the daughters were given their fathers' Christian names with "-datter" added. Hans Nielsen's children, for example, might be called Niels Hansen, Jørgen Hansen and Maren Hansdatter.

The city of Copenhagen is the principal seat of the national archives. The Danish State Archives office there keeps the records of the kingdom, together with large quantities of the old private collections, the older wills, and the archives of Copenhagen University, as well as those of the war office before 1868. Printed guides and finding aids for doing research in the archives are available.

The Danish State Archives holds lists of peasant sons liable for military service that date back to 1788. Until 1849 only peasant sons were conscripted into military service; their names were entered into the lists at birth by the manorial landlords. In 1849 the duty for military service was extended to all male children of age 15, and then in 1869 of age 17. These lists are helpful to genealogists because they give the name of the conscript's father, as well as information as to who moved away from or moved into a recruiting area. Special lists of navy conscripts were kept in the parishes that border the sea. The national archives also holds lists of the numerous veterans who received commemorative medals for their service in the wars of 1848–50 and 1864.

One interesting source of information is the servants' conduct books that date from 1832 and continue well into the 20th century. These books were issued to all servants in Denmark and were used to enter information, both positive and negative, about the various places where they served. Each book contains the holder's date and place of birth. Copies can be found in both the national and provincial archives.

The National Library of Denmark in Copenhagen has an extensive collection of both Danish and foreign books, while the municipal libraries of Frederiksberg have specialized in biography and genealogy. They house large collections on these topics. Two catalogs of these collections up to 1951 have been published and are available in any Danish library. A supplement was published in 1974 as the *Fortegnelse over slægtslitteratur 1948–1972* (Bibliography of Genealogical Literature 1948–1972), which can be found in the *Personalhistorisk Tidsskrift* (Review of Biography and Genealogy).

The largest collection of biographies of prominent Danish individuals is to be found in the three editions of the *Dansk Biografisk Leksikon* (Dictionary of Danish Biography). There are also a number of excellent directories, dealing with clergymen and members of the legal and medical professions. A list of these directories can be found in the *Haandbog i Slægtsforskning* (Manual of Genealogy) by Albert Fabritius and Harald Hatt.

Date Variations frequently occur in genealogical records. One of the main reasons is that Americans commonly place the month before the day, i.e., January 16, 1936, or 1/16/1936, and the Canadians, British, and other Europeans commonly place the day before the month, i.e. 16 January 1936, or 16/1/1936. If neither of the first two dates is greater than 12, it can be difficult to determine which format was used. For example, January 3, 1970 can be written as both 1/3/70 and 3/1/70. Whenever one runs into this problem, it is wise to look for other dates in the work being examined to find places where at least one of the first two numbers is greater than 12. This will indicate which system the author was using. To assure accuracy in any family history one must transcribe each date according to a single preferred method. Many genealogists recommend using the day, with a three-character month, followed by the full year, i.e., 10 Feb 1953. In this case there is no mistaking which is the month or year, and the date takes the least space because periods are not needed for the month abbreviation and no comma is required to separate the day from the year.

Another date problem occurs because a switch was made in 1752 from the Julian to the Gregorian calendar. The Julian calendar was established in 46 B.C. by Julius Caesar. It had March 25 as the first day of the year and each year was 365 days and 6 hours long. But in 1582, Pope Gregory XIII determined that the Julian calendar was incorrect in that each day was a bit too long and not in accord with nature's calendar. To solve the problem, the pope created what is known as the Gregorian calendar. This changed the first day of the year to January 1 and also jumped ahead by 10 days to make up for the lost time.

The genealogical aspect of this problem comes in the fact that the entire world did not adopt this Gregorian calendar at the same time. The Roman Catholic countries did so in 1582, but it was not generally adopted in the United States until 1752 (although the Dutch in New Netherland never used the Julian calendar) and Greece did not adopt it until 1923. Thus if a person was born while the Julian calendar was in use but died after the Gregorian calendar was adopted the dates on his or her tombstone may give conflicting data. For example, George Washington was born on 11 February 1731 in the British Colonies of America when the Julian calendar was still in use. His date of birth was later adjusted to 22 February 1732 to account for the changes caused by the adoption of the Gregorian calendar. This is the date we now celebrate.

By the time England and the colonies adopted the Gregorian calendar, the discrepancy between the two calendars was 11 days. The government then ordered that September 2, 1752, should be followed by September 14, 1752. Some people at that time also added 11 days to their birthdates (a fact that is never noted on their birth certificates). The general rule used by most genealogists is to add 11 days to any birthdate recorded contemporaneously for a child born before September 1752 so that the date will be in accord with the calendar practices that are now in effect.

These calendar differences are often referred to as "old style" and "new style" dates. The most thorough genealogical sources will indicate both dates recorded with the appropriate notations. Others just list them as double dates, i.e., 23 Jan 1731/2 (indicating the end of 1731 in the "old style" and the early part of 1732 in the "new style"). But many sources record the date as it is found in the original document, and it may be unclear whether the transcriber has written the date literally or made allowance for the modern calendar. However one decides to handle the problem, all researchers should be aware of the discrepancies. In most cases the genealogist does not need to calculate the exact day in new style form from the old style form. Perhaps only astronomers and mathematicians enjoy doing this. But if such a calculation is absolutely necessary, genealogical programs exist on the Internet that can do the work in a flash.

If the dates that are being used come from more diverse cultures, then one finds that the date now used in the West (the Gregorian calendar) may be quite different from that used in other cultures. For example 9

October 1998 in the West is the same date as 19 Eighth Month 4635 in China; 17 Jumada al-Ahiral 1419 in Islamic countries; 17 Asvina 1920 in India; 19 Tishri 5759 in Israel; and 26 September 1998 wherever the Julian calendar still holds sway.

A few other things the researcher should be aware of regarding dates are the fact that the Society of Friends (or Quakers), when it was established, did not approve of the month and day names that often were in honor of "pagan gods" (for example, January and March for the Roman gods Janus and Mars). The Quakers thus adopted the practice of referring to the months (and days of the week) by their relative positions; i.e., fourth month, third day, etc. This is easily understood and should not cause many problems.

The church records for many denominations often list the date on which a couple makes the announcement of their intention to marry, usually called the marriage banns. Be careful not to misinterpret the dates of such marriage intentions as the actual wedding date. The same thing can be found in church and cemetery records that may contain the date of the funeral rather than the date of death.

Daughters of the American Revolution Records are located in the Daughters of the American Revolution (DAR) Library in Washington, D.C. Founded in 1896 as a repository for genealogical and historical publications to be used by staff genealogists in verifying application papers for membership in the DAR, this library now has a book collection numbered at some 150,000 volumes. Approximately 5,000 new titles are added to its shelves each year.

Officially named the National Society of the Daughters of the American Revolution, the DAR was founded in Washington, D.C., in 1890, and was chartered by Congress in 1896. Its membership is open to women over 18 years of age who can prove their descent from any person who aided in establishing American independence. DAR programs promote appreciation for the past, patriotic service in the present, and educational training for the future. The organization helps preserve shrines that keep alive the memory of persons who served in the war for American independence.

Shortly after 1900 the library's growing collection was opened to the public and it has remained so ever since. Non-members of the DAR, as well as the Sons of the American Revolution, Sons of the Revolution, and Children of the American Revolution pay a small daily user fee to help maintain and expand the library's collection. Members of the 2,975 DAR chapters in the United States also support the library through donations of both books and money.

The period of the American Revolution is naturally the major focal point of this library, but the colonial era and the 19th century receive detailed coverage as well. Of particular interest to genealogists, since they are not found elsewhere, are the approximately 15,000 volumes of *Genealogical Records Committee Reports* that have been compiled by DAR members nationwide and constitute a unique source for family histories, cemetery record transcriptions, and Bible records.

Death Records, like birth records, provide concrete proof for the existence of a specific person at a particular period of time. They can be verified by death certificates, newspaper obituaries, coroner's records, cemetery records, and the Social Security Death Index. To obtain a facsimile copy of any available death certificate in the United States, one must write or go to the vital statistics office in the state or area where the death occurred. The small fees for this service vary according to the location.

The death certificates usually show the person's name, age at time of death, place and cause of death, and name and relationship of the informant. In some cases they also indicate when and where the person was buried, the witnesses at the funeral, where the person was married and to whom, age at the time of marriage, and the names and ages of living children and number of dead children. In many cases the newspaper obituaries are based on death certificates that are on file at funeral homes. But, as any experienced researcher knows, the death information is mostly provided by others who may be unsure about dates and places of birth, as well as the names of the deceased's parents. Thus they should always be checked against other records, if any are available.

Coroners' records, which are typically public records, can be a particularly rich resource of genealogical data related to a subject's death. They are usually held at one of the three governmental jurisdictions: state, county, or city. Some coroners' reports that were filed prior to the 20th century have been microfilmed and can be found in various genealogical libraries.

Cemeteries usually provide information on headstones, including the person's name and date of death. In some cases there may also be the year and place of birth as well as the person's occupation and spouse's name. Records in the office of a cemetery caretaker will likely add to the gravestone information by giving the names of the individual's children, parents, and other helpful data. It is important to remember that family groups are often buried together in some cemeteries, so that the location of one gravesite may lead to previously unrecorded information on a whole segment of a family tree.

The Social Security Death Index, beginning about 1935, gives a record of the individual's name, date of birth, date of death, and place where the death was reported. The records are readily available from the Social Security Administration, can be found in some genealogical libraries, and can be located on several Websites. *See also* **Cemeteries; Coroner and Mortician Records; Social Security Records; Vital Records**.

Deeds of trust, gifts, warrants, powers of attorney, and prenuptial agreements are among the most common and most useful types of deed records to a genealogist. These are not the only kinds of records found in deed books, but they are the ones that reveal various dates, relationships, marriages, former and new residences, and other pertinent details about the doings of a particular family. The affidavits found in deed books can also provide valuable genealogical information. Fortunately deeds are almost always indexed,

and in the case of land sale agreements, the deeds are indexed separately under the names of both the grantor (seller) and the grantee (buyer).

Deeds establish ownership and describe property. They sometimes indicate the circumstances of property transfer, and they can occasionally provide clues to the topography and ownership patterns in a given neighborhood or district. Deeds also often state relationships among individuals (son, daughter, child, wife, etc.) and for those that don't, the relationships can often be inferred from the transactions themselves. The records will also tell where the land came from, such as the estate of a parent or grandparent. The dower rights will include the name of a wife who must assent to the sale before witnesses to make the land title clear. Quit-claim deeds will list the married names of daughters and the signatures of heirs to undivided land, while deeds of gift may include the names of slaves given to grandchildren or aging parents. Security deeds reflect indebtedness of an ancestor and often list securities other than land. Deeds are thus indispensable in pedigree researches.

Yet working with the various kinds of deeds inevitably involves a genealogist in a great mass of records, many of which have legal language that is quite difficult for a novice to understand. To make a photocopy of every record that pertains to a person of interest may result in large quantities of rather useless information. Therefore the genealogist usually abstracts only the most pertinent data, such as the names of the parties to the deed, the places of residence for those parties, and the issue involved.

One particularly valuable feature of many deeds is the naming of the seller's wife. Sometimes the wife signed the deed with her husband. At other times, the wife might be taken aside by the appointees of the court to acknowledge the sale and relinquish her dower rights to the property. In many instances, the only place one might ever find the name of a wife is within a deed. Sometimes one will find the name of a wife that was not known to have existed. True, one won't find her maiden name, but there will be her first name.

There must be subscribing witnesses to the deed, and these may be friends, neighbors, or other members of the family.

Sometimes one will discover a difference between the spelling of a name in the body of the deed and the signature at the end of the document. This is because deeds were normally prepared by a lawyer, court clerk, or judge who wrote everyone's name as it was pronounced. The buyer, seller, seller's wife, and witness then signed the document in the way that they preferred their names to be spelled. Any man who signed his name with an X can be distinguished from others who could write their own names.

Deeds of trust are instruments made to secure the payment of a debt by the transference of a title to one or more trustees. Many such deeds were executed in the South after the Civil War when everyone was in debt and few had enough money to pay their debts. Warranty deeds are those used to transfer property with the guarantee of a good title. In the public land states, property conveyed by such deeds was identified by the section or fraction of a section, township, and range in which it lay. *See also* **Land Records**.

Delaware Records extend back to 1638 when the Swedes built a fort and established the first permanent European settlement in the region. Soon afterward the Dutch took control, followed by the English who ruled through James, Duke of York, until he granted the land to William Penn in 1682. The early colonial documents, printed copies of which can be found at various genealogical libraries, are found in archives of New York and Pennsylvania, as well as those of Sweden, the Netherlands, and Great Britain.

A complicating factor in the study of early Delaware records comes in the matter of boundary lines. The boundaries of Delaware did not reach their present configuration until 1760, due primarily to a long battle waged between the Penn family of Pennsylvania and the Calvert family of Maryland over who should control much of this territory. It is thus wise for a genealogist to check the records of both these states, plus Virginia, when researching early Delaware families.

The registration of births in Delaware began in 1861, stopped in 1863, and resumed in 1881. The Bureau of Vital Statistics, Division of Public Health, in Dover has these records, but they are filed by year rather than by name so that it is necessary to have the year of birth before any search of the records can be initiated. The registration of marriages began in 1847 and these can also be found at the Bureau of Vital Statistics. Delaware law stipulates that once birth records are at least 72 years old and marriage and death records at least 40 years old, they can be opened to public view. Copies of the birth, marriage, and death records can be obtained from the Vital Statistics Bureau for a small fee. Birth records up to 1930 and marriage and death records up to 1962 can also be found at the Delaware Public Archives in Dover. The Hall of Records in Dover has indexed birth records covering the years 1861–1913, death records for the years 1855–1910, baptisms for 1759–1890, and marriages for 1730–1850.

Unlike many other states Delaware never conducted a census of its own. However, there are records available from each of the 10-year national enumerations starting in 1800, located at the various National Archives sites. There is also a printed list of Delaware residents who were Loyalists during the American Revolution. It was compiled by the Historical Society of Delaware and can be found in many genealogical libraries. The Delaware Public Archives Commission of Dover, before 1919, collected a great deal of material relating to genealogical records and bound it in five volumes. Volumes two and three are in print and can be viewed at some libraries, particularly that of the Historical Society of Delaware in Wilmington. The Historical Society also has an alphabetically arranged card file of over 120,000 names that refer to births, baptisms, marriages, and deaths that were gleaned from newspapers printed before 1850, books, journals, church records, and other sources. Furthermore, the library has copies of the many Delaware cemetery lists compiled by the Work Projects Administration and the Delaware Genealogical Society.

Divorce records in Delaware are filed in

the superior court of each county, while guardianships are recorded in the county orphans' courts for minors and the county chancery courts for all others. Wills are filed in the county registers' courts, but all such probate records are then forwarded to the Hall of Records in Dover where they are indexed. Deeds are maintained by the county recorder of deeds, but access to them is restricted to attorneys at law. There is a collection of deeds in the Delaware Public Archives that can be viewed, as can the collection of Delaware tax assessments.

McCarter and Jackson's *Historical and Biographical Encyclopedia of Delaware* and J.M. Runk's *Biographical and Genealogical History of the State of Delaware,* found in various genealogical libraries, are quite useful for information about prominent Delaware families.

Through much of the colonial period, New Castle served as a major port of entry for ships from the British Isles. Yet because Delaware was part of the British Empire, the journey was considered one of internal migration, so immigration records were not kept. Thus, few passenger lists exist. The ones that do usually give the name of the ship and date of arrival, as well as the names of the passengers, but not their ages or towns of origin.

Researchers seeking information from county records can locate them at the following county seats: (Kent County) Dover, (New Castle County) Wilmington, and (Sussex County) Georgetown.

FOR FURTHER INFORMATION SEE:
- *Delaware Genealogical Research Guide.* Wilmington, DE: Delaware Genealogical Society, 1989.
- Delaware Public Archives Commission. *Delaware Archives.* 3 vols. Wilmington, DE: James and Walls, 1875.

Denmark *see* **Danish Genealogy**

Diaries *see* **Memoirs, Diaries, and Family Letters**

Disciples of Christ Records can be found in this denomination's Historical Society Library in Nashville, Tennessee, as well as in the records of each of its local churches. This Protestant denomination developed in the United States during the early 1800s under the leadership of Thomas Campbell, his son Alexander, and Barton W. Stone. The church now has about four million members; they adopted its present full name of Christian Church (Disciples of Christ) in 1968. Church headquarters are in Indianapolis, Indiana. The Historical Society Library has some 35,000 books and 50,000 files of personal and institutional records covering the 200 years of the Stone-Campbell Movement. Among these records is a wealth of genealogical information. Other information about the movement can be found in the Brite Divinity School Library in Fort Worth, Texas.

Divorce Records *see* **Marriage Records**

Documentation is as essential to genealogical information as it is to writing a history or producing a good research paper. In fact it is a common saying among genealogists: "Without proof there is no truth."

Only when a statement or date is backed up by a reference as to where it came from will other researchers have confidence in the accuracy of the information. Thus it is most important to cite sources. When there is no documentation the researcher is likely to repeat all the same steps with the same documents that a previous genealogist covered, thus wasting of a great deal of time and resources that could better have been used in seeking out areas no one has yet tackled.

Even in a researcher's own work, documentation is needed to avoid duplication of effort. Generally a researcher will do some work on one branch of a family line and then set this aside for many months while turning to another branch or even another family, only to return to the first task after most of the sources that were previously examined have been forgotten. If the citations are not written down, it is probable that the researcher will end up examining many of the same sources once again, only to find, or not find, what had already been learned. Taking time to document one's research will likely, in the long run, speed up the work.

Because much genealogical research is

based on the documented research of others, it is only right that one should cite the sources in any new study so as to aid those who might come afterward. This enables subsequent researchers to continue the work after a genealogist has decided to abandon further pursuit of any particular line of enquiry. No one has the time or energy to do unaided research on a family line, since for each person that is found there will be two more (his or her parents) to go after. The task is endless and can only be achieved in some measure through depending on the work that has been done in the past by others.

There are so many ways to cite sources that doing so takes little effort. Lineage societies, of course, require a certain level of documentation to constitute proof, and there are scholarly standards that are used in publications, but one does not need to follow those standards at the time of taking raw notes. As long as enough information is recorded so that others can determine what has been researched, this will be sufficient. The genealogist who later decides to publish the research can go back over the raw notes at that time and put the citations in proper form.

There is just one rule for documentation, whether in raw notes or established standards: record enough information so that any other researcher can determine what has been searched. It is not enough to simply say that the source is the U.S. Census. One needs to indicate, for instance, that the source is the U.S. Census of 1860 for Cook County, Illinois. It may also be wise to note the page and line number, as well as the microfilm roll number, because this may later be needed in the publication of a more formal scholarly work.

The six elements of a scholarly citation are: the author (who provided the information); the title; the publication information (publisher, location); the date of the information (usually the year); the location of the source used (library or archive) and the call number, and the reference number to the specific information (page, entry, line, etc.). A distinction is often made between primary sources and secondary sources. The primary records in genealogy include deeds, wills, court proceedings, and church or civil documents that record births, baptisms, marriages, and deaths or burials. The secondary sources include almost all published works, be they county histories, genealogies, or indexes and abstracts of original records. It is usually assumed that primary records are more exact than secondary ones, but for the researcher both are valid citations. It is simply impossible to assume that there will always be a precise primary record for every event in one's database. Thus a researcher will usually have to rely on secondary sources to document a work.

There are a number of excellent guides that show how to list citations in a scholarly form. These include *The Chicago Manual of Style*, published by the University of Chicago Press in many editions; Richard S. Lackey's *Cite Your Sources* (University Press of Mississippi, 1980); and Elizabeth Shown Mills's *Evidence: Citation & Analysis for the Family Historian* (Genealogical Publishing Co., 1997).

Domesday Book, a statistical survey of the property and people of England, was ordered to be compiled by William the Conqueror in 1085. This was the first census to be completed by any European nation, and it was designed to register all the landed wealth of the country in a systematic fashion. This listing was then used by William to determine the revenues due him as king. In collecting these records of all feudal estates, both lay and ecclesiastical, the Domesday Book also enabled the king to strengthen his authority by exacting oaths of allegiance from each of the tenants who lived on the land, as well as from all the nobles and churchmen.

Each place named in the Domesday Book includes the name of the person who was maintaining the estate at the time that King Edward the Confessor died in 1066, and each person who then acquired it after William redistributed the land among his own followers. Thus this census contains a great deal of genealogical information. But this, of course, was not the purpose for which this census was designed. William was only interested in having an accurate account of the nature of the land, its value, and the number and condition of the people living on it. The census was named the Domesday Book because no one was allowed to question its authority once the survey was completed. In fact its contents were considered to be as irreversible as the Last Judgement Day ("Domesday" is a corruption of the word "Doomsday").

The census was completed in 1086 by a group of commissioners, called legati, who were sent out by William to collect all the information. The data was eventually recorded in two massive Latin volumes that are still preserved in the Public Records Office in London. The legati were required to ask of the town and county representatives a specific set of questions that constituted the Inquisitio Eliensis; the answers they received were then recorded in the Domesday Book. Modern studies of this census have shown, as a rough estimate, that the number of persons then living in England totaled a million to a million and a half. The number of knights can be put at 5,500 and the number of great tenants directly holding their lands at the behest of the Crown at less than 200. It was the practice in feudal society for the King to actually own all the land and loan it out to tenants-in-chief who, in their turn, let out parts of this land to under-tenants, in subinfeudation as it was termed.

The first and larger of the two volumes, called the Great Domesday, included information on all England with the exception of three eastern counties and several northern ones. The surveys of the three eastern counties (Essex, Suffolk, and Norfolk) constitute the second volume, called the Little Domesday. No record, however, survives for the records from Durham, London, and Northumberland. The two volumes—Great and Little—were first published in 1783. An index was produced in a separate volume in 1811. An additional volume containing the Inquisitio Eliensis with surveys of the lands of Ely was published in 1816. Then, between 1861 and 1863, a facsimile edition of the original work was published. This edition can be found in many libraries of Britain.

The Domesday Book was frequently used in medieval law courts, and still today is occasionally used in cases involving matters of topography and genealogy.

Dutch Genealogy, prior to Napoleon's conquest in 1811, is primarily a matter of church registrations. As early as 1695 all churches were asked to keep duplicate copies of their baptismal and marriage records. Although many did, there were also many that did not. Thus there are churches with registers that don't go back very far, and many don't begin until 1772 when the churches were firmly ordered to keep duplicate records. These records can now be found in the archives of the 11 provincial capitals.

Fires, floods, and hostilities were responsible for the loss of many of the church records over the centuries. One will usually find that the minister or clerk responsible for keeping these records has made a note in the register that certain years are missing due to such calamities. Sometimes a clerk even put the records in a safe place and then later forgot where they were, and sometimes the records are missing because they were stolen.

One of the difficulties in searching through the Dutch records before 1811 is that there are few real surnames. Patronymics were then in use (names derived from the father, such as Peterson for the son of Peter), but not surnames. Napoleon's decree that every person should take a name and register it resulted in the establishment of some 87,000 family names that are now in use in Holland. Careful analysis of these names may give clues as to where in Holland a particular family came from.

People researching records in the Netherlands, however, do have some advantages over genealogists in many other countries. This is because all the witnesses to church baptismals are usually listed, including the grandparents, aunts, uncles, and older siblings, so that whole generations of a family can be found at once. In addition to the records of births, marriages, and deaths, the church records contain minutes of the church councils, which consisted of the minister, the elders, and the deacons. These records are usually divided into two parts, those dealing with the elder's decisions (ouderling) and those dealing with the deaconate (diaken). These minutes can be quite rewarding to a genealogist because they detail aspects of church life that cannot be found among the vital statistics, items such as who was censured for drunkenness or how a case of marital infidelity was handled by the elders.

The system of civil registration that began with Napoleon was maintained after Holland regained its independence in 1815. Records from that date are in the main center of archives, the Rijksarchief in The Hague. These include notarial records (legal records), court records (land registration, land transfers, orphan's court matters, civil marriages, etc.), and tax records (taxes on burials, marriages, cattle, hearth stones, etc.). Probably the most useful tax records are those on burials and marriages. These records often reveal several names in a single family.

It has been the practice in the Netherlands for guardians to be appointed for orphaned children or for children who might soon become orphaned because one of the parents was seriously ill. The family will then have a guardian (or guardians) appointed to make sure that the remaining spouse looks after the child or several children. In the court records one can often find the ages of the children as well as the names of the brothers, sisters, brothers-in-law, sisters-in-law, and sometimes even grandparents. Wills from about 1850 are held in the Central Testamenten Register, or Central Registry of Wills, at The Hague. Earlier wills must be sought in the provincial archives.

In 1945 the Dutch government and representatives of the business community established the Centraal Bureau voor Genealogie (CBG) at The Hague as a special place for genealogical research in the Netherlands. Since then, the CBG has achieved an international reputation as an excellent information center for genealogy, family history and heraldry. More than one hundred visitors make use of its reading rooms every day. It has a fine collection of resource materials and provides information about the newest developments in the field of genealogy to all interested parties.

Dutch Reformed Records *see* **Reformed Church Records**

E

Eastern European Genealogy deals with the records for Albania, Bulgaria, Czechoslovakia, Hungary, Poland, Romania, and Yugoslavia (Slovenia, Macedonia, Croatia, Bosnia and Herzegovina, Serbia, and Montenegro). Some of these records are quite limited due to the many political changes that have occurred in these nations. Others are much more extensive. Here is a brief description of what can be found in each of these countries:

Albania— Until 1929 all birth, marriage, and death records in this country — one of the smallest in Europe — were kept by the churches, both Roman Catholic and Orthodox. As for the Moslems, who make up 21 percent of the population, their records were not maintained as well as were those of the Christian churches. After Albania became a republic in 1929, civil registration came into force. The country had previously been occupied by the Austro-Hungarians, Italians, Serbs, and French. During the Communist period following World War II, many of the church records were destroyed so that there is limited likelihood of finding much genealogical information in Albania today.

Bulgaria— This is another country where the genealogical resources are rather scarce. Parochial registers were begun in 1860 when the Bulgarian Church became independent of the Greek Orthodox Church, and civil registration began in 1893. The records are kept in the 28 district archives. Wills have been deposited with the various notaries public. Older documents are stored at the Ministry of Justice in Sofia. There are also some records from earlier times at the Bulgarian National Library in Sofia. It is said that there are now about 200 members of the Bulgarian Genealogy Association that was founded in 1975. The association publishes a magazine in Bulgarian, titled *Rodoznanie* (Genealogy).

Czechoslovakia— Here there are both Catholic and Protestant parishes that have kept parish registers. Some of the Catholic ones extend back to 1620. The records can be found written in Czech, German, or Latin, and in some parishes there are records written in all three languages. In 1802 all of these records of births, marriages, and deaths, including the older ones, were indexed. This makes the individuals listed in the Czech records some of the easiest to locate. These parish registers were taken over by the state in 1950 and are now held in the National Archives in Prague. Civil registration began after 1918 but only for those persons who were not members of a church. Wills are kept by the state notaries who have offices in each town with a district administration.

A problem for persons working with Czech records is the handwriting and spelling forms that were used more than 70 years ago. Unless one is looking for quite recent names, the handwriting is likely to be in the style known as "Kurrent," which is a German script that cannot be read by most Czechoslovakians today without some instruction and experience. There are a number of letters in Kurrent that are easily confused with letters in the modern Czech script: "a" often looks like an "r," "e" like an "n," and the capital "S" like an "O." When Latin was used, elements of the Latin script often crept into Kurrent, making it doubly difficult to read. Add to this the problems of poor handwriting (in whatever style) and faded documents, as well as the fact that spelling in the past differed radically from modern practice.

The first Czech census was taken as early as 1158, but has been preserved only in fragments. It was recorded in Latin and can be seen at the National Archives. The first census complete enough to be useful as a genealogical tool is the Register of People by Denomination of 1651. It was completed following the Thirty Years War, and most persons then living were listed. The purpose, of course, was to obtain religious information so as to bring the country back into line with Catholicism. Various censuses were subsequently taken on a regular basis and have been ever since. The 1869 census, however, was the first to contain extensive information on each person in a household, such as the name, sex, birth year, marital status, occupation, religion, and place of birth. Many of the census records have been preserved, but many have also been destroyed or lost. Generally, such records are available at the district archives.

Four tax and land surveys were carried out by the state between about 1650 and 1848. They give the names of the owners of land, the serfs working the land, and a description of the land parcels. The primary advantage of these land records is that they go back further than the parish registers of births, marriages, and deaths. Often, the same land was passed from generation to generation, so it is possible to follow the various generations of a family line. The records are housed in the National Archives. Later land records are also deposited there, with some of them in regional archives and others in town archives. There are also local histories of varying quality that can be consulted. These histories can be found in the town halls of each community.

Hungary— As with many other Catholic countries, the registration of baptisms, marriages, and burials in Hungary began in the 16th century, and as early as 1515 for baptisms. However, Hungary has been devastated many times in various wars, and churches and castles have been burned so that many of the records have been lost. The ecclesiastical records were formerly kept in the parishes, but the older ones have now been placed in the National Center of Archives in Budapest. Civil registrations began in 1895, and those records are also kept in the National Archives. Besides this center there are 21 provincial archives situated in the regional centers, as well as magistrates' offices in each town that maintain some of the vital records. Not all of these are open to public access.

Budapest can be quite a challenge to the researcher. It is separated into 22 districts, each having its own bureau of vital statistics and at least one Reformed and one Catholic church. There are some indexes to the Budapest records on microfilm at the National Archives, but they are difficult to use if the researcher has no knowledge of the district from which the person being sought came or the religion that person practiced.

There are also census records at the National Archives. The first census was conducted in 1696 after the liberation of Hungary from the Turks. It was a census only of the residents of the city of Buda and was taken to determine how many Hungarian families had survived the 150-year occupation. Not until 1715 was a countrywide census conducted. It was followed by two other censuses in 1720 and 1728. The next was in 1747, but this was an ecclesiastical one only. Another census, in 1748, was resisted by the nobility of Hungary, who did not wish to give personal details to a foreign monarch (Jozsef II of the Austrian Habsburg line) and parts of it were soon destroyed. Queen Marie-Teresa authorized the next census in 1770, but it was mainly an enumeration of the nobility and the lands they owned. In contrast, the census of 1828 enumerated everybody except the nobility.

The national censuses taken from 1868 on are subject to secrecy rules, so the only information available from them is number of persons and occupations by district. One citywide census of Budapest is open to researchers and is stored in the city archives, rather than the National Archives. It was a survey of the residents taken on January 1, 1941, during the early part of World War II.

Records that are held in district archives are difficult to use because, unless one can show a direct relationship to the person being sought, they remain confidential for 90 years. Wills and cemetery records are also difficult to locate, partly because so many have been destroyed. It is the practice in Hungary for graves to be rented for 25 years, at which point, if the contract for the gravesite is not renewed, the bodies are transferred to an unmarked communal plot in the corner of the cemetery.

The National Library in Budapest and the Budapest City Archives are where the researcher can find information about persons who lived in that city in the late 1800s and early 1900s. These institutions have collections of city directories and the records of the city administration. The directories are of two types, one for private individuals and business owners and the other for civil servants and city administrators. The City Archives also have what remains of the city guild records that list the apprenticeships and careers of various tradesmen, such as carpenters and goldsmiths. A source for military records in Budapest is the Hadtortenelmi leveltar, or Archives of Military History.

Poland— Due to many wars and other catastrophes that Poland suffered prior to its once more becoming a political entity (1918), most early genealogical records have been lost. The remaining ones may be found in a variety of places, but the record keeping of the three partitioning powers (Russia, Germany, and Austria) varied according to the methods they used. In Russian-ruled Poland, the clergy were authorized to keep the usual records and vital statistics; in the Austrian-ruled districts, the parish clergy were treated as state officials and ordered to make duplicates of their registers to be delivered to the local authorities; and in the German areas, the records were kept by secular officials. These differences, existing for a century and a quarter, have produced quite a tangle for the inquirer to unravel.

Although the practice of registering births (baptisms), marriages, and deaths in the local parishes was observed for centuries, the few records that can be found before 1795 provide relatively little data. Those compiled afterward vary according to their location. The Roman Catholic Church records were written in Latin for the provinces of Posen and Galicia, in Polish for the Kingdom of Poland until 1868, in German for the other former Prussian provinces, and in Russian for the Kingdom of Poland after 1868. The Lutheran Church records were written in

German, as were the Prussian civil state office records. The Eastern Orthodox Church records were written in Russian and the Byzantine Catholic records were written in Latin or Ukrainian.

The Catholic Church records prior to the early 1900s are usually stored in the diocesan archives, but some have remained in the churches. Because many Lutheran churches from the former German provinces were transferred to the Catholics after 1945, some of the Protestant Church records can also be found in the Catholic archives. A large number of Catholic and Lutheran Church records, as well as some Jewish ones, are stored at the Central Archives in Warsaw, most of them 19th century civil duplicates.

The 19th century records usually indicate information about the parents, such as the father's profession in the birth and death records, age in the marriage and death records, and cause of death in the death records. In the latter, a list of the surviving family may be provided. In the records from Galicia, even the names of the baby's grandparents are listed with the birth records.

After Poland had become independent in 1918, the civil registration offices in the former Prussian provinces were retained, whereas the other areas continued the older practice of producing duplicates separately for every religion. In 1946, after World War II, civil registration offices were established throughout the rest of Poland. Only the Province of Poznan (Posen) has comprehensive lists of existing vital records. Another source for genealogical records of Poland is the National Library in Warsaw.

Romania— Registrations of births, marriages, and deaths began officially in Romania in the 19th century and were conducted by the Orthodox churches. In Walachia these registrations (*mitrici*) were introduced in 1831, in Moldavia in 1832, and in Transylvania in 1895. Other religious bodies in Romania have kept registers since the second half of the 18th century. The registers were not transferred by the churches to the appropriate sections of the mayoral departments until 1865. Wills are located in the archives of the tribunals and in the state archives of the ter-

ritorial zones to which the respective tribunals pertain. The most important documents of the whole country are concentrated in these state archives with an aim toward their preservation. Although there is some difficulty in obtaining genealogical information in Romania, records can also be found at the National Library in Bucharest.

Yugoslavia— With the fall of the Austro-Hungarian Empire at the end of World War I, the victors created a new country composed of more than 20 ethnic groups, and called it Yugoslavia. Just over 70 years later this piecemeal nation disintegrated and war broke out between the newly created states. One segment, Slovenia, was the first to secede. It is the most heterogeneous and prosperous region of the former country of Yugoslavia. The Slovenians have their own language, are mostly Roman Catholic, and have set up their capital at Ljubljana. Another part of former Yugoslavia is Macedonia with its capital at Skopje. Then there is Croatia. The capital of this Roman Catholic state is Zagreb. Yet another segment is the independent nation of Bosnia and Herzegovina, with its capital city being Sarajevo. But by far the largest part, composed of Serbia and Montenegro, has become the Federal Republic of Yugoslavia with its capital in Belgrade.

Because of the discordant nature of Yugoslavia and its subsequent breakup, the state of records leaves much to be desired. Civil registration began in the territory of Volvodina only after 1895. Before that all vital records were kept in the church registers. In 1946 civil registration began for all of Yugoslavia, operated under the State Secretariat for Internal Affairs. Each person was required to supply information concerning birth, marriage, divorce, annulment, death, adoption, etc.

Now with the area becoming five separate nations, what genealogical records there are can be found spread around a variety of sites. In Slovenia some can be found at the Slovene Archives in Ljubljana. The Archives of Macedonia are divided into nine districts: Bitola, Veles, Kumanovo, Ohrid, Prilep, Skopje, Strumica, Tetovo, and Shtip. Probably the most important of these is the one in Skopje, the capital.

As of 1945 all birth, death, and marriage records held by the Croatian churches were turned over to the civil authorities and deposited in the various city halls. Those older than 1860 were turned over to the historical archives in the various districts. The churches were able to keep their religious records, such as the baptismal records and those regarding the "Status of the Souls." The latter record the names of a man and his wife upon marriage, as well as the names of each child as it was born. This genealogical material remains with the churches today.

Although Bosnia and Herzegovina are one nation, their archives are separated. Bosnia's state archives and historical archives are in Sarajevo, while Herzegovina's archives are in Mostar. There are also regional archives in the cities of Banja Luka, Travnik, Tuzla, and Doboj. The Federal Republic of Yugoslavia also has its archives split into four centers. Those of Serbia are in the city of Belgrade. Those of Montenegro are in Kotor. The other two are in Pristina and Sremski Karlovci.

Eastern Orthodox *see* **Orthodox Church Records**

Ecuadorian Genealogy has two major locations where extensive amounts of genealogical data and family history records can be found, the National Archives and the National Library, both in the city of Quito. The Republic of the Equator was one of three countries that emerged from the collapse of Bolivar's Gran Colombia in 1830 (the other two being Colombia and Venezuela). Between 1904 and 1942, Ecuador lost some of its territory in a series of conflicts with its neighbors.

The civil records of births, marriages, and deaths are stored in the National Archives where there are indexes for all the records. When this data was collected, it was separated by province, canton, city, and parish. The archive records include adoptions, divorces, and annotations for legitimacy. They cover the years from 1901 to the present. Some are in script and not easy to read. There are also records filled out on a long form, and more recent ones entered on a short form.

The parish records of the Catholic churches in Ecuador have been maintained since the foundation of the country. Some of the earliest ones have been destroyed, but later ones are intact. They can be located at the various parish churches. Some of the cemetery records date back to 1800. They include names and birth and death dates, as well as information regarding the rents paid for the gravesites. Some of them also give the sex, cause of death, attending physician, address of the deceased at the time of death, and other biographical information that can be of great assistance to the genealogist.

For many years the notaries public in Ecuador acted as judges in civil and criminal court cases. Their records can be found in the archives of the major cities as well as in the palaces of justice of the cities and towns where the notaries usually have their offices.

Education, Genealogical *see* **Genealogical Courses**

Educational Records *see* **School Records**

Egypt *see* **African Genealogy**

Ellis Island Records cover some 5.4 million people who arrived in New York between 1820 and 1860, as well as some 12 million who came during the peak years of immigration (1892 to 1924). The island lies about a mile southwest of the tip of Manhattan, and was once the site of an old fort. In 1855 it was designated as the Castle Garden immigrant station, under the supervision of the state. By the 1850s, New York was receiving more than three-quarters of the nation's total of immigrants, and by the 1890s, more than four-fifths.

In 1891 the U.S. Bureau of Immigration began to use the island as a detention and deportation center. The bureau renamed and dedicated it on New Year's Day 1892 as the Ellis Island Immigration Center. That day Annie Moore, an Irish girl, was the first person to be processed there. Some 700 others also cleared that day. They had come on the ships *City of Paris* and *Victoria*. The passenger lists for these and all the other vessels that entered New York and other American ports have been preserved on microfilm and are available at the National Archives for those who wish to trace their ancestors' passage to the New World.

Ellis Island remained an immigrant receiving station until World War I, when the federal government began to enact various laws to stem the flow of immigrants. After the 1924 Immigration Act was adopted, the number of immigrants passing through Ellis Island dropped to a trickle. Then, in November 1954, the last immigrant and the last detainee were processed there, and the immigration center was then declared surplus property by the General Services Administration. A portion of the island had already been used as a Coast Guard station and then as a detention center for enemy aliens.

In 1990, Ellis Island was reopened as a museum. It is reported that it receives more than two million visitors annually. Recently a Website was established (EllisIsland.org) where searchers can look for the names of ancestors who were processed through Ellis Island. This Website had some 1.5 million hits in the first six months of its operation. *See also* **Passenger Lists.**

El Salvador *see* **Central American Genealogy**

English Genealogy records are quite well preserved compared to those of many other countries. Most of the parish records (baptisms, marriages, and burials) survive from the 17th century onwards, and some extend back to as early as 1538. Consequently there are documents available for research on most English ancestors, although the parish registers may sometimes be lost, damaged, or difficult to interpret.

Before 1837 all marriages had to be performed in parish churches related to the Church of England in order to be valid. Thomas Cromwell, the trusted advisor to King Henry VIII, rendered invaluable service for future genealogists with his order of 1538 making it mandatory for every parish clergyman to keep registers of baptisms, marriages, and burials. The process was somewhat disrupted during the Civil War that erupted in 1642, but after the monarchy was restored in 1660 this practice was continued

and the parish registers have been fairly well kept ever since. A useful source for locating these records is A.M. Burke's *Guide to the Parish Registers of England and Wales.* It is available in many libraries. In 1992 the Church of England required that copies of all parish registers of baptisms and burials with entries more than 150 years old should be open to be public and deposited in the county records offices. Many of these records have now been microfilmed to prevent damage.

Parish registration did not, however, take place for nonconformist religious groups, such as the Puritans, because they had been expelled from the established church. These groups usually maintained their own records. Members of the Society of Friends, or Quakers, who began to gather for independent worship services about 1646, were not even permitted burial in the parish churchyards, and so had to establish their own graveyards near their meeting houses. They seldom erected any gravestones. Other nonconformist religious groups included the Muggletonians (1651), Unitarians (1662), Calvinists (1735), Moravians (1736), Inghamites (1753), Swedenborgians (1783), Methodists (1784), Bible Christians (1815), Universalists (1792), Thomasites (1848), Salvation Army (1865), and Christian Scientists (1879). About 7,000 registers of the nonconformist records were eventually handed over to the government, and can now be found in the London Public Records Office. This office was created in 1838 by an act of Parliament to house various records that previously had been kept at the Tower of London in a highly unsatisfactory condition. Dirt, dampness, and even rats had begun to destroy these records. Thus a records commission was appointed to find ways to preserve and reprint some of the old documents.

Catholic and Jewish congregations also kept their own records. The Catholic Record Society in London has the registrations for Catholics, and those for the Jews still remain at the various synagogues in England.

Civil registration was introduced by an act of Parliament in 1837. The original repository for these civil records was Somerset House in London, but in recent years they were moved a short distance away to the Office for National Statistics. Copies of the birth, marriage, and death certificates may be procured by request from that office. In the early years of civil registration, the registrars had to gather the vast numbers of records (some 958,630 the first year) without mechanical assistance and in the face of much skepticism and opposition. The registrars were paid by the entry and some of these collectors are known to have created false entries in order to increase their income. However, in spite of all difficulties, the system was well in place within five years.

The 1837 act of Parliament allowed civil ceremonies of marriage, performed in a civil registry office, to be considered valid. Civil registrations of deaths also began in 1837 because burials were permitted only when a death certificate was issued, a certificate that would have been confirmed by the civil authorities. But the civil registrations of births did not begin until 1875 following an act of Parliament requiring those present at a birth or death to report it to a registrar.

The Statute of Wills, passed in 1540, gave the right to draw up a will to all males 14 years of age and older and females 12 years and older. These ages were raised to 21 by the Wills Act of 1875. Many wills can be found that were designed by unmarried women and widows, but none by married women. This is because married women could not have property in their own names until after 1882, when the Married Women's Property Act was passed. Before this, they and all their possessions were considered to be the property of their husbands.

The responsibility for granting probate on all wills passed from the Church of England to civil authorities in 1858. When this happened over 300 ecclesiastical courts turned their probate functions over to either the Principal Probate Registry in London or to one of the 30 district probate registries throughout England and Wales. Access to these records can be obtained through the Principal Probate Registry of Somerset House and the Public Record Office, both of which are in London. Up until 1929 all the district registries were provided with copies of the national indexes, and in most cases they have been deposited in local county record offices. Unfortunately, some of the wills and other records were destroyed by a fire bomb dropped during World War II.

Records of adoptions are held at the General Register Office at St. Catherine's House in London and are available only to adopted persons or their children. However, even with information from a birth certificate, an adopted person may find it difficult to locate the ancestry of his or her true parents, because the record may give the hospital or a temporary address of the mother as the place of birth. Furthermore, many adoption records have been lost or are still held in the files of various public or private adoption agencies.

Many adopted persons came from the poorest sections of the population, and the lot of these people was regulated by various poor laws that were passed from 1285 until 1929. The ostensible aim of these laws was to alleviate pauperism, but many of them were dreadful in their implementation. In 1288 a statute of Winchester required strangers in a parish to be arrested after sunset. In 1349 donations were forbidden to the poor who might be capable of work, and in 1388 all laborers, servants, and even those making pilgrimages were prohibited from departing their homes without written permission from a justice of the peace. In 1530 it was ruled that all beggars had to acquire licenses from the local justice of the peace. Those caught without such licenses were to be stripped and whipped or put in the stocks, after which they would be given a license. From 1575 on, houses of correction were set up in every county. The mothers of illegitimate children and fathers, if they could be identified, were required to pay for the upkeep of their "bastards begotten and born out of wedlock," or go to jail. Both the indigent as well as convicts were transported to America, Gibraltar, Bermuda, or Australia. The poor laws were administered by secular authorities, but within ecclesiastical boundaries so that many of the records of individuals prosecuted under the poor laws can be found in the parish records as well as the county records offices.

Many apprenticeship records can be found among the guild, parish, and taxation records. A boy or girl might be bound as an apprentice to serve a master or mistress for a specified number of years in return for instruction, food, and lodging. Such arrangements were generally private and quite informal, so that documentation is difficult to find. However, those contracted from 1710 to 1811, during the period of the stamp duty tax that was payable on the premium paid for the apprenticeship, are preserved in the Kew Public Records Office.

Registers of land title deeds were started in Middlesex and Yorkshire counties between 1704 and 1735, and then extended on a voluntary basis across the country in 1862. This practice allowed titles to be proved by an entry in a register. From 1899, certain areas became subject to compulsory registration. The registers listed a description of the property, the names of the owners since the date of first registration, and the details of any mortgages. These and other types of land records—manorial records, chancery proceedings, land taxes, maps, and lists of church lands—can be found in the county records offices.

Many records of taxation are held in the London Public Records Office and the various county records offices. Some taxes that were levied at various periods of English history were a yearly hearth tax on those who occupied property; a marriage duty tax on the occasion of births, marriages, and burials; a window tax on houses with 10 or more windows; a death duty tax, and an annual land tax on property owners. Such records are useful because the information can be compared with that in parish registers to help establish family links and to estimate an ancestor's status in the community. The records of taxes collected for local purposes were recorded in rate books that go back to the early 1600s. Sometimes these books contain more information about individuals than do the commercial directories or voters' lists, but they can be more difficult to use because the rate collectors usually had no pattern to their lists. Rate books can be found in local libraries and county records offices.

Some were destroyed to help alleviate the paper shortage during World War II.

Records of professions and tradesmen can be found in commercial directories, newspapers, and the archives of trade associations. A number of books have been published listing such persons by their trades or professions. For example there is *Bedfordshire Clock & Watchmakers 1352–1880* by C. Pickford; *The London Goldsmiths, 1200–1800, a Record of the Names and Addresses of the Craftsmen, Their Shop-signs and Trade Cards*, by A. Heal; and volumes concerning persons in the medical, architectural, and theatrical professions. These books and many commercial directories can be found in various libraries. Many trade associations also have their own collections of historical records concerning their areas of work.

Commercial directories were the forerunners of telephone directories. As early as 1677 one was published for the city of London that listed the merchants there. It was followed in 1734 by another London directory and subsequently thereafter by annual updates. By 1800 such directories were being published for most of the cities and large towns, and within a couple of decades later for small towns and rural areas as well. Advertisements from merchants were often included, and a researcher can trace the growth or decline of a business and the owner or owners by examining successive years of publication of these commercial directories. One useful guide to what is available is J.E. Norton's *Guide to the National and Provincial Directories of England and Wales, Excluding London, Published Before 1856*. The largest collection of London directories can be found at the Guildhall Library in London. They also have a large collection of the provincial ones. Some are now being reprinted in book form or on microfiche for the benefit of researchers.

In England the court of chancery had jurisdiction over civil disputes while criminal cases appeared in the common law courts. Over the centuries the court of chancery's procedures became increasingly complex and expensive to litigate. The surviving records are enormous. It is estimated that between

1600 and 1800 there were about 750,000 chancery actions. Many of the court's actions contain a great deal of genealogical information. The original manuscripts to these chancery proceedings are located in the Public Record Office in London, but indexes to them can be found in some libraries. The records of the court of exchequer can also be found at the Public Record Office, but few of them survive from before 1558. The three-volume *Guide to the Contents of the Public Record Office* can be helpful in locating desired records available from that office.

Poll books listing the men who voted in parliamentary elections survive from the early 18th century. They give the names of the voters and which way they voted up until the adoption of the secret ballot in 1872. A guide to these books can be found at the library of the Society of Genealogists in London. The guide indicates which copies of these records are in the library, as well as the appropriate county record office where the originals can be located.

During the 13th century, commissioners were appointed in each county to prepare lists of all men between the ages of 16 and 60 considered fit to bear arms. Some of these lists have been preserved in libraries and in family archives. The names of some officers and a few soldiers in the muster rolls and pay lists of the Civil War that began in 1642 are at the Public Record Office in London. More records are available from about 1660 and a large number survive from the early 18th century. These records are listed in M.J. and C. Watts's book, *My Ancestor Was in the British Army; How Can I Find Out More About Him?* (Society of Genealogists, 1992). There is also an index of over two million names of British soldiers in World War I that can be searched for a fee. Details about this index can be found in P. Saul and F.C. Maxwell's *Tracing Your Ancestors: The A–Z Guide* (Countryside Books, 1991).

There are many published works on the peers of England that can be found in English genealogical libraries and abroad. Two of them give the names of almost all the families in Great Britain whose pedigrees appear anywhere in print. The first is *The Genealo-gist's Guide to Printed Pedigrees*, by George W. Marshall. It was last updated in 1912. The second is *A Genealogical Guide; An Index to British Pedigrees in Continuation of Marshall's Genealogist's Guide*, by J.B. Whitmore, published in 1953. Another volume of note is *Burke's Landed Gentry of Great Britain and Ireland* (1952) that lists about 4,500 families in 3,000 pages. The featured families are indexed in *Burke's Family Index* (1976).

The title of baronet was initiated by King James 1 in 1611. The earliest persons awarded this title were all from landowning families, but it was later also conferred on persons distinguished in science, commerce, the arts, or the military. *The Complete Baronetage*, by G.E. Cokayne (1983), gives descriptions of all those who were created baronets up to the year 1800. J.B. Burke's *A Genealogical and Heraldic History of the Extinct and Dormant Baronetcies of England, Ireland, and Scotland* (1964) gives the lineage of men who held the title but whose lines later became extinct.

Vast collections of pedigrees are located at the College of Arms in London, but these are private collections and not available for public examination. However, for a fee the Heralds of the College of Arms will search the records on behalf of any researcher. *See also* **Burke's Peerage**; **Census, British**.

Episcopalian Records in the United States have often been lost, even though the individual churches originally did a relatively good job in recording the baptisms, confirmations, marriages, and burials. Records that have been preserved are held by the local churches and some, such as the Augusta Parish Protestant Episcopal Church in Augusta County, Virginia, extend back to colonial times. Such church records may contain genealogical information that cannot be found elsewhere, particularly in the case of Letters of Transfer that give information as to where each member family lived before joining the church.

The Episcopal Church grew out of the Church of England that was established in the New World by the English government. Because England claimed rights to the land in the New World, it could mandate that all colonies have an Anglican Church. This church was therefore established in all 13 of the original colonies. Now known as the Episcopalian Church or the Protestant Episcopal Church, it is a part of the Anglican Communion, an international organization of 23 self-governing churches. In the British Commonwealth nations the denomination is known as the Anglican Church.

The Episcopal archives in the United States are located on the campus of the Episcopal Seminary of the Southwest in Austin, Texas, and there is an Episcopal Records Administration Center in New York City. Unfortunately, neither of these archives holds much information of a genealogical nature, so it is wiser to go directly to the individual churches.

Records of the Anglican churches in England can be found not only in the church archives, which are under the direction of a vicar, but also in the London Metropolitan Archives, the Guildhall Library, and the Westminster Archives, all three of which house the older parochial records. In Canada the Anglican General Synod Archives are at church headquarters in Toronto, and in Australia, they are at the Church of England Historical Society of Sydney. Again it is probable that the most useful genealogical records of the Anglican denomination in Canada and Australia will be found in the individual churches.

Estonia *see* Baltic Region Genealogy

Ethnic Heritage societies provide genealogists with specialized information related to the various countries of family origin and to the ethnic enclaves that often developed in the New World. These societies are usually better equipped to provide information about the family trees of persons from specific national groups than are the more general genealogical organizations.

Here is a listing of many of these ethnic heritage societies with addresses, or pertinent research books, where available:

Armenians— Armenian Genealogical Society, P.O. Box 1383, Provo, UT, 84603

Austrians— Senekovic, Dagmar. *Handy*

Guide to Austrian Genealogical Records. Draper, UT: Everton Publishers, 1979.

Chinese— Chinese Historical Society of America, 650 Commercial Street, San Francisco, CA, 94111; Low, Jennie W. Chooey. *China Connection: Finding Ancestral Roots for Chinese in America.* San Francisco: JWC Low Co., 1994.

Croatians— Croatian Genealogical and Historical Society, 2527 San Carlos Avenue, San Carlos, CA, 94070.

Cubans— Cuban Genealogical Society, P.O. Box 2650, Salt Lake City, UT, 84110; Carr, Peter E. *Guide to Cuban Genealogical Research: Records and Sources.* Chicago: Adams Press, 1991.

Czechs (Bohemians)— Czechoslovak Genealogical Society International, P.O. Box 16225, St. Paul, MN, 55116; Schlyter, Danial. *Czechoslovakia: A Handbook of Czechoslovak Genealogical Research.* Buffalo Grove, IL: Genun, 1985.

Danes— Danish-American Genealogical Group, c/o Minnesota Genealogy Society, P.O. Box 16069, St. Paul, MN, 55116; Thomsen, Finn A. *Beginners Guide to Danish Research.* Bountiful, UT: Thomsen's Genealogical Center, 1984.

English— British Isles Family History Society in the U.S.A., 2531 Sawtelle Blvd., PMB 134, Los Angeles, CA, 90064; Milner, Paul, and Linda Jones. *A Genealogist's Guide to Discovering Your English Ancestors.* Cincinnati, OH: Betterway Books, 2000.

French— American-French Genealogical Society, P.O. Box 2113, Pawtucket, RI, 02861; Boudreau, the Rev. Dennis M. *Beginning Franco American Genealogy.* American French Genealogical Society, 1986.

Finns— Finnish Genealogy Group, 2119 Twenty-first Ave. S., Minneapolis, MN 55404; Choquette, Margarita, et al. *The Beginners Guide to Finnish Genealogical Research.* Bountiful, UT: Thomsen's Genealogical Center, 1985.

Germans— German Genealogical Society of America, P.O. Box 291818, Los Angeles, CA, 90029; Smith, Clifford Neal. *Encyclopedia of German-American Genealogical Research.* New York: R.R. Bowker, 1976.

Greeks— Greek Family Heritage Committee, 75–21 177th St., Flushing, NY, 11366; Koken, Paul, Theodore N. Constant and S.G. Canoutas. *History of the Greeks in the Americas, 1453–1938*. Ann Arbor, MI: Proctor Publications, 1995.

Hungarians— Hungarian Genealogical Society of Greater Cleveland, 7830 Sugar Bush, Ln., Gates Mills, OH, 44040; Suess, Jared H. *Handy Guide to Hungarian Genealogical Research*. Draper, UT: Everton Publishers, 1980.

Icelanders— Johansson, Carl-Erik. *Tracing Your Icelandic Family Tree*. Winnepeg, Manitoba: Wheatfield Press, 1975.

Irish— Irish Genealogical Foundation, P.O. Box 7575, Kansas City, MO, 64116; Mitchell, Brian. *Pocket Guide to Irish Genealogy*. Baltimore: Genealogical Publishing Co., 1991.

Italians— Italian Genealogical Society of America, P.O. Box 8571, Cranston, RI, 02920; Colletta, John Philip. *Finding Italian Roots: The Complete Guide for Americans*. Baltimore: Genealogical Publishing Co., 1996.

Japanese— Japanese American History Archives, 1840 Sutter Street, San Francisco, CA, 94115; Yamaguchi, Yoji. *A Student's Guide to Japanese American Genealogy*. Phoenix, AZ: Oryx Press, 1996.

Lithuanians— Lithuanian American Genealogical Society, Balzekas Museum of Lithuanian Culture, 6500 Pulaski Road, Chicago, IL, 60629

Mexicans— Society of Hispanic Historical and Ancestral Research, P.O. Box 490, Midway City, CA, 92655; Ryskamp, George P., and Peggy R. Ryskamp. *A Student's Guide to Mexican American History*. Phoenix, AZ: Oryx Publishers, 1996.

Norwegians— Norwegian-American Genealogical Society, 502 W. Water St., Decorah, IA, 52101; Carlberg, Nancy Ellen. *Beginning Norwegian Research*. Anaheim, CA: Carlberg Press, 1991.

Poles— Polish Genealogical Society of America, 984 N. Milwaukee Ave., Chicago, IL, 60622; Chorzempa, Rosemary A. *Polish Roots*. Baltimore: Genealogical Publishing Co., 1993.

Portuguese— Portuguese Historical and Cultural Society, P.O. Box 161900, Sacramento, CA, 95816; Pap, Leo. *The Portuguese-Americans*. New York: Twayne Publishers, 1981.

Puerto Ricans— Puerto Rican/Hispanic Genealogical Society, P.O. Box 260118, Bellerose, NY, 11426.

Russians— Russian-American Genealogical Archival Source, 1929 Eighteenth St., NW, Washington, DC, 20009; Magocsi, Paul R. *The Russian Americans*. Broomall, PA: Chelsea House, 1989.

Scots— The Scotch-Irish Foundation, P.O. Box 181, Bryn Mawr, PA, 19010; Irvine, Sherry. *Your Scottish Ancestry: A Guide for North Americans*. Salt Lake City: Ancestry, Inc., 1997.

Slovaks— National Slovak Society of the USA, 333 Technology Drive, Suite 112, Canonsburg, PA, 15317; Miller, Olga K. *Genealogical Research for Czech and Slovak Americans*. Detroit: Gale Research, 1978.

Spanish— Spanish-American Genealogical Association, P.O. Box 794, Corpus Christi, TX, 78403; Platt, Lyman D. *Hispanic Surnames and Family History*. Baltimore: Genealogical Publishing Company, 1996.

Swedes— Swedish Genealogical Group, c/o Minnesota Genealogy Society, P.O. Box 16069, St. Paul, MN, 55116; Johansson, Carl-Erik. *Cradled in Sweden*. Draper, UT: Everton Publishers, 1995.

Swiss— Wellauer, Maralyn A. *Tracing Your Swiss Roots*. Milwaukee, WI: The author, 1979.

Welsh and Cornish— Welsh-American Genealogical Society, 13 Norton Ave., Poultney, VT, 05764; Rowlands, John, ed. *Welsh Family History: A Guide to Research*. Baltimore: Genealogical Publishing Co., 1999.

Evangelical Covenant Records are kept in the various churches and also in the archives of the library at North Park University in Chicago, Illinois. This denomination has more than 600 churches in the United States and Canada, and was founded in 1885 by Swedish immigrants to the United States who were formerly members of the Lutheran State Church of Sweden.

The archives of the North Park Library include the denominational records of the church, the records of the university, the collections of the Swedish-American Archives of Greater Chicago, and the records of the Society for the Advancement of Scandinavian Study. There are also special collections written in the Scandinavian language that include some genealogical data.

Extended-Family Genealogy see **Cluster Genealogy**

F

Family Associations in genealogy are organizations formed by people who share a common ancestor or surname. They join together to exchange genealogical information, share current news about family members, have family reunions, and promote family pride. Some of these associations strive to collect genealogical information about those with the same surname all over the world, while others take an interest only in their relatively small family group living within a specific geographic area.

Many family associations maintain collections of their members' family trees, and almost all of these associations put out some sort of newsletter (annually, quarterly, or monthly) that can contain interesting tidbits about a family's history, announcements of current births and deaths, information on upcoming reunions, and even queries submitted by members or others.

Locating a family association organized around a particular surname is usually done through contact with others of the same name. Some of these people are likely to belong to one of these associations or to know of any that exist. Books listing family associations are also available in libraries or through genealogy booksellers. One example is Elizabeth Petty Bentley and Deborah Ann Carl's *Directory of Family Associations*, published in several editions by Heritage Books of Bowie, MD, which contains contact information for approximately 6,000 family associations across the United States, many of which by their very nature exist for only a brief time. There are more than one thousand of these associations that have Websites. They range from the Abercrombie Family Association to the Zelinski Family Journal.

Family Bibles have often been used to record births, christenings, baptisms, marriages, and deaths. This was particularly true in the 1700s and 1800s, although some families keep such records today. Sometimes these entries contain little more than just a comment such as: "Ma died yesterday." But more often they contain exact dates and lists of children. Unfortunately, many family Bibles have been lost or destroyed. Some can be found in secondhand bookshops. Where no documents can be located to verify vital record information, the items listed in a family Bible may be used to do so.

However, it is wise to be somewhat skeptical of the handwritten notes therein. If possible, this information should be checked against other records. One should particularly check the date of publication of the Bible to discover which information was written from memory or family traditions and which was likely written near the time of occurrence, since the latter will be more reliable. Of course, if any date entered in the Bible is earlier than that of the publication date, this obviously would have been added after the event occurred.

Another thing to check is whether or not all the entries made in the Bible are done in the same ink or by the same hand. If so, it is possible that the information was transcribed from another Bible or another source and was entered some time after the events that they record. A telltale clue may lie in entries that appear to be written with a ballpoint pen. If so, they might have been put there relatively recently. Ballpoint pens did not come into general use until the mid–1940s. A patent for their development was awarded in 1944 to Lazlo Biro, a Hungarian living in Argentina.

Then there is the matter of whether or not all of the entries are in chronological sequence. If not, it is probable that some entries were put there after the event. When an entry is squeezed in between others in order to force it into sequence, this indicates that it must have been entered at a later time. Finally, entries in a Bible published in the United States that include events occurring in another country, or vice versa, suggest that the person who made the entry obtained the information from elsewhere and was not in attendance at the event itself.

Family Group Records *see* Pedigree Charts

Family Histories are compilations of genealogical records of single families that include more than the vital records that are listed in a family tree. Hundreds of them have been published and many more have been written only for circulation among the members of the family. Some are well written and well documented; others are not. All libraries with genealogical collections have a section of printed family histories. Large libraries such as the Library of Congress in Washington, D.C., or the Newberry Library in Chicago have large collections of them.

Family histories often include photographs of ancestors, family stories about them and what they were like, details about their occupations, information about what life was like in the earlier days, and how economic and historical conditions affected their lives. The Library of Congress published, in 1992, a listing of its family history collection, *Genealogies Catalogued by the Library of Congress Since 1986: With a List of Established Forms of Family Names and a List of Genealogies Converted to Microfilm Since 1983*. The library has also microfilmed all the volumes in its collection that were printed before 1900. These films are available for purchase or interlibrary loan. Many family histories are also listed in the *Encyclopedia of American Family Names*.

Caution needs to be advised about books that are composed of pedigrees and biographical sketches contributed by persons who subscribe to the books. Commonly called "mug books" because they usually include photographs of those who have contributed the biographies, much of the material in these volumes may be bogus and should be checked against original records when possible. Although some of these books are quite factual, others are notoriously faulty. A great many of these mug books have been published in recent years, and can be found in every genealogical library. *See also* **Books.**

Family History Centers are branch facilities of the Church of Jesus Christ of Latter-day Saints' Family History Library in Salt Lake City, Utah. There are more than 3,400 such Mormon-operated centers worldwide, and most of them are located within the facilities of the various Mormon meeting houses. They are open to the public, are administered by local church members, and provide access to most of the microfilm and microfiche files stored in the Family History Library. The centers can also obtain books and films on loan from the Family History Library. There is a small fee for this service and the records must be examined at the center facilities; they cannot be taken elsewhere.

Family History Centers can be found in every one of the United States and in Puerto Rico, as well as in Canada, England, Australia, Brazil, most of the countries of Europe, and some of the countries of Asia. To locate any one of them, a researcher should telephone the closest Mormon meeting house, or look at the listing of them and their hours of operation on the Website operated by the Church of Jesus Christ of Latter-day Saints.

In most of these centers there is also a small collection of books related to genealogy, including research helps, family genealogies, histories, gazetteers, atlases, and maps. There is also a collection of computer files and programs to help individuals search for information about their ancestors. Patrons can arrange to have copies of most of the Family History Library microfilm and microfiche records not available at any particular center sent there on loan from the Family History Library. Members of the volunteer staff are usually available to help researchers, although the researchers must do their own investigations. Some of these centers also offer classes on a variety of genealogical research subjects. The members of the volunteer staff are likely to be aware of other libraries and institutions in the immediate area that can provide additional information in any particular area of genealogical research. *See also* **Family History Library.**

Family History Library in Salt Lake City, Utah, is without doubt the largest and best genealogical library in the world. It is operated by the Church of Jesus Christ of Latter-day Saints, better known as the Mormons, and has a collection of over 2.2 million rolls of microfilmed genealogical records; 742,000 microfiche records; 300,000 books, serials, and other formats; and 4,500 periodicals related to genealogical topics.

The library had its beginning in 1894 with the founding of the Genealogical Society of Utah. It grew slowly at first. The library's quarterly *Utah Genealogical and Historical Magazine* began publication in 1910. By 1919 the library boasted over 5,000 books. In 1934 it was moved to new facilities in the Joseph F. Smith Memorial Building, and by 1937 included over 19,000 books in its collection.

In 1938 the library was equipped with microfilm readers; the directors had purchased their own microfilm camera. Computer technology was added in the late 1960s. But as the library and its functions expanded, the need for more working space became acute. The library was then moved into the former Montgomery Ward building in Salt Lake City. Soon the number of library patrons doubled from 300 a day to 600. The church also authorized the construction of a vault tunneled into the mountainside some 25 miles southeast of Salt Lake City as a safe repository for the camera masters of the library's precious microfilmed records.

The library moved, in 1972, into the entire four floors of the west wing of the church's newly-completed office building and then, in 1985, into a new building devoted entirely to the library's facilities. At the time it was accommodating approximately 2,000 visitors each day. Plans were completed to significantly enlarge the library in 1993, and today it welcomes about 3,000 researchers each day, at no charge, from all over the world. The library's collection of genealogical records is estimated to be increasing each month by an average of 4,100 rolls of film and 700 books.

The Family History Library catalog has been duplicated on microfiche, and copies are available at all its family history center branches. This catalog describes the records at the library and allows one to search for a surname, locality, subject, author, or title. There is a brief video program at the library and the family history centers that explains how best to use the microfiche edition of the catalog. The library also conducts regular orientation classes and specialized research classes.

Those who are new to the services of this library often begin their visits by going to the nearby Family Search annex, located in the Joseph Smith Memorial Building. This facility has individual and group workstations at which visitors can use computers to access the library catalog, the Social Security Death Index, Scottish church records, the U.S. military index, the 1920 census, over 70,000 biographies and family history books from around the world, and other computer-based resources of the library. The helpful staff answers questions and gives individual assistance.

Finally, the computers at the Family History Library and its annex make readily available the library's International Genealogical Index, the Personal Ancestral File, and the Pedigree Resource File, which contains some 45 million names linked into families. These pedigree records can only be viewed outside of the Family History Library on some 30 or more compact disks and by using the GEDCOM genealogy computer program developed by members of the Latter-day Saints. *See also* **Genealogical Text Formats for Computers; International Genealogical Index.**

Family Reunions are popular events at which people with the same surname, including professional genealogists, gather to exchange information about their pedigrees and family history. There are hundreds of these events held throughout the United States each year, usually during the summer vacation months. These groups are united by a family name and possibly some common history on the part of their ancestors.

In the past, most such reunions were conducted as picnics at a park or on a farm where games were played and food was provided by the attendees. But many reunions are now planned by carefully-chosen committees and frequently last for as long as three days. Often participants coordinate their family vacations with the time for a family reunion so that the event becomes a significant part of their leisure experience.

Frequently there may be as many as 100 to 200 people in attendance at an American family reunion, some coming from great distances and from many different states. There will likely be games and races for children, as well baseball, volley ball, and swimming for the entire group. Raffles and auctions may offer diversions from the business meetings and discussions of genealogical heritage. Sometimes such events close with fireworks over a nearby lake, a session of picture taking, and decisions as to where the next such event might be held.

Cemeteries sometimes play an important role at these family reunions. They provide a place to contemplate, relax, and enjoy quiet. When the cemetery is or was once primarily the place of burial for the extended members of a single family, it gives the reunion participants an opportunity to learn about the people buried there and speculate about the significance of their lives many years ago. A visit to the cemetery can also provide an opportunity for family members to become involved in cleaning away debris, planting flowers, and perhaps taking photographs or making rubbings of the gravestones.

A number of books describe how to organize family reunions, how to raise funds to pay for them, and the types of activities that are best suited to such events. A quarterly magazine, *Reunions*, is devoted to just this subject. It is published in Milwaukee, Wisconsin. A series of audio tapes being marketed give step-by-step instructions for conducting a family reunion. Sources for these tapes can be found at some genealogical Websites.

Family Shields *see* **Heraldry**

Family Tree *see* **Pedigree Charts**

Finnish Genealogy begins during the 800 years when Finland was a part of Sweden. It remained a Swedish province until 1809, when the country was ceded to Russia and became a grand duchy of the Russian Empire. Finland did not achieve independence until 1917, and then it was again invaded by Russia in 1939. After World War II, Finland joined the United Nations and the Nordic Council. Approximately 95 percent of the Finns today belong to the Evangelical Lutheran Church. The next largest religious group in Finland is the Greek Orthodox Church.

Civil registration has been allowed in Finland since 1918, but it has never been compulsory. Either civil or church registration is allowed, but not both. Records of birth before 1918 are likely to be found in the parishes. However, the central archives in Helsinki has copies of all the available chronological lists of births, marriages, and deaths before 1850.

The Lutheran Church parish records go back to the late 1600s and provide more genealogical information than do most parish records elsewhere in the world. This is because the communion books (rippikirjat), also known as the main books, are organized by villages and owners of farms. The name of each farm owner appears in these records with all the other residents of that farm, along with their relationships to the farm owner. No one was ever missed. The parish records also include the births, baptisms, confirmations, banns, marriages, membership transfers, parish minutes, deaths, burials, and more.

In Finland wills are not often drawn up, but their place is filled by estate inventories. Such documents are in the district archives, and in some cases in the town records. None date before the 17th century. Military and court records can also be found at the Central Archives. The *Statistical Yearbook of Finland*, with text in English as well as Swedish and Finnish, and the *Finlands Statskalender*, which gives a list of the religious congregations, can be helpful in finding local records.

Florida Records that are useful to genealogists do not begin until the early 1820s, even though Spanish explorers arrived there in the early 1500s. The area belonged at various times to Spain and Britain until it was ceded to the United States in 1819 by Spain. Florida was declared an American territory in 1822 and a state in 1845. Two territorial censuses were conducted, one in 1830 and the other in 1840. They are stored in the Florida State Archives at Tallahassee, with copies in the National Archives in Washington, D.C.

The State Archives also has fragments of a number of state censuses, including Leon County (1825); Marion County (1855); Hernando, Madison, Orange, and Santa Rosa Counties (1867); Alachua County (1875); all the counties except Alachua, Clay, Nassau, and Columbia (1885); and all the counties with some missing precincts (1935 and 1945). In 1941 and 1942 the Work Projects Administration published two volumes relating to the vital statistics of Florida that can be found in many Florida libraries and some genealogical libraries elsewhere. They are titled *Guide to Public Vital Statistics Records in Florida,* and *Guide to Supplementary Vital Statistics from Church Records in Florida: Preliminary Edition*. The latter is in two volumes, the first covering Alachua County and the second covering Gilchrist County.

The State Archives claims to have a 7,000 volume collection of published materials relating to Florida and most other Southeastern states. These volumes include Florida service records from the Revolutionary War, Indian Wars, and the Mexican War; Confederate pension records; a compiled index of Civil War soldiers; state and county maps; Spanish land grant records; state tax records; cemetery records; militia records, and national guard records. Other sources for Florida genealogical material are the Florida State Library at Tallahassee and the Florida State Historical Society at Melbourne.

The Office of Vital Statistics of the Department of Health and Rehabilitative Ser-
vices has some birth records that date back to April 1865, and some death records dating back to August 1877, but the majority of its birth and death records date from January 1917. It has marriage and divorce records since June 6, 1927. Copies of the records at the Office of Vital Statistics can be obtained for a small fee. Divorce records prior to 1927 are in the circuit court clerk's office where the divorce was granted. Wills and guardianship records in Florida are registered in and controlled by the county judge's court, while divorce records are kept in the circuit court of each county where they were probated. This is also where the Florida land records are maintained. The state makes no distinction between equity and law actions so that the circuit courts in the various counties have jurisdiction.

One other resource for Florida records is the immigration passenger lists for various periods from 1899 to 1945 held in the National Archives in Washington, D.C. These lists cover the following ports of entry: Apalachicola, Boca Grande, Clarabelle, Fernandina, Jacksonville, Key West, Knights Key, Mayport, Miami, Millville, Panama City, Pensacola, Port Everglades, Port Inglis, Port St. Joe, St. Andrews, St. Petersburg, Tampa, and West Palm Beach.

Researchers seeking information from county records can locate them at the following county seats: (Alachua County) Gainesville, (Baker County) MacClenny, (Bay County) Panama City, (Bradford County) Starke, (Brevard County) Titusville, (Broward County) Fort Lauderdale, (Calhoun County) Blountstown, (Charlotte County) Punta Gorda, (Citrus County) Inverness, (Clay County) Green, (Cove County) Springs, (Collier County) East Naples, (Columbia County) Lake City, (Dade County) Miami, (De Soto County) Arcadia, (Dixie County) Cross City, (Duval County) Jacksonville, (Escambia County) Pensacola, (Flagler County) Bunnell, (Franklin County) Apalachicola, (Gadsden County) Quincy, (Gilchrist County) Trenton, (Glades County) Moore Haven, (Gulf Port County) St. Joe, (Hamilton County) Jasper, (Hardee County) Wauchula, (Hendry County) La Belle, (Hernando County) Brooksville, (Highlands County) Sebring, (Hillsborough County) Tampa, and (Holmes County) Bonifay.

Also at (Indian River County) Vero Beach, (Jackson County) Marianna, (Jefferson County) Monticello, (Lafayette County) Mayo, (Lake County) Tavares, (Lee County) Fort Myers, (Leon County) Tallahassee, (Levy County) Bronson, (Liberty County) Bristol, (Madison County) Madison, (Manatee County) Bradenton, (Marion County) Ocala, (Martin County) Stuart, (Monroe County) Key West, (Nassau County) Fernandina Beach, (Okaloosa County) Crestview, (Okeechobee County) Okeechobee, (Orange County) Orlando, (Osceola County) Kissimmee, (Palm Beach County) West Palm Beach, (Pasco County) Dade City, (Pinellas County) Clearwater, (Polk County) Bartow, (Putnam County) Palatka, (Santa Rosa County) Milton, (Sarasota County) Sarasota, (Seminole County) Sanford, (St. Johns County) St. Augustine, (St. Lucie County) Fort Pierce, (Sumter County) Bushnell, (Suwannee County) Live Oak, (Taylor County) Perry, (Union County) Lake Butler, (Volusia County) DeLand, (Wakulla County) Crawfordville, (Walton County) DeFuniak Springs, and (Washington County) Chipley.

FOR FURTHER INFORMATION SEE:
- Bodziony, Gill Dodd. *Genealogy and Local History: A Bibliography*. Tallahassee: Florida State Library, 1978.
- Taylor, Anne Wood. *Florida Pioneers and Their Descendants*. Tallahassee: Florida State Genealogical Society, 1992.

France *see* **French Genealogy**

Freedmen's Bureau, or more properly the Bureau of Refugees, Freedmen, and Abandoned Lands, was established in the War Department by an act of March 3, 1865. Its purpose was to assist freed slaves after the Civil War in dealing with the many changes they faced as a result of emancipation. The bureau supervised all relief and educational activities relating to the refugees and freedmen, including the issuing of rations, clothing, and medicine. Furthermore, it engaged in many other activities, including surveying, seizing, leas-

ing, and restoring to their owners "abandoned" lands in the former Confederate states.

Copies of the records of the Freedmen's Bureau are preserved in the National Archives in Washington, D.C., under the file name *Records of the Bureau of Refugees, Freedmen, and Abandoned Lands*. The originals are at various locations in Alabama, Arkansas, Florida, Georgia, Kentucky, Louisiana, Maryland, Delaware, Mississippi, Missouri, North Carolina, South Carolina, Tennessee, Texas, and Virginia. They contain information on both black and white residents of the Southern states, letters sent and received between the populace and the bureau offices, as well as indentures and contracts made with former slaves.

The records of the Freedmen's Bureau are a vital source of information for historians and genealogists. They contain a wide range of data about the African-American experience during slavery and freedom, including marriage records, labor contracts, government rations and back pay records, and indentured contracts for minors.

Freedom of Information Act was passed by Congress and signed into law in 1966. It provides the right for any person to gain access to federal agency records or information, except when such records are protected from disclosure by specific exemptions and exclusions. A person exercising this right must make a request in writing and pay a fee for obtaining a copy of the requested document. The right of access is enforceable in court, and the act only applies to federal records. Many states have their own laws regarding access to local records.

It is relatively rare that any genealogist must resort to this act in order to obtain desired information. The vast majority of federal records of use to genealogists can be easily accessed without having to go through such procedures. However, there are occasions when documents about known individuals who were illegal or undesirable immigrants, federal prisoners, suspected political dissidents, etc., have been hidden from public view. Then the Freedom of Information Act may be the only recourse that a genealogist has. Before making applications under this statute, the researcher might study *A Citizen's Guide on Using the Freedom of Information Act and the Privacy Act to Request Government Records*, available from the U.S. Government Printing Office.

A Freedom of Information request can be made for any federal record. This does not mean, however, that the Justice Department or other agency will disclose whatever record is being sought. As noted above, there are statutory exemptions that authorize the withholding of information of a sensitive nature. Yet when an agency does withhold information, it must specify which of the listed exemptions permits the withholding of the requested information.

The exemptions authorize federal agencies to withhold information covering: 1) classified national defense and foreign relations information; 2) internal agency rules and practices; 3) information that is prohibited from disclosure by another federal law; 4) trade secrets and other confidential business information; 5) inter-agency or intra-agency communications that are protected by legal privileges; 6) information involving matters of personal privacy; 7) certain types of information compiled for law enforcement purposes; 8) information relating to the supervision of financial institutions; and 9) geological information on wells. Three other exclusions, which are rarely used, pertain to especially sensitive law enforcement and national security matters.

Some Freedom of Information records have been requested so often that they are now available for public viewing at the many Justice Department reading rooms in the offices of each of this agency's departments in Washington, D.C. Wherever the number of pages of these documents is voluminous, only summaries are available. These summaries include documents about such prominent individuals as Josephine Baker (singer); Lucille Ball (actress); Cesar Chavez (union leader); Clarence Seward Darrow (lawyer); W.E.B. Herbert DuBois (historian); William Faulkner (author); Errol Flynn (actor); Henry Ford (industrialist); Jacqueline Kennedy (first lady); Martin Luther King, Jr. (leader of civil

rights movement); John Lennon (rock star); Mickey Mantle (baseball player); Thurgood Marshall (supreme court justice); Eleanor Roosevelt (first lady), and many others. Many of them can also be downloaded from the Justice Department's Website (http://www.usdoj.gov/). *See also* **Privacy Act.**

French Genealogy records, though for the most part accurate and well indexed, are spread among many different departmental archives located at various places throughout France. For this reason, the researcher tracing the ancestry of a particular individual must know the department of origin in order to find the information desired. The departmental archives of France are open to the public. Each one has a reading room in which researchers can do their own research and each usually has an inventory or guide to its collections.

The earliest vital records in France were recorded by the churches at the request of French kings. These parish records are often the only source of family data before civil registration was initiated in France. They include listings of births, christenings, marriages, and burials, as well as other types of information desired by the Catholic Church. Some of the earliest ones, recorded in either French or Latin, are those of Givry (Saône-et-Loire) covering the period from 1334 to 1357, and those of Roz Landrieux (Ille-et-Villaine) from 1451 to 1528. Most of the parish registers, however, date from the mid–1600s, and many have gaps, especially before 1736.

Civil registration began in 1792 when the French Revolution was in full force, and everything in the old regime needed to be changed. The revolutionary government designated civil officers to be responsible for keeping vital records and required all people to report births, marriages, and deaths to a civil registration office. This demand was well received, and soon almost all of the people in France at that time were recorded. This practice has been followed ever since, so that the French civil registration offices are excellent sources for accurate information on names, dates, and places of birth, marriage, and death in the areas where each of the departmental archives is located. The civil records are indexed and easily accessible. They provide more information than do the church records, and unlike the church records, they include persons of all denominations. Furthermore, these archives sometimes include divorce records. These civil registers may be the only available source of information about many families.

Duplicates were made by the churches of their baptism, marriage, and death records before 1792. They can usually be found in the departmental archives, or occasionally in the town's civil registration office. After the civil registration system began, the clergy continued to keep their own parish registers separate from civil registers, but such records are often incomplete and less accurate than are the civil ones. Two copies have also been made of all the civil records, one of which was deposited in the local town or city archives and the other in the departmental archives.

The civil registration birth records give a child's name, sex, date and place of birth, and the name of the parents, including the mother's maiden surname. They sometimes may provide additional information, such as the ages of the parents and occupation of the father. The births are usually registered within two or three days of the event and usually by the father, though sometimes by a relative or friend. The parents of a single mother are usually listed as well to provide a more complete identification of the mother. Births entered in the civil register usually are indexed yearly along with the regular 10-year indexes.

Following the establishment of the civil registration offices in 1792, every marriage in France had to be performed by civil authorities before the couple could be married in a church. The church wedding usually took place in the town where the bride lived and was recorded there in the church records; the civil marriage might be recorded in a registration office in another town.

Other records that document marriages include published marriage banns, marriage certificates, and contracts created for the protection of property. The latter are documents sworn before a notary and would likely have remained in the office of the notary's successors. Sometimes the marriage certificate will indicate the name of the town of the notary hired to write the contract and the date on which it was written. One can obtain marriage certificates issued during the last hundred years in person from the registrar's office at the town hall. A copy will be sent by mail only to direct descendants.

Occasionally one finds marriage supplements that were filled out by the bride and groom in support of their application to be married. These supplements may include records of birth for both the bride and groom, death certificates for the parents, divorce decrees of a previous union, certificates of residence, records legitimating children, the military status of the groom, parents' consents, and sometimes documentation relating to earlier generations. Some of these marriage supplements can be located in the departmental archives.

Civil officials recorded the marriages they performed in a bound book that was kept in the registrar's office. This book is known as the marriage register (*registre des actes de mariage*). It includes the birthdate and birthplace of the bride and the groom, as well as their parents' names, including mother's maiden surname. These registers also include the names of the four witnesses, their ages, occupations, residences, and relationships to the bridal couple. More recent marriage registers may even include pertinent information about grandparents.

From 1877 on the civil registrar gave each couple he married a marriage booklet that contained an extract of the marriage record and references to the marriage contract. The couple was then responsible for taking this booklet to the registrar after each of their children was born. The registrar would then enter the child's birth information and return the booklet to the parents. The registrar would also record deaths in this booklet. French families generally keep these family civil registration booklets and often hand them down as mementos to their children.

Divorce was permitted in France from 1792 to 1816 and after 1884. A few divorce records can be found with the marriage records in the early period. This information is obtainable from the registration office in the town hall where the divorce took place. When wills were drawn up, the custom was for a copy to remain with the notary who performed the service. Finding such records requires knowing the name of the notary, even though a copy of the will may be stored in one of the departmental archives.

Notaries are particularly important officials in France and other nations where a civil code based on Roman law is in force. These persons handle matters that deal with contracts, estates, inheritances, and guardianship agreements, and their records sometimes cover genealogical matters that are earlier than the church records. But their records are difficult to find, and difficult to use because they are seldom indexed. Notaries are required to deposit records that are more than 125 years old in the departmental archives, but compliance with this rule is sometimes ignored. Furthermore, most of the notarial records are tied in bundles or put in boxes labeled by the name of the notary and his town of residence so they have to be searched systematically, one by one.

Death records can be quite helpful because they probably contain information about a person's birth, spouse, parents, age, and birthplace. Death records often exist for persons on whom there are no birth or marriage records, and they were usually recorded within a day or two of the death at the town or city where the person died. The names of children who died before a declaration of birth had been recorded may be found only among the death records.

Cemeteries in France can also provide a modest amount of genealogical information through their tombstones with inscriptions. These inscriptions can be found from the early 18th century up to today, and may apply to entire families, since members of the same family are often buried in the same grave at various levels. A cemetery keeper at the entrance may have an alphabetical list of the graves that gives detailed information as to the age of the deceased, birthdate, death date, and sometimes even marriage information. Where there is no keeper, cemetery records can usually be found at the town hall. Remem-

ber that it is illegal to photograph French tombstones without permission of the cemetery keeper.

Roman Catholicism has been the predominant religion of France since the sixth century, but a few other religious groups have also been formed there, such as the Huguenots, Waldensians, and Mennonites. The Huguenots, who began to worship together in 1541, followed the teachings of John Calvin in Switzerland. They were persecuted by the Catholics until 1598, when the Edict of Nantes granted them a period of religious freedom. Most Protestant records in France date from that year. However, the Edict of Nantes was revoked in 1685 and the members of this Protestant denomination had to flee by the thousands to various foreign nations. Those who could not leave were converted under pressure to Catholicism. Many Protestant records were then destroyed. It was not until 1787, when Louis XVI signed the Edict of Tolerance, that freedom of religion for the Protestants was again granted.

The Waldensians were founded by Pierre Valdo (or Waldo) at the end of the 12th century in the city of Lyon. The movement soon spread into Germany, Flanders, and Aragon, but in 1545 hundreds of French Waldensians were executed in the towns of Cabrières and Merindol. These persecutions caused the members to leave France and move to Uruguay and Argentina. A small branch of this religious group now lives in Merindol, France, where it publishes a bulletin related to studies of its history.

The Mennonites, another Protestant group, have existed in France since 1523. They are found mostly in Alsace-Lorraine and in the former principality of Montbéliard. Finding information about these Protestant groups in France is difficult because the people moved frequently and many fled the country. In most cases one must start the search from the places to which the families emigrated and work backwards into the French records. In some genealogical libraries there are name indexes for the Huguenots, Waldensians, or Mennonites that also give information about their religious beliefs and migrations. One can also write to the Library of French Protestantism in Paris for assistance.

Census records in France are seldom used for genealogical research because they are not indexed, so it is not easy to find any specific names in them. The indexed civil registration records and church records are much better sources for finding ancestors. The first national census that listed names in France was taken in 1772. The national censuses taken from 1795 to 1836 are without names and show only the number of persons in the towns or rural areas. These censuses were taken primarily for military purposes, taxation, or the identification of the poor. From 1836 to 1936 a national census with names, ages, occupations, heads of household, nationality, and sometimes birthplaces was taken every five years except for the year 1916, which was skipped.

In some cases one may find that the earlier censuses have been destroyed because of an 1887 decree authorizing this destruction, but the law was not applied everywhere; portions of the destroyed census records are still available. They can be found in the departmental archives, as can various town and provincial censuses that covered portions of the local population. Wherever census records are located they are only open to the public if they are at least one hundred years old. Those of a later date remain confidential, although a few departmental archive administrators will allow researchers access to census records up to the last 30 years.

Thousands of brief biographies of notable French persons have been collected and published in various biographical dictionaries. One of the most useful is the *Nouvelle Biographie Générale Depuis les Temps les plus Reculés Jusqu'à 1850–1860* (New Biographical Dictionary). This dictionary contains articles about various people that run from just a few lines to several pages. Another well-known source is *Archives Biographiques Françaises* (French Biographical Archives), which lists 140,000 pre–1914 individuals from France, Switzerland, Belgium, Luxembourg, Quebec, and many French colonies. An index to these biographies was published in four volumes in 1993 by Helen and Barry Dwyer under the title *Index Biographique Français* (French Biographical Index).

Some French military records go back to the 1500s, giving information about a person's military career, including promotions, places served, pensions, and conduct. In addition, such records may include information about the person's age, birthplace, residence, occupation, physical description, and family members. Many of these records have been centralized at the Military Archives at Vincennes, but the conscription records are kept in the departmental archives. Again, these records are difficult to access and few have been indexed. To find a desired name one must first determine the soldier's specific regiment or the ship on which a sailor served.

Some French families have produced histories of several family generations that may include photographs and other excellent information. Unpublished family histories can sometimes be found in the possession of private individuals, but such materials are accessible only by contacting the appropriate person. An index of the published family histories is the *Répertoire de Généalogies Françaises Imprimées* (French Genealogical Bibliography), compiled in thee volumes by Étienne Arnaud. This book indexes many periodical articles and published genealogies, with each listing citing a home area in France.

The Genealogical Library in Paris (Bibliothèque Généalogique) has a name index, a list of genealogical books, and genealogical periodicals from all parts of France. The library also holds genealogical instruction classes in French for beginners. The first visit to this library is free; thereafter a yearly membership fee of 220 French francs is required.

The National Archives (Archives Nationales) in Paris contains five sections. The old section has a great deal of information relating to the nobility and royal family, reports from notaries, military matters, the clergy, and the orders of chivalry. The modern section is composed mostly of political and governmental matters from 1791 onwards. The other three sections contain the microfilm archives, wills that have been deposited there by notaries, and heraldic information. Many of the microfilms contain genealogical materials. The National Archives has published a family history research guide (*Guide des Recherches sur l'histoire des Familles*) that can be consulted in many French libraries.

Finally, the Public Library of Information in Paris (Bibliothèque Publique d'information) has a collection of 300,000 volumes and 2,400 periodicals. It is a self-service library with many books related to genealogy.

There is also a computerized surname file available here, the *Géopatronyme*.

Fraternal Organizations *see* **Societies and Fraternal Organizations**

Friends, Society of *see* **Quaker Records**

FTP *see* **Computer Genealogy Files**

Funeral Directors' Records *see* **Coroner and Mortician Records**

G

Gazetteers *see* **Maps**

GEDCOM *see* **Genealogical Text Formats for Computers**

Genealogical Charts *see* **Pedigree Charts**

Genealogical Courses are offered by many specialist libraries and family associations. Some colleges also give credit for such studies, and one can participate in genealogical training through various Websites. Some of the courses are directed toward accreditation as a professional genealogist; others are for improving the skills of the amateur. And, of course, there are programs to interest the beginner.

The college courses cover subjects such as Scandinavian family history research, Germanic language handwriting and documents, and Slavic research. Brigham Young University in Utah offers an 18-credit-hour program of six courses to provide a solid foundation in family history principles, and the Samford University Institute of Genealogy and Historical Research in Alabama provides a week of intensive genealogical study led by prominent family history specialists. Genealogical courses are also taught at the University of Toronto, the University of London, University College in Dublin, and a number of colleges and universities in the United States.

Some of the courses available at Websites include beginning genealogy, tracing immigrant origins, and Internet genealogy. The International Internet Genealogical Society offers online courses ranging from introductory classes for beginners to more complex classes for experienced students. E-mail courses cover subjects such as biographical reference works, using Jewish genealogical sources, Jewish genealogy in the United States, and Jewish genealogy in the former German regions. Some of these are free; others are available for a relatively small fee.

Genealogical Mailing Lists And Newsgroups can be a good source of information for most researchers. They are also a place on the World Wide Web where genealogical information can be exchanged among those interested in one or more of the many aspects of family research. Some newsgroups are even "gatewayed" or "mirrored" with mailing lists. This means that the same messages appear in both a mailing list and on one of the newsgroups.

The mailing lists are electronic discussion groups based on e-mail messages. Any user can subscribe to one of the many mailing lists, such as the ROOTS-L list that now has more than 10,000 subscribers. The locations of such mailing lists can be found on various genealogical Websites, and there is a catalog of them on the Cyndi's List Website (www.cyndislist.com). *See also* **Computer Genealogical Sites**.

To participate in any mailing list one sends an e-mail message that just says "subscribe" to a program (i.e., Listserv, Smartlist, etc.) in order to be automatically added to the list. The subscription service for any such list is free, but one should wisely avoid subscribing to too many of them, because reading the huge amount of incoming mail may prove quite daunting. One can unsubscribe from a list in the same way that one subscribes, by e-mailing the word "unsubscribe." To communicate with the other subscribers, one sends e-mail messages to a different address from that used to subscribe. The researcher, after subscribing to a list, will receive all the e-mail that is sent to that list, and any message the subscriber sends in return will be relayed to all other subscribers so they can read it and respond if they wish to. Generally the mailing list ROOTS-L posts about 200 messages each day.

Many of the mailing lists are completely automated, with an electronic program taking care of subscribing people to the list, forwarding messages, and removing people from the list. Other mailing lists involve humans in the loop, persons who handle any and all of the mailing list functions that the electronic programs do. Such moderated mailing lists may have restricted membership (only for adoptees, for example), or the human moderator will review each incoming message before it gets distributed, thus preventing inappropriate material from making it onto the list.

A good number of mailing lists focus specifically on genealogy. In addition, many more lists although not specifically for genealogists, cover topics of interest to genealogists, such as ethnic groups or historic events. A few of the popular mailing lists are: SUR-NAMES-USA; SURNAMES-CANADA; Genealogy Today Newsletter; Heritage Quest eNewsLETTER; Eastman's Online Genealogy Newsletter; Family Tree Finders; and the GEN_SOCIETIES Mailing List for persons involved in establishing local genealogical societies.

Those who have never accessed any mailing lists may find the following sites the most helpful:

http://members.aol.com/johnf14246/gen_mail.html — a list of genealogical mailing lists.

http://listserv.indiana.edu/archives/index.html — has a listing of several different genealogy discussion lists, any of which can be subscribed to by sending the following message: SUB (name of selected list) and then your name.

http://www.ancestry.com/home/times.htm — a weekly newsletter on genealogy topics that can be subscribed to by sending a message to subscribe@ rootscomputing.com with the subject line saying: SUBSCRIBE.

http:/www.enoch.com/genealogy/newslet.htm — a monthly newsletter with tips and information for genealogists. Subscribe by sending the word SUBSCRIBE in the subject line to ROOTS WEB-REVIEW-request@ rootsWeb.com.

http://www.rootsWeb.com/-mlnews/index.htm — weekly online newsletter for genealogists. To subscribe, send an e-mail message with the word SUBSCRIBE in the subject line to MISSING-LINKS-L-request.rootsWeb.com.

Newsgroups, known also as Usenet (User Network) groups, are more manageable than mailing lists because one can search through all the postings by title and only read those few that might seem of interest. As with mailing lists, one can post messages on a newsgroup for others to read. But the user needs a special news reader, such as the excellent *Free Agent* program, to access any of the Usenet groups. Fortunately, popular programs such as *Outlook Express* and *Netscape* include news readers as part of their Internet service. The browser itself will, on request, download the complete list of more than 100,000 newsgroups. One can then mark all the newsgroups one wishes to look through. The downloading process can take as long as half an hour, depending on the speed of one's modem, but it only needs to be done once.

Most newsgroups are devoted to subjects other than genealogy, but there are some that specialize in this area. Here are a few of them:

alt.scottish.clans — devoted to Scotch and Irish tartans
soc.genealogy.african — specializes in African families

soc.genealogy.australia+nz — devoted to genealogy in Australia and New Zealand

soc.genealogy.britain — devoted to genealogy in the British Isles

soc.genealogy.computing —for genealogical programs, bugs, and how-to instructions

soc.genealogy.french —for students of French genealogy (most messages in French)

soc.genealogy.german — devoted to German genealogy

soc.genealogy.hispanic — devoted to Hispanic genealogy

soc.genealogy.jewish — devoted to Jewish genealogy

soc.genealogy.marketplace —for buying, selling and trading genealogical materials

soc.genealogy.medieval — devoted to medieval times

soc.genealogy.methods— tips on doing genealogy

soc.genealogy.misc — various clues to genealogy and other subjects

soc.genealogy.surname.global —for sending queries and answers about surnames

soc.genealogy.uk+ireland — devoted to British Isles genealogy

wales.genealogy.general — all aspects of genealogy with emphasis on Wales.

Genealogical Periodicals are published in many different forms— as monthlies, bi-monthlies, quarterlies, semi-annuals, and annuals. Many are distributed on a quite restricted basis; copies can be almost impossible to obtain. No library has all such publications, though several preserve all the most reputable ones. The New York Public Library receives some 600 genealogical periodicals annually. The Allen County Public Library in Fort Wayne, Indiana, claims to have some 3,500 genealogical and local history periodicals. They vary from highly-popular national genealogical magazines to four-page mimeographed newsletters distributed by various family associations.

Some genealogical periodicals are connected to a society and are part of the society's membership benefits, such as *The New England Historical and Genealogical Register*,

the *National Genealogical Society Quarterly*, the New York Genealogical and Biographical Society's *New York Genealogical and Biographical Record*, and the Federation of Genealogical Societies newsletter, *FORUM.* Others that can be subscribed to by any interested person include the popular national magazines *Ancestry, Heritage Quest, Everton's Genealogical Helper, Family Tree Magazine, The American Genealogist, The Colonial Genealogist,* and *Family Chronicle.*

Many of these periodicals contain a wealth of genealogical and historical information. There may be family histories, biographical sketches, indexes to otherwise unindexed records, copies of lost records, genealogical queries, guides to research, and sometimes whole genealogies. The *Boston Evening Transcript,* a newspaper published twice weekly from 1906 until 1941, had an excellent genealogical department that contained notes, queries, and answers provided by skilled genealogists and, more often, less experienced amateurs. Valuable clues and much dependable data can still be gleaned from the pages of this journal. Much of the information in these periodicals, however, remains little known because of the publications' limited circulation and, for the most part, lack of indexes.

Fortunately, there are a number of indexes to the better-known periodicals. Among them are Donald Lines Jacobus's *Index to Genealogical Periodicals* (Genealogical Publishing Co. 1988); and the *Genealogical Periodical Annual Index,* volumes 1–4 (1962–1965), edited by Ellen Stanley Rogers, volumes 5–8 (1966–1969), edited by George Ely Russell, volumes 9–12 (not yet published) and volumes 13–30 (1974–91), edited by Laird C. Towle. These indexes have been published by Heritage Books of Bowie, MD, and more volumes with later material are being published each year.

Genealogical Societies exist in many counties throughout the United States, as they do in all the countries of the world where there are persons interested in genealogy and family history. Most of them publish newsletters and can be helpful in locating information about relatives who lived in the areas they service. Often these newsletters have articles on specific research topics, book reviews, extracts from cemeteries, lists of new books in the society libraries, member queries, and pointers to source materials. The societies also offer genealogy classes and access to special conferences, as well as an opportunity to network with other researchers in the club.

There are a number of different types of genealogical societies, each with a specific goal and area of coverage: local (city or region), county, state, national, international, lineage, ethnic, area-specific (out of the country), historical, specialty (such as royalty, medieval, and Civil War reenactment groups), and surname-specific. Some are listed in Elizabeth Petry Bentley's *The Genealogist's Address Book,* Ancestry's *The Source,* and Everton's *Handybook for Genealogists.*

The Federation of Genealogical Societies, located in Austin, Texas, coordinates the activities of many genealogical societies. It was founded in 1976. This organization is composed of hundreds of genealogical and historical societies, family associations, and libraries. It has a combined membership of over 500,000, and acts as the collective voice for genealogists at the national level. The federation provides lecturers for society meetings and keeps members abreast of current news and events. Such services improve family history skills and provide a network of people to help break through research barriers. According to the federation, it has three major purposes: to serve the needs of its member societies, to provide products and services needed by the member societies, and to marshal the resources of the member organizations. *See also* **Books.**

Genealogical Text Formats for Computers provide a compact way of recording the information in a family database so that it can be scanned visually or by computer. The text format standard used in many genealogical programs for the computer was developed by the projects and planning division of the Church of Jesus Christ of Latter-day Saints. It is called GEDCOM (GEnealogy Data COMmunications), and was created to allow the sharing of genealogical information between two potentially dissimilar computer systems.

GEDCOM is continually being improved and updated, and is now becoming the de facto standard for data exchange among most genealogy software programs and systems. It is unique in that it allows the exchange of genealogical data among widely different software programs and operating systems. All vital information regarding each individual in the database is collected and put in a structured format that the receiving computer will understand. The program utilizes numbers to indicate the hierarchy of persons in the pedigree line and tags to indicate individual pieces of information within the file.

Another text formatting system, developed earlier than GEDCOM, is the Tiny Tafels standardized file format that was created to provide a compact way of describing a family database so that surnames of interest can be exchanged by computer among interested genealogists. Tiny Tafels are brief "shorthand" records of what an originator has researched. All data fields are set at a fixed length for easy parsing by the computer software, with the obvious exception of the surnames and optional places; the data is limited to surnames, beginning and ending dates, and beginning and ending locations.

Tiny Tafels can be created and compared by using freely available software. They can then be submitted to one of the Tafel Matching Services around the world that will compare them with all others that have been submitted and then report back any matches. One Tiny Tafel matching service is located on the GenealogySF World Wide Website.

Genealogical Websites on the World Wide Web are growing every day, and there are Web pages for virtually every aspect of genealogy. In 1999 there were over 55,000 of these Web-based genealogical sites, and now it is said there are more than one million. On the Web one can find census lists and vital statistics for many cities, states, and other countries, as well as information on genealogical organizations, libraries, databases, record abstracts, and various images. There are also numerous articles and clues to use in further research. And at some sites there are whole family trees, as well as biographies of noted family members.

Until relatively recent times, researching a family tree was a pursuit requiring much patience and travel over great distances to glean bits of often unrelated information. Writing to far-off places for copies of genealogical records and awaiting the reply could take months. Long-distance telephone calls to contact relatives in adjoining states and nearby cities could result in towering telephone bills. But now much of this research can be done on a computer with an attached or internal modem. Many of the most crucial sources of information have been digitized for computer use, and mountains of historical data are now available online for public perusal and downloading.

Perhaps the best place to start finding Web-based genealogical information is at the Cyndi's List Website. This is by far the largest online collection of genealogical links, and it is being updated all the time. The organization and indexing system used at this site make it a joy to browse there. Cyndi's List can be found at *www.cyndislist.com*.

Other fine Websites include:

About.com: Located at genealogy.about. com, this site is filled with many original articles and links to other genealogical sites that will prove useful to any serious genealogist.

Afrigeneas.com: This is a site focused on genealogical research and resources in general and on African ancestry in particular. It is a great tool for the growing number of African-American genealogists.

Ancestry.com: This massive site is related to MyFamily.com (listed below). It contains an extensive library, a great many free searchable databases, and many more that can be accessed for a fee.

Canadian Genealogy Links: *www.50mgs. Com/genealogy/* is an excellent source for finding data on one's Canadian forebears.

Dear Myrtle's Genealogy Lessons: *www. dearmyrtle.com/lessons.htm* gives practical,

down-to-earth advice from a daily newspaper genealogy columnist.

Everton.com: This site includes a tutorial for genealogy beginners and links to many online resources.

Familysearch.org: This database, compiled by the Church of Jesus Christ of Latterday Saints archives, contains over 320 million records and 600 million names from all over the world. The site is free and non-denominational.

Familytreemaker.com: This site boasts a FamilyFinder Index that allows a search of more than 153 million names, as well as a 1,200-page guide to genealogy.

Genealogy for Teachers: *http://www. polaris.net/~legend/genealogy.htm* provides resources, guides, and tutorials for genealogy teachers.

Genealogy Glossary: If the many acronyms and other confusing terms and concepts is getting you down, turn to *www.personstech.com/genealogy/def.html* for handy definitions.

Genealogy Online: *http://genealogy. emcee.com/* provides many resources for genealogists as well as an online copy of the 1880 U.S. census.

Genealogy Resources on the Internet: *http://users.aol.com/johnfl4246/internet.htm* may be the place to go when looking for a comprehensive list of resources on the Internet. The site will direct one to mailing lists, news groups, e-mail lists, FTP sites, and more.

Gentech.org: This site is operated by a nonprofit group that provides a forum where tech-minded genealogists can communicate with each other.

GenTree.com: This site accesses the Online Genealogical Database Index, listing over 1,000 searchable databases. There is much information, but the site is not well organized, so any search here may involve a great deal of time.

German.genealogy.net/gene provides information for those working in the field of German genealogy and German immigration.

Global: *http://www.globalgenealogy.com/* is a supply shop for maps, forms, software, and other tools the genealogist may need.

Hispanic Genealogy: *http://users.aol.com/mrosado007/* is a special interest group for those specializing in Hispanic genealogy.

Italian Genealogy: *http://www.italgen.com/* specializes in Italian genealogy and family names.

Jewish.Gen.org: This is the premiere site for Jewish genealogy, including Family Finder, which catalogs over 70,000 surnames and towns around the world. It has discussion groups, information files, and numerous databases.

Marston Manor: *http://www.geocities.com/Heartland/Plains/1638/* offers many on-line items for genealogists, including a detailed discussion on obtaining proof and evidence.

MyFamily.com: The purpose of this site is to bring families closer together. Those accessing the site can post photos, calendars, reminders, instant messages, and e-mail, and even engage in chat sessions.

National Archives and Record Administration: *www.nara.gov/genealgy/genindex.html* provides an overview and guide to the National Archives' bountiful resources both on the Internet and off.

Native America Genealogy: *www.geneasearch.com/ethnic/ethnicafam.htm* specializes in Native American records.

RootsWeb.com: This is one of the oldest and largest of the Websites. It contains a database of roughly 250,000 surnames and 30,000 genealogists researching them, In addition, searches can be done of the data using the Soundex system (q.v.) that finds items based on how a name sounds rather than its literal spelling.

Social Security Death Index: *http://www.ancestry.com/ssdi/advanced.htm* allows for a search of the SSI records for birth and death dates.

Surnames: *http://clanhuston.com/name/name.htm* contains a large collection of surnames and their meanings.

Thousand Genealogy Links: *http://members.tripod.com/surnames* provides some 2,000 links to various genealogical databases.

UsgenWeb.org: This site includes research topics, answering questions, and sending out records.

Genealogists, Professional *see* **Genealogy As a Profession; Professional Genealogists**

Genealogy is the process of reconstructing a family lineage by using records that can be found in one's own family as well as in many archives and other facilities that house historical records. The term comes from a combination of two Greek words—*genea*, meaning descent, and *logos*, meaning discourse. At one time the preserve of just a handful of enthusiastic amateurs and a few professionals, genealogy now offers countless hours of fascination to those who like an intellectual challenge as well as those who wish to make a living in serious research. As a form of recreation, genealogy is believed to be the third most popular hobby in America, only exceeded in interest by stamp and coin collecting. A survey conducted in 1995 by the Maritz Marketing Research company showed that about 19 million Americans are "involved a great deal in tracing their lineage."

Compiling genealogical records is an ancient craft. In the earliest days its purpose was to establish proof of ancestral rights and to assert the privileges of an hereditary aristocracy. Only much later did people, out of curiosity, begin to compile private genealogies of their own families. In the United States the development of genealogy was closely associated with the organization of patriotic societies. Many such societies were organized shortly after the celebration of the centennial of American independence. The first family genealogy in America was published in 1771, and titled *The Genealogy of Mr. Samuel Stebbins and Hannah his wife from 1701 to 1771.*

For a long time the work of the genealogist had the taint of inaccuracy tempered with forgery, a problem from which it has not yet been completely cleansed. The medieval kings, much like the English and French gentry of later ages, displayed tracings of their family lines all the way back to Adam and Eve, while lesser men, even as early as the 14th century, eagerly asserted their descent from one of the companions of William the Conqueror. Such genealogies were characterized by inexperience, over-zealousness, and a great deal of dishonest research.

One driving force in the development of genealogical research was the desire to conform to the laws of inheritance, particularly those that govern the distribution of real estate. As early as 1385 genealogical records became the primary documents used in a celebrated court suit in England known as Scrope vs. Grosvenor. It was initiated after Sir Richard Scrope, Lord of Bolton, discovered that his own coat of arms was being displayed on a banner by Sir Robert Grosvenor, a participant in an invasion force marching into Scotland. Scrope brought his complaint against Grosvenor's use of this emblem to a court of chivalry and won the suit. The judgment was later confirmed on appeal to the king. Scrope claimed that his ancestors had borne that coat of arms since the days of King Arthur's Round Table. Grosvenor, on the other hand, argued that he had derived his right to bear that banner from an ancestor, Sir Gilbert Grosvenor, who had come to England with William the Conqueror. Neither genealogical claim was based on any firm evidence, just on family traditions.

Many genealogies are found in English manuscripts and printed volumes from the time of King Henry VIII in the 16th century. Henry awarded commissions to a group of heralds who traveled the countryside to interview nobles and other landowners and record their family heritages. The notes that the heralds recorded in their Visitation Books range from a simple registration of the interviewee's name and arms to entries of pedigrees many generations long. These pedigrees were subsequently registered by the king and are now located at the College of Arms in London. To the heralds, these visitations were rare opportunities to obtain fees from the persons they visited, and thus the value of the pedigrees they designed are notably unequal. Such heralds continued to be employed in this visitation process throughout the reigns of Elizabeth I, James I, and Charles II. No royal registrations have been issued since. Yet from that time onward large numbers of genealogies have been preserved at the College of Arms. The modern ones,

fortunately, have been compiled with a great deal of care in contrast to the unsupported statements recorded by the Tudor heralds.

Today no European family makes a serious claim to be able to trace its roots back through the Dark Ages to Roman or Greek times. Anyone who might try to claim descent from the Garden of Eden or a direct line to one of the sons of Jacob would be dubbed a lunatic. The ancient sovereign houses of Europe are, for the most part, content to attach themselves to some ancestor who rallied a group of spearmen together to forge a nation sometime after the 11th century.

No longer does the mere possession of a surname shared by a dozen families constitute a tie of kinship. A man with the family name of Howard may be presumed to have descended from an ancestor for whom Howard was a personal name; it cannot be presumed that this ancestor was the same as the one from whom the dukes of Norfolk trace their origin. Genealogy can no longer be allowed to stray from facts that are supported by evidence. Any new pedigree should be backed up by the statements of living members of a family, and should contain a collation of records based on family Bible entries, letters, and diaries. It should also be supported by data gathered from census records; parish registers; county histories; birth, marriage, and death certificates; wills and administrations registered in various probate courts, and other legal documents. The publication of such records from the 19th century to the present has made the matter of genealogical research and verification much easier.

Professional and amateur genealogists often fail to appreciate or understand each other, even though each usually benefits from the work of the other. Whatever the case, it is a fact that amateurs in the field are becoming increasingly more professional in their standards, even though they are not paid for what they do. They recognize that the greater their understanding of genealogy in all its breadth and depth, the greater will be their likelihood of solving seemingly intractable pedigree problems.

Today the study of genealogy is growing

rapidly in both America and Europe. Individuals and genealogical societies are publishing vast numbers of pedigrees and family histories. In fact, genealogical works are now published in such abundance that the bibliographies on this subject are already filling substantial volumes on library shelves.

The end result of each investigation is finally more than just a timeline. It becomes an incredible journey into the past that builds a bridge into the future —for oneself, for one's family, and for future generations. *See also* **Genealogy for Beginners; Pedigree Charts.**

Genealogy as a Profession requires good training, a great deal of practical experience, and the ability to remember and categorize many details. Professionals also must be particularly painstaking in their recording of information and details, and be able to do this rapidly. Furthermore, in recent years, the genealogical profession has begun to require the knowledge of many computer skills.

Most professionals are engaged in freelance research conducted on behalf of clients seeking specific genealogical information. They build up their client base through reputations for good work. Many claim to have several months' work ahead of them all the time. They are generally persons who have been accredited through their experience and the courses they have taken.

Some free-lance genealogists search records for others who cannot travel to places where the records are stored or who do not have personal access to particular archives. They take on assignments to look for a few specific records needed by their employers rather than locating whole groups of records to fill out a pedigree chart. These free-lancers may not make as much money as the others, but good searchers, especially those able to travel, are in great demand. Often they are employed to go into courthouses and city repositories where the working conditions are dusty, cramped, and uncomfortable in order to find the needed materials.

Many libraries, historical societies, and hereditary organizations now employ professionals to take care of their collections and to answer the many questions that come in

by phone and correspondence. For such work it is not only important to have genealogical knowledge but also some library training.

Finally, there are some teaching and writing jobs available for professional genealogists. The writers are usually hired to edit family histories that others have composed, or to put the records of others into readable form. Teaching jobs, though relatively few, are sometimes available at schools that offer genealogical courses.

A useful book for persons interested in the profession is *Genealogy as Pastime and Profession*, by Donald Lines Jacobus. Baltimore: Genealogical Publishing Co., 1996. The Association of Personal Historians is a professional alliance of genealogists and other individuals whose mission is to assist in the preservation of life stories and memories. Many of the members have expertise in journalism, non-fiction writing, publishing, genealogy, history, storytelling, gerontology, counseling, and the making of video documentaries. *See also* **Genealogical Courses; Professional Genealogists.**

Genealogy Done by Computers is no different from the way such research was done otherwise. The only difference is in the tools that are used and the fact that many weeks work can now be accomplished in a matter of minutes. Instead of having to use a copying machine to acquire documents, one can download files from the World Wide Web. Instead of sending questions and requests by mail, one can send them in an instant by e-mail. Instead of going to the library to look through a card catalog, one can visit the same catalog by using a modem. And instead of reading a page in a book or magazine, one can find and read it on the computer screen with a browser.

More and more genealogical materials are being added to the World Wide Web every day. In fact, most of the basic data that a genealogical researcher might want to locate can now be accessed by a computer and a good search engine. There are Websites that hold vital records from every state in the Union. Others provide U.S. Census listings and Social Security death lists. There are also county histories and family trees, and some Websites specialize in family history research throughout the world. Some researchers have even designed their own Websites to enable others to view their genealogical accomplishments.

But in doing genealogy by computer one must be aware of the fact that just because something appears on a computer screen, this does not mean it is infallible. Everything that pops up there is based on the input of human beings, who make many mistakes. As the saying goes, "garbage in, garbage out." Thus the researcher needs to raise several questions when doing online genealogical research.

First, one needs to ask who created the data found on a particular Web page. There are resources on the Internet from the national and state governments, from universities, from libraries and research institutions, and from highly reputable genealogical societies. But there are also many documents based on family traditions and poorly-done research by persons to whom genealogy is just a spare-time hobby. Obviously one can have more confidence in the information provided by some of these sites than by others.

Second, one must ask how long the material has remained unchanged on the Internet page. If the page has been frequently updated, it is more likely that the information it contains will be valid. Of course, a page devoted to the 1880 census records does not usually need any updating, but a family history that is put online probably needs to be revised regularly as more information is uncovered through further research.

Third, one should consider the source of the information. If the author of the material or owner of the Website gives no sources, it may be wise to contact that person to get such information. If sources are cited on the screen, then it is up to the viewer to determine if they can be trusted. Many errors in genealogy appear on computer screens, just as they do in some books and magazines.

Finally, one must consider whether the information found on any Website makes sense in comparison to what one already knows. If the documentary evidence already gathered conflicts with that on a Web page, then it may be that one or the other is a mistake and should be treated as such. Most researchers will contact the author of the Web page in order to reconcile the differences or to urge them to correct the data. This sort of exchange is, after all, one of the advantages of genealogy done by computer.

Genealogy for Beginners requires basically the same research steps followed by professional genealogists and hobbyists with many years of experience. The method is to begin with what is known and easily verified and then to work backwards, one generation at a time, until all the pertinent records have been examined and verified. Whether genealogy is pursued as a fascinating hobby or as a profession, it uses family and historical records to prove or disprove that an individual or group of individuals are connected through kinship or genetically. The process results in the next best thing to DNA evidence.

Step One begins with oneself and all the information already at hand about one's family. The genealogist lists all the known names of parents, grandparents, great-grandparents, and so on, together with their birth, marriage, and death dates, as well as the locations of these events if possible. Once listed, it becomes important to determine how much of the information can actually be proved. Are there copies of records? A birth certificate can provide evidence of an exact birthdate, place, parents' names, address, ages, occupations, birthplaces of both parents, as well as additional clues that can later be used to link these names to other records as one searches further. "In working up a pedigree you should always begin with the earliest undoubted fact in your possession," said Walter Rye in his 1897 book, *Records and Record Searching.*

Experienced genealogists find it best to keep all their records and miscellaneous notes on sheets of paper or file cards that are the same size and shape. Keeping notes on any handy piece of paper — the backs of envelopes, credit card receipts, and odd-sized note pads— only assures that they will soon get lost, and if not, will inevitably result in a confusing mess. When the records are all put on the same type of paper or cards they can easily be filed according to whatever system a researcher prefers. Writing surnames with all caps helps the eye to scan more easily over the genealogical records (example: Frank Paul JONES). Furthermore, always listing dates by the day-month-year system (17 Feb. 2001), rather than the month-day-year system (2-17-01), helps to keep the numbers from getting jumbled, and listing places in the order of city/township, county, state, country (Chicago, Cook, Illinois) usually proves the best.

The family member names accompanied by their birth, marriage, and death dates are to be listed in order on a pedigree chart or series of pedigree charts. Blank spaces are left unfilled wherever such information about a family member is unknown. This enables the researcher to quickly recognize what yet needs to be found.

Step Two moves to interviews of all living relatives by mail or in person to find out if they have additional information about the family line. It is always possible that some family member has already begun to gather genealogical information. That information will save the researcher many hours of searching through records that another has already examined. Other family members may have old photographs, baby books, family Bibles, certificates, old letters and journals, Army discharge papers, deeds, mortgages, diplomas, insurance records, naturalization papers, newspaper clippings, school records, wills that were not discarded when new ones were made, a life insurance policy with family background, and scrapbooks that contain names and locations that can be added to the notes and pedigree chart.

Step Three requires the examination of any published materials about families with the same surname that may be borrowed from or perused at a library. Such works about persons of the same family name can sometimes be enormously helpful to one's research. A good guide to what is available is Robb and Chesler's *Encyclopedia of American Family Names* (HarperCollins, 1995), which alpha-

betically lists the printed genealogies of most U.S. families. This book can be found in many large libraries. Another source for published family trees is the genealogical magazines, many of which are put out by genealogical societies. Many of the leading magazines have indexes that list the families alphabetically. Occasionally, in a moment of great luck, a genealogist will find a family branch in one of these publications that links directly to the line being currently investigated.

There are two main types of genealogical records: original records and compiled records. Original records were created at or near the time of an event, such as birth, death, and marriage registers; census records; land and property records, or probate records. Compiled records have been researched by others. They include biographies, family histories, or genealogies that may be on microfilm, on microfiche, or in books. By looking in the compiled records first, a genealogist saves time, even though some mistakes may have crept into those records. Indeed, it is a common piece of advice given to all novice researchers that they should check for previous research before going further when looking for details about their own family trees.

Step Four is an examination of the microfilmed census records that can be found at the various National Archives locations and in some genealogical libraries. Clues as to which years and where to look in these records will come from the locations that have previously been recorded on the pedigree charts. Wherever a person is found in these census records listed as a farmer, it is likely that his father will be found at much the same location in an earlier census listing. Finding the father's name and location in that listing adds one more level to the pedigree chart. The researcher should remember that ancestor's names may be spelled in a number of different ways on the census lists. For example the 1790 census has these spellings for members who were all probably from the same family line: Fitzgerald, Fichgerrel, Fitchgearld, Fitchgerrel, Fitsgarrel, Fitsgerald, Fitsgerel, Fitsgorrel, Fitsjarald, Fitsjerald, Fitts Gerald, Fitzarrell, Fitzgarald, Fitzgarrold, Fitzgearld, Fitzgeral, Fitz Gerald,

Fitzgerrald, Fitz Gerrald, Fitzgerrel, Fitzger-rold, Fitzjarald, and Fitzjerald. A count of the surname Reynolds in the same census reveals 34 different forms.

Step Five moves into searching through such sources as the relevant county histories, city directories, church records, and vital statistics for other information related to the family line. The researcher must become very familiar with the various types of reference books that he or she will use over and over again. What notes the researcher has already recorded and what sections of the pedigree charts have been completed will suggest the directions in which further research of this type should be conducted. Much of the task at this point will be done in libraries, in searching Websites, and through correspondence with the state or county vital records departments. Most genealogical records are waiting to be found, if one knows where to look. The scribes of the past — census enumerators, county clerks, a minister, a ship captain, a newspaper editor, and perhaps even a neighbor — may have recorded exactly what one wishes to know.

It is important for the researcher to keep in mind that the primary purpose in building a family tree is to establish links from one generation to the next. Although it may be satisfying to "fill in all the blanks" on a family group sheet, that's not the real aim. Many times a genealogist is neither able to prove or disprove an event because no substantial evidence can be found. Then the researcher has to rely on surmise. For example, if William and Mary Jones are listed as a married couple in several records but no marriage certificate can be found stating that the event indeed took place on a specific date at a specific place, then the researcher can still conclude that William and Mary Jones were probably married, but the record cannot be located for a number of reasons, such as the fact that the county was not recording marriages at the time. One also has to accept the fact that verified records frequently list conflicting dates. A conflict in dates is somewhat irrelevant unless they create an anachronism.

There are three ways to build a credible case in genealogy: by direct evidence, by in-direct evidence (circumstantial evidence), or by a combination of both. Whenever records conflict, each piece of evidence must be weighed and evaluated for authenticity. One needs to ask "Who" created the record, "When" it was created, and "Why" it was created. For this reason the researcher must keep an accurate record of all the work he or she has done. Relevant documents should be copied by hand or by duplicating machine, labeled with the date and place where they were found, and filed in the appropriate order. Then they will be available for later reference.

It is highly important that all sources be cited so that if the particular document is required again it can be easily relocated. Accurate citation will be important to other researchers who might want to examine the evidence. If one doesn't cite sources, it will be difficult to reconstruct the proof for any stated fact. Many experienced genealogists even say that it is wise to keep a record of all sources, including those that have produced negative results as well as positive ones. Putting a genealogy together requires more than just knowing that records containing family information exist. A well-written genealogy will detail the useful genealogical records and direct others to the information sources.

The beginner should be aware of the great temptation among ancestor hunters to see how far back they can go rather than to see how accurate and complete they can be. The beginner also must be wary of the myths that usually develop as families retell their oral histories. One of these is that the family has an American Indian ancestor (usually Cherokee). Although some families do have such an ancestor, this is a relatively rare event and almost always is dispelled as documents are uncovered and verified. Perhaps the myth develops because there is an admirable strain of heroism and courage in the history of the American Indians. Related to this myth is the "coat of arms myth" that claims an ancestor of noble blood who had the right to display a particular coat of arms bearing the family surname. In most cases this myth derives from the discovery that there once was a coat of arms for a person with that surname.

However, not all Talbots are descended from the Earl of Shrewsbury and not all Staffords are descended from the Duke of Buckingham. Again, following the documents backward will reveal a large number of commoners named Talbot or Stafford, or whatever, who were never awarded any right to bear a coat of arms. As J. Gardner Bartlett, a noted specialist in tracing English roots among American immigrants has pointed out, "Of the 5,000 heads of families who came between 1620 and 1640, less than fifty or not one percent are known to have belonged to the upper gentry of England."

Then there is the "claim to fame myth" that attempts to relate all Bradfords and Aldens to William Bradford and John Alden of the *Mayflower*. This myth spills over into families with the surnames of U.S. presidents and even sometimes movie stars. It seems that having a noted name on one's family tree gives more prestige to that listing than otherwise. If no ancestor with a noted name is available, then "the stowaway myth" may offer a replacement. This myth has it that an ancestor came to America as a stowaway on a ship rather than as a paying passenger. Cleverness is here replaced for notoriety. But just because passenger records cannot be found there is no reason to assume that the particular surname was not among the ship passengers.

Less common is the "three brothers myth" that holds to the idea that three brothers — never two or four or six — immigrated to America at the same time. For immigrants there is "the Ellis Island baptism myth" that claims the immigrant ancestor's surname was changed by officials during processing at Ellis Island. Such name changes did happen sometimes with unique foreign names at some ports where the officials could not interpret the applicant's pronunciation, but the Ellis Island officials were better equipped to do this. In most cases, when the immigrant records are traced to the point of embarkation it is found that the family name was the same at both ports. Finally, there is "the ethnic identity myth" that makes all German ancestors Hessians who fought in the American Revolution, all French ancestors Huguenots expelled from France, and all Hispanic ancestors Mexicans.

More experienced genealogists find that in searching for the parents of an ancestor who was born in one place and died in another the best course is to start the search at the place where the ancestor was born. Then one should work systematically backwards through the person's life from death to birth, starting with the will and any other records of the individual's estate, including the inventories and accounts of sales, for clues as to occupation, social and economic status, ethnicity, and religion of the individual. One should also try to identify all the children, administrators or executors, bondsmen, and estate-sale purchasers (they may be relatives, friends, and neighbors who moved there with the ancestor). The deeds for a land division among heirs, for acquisition of that land, and the earliest deed may point to the place of origin. Any marriage, tax, and other court documents may also provide clues.

Problem-solving in genealogy is somewhat like detective work. It depends on a mixture of methodical plodding, inspired guesswork, and luck. Every individual can, with the proper training, become proficient at it and achieve the deep and satisfying experience of relating oneself to the lives of one's ancestors. *See also* **Books; Correspondence; Documentation; Geographical Context; Historical Context; Pedigree Charts; Research Methods.**

Genealogy, Uses of *see* **Uses of Genealogy**

Geographical Context is important for the interpretation of genealogical records. The exact place of a birth, marriage, death, or other event should be located on a map that was published around the time of that happening. Boundary lines on maps change over time as county, state, and even country borders are sometimes moved, and the place names also change when towns are renamed. One can waste hours of precious time searching for records in the wrong place if one assumes that a particular ancestor lived in a certain town in 1850 just because that's where the town is located now. Both the town name and county name may have changed over the last 150 years. At the very least one must know the name of the county at the time in which an event took place because most vital records (yet certainly not all) are preserved on a county basis.

Gazetteers, postal directories, and encyclopedias may include good maps for this purpose. However, unless a map is quite detailed, it may not show small towns. Older maps are also usually more useful than the recent ones because they show the old names. One of the best collections of American period maps is in the Library of Congress in Washington, D.C. This repository includes a vast inventory of land-ownership maps for U.S. counties during the 1800s. A listing of these maps is available from the U.S. Government Printing Office in Washington. It was prepared by the Library of Congress. Most libraries also have the *Rand McNally Commercial Atlas and Marketing Guide* (updated frequently) that has excellent maps of all the states and their counties as they exist today.

Maps are an aid to understanding the geographical and physical features that often have an important effect upon genealogical development. They may suggest patterns of settlement and migration, and at the same time rule out other possibilities. Topographical maps show the hills and valleys, waterways, and other natural features. A range of mountains becomes a barrier to migration, while a river may provide a way to travel. Historical maps provide the details on transportation lines in the counties where ancestors may have lived and worked. Maps show the relationship of one town or county to other towns and counties in the same general area. Such relationships may point one in the direction to go in order to find further genealogical data. A simple obstacle, such as a river, between an ancestor's land and the county seat, may prove to be the reason that this ancestor would go to a neighboring county for a marriage certificate or other documents that required registration. *See also* **Historical Context; Maps.**

Georgia Records begin about 1730, when a few Englishmen made plans to establish a separate colony in the region. The group was led by James Oglethorpe, and arrived at Yamacraw Bluff, the site of present-day Savannah, on November 17, 1732. Tomochichi, a Creek Indian chief, whose tribe lived nearby, aided the colonists. Within 21 years more than 4,000 settlers had come to Georgia from England. By 1775 many of the colonists joined the revolution against British rule, and after the war Georgia became the fourth state to ratify the U.S. Constitution, in 1788. By 1838 all the Indian tribes that had once lived here, including the Creeks and the Cherokees, had been forced to leave. Georgia seceded from the Union in 1861, siding with the Confederacy in the Civil War. It was readmitted into the Union in 1870. By 1900 the state had over 2.2 million residents.

Many families became permanent settlers in Georgia in the early 1800s because of the land lotteries that were held in 1805, 1807, 1820, 1821, 1827, and 1832. Families who had lived in the territory for at least one year were allowed to draw lots for parcels of land as large as 400 acres. Lists of these lottery participants are now located in the office of the secretary of state.

There are 159 counties in Georgia and each one has its vital records registrar and vital records custodian appointed by the state registrar. Each of these county records offices is authorized to prepare certified copies of birth and death certificates in its specific county. Depending on which county is considered, the custodian of vital records may be located at the county health department or in the office of the probate judge. Birth and death records from 1919 to the present can also be found at the Vital Records Service in Atlanta, where copies can be obtained for a small fee. Marriage records are available from the county clerk's office as well as the county clerk of the Ordinary Court. The latter is where voter registration lists are also to be found.

The first federal census in Georgia was conducted in 1820. The listings for this and each of the subsequent censuses conducted at 10-year intervals can be viewed at the various National Archives sites. There are printed indexes for the census years of 1820 and 1840.

The state conducted its own series of censuses in a number of other years. Those for 1799 and 1804 give the names of the heads of households and the number of persons living with them. These censuses and fragments of others can be found at the Georgia State Archives in Atlanta. For 1838 there are records from Laurens, Newton, and Tatnall counties; for 1845, records from Dooly, Forsyth, and Warren counties; and for 1859, records from Columbia county. School censuses exist for Talafero county (1827), Lumpkin county (1838), and Chatham county (1845).

Georgia maintains a clear distinction between its law and equity courts, though both are under the jurisdiction of the superior courts in the various counties. Divorce records can be found in the superior courts, which will provide information on any that have been enacted since June 9, 1952. Wills are probated in the county ordinary courts and exist from 1777 to 1798 and after 1852, while guardianship records are in the county courts of chancery. State land records are with the clerk of the county superior courts.

Records of Georgia land-grants made to veterans after the Revolutionary War can be found in the state land offices. But the listing of Confederate war pensioners will be found at the Confederate Pension and Record department in the state capitol at Atlanta.

Because the cities of Savannah and Brunswick are port cities, some ship passenger lists are stored in the National Archives in Washington, D.C. They include passenger lists for Savannah from June 5, 1906, to December 6, 1945. The ones for Brunswick go from November 22, 1901, to November 27, 1939.

A publication that may be of use to anyone looking for records in Georgia is the *Guide to Public Vital Statistics Records in Georgia* compiled and published in 1941 by researchers working for the Work Projects Administration. This guide can be found in some genealogical libraries both in Georgia and elsewhere. The booklet *Genealogical Research in Georgia* is available from the Georgia Department of Archives and History in Atlanta. Other places in Georgia that have genealogical records are the Georgia State Library and the Georgia Genealogical Society, both in Atlanta, and the Georgia Historical Society in Savannah.

Researchers seeking information from county records can locate them at the following county seats: (Appling County) Baxley, (Atkinson County) Pearson, (Bacon County) Alma, (Baker County) Newton, (Baldwin County) Milledgeville, (Banks County) Homer, (Barrow County) Winder, (Bartow County) Cartersville, (Ben Hill County) Fitzgerald, (Berrien County) Nashville, (Bibb County) Macon, (Bleckley County) Cochran, (Brantley County) Nahunta, (Brooks County) Quitman, (Bryan County) Pembroke, (Bulloch County) Statesboro, (Burke County) Waynesboro, (Butts County) Jackson, (Calhoun County) Morgan, (Camden County) Woodbine, (Candler County) Metter, (Carroll County) Carrollton, (Catoosa County) Ringgold, (Charlton County) Folkston, (Chatham County) Savannah, (Chattahoochee County) Cusseta, (Chattooga County) Summerville, (Cherokee County) Canton, (Clarke County) Athens, (Clay County) Fort Gaines, (Clayton County) Jonesboro, (Clinch County) Homerville, (Cobb County) Marietta, (Coffee County) Douglas, (Colquitt County) Moultrie, (Columbia County) Appling, (Cook County) Adel, (Coweta County) Newnan, (Crawford County) Knoxville, and (Crisp County) Cordele.

Also at (Dade County) Trenton, (Dawson County) Dawsonville, (DeKalb County) Decatur, (Decatur County) Bainbridge, (Dodge County) Eastman, (Dooly County) Vienna, (Dougherty County) Albany, (Douglas County) Douglasville, (Early County) Blakely, (Echols County) Statenville, (Effingham County) Springfield, (Elbert County) Elberton, (Emanuel County) Swainsboro, (Evans County) Claxton, (Fannin County) Blue Ridge, (Fayette County) Fayetteville, (Floyd County) Rome, (Forsyth County) Cumming, (Franklin County) Carnesville, (Fulton County) Atlanta, (Gilmer County) Ellijay, (Glascock County) Gibson, (Glynn County) Brunswick, (Gordon County) Calhoun, (Grady County) Cairo, (Greene County) Greensboro, (Gwinnett County)

Lawrenceville, (Habersham County) Clarkesville, (Hall County) Gainesville, (Hancock County) Sparta, (Haralson County) Buchanan, (Harris County) Hamilton, (Hart County) Hartwell, (Heard County) Franklin, (Henry County) McDonough, (Houston County) Perry, (Irwin County) Ocilla, (Jackson County) Jefferson, (Jasper County) Monticello, (Jeff Davis County) Hazlehurst, (Jefferson County) Louisville, (Jenkins County) Millen, (Johnson County) Wrightsville, (Jones County) Gray, (Lamar County) Barnesville, (Lanier County) Lakeland, (Laurens County) Dublin, (Lee County) Leesburg, (Liberty County) Hinesville, (Lincoln County) Lincolnton, (Long County) Ludowici, (Lowndes County) Valdosta, and (Lumpkin County) Dahlonega.

As well as at (Macon County) Oglethorpe, (Madison County) Danielsville, (Marion County) Buena Vista, (McDuffie County) Thomson, (McIntosh County) Darien, (Meriwether County) Greenville, (Miller County) Colquitt, (Mitchell County) Camilla, (Monroe County) Forsyth, (Montgomery County) Mt. Vernon, (Morgan County) Madison, (Murray County) Chatsworth, (Muscogee County) Columbus, (Newton County) Covington, (Oconee County) Watkinsville, (Oglethorpe County) Lexington, (Paulding County) Dallas, (Peach County) Fort Valley, (Pickens County) Jasper, (Pierce County) Blackshear, (Pike County) Zebulon, (Polk County) Cedartown, (Pulaski County) Hawkinsville, (Putnam County) Eatonton, (Quitman County) Georgetown, (Rabun County) Clayton, (Randolph County) Cuthbert, (Richmond County) Augusta, (Rockdale County) Conyers, (Schley County) Ellaville, (Screven County) Sylvania, (Seminole County) Donalsonville, (Spalding County) Griffin, (Stephens County) Toccoa, (Stewart County) Lumpkin, (Sumter County) Americus, (Talbot County) Talbotton, (Taliaferro County) Crawfordville, (Tattnall County) Reidsville, (Taylor County) Butler, (Telfair County) McRae, (Terrell County) Dawson, (Thomas County) Thomasville, (Tift County) Tifton, (Toombs County) Lyons, (Towns County) Hiawassee, (Treutlen County) Soperton, (Troup County) La-

Grange, (Turner County) Ashburn, (Twiggs County) Jeffersonville, (Union County) Blairsville, (Upson County) Thomaston, (Walker County) La Fayette, (Walton County) Monroe, (Ware County) Waycross, (Warren County) Warrenton, (Washington County) Sandersville, (Wayne County) Jesup, (Webster County) Preston, (Wheeler County) Alamo, (White County) Cleveland, (Whitfield County) Dalton, (Wilcox County) Abbeville, (Wilkes County) Washington, (Wilkinson County) Irwinton, and (Worth County) Sylvester

FOR FURTHER INFORMATION SEE:
• Adams, Marilyn. *Georgia Local and Family History Sources in Print.* Clarkston, GA: Heritage Research, 1982.
• Davis, Robert Scott, Jr. *A Researcher's Library of Georgia History, Genealogy, and Records Sources.* Greenville, SC: Southern Historical Press, 1991.

German Genealogy research is made difficult by the country's division until the 1870s into different kingdoms, as well as by religious differences that pitted the Protestants and Catholics against each other for several hundred years. In 1555, after much conflict, an agreement was reached that gave each Lutheran and Catholic ruler the right to force those under him to accept his religion.

Parish registers were first kept in the southern parts of Germany as early as the 16th century. These registers were initiated by the Lutherans in 1540 and by the Catholics in 1563. Many of these church records were later destroyed during various wars, particularly the Thirty Years War that took place from 1618 to 1648. However, some from the area along the river Saale have survived, including the parish register of St. Catherine's in Brandenburg, which dates to 1566, one in Hanover that dates to 1562, and one in Mecklenburg that dates to 1580.

The parish records of the Evangelical Lutheran churches were written either in German or Latin, but most of them in an old German script that researchers find difficult to read. An archive center for the Lutherans at Hanover, the Archivant der Evangelischen Kirche Deutschland, may be of help in locating the Lutheran parish records. The Catholic churches were ordered to start keeping their parish records by the Council of Trent, but recorded them only in Latin. Today, in each of the district archives there is a catalog of the parish records available.

Civil registration began with the enactment of a law in 1875. Every city, town, and village from January 1, 1876, was required to set up a Standesamt (registry office) where records of births, marriages, and deaths could be kept. Duplicates were made of these for the superior authorities. Unfortunately, there is no national archives repository, as there is in many other countries. Every city keeps its own archives of births, marriages, and deaths, as well as other records that may be useful to a genealogist. Each province also has its own Staatsarchiv (state archives office) to hold the state records for that province.

To find data for any individual, one must know in which city the person lived. Then one can go directly to the registry office of that city. The best advice for the researcher wanting records of German ancestry is to consult the main German Genealogical Society in Wiesbaden: Der Herold Verein für Heraldik, Genealogie und verwandte Wissenchaften. There are also many other genealogical societies that specialize in particular regions of Germany.

One source of genealogical information that is sometimes overlooked is the listing of ship sailings from the German port of Hamburg. These records give the last residence for each passenger. In the past there were also such records for ships from Bremen, but those have mostly been destroyed. Only a few remain. One can find a listing of these passenger manifests at the National Library of Germany in Frankfort.

There has always been much interest in Germany in the nobility and heraldry. This interest has resulted in an elaborate system of aristocracy because of the German insistence on the doctrine of the 16 quarters (*seizième quartiers*) — which means that all one's great-great-grandparents have to be noble in order to be considered a part of the standing aristocracy. The extensive records about German nobility are stored at the Deutsches

Adelsarchiv in Marburg. This institution publishes the *Genealogisches Handbuch des Deutschen Adels* (Genealogical Handbook of the German Nobility). There is also the *Almanach de Gotha*, which was begun in 1763 and was published in various editions at the town of Gotha, a residence for the former Dukes of Saxe Coburg Gotha. This volume of more than 1,200 pages deals with the sovereign royal houses of Europe, including those of the German princes.

Grand Army of the Republic Records can be found mainly at the Grand Army Museum and Library in Philadelphia and at various state and university libraries. The Grand Army of the Republic (G.A.R.) was a society of men who fought for the North during the Civil War. It was founded by Benjamin F. Stephenson in Illinois, in 1866, to strengthen fellowship among those who fought to preserve the Union. Membership was only open to honorably discharged soldiers, sailors, or marines who had served in the war. Its last member, Albert Woolson, died in 1955, and the organization was discontinued in 1956. The G.A.R. reached its largest membership of 490,000 in 1890.

During its most active years, the G.A.R. had a great influence in the politics, law, and social life of the United States. Its members were instrumental in electing several presidents of the United States, and a campaign of its membership led to the establishment of Memorial Day as a national holiday. At one time there were more than 8,600 community-level posts that were part of state-level departments. The great majority of G.A.R. records were maintained by the local posts. After the organization was disbanded, these records were treated as personal property, and many were thrown out or burned by uninterested executors. The records that did survive were often given to local, state, and national archives, as well as to historical societies and college libraries. Some ended up at the G.A.R museum. Others were inherited through default by later veterans' organizations, such as the Veterans of Foreign Wars and the American Legion. Still others probably remain stored — unknown — in attics. To locate such records, one first must determine to which post a particular member belonged. It then may be possible to discover what happened to that post's records. Most of these records, when found, only list the member's name, place of enlistment, unit name, service wound (if any), and place of birth.

Grants and Patents *see* **Land Records**

Gravestones are meant to be lasting memorials, but old cemeteries suffer from the ravages of time and weather. Old gravestones can be difficult to read, and others are already so faint that deciphering them is impossible. Many of these stones give vital information that cannot be found elsewhere because records are missing; some old markers read like entries on a pedigree chart, although most of them give no more than initials or a name and perhaps a date of death or age at time of death. However, gravestone inscriptions should never be accepted as the most accurate source of information. The dates of deaths on any stones should be compared with records that give the dates of burial. Dates of birth should be compared with christening or other pertinent information records.

A number of genealogical societies have made it a project to survey surrounding cemeteries and to locate, repair, clean, and make rubbings of or otherwise transcribe the inscriptions found on the gravestones. This is a valuable service because it needs doing before the information on more stones is lost forever to wind, rain, and vandalism. Of course, one should check with the cemetery sexton before trying any method of headstone cleaning.

The date when a gravestone was placed can be important, because the information on one set there a few days after a funeral will likely be more reliable than that on one placed there 25 to 50 years later. Most older graves also tend to sink, leaving a slightly depressed area that outlines the dimensions of the grave. If no age or birthdate is given for children, one can possibly determine which are those of the adults and which are their children by measuring the depressions. Those that are more than five feet long in a family group will likely be the parents.

Gravestone designs often provide a particularly interesting record of cultural changes. Two archaeologists, James Deetz and Edwin Dethlefsen, have studied the gravestones within a hundred miles around Boston and have measured how the styles varied according the changing religious climate over the 17th and 18th centuries. They found that the earliest designs to appear on the gravestones are those of a winged death's head with black eyes and a grim, grinning mouth. Sometime in the 18th century these death's head designs were replaced by winged cherubs, and by the late 1700s and early 1800s the winged cherubs had been replaced by willow trees overhanging pedestaled urns. Because all these gravestones bear the date of death (and usually the date of birth), the design changes could be accurately dated.

At the time that the death's heads were popular, orthodox Puritanism, with its strict rules governing everyday life, was the universal religious outlook in New England. Apparently the death's head was grim enough to make it acceptable as a motif to the Puritans, who frowned on the use of icons, which they interpreted to be idol worship. The winged cherubs began to appear as the religious rules relaxed and became less stringent. Cherubs are considered heavenly beings, and their use reflects a more cheerful, optimistic outlook on the part of the New Englanders of that time. The rise in popularity of the urn and willow designs coincided with the growth of less emotional, more intellectual religions, such as Unitarianism.

The styles of epitaphs also changed in much the same way the designs did. During the orthodox Puritan period, the stones merely had the words "Here lies" or "Here lies buried" written on them, thus emphasizing life's brevity. Many of the ones accompanying the cherubs read "Here lies the body of," suggesting that although the physical body remained behind, the soul would have fled to heaven and immortality. In the urn and willow designs, the words were mostly phrases such as "Sacred in the memory of." The epitaphs at this point were sometimes more sentimental, and combined such feelings with some sort of eulogy.

The kinds of stones used at different times were also varied, some of them better equipped to resist the ravages of time than were others. During the 18th and early 19th centuries, most gravestones were made of a soft, dark slate that weathered easily and tended to develop cracks and split off pieces as water, snow, and ice expanded in the dents and crevices. The stones erected between 1800 and 1850 generally were of a kind of grayish-blue slate that is harder and took a better polish. But engravers during this period tended to employ an italic script for their lettering that is sometimes quite difficult to read. After 1840 the gravestone makers began to turn to a type of hard marble that endured better, and they returned to the roman lettering they had used earlier. Then by the late 19th century gravestone carvers were using granite and raised lettering that is sometimes as difficult to read as the previous incised lettering. This is particularly true when the light is coming from the wrong direction or when the stone has become overgrown with lichens. Yet when sandblasting is used to deeply incise the lettering, as it is now, the wording probably will last much longer.

For those with a particular interest in researching gravestones, the Association for Gravestone Studies in Massachusetts gives advice as to the symbolism on grave markers as well as the tools and materials that can be used for gravestone cleaning. *See also* **Cemeteries.**

Graveyards *see* **Cemeteries; Gravestones**

Greek Genealogy includes many long pedigrees of noted Greek families, and almost every town and city has its published history. It is therefore wise for researchers to have a good grasp on the history and geography of Greece before they begin to conduct research into the genealogical records of this country. For example, one should recognize that various parts of today's Greece were under foreign rule before the Balkan War of 1912. A person moving from Crete to Athens in 1897 or before would have been designated an immigrant.

Some church registers in Greece have been maintained since the late 1700s, although it is not certain how far backward such records extend. These are diocese registers rather than the parish registers that are found in most other countries. In other words, the churches in Greek towns will not have any old records. They can only be found at the diocese (*Irea Mitropolis*), which will be in a large city. Since 1912 it has been obligatory for all churches to record the births, baptisms, marriages, and deaths in their parishes and to send them to the diocese. One also finds that many homes in Greece display one or more icons that depict saints. These icons often have personal information, such as the birthdates of family members, written on the back side.

Civil registration dates from about 1856 but was incomplete until 1931, when the civil registration process was extended throughout the whole country. Local archives are maintained with the names of all Greek citizens, a system that began in 1933. These archives can be found in the town hall (*Dimarheion*) as well as in the county office (*Nomarheion*) and district office (*Eparheion*). A few date back to 1830, but the ones of such an early date are all constructions written at a later date. Knowing the former name of a municipality in which a town of a later name belongs can be important. Old records were usually written in books that bear the name of the old municipality, and those books are now in the town hall of the new municipality. In the large cities there are also military archives (*Stratiotika Arheia*), and in the capital districts there are general archives (*Genika Arheia tou Kratous*) where select, old documents are cataloged and preserved.

Notaries public maintain both the public and secret wills. On hearing of the death of a testator, the notary sends a copy of the will to the secretary of the Court of First Instance at Athens. Another type of will, known as a written will as distinct from a public or secret will, is also sent on the testator's death to the Court of the First Instance, where copies of all wills are held. The notarial archives (*Symvolaiografika Arheia*) in Athens also store contracts of land transfers, dowry contracts, and other documents.

The first census conducted by the Greek

government was completed in 1828. Prior to that some censuses were conducted in Greece by other countries. From 1836 to 1845 the Greek government took censuses yearly. After that they were done every three to five years until it was decided to hold them only every 10 years. The census records can be found in the district offices; some of these records are in the National Library of Greece in Athens.

Finally, in looking through the names of females in Greece, one should know that a woman before marriage uses the initial letter of her father's last name as her own middle initial. After marriage, that same woman replaces this middle initial with the initial letter of her husband's surname. Thus the same woman may be taken to be two different persons because of the two different middle initials.

Some help in locating specific names in the civil registrations of Greece can sometimes be provided by the Civil Registration Division of the Ministry of the Interior in Athens. The Greek Orthodox Archdiocese, also in Athens, may be of help in locating specific church records. *See also* **Ancient Greek and Roman Genealogy.**

Guardianship Records, also known as guardian bonds or orphan's bonds, are closely related to probate records and the probate process, because when a person dies and is survived by minor children, such children are not considered capable of managing their own properties. Thus a guardian must be appointed to protect the child's rights to any estate, and the court records arising out of such guardianship matters may be kept in the probate record books. But whether this happens or not, in most states in the United States probate and guardianship matters are handled by the same courts. Apprenticeship records are also sometimes included among the guardianship records.

Guardianship proceedings take place when minor children are orphaned or when a father dies. The mother is then allowed to retain guardianship if officials consider her circumstances sufficient to provide for the children. Guardianship records can thus establish the parentage of a person who is a minor and help to establish the dates of death for the parent or parents. Another person who may be appointed as guardian is a relative, friend of the family, or someone that the court believes would raise the children adequately so that the minors might become contributing members of the community rather than wards of the county or state.

Some cases have been found among the guardianship records in which the person named as guardian for an orphan is actually the father. This man is named guardian after the mother dies so that he can take custody of the orphan's portion of the mother's inheritance from her father's estate.

Guardianship records usually give the name of the deceased parent(s), the names and ages of the minor children, the name and residence of the guardian, the date on which the inheritance was paid to the ward or minor, and the status of the ward at the time this payment was paid. In most cases the records are kept by clerks of the county courts, and they are usually not indexed. However, any genealogist would be wise to try to locate the guardianship records whenever a person is known to have died with minor children and some real property, regardless of whether the spouse survived him or her.

Before 1900, the wife of a deceased spouse was not normally appointed guardian for the underage children. Usually some close male family member or friend was appointed to this position. As such he assumed the responsibility and duties for managing the affairs of the children until they reached their majority. Guardians were required to attend court on a regular basis and account for the income and expenditures of all monies belonging to the children. If real property was involved, the guardian was responsible for maintaining it in the interest of the children. The guardianship remained in force until the youngest child came of age.

Because guardians have to make various court appearances, there are several kinds of records and varying kinds and amounts of information that such records can provide. The first document will be the appointment procedure. Then the guardian must be bonded, which entails another document, as does the inventory that the guardian has to provide as to the child's assets. Finally, when the guardianship terminates, an account of this

event will be filed with the court. *See also* **Indenture and Apprenticeship Records.**

Guatemala *see* **Central American Genealogy**

H

Handwriting Errors occur in many genealogical records both because a record keeper sometimes produces spelling mistakes and because letter formation often leads to difficulties, particularly in the reading and interpreting of surnames. Curlicues and flourishes may render some letters more or less indecipherable. A poorly written G looks like an S; R and K can resemble each other, and a capital B that is left open at the bottom is easily mistaken for an R. Other letters that can also be confusing are M and N; N and H; V and U; and S and L. Furthermore, the handwriting of some record keepers vies with that found on a doctor's prescription and leads one to suspect that the most important qualification for such a scribe may be that he or she could write in a way that no one else could read.

When one is looking at American records composed during the 1600s and even in the early 1700s, one may find enough carry-over from Middle English forms of writing to suggest that a study of the somewhat simpler Middle English alphabets might prove of value to any genealogist. In reading documents where there are such confusing words and letters, it can be useful to locate other words elsewhere in the document that, because of their context, are recognizable and then use them to resolve the problems.

Of course, handwriting in any generation can be a problem. Many people write in a way that is quite difficult for others to interpret. Almost everyone sometimes finds it confusing to interpret one's own writing after it has been put aside for a number of years. Fortunately, most records today are produced on a typewriter or computer, both

of which produce extremely legible alphabets. *See also* **Spelling Variations.**

Hawaii Records begin with the Protestant missionaries from New England who came to Hawaii in 1820 to convert the Polynesian Islanders to Christianity. After a revolution, led by nine Americans and four Europeans, that removed the Polynesian Queen Lilluakalani from the throne, the Islanders established the Republic of Hawaii in 1894. The United States annexed Hawaii in 1898 and established the Territory of Hawaii in 1900. In 1959 Hawaii became the 50th state of the Union.

A census was taken in 1900 and thereafter every 10 years as part of the United States national census. The records are stored in the National Archives in Washington, D.C., and can be viewed on film at any of the National Archives locations throughout the United States. There are also some fragments of earlier special censuses that can be seen at the Hawaii State Archives in Honolulu. These items include records from 1866 (mostly Maui), from 1896 (part of Honolulu only), and from 1878 and 1890 (scattered districts on various islands). None of these special Hawaiian censuses are complete.

The Vital Records Section of the State Department of Health in Honolulu has birth and death records since 1853, and divorce records since July 1951. It also has marriage records from 1832 to 1949. Copies can be obtained from the Vital Records Section for a small fee. The Hawaii State Archives also has copies of the Hawaiian census records from 1866, 1878, and 1890; a collection of photographs; maps; immigration records from pre-

1900 (divided by nationalities); immigration records from 1900 to 1921; collections of books about Hawaii, and Hawaiian city directories.

In Hawaiian courts, there is no distinction between equity and law actions. The jurisdiction for both is in the circuit courts. That is where guardianship and probate records can be located. Land records, however, are under the jurisdiction of the Registrar of Conveyances in Honolulu. The Hawaii State Archives is the repository for legislative records from 1840 to the present, judiciary records from the 19th and early 20th centuries, governors' records from 1900 to 1986, and the Maui Historical Society Archives. These records are arranged mostly by the agency, organization, or individual that created them, rather than by subject. Other places where genealogical materials can be found include the Hawaiian Historical Society and the University of Hawaii Library at Manoa, both in Honolulu.

Researchers seeking information from county records can locate them at the following county seats: (Hawaii County) Hilo, (Honolulu County) Honolulu, (Kauai County) Lihue, and (Maui County) Wailuku (includes Kalawao).

FOR FURTHER INFORMATION SEE:
* Conrad, Agnes C. *Genealogical Sources in Hawaii.* Honolulu: Hawaii Library Association, 1987.
* Luster, Arlene D.C. *A Directory of Libraries and Information Sources in Hawaii and the Pacific Islands.* Honolulu: Hawaii Library Association, 1972.

Headstones *see* **Gravestones**

Health Records *see* **Public Health Records**

Heraldry is the branch of knowledge dealing with the history and description of designs that are used to distinguish individual families and to authenticate official documents. Although these images are of little use in the construction of family pedigrees, some genealogists find delight in identifying and collecting heraldic designs, also known as coats of arms. The term "coat of arms" comes from the custom of embroidering the emblem of a knight on the surcoat worn over his armor.

Ornamental figures similar to those of heraldry have been used as tribal and national emblems since ancient times. For example, the Old Testament refers to the separate symbols used by each of the 12 tribes of Israel — a lion for the tribe of Judah and a wolf for the tribe of Benjamin, for example. The early Romans used the symbol of an eagle when they went into battle, and the French used the symbol of a lion and later the fleur-de-lis. In England, the Venerable Bede, writing in the early eighth century, tells of the banners of King Edwin of East Anglia that "were not only borne before him in battle, but even in time of peace, when he rode about his cities, towns or provinces."

During the thirteenth century, the practice of using emblems to identify individuals in battle evolved into a complex system for marking social status that was inherited from generation to generation. Most of the terms that are used to describe this system are derived from the language of the French court, although the process of designing coats of arms developed all over Europe. A seven-volume work of reference, the *Grand Armorial de France*, contains references to about 40,000 different coats of arms. This work is published in Paris; one of the latest editions is that of 1975.

At first coats of arms were largely self-assumed by members of the knightly class. But in 1483 King Richard III of England established the College of Heralds (also known as the College of Arms) in London to supervise the granting of such armorial bearings. Over time, many prominent individuals, families, kingdoms, lordships, towns, Episcopal sees, abbeys, and even corporations have been awarded their own coats of arms. In the United States and Canada the national seals and the seal of each state and province bear such heraldic designs.

A complete coat of arms consists of a shield, crest, and motto. The fundamental element is the shield, or escutcheon from the French word *écusson*. To facilitate description, the shield is divided from right to left (from the wearer's viewpoint) into the dexter side, middle or pale, and sinister side. It is also divided from top to bottom into three areas—

chief, fess, and base. All the terms used in heraldry have an exact meaning in order to avoid confusion when giving a verbal description.

The designs on a shield are known as charges. These consist of almost anything that can be symbolized: representations of divine beings, people, monsters, animals, and natural and man-made objects. One often sees charges that depict a bear, bull, boar, deer, goat, dog, horse, hedgehog, or even occasionally an elephant, camel, mole, ape, eagle, cat, or mouse. Some of them are given special names, such as the "rampant" lion standing on one hind leg with front paws held high as if warding off an enemy. A beast looking toward the observer is known as gardant, and if looking backwards is known as regardant. The animal symbols are often crowned or collared (gorged) with a wreath (torse) or coronet. In listing the elements of a coat of arms, the color (tincture) of the charge follows the description of it, as in "two lions crowned, azure."

The colors can be white (silver), yellow (gold), red, blue, black, and green. In small amounts one also occasionally finds orange, purple, and crimson. These colors all go by the language of the French court, but there is really no need of saying "gules" instead of "red," "azure" instead of "blue," or "sable" instead of "black." However, when the whole design of a particular coat of arms is described, as it will be in any dictionary of heraldry, there is some advantage in saying "azure a bend gold" instead of "a blue shield crossed diagonally by a yellow straight-sided band running from the upper left corner to the lower right side."

The crest is the topmost element of the heraldic emblem. It usually extends above a helmet that, in turn, stands above the shield. The crest is the most ancient part of armorial bearings, and in Greek and Roman antiquity it served as a conspicuous object around which soldiers might rally. Usually the crest in heraldry is referred to as the most important part of the mantling, which includes all the ornamental accessories surrounding the helmet and top of the shield. Its base is frequently surrounded by a wreath, or circlet of twisted ribbons in the principal color of the shield.

The motto is placed in a scroll below the shield or sometimes above the crest. Such mottoes grew out of the war cries once used in battle, though they are now just a phrase or sentence alluding to the family that possesses the right to bear that coat of arms. There are other elements of a coat of arms such as the helm, supporters, and compartment, but space limits their description here. It might be advisable for readers to find descriptions of all these and other elements in one of the many dictionaries and books on heraldry found in most libraries.

Just as England has its College of Arms, many other nations have special officials who are responsible for creating and maintaining the country's heraldic symbolism. In Scotland, the matter has long been regulated by Parliament. Nobody there is allowed to display arms without approval by the Lyon Office, which stipulates an exact design. In Switzerland there are coats of arms for every canton and for the great majority of towns, and any Swiss individual has a right to use whatever arms he or she might desire, whether inherited or personally assumed. Even in the United States, the standing Committee on Heraldry was appointed in 1864 by the New England Historic Genealogical Society. Its purpose was to examine the validity of arms used in this country and to discourage the use of unauthorized forms. Today that task has passed to the American College of Heraldry at Tuscaloosa, Alabama.

In the Republic of Ireland the heraldic archives are located at Dublin Castle. But for Austria the official use of any coats of arms has been forbidden since 1919, and before that they were restricted to use by the nobility. In Belgium the coats of arms are regulated by Le Conseil Héraldique in Brussels, and in France by the Conseil Historique et Heraldique in Paris. The records for the German coats of arms are kept by the genealogy archives in Berlin; for those in Italy by the Collegio Araldico in Rome; for those of Spain by the Cronistas de Armas in Madrid, and for those in Switzerland by the Schweizerische Hearldische Gesellschaft in Fribourg.

Since the early days of heraldry, only the head of a family had the right to inherit unchanged the entire paternal arms, and this is still true in England and a number of other European countries. Junior branches of the family can use that coat of arms only if they change certain colors or make small substitutions to the charges. But in America it is often assumed that coats of arms belong to specific surnames or families rather than to particular individuals. Actually this is not the case, and it tends to spread confusion among family history researchers. Companies that advertise the ability to provide "your coat of arms" are really only providing a copy of a heraldic design that was granted to one individual sometime in the past. One such coat of arms provider claims to have over a million different designs from which it can locate any particular one that belongs to a specific surname, thus deceiving or misleading the public. *See also* **College of Arms.**

Hereditary Society *see* Lineage Societies

Hispanic-American Records can be difficult to locate and piece together, even though Hispanic-American settlers were already living in Saint Augustine, Florida, as early as 1565 and in parts of New Mexico as early as 1598. Spaniards came to what later became the United States by way of the Caribbean islands, Central America, and Mexico. Later Hispanic immigrants arrived here from South America as well. From 1820 to 1906 approximately 20,000 legal Hispanic immigrants arrived from South America. More came between 1906 and 1926, and it is estimated that from 1951 to 1975 a total of 421,000 South Americans came into the United States. These figures do not include the many Hispanics who have continued to come from Cuba, Puerto Rico, Mexico, and various Central American countries during this time and ever since.

Hispanics also came to the United States directly from Spain. For example, many from the Andalucia and Valencia regions of Spain went to Hawaii to work in the sugar fields, their families later migrating to California and other parts of the western United States. Spanish and French Basques also arrived as sheepherders to work in California and Nevada.

The U.S. federal census records have a column that indicates the country of birth, which can be useful in locating Hispanic-American records. But in some of the Southwestern states the census takers often listed the name of a Mexican state as the place of birth rather than the country Mexico, a listing that can sometimes be rather confusing. In any case, the census records should be carefully studied even though they may provide little more than the country where a particular Hispanic came from. Starting with the 1920 census, columns indicate whether or not an individual was a naturalized citizen and how long he or she had lived in the United States.

If they can be located, naturalization and citizenship records are useful in identifying the place of birth, age, physical characteristics, and some information about other members of the family. Some Hispanic families have also retained work permits among the family papers that may provide good information. Ship passenger lists as well as border crossing lists for some years are available at the National Archives in Washington, D.C. These lists include the U.S. Immigration and Naturalization Service records for some 1,500,000 persons who, from 1903 to 1953, crossed the border from Mexico into the United States at El Paso, Texas.

Perhaps the best Spanish-language sources for information about Hispanic-Americans are the records of the local parishes of the Roman Catholic Church. Such records of baptisms, marriages, deaths or burials, and confirmations can provide a great deal of information about particular families. For example, before any marriage there would need to be a marriage petition that would include proof of the good standing of a couple in the Catholic Church (often baptismal certificates for both the bride and groom), written permission from the parents if either party was under the age of 21, and the priest's permission for the marriage to take place. If the father of the bride or groom was dead and so could not give his consent, then the date of the death of the father would also be a part of the marriage petition, as would any special dispensations required from the bishop. The researcher should always check these records in their original forms. Extracts and indexes usually omit details that may be of the greatest use.

Library collections of documents related to Hispanic-Americans can be seen at the University of Texas in Austin (Benson Latin American Collection) and the University of Texas Pan American Library in Edinburg; at the San Antonio Public Library in Texas (Texana Department); at the University of Arizona at Tucson (Documentary Relations of the Southwest), and at the University of California in Berkeley (Bancroft Collection of Western and Latin Americana). A book that may be useful in Hispanic research is George R. Ryskamp's *Finding Your Hispanic Roots* (Baltimore: Genealogical Publishing Co., 1997).

An interesting side issue in the field of Hispanic genealogy is the origin and original meaning of many Hispanic surnames. A number of books and dictionaries are helpful in this area. Some names originated from physical characteristics: Juan el Gordo (John the Fat) as opposed to Juan Delgado (Thin John), Juan Gran (Big John) as different from Juanito (Little John). Parentage was another source, as it has been in many cultures. The Hispanic names of this sort include: Mendez (son of Mendo), Alvarez (son of Alvaro), Gonzalez (son of Gonzalo), Ortiz (son of Ortun), Ibañez (son of Iban), and Jimenez (Son of Ximena). And then there are, of course, names associated with occupations: Carillero (cart maker), Molina (miller), Marrero (hoe maker), Guerrero (warrior/soldier), Torrero (bullfighter), Escudero (Squire), and Escobedo (sweeper). There are also surnames that originated from likenesses to animal characteristics—Garcia (like a fox) and Aguila or Aguilar (eagle/eagle like). Many other Hispanic names originated, of course, in other identifiable ways.

Historical Context is important in genealogical research because the times, places, and events through which family members lived, as well as the conditions at the time,

give meaning to their lives. A knowledge of historical events such as weather disasters, pestilence, and wars can lead one to additional records or even provide answers to puzzling questions. Of course, genealogy in its most basic form tries only to identify individuals and their relationships. But if one limits research to this approach, nothing much can be learned about any of the ancestors who are identified. The best genealogical research always employs a good understanding of history and sociology along with that of basic genealogy. As Dr. Amandus Johnson said in a lecture to members of the National Genealogical Society, "History is based upon biography, and biography is based upon genealogy."

Many examples can be amassed to show the importance of understanding history. For example, earlier ancestors probably traveled by horse and wagon, steamer ship, sailing ship, rowboat, or even by pole boats. It would have been extremely difficult for them to go the great distances that people do today. Then suppose family tradition says an ancestor was born Catholic but was adopted at the age of six by a Quaker family after the French and Indian War. Only by studying history will the researcher find out that adoption did not exist under colonial law and that the earliest adoption law in the United States was a Massachusetts statute of 1851. Probably this "adoption" was really a guardianship arrangement. Furthermore, if this event took place in the state of New York, then the historical records would show that in 1763 it was illegal to practice Catholicism there. Yet Catholic worship was permitted in nearby Pennsylvania.

Though it is important to develop historical and geographical context, it is also essential to flesh out the details of what the physical environment would be like at the time. Pictures can often provide visual details that capture the "flavor" of the time, place, and people involved. Some of these pictures can be found in the line drawings published in old magazines and newspapers during the early years under investigation. For persons in the early years of the 20th century there are a multitude of picture postcards that reproduce drawings and old photographs. Postcards can be found in family albums, antique stores, and on Web-based auction sites. There are also old stereographs that were popular before postcards. Tens of millions of such stereographic cards were printed and sold. Not surprisingly, a wealth of the cards and viewers still survive.

Finally, the best advice for any genealogist is that one can never know too much about what records are available. One should look beyond the standard genealogical records to what the economic, political, and social historians use. Find where such records are kept, where copies may be found, and in what format. Then one's genealogy will be more than a flat, two-dimensional chart. It will have vitality. *See also* **Geographical Context.**

Historical Societies have been founded in every one of the 50 states, many counties, and also many cities. Most of them have libraries containing books relating to the history of the areas that they serve, and some of these books and other records may be useful to the genealogist. Some of the societies operate on a limited budget with volunteer staffs. Others are supported by state funds and have paid administrators. Although one can often find the records these societies maintain in various court archives, town libraries, and vital statistics offices, they are usually found more quickly at the historical societies' libraries. The staff of these may be very helpful.

One of the earliest historical societies formed in Philadelphia, the Historical Society of Pennsylvania. It is particularly famous for its collection of ships' registers from 1682 to 1924. Its library is also the home of the Genealogical Society of Pennsylvania.

The American Association of State and Local History (AASLH) provides leadership to the historical societies. It is located at Nashville, Tennessee, and was initiated in 1904 by the American Historical Association. The association publishes a biennial directory of the various historical societies that belong to its membership.

History and Genealogy cannot be separated. The events of history have always determined what types of records were collected and kept, together with the format and content of those records. Religious, economic, political, and social happenings have thus had a profound effect on genealogy and genealogical records in America and throughout the world.

For the genealogist it is impossible to fully understand the actions of individual ancestors without some knowledge of the times in which they lived. The events of history dictate the social stratification, migration patterns, locations of settlements, and even the occupations of all the members of one's family tree. If the researcher can understand the forces that shaped people's lives, then he or she will better understand the actions of those people. For example, if an ancestor lived at the time of the Civil War and participated in it, then an investigation of the records of that war will likely help to fill in gaps in the understanding of that individual's life. At the same time, if the person did not participate in the war and avoided the military draft, it may have been because he was a conscientious objector on religious grounds (as were members of the peace churches, such as the Quakers), and this religious connection would be worth further investigation.

For the historian genealogical information is equally important. The British historians Sir Frank Stenton and his wife, Lady Stenton, have used the rich resources of English genealogy to develop particular aspects of medieval history. So also has the historian Lewis Namier in unraveling the intricacies of 18th-century British politics. For those who write modern biographies, the genealogical background of their subjects is now considered essential to broadening an understanding of the family relationships.

Family historians have been anxious to move beyond the constraints of mere pedigree-listing so as to arrive at an understanding of their ancestors within the broader context of time and place. Little wonder, therefore, that demographers and social historians are increasingly open to developing lines of communication between themselves and the family historians. This work is providing ample opportunities for establishing mutually beneficial relationships between these and other disciplines. *See also* **Historical Context.**

Homestead Act was passed by the U.S. Congress in 1862 after more than 70 years of controversy over the distribution of public lands. The act declared that any citizen or intended citizen was eligible to claim 160 acres—one quarter of a square mile—of surveyed government land in the Western territories. But all claimants had to "improve" the plot by erecting a dwelling on it, digging a well, fencing part of it, and growing crops. After five years, if the original claimant was still living on the land, it became the claimant's property, free and clear. Women, as well as men, were permitted to be homesteaders.

One of the first claimants was a scout from the Union Army named Daniel Freeman. He and his wife, Agnes, joined the post–Civil War wave of homesteaders who hailed mostly from the Ohio and Mississippi valleys. Later homesteaders included European immigrants who came from Norway, Germany, Finland, and other countries lured to America by the promise of grant land. But the act's lenient terms proved the undoing of many settlers, particularly those who knew nothing about farming. The quarter sections, though adequate for farming in humid regions, were too small to support farms in the plains areas west of the 100th meridian, where water scarcity reduced yields. Later laws allowed homesteaders there to obtain additional land if they planted 40 acres of trees, a practical impossibility. Speculators also obtained some of the homestead lands by hiring bogus claimants. They also made it a practice to buy up homestead farms that had been abandoned.

The settlers built sod homes and withstood hailstorms, drought, prairie fires, and blizzards. Added to the natural disasters were human struggles with cattlemen who resisted the dividing up of the open range by farmers. Furthermore, the farmers faced heavy debts, expensive rail transportation and grain storage, and market fluctuations. But eventually frame and brick houses replaced the soddies, and trees grew high to shield the dwellings. At the same time windmills pumped water from deep underground, and a host of technological advances made the farming profitable for those who had endured the early years of deprivation.

The passage of the Homestead Act brought an end to the many years of controversy over the issue. Attempts to pass the legislation had been constantly blocked by Southerners who opposed such a land giveaway because they believed it would benefit working-class whites who were likely to vote against slavery in the newly created Western states. Among the strong promoters of the bill were Missouri Senator Thomas Hart Benton and Tennessee Congressman Andrew Johnson. It became law only after the Southern states had left the Union, and it was signed by President Abraham Lincoln in 1862. The Homestead Act remained in effect until 1977 when it was repealed. By 1900 about 600,000 farmers had received clear title to lands covering about 80 million acres.

The case files for the homestead lands vary, but nearly all have valuable genealogical information, such as the age and address of the person applying for the land, family members, descriptions of the land, and testimony of the witnesses. For a naturalized citizen, one can find information about the person's immigration date and port of arrival, as well as the date and place of naturalization. Some of the files even have copies of discharge from Union service in the Civil War, because a subsequent act gave special privileges to those veterans.

The homestead files are in two series: one for completed land entries and one for canceled land entries. Both are useful. The completed land entry files are in the custody of the National Archives in Washington, D.C. The canceled land entry papers are scattered among a variety of repositories, but they can yield clues to why the requirements were not fulfilled. Copies are obtainable from the Bureau of Land Management in Springfield, Virginia. Some of the records have been indexed and recorded on a CD-ROM, but for others one must know the legal description of the land before the records can be located. The section number, township number, and range number are required, since they were recorded in that fashion. The CD-ROM includes the particulars of each claim with a reference number that can be used to get copies of the actual records. The location for purchase of the CD-ROM can be found by searching pertinent Websites. *See also* **World Wide Web.**

Honduras *see* **Central American Genealogy**

Hospital Records *see* **Medical Records**

Huguenot Records are maintained at the library of the Huguenot Society of London, and include a large collection of pedigrees. The Huguenots were a group of Protestants who became the center of political and religious quarrels in France during the 14th and 15th centuries. They followed the teachings of John Calvin and were members of the Reformed Church. In 1572, thousands of them were massacred by Catholics in France, and in 1685, after the repeal of the Edict of Nantes that had given them some political freedom, many of the Huguenots fled to England, Prussia, the Netherlands, and America. Some of them settled and prospered in South Carolina, Virginia, Massachusetts, and New York.

The total emigration is thought to have been between 400,000 to one million Huguenots, with about one million remaining in France. Thousands of them settled in the mountainous Cévennes region of France, where they became known as Camisards. Many of those who found refuge in Ireland settled in the town of Lisburn in the province of Ulster. The Huguenots were primarily textile workers, and they had a large part in building up the English textile industry. Some of their families were named DeLancey, Jay, Legaré, Maury, Petigru, and Revere.

Today there are Huguenot societies in England, Germany, Australia, Canada, and the United States that are dedicated to perpetuating the memory of the Huguenot settlers and to collecting and publishing materials about their history and accomplishments. The Huguenot Society of London has a library of some 6,000 books, periodicals, manuscripts, prints, and engravings relating to their heritage. Many of these publications can also be found in the New York State Library in Albany, Library of Congress in Washington, D.C., Cornell University Library in Ithaca, New York, and Newberry Library in Chicago.

Hungarian Records *see* **Eastern European Genealogy**

Hutterite Records *see* **Mennonite Records**

Hypertext *see* **World Wide Web**

I

Icelandic Genealogy is extensive and well organized because the country's population is relatively stable and its social fabric has always remained somewhat insulated from the stresses that have overwhelmed many other cultures around the world. Few people have come to this island nation over the past 11 centuries and few people have left, except for a brief period following a series of violent and protracted volcanic eruptions in the late 19th century. In its earliest days Iceland was an independent republic, but it came under Norwegian rule in 1264 and the rule of Denmark in 1380. By 1944 it had once again become an independent republic.

None of the nation's genealogical records has been destroyed by wars or floods. Some extend all the way back to the ninth century. As with other Scandinavian states, the Icelandic records of births, deaths, confirmations, and marriages have been kept by some of the clergy in their churches from the time of the establishment of these congregations to the present day. In 1746 a Danish royal decree instructed the parochial clergy to keep meticulous registers of their membership.

Thus the congregational records from that date are generally unbroken. The practice is for the clergy to send annual reports to the Statistical Bureau of Iceland in Reykjavik, the capital, and for copies of all the parish records to be eventually deposited in the National Archives, also at Reykjavik. The National Archives were established in 1899. Wills are kept there as well.

The first census in 1703 listed the names, ages, residences, and occupations for every person in Iceland. The census of 1816 added places of birth to this information. From 1835 on, censuses have been taken every five or 10 years. These censuses are held at the Statistical Bureau. Some copies can also be found in the Danish National Archives in Copenhagen. It comes as a surprise to those who think that only Vikings and Danes settled Iceland when they might find a number of Scotch and Irish names also listed in the census records.

Although the genealogical trail shows no major interruptions, the volcanic eruptions in the late 19th century drove about 20 percent of the population to Nova Scotia, Canada, and the Northern United States. Some of the resulting Icelandic settlements in North America bequeathed Icelandic names to their communities. Thus there is the town of Hallson in North Dakota; the villages of Baldur, Gimli, Hecla, Hnausa, Husavick, Markland, and Reykjavik in Manitoba; Hekkla in Ontario, and Kristnes in Saskatchewan.

The National and University Library of Iceland in Reykjavik has a collection of genealogical materials; a work that may prove useful to North Americans of Icelandic descent is *Almanach Fyrie,* by Olafur S. Thorgeisson, published in 1895. It contains a great deal of historical and genealogical data about the Icelandic settlers in Canada and the United States.

Idaho Records extend back to about 1860 when the residents of this area were listed in parts of the Utah and Washington territory population schedules. Idaho didn't become a territory of its own until three years later. Then it included small parts of what are now Montana and Wyoming, as well as the entire area that is now the state of Idaho. The first censuses conducted for the Idaho territory were in 1870 and 1880. It became the 43rd state in 1890. Some special Indian censuses for tribes in Idaho can be found in the National Archives in Washington, D.C. They include the Shoshone and Bannock Indian census for the Fort Hall Agency from 1885 to1939; the Nez Percé Indian census for the Fort Lapwai Agency from 1902–1933; and the Coeur d'Alene Agency Indian census from 1906 to 1937; the latter contains birth, marriage, and death information for the years 1931 to 1937.

Indians lived in the Idaho region for more than 10,000 years before the first white men arrived, according to evidence uncovered by archaeologists. When the explorers Meriwether Lewis and William Clark crossed the region in 1805, there were six different Indian tribes in the area — the Nez Percé, Coeur d'Alene, Pend d'Oreille, Shoshoni, Kutenai, and Bannock Indians.

In 1911 the state of Idaho began to keep birth and death records, although some Idaho counties had been keeping them from as early as 1900. To find them one must look at the archives in the county where the event occurred. The registers of births start in 1900 for Nez Perce County, and the county clerk there also has some that date from as early as 1880, which were added later. Idaho started to keep marriage and divorce records in 1947. These can be located at the Bureau of Vital Statistics in Boise, and copies can be obtained for a small fee. Again, earlier ones can be found in some of the counties, and the ones from Nez Perce County begin in 1863. The mortality schedules for 1870 and 1880 are in the Idaho State Library at Boise.

The records of will probates can be found in the district courts, of which there are seven. All the county probate courts were absorbed into these district courts on January 11, 1971. Guardianship records are also held by the district courts, while land records are under county jurisdiction and are maintained by the various county recorders.

The *Guide to Public Vital Statistics Records in Idaho: State and County* (Work Projects Administration, 1942) can be helpful for any researcher looking for genealogical information from this state. Libraries in Idaho and elsewhere may own it. The Idaho State Historical Society and Archives in Boise has death certificates from 1911 to 1937, as well as an excellent collection of Idaho newspapers, and copies of many county records, including cemetery records and birth, marriage, and death registers, all on microfilm. Two other places in Idaho that have genealogical records of note are the University of Idaho Library at Moscow and the Idaho State Genealogical Society at Boise.

Researchers seeking information from county records can locate them at the following county seats: (Ada County) Boise, (Adams County) Council, (Bannock County) Pocatello, (Bear Lake County) Paris, (Benewah County) St. Maries, (Bingham County) Blackfoot, (Blaine County) Hailey, (Boise County) Idaho City, (Bonner County) Sandpoint, (Bonneville County) Idaho Falls, (Boundary County) Bonners Ferry, (Butte County) Arco, (Camas County) Fairfield, (Canyon County) Caldwell, (Caribou County) Soda Springs, (Cassia County) Burley, (Clark County) Dubois, (Clearwater County) Orofino, (Custer County) Challis, (Elmore County) Mountain Home, (Franklin County) Preston, (Fremont County) Saint Anthony, (Gem County) Emmett, (Gooding County) Gooding, (Idaho County) Grangeville, (Jefferson County) Rigby, (Jerome County) Jerome, (Kootenai County) Coeur d'Alene, (Latah County) Moscow, (Lemhi County) Salmon, (Lewis County) Nezperce, (Lincoln County) Shoshone, (Madison County) Rexburg, (Minidoka County) Rupert, (Nez Perce County) Lewiston, (Oneida County) Malad City, (Owyhee County) Murphy, (Payette County) Payette, (Power County) American Falls, (Shoshone County) Wallace, (Teton County) Driggs, (Twin Falls County) Twin Falls, (Valley County) Cascade, and (Washington County) Weiser.

FOR FURTHER INFORMATION SEE:
• Idaho Genealogical Society. *Footprints Through Idaho*. 3 vols. Boise, ID: Idaho Genealogical Society, 1989.
• Southern California Genealogical Society. *Sources of Genealogical Help in Idaho*. Burbank, CA: The Society, [n.d.].

Illinois Records begin about 1720 when the first African slaves were brought to the French settlements along the Mississippi. Not until 1800, when this section of the United States was included as part of the Indiana Territory, was a census conducted that listed much of the population of what is now Illinois. The General Assembly of the Indiana Territory authorized another census in 1807 to apportion better the territory's representation. The surviving part of this 1807 census for what is now Illinois enumerates persons only in Randolph County, which then composed the southern quarter of Illinois. These 1807 records have been indexed and can be viewed at the various National Archives locations and at the Illinois State Archives in Springfield.

It was not until 1809 that Illinois was separated from Indiana. Then there was an 1810 Illinois Territorial census, but the only portion still in existence is again that for Randolph County. There was another territorial census conducted in 1818, shortly before Illinois became the 21st state. This includes 14 of the 15 counties in existence at that time; the enumeration for Edwards County is missing. The first available census of Illinois as a state took place in 1820 as part of the regular national decennial census. In the case of one of these decennial censuses— the 1890, most of which was destroyed by fire in Washington, D.C.— the portion covering Mound Township in McDonough County has survived.

The state itself conducted special census enumerations in 1818, 1825, 1835, 1845 (only fragments of which remain), as well as in 1855 and 1865, which have a few counties missing. The 1865 state census is partially indexed. It names the heads of households, and it can be seen at the Illinois State Archives. Other locations in Illinois that have copies of these census records are the Illinois State Library in Springfield and the Newberry Library in Chicago. The Work Projects Administration's 1941 *Guide to Public Vital Statistics Records in Illinois* may prove valuable in researching materials concerning this state.

The Illinois State Archives and its seven

regional archives depositories hold various records that provide information on servitude and emancipation. These records encompass the colonial era of French and English occupation (1720–1790) as well as the American period (1790–1865). The archives has produced a name index of all the persons appearing in these servitude and emancipation records.

The records indicate that the English victory in the French and Indian War and subsequent seizure of the Illinois country did not significantly alter the practices of French slavery. When George Rogers Clark and his Virginia militia conquered the Indiana-Illinois area in 1778, the slave population totaled some 1,000. Despite an ordinance passed in 1787 prohibiting slavery, many African-Americans remained in a state of de facto slavery as indentured servants. The 1800 census lists 135 slaves and 163 free persons of African descent. By 1810 the Illinois Territory itself had 781 African-American residents, of whom 168 were registered as slaves.

After Illinois achieved statehood in 1818, the Illinois General Assembly began enacting a series of laws known as the "black codes." These restrictive laws continued the practice of indentured servitude, denied legal protection to African-Americans, and required local governmental officials to maintain registers of indentured servants and free Negroes and mulattoes. The 1820 federal census lists 917 slave and 457 free African-Americans. Ten years later the numbers are 747 slave and 1,637 free. The 1840 census was the last one to record free and slave African-Americans in Illinois. For that year there were 331 slave and 3,598 free African-Americans in Illinois. The 1850 and 1860 censuses enumerated 5,436 and 7,628 African-Americans respectively. Illinois repealed the "black codes" after the Union victory in 1865.

The listings of Illinois births and deaths started about 1843 when the Illinois General Assembly passed legislation providing for the registration of such information by county clerks. But because this act made such listings a voluntary process, few counties complied. It was not until 1877 that new legislation was passed making it mandatory for the county clerks to do so. Yet the law still provided for no enforcement of this rule, so many counties recorded the data irregularly. A 1915 statute provided for the first effective system of registration of births, deaths, and stillbirths. This law required both the State Board of Health and the county clerks to record these events, and provided a system of financial incentives for local registrars. In 1919 the Illinois Department of Public Health was established as the successor agency to the State Board of Health. It is located in Springfield.

The seven Illinois Regional Archives Depositories now hold copies of the birth records up through 1915 for the surrounding counties. The archives are located at Eastern Illinois University in Charleston, Illinois State University at Normal, Northeastern Illinois University at Chicago, Northern Illinois University at DeKalb, Southern Illinois University at Carbondale, University of Illinois at Springfield, and Western Illinois University at Macomb. If these depositories don't have a particular birth record prior to 1915, then a researcher should contact the county clerk's office in the county where the birth occurred. All birth records after 1915 are located at the Illinois Department of Public Health, Division of Vital Records, in Springfield. Copies of these records can be obtained for a small fee.

The Illinois Regional Archives Depositories also have copies of the marriage records for many counties in Illinois. These archives, in cooperation with the Illinois State Genealogical Society, are creating a database for all Illinois marriages that took place prior to 1901. Again, if these archives do not have a copy of the specific marriage record being sought, the researcher should contact the county clerk's office in the county where the marriage occurred.

Beginning in 1916 the Illinois Department of Public Health, along with the county clerks, jointly maintained the state's death records. Copies of these records are also in the seven Illinois Regional Archives Depositories. The death certificates usually show the name, age, sex, marital status, and race of the deceased; as well as the place of birth, death, and burial; date of death and burial;

cause of death; date filed and the signatures of the attending physician and registrar. An index on microfiche to the deaths in Illinois from 1916 until 1950 is in the Illinois State Archives. It can also be downloaded from the Internet at the Illinois State Archives Website. Photocopies of death records not less than 20 years old can be obtained for a small fee from the Department of Public Health or from the county clerks where the event took place.

The Illinois General Assembly granted probate jurisdiction to the clerks of the county commissioners' court in 1819. Their duties included issuing letters of administration for interstate (without a will) estates, distributing the estates of individuals who died interstate, recording all wills and letters relating to probate matters, ruling on contested wills, receiving bonds from administrators, paying witnesses, ordering final distributions, ordering property sales for payments of debts, making pro rata distributions of assets to creditors, appointing guardians for children under the age of 14, approving guardians selected by children age 14 and over, and receiving bonds from those guardians. These functions were transferred to the county probate courts in 1821, then to the newly created county courts in 1848, and finally to circuit courts in 1964.

Thus the probate records can now be found at the various circuit courts, and some duplicate copies can be found in the Illinois Regional Archives Depositories as well as at the Illinois State Archives building in Springfield. A photocopy of any available record requested will be provided by the appropriate regional depository, if it can be located. Divorce records are also kept in the circuit courts, and those that have been administered since 1962 are available to researchers.

At the Illinois State Library, as well as at many other genealogical libraries, one can find *The Honor Roll of Veterans Buried in Illinois,* published in 1956 on the instructions of the Illinois General Assembly. It covers the years 1774 to 1955. Entries include the veteran's name, rank, service branch, war served in, unit or organization, date of death, cemetery name and county location, and occa-

sionally the grave location within that cemetery. The Illinois Department of Veterans' Affairs maintains a record of all Illinois war veterans buried after 1955.

The Illinois State Archives has copies of the report on Illinois Territory residents who served in the Army on the western frontier during the War of 1812; the list of War of 1812 pension applications; the muster rolls of Illinois volunteers in the Black Hawk War (1831–1832); the muster rolls of Illinois volunteers in the Mexican War (1846–1848); the muster rolls of those who served in the Civil War (1861–1865); the muster in and muster out rolls for those who served in the Spanish-American War (1898–1899); and the draft registration card lists for the Illinois men registered with the Selective Service System during World War I (1917–1918). Records of those who served in World War II, the Korean War, and the Vietnam War are at the Illinois Department of Veterans' Affairs, but the only information available to the public from these records is a veteran's branch of service and dates of service.

The sale of Illinois land began in the late 17th century, nearly one hundred years before the establishment of the United States. While under the control of three separate and distinct governmental authorities— France (1678–1763), England (1763–1778), and the state of Virginia (1778–1784)—individuals residing in what was to become the state of Illinois received and conveyed title to the lands there. Throughout all these periods respective government agents registered the land transactions. After the United States established its control over Illinois in 1784, the federal government began a review process to determine the legitimacy of the preexisting land claims. By the time these examinations were completed in 1814, the federal authorities had confirmed title to less than half of the claims presented to them.

Today these records of Illinois land sales are located at the Illinois State Archives. The records include the sales of the vast amount of public land in Illinois beginning in 1814. Ten U.S. General Land Offices located across the state conducted 538,750 sales up to 1876, when the last remaining Illinois federal land office was closed. The large bulk of sales had taken place by the mid–1850s. With the assistance of a grant from the National Endowment for the Humanities, archivists have indexed the first purchasers of the Illinois public lands. The resulting massive file of 538,750 entries has been generated on 144 microfiche cards. Each entry gives the name, sex, county or state residence of purchasers; sale type; legal description of the land; the number of acres; price per acre; and total cost of the purchase.

For more recent land records, a researcher needs to contact the office of the county recorder in all Illinois counties with populations of 60,000 or more, and the county clerk in counties with a smaller population. Deed records generally show the names of the grantee and grantor, legal description of the property, date and type of instrument, amount of consideration, and date filed.

Researchers seeking information from county records can locate them at the following county seats: (Adams County) Quincy, (Alexander County) Cairo, (Bond County) Greenville, (Boone County) Belvidere, (Brown County) Mt. Sterling, (Bureau County) Princeton, (Calhoun County) Hardin, (Carroll County) Mt. Carroll, (Cass County) Virginia, (Champaign County) Urbana, (Christian County) Taylorville, (Clark County) Marshall, (Clay County) Louisville, (Clinton County) Carlyle, (Coles County) Charleston, (Cook County) Chicago, (Crawford County) Robinson, (Cumberland County) Toledo, (DeKalb County) Sycamore, (DeWitt County) Clinton, (Douglas County) Tuscola, (Du Page County) Wheaton, (Edgar County) Paris, (Edwards County) Albion, (Effingham County) Effingham, (Fayette County) Vandalia, (Ford County) Paxton, (Franklin County) Benton, (Fulton County) Lewistown, (Gallatin County) Shawneetown, (Greene County) Carrollton, (Grundy County) Morris, and (Hamilton County) McLeansboro.

Also at (Hancock County) Carthage, (Hardin County) Elizabethtown, (Henderson County) Oquawka, (Henry County) Cambridge, (Iroquois County) Watseka, (Jackson County) Murphysboro, (Jasper County) Newton, (Jefferson County) Mt. Vernon, (Jersey County) Jerseyville, (Jo Daviess County) Galena, (Johnson County) Vienna, (Kane County) Geneva, (Kankakee County) Kankakee, (Kendall County) Yorkville, (Knox County) Galesburg, (La Salle County) Ottawa, (Lake County) Waukegan, (Lawrence County) Lawrenceville, (Lee County) Dixon, (Livingston County) Pontiac, (Logan County) Lincoln, (Macon County) Decatur, (Macoupin County) Carlinville, (Madison County) Edwardsville, (Marion County) Salem, (Marshall County) Lacon, (Mason County) Havana, (Massac County) Metropolis, (McDonough County) Macomb, (McHenry County) Woodstock, (McLean County) Bloomington, (Menard County) Petersburg, (Mercer County) Aledo, (Monroe County) Waterloo, (Montgomery County) Hillsboro, (Morgan County) Jacksonville, and (Moultrie County) Sullivan.

As well as at (Ogle County) Oregon, (Peoria County) Peoria, (Perry County) Pinckneyville, (Piatt County) Monticello, (Pike County) Pittsfield, (Pope County) Golconda, (Pulaski County) Mound City, (Putnam County) Hennepin, (Randolph County) Chester, (Richland County) Olney, (Rock Island County) Rock Island, (Saline County) Harrisburg, (Sangamon County) Springfield, (Schuyler County) Rushville, (Scott County) Winchester, (Shelby County) Shelbyville, (St. Clair County) Belleville, (Stark County) Toulon, (Stephenson County) Freeport, (Tazewell County) Pekin, (Union County) Jonesboro, (Vermilion County) Danville, (Wabash County) Mt. Carmel, (Warren County) Monmouth, (Washington County) Nashville, (Wayne County) Fairfield, (White County) Carmi, (Whiteside County) Morrison, (Will County) Joliet, (Williamson County) Marion, (Winnebago County) Rockford, and (Woodford County) Eureka.

FOR FURTHER INFORMATION SEE:

- Beckstead, Gayle, and Mary Lou Kozub. *Searching in Illinois: A Reference Guide to Public and Private Records.* Costa Mesa, CA: ISC Publications, 1984.
- Gooldy, Pat, and Ray Gooldy. *Manual for Illinois Genealogical Research.* Indianapolis: Ye Olde Genealogie Shoppe, 1994.

Immigrants have come to the United States and settled here from more than one hundred different countries throughout the world. This immigration has given the nation one of the richest and most varied of cultures. It is indeed one of the strengths of America, and the solving of every national crisis or problem brings together viewpoints as varied as the history of all the nationalities that have made their way to these shores.

Immigration has been constant, but its numbers have ebbed and flowed over the centuries. Historians generally tend to divide the periods in which the more than 50 million immigrants have arrived into six major groups. These are:

First, the colonial period (late 1500s to 1776) in which the primary groups arriving were African slaves, Dutch, English, Finnish, French, German, Scottish, Scotch-Irish, Spanish, and Welsh.

Second, the period from 1776 to 1820 in which the primary groups arriving were the same as those of the colonial period, but they came in decreasing numbers because of attempts by the U.S. government to restrict immigration and because of wars taking place in Europe.

Third, the period from 1820 to 1880 in which the primary groups arriving were Catholic Irish, Chinese, Danish, French Canadian, German, Japanese, Norwegian, and Swedish.

Fourth, the period from 1880 to 1920 in which the primary groups arriving were Arab, Armenian, Austrian, Czech, European and Russian Jews, Greek, Hungarian, Italian, Japanese, Polish, Romanian, Russian, Slovakian, and Yugoslavian.

Fifth, the period from 1920 to 1945 in which the primary groups arriving were British (English, Scottish, Welsh), Canadian, Czech, German, Irish, Italian, Mexican, Polish, and refugees from Nazi Germany. Immigration during this period was limited by quota systems and literacy tests enacted by the government, as well as by the Great Depression.

Sixth, the Post–World War II period in which the primary groups arriving have been Cambodian, Caribbean, Central and South American, Korean, Laotian, Mexican, Middle Eastern Arab, Soviet Jews, and Vietnamese.

It was not until 1819 that the U.S. government first mandated the keeping of immigrant arrival lists. Before then no one thought there was any need to do so, and, of course, before the American Revolution there was no national government to do so. The control of immigration at the time was left to the 13 original colonies, and inasmuch as these were British colonies, and close to 80 percent of the white immigrants before 1790 came from British countries, there was no need to record any arrivals. Laws dealing with immigration were later passed in 1847, 1848, and 1855, but these laws had little effect on the manner in which immigrant arrival lists were kept. Little or no information was ever recorded about the immigrants' home towns, so the lists are of limited use to genealogists searching for the origins of their ancestors.

The Immigration and Passenger Acts of 1882 provided the foundation for the later, more detailed immigration lists. The Passenger Act called for the records to include, in addition to the name, age, sex, and occupation of a passenger, the native country and intended destination. In 1891 another immigration act created the Bureau of Immigration, which since 1933 has become known as the Immigration and Naturalization Service, or INS. Two years later, in 1892, still another act, designed to improve the enforcement of the existing law, required more than twice as much information from each passenger. Some of the important additions now were the immigrant's last residence, the address and relationship of any relative the passenger might be joining, the immigrant's ability to read and write, the name of the person who paid for the passage, and the state of the immigrant's health.

Such records were usually filled out by agents of the steamship lines on forms provided by the Bureau of Immigration. They were then given to the government inspectors at the receiving stations. Because the information came from the steamship agents, who collected it from the immigrants often at the beginning of a voyage, it is unlikely that there were many of the name changes that some Americans insist took place at the ports of entry. Although a few immigrants did change their names, such changes were generally quite minor and were typically just the Anglicization of a foreign name (i.e. Smith for Schmidt). The name changes also seldom took place at the port of arrival, but rather evolved as the immigrant became part of American society.

During the colonial period, Philadelphia was the most popular port for immigrants arriving in the British colonies, but by 1840 New York had overtaken Philadelphia and all the other ports of entry. Soon, New York was receiving more immigrants than all the other ports combined. After 1855 New York's Ellis Island port processed some 90 percent of all the immigrants who were then arriving.

At various times groups of immigrants were denied entry to the U.S. because of changing American attitudes toward various nationalities. For example, although Chinese immigrants had been enthusiastically welcomed in the 1840s because they were willing to do the heavy labor of building our railroads and working our gold mines, during the economic depression of the 1870s, they were accused of unfair competition in business, of lowering wages, and of immoral and unsanitary habits. A series of acts passed by Congress in 1882, 1888, and 1892 prohibited Asians from entering the United States. At first these acts were intended to be only temporary, but Congress made the exclusion permanent in 1902. It was not until World War II that Congress repealed these laws against the Chinese. They may now enter the United States on a quota basis. The National Archives in Washington, D.C., has the Chinese Immigration Records, 1882–1925, which are available to public access.

Much the same kind of discrimination was directed against the Japanese. During World War II roughly 120,000 Japanese Americans living on the West Coast were relocated and placed in internment camps, between 27 August 1942 and 2 January 1945, in the belief that some of them might be "enemy agents." Yet 64 percent of these Japanese were American citizens of Japanese ancestry. The records of the Japanese internments may

be found at the National Archives. Some, however, have restricted access.

Besides the internment of Japanese during the war, approximately 4,000 Italian and 6,000 German "enemy" aliens were also interned in 1941 and 1942. These were mostly immigrants who had never become U.S. citizens, even though they may have resided in the United States for half their lives. As of this writing these German and Italian records, also stored at the National Archives, are still restricted and accessible only by an internee, spouse of an internee, or upon proof of the internee's death.

Family lines for immigrants are traced in the way that they can be for any other family lines, at least back to the point of entry into this country. At that point the task becomes more difficult, because all a researcher often has to go on is a series of passenger lists that give no more than the names of passengers and the ports of entry. However, the desired information may sometimes be found by consulting a number of sources both in this country and abroad. Depending on the immigrant's ethnic group, religious preference, date of immigration, and other factors, the information regarding his or her point of origin may be found in any of a dozen or more different sources. Fortunately, the passenger lists provided after 1882 do provide more information about the immigrants and their families than the earlier ones did.

In seeking the overseas town in which an immigrant once resided, a researcher must first determine the exact name used by the immigrant at the port of entry and the approximate time of entry. This task may seem relatively easy, but many family members today are only able to provide a vague tradition about somebody who immigrated sometime in the past. If the immigrant Anglicized the family name after arriving in this English-speaking country, then it becomes important to uncover the original foreign version. The task of locating the origin of a specific immigrant is somewhat easier if one or two dates for that individual can be found, such as an exact date of birth or marriage.

A passenger list will likely give the port of ship departure as well as the port of entry, and thus can be a guide as to what country the immigrant probably came from. These lists generally include information as to the name of each ship, its captain, ports of departure and arrival and the date of arrival, as well as the names of the passengers.

The next task is one of determining what likely city or town in that country was the immigrant's original home. Here the family surname can provide clues. In some towns there were usually many people who shared the same name, and that is a likely place to start. The researcher may even find relatives of the individual still living in that town, and there are likely to be records of members of that family in the town archives. It is virtually impossible to find any nation-wide indexes in foreign countries.

Another source of information about immigrants' backgrounds that sometimes proves useful to researchers is the records of a union or fraternal benefit-life insurance society, such as the Sons of Italy or the Polish Union of the United States of North America. Immigrants often joined such organizations after their settlement in America. A book that lists the various fraternal organizations is *The Immigration History Research Center: A Guide to Collections* by Suzanne Moody and Joel Wurl (Westport, CT: Greenwood Press, 1991), which can be found in most genealogical libraries. Also helpful may be Nicholas V. Montalto's *The International Institute Movement: A Guide to Records of Immigrant Society Agencies in the United States* (Minneapolis: Immigration Research Center, 1978), which gives state-by-state listings of the immigrant women's aid societies.

For those who came during the colonial period and the earlier years of this nation, one can consult P. William Filby's *Passenger and Immigration Lists Index* (Detroit: Gale Research, 1981). This multi-volume bibliography and index includes more than two million names from published passenger lists and naturalization records. Each entry gives the name of the immigrant, his or her age, the place and year of arrival, and sometimes the family members accompanying the immigrant. A companion volume by the same author and also published by Gale Research,

Passenger and Immigration Lists Bibliography, 1538–1900, annotates over 2,550 published sources of information. Both books can be found in most genealogical libraries.

Another source for identifying immigrants are the lists of early land grants of one kind or another. Such records are the basis for Gust Skordas's *The Early Settlers of Maryland: An Index to the Names of Immigrants Compiled from Records of Land Patents, 1633–1680* (Baltimore: Genealogical Publishing Co., 1968). This is an alphabetical index of more than 25,000 settlers, virtually all of whom remained in Maryland after their arrival. The book provides each immigrant's full name, approximate date of immigration, residence, and the basis for the immigrant's claim of land.

The largest single collection of colonial passenger arrival lists is Ralph Beaver Strassburger and William John Hinke's three-volume transcription of *Pennsylvania German Pioneers: A Publication of the Original Lists of Arrivals in the Port of Philadelphia from 1727 to 1808* (Pennsylvania German Society, 1934). This collection has been reprinted several times and can be found in most genealogical libraries. Because only males over 16 are named in these lists, the editors have estimated that the 29,800 names represent upwards of 70,000 German immigrants. As for the colonial immigration into Virginia, the early land records are the only way to document them. George Greer's *Early Virginia Immigrants, 1623–1666* (Genealogical Publishing Co., 1912), provides much helpful information on this area of research. *See also* **Ellis Island Records; Immigration Records; Naturalization and Citizenship Records; Passenger Lists.**

Immigration Records have been maintained by the U.S. government in order to keep track of foreign nationals entering and residing in America. Most of these records are naturalization documents and passenger arrival lists. With the exception of some baggage and cargo manifests, few actual passenger lists were kept until federal law required them in 1819. Yet some customhouse records were kept: the slave manifests that identified the vessels and dates of arrival, as well as the name, age, and sex of slaves, and the name and address of the consignee. The National Archives in Washington, D.C., has some of these records.

In 1790 the first federal naturalization laws were passed. Prior to this, each state established its own residency requirements for aliens to become naturalized citizens. An applicant for citizenship in 1790 had to be a free white male of 21 years of age or older, living in the United States for two years and in the state where he applied for citizenship for a least one year. However, he could apply for his citizenship in any court, whether federal, state, or local.

In 1795 a two-step process to obtain citizenship was instituted. First, an applicant had to declare an intent to obtain citizenship in the future, and second, after at least three years, a court would grant the naturalization right. This procedure was amended in 1824 to just two years following the declaration. In the same 1824 law it was stipulated that the process could be completed in one step for any applicant under the age of 18, if he or she had resided in the United States for three years before petitioning for citizenship. This was called a "minor naturalization." Between 1855 and 1922 an alien wife automatically became a citizen when her husband did, or when she married an American citizen.

Some courts did not make an applicant file a request for naturalization, even though it was formally required, until after 1903 when the Justice Department created a special form for this purpose. It had places for the applicant's name, birthplace, date of birth, country of birth, date and port of arrival, date of application, occupation, residence, and signature. In the long run, more aliens applied for citizenship at county and state courts than at federal courts because the fees were usually smaller and the standards may have been somewhat more lax. Yet, as with any bureaucratic process, some people found ways to obtain citizenship papers without going through the legal process. For example, some local election workers made copies of legitimate citizenship papers and passed them out at election time so that aliens could vote for their party candidates.

Following the Civil War all former slaves were automatically granted citizenship. Laws passed in 1887 and 1924 made all American Indians citizens. Asians were not permitted to become citizens from 1882 to 1943, and Filipinos and Asian Indians were banned from citizenship until 1946.

No records were kept on those who crossed the border from Canada into the United States until 1895, or on those who crossed from Mexico until 1913. Records for Canadian crossings after 1895 are available at all the various National Archives centers. They cover the period from 1895 to 1952, and include those who entered the United States at the border crossing points in Washington, Montana, Michigan, New York, North Dakota, and Minnesota. Most of the records have been microfilmed and arranged by the Soundex code for easy access. The Immigration and Naturalization Service records covering those who crossed from Mexico between 1913 to 1953 are not Soundexed, but some have been alphabetized and can be seen at the National Archives in Washington, D.C.

The Bureau of Immigration and Naturalization, now called the Immigration and Naturalization Service (INS), was established in 1906. All copies of naturalization papers after that date have been forwarded to this agency. However, to obtain naturalization records, one should check for them in the archives of the municipal, county, state, and federal courthouses where the immigrant settled or was living at the time of application. If no such records can be found in any of these places, then one might write to the Immigration and Naturalization Service in Washington, D.C. To get information from this last source, one must put "FOIA/PA request" on the envelope as well as in the letter. This indicates that the request is being made under the Freedom of Information Act/Privacy Act. *See also* **Freedom of Information Act; Soundex System.**

Indenture and Apprenticeship Records can sometimes contain a great deal of genealogical information. In addition to the name and age of the individual (often a child), indenture records usually contain the names of family members and their relationships, the reason for the indenture, and possibly the original residence of the indentured person. These agreements, of course, bound one individual to another for a set time as payment for some service. Some were enacted by persons who agreed to work for others for a specific time to pay for the passage from the country of origin. Others were set up by the English government as a means of letting their prisoners work off their sentences in the New World. More often, however, they were agreements made by the parents of a youth so that the boy or girl might learn a trade. As such these agreements are usually referred to as apprenticeships.

Many of our early ancestors learned their professions through apprenticeships. Some of the most famous ones got their start this way. This is how Paul Revere learned the art of silver smithing, and Benjamin Franklin was apprenticed to his brother James as a printer. That a child would be apprenticed to a total stranger was actually an unusual happening. Often fathers took on their own sons as apprentices.

Generally an apprentice was bound until the age of 21. By reading the indenture agreement, one can estimate how old the child was at the beginning of the apprenticeship and then estimate what year he or she was born. Apprenticeships in New England often began for children who were under 10; such agreements continued long after the colonial period. Children continued to be indentured so that they might learn a trade up through the 1800s.

Some of the indenture and apprenticeship records, such as those for Connecticut and Virginia, have been published, and the books can be found in various genealogical libraries. Additionally, one can sometimes find indenture records in manuscript collections and heritage society holdings, as well as in the offices of county clerks.

Indian Genealogy includes long pedigrees of various Hindu and Muslim kings and royal families of India. Some go back to periods well before the beginnings of the Christian era, and many of them include various mythical happenings and have origins that are ascribed to some divine god. However, there is little interest in India in the process of charting pedigree lines outside of these royal families.

Since India has no birth, marriage or death records, the search for genealogical information must begin with various institutional records, such as those for hospitals, ashrams, schools, or temples where an individual might have been cared for, lived, gone to study, or performed religious ordinances. In the case of Hindu families, who cremate their dead, one may have to obtain any information about a deceased member from living relatives or from persons in the villages or towns in which the individual once lived. If the individual converted to Christianity, then it may be possible to find cemetery records. The British Association of Cemeteries in South Asia, in London, England, has records for many of the Christian cemeteries in India.

Another area relating to genealogy in India is that of the families of the British military personnel and civil authorities who ruled India from 1858 to 1947. Here the records are kept in the Oriental and India Office Collections of the British Library in London. These records comprise the archives of the East India Company (1600–1858), the Board of Control or Board of Commissioners for the Affairs of India (1784–1858), the India Office (1858–1947), and a number of related British agencies overseas. The records are open for public consultation under the provisions of the British Public Records Act.

Indians, American *see* **Native American Records**

Indiana Records of births, deaths, marriages, and divorces can be seen at a number of libraries in the state, or certified copies can be obtained for a small fee from the Indiana Vital Records Department in Indianapolis. This state covers the smallest area of any in the Midwest, but it has a very large population. Although it ranks 38th in geographic size among all the states of the Union, it is 11th in population. It became a part of the Northwest Territory in 1787, was then designated as the separate Indiana Territory in 1800, including not only what is now the state of Indiana but also Illinois, Wisconsin, Michigan, and Eastern Minnesota. It became the 19th state in 1816.

At the time the first white explorer, Sieur de la Salle, arrived in Indiana in 1679, the area had only a relatively few Indians, most of whom belonged to the Miami tribe. However, many more Indian groups soon began to move there as they were pushed out of the Eastern parts of America by the incoming white settlers. The Delaware, Mohican, Munsee, and Shawnee tribes came first. Then the Huron, Kickapoo, Piankashaw, Potawatomi, and Wea followed. But as whites began to move into Indiana, they forced these Indians to sell or surrender all their lands and move farther west.

The records of the federal territorial census of 1810 no longer exist, except for the enumerations of Clark, Dearborn, Harrison, and Knox counties. However, there was a special census taken in 1807 that can be found in the Allen County Public Library at Fort Wayne and at the Indiana Historical Society in Indianapolis. The Indiana State Archives in Indianapolis has none of these early census records. In 1851, the newly designed Indiana constitution stipulated that an enumeration of white males over the age of 21 should be completed every six years. The first of these state censuses was taken in 1853. None of these special censuses listings is complete except for the counties of Hendricks and Jennings for the year 1853. The parts that still exist of the ones taken in 1857, 1871, 1877, 1883, 1889, 1901, 1913, 1919, and 1931; they can be found at the Indiana State Library in Indianapolis.

The enumerations of the federal census that has been taken every 10 years since 1920 can, of course, be seen at the various National Archives sites throughout the country, as well as at the Indiana State Library and the Allen County Public Library. There are indexes for some of the years, and the Indiana Genealogical Society in Fort Wayne is compiling an index for the 1870 census of Indiana. It is unknown when this project will be completed.

Indiana birth and death records were kept as early as 1882 for most of the counties. Although it was the law to do so, some doctors, undertakers, and midwives did not comply. Where these statistics do exist they can be obtained from the health officers of the city or county where the event occurred. Birth and death records since October 1907 can be acquired from the Indiana Vital Records Department. Certified copies of any marriage record must be obtained from the county where the marriage took place, but the Vital Records Department does maintain a marriage index of the events that have taken place since 1958 for many of the counties. For certified copies of divorce records, one must write to the county clerk in the county where the divorce was granted. These divorce records have been stored in either the circuit court or the superior court of each county. Guardianship records are in the particular court that has probate jurisdiction in each county.

From 1936 to 1940 the Indiana Works Progress Administration, renamed the Work Projects Administration (WPA) in 1939, indexed many of the birth, marriage and death records for 68 out of Indiana's 92 counties. The marriage records that were indexed covered the years from 1850 through 1920, and the birth and death records were indexed from 1882 through 1920. These WPA indexes are in both book form and on microfilm. They can be found at the Indiana Historical Society and at the Allen County Public Library. The following counties were not included in the WPA indexes: Blackford, Brown, Crawford, Dearborn, Decatur, DuBois, Fayette, Grant, Jefferson, Jennings, Lawrence, Marshall, Noble, Ohio, Porter, Randolph, Ripley, Rush, Scott, Steuben, Switzerland, Tipton, Union, Wabash, and Whitley. There are only partial WPA indexes for the counties of Fulton, Kosciusko, and Pulaski.

The county probate courts have the exclusive jurisdiction over wills in Marion, St. Joseph, and Vandenburgh counties, while in Allen, Madison, and Hendricks counties the superior courts have the exclusive jurisdiction. In all the other counties the circuit court of the county has the jurisdiction. However,

in Bartholomew, Elkhart, Grant, Lake, La-
Porte, and Porter counties the superior courts
and the circuit courts have concurrent jurisdiction.

Land records can generally be obtained
from the county recorders, although there
are also records of the private land claims for
Indiana at the National Archives in Washington, D.C. The mortality schedules for the
years 1850, 1860, 1870, and 1880 are available
at the Indiana State Library. A useful *Guide
to Public Vital Statistics Records in Indiana*
(Work Projects Administration, 1941) can be
found in various Indiana libraries and some
genealogical libraries in other states.

Researchers seeking information from
county records can locate them at the follow-
ing county seats: (Adams County) Decatur,
(Allen County) Fort Wayne, (Bartholomew
County) Columbus, (Benton County) Fow-
ler, (Blackford County) Hartford City, (Boone
County) Lebanon, (Brown County) Nash-
ville, (Carroll County) Delphi, (Cass County)
Logansport, (Clark County) Jeffersonville,
(Clay County) Brazil, (Clinton County)
Frankfort, (Crawford County) English,
(Daviess County) Washington, (Dearborn
County) Lawrenceburg, (Decatur County)
Greensburg, (DeKalb County) Auburn,
(Delaware County) Muncie, (Dubois County)
Jasper, (Elkhart County) Goshen, (Fayette
County) Connersville, (Floyd County) New
Albany, (Fountain County) Covington,
(Franklin County) Brookville, (Fulton
County) Rochester, (Gibson County) Prince-
ton, (Grant County) Marion, and (Greene
County) Bloomfield.

Also at (Hamilton County) Noblesville,
(Hancock County) Greenfield, (Harrison
County) Corydon, (Hendricks County) Dan-
ville, (Henry County) New Castle, (Howard
County) Kokomo, (Huntington County)
Huntington, (Jackson County) Brownstown,
(Jasper County) Rensselaer, (Jay County)
Portland, (Jefferson County) Madison, (Jen-
nings County) Vernon, (Johnson County)
Franklin, (Knox County) Vincennes, (Kos-
ciusko County) Warsaw, (Lagrange County)
Lagrange, (Lake County) Crown Point, (La-
Porte County) LaPorte, (Lawrence County)
Bedford, (Madison County) Anderson, (Mar-
ion County) Indianapolis, (Marshall County)
Plymouth, (Martin County) Shoals, (Miami
County) Peru, (Monroe County) Blooming-
ton, (Montgomery County) Crawfordsville,
(Morgan County) Martinsville, (Newton
County) Kentland, (Noble County) Albion,
(Ohio County) Rising Sun, (Orange County)
Paoli, (Owen County) Spencer, (Parke
County) Rockville, (Perry County) Cannel-
ton, (Pike County) Petersburg, (Porter
County) Valparaiso, (Posey County) Mount
Vernon, (Pulaski County) Winamac, (Put-
nam County) Greencastle, (Randolph
County) Winchester, (Ripley County) Ver-
sailles, (Rush County) Rushville, (St. Joseph
County) South Bend, (Scott County) Scotts-
burg, (Shelby County) Shelbyville, (Spencer
County) Rockport, (Starke County) Knox,
(Steuben County) Angola, (Sullivan County)
Sullivan, (Switzerland County) Vevay, (Tippe-
canoe County) Lafayette, (Tipton County)
Tipton, (Union County) Liberty, (Vanderburg
County) Evansville, (Vermillion County)
Newport, (Vigo County) Terre Haute, (Wa-
bash County) Wabash, (Warren County)
Williamsport, (Warrick County) Boonville,
(Washington County) Salem, (Wayne
County) Richmond, (Wells County) Bluff-
ton, (White County) Monticello, and (Whit-
ley County) Columbia City.

FOR FURTHER INFORMATION SEE:
- Beatty, John D. *Research in Indiana.* Ar-
  lington, VA: National Genealogical Society,
  1992.
- Carty, Mickey Dimon. *Searching in Indiana:
  A Reference Guide to Public and Private
  Records.* Costa Mesa, CA: ISC Publications,
  1985.

Industry Schedules *see* **Census, United
States**

Insurance Records can provide useful genealogical information, with the application
forms being the most helpful in providing
family information. However it is often difficult to discover which particular insurance
company covered an individual, and most of
these companies are unwilling to search
through their large collections of files for a
family historian. Some 16 life insurance com-

panies were formed in the United States between 1843 and 1852, and 19 more had been founded by 1875. The oldest surviving one, the Presbyterian Ministers Fund, was established as early as 1758.

Even the earliest insurance records, which can be loosely worded, contain some information about the client's health, age, residence, and the beneficiaries who were most likely to be relatives. Medical information about the client's diseases and general health became a part of every insurance application by 1865.

Often the researcher may learn which company insured an individual from other family members, but it can be much more difficult for a researcher to persuade that company to allow any search through its records. One may have to prove legitimate descent from the deceased whose records one wishes to view. It is most likely that the researcher will have to do the searching through the files personally, since this work can involve a great deal of time and effort. Yet difficult as it may be to pursue such information, data in insurance records are often most rewarding.

International Genealogical Index (IGI) is a microfiche index of births, baptisms, and marriages from all over the world that has been compiled by the Church of Jesus Christ of Latter-Day Saints (Mormons). It includes records from as early as 1538 for Great Britain to the late 19th century for many other countries. This database contains approximately 600 million individual names. An addendum to it contains an additional 125 million names. The records may be seen on microfilm at the various Family History Centers, most of which are located in Mormon meeting houses. All these Family History Centers also have copies of the Family History Library Catalog (FHLC) that lists all the materials held in the main Mormon library in Salt Lake City, Utah. The IGI can also be accessed by computer on a Website maintained by the Church of Jesus Christ of Latter-Day Saints, and it is contained on the FamilySearch series of CD-ROMs that are marketed by the Family History Library.

The index includes each person's name in alphabetical order, as well as the names of parents for baptisms or the name of a spouse for marriages. A batch serial number facilitates tracing the original documents from which the information was derived. The index is occasionally unreliable, so researchers should check any entries that are found against the much more accurate original transcripts.

The names in the IGI come from two main sources: materials supplied by researchers from the family records they have researched, and materials extracted from selected sources by trained volunteers. These sources include church registers, probate and census documents, and birth and marriage records from around the world. *See also* **Mormon Records.**

Internet *see* **World Wide Web**

Iowa Records begin a little before 1840, although the first white settler, Julien Dubuque, started to mine lead near present-day Dubuque as early as 1788. In 1673, the earliest explorers found both Woodland and Plains Indians living here, including members of the Illinois, Iowa, Miami, Ottawa, Sioux, Omaha, Oto, and Missouri tribes. Sauk and Fox Indians later fled into this area in 1733 after the French forced them out of Wisconsin. The United States acquired Iowa in 1803 as part of the Louisiana Purchase. The U.S. Army then built Fort Madison, and by 1833 a few permanent settlements had been established in the Iowa region.

Congress attached the area to the Territory of Michigan in 1834 and then reorganized the Territory of Wisconsin in 1836 to include Iowa, Minnesota, and most of the Dakotas. In 1838 Congress established the Territory of Iowa, still combining it with Minnesota and about two-thirds of North and South Dakota. In 1846 Iowa was declared a state in its own right, the 29th. The Iowa legislature adopted its present constitution in 1857.

The federal government conducted a census of the Territory of Iowa in 1840. This was followed by an 1850 census of the state and regular censuses every 10 years thereafter. The records of these national censuses can be found at the various National Archives locations. The mortality schedules for 1850, 1860, 1870, and 1890 can be found at the Iowa

State Historical Museum in Des Moines. Separate state-sponsored census enumerations were conducted in 1836, 1856, 1895, 1905, 1915, and 1925. Most of them can also be found at the State Historical Museum.

The Iowa State Board of Health, established on July 1, 1880, created an Iowa Vital Records system of birth, death, and marriage record keeping. Yet the registration responsibilities were not well defined, which resulted in poor record keeping in some areas of the state. A few events, primarily marriages, were recorded in some counties before 1880, but little information is included on those records. For a fee the Bureau of Vital Records in Des Moines will search for death records between the years 1880 and 1895 and marriage records between the years 1880 and 1915.

The vital records maintained at the state level are closed to inspection. At the county level, all vital records occurring in a county (excluding fetal deaths, adoptive records, and out-of-wedlock births prior to July 1, 1995) are open to the public for inspection. Applicants must have a direct or tangible interest in the record in order to secure a certified copy. In other words, the applicant must have a lineal relationship to the persons whose record is being sought, such as being a legal parent, grandparent, spouse, brother, sister, child, legal guardian, or legal representative. All requests for any certificate must be in writing and must include the purpose for which the certificate is being sought. The Iowa Genealogical Society in Des Moines may be of help to those seeking vital records information. The Work Projects Administration's 1941 *Guide to Public Vital Records in Iowa* can be found at the Iowa State Library in Des Moines as well as in some other libraries in the state and in some genealogical libraries elsewhere.

Divorce records since 1906 are held by the district courts in each county where the actions took place, as are the guardianship and probate records. Both equitable and ordinary civil actions are under the jurisdiction of the district courts in Iowa; the state is divided into 18 judicial districts.

The National Archives in Washington, D.C., has records of private land claims for Iowa when it was part of the Louisiana Purchase. Land records since that time rest with the various county recorders of deeds.

Researchers seeking information from county records can locate them at the following county seats: (Adair County) Greenfield, (Adams County) Corning, (Allamakee County) Waukon, (Appanoose County) Centerville, (Audubon County) Audubon, (Benton County) Vinton, (Black Hawk County) Waterloo, (Boone County) Boone, (Bremer County) Waverly, (Buchanan County) Independence, (Buena Vista County) Storm Lake, (Butler County) Allison, (Calhoun County) Rockwell City, (Carroll County) Carroll, (Cass County) Atlantic, (Cedar County) Tipton, (Cerro Gordo County) Mason City, (Cherokee County) Cherokee, (Chickasaw County) New Hampton, (Clarke County) Osceola, (Clay County) Spencer, (Clayton County) Elkader, (Clinton County) Clinton, (Crawford County) Denison, (Dallas County) Adel, (Davis County) Bloomfield, (Decatur County) Leon, (Delaware County) Manchester, (Des Moines County) Burlington, (Dickinson County) Spirit Lake, and (Dubuque County) Dubuque.

Also at (Emmet County) Estherville, (Fayette County) West Union, (Floyd County) Charles City, (Franklin County) Hampton, (Fremont County) Sidney, (Greene County) Jefferson, (Grundy County) Grundy Center, (Guthrie County) Guthrie Center, (Hamilton County) Webster City, (Hancock County) Garner, (Hardin County) Eldora, (Harrison County) Logan, (Henry County) Mount Pleasant, (Howard County) Cresco, (Humboldt County) Dakota City, (Ida County) Grove, (Iowa County) Marengo, (Jackson County) Maquoketa, (Jasper County) Newton, (Jefferson County) Fairfield, (Johnson County) Iowa City, (Jones County) Anamosa, (Keokuk County) Sigourney, (Kossuth County) Algona, (Lee County) Fort Madison and Keokuk, (Linn County) Cedar Rapids, (Louisa County) Wapello, (Lucas County) Chariton, (Lyon County) Rock Rapids, (Madison County) Winterset, (Mahaska County) Oskaloosa, (Marion County) Knoxville, (Marshall County) Marshalltown, (Mills County)

Glenwood, (Mitchell County) Osage, (Monona County) Onawa, (Monroe County) Albia, (Montgomery County) Red Oak, and (Muscatine County) Muscatine.

As well as at (O'Brien County) Primghar, (Osceola County) Sibley, (Page County) Clarinda, (Palo Alto County) Emmetsburg, (Plymouth County) Le Mars, (Pocahontas County) Pocahontas, (Polk County) Des Moines, (Pottawattamie County) Council Bluffs and Avoca, (Poweshiek County) Montezuma, (Ringgold County) Mount Ayr, (Sac County) Sac City, (Scott County) Davenport, (Shelby County) Harlan, (Sioux County) Orange City, (Story County) Nevada, (Tama County) Toledo, (Taylor County) Bedford, (Union County) Creston, (Van Buren County) Keosauqua, (Wapello County) Ottumwa, (Warren County) Indianola, (Washington County) Washington, (Wayne County) Corydon, (Webster County) Fort Dodge, (Winnebago County) Forest City, (Winneshiek County) Decorah, (Woodbury County) Sioux City, (Worth County) Northwood, and (Wright County) Clarion.

FOR FURTHER INFORMATION SEE:
- Harris, Katherine, comp. *Guide to Manuscripts.* Iowa City, IA: State Historical Society of Iowa, 1973.
- Peterson, Becki. *Iowa County Records Manual.* Iowa City, IA: State Historical Society of Iowa, 1987.

IRC *see* **Computer Chat Programs**

Irish Genealogy includes reliable pedigrees that go back as far as A.D. 600, and unreliable ones that are based mainly on mythology and extend back to the fifth century, or about 1,500 years ago. There are irreparable gaps in many of these records because of Ireland's turbulent history and because the Public Record Office at Four Courts in Dublin was burned on April 13, 1922, destroying about a thousand Protestant parish registers, as well as bishops' transcripts, census returns, civil registrations, wills, and estate papers.

Until 1921 Ireland was one country and the registrar general in Dublin kept the records of births, marriages, and deaths. But Ireland was divided by Great Britain into two parts in 1921; the larger part became the Irish Free State in 1921 and then the Republic of Ireland in 1949. The smaller part composed of six counties in the north, known as Northern Ireland, now has its own registrar general at Belfast. This Belfast office has all the records of the births, marriages, and deaths recorded in the north since 1921, as well as the census returns for 1931 and 1951.

Because Ireland was administered until 1921 by English monarchs, after Henry VIII forced Ireland's parliament to declare him king of Ireland in 1541, many of the records of Irish ancestors are held in the Public Record Office in London. The ones that are held at Joyce House in Dublin include the civil registrations of births, marriages, and deaths starting in 1864 and continuing to the present, with the exception of those for Northern Ireland after 1921. These birth certificates include the date and place of birth; name and sex of the baby; name, surname and residence of the father; name, surname, and maiden surname of the mother; rank, profession, or occupation of the father; and the name and qualifications of the informant, usually a family member. The records are indexed and are an excellent source for the researcher.

Since England governed all Ireland until 1921, the favored religious denomination was that of the Protestant Church of Ireland, the Anglican body. However, the civil registrations of Protestant marriages actually began in April 1845. Catholic and Church of Ireland records are relatively sparse due to the depressed state of the Catholics. Few of their priests were able to keep registers and those that do exist are generally in the hands of the particular parish priest. There are, however, a few that go back some 200 years. Some microfilm copies of church registers, both Catholic and Protestant, are at the Public Record Office of Ireland in Dublin. There are also microfilm copies of most of the surviving Catholic registers up to 1880 at the National Library in Dublin. Some of these, however, are only open to the public with the permission of the relevant bishop.

The Protestant Church of Ireland parish registers of baptisms, marriages, and burials before 1871 are public records; copies are available for about one-third of Irish parishes from the Public Record Offices either in Dublin or Belfast. Many of these Protestant records, however, are still held by the local clergy, and a researcher should contact the relevant church officials for access to them.

The National Archives in Dublin holds many records relating to Irish genealogy and local history, while the register general in Dublin has many other useful registers, such as those for adopted children (since 1953), births at sea to Irish parents (since 1864), and deaths at sea of Irish-born persons (1864–1921). The register general in Belfast holds registers of adopted children (since 1931), marine births and deaths (since 1922), war deaths (1939–48), and British Consulate records of Irish births, marriages, and deaths abroad (since 1922).

The Public Record Office in Belfast has some materials of genealogical interest that date before 1922, such as wills and probate records, tithe apportionment books, poll tax records, militia yeomanry and muster rolls, voters polls, and some of the earlier census records. The National Library of Ireland in Dublin also has a substantial collection of printed and manuscript materials relating to Irish family history.

Many Presbyterian, Methodist, Quaker, and other non–Anglican and non–Catholic records have also survived in Ireland. The Presbyterian Church of Ireland was established there in the later 1700s and early 1800s principally by Scotch settlers. Unfortunately few Presbyterian congregations kept registers until about 1820. The Public Record Office in Belfast has copies of most of these registers that were kept in the provinces of Northern Ireland. For information about other Presbyterian records, one should contact the Presbyterian Historical Society in Belfast.

The Methodists established churches in Ireland about 1820, and most of these churches still hold their own records, although some of them can be found at the Public Record Office in Belfast. There were also a few Baptist and Congregational chapels in Ireland, but most of their records remain in the custody of their ministers. Many of the Quaker records for those areas now in Northern Ireland are in the Public Record Office in Belfast. Quakers emigrated from England to Ireland about 1653. There are also extensive Quaker records in the Friends Historical Library in Dublin, Ireland, and at the Friends Meeting House in Lisburn, Northern Ireland.

Up to 1858 all Irish probates of wills were handled by the ecclesiastical courts in each diocese. After 1858 the testamentary jurisdiction was transferred to the civil courts, but the 1922 fire in Dublin destroyed most of these records. Fortunately many of these wills had been indexed, and these indexes are now in the National Archives of Northern Ireland. They include the deceased's name, address and occupation, date and place of death, the estate's value, and the executors' or administrators' names and addresses. The National Archives has tried to replace some of the lost probate records by collecting copies from family or solicitor's archives, and now holds over 20,000 probate items, many of which are wills that were never proved.

In the National Library in Dublin there are many published and manuscript versions of Irish family histories. An excellent guide to these and other genealogical records in Ireland is Margaret Dickson Falley's two-volume *Irish and Scotch-Irish Ancestral Research: A Guide to the Genealogical Records, Methods and Sources in Ireland* (Baltimore, MD: Genealogical Publishing Co., 1981).

Most of the Irish court records were also destroyed in the 1922 fire. What records survived can be found in the Public Record Office in Dublin and at the National Archives of Northern Ireland in Belfast, which has the largest number of such documents, including deeds and estate records, tithe payments for land, hearth tax records, and military records. The most important tax records for Irish researchers are the Tithe Applotment Books and Griffiths Primary Valuation, which usually give the place of residence at the time of the tax record. Both of these tax record sources serve as census substitutes, and can be found at the Public Records Office in Belfast.

Many records survive concerning poor relief granted by the poor law unions that were created after the passage of the Poor Law Act in 1838. These Irish records cover a much larger proportion of the population than similar ones do in England primarily because of the poverty and distress Ireland suffered in the mid–19th century. The records can be found in the National Archives in Dublin and are on microfilm at the National Library there. Military archives also contain the records of the Royal Irish Constabulary, as well as the service records for the Irish soldiers and sailors who served in various wars. Some of these records can be found at the National Archives in Dublin and at the Public Records Office in Belfast, yet the largest collection of them is not in Ireland, but in London at the Public Record Office.

There were directories of the cities of Dublin and Limerick published in the mid–18th century; many other town directories were published later. The largest collection of these is in the National Library in Dublin. They can be helpful in locating particular streets and buildings that may no longer exist or whose names have changed. The library also has an 1837 topographical dictionary for Ireland. The large collection of Irish newspapers at the National Library can also help in finding information about people and events for which the records were destroyed in the fire of 1922.

Some published registers of Irish schools date to as early as the 17th century, and registers of the independent and charity schools that date to the 18th century. Such school records may contain valuable information regarding alumni lists and other registers. These records can include information about names, birthplaces, residences, and fathers' names and occupations. The registers of students at Trinity College in Dublin from 1593, when it was founded, up to 1860 have been published and can be found in a number of Irish libraries, including the Trinity College Library itself. This is the greatest library in Ireland, and it has many books and manuscripts of genealogical interest. It is also one of the six libraries in the United Kingdom that are authorized under the Copyright Acts to receive one copy of every book published in the United Kingdom.

The various family history and genealogical societies from all parts of Ireland are involved in the Irish Genealogical Project, which aims to transcribe and computerize all the Irish genealogical records. The project is being coordinated by the Association of Professional Genealogists of Ireland in Dublin and the Association of Ulster Genealogists and Record Agents in Belfast. *See also* **Census, Irish.**

Islamic Genealogy has deep roots in the tribal origins of the pre–Islamic groups that were converted to the teachings of Mohammed sometime after the year A.D. 610. The followers of the religion of Islam are called Muslims, an Arabic word meaning one who submits (to God). The religion spread rapidly, and today Islam is one of the world's largest religions, with more than 500 million followers. The principal Muslim communities are in the Middle East, North Africa, Indonesia, Bangladesh, and Pakistan. In Europe, Islam is the principal religion in European Turkey and Albania.

Instead of having a hierarchy of priests and a complex structure of churches and cathedrals, the Muslims depend only on the teachings of holy men. They can pray wherever they may be with nothing more cumbersome than prayer mats. One of the tenets of Islam considers all men brothers who are True Believers. The proudest sultan has as much of a chance of gaining paradise — and no more — than the humblest believer.

The Muslims are well known for their concern for family traditions and genealogy. Their detailed and complete preservation of people's genealogies begins with the assumption that the tribe is a family on a larger scale. Thus throughout history there has accumulated an enormous legacy of writings on genealogy, preserving the lineages of numerous tribes and their branches. In pre–Islamic days there were various genealogical listings that resemble those found in the Book of Genesis and other parts of the Old Testament. The Arabs of the north claimed their descent from Adnan, a reputed descendant of Ishmael, who was in turn supposedly the elder son of Abraham. Those of the south traced themselves back to Qahtan, identified as Joktan, son of Eber and a descendant of Noah.

The Prophet Mohammed, himself, belonged to a notable tribe of Mecca, the Khoreish, and many of the genealogies of Islam spring from that fact. Mohammed was the son of `Abd Allah, the son of `Abd al-Muttalib, the son of Hâshim, the son of `Abd al-Manâf, the son of Qusayy, the son of Kullâb, the son of Mirrah, the son of Ka`b, the son of Lu'ay, the son of Ghâlib, the son of Fahr (known as Quraysh, the man whom the entire tribe is related to), the son of Mâlik, the son of Nadir, the son of Kinânah, the son of Khuzaymah, the son of Mudrikah, the son of Iyâs, the son of Mudar, the son of Nazzâr, the son of Ma`d, the son of `Adnân. It is said that when Mohammed was a young man, he worked as a shepherd for the flocks of Quraysh. This occupation had, indeed, been the practice of the prophets who came before him.

The Islamic chronicler al-Tabari (died A.D. 923) included the genealogies of the pre–Islamic tribes in his writings, and Ibn Durayi (died A.D. 934) wrote a complete treatise on the genealogies of the Arabian tribes. The rapid growth of Islamic power encouraged the pursuit of Arabic genealogy and naturally supported the traditional records of the conquering tribes. The first three caliphs who succeeded Mohammed — Abu Bekr, Omar, and Othman reigned without disturbance. But on Othman's death, four candidates came forward to assume the office. One was Ali, the Prophet's cousin and son-in-law, being the husband of the Prophet's daughter, Fatima. The competition for leadership eventually resulted in several different branches of Islam ruling in various parts of the Muslim world.

During Medieval times the pedigrees of the ruling families throughout the Islamic world were committed to writing, and can be found in a number of libraries, such as the Greater Cairo Library in Egypt. Some of them have been posted on the World Wide Web. During this period certain people of Arab descent, who claimed ancestry directly from Mohamed, also traveled and settled in various Asian countries ruled by Moslems. They carried warrants from the Islamic authorities of the countries they departed in order to establish their credentials. The genealogies of these persons can be found in the libraries of the countries to which they emigrated.

Documentation of vital statistics is not available until 1897 in Egypt, when the first census was conducted under British suzerainty. The process has been continued there periodically ever since. In Turkey the first census was in 1927, although one had been proposed, yet never implemented, during the reign of Suleiman the Magnificent (Sultan from 1520 to 1566). Algeria conducted its first census in 1966 after achieving its independence from France. Tunisia, Syria, Iraq, Iran, and other Muslim countries have yet to conduct censuses, so the population figures for these countries remain only estimates.

Some of the difficulties that arise in Islamic genealogical research come from the extremely common use of the same forenames. One will find in traveling to Islamic lands that a large number of men bear the name Mohammed and a large number of women have the name of the Prophet's daughter, Fatima. Many surnames are also common, and the Turks, in many cases, have adopted surnames only recently. Furthermore the seclusion of Islamic women in the past has prevented the development of maternal lines of descent.

Italian Genealogy is somewhat fragmented since for many centuries the country was split into a large number of states. However, in most of the southern regions (the former Kingdom of the Two Sicilies), the civil records date from the early 1800s. The same is true for certain northern localities. Elsewhere (in most of the former Kingdom of Sardinia, the Papal States, etc.), such civil records were only instituted around 1860.

Italian church records date from a much earlier period. Catholic priests were required, as early as 1563, to keep records of baptisms, marriages, and deaths. In cities such as Palermo these records begin in the 1300s. But access to parochial archives in Italy is notoriously difficult. Obtaining the right to examine any of them is a bureaucratic exercise requiring months or even years of negotiations. These parochial records were usually written in Latin, yet some can also be found in modern Italian or in the local dialect. A degree of knowledge and practice is needed to render accurate transcriptions and translations. After the 1900s duplicates of the church records were sent to the diocesan archives. Besides vital statistics, the records include the church censuses, known as the state of the souls (*stato delle anime*).

There was a brief period at the beginning of the 19th century when Napoleon's troops occupied much of Italy and instituted the maintenance of civil records. The French had a system of law that included the recording of all births, marriages, and deaths. These so-called Napoleonic records begin about 1806 or later, depending on the area of Italy. When Napoleon lost power in 1815, most of the areas under his control stopped keeping these civil registers.

In southern Italy and Sicily (a state Napoleon never occupied), these Napoleonic records are printed in Italian, are fairly uniform, and are relatively easy to read. They start about 1809 and extend to 1820. In northern Italy, however, the records are handwritten and not as easy to use. They end in 1815 when the French departed. There are a few northern areas such as Veneto, Trento-Alto-Adige, and parts of Lombardia, in which the parish priests kept separate civil registrations along with their parish registrations long after the Napoleonic period ended. These post–Napoleonic records date from 1809 to 1865. In a few of the southern areas records were generally kept just as long. This was the case for Abruzzo, Naples, Campania, and Sicily.

The first attempt to conduct a national census took place in 1861, nine years before the country was unified under King Victor Emmanuel II. Every 10 years since then national censuses have been conducted. There has been some civil registration of births, marriages, and deaths since 1851, but it is only since 1870 that such civil records have been preserved in good order. These vital statistics are kept by the local registrar's office (*anagrafe*) of each city or town. Records before 1865 are at the state archives in each province, which are usually located in the major city of that province. There is also a center for the national archives, the Archivio Centrale della Stato, in Rome. Census information can be provided by the Istituto Centrale de Statistica in Rome.

Generally the records are not open to the public view unless they are over 75 years old, and even then a researcher must have written permission from either a provincial authority or the mayor of the town in order to view the records. One can request for a fee an extract that will give much of the information contained in the original copy. These extracts are fairly easy to read with an Italian genealogical word list or dictionary. The earliest marriage and death records often contain the names only of the marriage couple or of the deceased, with no other identifying information concerning the persons involved. But the later records typically include professions, approximate ages, and other information unavailable in the older primary records. The death records will often give the names of the deceased's parents and their ages and professions, as well as the names of two witnesses who came to the town official to report the death. These are often the relatives of the decedent. Wills in Italy are deposited with the notaries. Information about them can be obtained from the Archivio Notrale, Ispettatore Generale in Rome.

Given and surname patterns in Italy sometimes provide clues to an individual's ancestry. In Italy, a couple's first son was traditionally named for the paternal grandfather. The second son would then be named for the maternal grandfather, and the first daughter would be named for the paternal grandmother while the second daughter would be named for the maternal grandmother. If a couple had more than four children, the others might have been given the names of aunts, uncles, cousins, or even close friends. When a child died in infancy, a couple may have given their next baby the same name to preserve the naming patterns. Furthermore, some surnames are found only in specific regions or towns of Italy.

Genealogical collections in the various town libraries often provide good information relating to the history of local families. A particularly useful tool for correctly identifying communities and court jurisdiction is the *Nuovo Dizionario dei comuni e frazioni di comuni*, a gazetteer of villages and hamlets in Italy that can be found in most Italian libraries. *See also* **Ancient Greek and Roman Genealogy.**

J

Japanese Genealogy is closely related to the country's samurai tradition, which began in the early 17th century. The various clans at that time established private academies to train their samurai soldiers, and most of these academies had libraries to preserve their genealogical materials. Buddhist monasteries in Japan have also preserved genealogical records. However, gaining access to the clan records can be difficult and often impossible to achieve. It is easier to obtain access to the Buddhist records that are kept by each individual monastery.

A Family Registration Law was passed by the Japanese Diet in 1947 that requires the registration of all births, adoptions, marriages, divorces, guardianships, deaths, and disappearances in Japan. These records are kept by the city, ward, town, or village where the events took place, rather than by any centralized national public record office. The researcher who wishes to obtain information from these various local archives must correspond with the Civil Affairs Bureau of the Ministry of Justice in Tokyo.

Wills are the established way in which inheritances are transferred in Japan, and this has been the case since the early seventh and eighth centuries. The making of a will does not necessarily require the presence of a notary, and the records are kept either by the person who makes the will or by the person to whom it has been entrusted. In situations where a will has been drawn up by a notary and for which the family court has authority for attestation, a photostat can often be obtained from the court of jurisdiction.

In July 1971 the Japanese government established a National Archives center to receive and preserve important official documents and records from the various ministries and agencies that had been preserving them for long periods. These included the records from the Meiji period (1868–1912) and those related to the Tokugawa Shogunate (1603–1867). The National Archives is located in Tokyo.

Japanese Internment Records *see* **Immigrants**

Jewish Records can be found in various libraries and repositories in the United States, in Israel, and in a few other countries, as well as in various synagogues and cemeteries around the world. Synagogues, whether Orthodox, Conservative, or Reform, have always been the heart and soul of the Jewish communities, although many Jews who have left their homelands have also joined landsmanshaftn societies (organizations of people from the same ancestral town). Until 1900 about 81 percent of the world's Jews lived in Europe. But today roughly 46 percent reside in the United States. Another 28 percent live in Israel. Jews classify themselves on the basis of historical origins as being Sephardic (pre-inquisition Spain), Ashkenzsic (Germany and Eastern Europe), Oriental (Iran, Iraq, India, and China), or Ethiopian (African).

Most Jews in medieval times kept few records, but their rabbis did keep records, and they considered it a sacred duty to do so. Such records that still survive — in commentaries and responses (answers to questions regarding Jewish law) that the rabbis and rabbinical students wrote — can be found in various printed books and manuscript collections, many of which contain genealogical information about their authors. Most of these are in Hebrew or one of the various European non–English languages, although a few can be found in English.

A large number of records relating to

Jews, Jewish families, Jewish congregations, and Jewish communities both in America and elsewhere can be found in a number of key libraries in New York City, Cincinnati, Ohio, and Waltham, Massachusetts. By some estimates the YIVO Institute for Jewish Research in New York contains the largest collection of Judaic volumes in the world. It was started as the official Jewish archive for Lithuania, and part of its collection came from a library in the city of Vilnus (now Vilnius) in Lithuania. However, it is now the repository for anything related to Yiddish life in Europe and America. The library is said to contain about 300,000 volumes, including the complete records of the Hebrew Immigrant Aid Society, more than a thousand autobiographies written by East European Jews, and the records of numerous Lithuanian, Russian, and Polish communities that no longer exist. The records are not well indexed, and the library catalogs are separated into four different languages: Roman (English, French, German, etc.), Hebrew, Yiddish, and Cyrillic (Russian, Ukrainian, etc.).

While YIVO is one of the best sources for material from the Eastern European countries, the Leo Baeck Institute, also in New York, is the best place in America to find records from the German-speaking countries. Most of its materials are in German and the staff does no translations, but it does have a large collection of family histories, family trees, and other genealogical information. Microfilmed records pertain to 446 destroyed synagogues in the states of Bavaria, Hesse, and Bremen. The collection of 50,000 volumes is well indexed, and there is a computerized index that allows the researcher to search by family names.

The American Jewish Historical Society in Waltham, Massachusetts, located on the Brandeis University campus, has about four million items relating to American Jewish history, including a wide variety of family papers, family histories, and immigration and synagogue records. Records for Jews in the Western Hemisphere, particularly those in the United States, Canada, Mexico, the West Indies, and South America can be found in the American Jewish Archives in Cincin-

nati, Ohio. Other sources for Jewish genealogical information in the United States include the National Archives in Washington, D.C., the Mormon Family History Library in Salt Lake City, Utah, and several universities throughout the country. A complete listing of these sources can be found in Dan Rottenberg's *Finding our Fathers* (Baltimore, MD: Genealogical Publishing Co., 1977). Rottenberg also lists a number of libraries and archives of Jewish records located in Canada.

In Israel some 20 major archives and about 15 minor ones deal with matters of Judaica. Many don't have much information of use to genealogists, but a few do have important family records. The Central Archives for the History of the Jewish People in Jerusalem has a series of microfilmed records from different countries that include birth, marriage, and death records, as well as circumcision books, gravestone registrations, and so forth. The Central Archives also has nearly 200 lists describing the records of Jewish interest in other countries. A large collection of documents of Eastern Jews in Palestine (Greek, Turkish, North African, etc.) beginning with the Ottoman conquest of Palestine in the 16th century can be found in the Archives of the Sephardi Community, also in Jerusalem. This repository has various Muslim court documents and letters sent by Sephardic Jews to Jewish communities throughout the world.

Until the 19th century, Italy was the leading center for Jewish libraries. It still houses many important Jewish book and manuscript collections. These can be found in the Hebrew department of the Library of Parma, which has over 2,000 old manuscripts; at the Vatican Library; and at a number of other public, private, and university libraries. Some Italian Jews claim to be descendants of those who lived in Italy in the first century, though Jewish family names didn't come into use in Italy until early in the Middle Ages. Spain, prior to the 15th century Inquisition, had the largest number of Jews in Europe, but relevant records were destroyed when the Jews were expelled from Spain in 1492; all that remains are the records of the trials during the Spanish Inquisition. Some of these, however, contain genealogical information about those being tried. They are preserved on microfilm at the Central Archives for the History of the Jewish People in Jerusalem.

Jews lived in England when William the Conqueror arrived in 1066, but they were expelled in 1290 and none returned until after 1680. By 1738 there were said to be about 6,000 Jews living once again in England. However, they were not allowed to become barristers in England until 1833, to vote until 1835, to obtain military commissions until 1846, or to enter Oxford or Cambridge universities until after 1871. There are now about 400 synagogues in Great Britain, as well as many Jewish cemeteries. Each has records of its congregation that can be viewed by a researcher. Some of the synagogue registers have been published, including those from the Synagogue of London for the years 1687 to 1837. The British Museum in London also has a very fine collection of Jewish materials, including some records of Jewish businesses and taxation from before 1290. However, there are no synagogue registers from that early period. The Jewish Historical Society of England, located in London, has a great deal of material as well, including many Anglo-Jewish genealogies. Ireland has very few synagogues, but information on Jewish records there can be obtained from the Irish Jewish Museum in Dublin.

Most of the Jews who have immigrated to the Western Hemisphere have come from Poland. The Jewish population of that country before World War II was approximately 3.25 million. Virtually all the Russian Jews— 2.8 million at that time—lived in areas that had once been a part of Poland. So many Jews were living in that area because Poland and Lithuania were among the last countries of Europe to be Christianized. The pagan kings were much more tolerant toward the Jews than were the Christian kings, who mounted major campaigns to eliminate heretics. Much of the genealogical material from Poland that may interest researchers has been microfilmed and can be found in the Central Archives for the History of the Jewish People in Jerusalem.

In Czarist Russia, the Jewish synagogues kept their own circumcision books, marriage and divorce registration, cemetery lists, and other records. But few of these have survived. The government had no bureaus to register births, marriages, and deaths prior to the Communist victory in 1918. What Russian Jewish records do exist can be found at the Central Archives in Jerusalem. Another valuable source of information on Russian Jews is the Helsinki University Library in Finland. Helsinki was part of the Russian Empire prior to 1917, and the Czar required the Helsinki Library to keep a copy of every official publication produced in the empire. Because of its completeness, this library has perhaps the largest Russian collection of Jewish materials outside the former Soviet Union.

The Jewish vital registers from the period of 1880 to 1944 in Prague, Czechoslovakia, were destroyed by the Nazis in 1945, but earlier records do exist. The earliest of these Czechoslovakian records are the circumcision books of 1677 and 1779. There are birth records for females from 1783. These Jewish registers are located in the Státní ústřední archiv (Czech Central Archive) in Prague. A few records have been found for Bulgarian Jews as early as 811 A.D., located in various libraries in New York and Israel. The Budapest National Library has a good-sized collection of records for Hungarian Jews. Guidance can also be obtained from the World Federation of Hungarian Jews in New York City. The best source for Jews in Lithuania is the YIVO Institute in New York City. The Central Archives for the History of the Jewish People in Jerusalem has an inventory of records that can be found in several libraries and archives in Yugoslavia.

Despite German attempts to exterminate the Jews, the Germans have kept meticulous records of Jewish births, marriages, and deaths. These records are available in the archives of countless numbers of communities throughout Germany. Both the Leo Baeck Institute in New York City and the Central Archives for the History of the Jewish People in Jerusalem have genealogical data and information regarding these German records. The same is true for the Austrian records of

Jews, though for such Austrian records one can also contact the Jewish Record Center in Vienna.

The best source for Jewish records in Belgium is the synagogues, of which there are three in Brussels and two in Antwerp. In Denmark, records of Jewish interest can be obtained from the Danish State Archives in Copenhagen as well as from the Central Archives for the History of the Jewish People in Jerusalem. Most of the records of the Jewish communities in France are still preserved in the various city and village archives, in the departmental archives, and in the National Archives in Paris. The Central Archives for the History of the Jewish People in Jerusalem has extensive material about the Jews of Amsterdam as well as some of the other cities in the Netherlands. The Leo Baeck Institute in New York City has a large collection of genealogical materials concerning Swedish-Jewish families.

One other source for Jewish records from Europe is the Holocaust lists. The Holocaust has been called the most documented event of the 20th century. Tens of thousands of books and other resources exist. However, these are not conveniently organized for genealogical research, and there are few general indexes. The library at the Yad Vashem museum in Jerusalem is the principal repository for such information. Its 100,000 volumes include over a thousand yizkor books (published histories of individual Eastern European Jewish communities). There is also a list of over 170,000 survivors and their children in the U.S. and Canada, maintained by the U.S. Holocaust Memorial Museum in Washington, D.C. The Dallas Memorial Center for Holocaust Studies in Texas also has a fairly large library with lists of Jews from Belgium, Rumania, France, Holland, Poland, Hungary, and Germany.

Dan Rottenberg's *Finding our Fathers* includes some 8,000 Jewish family names with sources where more information can be found about each. Other books of Jewish surnames can be found in many libraries, and David S. Zubatsky and Irwin M. Berent's *Sourcebook for Jewish Genealogies and Family Histories* (Bergen, NJ: Avotaynu, Inc.,

1996) lists over 22,000 printed and manuscript genealogies in archives and libraries worldwide. Most Jews did not have hereditary surnames until the early 19th century. Before that, people were known only by their first names and patronymics (their father's given name), e.g., "Mendelsohn" = son of Mendel, or "Abramowitz" = son of Abram. They were required to take surnames by various governments at various times: Austrian Empire (1787), Russia (1804, not enforced until 1835/1845), Russian Poland (1821), West Galicia (1805), France (1808), and the various German states, Frankfurt (1807), Baden (1809), Westphalia (1812), Prussia (1812), Bavaria (1813), Wuerttemberg (1828), Posen (1833), and Saxony (1834).

At the same time, spelling was somewhat haphazard. It is only during the 20th century that consistent spelling has become an obsession. In the Jewish records it is not unusual to find the same person's name spelled in several ways. For example, Meyerson, Meirzon, and Majersohn are all spellings of the names of the same person. Furthermore, transliteration from one language to another creates a wide range of spelling variances. The Yiddish "H" became the Russian "G" and the Polish/German "W" became the English "V." Many Jewish immigrants changed their names when they moved from one country to another, and after they arrived in America, they frequently changed their first names, usually to something with the same initial letter or sound. Thus someone named "Moshe" or "Mendel" or "Mordcha" or "Mayer" might take the American name "Max" or "Morris" or "Milton" or "Murray" or even "Mel."

There was great pressure on families to remain intact, so Jews generally had a low divorce rate. Marriages of first cousins were common and legal according to Jewish law. A study in England in 1875, for example, indicated that 7.5 percent of all English Jewish marriages were among first cousins—a proportion that was about three times that among gentiles. The proportion of such marriages has generally been much greater among the Sephardic Jews than among the Ashkenazic. Ashkenazic Jews traditionally name their children after deceased relatives. Sephardic Jews traditionally name their children after

grandparents, whether living or dead. *See also* **Biblical Genealogy**.

K

Kansas Records of births, marriages, and deaths are obtainable for a small fee from the Office of Vital Statistics in Topeka. This area was part of the Louisiana Purchase when it was annexed to the United States in 1803. It then became part of the Missouri Territory from 1812 to 1821, and for the following 33 years it was known as an unorganized territory, inhabited mainly by Indians. These Indians were then gradually pushed into the Oklahoma area. Then in 1854 the area became the Territory of Kansas, with its western boundary including the part of Colorado east of the Continental Divide, and in 1861 Kansas was designated the 34th state of the Union. At that time the population consisted of about 110,000 persons, mostly Southerners and New Englanders, with a sprinkling of settlers from Illinois, Indiana, Missouri, Ohio, and Kentucky. Many veterans took up homesteads in Kansas following the Civil War.

Fort Leavenworth, established in 1827, was the first organized community in Kansas. It was a welcome stopover and outfitting place for the thousands of persons traveling in wagon trains to the valleys of Utah, the gold fields of California, and the beckoning Oregon country. The passage of the Kansas-Nebraska Act in 1854 opened the Territory of Kansas to settlement and for the construction of a transcontinental railway. But the Kansas-Nebraska Act, by incorporating popular sovereignty, also opened the territory to a bitter dispute over the question of slavery. The proximity of Kansas to slave-owning Missouri and the lack of any natural border between the two regions prompted a large influx of pro-slavery individuals into the new territory. At the same time the New England Emigrant Aid Society in Boston, which was interested in peopling the frontier with anti-slavery settlers, helped to found the town

Lawrence (named after Amos A. Lawrence, promoter of the Emigrant Aid Society), which then became the center of Free-State activities. The often violent conflict between the pro- and anti-slavery forces resulted in the territory becoming known as "Bleeding Kansas."

A territorial census was conducted by the national government in 1860, and state censuses were conducted in 1865, 1875, 1885, 1895, 1905, 1915, and 1925. The original copies of the 1870 and 1880 national census enumerations for Kansas can be found at the State Historical Society in Topeka. Copies of these and later national census records are, of course, at the various National Archives locations. The mortality schedules for 1860, 1870, and 1880 are also in the State Historical Society Library.

Although copies of the Kansas records of births, marriages, and deaths can be obtained from the Office of Vital Statistics, to obtain a death certificate, one must be a member of the individual's immediate family. Vital records earlier than those held by the Office of Vital Statistics are obtainable from the county clerks in the counties where each event took place. The *Guide to Public Vital Statistics Records in Kansas* (Work Projects Administration, 1942) is available at the Kansas State Library in Topeka, as well as at some other libraries in the state, and elsewhere in some of the largest genealogical libraries.

Divorce records since July 1951 are also maintained at the Office of Vital Statistics, and those registered before 1951 in the district courts in the various counties. In Kansas there is no distinction between equity and law actions. Therefore, judgments under $1,000 can be found in the county courts; actions that result in larger judgments are in the district courts. Guardianship and probate records are in the county probate courts. Land records lie with the county clerk, who maintains the transfer books in which are recorded all the transfers that must be made before deeds can be registered by the county register of deeds.

One other location for valuable genealogical records is the library at the University of Kansas in Lawrence. It maintains the Kansas Heritage Center for Family and Local History.

Researchers seeking information from county records can locate them at the following county seats: (Allen County) Iola, (Anderson) Garnett, (Atchison) Atchison, (Barber) Medicine Lodge, (Barton) Great Bend, (Bourbon) Fort Scott, (Brown) Hiawatha, (Butler) El Dorado, (Chase) Cottonwood Falls, (Chautauqua) Sedan, (Cherokee) Columbus, (Cheyenne) St. Francis, (Clark) Ashland, (Clay) Clay Center, (Cloud) Concordia, (Coffey) Burlington, (Comanche) Coldwater, (Cowley) Winfield, (Crawford) Girard, (Decatur) Oberlin, (Dickinson) Abilene, (Doniphan) Troy, (Douglas) Lawrence, (Edwards) Kinsley, (Elk) Howard, (Ellis) Hays, (Ellsworth) Ellsworth, (Finney) Garden City, (Ford) Dodge City, (Franklin) Ottawa, (Geary) Junction City, (Gove) Gove, (Graham) Hill City, (Grant) Ulysses, (Gray) Cimarron, (Greeley) Tribune, (Greenwood) Eureka, (Hamilton) Syracuse, (Harper) Anthony, (Harvey) Newton, (Haskell) Sublette, (Hodgeman) Jetmore, (Jackson) Holton, (Jefferson) Oskaloosa, (Jewell) Mankato, (Johnson) Olathe, (Kearny) Lakin, (Kingman) Kingman, (Kiowa) Greensburg, (Labette) Oswego, (Lane) Dighton, (Leavenworth) Leavenworth, (Lincoln) Lincoln, (Linn) Mound City, (Logan) Oakley, and (Lyon) Emporia.

Also at (Marion) Marion, (Marshall) Marysville, (McPherson) McPherson, (Meade) Meade, (Miami) Paola, (Mitchell) Beloit, (Montgomery) Independence, (Morris) Council Grove, (Morton) Elkhart, (Nemaha) Seneca, (Neosho) Erie, (Ness) Ness City, (Norton) Norton, (Osage) Lyndon, (Osborne) Osborne, (Ottawa) Minneapolis, (Pawnee) Larned, (Phillips) Phillipsburg, (Pottawatomie) Westmoreland, (Pratt) Pratt, (Rawlins) Atwood, (Reno) Hutchinson, (Republic) Belleville, (Rice) Lyons, (Riley) Manhattan, (Rooks) Stockton, (Rush) La Crosse, (Russell) Russell, (Saline) Salina, (Scott) Scott City, (Sedgwick) Wichita, (Seward) Liberal, (Shawnee) Topeka, (Sheridan) Hoxie, (Sherman) Goodland, (Smith) Smith Center, (Stafford) Saint John, (Stanton) Johnson, (Stevens) Hugoton, (Sumner) Wellington, (Thomas) Colby, (Trego) WaKeeney, (Wabaunsee) Alma, (Wallace) Sharon Springs, (Washington) Washington, (Wichita) Leoti, (Wilson) Fredonia, (Woodson) Yates Center, and (Wyandotte) Kansas City.

For FURTHER INFORMATION SEE:
- Rooney, Doris Dockstader, et al. *Kansas Genealogical Society Six-Generation Ancestor Tables*. Dodge City, KS: Kansas Genealogical Society, 1976.
- Smith, Patricia D. *Kansas Biographical Index: Statewide and Regional Histories*. Garden City, KS: The Author, 1994.

Kentucky Records of births, marriages, and deaths are available for a small fee from the Office of Vital Statistics in Frankfort. Some of them have been indexed and are available at the Kentucky Department for Libraries and Archives, Public Records Division, also in Frankfort. The area was occupied by Cherokee, Chickasaw, Delaware, Iroquois, and Shawnee Indian tribes at the time that the first white explorers visited the region during the late 1600s and early 1700s.

It was considered to be a part of Augusta County, Virginia, before 1584, and after that a part of Fincastle County, Virginia. The early settlers even called the area that now constitutes the state by the name "Transylvania." Around 1774, as more people entered the state to build homes there, they established the first permanent white settlement at Harrodsburg. It was then known as the Kentucky County of Virginia. In 1776 the Kentucky area was divided into three counties—Fayette, Jefferson, and Lincoln—and in 1790 it was divided once more into nine counties. In 1792 Kentucky became the 15th state of the Union. The western tip of Kentucky has been called the Jackson Purchase Region because it was purchased by President Andrew Jackson in 1818, during his presidency, from the Chickasaw Indians.

Although there have been several state censuses, none of them listed the heads of household or family names. The first census to do so was the national census of 1810; there have been such census listings in each of the decennial years since then. All of them can be seen at the various National Archives locations.

Most of the birth and death records at the Office of Vital Statistics date from 1911, although there are earlier ones from the cities of Louisville, Lexington, Covington, and Newport. Some of the earlier birth and death records from other places in Kentucky will be found at the Kentucky Historical Society in Frankfort. Most of the marriage records can be obtained from the county clerks in the counties where such events took place, although such records beginning in 1958 will be found at the Vital Statistics Office. Prior to 1849 divorces could be granted only by the state legislature. The records for divorces after that date are in the circuit courts of each county. So are the guardianship records and land records.

Wills and other court records can be found in all the county courts, while naturalization records are filed in the district courts at Bowling Green, Catlettsburg, Covington, Frankfort, London, Louisville, Owensboro, and Peducah. There is no distinction between equity and law actions in the Kentucky courts. The quarterly courts in the counties handle legal matters that involve no more than $500 judgements, and the circuit courts in the counties have jurisdiction over the more severe cases.

The useful *Guide to Public Vital Statistics Records in Kentucky* (Work Projects Administration, 1942) can be consulted at the Kentucky Department for Libraries and Archives, the University of Kentucky Library, and some other libraries in the state, as well as at a few of the larger genealogical libraries in other states. Other sources for genealogical information in Kentucky are the Kentucky Historical Society, the Kentucky Genealogical Society in Frankfort, and the Ancestral Trails Historical Society in Vine Grove.

Researchers seeking information from county records can locate them at the following county seats: (Adair County) Columbia, (Allen County) Scottsville, (Anderson County) Lawrenceburg, (Ballard County) Wickliffe, (Barren County) Glasgow, (Bath County) Owingsville, (Bell County) Pineville, (Boone County) Burlington, (Bourbon County) Paris, (Boyd County) Catlettsburg, (Boyle County) Danville, (Bracken County) Brooksville, (Breathitt County) Jackson, (Breckinridge County) Hardinsburg, (Bullitt County) Shepherdsville, (Butler County) Morgantown, (Caldwell County) Princeton, (Calloway County) Murray, (Campbell County) Alexandria, (Carlisle County) Bardwell, (Carroll County) Carrollton, (Carter County) Grayson, (Casey County) Liberty, (Christian County) Hopkinsville, (Clark County) Winchester, (Clay County) Manchester, (Clinton County) Albany, (Crittenden County) Marion, (Cumberland County) Burkesville, (Daviess County) Owensboro, (Edmonson County) Brownsville, (Elliott County) Sandy Hook, (Estill County) Irvine, (Fayette County) Lexington, (Fleming County) Flemingsburg, (Floyd County) Prestonsburg, (Franklin County) Frankfort, (Fulton County) Hickman, (Gallatin County) Warsaw, (Garrard County) Lancaster, (Grant County) Williamstown, (Graves County) Mayfield, (Grayson County) Leitchfield, (Green County) Greensburg, and (Greenup County) Greenup.

Also at (Hancock County) Hawesville, (Hardin County) Elizabethtown, (Harlan County) Harlan, (Harrison County) Cynthiana, (Hart County) Munfordville, (Henderson County) Henderson, (Henry County) New Castle, (Hickman County) Clinton, (Hopkins County) Madisonville, (Jackson County) McKee, (Jefferson County) Louisville, (Jessamine County) Nicholasville, (Johnson County) Paintsville, (Kenton County) Independence, (Knott County) Hindman, (Knox County) Barbourville, (Larue County) Hodgenville, (Laurel County) London, (Lawrence County) Louisa, (Lee County) Beattyville, (Leslie County) Hyden, (Letcher County) Whitesburg, (Lewis County) Vanceburg, (Lincoln County) Stanford, (Livingston County) Smithland, (Logan County)

Russellville, (Lyon County) Eddyville, (Madison County) Richmond, (Magoffin County) Salyersville, (Marion County) Lebanon, (Marshall County) Benton, (Martin County) Inez, (Mason County) Maysville, (McCracken County) Paducah, (McCreary County) Whitley City, (McLean County) Calhoun, (Meade County) Brandenburg, (Menifee County) Frenchburg, (Mercer County) Harrodsburg, (Metcalfe County) Edmonton, (Monroe County) Tompkinsville, (Montgomery County) Mt. Sterling, (Morgan County) West Liberty, and (Muhlenburg County) Greenville.

As well as at (Nelson County) Bardstown, (Nicholas County) Carlisle, (Ohio County) Hartford, (Oldham County) La Grange, (Owen County) Owenton, (Owsley County) Booneville, (Pendleton County) Falmouth, (Perry County) Hazard, (Pike County) Pikeville, (Powell County) Stanton, (Pulaski County) Somerset, (Robertson County) Mt. Olivet, (Rockcastle County) Mt. Vernon, (Rowan County) Morehead, (Russell County) Jamestown, (Scott County) Georgetown, (Shelby County) Shelbyville, (Simpson County) Franklin, (Spencer County) Taylorsville, (Taylor County) Campbellsville, (Todd County) Elkton, (Trigg County) Cadiz, (Trimble County) Bedford, (Union County) Morganfield, (Warren County) Bowling Green, (Washington County) Springfield, (Wayne County) Monticello, (Webster County) Dixon, (Whitley County) Williamsburg, (Wolfe County) Campton, and (Woodford County) Versailles.

FOR FURTHER INFORMATION SEE:
- Cox, Mrs. Edgar L., and Thomas W. Westerfield. *Kentucky Family Records*. 19 vols. Owensburg, KY: West Kentucky Family Research Association, 1970–95.
- Fowler, Ila Earle. *Kentucky Pioneers and Their Descendants*. Baltimore, MD: Genealogical Publishing Co., 1967.

Korean Genealogy, known as Chokpo, includes many lengthy pedigrees for elite families. In the past commoners did not record their genealogies and slaves had no names of their own to record. (Slavery was not ended in Korea until 1894.) Interest in tracing family origins and compiling genealogical tables

began in Korea around the 16th century. The purpose was to have records that could be passed down to succeeding generations.

During the Choson Dynasty (1392–1910) Confucian influences from China penetrated all aspects of social life, and the gathering together under one roof of an extended family of two or three generations was considered the ideal. To ensure the continuation of the family lineage, the oldest son was chosen to succeed the father as the head of the family, as dictated by the Confucian stress on the importance of the paternal line. Prior to this, daughters and wives had been just as likely to inherit as were the sons, but now daughters were pushed into the background. In fact a daughter didn't even merit a name any longer before she was betrothed. In the unlikely event that a couple divorced, her name would be immediately expunged from the genealogical record.

At the top of society were the yangban (military and civilian figures) who staffed the Choson Dynasty. They were persons of landed wealth and political power, and were the persons to whom pedigree lines had great significance. Records showing how many people were part of the yangban are scattered, but it has been estimated that during the Choson Dynasty from nine to 16 percent of the population considered themselves to be a part of this elite class. The children of the yangban were given a rigorous and extensive education in the Confucian classics, and the examination system for public office required of every candidate began with his family pedigree, that is, the name and rank of the last three generations of his father's line and the clan home of his mother's line.

According to the regular format, a Chokpo starts with the originator of a family name and continues into its later generations. Each relative within the sphere of kinship is identified by a specific title given to his position within the family. This is more than just a matter of identifying different generations by adding the word great, as in great-great grandfather, or designating the children of an uncle as cousins. The Koreans have specific names to distinguish each generation from the next and each cousin from the others. The designations allow for no confusion as to which relative is being named. Over time the ancestors to be remembered through family rituals became so great in number that it was impossible to conduct rituals for every one of them. Therefore, prominent ancestors, usually high-ranking government officials or scholars of outstanding merit, were selected to be worshipped on a regular basis. These ancestors were regarded as the founders of the family clan.

The recording of entries into a family's genealogical table always followed a given format. A man's name (child name or penname included, if any), his dates of birth and death, government positions occupied, scholarly works in the form of an essay or poem that verified that he passed the high civil examination, and the grave site were clearly written down. Paralleling this were the records of his spouse, including her family name and its place of origin, government positions occupied by her father or grandfather, the dates of her birth and death, and so on. Thus the Chokpo records always contain the history of the family and the records of important historical events and achievements of ancestors who distinguished themselves as officials or scholars. It was through the Chokpo that one could ensure the continuity of one's family into the future — a boundless time line that dates back to a remote past and looks to the immortality of the family.

For the most part, these genealogical records are kept within the family circle and are not open to public inspection. What records do exist that can be viewed are found at the National Library in Seoul, where a researcher can also find materials relating to the development and perpetuation of the Chokpo system in Korea.

L

Labor Union Records can sometimes be obtained from the specific union to which a particular member belonged. Before the development of unions, individual laborers had almost no voice in determining their wages, hours of employment, or working conditions. The competition for jobs forced poor people to work under almost any conditions. Workers formed unions because their bargaining as a group was greater than it could be for unorganized individuals. Labor unions became generally accepted as necessary organizations in the United States during the 1930s, after a series of violent and often bloody struggles to improve working conditions. The National Labor Relations Act of 1933 and other laws made it a requirement for employers to bargain with unions. There are many different unions today, representing many different industries.

Because accurate membership lists are vital to the maintenance of union activity, most unions have many volumes of records that may contain information relevant to a genealogist's research. The researcher, of course, must identify the particular union and local of that union to which person belonged before any search of the records can be made. Many unions are reluctant to release such materials for obvious reasons, but they will permit the researcher to examine bound copies of the union newspapers they publish. These newspapers contain extensive details about the union activities, lists of elected officers, and often obituaries about prominent members. Most such records will be at union local headquarters.

If one's ancestor was an active leader in one of the 19th or 20th century unions, one can often find records relating to that individual in the Archives of Labor at the Walter P. Reuther Library of Wayne State University in Detroit, Michigan. The holdings include records of the American Federation of Labor (AFL); Congress of Industrial Organizations (CIO); Industrial Workers of the World

(IWW); American Federation of State, County, and Municipal Employees; American Federation of Teachers; Newspaper Guild; Union of Farm Workers, and other labor organizations.

Labrador Records *see* **Newfoundland and Labrador Records**

Land Records are of many different types and every genealogical researcher eventually must consult some of them to locate information not obtainable elsewhere. Deed books, for example, can provide a wealth of information by locating individuals on particular pieces of property and thus distinguishing the difference between two persons with the same surname. For someone looking for African American ancestors, the deed books compiled before the Civil War usually contain records of the transfer of ownership of slaves. Yet land records are not the kind of sources that provide names with birthdates and birthplaces, and names of parents, and it may appear somewhat tedious to have to wade through volume after volume of land records in order to find just one bit of information. However, the results will often prove worth the time.

Land records exist from the first permanent settlements in America, and they are usually among the few records that relate to those who occupied these settlements. It is also generally true that the older the records, the more genealogical information (especially concerning relationships) they may contain. This is the opposite of the situation for most other genealogical sources.

The land in each of the 13 original colonies was owned by a group of proprietors who had been granted the land by the English king. The proprietors, in turn, sold this land to individuals, who in turn may have resold it, from time to time, to other individuals. In the course of all these actions, land records were generated.

After the Revolutionary War, Congress opted for a policy of land settlement with the adoption of the Land Ordinance of 1785. This ordinance provided for a survey and the auction of public lands. The government allowed the original 13 colonies to retain the rights to all undistributed land within their own borders. These states, along with Texas and Hawaii, are now called "State Land States." The land in the other areas that the federal government controlled is referred to as public land (or the public domain). These are the parts of the United States acquired by the federal government by treaty or purchase from another government, or by the appropriation of Indian territory. The formerly public lands now constitute the states of Alabama, Alaska, Arizona, Arkansas, California, Colorado, Florida, Idaho, Illinois, Indiana, Iowa, Kansas, Louisiana, Michigan, Minnesota, Mississippi, Missouri, Montana, Nebraska, Nevada, New Mexico, North Dakota, Ohio, Oklahoma, Oregon, South Dakota, Utah, Washington, Wisconsin, and Wyoming.

The first public-domain surveys (1785–88) were in Ohio, and all the land there was then put up for cash sale or for purchase with bounty land warrants. In 1803, the Louisiana Purchase added more than 500 million acres of land to the public domain. In 1812, the U.S. Congress passed its first act for military bounty land in the public domain. Those bounties were situated in special districts in Arkansas, Illinois, and Missouri. Four more acts of this sort were passed between 1847 and 1856, providing for bounty lands first to any veteran of the Mexican War, then to veterans of the various Indian wars, and finally for service in any war since (and including) the Revolution.

The federal government began selling the public domain land in 1785 in 36-section townships (23,040 acres) and in sections (640 acres) for a minimum of $1 per acre, payable within one year. In 1786 the price was raised to $2 per acre and in 1800 the size of a sale tract was reduced to a half section (320 acres). Other acts of Congress changed both the size of tracts and price per acre again and again. At one point the tracts were being sold for as little as 12½ cents per acre.

The records of sales of these public domain lands are in the various National Archives centers. They include Credit Entry File Certificates, Cash Entry Files, Donation Entry Files (for Florida, Oregon, Washington, and

New Mexico), Military Bounty Land Entries, Homestead Entry Papers, and private land claims.

Texas never came under the government's public land policies because of the way the territory was annexed after the war with Mexico. Under its agreement with Congress, the residents of the Republic of Texas assumed responsibility for their own public debts and thus retained control of their public lands. Texas then offered every family that would settle within the boundaries of the republic 120 acres of free land, a highly popular offer. The state soon grew rapidly in population. All the Texas land grants are filed in the Texas Land Office in Austin.

For any land acquisition there were (and still are) three steps that had to be followed, each of which produced a document or documents related to that action. The first was the application or petition to take up a specified portion of land. Such applications would include information about the person's place of residence, length of time lived there, and often the depositions of several neighbors stating that they knew this person for a certain length of time. The appropriate document would include a statement about the basis for obtaining the land, such as paying the purchase price, being promised land for military service, bringing an immigrant into the colony and thus becoming eligible for the headright land bounty (especially used in the South), or being able to produce a government order for a specified amount of land.

Second, a warrant would be issued that certified the right to a specific acreage and authorized an official surveyor to survey it, assuming there were no prior and conflicting claims. The survey would then be conducted to set up the boundaries to the land. These surveys often contain a map of the tract, but these maps may no longer be of much use because surveying in the earlier days was not done as it is now. For example, a boundary may be listed as a water course that has long since dried up; another might be a red oak stump.

The third step was the issuance of a Patent/Grant. This was the government's or proprietor's passing of title to the patentee or grantee. In essence this is the first-title deed, or deed of ownership, and the true beginning of the private ownership of the land. These patents/grants are well documented for all the public domain states and can be found in the appropriate Bureau of Land Management Offices. For the original 13 colonies, Texas, and Hawaii, their land patents/grants are usually found in their state archives or state land offices. All property in the U.S. can be traced back to such a first-title deed.

In the old land records there are often measurements that may not be familiar to the researcher. The most common units are as follows:

Acre: 43,560 square feet, or 160 square rods

Chain: 66 feet or 22 yards (100 links)

Furlong: 660 feet or 220 yards (10 chains)

Link: 7.92 inches (25 links in a rod and 100 links in a chain)

Mile: 5,280 feet (80 chains, 32 rods, or 8 furlongs)

Perch: 5½ yards or 16½ feet, also called a Rod or a Pole

Rood: varies depending on locality from 5½ yards (rod) to 8 yards

Fortunately, most land records are well indexed, both by the names of the grantors (sellers) and names of the grantees (buyers). These names are usually in separate index books, but sometimes the indexes are combined into one. A particular name being looked for can usually be found relatively easily in such indexes unless someone else is the first one named in the document (trustee, guardian, attorney, executor, or other legal agent). In such cases the name first found in the document will be the one listed in the index.

The primary land documents of interest to the genealogist are deeds. These are the documents that transfer the ownership of a piece of property from one person to another. In order to make any transfer legal, the deed must describe the property in such a manner that it will never be confused with another piece of property. Thus, in the case of public lands, the description on a deed will list the amount of land and the section, township, and range in which the property is located. It will also include a description of the natural features of the property such as the name of a creek or road, as well as the names of neighbors. When the land is being resold, it will likely list the name of the former owner. A deed may also state that the land was granted by the state or federal government in exchange for a patent or warrant. Whatever wording is used, the land will be fully described.

Most early Americans were farmers who left few records other than deeds. Their names didn't make newspaper headlines and they participated only marginally in town and county politics. However, most of them owned property in the form of houses and farms. Even when they were store owners, doctors, lawyers, or local pastors, they usually owned some property that left a record in the deed books. Frequently this is the only record that can locate an individual at a particular place and time. Thus deed records are of vital interest to any genealogist.

There are many types of deeds—trust deeds, deeds of division, gift deeds, deeds of release, quitclaim deeds, and many more. These distinctions are important to lawyers, but are not of much use to genealogists. A similar type of document in its format is the lease, an agreement that creates a landlord-tenant relationship. One major difference between the two is that a lease usually specifies the duration of the agreement. Legally such an instrument is referred to as leasehold or as an estate for years.

A mortgage, again, is much like a deed in form. However, it is a conditional transfer of legal title as security for the payment of a debt. When the conditions listed in the document are met (the debt is paid), the mortgage terms become void.

Tax records are also a part of land records, and have long been recognized as important genealogical sources. Whenever early census schedules have been lost or destroyed by fire, tax lists have been used as substitutes. Some tax lists have been published and others have been microfilmed. They can be consulted in various genealogical libraries. One can often follow a family through several generations by consulting

the tax lists alone. *See also* **Bounty Land Warrants; Deeds; Homestead Act; Public Domain Lands; Tax and Real Estate Records.**

Latin American Genealogy *see* **Argentine Genealogy; Bolivian Genealogy; Brazilian Genealogy; Central American Genealogy; Chilean Genealogy; Colombian Genealogy; Ecuadorian Genealogy; Mexican Genealogy; Paraguayan Genealogy; Peruvian Genealogy; Uruguayan Genealogy; Venezuelan Genealogy**

Latvia *see* **Baltic Region Genealogy**

Lease *see* **Land Records**

Legal Records *see* **Court Records**

Letters *see* **Correspondence; Memoirs, Diaries, and Family Letters**

Liberia *see* **African Genealogy**

Libraries, Genealogical, are vital resources to those working in family history and family pedigrees. Some, such as the National Archives in Washington, D.C., Family History Library of the Church of Jesus Christ of Latter-day Saints in Salt Lake City, and the Library of Congress, also in Washington, have vast collections of primary records, both originals and on microfilm. Many libraries in the United States also have large and important collections of books, manuscripts, and printed materials relating to genealogical interests. Many of them also have local or regional manuscripts, maps, and newspaper collections and documents from federal and state governments. Regardless of the size of their collections, all these libraries are worth a visit. One website lists more than 1,000 libraries of this sort, without including any of the university or college libraries that also have both large and small collections of genealogical books. And, of course, there are libraries all over the world with fine national collections of historical and genealogical materials.

The major libraries have enough material to keep researchers busy for weeks or even months. Room prevents the listing of all those with genealogical records in the U.S., but some of the best are:

Allen County Public Library, Fort Wayne, IN

American Antiquarian Society Library, Worcester, MA

Bancroft Library at the University of California, Berkeley, CA

Boston Public Library, Boston, MA

California State Library (Sutro Branch), San Francisco, CA

Connecticut State Library, Hartford, CT

DAR Library, Washington, D.C.

Denver Public Library, Denver, CO

Detroit Public Library, Detroit, Ml

Historical Society of Pennsylvania Library, Philadelphia, PA

Holland Society of New York Library, New York City, NY

Indiana State Library, Indianapolis, IN

Long Island Historical Society Library, Brooklyn, NY

Los Angeles Public Library, Los Angeles, CA

Maryland Historical Society Library, Baltimore, MD

Mid-Continent Public Library, Independence, MO

National Genealogical Society Library, Arlington, VA

New England Historic Genealogical Society Library, Boston, MA

New York Public Library, New York City, NY

New York State Library, Albany, NY

Newberry Library, Chicago, IL

Seattle Public Library, Seattle, WA

St. Louis Public Library, St. Louis, MO

Western Reserve Historical Society Library, Cleveland, OH

Wisconsin Historical Society Library, Madison, WI

See also **Daughters of the American Revolution Records; Family History Centers; Library of Congress; and National Archives and Records Administration.**

Library of Congress, often referred to as the largest library in the world, is the nation's oldest federal cultural institution. It contains more than 120 million items resting on approximately 532 miles of bookshelves. The collections include more than 18 million books, 2.5 million recordings, 12 million photographs, and 54 million manuscripts. Among these resources is a large collection of books and resource materials related to genealogy.

The geography and map division provides direct access to almost four million maps, 51,000 atlases, 8,000 reference works, and a large number of related materials in other formats. This is an unrivaled cartographic and historic record of America's urban settlement and growth over more than a century. The atlas collection includes representative volumes of all significant publishers of atlases over the past five centuries. These atlases cover individual continents, countries, states, counties, cities, and other geographic regions. They range in scope from the general to the topical. Among the many county maps and city and town plans are some 700,000 large-scale Sanborn fire insurance maps.

The library simultaneously serves as a legislative library and as the major research arm of the U.S. Congress, the copyright agency of the United States, a center for scholarship that collects research materials in more than 450 languages from all over the world, and a public institution that is open to everyone over high school age. Its books can only be used on the premises.

After its founding in 1800, the library was first housed in a boarding house and later in the Capitol building. Its first permanent building — now called the Thomas Jefferson Building — was opened in 1897. The John Adams Building was completed in 1939, and the James Madison Memorial Building in 1980. In late 1851 the library suffered a serious fire that destroyed about two-thirds of its 55,000 volumes, but by the end of 1901 these books had been restored and the Library of Congress had become the first American library to reach the goal of housing one million volumes. Since then its collections have grown to an enormous size.

The Library of Congress maintains a Website where viewers can access its online library catalog. A brochure about the library's local history and genealogy collection can be obtained by writing to that section of the library, in care of the Library of Congress. There is also a useful guide, *The Library of Congress: A Guide to Genealogical and Historical Research* (Salt Lake City, UT: Ancestry Pub., 1990).

Lineage Societies based on one's descent from veterans of various wars, from pioneers, from specific trades, or from other groups are popular organizations for persons with a genealogical interest. One of the best known of these is the Daughters of the American Revolution (DAR), with branches located in many cities throughout the country. There are hundreds of others in the United States, including such groups as the Society of the Descendants of the Signers of the Constitution; National Society of the Sons of Colonial New England; Military Society of the War of 1812; Welsh Society of Philadelphia, and the Society of Descendants of the Alamo. According to the *Heredity Society Blue Book*, the first lineage society in America was established as early as 1637. This was the Ancient and Honorable Artillery Company of Massachusetts.

Some of these American lineage societies focus on ancestors who were notable long before the American colonies were established. Therefore, those who wish to join such a lineage group have to trace their ancestry back to qualifying ancestors in the old country (called the "gateway" ancestors), often one who was a part of British royalty or nobility. One such society is the Order of the Crown of Charlemagne in the United States of America. This organization requires documented proof of descent from that early emperor. Other ancestral groups of this type include those of royal descent (the Order of the Crown in America) and those who trace their ancestry back to one of the Crusaders (the Military Order of the Crusades). There is even a lineage society for the descendents of the illegitimate sons and daughters of the kings of Britain that has extremely strict standards of proof to obtain membership.

Among the societies for descendents of earliest settlers in America is the Order of Descendants of Ancient Planters. The term "ancient" is here applied to those persons who arrived in Virginia before 1616, remained for three years, paid their passage, and survived the massacre of 1622. This society lists only about 150 known, qualifying planters. Then there are societies for the descendants of persons who arrived on a specific ship. Two of these include the Welcome Society of Pennsylvania for those who arrived on the ship *Welcome* in 1682 and other ships up to the end of 1682, and the Society of the Ark and the Dove for those arriving on ships in Maryland in 1634.

Lineage societies such as the DAR have been in the forefront in developing interest in American genealogy and family history. They are devoted to accurate and well-documented lineages, and as such, serve as examples to all family historians. Many of these societies publish books listing the lineages of their members back to the qualifying ancestor. Such books can be found in most major genealogical libraries. Some examples are the *National Society of the Colonial Daughters of the Seventeenth Century, Lineage Book* series; *Mayflower Families Through Five Generations* series; *The Order of Founders and Patriots of America Registers*; and *Lineages of Members of the National Society of the Sons and Daughters of the Pilgrims*.

Because membership in any lineage society requires documented records of descent from a specific individual whose presence or action qualifies his descendants for membership, there is significant genealogical information contained in the application papers that have been filled out for membership in a lineage society. But a few of the societies have restrictions on releasing application papers. For example, to obtain such papers from the Daughters of the American Revolution, one must be a prospective member.

Most lineage societies are small organizations run by volunteers. Often their addresses may change with the officers. However, they are usually willing to help any genealogical researcher because they presume that the researcher might be interested in membership. Yet some societies are open by invitation only. *See also* **Daughters of the American Revolution Records; Mayflower Descendants; Sons of the American Revolution; Society of the Cincinnati.**

Lithuania *see* **Baltic Region Genealogy**

Louisiana Records begin in 1714 when Louis Juchereau de St. Denis, a French trader, established Natchitoches on the banks of the Red River. This settlement became the first permanent town in Louisiana. In 1718 the French governor of Louisiana began building the town of New Orleans. This became the capital of the region in 1722. Before the French came to this region, the area had been the home to about 30 different Indian tribes, including the Atakapa, Caddo, Chitimacha, and Tunica. They lived mainly in villages along the banks of Louisiana's rivers and bayous.

The United States purchased Louisiana from the French in 1803 as part of the Louisiana Purchase, and on April 30, 1812, what was then called the Orleans Territory became the 18th state of the Union. The British tried to capture New Orleans during the War of 1812, but were defeated at the Battle of New Orleans in 1815. Today the influence of the early French settlers remains in the various Cajun communities located in the southern part of the state.

The first census of the Orleans Territory was conducted during the national census of 1810, and every 10 years thereafter there have been national censuses conducted in this state. They can be seen at the various National Archives locations. Louisiana itself, however, has never conducted a separate state census. There was no state-wide registration of births until 1914, although there are birth records for the city of New Orleans as early as 1790 and death records for that city from 1803. These vital records are available for view at the Louisiana State Archives if they are over a hundred years old for births and over 50 years old for deaths. Copies of these records can be obtained for a small fee. Later records of births and deaths are available from some of the individual parishes (counties) where the events occurred. Marriage records are available from 1870 to 1946 for Orleans Parish, but certified copies of other marriages or divorces must be obtained from the clerks of the district courts in the parishes where the marriage license was issued. Current vital records may also be obtained through the Louisiana Department of Health and Hospitals in Baton Rouge. Guardianship records, which in Louisiana are called tutorships, are available from the district courts of the various parishes, and in Orleans Parish from the civil district court.

In 1942 the Work Projects Administration published two guides to the vital statistics of Louisiana that can be found in the Louisiana State Library, New Orleans Public Library, and some genealogical libraries elsewhere in the United States. These are the *Guide to Public Vital Statistics Records in Louisiana* and the *Guide to Vital Statistics Records in Church Archives in Louisiana*.

There has never been any distinction between law and equity actions in Louisiana, and the district courts in all the parishes have jurisdiction over such actions. The clerk of the court in the various parishes maintains the records of all mortgages and title conveyances. Immigration records, such as the ship passenger lists of those who arrived in New Orleans, can be found at the National Archives in Washington, D.C.

The New Orleans Public Library has a fine collection of Louisiana cemetery records, census records, church records, land records, military records, newspapers, and books relating to genealogy. The New Orleans City Archives, which are located in the same library building, also has marriage, probate, cemetery, census, naturalization, emancipation, hospital, court, and voter records for the city of New Orleans.

Researchers seeking information from parish records can locate them at the following parish seats: (Acadia Parish) Crowley, (Allen Parish) Oberlin, (Ascension Parish) Donaldsonville, (Assumption Parish) Napoleonville, (Avoyelles Parish) Marksville, (Beauregard Parish) De Ridder, (Bienville Parish) Arcadia, (Bossier Parish) Benton, (Caddo Parish) Shreveport, (Calcasieu Parish) Lake Charles, (Caldwell Parish) Columbia, (Cameron Parish) Cameron, (Catahoula Parish) Harrisonburg, (Claiborne Parish) Homer, (Concordia Parish) Vidalia, (De Soto Parish) Mansfield, (East Baton Rouge Parish) Baton Rouge, (East Carroll Parish) Lake Providence, (East Feliciana Parish) Clinton, (Evangeline

Parish) Ville Platte, (Franklin Parish) Winnsboro, (Grant Parish) Colfax, (Iberia Parish) New Iberia, (Iberville Parish) Plaquemine, (Jackson Parish) Jonesboro, (Jefferson Parish) Gretna, (Jefferson Davis Parish) Jennings, (La Salle Parish) Jena, (Lafayette Parish) Lafayette, (Lafourche Parish) Thibodaux, (Lincoln Parish) Ruston, and (Livingston Parish) Livingston.

Also at (Madison Parish) Tallulah, (Morehouse Parish) Bastrop, (Natchitoches Parish) Natchitoches, (Orleans Parish) New Orleans, (Ouachita Parish) Monroe, (Plaquemines Parish) Pointe a la Hache, (Pointe Coupee Parish) New Roads, (Rapides Parish) Alexandria, (Red River Parish) Coushatta, (Richland Parish) Rayville, (Sabine Parish) Many, (St. Bernard Parish) Chalmette, (St. Charles Parish) Hahnville, (St. Helena Parish) Greensburg, (St. James Parish) Convent, (St. John the Baptist Parish) Edgard, (St. Landry Parish) Opelousas, (St. Martin Parish) St. Martinville, (St. Mary Parish) Franklin, (St. Tammany Parish) Covington, (Tangipahoa Parish) Amite, (Tensas Parish) St. Joseph, (Terrebonne Parish) Houma, (Union Parish) Farmerville, (Vermilion Parish) Abbeville, (Vernon Parish) Leesville, (Washington Parish) Franklinton, (Webster Parish) Minden, (West Baton Rouge Parish) Port Allen, (West Carroll Parish) Oak Grove, (West Feliciana Parish) St. Francisville, and (Winn Parish) Winnfield.

For further information see:
• Boling, Yvette G. *A Guide to Printed Sources for Genealogical and Historical Research in the Louisiana Parishes.* Jefferson, LA: The author, 1985.
• *Dictionary of Louisiana Biography.* 2 vols. New Orleans, LA: Louisiana Historical Association, 1988.

Loyalists *see* **Military Records; New Brunswick Records; Ontario Records**

Lutheran Records can be found in various libraries and archives in the United States and elsewhere, as well as in the files of local congregations. The Lutherans compose the largest Protestant church in the world and the majority of the members live in traditionally Lutheran countries of central and northern Europe. They were among the earliest settlers in the American colonies, primarily settling in New York and Pennsylvania. In the 1800s many Lutherans came from Germany, Norway, and Sweden and established churches in the Midwest and upper Midwest. Although there are a number of different branches of Lutheranism, some with bishops and some insisting on the sovereignty of the local congregations, most of the Lutherans in the United States belong to one of the three major synods: the Evangelical Lutheran Church of America (ELCA); the Wisconsin Evangelical Lutheran Synod; or the Lutheran Church—Missouri Synod. The Lutheran World Federation (LWF), based in Geneva, coordinates the activities of almost all the various Lutheran churches in the world. It oversees ecumenical relations, theological studies, and world service and is guided by an international executive committee.

For the most part, the Lutheran records in America are preserved by local congregations of the churches and include a register of member families, lists of communicants, lists of confirmations, and lists of marriages, baptisms, and deaths. Other parish records include annual congregational and council meeting minutes, financial and legal documents, parish newsletters or other printed items, including congregational histories, as well as similar records for various congregational organizations, such as women's, men's or youth groups. No centralized lists of members exist in churchwide or synodical archives.

There are, however, several Lutheran archives in which the records of various congregations exist on microfilm and are available to researchers. One of these is Evangelical Lutheran Church of America (ELCA) Archives in Chicago. The Lutheran Church—Missouri Synod has its historical archives in St. Louis. There is also an ELCA Lutheran Historical Society in Gettysburg, Pennsylvania, and a collection of archive materials at the Pacific Lutheran University in Tacoma, Washington.

M

Mailing Lists *see* **Genealogical Mailing Lists and Newsgroups**

Maine Records begin around 1677 when the Massachusetts Bay Colony purchased title to the area from Fernando Gorges, one of two persons who had been given a large tract of land between the Merrimac and Kennebec rivers by the English government. The tract included present day Maine and New Hampshire. Massachusetts, in 1693, designated Maine as York(shire) county and then, in 1760, this county was divided into three counties. Maine at that time was primarily a source of furs, timber, and forest products. During the American Revolution the British established a base near present-day Castine on Penobscot Bay. The Massachusetts attempt to expel the British proved to be a failure.

After the Revolution, a movement began to separate Maine from Massachusetts. It did not pick up momentum until 1816, when persons who favored separation began to win election to the Massachusetts legislature. In 1819, the Massachusetts General Court agreed to an Act of Separation and a state constitutional convention was held in Portland. Maine was admitted to the Union as the 23rd state in 1820. By the time Maine won independence, about half its total land area had been distributed; much of the remainder was still unsurveyed. There was a great deal of disagreement about the boundary separating Maine from the Canadian province of New Brunswick, and this was not resolved until 1842.

The first census that included Maine was the 1790 census of Massachusetts. Maine was also included with Massachusetts in the 1800 and 1810 censuses, but from the 1820 census onward it was enumerated in the national census as the state of Maine. These census records can be seen at any of the National Archives locations throughout the United States. There was also a state census of Maine in 1837, only fragments of which have survived. The parts for Bangor, Portland, and some unincorporated towns can be found in the Maine Archives in Augusta. The part for the town of Eliot is at the Maine Historical Society in Portland.

The Maine Historical Society Library is a research facility in which materials must be used on site. The library has a good collection of books, manuscripts, microfilms, newspapers, maps, and other materials related to the genealogy of Maine. The Maine Historical Society also has an index to the vital records of Maine up to the year 1892, listed under the name of each town. It covers 80 towns in the state. The society has published records for 17 of these towns, each volume named after the town, which can be found in various libraries throughout the state as well as in many genealogical libraries elsewhere.

An index of Maine marriages from 1895 to 1996 (1967 to 1976 missing) is located at the Maine Vital Records Office in Augusta. Death records for 1960 to 1996 are also available from the Vital Records Office, as are divorce records since 1892. Copies of these records can be obtained for a small fee. For births, marriages, and deaths prior to 1892 contact the town clerk where the birth, marriage, or death occurred. Prior to 1892, however, there was no requirement for these events to be recorded, and many were not.

Probate and guardianship records can be found in the county probate courts, while land records are with the register of deeds in each county except for those of Aroostook and Oxford counties. In Aroostock County there is a northern registry district at Fort Kent and a southern registry district at Houlton. In Oxford County there is a western registry district at Fryeburg and an eastern registry district at South Paris. Finally, the records of immigration from the ports at Portland and nearby Falmouth can be found in the National Archives in Washington, D.C.

One other source for extensive genealogical materials in Maine is the Maine State

Library, which is located in the same building as the State Archives in Augusta.

Researchers seeking information from county records can locate them at the following county seats: (Androscoggin County) Auburn, (Aroostook County) Houlton, (Cumberland County) Portland, (Franklin County) Farmington, (Hancock County) Ellsworth, (Kennebec County) Augusta, (Knox County) Rockland, (Lincoln County) Wiscasset, (Oxford County) South Paris, (Penobscot County) Bangor, (Piscataquis Dover-Foxcroft, (Sagadahoc County) Bath, (Somerset County) Skowhegan, (Waldo County) Belfast, (Washington County) Machias, and (York County) Alfred.

FOR FURTHER INFORMATION SEE:
- Burrage, Henry Sweetser. *Genealogical and Family History of the State of Maine.* 4 vols. New York: Lewis Historical Publishing Company, 1909.
- Frost, John Eldridge. *Maine Genealogy: A Bibliographical Guide.* Portland, ME: Maine Historical Society, 1985.

Manitoba Records, at least the earliest ones, are closely related to those of the Hudson's Bay Company that was granted trading rights in the region in 1670 by King Charles II of England. At that time five Indian tribes lived there: the Chipewyans, the Woods Cree, the Plains Cree, the Assiniboin, and the Chippawa. The first English explorer to enter the region was Sir Thomas Burton, who sailed down the west coast of Hudson Bay in 1612.

The Hudson's Bay Company initially sent Henry Kelsey into Manitoba, then called Rupert's Land, to find new sources for fur. Kelsey persuaded many of the Indians to bring furs to the company trading posts that he established. In 1811, Thomas Douglas, the Earl of Selkirk, obtained a land grant from the Hudson's Bay Company and sent several groups of Scottish Highlanders and Irishmen into the area to begin a farming and fur-trapping community that was called the Red River Colony. The records of the members of this colony are in the Hudson's Bay Company Archives in Winnipeg. Manitoba became Canada's fifth province in 1870. By 1876 the resident farmers were exporting wheat to other parts of Canada.

The Hudson's Bay Company Archives, which are located in the Archives of Manitoba at Winnipeg, include the genealogical records of most of the individuals who worked for the Hudson's Bay Company as well as its fur-trading rival, the North West Company. In many cases these genealogical records contain the parish of origin or place of birth for each individual; the positions, posts, and districts in which the individuals served; and some family information and references to photographs or drawings of the individuals. There are also 3,500 log books of the various ships that from 1750 up to the 1970s transported people across the ocean and across Hudson Bay into Manitoba. These log books include the names of the ships and areas of service, lists of the commanders or masters, and the records and photographs of the various vessels. There are also histories of the various trading posts that were established by the Hudson's Bay Company, as well as lists of the post managers.

One set of records in the Hudson's Bay Archives includes the immigration list of those who came to Manitoba on the *Prince of Wales* in 1813. This ship left from Stromness, Orkney, Scotland on June 28 and arrived two months later at York Factory on the western shore of Hudson Bay. After several years of great difficulty and violence in which the North West Company tried to force the settlers to leave because they were interfering with the company's fur-trading operations, many of these early settlers departed Canada to move to Iowa, Illinois, Nebraska, and other parts of the United States.

Manitoba is divided into five judicial districts that hold the probate records, bills of sale, and chattel mortgages. The Eastern Judicial District is located at Winnipeg, the Central Judicial District at Portage la Prairie, the Western Judicial District at Brandon, the Dauphin Judicial District at Dauphin, and the Northern Judicial District at The Pas. A child in Manitoba can be disinherited by not being named in a will. Manitoba land records are in separate land registration districts located at Boissevain, Brandon, Carman,

Dauphin, Morden, Neepawa, Portage la Prairie, and Winnipeg.

The Vital Statistics Branch of the Department of Health in Winnipeg has the records of births, marriages, deaths, adoptions, and divorces that have taken place since 1882. Prior to Manitoba becoming a Canadian province in 1870, there were censuses taken that show the heads of families in 1832, 1834, 1835, 1840, 1843, 1846, and 1849.

The Archives of Manitoba has published a *Guide to Family and Community History* that is available there for researchers, as well as a *Guide to Government Records in the Archives*. Both publications provide keys to the archive resources that may be useful in genealogical research, including provincial court records, land records, educational records, and municipal records. A *Freedom of Information and Protection of Privacy Act — Access and Privacy Directory* identifies the full range of active and archival records created by Manitoba government departments and Crown agencies. The directory is published in English and French and is available for consultation at the Archives of Manitoba and in various public libraries throughout the Province.

At the Archives of Manitoba can be found the records and registries of all births, deaths, marriages, and stillbirths that have taken place in Manitoba. Citizens of Manitoba or their representatives (lawyers, for example) can obtain certificates or certified copies of these records by applying to the archives' administration. The archives also has microfilm census records and many other types of government documents. *See also* **Census, Canadian**.

Maps are an essential part of genealogical research because they are often the one source needed to complete a family tree. Maps can provide clues as to where particular ancestors may have lived and thus where to look for written records about them. Maps may also suggest a particular pattern of settlement and migration, thus completely ruling out others. For example, a range of mountains may present a barrier to further migration while a river can often be an aid to the traveler.

Old maps are particularly useful because the names of many towns, counties, cities, and even countries may have experienced name changes over the years. The names of these places will be found on an old map and the location of others may be found in lists of abandoned post offices, local histories, government records, microfilm records, clippings from old newspapers, old city directories, or old county atlases kept in the library archives of a town, city, or county in the region. A plat book in a town hall or county courthouse or an old fire insurance map may even show the outline of an ancestor's house and its placement on the property.

Changes in place names are not the only challenge. The boundaries of many political jurisdictions where ancestors once lived have probably changed one or more times over the years. Some American families lived in the same place for hundreds of years, yet the names of the area in which their homes were located may have moved back and forth a number of times between different political jurisdictions — towns, provinces, states, or, in a few cases, even countries. This can greatly complicate one's research. In one known case, the place where a family lived for the entire 19th century was at various times part of seven different counties.

In the United States and many other countries, birth, death, property, and some other kinds of records are normally kept by the various county governments. If one can determine the place where an ancestor lived, then the new and old maps of that place will probably reveal the county seat where data about that person can be found. In the case of an 1820 marriage record from Tennessee, for example, the county name at that time may be different from what it is now and the records of that marriage will be in the county that had jurisdiction over the area at that time.

Similar but even more complex problems arise when one tries to find personal records in the archives of faraway lands. The names and boundaries of countries sometimes appear to be constantly in flux, and many public and private record centers disappear or move from place to place.

Various kinds of maps can be found at local, state, or regional libraries, museums, or historical archives. Most local librarians can help the researcher learn how to access the rich holdings of the U.S. Geological Survey (USGS), the National Archives, and the Library of Congress, as well as to international sources for maps and other resources needed by genealogists. The best maps for genealogical purposes show in great detail the areas surrounding where specific people once lived, the exact location within a county or other jurisdiction, and the names and borders of neighboring areas.

Any map, of course, is a representation of a geographical area, although it may be designed in many different ways, from a traditional map printed on paper to a digital map built out of pixels on a computer screen. Depending on the purpose for which it is designed, a map can show anything from the electricity supply grid of an area to the terrain in the Himalayan Mountains or the depths of the ocean floor. Maps can also be drawn in many different styles, each showing different faces of the same subject, thus allowing the researcher to visualize the world in a convenient and informative way.

The size of a map in relation to the Earth is called its scale. This is usually stated as a fraction or ratio. For example, a scale of 1/10,000 means that one centimeter on the map is equivalent to 10,000 centimeters on the ground. As a ratio, this scale would be shown as 1:10,000. Usually there will be a legend at the top or bottom of any map indicating the scale used by the designer of the map.

More than 55,000 large-scale and topographic maps are published and updated on a regular basis by the USGS. The ones for the United States and its territories are scaled at 1:24,000, 1:25,000, 1:20,000 for Puerto Rico, and 1:63,360 for the 2,400 maps of Alaska. Each map names and shows in fairly rich detail every settled area and other features within the map's boundaries. To cover the state of Virginia in maps scaled at 1:24,000 requires approximately 800 separate sheets. The USGS publishes an *Index to Topographic and Other Map Coverage* and a *Catalog of Topographic and other Published Maps*. The maps can be purchased from the United States Geological Survey in Reston, Virginia, as well as through local map dealers.

When a group of maps is printed in book form, the volume is called an atlas. Gazetteers are books that list geographical names in alphabetical order. There are many different editions of both kinds of such books that can be helpful to any genealogist. Among the atlases, some of the best are the five-volume *Historical Atlas and Chronology of County Boundaries 1788–1980* (Boston: G.K. Hall, 1984); *A Genealogical and Historical Atlas of the United States of America* (Logan, UT: Everton, 1976); the *Atlas of American History* (New York: Scribner's, 1943); and the *Rand-McNally Commercial Atlas and Marketing Guide* that is revised annually and published in Chicago. It shows geographical locations in every state as they exist today, and can be found in most libraries of medium size and larger.

Some of the leading gazetteers include the *Chambers World Gazetteer: A–Z of Geographical Information* (New York: Chambers/Cambridge, 1988); and the *Columbia Lippincott Gazetteer of the World* (New York: Columbia University Press, 1962); as well as Sealocks' and Powell's *Bibliography of Place-Name Literature, United States and Canada* (Chicago: American Library Association, 1982); and *Webster's New Geographical Dictionary* (Springfield, MA: G. & C. Merriam, 1999).

For a comprehensive reference to county changes in the United States beginning with the 1790 census, one can refer to William Thorndale and William Dollarhide's *Map Guide to the U.S. Federal Censuses, 1790–1920* (Baltimore, MD: Genealogical Pub. Co., 1988). This 445-page book shows all U.S. county boundaries from 1790 to 1920. On each of the nearly 400 maps, old county lines are superimposed over modern ones to highlight the boundary changes made in 10-year intervals. Two fine map catalogs include *The Map Catalog* (New York: Random House, 1990); and *Map Collections in the United States and Canada: A Directory* (New York: Special Libraries Assoc., 1984).

Finally one can write to the Geographic Names Center of the United States Geological Survey in Reston, Virginia, for information on place name changes. The center maintains a database of more than two million entries called the Geographic Names Information System (GNIS). This free service provides the names of places that no longer exist, as well as variant names for existing places.

Marine Corps Records *see* **Military Records**

Marriage Records in the United States are generally recorded by county or town officials and are preserved in local archives, although copies can be stored in statewide archives as well. However, many marriage returns were never submitted to the civil authorities, and it is estimated that some 30 percent of those that were submitted are incomplete. Marriages also can be recorded and kept by churches, ministers, military personnel, and sometimes even by colonial governments. Family records such as Bibles, diaries, journals, and personal histories often include marriage documents or references to marriages.

An exact marriage date can be found on the certificate of marriage or on the duplicate copy that was given to a couple when they presented their license and were married (often found among family papers). Perhaps an even more valuable source for the genealogist is the original application for a marriage license. Together, the certificate and application will likely contain the names of parents, dates and places of birth for both the bride and the groom, relatives who appeared as witnesses or bondsmen, places of residence, and clues as to religious affiliations. The religious affiliation could lead to church records of children, burial records of other family members, and other information.

A genealogist can usually obtain a copy of the original marriage certificate by writing to the vital records office in the state where the couple was married. Earlier marriage records may have been compiled and printed in book form, and such volumes can usually be found in the larger genealogical libraries. For example, the book *35,000 Tennessee Marriage Records and Bonds 1783–1870* contains the marriage bonds and marriage records that can be found on index cards at the Tennessee State Library and Archives in Nashville. The records are listed alphabetically and cover the period 1783 to about 1870.

When a researcher has no idea of where a marriage might have occurred, the first place to look for such information is probably in a family Bible. When vital statistics are recorded in Bibles, they usually include the family members' marriage places. In looking at Bible records, the researcher should check under both the maiden name and married name. Often family members no longer have any Bibles containing family records because they have been discarded or donated to a local genealogical society. The researcher might be wise, then, to contact the local society to see if it has such a Bible. The DAR Library in Washington, D.C. also has a series of transcribed Bible records that might be consulted.

Marriage dates may be found in a many places besides the actual marriage certificate. Sometimes they are recorded in newspapers, in various court records, and in private collections of family papers. Applications for marriage licenses, which were instituted in the mid–1800s, can provide useful information not found on any marriage license. Modern ones, for example, will list family relationships, ages, residences, and the fact that a couple is free of disease.

Another source of marriage information is the consent affidavits that deal with transcripts of permissions slips given to a licensing authority at the time a couple intends to be married, or when bonds are posted, banns published, or licenses issued. Usually such permissions must be obtained by underage persons who want to be married. The consent affidavits are a good source for identifying parents, proving whether the parents are deceased or living, determining relationships of guardians to marriage partners, and indicating the ages of the couple.

Declarations of intent to marry are often required before the ceremony can be performed. These are filed and recorded with the county or town clerks. It was an ecclesiastical practice during the 17th and 18th centuries in almost every state to have persons intending marriage post a bann. This posting gave people in the area an opportunity to step forward and submit any reason why the marriage should not take place. Bonds were usually paid by a father, brother, or some other relative of the bride, and they had to be posted before a license could be issued.

In order to protect the property of a wife and sometimes even a husband, a couple might enact a marriage contract, often known as an antenuptial or prenuptial agreement. This is frequently done between well-to-do individuals to protect their individual interests in the property that each possesses at the time of the marriage. Such agreements are generally made prior to a second marriage and are often enacted to secure certain properties for the children of former unions, although this is not always the case. Many relationships have been determined by genealogists using these records in unison with probate records, since the marriage contract does not necessarily provide proof that the marriage took place.

Divorce, or the legal ending of a marriage, can only be granted by the county courts that have control over equity matters. This is also where the records are kept after a divorce is granted. If the couple seeking a divorce have children, their names and ages can be found in these records. The dates of birth (or ages) of both the wife and the husband, the state or country of their births, the place and date of their marriage, and the date and grounds for the divorce itself will also be found in these documents. Experts estimate that about 35 percent of all U.S. marriages end in divorce. *See also* **Daughters of the American Revolution Records; Marriage Records; Vital Records.**

Maryland Records, in most cases, can be found at the Maryland State Archives in Annapolis. This state was one of the original 13; it formally adopted statehood in 1788 and was the seventh one to ratify the Constitution. Prior to that the area had been chartered to

Lord Baltimore, in 1632, by the English King Charles I. Under Lord Baltimore's leadership, Maryland passed a religious toleration act in 1649, one of the first colonies in America to do so. In 1774 some Marylanders burned the ship *Peggy Stewart* and its cargo of tea in protest against the English Port Bill. Then in 1776 its citizens declared their independence from England. Almost a hundred years later, in 1864, they adopted a constitution that abolished slavery.

The first census enumeration in this state was that of the 1790 national census, and these census enumerations have continued every 10 years since. They can be seen at the various National Archives locations. There have been no separate censuses instituted by the state alone. The mortality schedules for 1850 through 1880 can be found in the Maryland State Library at Baltimore.

The first act in Maryland for the recording of births, marriages, and burials was passed in 1650 (revised in 1654, 1658, 1678, and 1692). County clerks were required to record these events in their registers. The 1678 act exempted blacks, Indians, and mulattos, but after the 1692 act, their vital events were recorded if their mothers were white women. A 1695 law, revised in 1696, transferred the recording of vital records to the vestries of the Protestant Episcopal parishes in the colony. For a short time afterwards, the clerks of the county courts continued to register burials concurrently with the clerks of the vestries. By the early 1700s, the registration of all burials, regardless of a person's denomination, was the sole responsibility of the Protestant Episcopal Church. The 1695 law regarding the recording of records lost its effect in 1776 when Maryland enacted its first constitution. Most churches, however, continued the practice of registering burials though the 19th century and into the 20th.

The extant parish registers, available at the Maryland State Archives, constitute the official marriage records during most of the colonial period. The archives also holds other church records for many churches in Maryland. At the Hall of Records in Annapolis there are indexes for all births occurring between 1801 to 1877, and for deaths from 1865 to 1880 for Anne Arundel County. The Hall of Records also has some death records for the 1600s from Charles, Kent, Somerset, and Talbot counties. There is a card index to pre–Revolutionary marriages in Charles, Kent, and Somerset counties and later marriages in Anne Arundel, Caroline, Cecil, Dorchester, Frederick, and Prince George's counties, as well as a separate index for Baltimore County marriages.

In 1910 the Maryland General Assembly created the Bureau of Vital Statistics as an agency under the State Department of Health. It was given the responsibility for supervising the registration of births and deaths in Maryland. From 1914 to 1940 the Bureau of Vital Statistics maintained one series of marriage certificates for the counties and another series for the city of Baltimore. In 1941, the bureau began filing the Baltimore certificates with those of the counties, thus creating a single series of records. Unfortunately for researchers, the bureau did not begin indexing the certificates until 1951, when the General Assembly authorized it to provide certified copies of all marriages performed after June 1, 1951. Also in 1951, the bureau was given its current name, the Division of Vital Records.

The Division of Vital Records in Baltimore has the birth and death records since August, 1898, and those for the city of Baltimore since January, 1875. There is an index for the Baltimore City births from 1875 to 1941, and an index for births elsewhere in the state from 1875 through 1950. The early index (1875–1919) is arranged alphabetically by the surname of the child, or by the parents' surname if the child's name is not given. The index provides the child's name, the names of the parents, the date of birth, and the county in which the birth occurred. The later index (1920–1950) is in Soundex order by the surname of the child. Actual copies of the birth certificates, however, are available only for persons born more than 100 years ago. They can be obtained for a small fee. The Maryland State Archives holds card indexes to the earlier birth records and for some church records.

The Division of Vital Records has marriage records since June 1951. Earlier ones can be located in the circuit courts of the counties where the marriages took place, and in the Baltimore Court of Common Pleas for those of the city of Baltimore. A 1664 law prohibited marriages between white women and black men. This act remained in effect for over three hundred years, finally being repealed in 1967. In 1951, after the General Assembly authorized the Division of Vital Records to provide certified copies of marriage records, this body began to file the certificates numerically by certificate number. In order to facilitate access to these certificates, the agency created two indexes, one for the brides and one for the grooms. Since the groom index contains some missing or torn pages, the bride index is more complete. The State Archives has copies of these indexes on microfilm. Divorce records have been kept at the Division of Vital Records since January 1961, and earlier ones are in the various county clerks' offices. The State Archives has divorce records for the city of Baltimore and several of the counties.

Death records from 1924 to 1930 are at the Division of Vital Records office arranged first by year, then by county, and then alphabetically by surname. However, the State Archives does have indexes by which to look up the date and place of death, if that information is uncertain. Beginning in 1950 the city of Baltimore death certificates were indexed under the Soundex system. Wills in Maryland are maintained in the county orphans' courts. Those prior to 1788, and in fact all Maryland probates and official records before that date, are in the Hall of Records at Annapolis. Guardianship records are in the county equity courts. In Maryland there is a distinction between law and equity actions, but the circuit courts in the counties have jurisdiction over both.

All land records for Maryland before the U.S. Constitution was ratified in 1788 are in the Hall of Records. Some of them were previously housed in the State Land Office at Annapolis, but that office was recently abolished and the records were then transferred to the Hall of Records. Later land records are with the clerks of the circuit courts in the various counties, and in Baltimore County they are with the clerk of the superior court. The immigration records for the port of Baltimore from 1891 to 1909 can be found at the various National Archives centers.

Researchers seeking information from county records can locate them at the following county seats: (Allegany County) Cumberland, (Anne Arundel) Annapolis, (Baltimore County) Towson, (Calvert County) Prince Frederick, (Caroline County) Denton, (Carroll County) Westminster, (Cecil County) Elkton, (Charles County) La Plata, (Dorchester County) Cambridge, (Frederick County) Frederick, (Garrett County) Oakland, (Harford County) Bel Air, (Howard County) Ellicott City, (Kent County) Chestertown, (Montgomery County) Rockville, (Prince Georges County) Upper Marlboro, (Queen Annes County) Centreville, (St. Marys County) Leonardtown, (Somerset County) Princess Anne, (Talbot County) Easton, (Washington County) Hagerstown, (Wicomico County) Salisbury, and (Worchester County) Snow Hill. *See also* **Soundex System.**

For further information see:
- Heisey, John W. *Maryland Genealogical Library Guide.* Morgantown, PA: Masthof Press, 1998.
- *Maryland Genealogies.* Baltimore, MD: Genealogical Publishing Co., 1997.

Massachusetts Records include not only those for the early Massachusetts Bay Colony and the Plymouth Colony, which were not united until 1692, but also for those of early Maine, which was part of Massachusetts from the colonial period through 1820. Settlement in this area began in 1620 with the landing of the Pilgrims at Plymouth and the founding of Boston by the Puritans in 1630. Massachusetts became a state in 1788 when it was the sixth among the original 13 colonies to ratify the Constitution.

The Massachusetts State Archives in Boston has records that date from the beginning of the Massachusetts Bay Colony in 1628 and document the settlement of lands in Maine and Massachusetts, the arrival of immigrants, and the development of the state government. It also has a limited selection of books and microforms to aid genealogists and other researchers. Among them is a special collection of early documents that have been bound into 328 volumes, known as the Felt Collection. These volumes describe the development of the Massachusetts Bay government and settlement of its lands between 1630 and 1800. They also include the early records of land grants, divorces and contested estates, legislative papers, military records from 1643 through 1775, records of mercantile affairs, and tax valuation lists. Most of the volumes have a table of contents and many have been indexed.

The Plymouth Colony, also known as the Old Colony, existed as a separate entity until 1686. It was then officially merged into the Province of Massachusetts Bay in 1692. The original colony records, including wills and deeds, are maintained at the Plymouth County Commissioners' Office in Plymouth, although the Massachusetts State Archives has transcriptions of these records. Most of the files, along with records from the Commissioners of the United Colonies, were published between 1855 and 1861 in a 12-volume set titled the *Records of Plymouth Colony.* This set of books is available at the State Archives and at the Massachusetts State Library in Boston.

Since Maine was part of Massachusetts from the early colonial period up to 1820, there are many records in the State Archives that pertain to the settlement and settlers of Maine. These records are not grouped separately from those of Massachusetts, but are distinguished by their counties. They include court records, both passed and unpassed legislation, petitions, remonstrances, reports, and correspondence relating to Maine from 1780 to 1820. Researchers will also find copies of deeds for land conveyed by the Committee for the Sale of Eastern Lands and the land agent, the establishment of land titles in disputed areas, and extensive correspondence regarding road construction, land settlement, and the development of Maine's natural resources. The archives holds indexes to several volumes of the deeds and the correspondence dating from 1783 through 1867.

The federal census schedules for Massachusetts date from 1790 and continue every 10 years thereafter. They can be seen at the various National Archives locations throughout the United States. The 1890 population schedules were destroyed by fire in Washington, D.C., in 1921; however, a special census of Union war veterans and widows of veterans was taken in 1890 and is available on microfilm at the State Archives. Printed indexes for the census schedules through 1850 and the War Veterans Census are also available. There were state censuses held in 1855 and 1865. These records are not only available at the State Archives, but also at the library of the New England Historic Genealogical Society in Boston. A name index for these state census schedules exists for many of the small towns in Essex, Middlesex, and Norfolk counties, as well as for Charlestown. The mortality schedules for 1850 to 1880 are also at the State Archives.

The Work Projects Administration published a *Guide to Public Vital Statistics Records for Massachusetts* in 1942 that is available in some libraries in the state as well as in the largest genealogical libraries elsewhere. Church, cemetery, town meeting, and vital records prior to 1850 for more than two hundred towns in Massachusetts have been collected and published by the New England Historic Genealogical Society. These volumes are also found in the Massachusetts State Library in Boston, as well as in other Massachusetts libraries and in various genealogical libraries elsewhere.

The Massachusetts State Archives holds the registration books of births, marriages, and deaths for all Massachusetts cities and towns from 1841 through 1910. Municipal clerks are required to submit their vital registration pages to the state annually. Although there is some variation in the information provided, these books generally give names, dates, residences, occupations, and parental information. Some death records include the place of burial. The archives also has microfilm rolls of the entries and corrections to vital records covering the same period, and there is an index to aid researchers.

Copies of the vital records after 1910, such as birth and death certificates, marriage licenses, and divorce decrees are available at the municipal clerks' offices in each city or town or at the Massachusetts State Vital Records Office in Dorchester. Copies can be obtained from the Vital Records Office for a small fee. An index to these vital records from 1910 through 1971 is available at the State Archives, but there are no copies of the actual records there. Guardianship records are held in the county probate courts, as are the divorce records since 1952.

Divorce cases were heard in the Massachusetts courts starting as early as 1639. At that time divorce petitions were filed in a variety of courts, including the county courts, the general court and the court of assistants. The records for the cases that appeared before the general court and the court of assistants have been published and are available at the Massachusetts State Archives and in the county courts. During the provincial period (1692–1775), the primary jurisdiction for divorces was with the governor and the council, although from 1755 to 1757 six petitions were heard by the general court. Again, the original records can be found in the Massachusetts State Archives, as can those from 1775–1785 in which the council had jurisdiction. In 1786, the Supreme Judicial Court was given jurisdiction over all the divorce cases; that jurisdiction was changed in 1887 to the superior courts and finally, in 1922, to the county probate courts. There is an index for the divorce cases since 1952 at the Registry of Vital Records and Statistics in Boston.

Probate records, including the administration of estates, probate of wills, and the appointment of guardians are under the jurisdiction of the county probate courts. These courts are also responsible for adoptions, name changes, and disputes over domestic relations. The records are indexed by county; there is no statewide index. There is, however, a book titled *List of Persons Whose Names Have Been Changed in Massachusetts* that covers all the name changes granted by the courts between 1780 and 1900. It is well indexed and can be found in the Massachusetts State Library.

Land records are maintained by the registrar of deeds in each county, except for five of the counties that have more than one registry office, including Berkshire County, which has a northern district at North Adams, a middle district at Pittsfield, and a southern district at Great Barrington; Bristol County, which has a northern district at Taunton and a southern district at New Bedford; Essex County, which has a northern district at Lawrence and a southern district at Salem; Middlesex County, which has a northern district at Lowell and a southern district at Cambridge; and Worcester County, which has a northern district at Fitchburg and a Worcester district at Worcester. The deeds for Suffolk County from 1689 to 1800 are held at the State Archives. There are also many maps at the archives, especially those for the towns in Maine that include settlers' names with their residences or lots.

The National Archives in Washington, D.C., and the New England Regional Branch of the National Archives in Waltham have the immigration lists for the ports at Boston, Charlestown, Gloucester, and New Bedford. The State Archives has the lists for Boston only. However, the archives does have naturalization records for all those naturalized in the state superior courts and some district courts. These records usually include the individual's declaration of intent and naturalization petition. The later ones also include a photograph of the applicant.

Two other places where extensive genealogical information for Massachusetts can be found are the Massachusetts Historical Society, which has many letters, diaries, and other personal papers of individuals, and the Boston Public Library, which has a fine section of genealogical resource books. The material at the Boston Public Library includes an extensive index to names found on the genealogical pages of various Boston newspapers. The Adjutant General's Office oversees a large collection of military records which are particularly strong in the areas of the Mexican, Civil, Spanish-American, and 20th century wars. These records are stored in Office of the State Quartermaster in Worcester.

Researchers seeking information from county records can locate them at the following county seats: (Barnstable County) Barnstable, (Berkshire County) Pittsfield, (Bristol County) Taunton, (Dukes County) Edgartown, (Essex County) Salem, (Franklin County) Greenfield, (Hampden County) Springfield, (Hampshire County) Northampton, (Middlesex County) Cambridge, (Nantucket County) Nantucket, (Norfolk County) Dedham, (Plymouth County) Plymouth, (Suffolk County) Boston, and (Worcester County) Worcester.

FOR FURTHER INFORMATION SEE:
- Central Massachusetts Genealogical Society. *A Guide to Genealogical and Historical Holdings of Massachusetts Libraries.* Westminster, MA: Central Massachusetts Genealogical Society, 1997.
- Schweitzer, George K. *Massachusetts Genealogical Research.* Knoxville, TN: The author, 1990.

Mayflower Descendants, or the Society of the Descendants of the Mayflower, is one of the best-known of the lineage societies in America. It was established in 1890 by some of the social leaders of Boston, New York, Philadelphia, and Newport. At that time proof of lineage was not as painstakingly checked as it is today, and many of the early members of this organization assumed they were descended from one of the 1620 passengers on the *Mayflower* because they shared one of the surnames. In other words, anyone with the surname of Cooke, Rogers, or Brewster assumed his or her ancestor was on the *Mayflower*. Most of these spurious pedigrees have since been disproved.

Only a handful of the *Mayflower* passengers left descendants, who lived in just a few localities for several generations. According to the records of this society, there were 104 passengers on the *Mayflower* when it landed in 1620 and only 26 men and their wives left any issue from whom one can today trace a descent. Despite all the research that has been undertaken over the years, the English origins have been established for only 12 of those 26 passengers, although there are three others with suspected English origins.

Great as was the role played by those who came to America on the *Mayflower*, the importance of this heritage has certainly been overemphasized, and it is no basis for the establishment of any kind of American aristocracy. Just as significant were many of the people who came on later ships. So it is somewhat of a mystery as to why Americans of colonial descent should be so anxious to trace their ancestry to one of the *Mayflower* passengers.

For many years the Society of the Descendants of the Mayflower has published a journal as well as a series of books detailing the genealogies of the known descendants of the *Mayflower* passengers. Its main headquarters is at Plymouth, Massachusetts, although there are branches in a number of other states as well as in Canada.

Medical Records

Medical Records are excellent sources of genealogical information. But because they are confidential documents, they are difficult to obtain and are often not available even to immediate family members. Such records are held by hospitals, nursing homes, physicians, dentists, and other health care practitioners and facilities. For the most part information from such records will normally be released only to a physician, although that physician may pass the information on to the person involved. Thus privacy and record retention are major stumbling blocks to any genealogist's gaining access to such records.

An exception to these privacy rules comes in the case of birth mothers, who are usually entitled to copies of their hospital records and to those of their children. But if the hospital case file indicates an adoption, even this access will probably be denied.

When medical records can be located, they will likely indicate a patient's name, age, birthplace, date of admission to the medical facility, illness or disease, and the date of discharge or death. If the medical records have been destroyed, there may still be an admittance record that gives the name of the patient, age, residence, date of admittance, and financial arrangements.

Some hospital records from the 19th century have been released and microfilmed by the Genealogical Society of Utah. They include the early records of the St. Louis City Hospital. There are also a series of indexed hospital admission registers that are available at the Queensland State Archives in Australia. These are early records from hospitals in the cities and towns of Brisbane, Burketown, Cooktown, Croydon, Ingham, Muttaburra, and Toowoomba. The places of birth for some of those listed include the United States, Canada, the West Indies, India, South Africa, China, New Zealand, Germany, Scandinavia, and some other parts of Europe.

Memoirs, Diaries, and Family Letters are highly valued by family historians because they often provide information that is unavailable elsewhere. All of them are records of facts and events written from personal knowledge or special information. Although the facts presented in these documents may sometimes be questionable, it is easy to verify the accuracy of such things as the weather and local happenings by comparing the facts and events described in the memoirs and diaries with published reports in newspapers and elsewhere. For the most part, what is described by the authors will prove to be most accurate.

Diaries are wonderful sources for understanding the day-to-day events that shaped an ancestor's life. Some are merely terse "account books" rather than detailed descriptions of private observations or feelings. But even the tersest ones can reveal patterns of daily and seasonal activity, the workings of both cash and barter economies, and private and public events that warranted notice. They provide the stories that help descendants relive the hardships and hopes and the ups and downs of an ancestor's day-to-day life. Such life stories add more to a family's history than to a family's tree, and learning how early relatives lived is one of the most rewarding parts of genealogy research.

If memoirs, diaries, and letters still exist, genealogists immediately know that their ancestors had enough forethought and appreciation of history to preserve these documents for future generations. Many family historians are not that lucky, since these types of papers do not exist for them. Yet genealogists can still use the papers of other families and individuals to understand what life was like in the past.

If a researcher finds an old diary, it would be wise to handle it as an object of great value. Pages, bindings, and wrappings can rip easily, especially in old diaries with fragile pages. The volume should be protected from sunlight, which can fade certain types of ink and be harmful to cloth, paper, and photos. One can date the diary by examining it for any dates inserted inside or out. Other clues may be found in the kind of paper it is written on, the type of ink, style of writing, and the writing instrument used, as well as the events talked about in the entries. A name written on the inside or outside of the diary may provide the identification of the author, as may the names and relationships of people mentioned in the entries.

It is often useful to create a chronology of facts and events that one finds in a diary to help make order and sense of the written information. Transcribing a hand-written diary usually makes the entries more readable. Sometimes taking the time to transcribe each page into a computer database program will make it possible to search and rearrange the entries according to one's research needs. The same is true of a batch of letters written by one person.

Mennonite Records can be found in the Mennonite Library at North Newton, Kansas, in the college library at Goshen, Indiana, and at a Mennonite heritage center in Winnipeg, Canada. This Protestant religious group was founded in Switzerland in 1525 as the Swiss Brethren. They rejected the concept of a state church and refused to sanction war or to accept military service. Thus they were persecuted by the Swiss government. They also rebaptized those who joined them and accepted their beliefs, and so these church members were soon nicknamed Anabaptists, meaning rebaptizers. The name Mennonite came from Menno Simons, a Roman Catholic priest in the Netherlands, who held to similar beliefs after he left the Catholic Church and began,

in 1537, to preach throughout northern Europe. Other groups of this sort sprang up in southern Germany and also in Austria, where they were led by Jakob Hutter and were called Hutterites. The Mennonites later split into several groups, including the Amish who were led by a Swiss Mennonite bishop by the name of Jakob Amman. Most of the Amish eventually moved to Pennsylvania, where many still live and are recognized by their very conservative dress, use of horses and buggies rather than automobiles, and other customs—especially their practice of shunning as a method of discipline.

Due to persecution, the various Mennonite groups began to emigrate to America, where in 1683 William Penn offered them religious liberty. Some went eastwards to Prussia and Poland, and from there to Russia at the invitation of Catherine the Great, who wanted them to settle lands in the Ukraine that the Russians had just taken from the Turks. Later, most of those who had settled in Russia came to the United States, Canada, Paraguay, Mexico, and Brazil. Throughout much of their history, the Mennonites have been a rural people, traditionally farmers.

Today the largest number of Mennonites lives in the United States and Canada, followed by large groups in Zaire and India. The major Mennonite churches in North America today include the Mennonite Church, sometimes referred to as the "Old Mennonites," which is the largest Mennonite body; the General Conference Mennonite Church; the Mennonite Brethren Church; the Amish; the Hutterites; the Church of God in Christ, Mennonite; and the Brethren in Christ. The Hutterites have established communal farm settlements in a number of Midwestern states, and, unlike the Amish, do not shun technology; in fact they welcome it. The benefits of that technology, however, are always held as the property of the community, rather than of the individual.

The Mennonite Library and Archives in North Newton, Kansas, is operated by both Bethel College and the Historical Committee of the Mennonite Church. It houses about 30,000 books, 5,600 volumes of bound periodicals, audio and video recordings, microforms, photographs, motion pictures, maps and other items. Many of these items are of interest to genealogists, such as obituaries, diaries, and census records. The library at Goshen, Indiana, also contains much archival material about the Mennonite movement. It is operated by Goshen College, a Mennonite training school.

In Canada the Mennonite Heritage Centre, an inter–Mennonite facility, holds the records of the Mennonite Church of Canada, Mennonite Central Committee, Canadian Mennonite Board of Colonization, Evangelical Mennonites Mission Conference, Prussian and Russian Mennonite community documents, and personal papers of many individuals. The facility is located in the city of Winnipeg.

Those particularly interested in locating Hutterite genealogical records should contact the Heritage Hall Museum and Archives in Freeman, South Dakota. *See also* **Paraguayan Genealogy.**

Merchant Marine Records are on file with the U.S. Coast Guard records at the National Archives in Washington, D.C. The files regarding discharged, deceased, and retired personnel in the Merchant Marine force are in the custody of the National Personnel Records Center in St. Louis. But the files on Merchant Marine officers and active or reserve personnel who served before 1929 are in the custody of the Commandant of the U.S. Coast Guard in Washington, D.C.

Methodist Records can be obtained from local churches or from their administrative bodies, known as conferences, as well as from national church archives. Although there are 22 different branches of Methodism in the United States, by far the largest is The United Methodist Church, which is divided into some 60-plus conferences, each of which is presided over by a bishop and each of which has its own archive center. The United Methodist Archives and History Center at Drew University in Madison, New Jersey, maintains a collection of various church records.

Generally the baptism, marriage, and funeral records are kept by the local church until it merges with another church. Then the records go to the new church. If the local church is formally closed, the records go to the conference archives or to a local college or university. For example, Wright State University in Dayton, Ohio, now has on microfilm the 1832–1985 records of the Crosby United Methodist Church in New Haven, Ohio, as well as the 1823–1986 records of the Greene Street United Methodist Church in Piqua, Ohio.

The United Methodist Church is the descendent of several predecessors. These were: Methodist Episcopal Church (1784–1939); Methodist Episcopal Church, South (1845–1939); Methodist Protestant Church (1828–1939); Methodist Church (1939–1968); United Brethren in Christ (1800–1946); Evangelical Association (1803–1922); United Evangelical Church (1894–1922); Evangelical Church (1922–1946); and Evangelical United Brethren (1946–1968). Since 1968 these combined denominations have been known as The United Methodist Church.

Some of the other branches of Methodism are: the Primitive Methodist Church, the Congregational Methodist Church, the Calvinistic Methodist Church, the Free Methodist Church of North America, the African Methodist Episcopal Church, the African Methodist Episcopal Zion Church, and the Christian Methodist Episcopal Church (formerly the Colored Methodist Episcopal Church). To obtain records of any of these smaller denominations it is best to contact the various local churches.

Addresses for existing local United Methodist churches can be found by contacting the particular conference that oversees the area in which the church is located. All these conferences have Websites where it is likely there is a list of addresses for the churches under their jurisdiction. One can then write directly to the church secretary or, if possible, visit the church itself to obtain answers to questions regarding its vital records. It may also be wise to contact local libraries in the county where the church is located, or historical societies to see if they have any of the records for that particular local church. When the name for the local church is not listed, it is likely that it has closed, changed its name, or merged with another church. Then one should contact the administrator of the conference archives to learn more about the status of that particular church and how to find its records. Again, the conference headquarters will tell how to contact the administrator.

One often finds a tradition in Methodist families that some deceased member was a preacher. Such family history may or may not be accurate. During the 19th century, the term preacher could refer to an ordained minister or to a lay person who had many of the duties of an ordained minister, yet only in a specific locale. If the person was an ordained minister, then records held by the General Commission on Archives and History in Madison, New Jersey, will probably have proof of this. If the person being sought was a missionary, the same body will probably also have data about him or her. Obituaries for many of the denomination's missionaries and reports that they filed about their work can also possibly be found at the Madison archives.

Other libraries with extensive collections of Methodist materials are those at Duke University in Durham, North Carolina; Emory University in Atlanta, Georgia; Garrett Evangelical Theological Seminary on the campus of Northwestern University in Evanston, Illinois; and the Perkins School of Theology in Dallas, Texas. Furthermore, the Interdenominational Theological Center in Atlanta, Georgia, has a large collection of materials about African American Methodists.

Mexican Genealogy includes a rich assortment of genealogical and historical materials. Civil registration of births, marriages, and deaths began as early as 1859, and in some municipal areas even earlier than that. The records also include information about divorces, annulments, adoptions, fetal deaths, and acknowledgement by fathers of illegitimate children. These are among the best family records in all Latin America because the birth listings often include information about grandparents as well as the parents.

Each state in Mexico has its own major archives center, though by far the largest and most important one is in the National Palace of Mexico City, the Archivo General de la Nación. Besides this data gathered by the state, some Roman Catholic parish registers also contain a great quantity of family history material. There are several thousand parishes throughout Mexico and, though some of the files have been destroyed and others have poorly written records, most of the parish files are in good condition. Because so many families in Mexico are Catholic, these records provide quantities of information that can be added to that obtained from the state archives, such as baptismal dates, confirmation dates, marriage dates, and dates of burial.

Another important source of material that can be of use to genealogists working in Mexico are the legal registers kept by the notaries public. There are some eight hundred notarial archives in Mexico, most of which are housed in the various state archive centers or in special notarial archives. They contain letters of administration, letters of indebtedness, wills, records relating to the buying and selling of land, mortgages, and property titles.

The researcher should not overlook the thousands of cemeteries scattered throughout Mexico. A great deal of information can be gained from an examination of the tombstone inscriptions. Few of these cemeteries, however, have any written records concerning those who were buried there prior to 1900.

Michigan Records of births, deaths, and marriages can best be found at the Michigan Vital Records Office at Lansing. Before the first European explorers came to this area, the region was occupied by various Indian tribes belonging to the Algonkian language group. They included the Chippewa and Menominee tribes in the Upper Peninsula, and the Miami, Ottawa, and Potawatomi tribes in the Lower Peninsula. There were also Wyandot Indians, belonging to the Iroquois language group, living around what is now the city of Detroit. The French were the first European explorers to come into Michigan. They entered the area around 1620. In 1791 the French founded Fort Pontchartrain at the place that later became the city of Detroit. The British, however, took possession of Michigan in 1763 and then lost it to the United States in 1783, following the Revolutionary War. Congress designated Michigan as part of the Northwest Territory in 1787, and then as part of the Indiana Territory in 1800. In 1805 Congress established the Territory of Michigan, but during the War of 1812, the British once again occupied Detroit as well as Fort Mackinac. These sites were returned to the United States in 1814, and in 1837 Michigan became the 26th state.

The first census taken by the U.S. government in Michigan was that of 1820, and censuses have been enumerated there every 10 years since. These censuses can be seen at any of the National Archives centers in the United States. There were also a series of state censuses conducted in 1845, 1854, 1864, 1874, 1884, 1894, but only a few of these records survive. Some of them can be found at the Library of Michigan in Lansing, at the University of Michigan Library in Ann Arbor, and at various county courthouses and local libraries elsewhere in the state. The mortality schedules for 1850 to 1880 are stored at the Michigan Historical Center at Lansing.

The Work Projects Administration (WPA) published a series of books in 1941 and 1942, *Vital Statistics Holdings by Government Agencies in Michigan*. One covered birth records, and the other three covered marriage, death, and divorce records. The WPA also published a *Guide to Church Vital Statistics Records in Michigan: Wayne County* in 1942. These volumes can be found in the Library of Michigan and in the University of Michigan library system.

Copies of the births and deaths that have taken occurred since 1867 are available from the Michigan State Vital Records Office for a small fee, or from the county clerks in the counties where the events occurred. Note, however, that some of these records, especially of births before 1906 and deaths before 1897 were never filed with the state. Records of Detroit births occurring since 1893 and deaths since 1897 may be obtained from the City of Detroit Health Department. Marriage records since 1867 can be found at the Vital Records Office, as can divorce records, though some of these before 1926 were never filed. The Vital Records Office also has immigration, naturalization, and military records. Guardianship records can be found in the county probate courts, as can the probates of any wills. Land records can be found in the offices of the county registers of deeds. In Michigan there is no distinction between equity and law actions, and the district courts in each county have jurisdiction over both.

One other place where various Michigan genealogical records and books of note may be found is in the Burton Historical Collection at the Detroit Public Library.

Researchers seeking information from county records can locate them at the following county seats: (Alcona County) Harrisville, (Alger County) Munising, (Allegan County) Allegan, (Alpena County) Alpena, (Antrim County) Bellaire, (Arenac County) Standish, (Baraga County) L'Anse, (Barry County) Hastings, (Bay County) Bay City, (Benzie County) Beulah, (Berrien County) St. Joseph, (Branch County) Coldwater, (Calhoun County) Marshall, (Cass County) Cassopolis, (Charlevoix County) Charlevoix, (Cheboygan County) Cheboygan, (Chippewa County) Sault Ste. Marie, (Clare County) Harrison, (Clinton County) St. Johns, (Crawford County) Grayling, (Delta County) Escanaba, (Dickinson County) Iron Mountain, (Eaton County) Charlotte, (Emmet County) Petoskey, (Genesee County) Flint, (Gladwin County) Gladwin, (Gogebic County) Bessemer, (Grand Traverse County) Traverse City, and (Gratiot County) Ithaca.

And at (Hillsdale County) Hillsdale, (Houghton County) Houghton, (Huron County) Bad Axe, (Ingham County) Mason, (Ionia County) Ionia, (Iosco County) Tawas City, (Iron County) Crystal Falls, (Isabella County) Mt. Pleasant, (Jackson County) Jackson, (Kalamazoo County) Kalamazoo, (Kalkaska County) Kalkaska, (Keweenaw County) Eagle River, (Kent County) Grand Rapids, (Lake County) Baldwin, (Lapeer County) Lapeer, (Leelanau County) Leland, (Lenawee County) Adrian, (Livingston County) Howell, (Luce County) Newberry,

(Mackinac County) St. Ignace, (Macomb County) Mt. Clemens, (Manistee County) Manistee, (Marquette County) Marquette, (Mason County) Ludington, (Mecosta County) Big Rapids, (Menominee County) Menominee, (Midland County) Midland, (Missaukee County) Lake City, (Monroe County) Monroe, (Montcalm County) Stanton, (Montmorency County) Atlanta, (Muskegon County) Muskegon, and (Newaygo County) White Cloud.

As well as at (Oakland County) Pontiac, (Oceana County) Hart, (Ogemaw County) West Branch, (Ontonagon County) Ontonagon, (Osceola County) Reed City, (Oscoda County) Mio, (Otsego County) Gaylord, (Ottawa County) Grand Haven, (Presque Isle County) Rogers City, (Roscommon County) Roscommon, (Saginaw County) Saginaw, (Sanilac County) Sandusky, (Schoolcraft County) Manistique, (Shiawassee County) Corunna, (St. Clair County) Port Huron, (St. Joseph County) Centreville, (Tuscola County) Caro, (Van Buren County) Paw Paw, (Washtenaw County) Ann Arbor, (Wayne County) Detroit, and (Wexford County) Cadillac.

FOR FURTHER INFORMATION SEE:
• Anderson, Alloa Caviness. *Genealogy in Michigan: What, When, Where*. Ann Arbor, MI: A. Anderson, P. Bender, 1978.
• McGinnis, Carol. *Michigan Genealogy Sources and Resources*. Baltimore: Genealogical Publishing Co., 1987.

Middle Eastern Genealogy *see* **Islamic Genealogy**

Military Records of the participants in the various colonial and U.S. wars are located, for the most part, at the National Archives in Washington, D.C., although copies of the abstracts can be found at all the National Archives centers outside of Washington; some of these are in the various state libraries and archives. There is another set of records at the National Personnel Records Center in St. Louis, Missouri. Most of the military records that have genealogical interest comprise two groups: compiled service records and veterans' benefits. However, these records give lit-

tle more than the serviceman's name, rank, unit, and dates of muster rolls or rosters. Some do show the serviceman's age, birthplace, physical description, and residence, as well as any imprisonment or medical information. They are arranged by period of service and then by state and unit, with the surnames listed in alphabetical order for each unit. Military discharge papers are often filed in county courthouses, and can provide some information for the genealogist.

There are indexes for many of the records in the National Archives; two published resources may also aid the researcher in locating specific record files. These are James C. Neagles's, *U.S. Military Records: A Guide to Federal and State Sources, Colonial America to the Present*, which is an introduction to the military files of the National Archives, and the National Archives catalog, *Military Service Records: A Select listing of National Archives Microfilm Publications*. The military records are so numerous that it may be best to list them in chronological order.

COLONIAL PERIOD: There are no official records of the wars that took place before the American Revolution because the United States did not exist at that time. However, even the earliest colonists felt the sting of war because of the many battles that were fought against the Indians and the French during the more than a century that the colonial period lasted. The Massachusetts State Archives in Boston has a variety of military rolls and accounts relating to military service in the colonial wars (circa 1643–1774). These records are indexed by name and are available on microfilm. The major wars are known as King Phillip's War (1675–1676), King William's War (1689–1697), Queen Ann's War (1702–1713), King George's War (1744–1748), and the French and Indian War (1754–1763). Many of the militia records from the colonial period have also been published in book form and can be found in various genealogical libraries. The genealogist in search of records for sailors during the colonial period, however, will be disappointed, since any records that may exist will be listed by the name of the ship and not by the names of the crew.

AMERICAN REVOLUTION (1776–1783): The

personnel records of this war are incomplete, since it was fought before the country was yet organized. Many of the muster rolls were kept by the officers as their personal property. The records do not include those who served in the militia. Such records, if available, must be procured from the archives of the states in which the individuals served. The muster rolls that do exist are at the National Archives, accessible through both a general index and one by states.

It is estimated that as many as one-third of the colonial population sided with the British during the Revolutionary War; most of these people departed for Canada, though some went to Florida and the West Indies. They included British officials and their friends, Anglican Church ministers, and persons whose positions or wealth depended on British sovereignty. They are known as Loyalists, and many of them returned to the United States after the war ended. Most genealogical libraries have books that list some of these Loyalists and the New York Public Library and the New Jersey State Library both have collections of records relating to the American Loyalists.

There are also Revolutionary War pension and bounty land warrant applications that include the veteran's name, rank, military unit, period of service, residence, birthplace, date of birth or age, and, if the claim was based on need, a listing of property owned. For widows and heirs such applications additionally include marriage dates and places and a veteran's date and place of death. In these instances supporting documents such as affidavits of witnesses, discharge papers, and marriage and birth certificates are sometimes included. The Massachusetts State Archives holds records of state pensions and bounties of Maine land grants for Revolutionary War veterans or their heirs. At the Massachusetts State Archives and some genealogical libraries both in Massachusetts and elsewhere there is a 17-volume set *Massachusetts Soldiers and Sailors of the Revolutionary War. See also* **Bounty Land Warrants; Pension Claims.**

RECORDS FROM SHAYS' REBELLION (1786–87), a period of internal turbulence, are included in the Massachusetts Archives collec-tion. This series of letters, orders, warrants, petitions, special reports, military payrolls, service certificates, financial records, and oaths of allegiance provide extensive documentation for Shays' Rebellion. A partial index exists with the names of soldiers and individuals who supplied or housed the Army at that time. As with the colonial records, there are none for the sailors of the Continental or United States Navy because no naval records were filed for more than 40 years after the organization of this country. If one knows the ship on which a man sailed in the early days of the Navy, his name and rating (the only information) can be found on the microfilm roll of that ship, if that roll is in the National Archives Navy files.

WAR OF 1812 (1812–1814): The records of the War of 1812 give a little more information than the previous records, such as the distance between the place of discharge and the soldier's residence. There is also a special index of the names of volunteers who served the Army but were not a part of it. The great majority of soldiers who served at that time were volunteers or members of state militia who were federalized for portions of the war period. At the National Archives these records are arranged by state or federal volunteer unit, and then alphabetically by the names of soldiers. The service records show the soldier's name, rank, regimental unit (usually showing the last name of the regimental commander), the company commander's name, dates of service and pay, whether the soldier was a substitute, and date of discharge. Other information such as date of death, if applicable, and periods of sickness, if recorded on the muster rolls, is noted. If a soldier's name does not appear in the index for volunteer soldiers, he might have served in the regular Army. Most of the names of regular Army soldiers who served during the War of 1812 appear in the 15 volumes of enlistment registers that show the names of soldiers enlisting for the period 1798–1815. The names are arranged alphabetically by the initial letter of surname, and thereunder alphabetically by given name.

Naval service for enlisted men is more difficult to establish than it is for those in the

Army, but establishing service for a Marine Corps soldier is somewhat easier. The records of the U.S. Marine Corps include comprehensive card indexes listing all officers and enlisted men who served before 1900. The information on these cards is slim, but it does show the dates of appointment and enlistment. There are also records relating to naval and other American prisoners of war captured and incarcerated by the British in England, Nova Scotia, or on prisoner of war ships. These lists show the names, dates of capture, ship from which taken, and the location of the prisoner.

Perhaps the most genealogically rich records for this period are the pension application files at the National Archives. Federal legislation passed in 1871 and 1878 provided that the War of 1812 veterans or their heirs receive pension benefits in addition to bounty land grants that had been awarded in 1812. The index listings of these pension awards include the veteran's name, pension application and certificate number, bounty land warrant application number, and the name or number of the unit in which he served. The data about marriages before 1815 found in some of the files may not be available anywhere else.

INDIAN AND MEXICAN WARS: The National Archives records of the Indian and Mexican wars do not give a great deal of information about the soldiers involved, but they do prove that each individual served during one of these wars. In the Illinois Archives at Springfield there are the original muster rolls of Illinois volunteers who fought in the Black Hawk War (1831–1832). These rolls include the soldier's name, rank, date and length of enrollment, county residence, amount of pay due, and number of traveling rations drawn. The Illinois Archives also has the original muster rolls for Illinois volunteers who served in the Mexican War (1846–1848).

CIVIL WAR (1861–1865): Over 2.8 million men (and a few hundred women) served in the Union and Confederate armies during the Civil War. For Union Army soldiers, there are three major record archives in the National Archives and Records Administration that provide information on military service: the compiled military service records (CMSR); the pension application files; and the records as reproduced on microfilm. There is no overall general name index for the Union soldiers, but there are microfilmed name indexes for each state. There are also some compiled lists of the Union soldiers buried at the U.S. Soldiers' Home in Washington, D.C. and for those buried in the various national cemeteries. For records of the state or local militias or National Guard units that were not federalized one should consult the various state archives. The voluntary militia lists give the soldier's name, residence, age, birthplace, occupation, and date and term of enlistment.

Most Union Army soldiers or their widows or minor children eventually applied for pensions. The pension files are indexed at the National Archives and Records Administration, and often contain more information about what the soldier did during the war than do the service records; some even contain medical information about the pensioners who lived for a number of years after the war. To obtain a widow's pension, the wife had to provide proof of marriage, such as a copy of the record kept by county officials, or by affidavit from the minister or some other person. Applicants on behalf of the soldier's minor children had to supply both proof of the soldier's marriage and proof of the children's births.

Some government publications that may be of help in locating information about those who served in the Civil War include *The Union: A Guide to Federal Archives Relating to the Civil War*, reprinted by the National Archives and Records Administration in 1986; the 128-volume *War of the Rebellion: A Compilation of the Official Records of the Union and Confederate Armies* (Government Printing Office, 1880–1900); and the 30-volume *The War of the Rebellion: A Compilation of the Official Records of the Union and Confederate Navies* (Government Printing Office, 1874–1922).

For Confederate army soldiers, there are two major record archives at the National Archives and Records Administration: the compiled military service records (CMSR), and the compiled records showing service in

Confederate military units. Records relating to Confederate soldiers are typically less complete than those relating to Union soldiers because many Confederate records did not survive the war. The ones that are available give the soldier's age and birthplace, and some indicate that the man was taken prisoner or paroled on particular dates.

Confederate pension records are not at the National Archives, but must be found in the archives of each of the states where the veterans lived after the war. These pensions were based on military service for the Confederate States of America and were granted by the states of Alabama, Arkansas, Florida, Georgia, Kentucky, Louisiana, Mississippi, Missouri, North Carolina, Oklahoma, South Carolina, Tennessee, Texas, and Virginia.

A helpful guide to the Confederate records that was reprinted in 1986 by the National Archives and Records Administration is *The Confederacy: A Guide to the Archives of the Confederate States of America.*

SPANISH-AMERICAN WAR (1898): The Spanish-American War took place in Cuba and was followed by the Philippine Insurrection (1899–1902), ending with the U.S. obtaining Guam, Puerto Rico, and the Philippine Islands. The National Archives holds a wealth of information for genealogists who are researching individuals who served in the U.S. Army during these two wars. Several of its record groups contain material related to Regular Army officers, enlisted men (soldiers, sailors, and marines), volunteers, physicians, contract surgeons, nurses, and, in the case of the Philippine Insurrection, the Philippine scouts.

The records of the Spanish-American War give each man's age, birthplace, and the name of the next of kin. Altogether 280,564 sailors, marines, and soldiers served, of whom 2,061 died from various causes. The number is not large compared to the approximately three million men who served in the Civil War or the 16 million men and women who served in World War II. The smaller numbers are in part due to the short length of the Spanish-American War. It ended before many soldiers had even been transported to the war zone. At this time some African-Americans served in the U.S. Navy and U.S. Army but not in the U.S. Marine Corps. Women served in the U.S. Army Nurse Corps, but there are no known records at this time of any women in the U.S. Navy or U.S. Marine Corps. There were also Native Americans who fought in the Spanish-American War as volunteers, especially in the First Volunteer Cavalry (Rough Riders) and First Territorial Volunteer Infantry.

On board Navy ships, African-Americans were integrated with sailors of all nationalities. (Many aliens, including Japanese, Chinese, and Filipinos, served on U.S. Navy ships during that era. Some of them enlisted while the ships were in foreign ports.) Of the 260 men who died on board USS *Maine*, 22 were African-American. They typically worked in the engine rooms; as firemen, oilers, and coal passers; or as mess attendants and landsmen. However, there were also five African-American petty officers, three seamen (experienced sailors), and one ordinary seaman. Over the ensuing years, a resurgence of racism led the Navy to relegate blacks to ratings of mess attendants, including some men who had held much higher ratings during the Spanish-American War.

The personnel files for enlisted sailors who served after 1885 are at the National Personnel Records Center in St. Louis, Missouri. The National Archives in Washington, D.C., does not have an index of these personnel records or compiled or consolidated records of any type for enlisted sailors. If one knows the names of ships on which a veteran served, one can examine the U.S. Navy muster rolls and conduct books. Both are arranged alphabetically by the names of the ships. The officers' records can be found in the U.S. Navy logbooks. For biographical records of Army and Navy chaplains, there are Chaplains Division records; the records of medical officers are located among records of the Bureau of Medicine and Surgery in Washington, D.C. Personnel records for the Marines who fought in the Spanish-American War can be found at the National Archives and at the National Personnel Records Center.

The pension index for this war, also in the National Archives center, includes veterans who served in the regular Army, state volunteers who were called into federal service, U.S. volunteers (e.g., Rough Riders), regular U.S. Navy, temporary naval personnel, naval militia, U.S. Coast Signal Service, and U.S. Marine Corps.

Approximately 125,000 U.S. troops served during the Philippine Insurrection. After more than three years of fighting, at a cost of $400 million and approximately 4,200 American dead and 2,900 wounded, President Theodore Roosevelt proclaimed an end to it on July 4, 1902. Despite Roosevelt's proclamation, isolated and sporadic guerilla activity continued throughout the period of American rule, which lasted until 1946, when the Philippines finally gained their independence.

The compiled military service records for the individuals who served in the Philippine Insurrection have not been copied onto microfilm. However, the register of enlistments is arranged at the National Archives chronologically and thereunder alphabetically by first letter of surname, and usually shows the individual's name, military organization, physical description, age at time of enlistment, place of birth, enlistment information, discharge information, and remarks. At the time there were four units of African-American soldiers who served in the Ninth U.S. Cavalry, 10th U.S. Cavalry, 24th U.S. Infantry, and 25th U.S. Infantry. Information related to Filipinos who served as scouts for the U.S. Army can be found among the Regular Army Enlistment Papers. The records for women who served as contract nurses in the Philippines include the full name, address, education, hospital experience, age, date, place of birth, and marital status.

BOXER REBELLION (1900–1901): In the fall of 1899, Secretary of State John Hay wrote that the United States wanted to maintain an "open door policy" in China. But if the Boxer Revolution succeeded in pushing the United States and other foreign countries out, this newly opened door would soon be shut. Thus two ship detachments of U.S. Marines were ordered to go to Peking to protect the foreign legations from the advancing Boxers. The total number of Marines sent to China during the Boxer Rebellion included 49 officers

and 1,151 enlisted men. The service records of these Marines are at the National Archives in Washington and at the National Personnel Records Center in St. Louis. When the Boxer threat subsided, the Marines in China were ordered back to the Philippines.

WORLD WAR I (1917–1918): Draft registration cards for World War I are located at the National Archives branch in East Point, Georgia. The information on the registration may include the name, age, sometimes the birthdate and birthplace, citizenship status, occupation and name of employer, name and address of the nearest relative, marital status, physical description, and signature. There is no indication if the registrant did or did not enter military service. The state archives in a number of states may have copies of the draft registration cards for their particular states. This is true, for example, of the Illinois State Archives.

The service records are in the St. Louis National Personnel Records Center, but they are not open to the public. The only information that is available as a public record is a veteran's branch and dates of service. Records of living World War I veterans, however, are maintained by the Departments of Veterans' Affairs in each state. The United States Army did not begin operating an independent air service until April 1918. At that time the air service consisted of only three squadrons for use in the front lines. By the time of the November 11, 1918, armistice, 45 American squadrons, consisting of 740 planes, were operating. A total of 7,726 officers and 70,769 men served in the air service.

National Guard unit records are not federal records and are in the custody of the various state repositories. Researchers should contact a Department of Veterans' Affairs (VA) office in their vicinity to determine if a World War I veteran received a pension or other government benefits. Addresses for many of these offices can be found in the *Genealogist's Address Book,* by Elizabeth Petty Bentley.

WORLD WAR II (1941–1945), KOREAN WAR (1950–1953), and VIETNAM WAR (1959–1973): To find records on the veterans of these wars, a researcher must consult the National Personnel Records Center in St. Louis. This office requires the veteran's name, war and branch of service, and, if possible, Social Security or serial number for any records search. Releasable information for living veterans is restricted to a person's unit, location of service, schools attended, and awards and decorations. It is also possible to obtain information about the veterans of these wars from each Department of Veterans' Affairs in the states from which the veterans joined the service.

COAST GUARD: The National Archives has records relating to the Coast Guard and its predecessor agencies: the Lighthouse Service, Revenue Cutter Service, and the Lifesaving Service. The muster rolls for the Revenue Cutter Service, and then the Coast Guard, 1833–1932, provide for each crew member name, rating, date and place of enlistment, place of birth, age, occupation, personal description, and number of days served during the reported month, along with notes if the crewman was detached, transferred, or discharged, or if he deserted or died during the report period. The records are arranged alphabetically by the names of the vessels.

Finally, in searching for the records of veterans, one should not overlook the veterans homes and veterans hospitals in many states, which have records of their residents and, in some cases, will provide genealogical information to the researcher. Since 1903 a few of them have admitted qualified wives and daughters of the veterans.

Minnesota Records of interest to genealogists may be found at the Minnesota Department of Health Vital Records Office in Minneapolis, the Minnesota Historical Society in St. Paul, the University of Minnesota's Wilson Library in Minneapolis, and at a number of other locations in the state. When French explorers first entered what is now Minnesota in the 1660s, they found Sioux Indians in the northern forests. Yet by 1750 large numbers of Chippewa Indians had moved into this area and forced the Sioux to move to the southwest. The Sioux and Chippewa tribes remained enemies for many years thereafter. In 1763 the French and Indian War came to an end with Great Britain the victor, and the part

of Minnesota east of the Mississippi River was soon occupied by various British fur-trading companies. Great Britain lost this territory after the American Revolution in 1783, and the part of Minnesota west of the Mississippi River was obtained by the United States in the Louisiana Purchase of 1803.

In 1820 soldiers under the leadership of Colonel Josiah Snelling began the construction of Fort St. Anthony on the site of present-day St. Paul. It was later renamed Fort Snelling. Congress designated the Minnesota area as part of the Michigan Territory in 1830, then as part of the Wisconsin Territory in 1840, and finally as the Minnesota Territory in 1849. As a territory, Minnesota extended west to the Missouri River and included much of what later became the Dakota Territory. In 1858 Minnesota became the 32nd state.

The first federal census was conducted in Minnesota in 1830, when it was still part of the Michigan Territory; the enumeration can be found among the Michigan records as Chippewa and Crawford counties. The 1840 census of the Wisconsin Territory includes the northeastern part of Minnesota, while the 1840 census of the Iowa Territory includes the southern and western parts of Minnesota. It was not until the 1850 census that Minnesota stood by itself as the Minnesota Territory. The fire that destroyed most of the 1890 census did not, however, destroy the enumeration for the town of Rockford in Wright County. The federal census records can be found at any of the National Archives locations. There were also a series of Minnesota state censuses taken in 1849, 1857, 1865, 1875, 1885, 1895, and 1905, which can be seen at the Minnesota Historical Society. They are also available at the National Archives in Washington, D.C., with the exception of the 1849 one. The mortality schedules for 1850 to 1880 are at the Minnesota State Library in St. Paul.

In 1941 the Work Projects Administration published the *Guide to Public Vital Statistics records in Minnesota*, and in 1942 it published two volumes under the title *Guide to Church Vital Statistics Records in Minnesota*. The first volume covered public archives and the second, church archives. These books can be found at the State Library, the State Historical Society, and some other libraries in Minnesota.

Records of Minnesota births that took place before 1935 and deaths that took place before 1997 may be obtained from the Minnesota Department of Health in Minneapolis for a small fee. For births or deaths that took place after those dates, the researcher should go to the registrar's office in the particular county where the birth or death took place. Marriage and divorce decrees are issued through the counties where the events took place, so the researcher should consult the appropriate clerks of the county district courts. Guardianship records are also held in the district courts, and the probate records can be found in the county probate courts.

Minnesota records relating to land transactions are located in the various counties, with the county register of deeds. There is no distinction in Minnesota between equity and law actions. The records for both are in the district courts of the counties that have jurisdiction.

Perhaps the most complete genealogical library in this state can be found at the Minnesota Historical Society. Its collection, besides the federal and state census rolls, includes histories of Minnesota as well as its counties, cities, towns, communities, and churches; many city directories; various family histories; and the publications of state and local historical societies.

Another good collection of genealogical materials can be found in the Wilson Library of the University of Minnesota in Minneapolis. It has an excellent collection of newspapers from around the state, including the major ones in Minneapolis and St. Paul. It also has a guide to genealogical resources, *Tracing Your Ancestors in Minnesota*. Another library that is worth visiting is that of the Minnesota Genealogical Society in Golden Valley. It has a growing collection of genealogical materials, including CD-ROM resources.

Researchers seeking information from county records can locate them at the following county seats: (Aitkin County) Aitkin, (Anoka County) Anoka, (Becker County)

Detroit Lakes, (Beltrami County) Bemidji, (Benton County) Foley, (Big Stone County) Ortonville, (Blue Earth County) Mankato, (Brown County) New Ulm, (Carlton County) Carlton, (Carver County) Chaska, (Cass County) Walker, (Chippewa County) Montevideo, (Chisago County) Center City, (Clay County) Moorhead, (Clearwater County) Bagley, (Cook County) Grand Marais, (Cottonwood County) Windom, (Crow Wing County) Brainerd, (Dakota County) Hastings, (Dodge County) Mantorville, (Douglas County) Alexandria, (Faribault County) Blue Earth, (Filmore County) Preston, (Freeborn County) Albert Lea, (Goodhue County) Red Wing, (Grant County) Elbow Lake, (Hennepin County) Minneapolis, (Houston County) Caledonia, (Hubbard County) Park Rapids, (Isanti County) Cambridge, (Itasca County) Grand Rapids, (Jackson County) Jackson, (Kanabec County) Mora, (Kandiyohi County) Willmar, (Kittson County) Hallock, (Koochiching County) International Falls, (Lac Qui Parle County) Madison, (Lake County) Two Harbors, (Lake of the Woods County) Baudette, (Le Sueur County) Le Center, (Lincoln County) Ivanhoe, and (Lyon County) Marshall.

Also at (Mahnomen County) Mahnomen, (Marshall County) Warren, (Martin County) Fairmont, (McLeod County) Glencoe, (Meeker County) Litchfield, (Mille Lacs County) Milaca, (Morrison County) Little Falls, (Mower County) Austin, (Murray County) Slayton, (Nicollet County) St. Peter, (Nobles County) Worthington, (Norman County) Ada, (Olmsted County) Rochester, (Otter Tail County) Fergus Falls, (Pennington County) Thief River Falls, (Pine County) Pine City, (Pipestone County) Pipestone, (Polk County) Crookston, (Pope County) Glenwood, (Ramsey County) St. Paul, (Red Lake County) Red Lake Falls, (Redwood County) Redwood Falls, (Renville County) Olivia, (Rice County) Faribault, (Rock County) Luverne, (Roseau County) Roseau, (St. Louis County) Duluth, (Scott County) Shakopee, (Sherburne County) Elk River, (Sibley County) Gaylord, (Stearns County) St. Cloud, (Steele County) Owatonna, (Stevens County) Morris, (Swift County)

Benson, (Todd County) Long Prairie, (Traverse County) Wheaton, (Wabasha County) Wabasha, (Wadena County) Wadena, (Waseca County) Waseca, (Washington County) Stillwater, (Watonwan County) St. James, (Wilkin County) Breckenridge, (Winona County) Winona, (Wright County) Buffalo, and (Yellow Medicine County) Granite Falls.

FOR FURTHER INFORMATION SEE:
- Kirkeby, Lucille L. *Holdings of Genealogical Value in Minnesota's County Museums.* Brainard, MN: The author, 1986.
- Lind, Marilyn. *Continuing Your Genealogical Research in Minnesota.* Cloquet, MN: The Linden Tree, 1986.

Mississippi Records of births, deaths, and marriages may be found at the state's vital records office and at the Mississippi Historical and Genealogical Association, both of which are in Jackson. Between 25,000 and 30,000 Indians lived in the Mississippi region when the first Spanish explorers arrived there in 1540. Three powerful Indian tribes—the Chickasaw, Choctaw, and Natchez—ruled the region at that time. In 1763 the English took control, following the end of the French and Indian War. In 1798 it became part of the United States as the Mississippi Territory, and in 1817 Mississippi became the 20th state.

The first federal census was conducted in Mississippi in 1820 and these federal censuses have been taken every 10 years since. They can be seen at the various locations of the National Archives records. Territorial and state censuses were held in 1792, 1801, 1805, 1808, 1810, 1813, 1816, 1822–1825, 1833, 1837, 1841, 1845, 1853, and 1866, but none of these are complete for the entire state. Parts of them have been published in several Mississippi journals, and the 1805 and 1810 schedules are available in the state archives. The 1810 census covers Amite, Baldwin, Claiborne, Franklin, Jefferson, Warren, and Washington counties. The mortality schedules for 1850 to 1880 are in the Department of Archives and History in Jackson.

In 1942 the Work Projects Administration published two volumes relating to the vital records of Mississippi: the *Guide to Public Vital Statistics Records in Mississippi* (Vol. 1, *Public Archives*; Vol. 2, *Church Archives*). The books can be found at the Mississippi State Library in Jackson as well as in some other libraries in the state and some genealogical libraries elsewhere.

Other genealogical materials at the State Library include Confederate army records, War of 1812 records, an index to naturalization records, property records, maps, photos, family histories (both published and unpublished), and private manuscripts. The Vital Records Office has birth and death records since 1912, copies of which can be obtained for a small fee, but its marriage records are basically statistical ones from 1926 to 1938 as well as since 1942, so certified copies are not available. The researcher would best contact the clerk of the county circuit court where a marriage license was issued to get a copy; for divorce records since 1926 the researcher should contact the clerk of the chancery court in the county where the divorce was granted. Guardianship records will also be found at the chancery courts, as will probate records. Immigration passenger lists for the port of Pascagoula, Mississippi, are at the National Archives in Washington, D.C.

In Mississippi there is a strict distinction between the county chancery courts, which have jurisdiction in equity matters, and the county circuit courts that have jurisdiction in law matters. All land transfers and other land transactions reside with the clerks of the county chancery courts.

Researchers seeking information from county records can locate them at the following county seats: (Adams County) Natchez, (Alcorn County) Corinth, (Amite County) Liberty, (Attala County) Kosciusko, (Benton County) Ashland, (Bolivar County) Rosedale and Cleveland, (Calhoun County) Pittsboro, (Carroll County) Vaiden and Carrollton, (Chickasaw County) Houston and Okolona, (Choctaw County) Ackerman, (Claiborne County) Port Gibson, (Clarke County) Quitman, (Clay County) West Point, (Coahoma County) Clarksdale, (Copiah County) Hazlehurst, (Covington County) Collins, (De Soto County) Hernando, (Forrest County) Hattiesburg, (Franklin County) Meadville, (George County) Lucedale, (Greene County) Leakesville, (Grenada County) Grenada, (Hancock Bay County) St. Louis, (Harrison County) Biloxi and Gulfport, (Hinds County) Jackson and Raymond, (Holmes County) Lexington, (Humphreys County) Belzoni, (Issaquena County) Mayersville, (Itawamba County) Fulton, (Jackson County) Pascagoula, (Jasper County) Bay Springs and Paulding, (Jefferson County) Fayette, (Jefferson Davis County) Prentiss, (Jones County) Laurel and Ellisville, (Kemper County) De Kalb, (Lafayette County) Oxford, (Lamar County) Purvis, (Lauderdale County) Meridian, (Lawrence County) Monticello, (Leake County) Carthage, (Lee County) Tupelo, (Leflore County) Greenwood, (Lincoln County) Brookhaven, (Lowndes County) Columbus, (Madison County) Canton, (Marion County) Columbia, (Marshall County) Holly Springs, (Monroe County) Aberdeen, (Montgomery County) Winona, (Neshoba County) Philadelphia, (Newton County) Decatur, (Noxubee County) Macon, (Oktibbeha County) Starkville, (Panola County) Sardis and Batesville, (Pearl River County) Poplarville, (Perry County) New Augusta, (Pike County) Magnolia, (Pontotoc County) Pontotoc, (Prentiss County) Booneville, (Quitman County) Marks, (Rankin County) Brandon, (Scott County) Forest, (Sharkey County) Rolling Fork, (Simpson County) Mendenhall, (Smith County) Raleigh, (Stone County) Wiggins, (Sunflower County) Indianola, (Tallahatchie County) Charleston and Sumner, (Tate County) Senatobia, (Tippah County) Ripley, (Tishomingo County) Iuka, (Tunica County) Tunica, (Union County) New Albany, (Walthall County) Tylertown, (Warren County) Vicksburg, (Washington County) Greenville, (Wayne County) Waynesboro, (Webster County) Walthall, (Wilkinson County) Woodville, (Winston County) Louisville, (Yalobusha County) Water Valley and Coffeeville, and (Yazoo County) Yazoo City.

FOR FURTHER INFORMATION SEE:
- Henderson, Thomas W., and Ronald E. Tomlin, comps. *Guide to Official Records in the Mississippi Department of Archives and History*. Jackson, MS: Mississippi Department of Archives and History, 1975.

- Liscomb, Anne S., and Kathleen S. Hutchinson. *Tracing Your Mississippi Ancestors*. Jackson, MS: University Press of Mississippi, 1994.

Missouri Records relating to vital statistics are maintained in the Bureau of Vital Records in Jefferson City. This region was originally the home of a diverse group of American Indian peoples, and its name was taken from one tribe, the Missouri. There are numerous mounds and other archaeological remains that indicate a large, prosperous settled population of Indians. French lead miners and hunters established the first permanent white settlement in Missouri in 1735 at Ste. Genevieve. St. Louis was founded in 1764, and Missouri became a U.S. possession in 1803 as part of the Louisiana Purchase. At that time its non–Indian population was about 10,000, most of whom were French. After the early French settlers, immigration came largely from other, especially the Southern, U.S. states.

In 1812 Congress established the Missouri Territory, and then in 1821 designated it as the 24th state. Immigration from abroad, mainly German, Irish, and English, increased after 1820. In the 1850s, there was increasing dissension between slave- and free-state advocates in Missouri, but the influx of immigrants from the Northeast and from Europe was influential in keeping the state within the Union. Citizens of this state fought on both sides during the American Civil War, but its Union soldiers outnumbered the Confederates by nearly four to one.

The first federal census of Missouri was taken in 1830. This and the later federal census records can be found at the various National Archives locations. A number of state censuses have also been taken, but they are preserved for only a few counties. The most complete one is the 1876 census. Its results can be found county by county in the individual county archives. The same is true for the 1844 state census. At the Missouri Historical Society in Columbia there are state census record for 1787 of St. Louis and Ste. Genevieve, for 1791 of St. Louis, for 1803 of New Madrid and Cape Girardeau, and for

1845 of St. Louis. The mortality schedules for 1850 to 1880 are located in the Missouri State Historical Society Archives in St. Louis.

Two guides to the vital records of Missouri were published by the Work Projects Administration that can be found in the Historical Society library as well as in several other libraries in the state and some genealogical libraries elsewhere. These are the *Guide to Public Vital Statistics Records in Missouri* (1941), and *Guide to Vital Statistics: Church Records in Missouri* (1942).

Certified copies of Missouri birth records and death records from 1910 to the present and certified statements relating to Missouri marriages and dissolution of marriages from 1948 to the present are available from the Bureau of Vital Records in Jefferson City for a small fee. Certified copies of most Missouri birth and death records are also available from local county health departments or the city health departments in St. Louis City and Kansas City. Certified copies of the actual marriage licenses or decrees can only be obtained from that appropriate county recorder or circuit clerk's office. Guardianship and probate records are located in the county probate courts, while matters relating to the transfer of lands are with the recorders of deeds in each county. The circuit court in each county has jurisdiction over all matters of equity and law.

The Missouri State Archives in Jefferson City were created in 1965 as the officially designated repository for all state records of permanent value. Among its holdings are documents relating to French and Spanish colonial rule, the New Madrid Earthquakes, Missouri Supreme Court case files, the Civil War, and other records that may be of interest to genealogists.

The holdings in the Missouri State Historical Society on the campus of the University of Missouri in Columbia include many letters, diaries, memoirs and photographs that provide a glimpse into the past and reveal some of the innermost thoughts and feelings of the people that lived before us. Genealogists may find love letters between great-grandparents that describe their courtship days or diaries that express political views, religious beliefs, or the adversities experienced by an immigrant. The library also has numerous Civil War letters and diaries that provide vivid descriptions of the carnage during battle.

Researchers seeking information from county records can locate them at the following county seats: (Adair County) Kirksville, (Andrew County) Savannah, (Atchison County) Rockport, (Audrain County) Mexico, (Barry County) Cassville, (Barton County) Lamar, (Bates County) Butler, (Benton County) Warsaw, (Bollinger County) Marble Hill, (Boone County) Columbia, (Buchanan County) St. Joseph, (Butler County) Poplar Bluff, (Caldwell County) Kingston, (Callaway County) Fulton, (Camden County) Camdenton, (Cape Girardeau County) Jackson, (Carroll County) Carrollton, (Carter County) Van Buren, (Cass County) Harrisonville, (Cedar County) Stockton, (Chariton County) Keytesville, (Christian County) Ozark, (Clark County) Kahoka, (Clay County) Liberty, (Clinton County) Plattsburg, (Cole County) Jefferson City, (Cooper County) Boonville, (Crawford County) Steelville, (Dade County) Greenfield, (Dallas County) Buffalo, (Daviess County) Gallatin, (DeKalb County) Maysville, (Dent County) Salem, (Douglas County) Ava, (Dunklin County) Kennett, (Franklin County) Union, (Gasconade County) Hermann, (Gentry County) Albany, (Greene County) Springfield, (Grundy County) Trenton, (Harrison County) Bethany, (Henry County) Clinton, (Hickory County) Hermitage, (Holt County) Oregon, (Howard County) Fayette, and (Howell County) West Plains.

Also at (Iron County) Ironton, (Jackson County) Independence, (Jasper County) Carthage, (Jefferson County) Hillsboro, (Johnson County) Warrensburg, (Knox County) Edina, (Laclede County) Lebanon, (Lafayette County) Lexington, (Lawrence County) Mount Vernon, (Lewis County) Monticello, (Lincoln County) Troy, (Linn County) Linneus, (Livingston County) Chillicothe, (Macon County) Macon, (Madison County) Fredericktown, (Maries County) Vienna, (Marion County) Palmyra, (McDonald County) Pineville, (Mercer County)

Princeton, (Miller County) Tuscumbia, (Mississippi County) Charleston, (Moniteau County) California, (Monroe County) Paris, (Montgomery County) Montgomery City, (Morgan County) Versailles, (New Madrid County) New Madrid, (Newton County) Neosho, (Nodaway County) Maryville, (Oregon County) Alton, (Osage County) Linn, (Ozark County) Gainesville, (Pemiscot County) Caruthersville, (Perry County) Perryville, (Pettis County) Sedalia, (Phelps County) Rolla, (Pike County) Bowling Green, (Platte County) Platte City, (Polk County) Bolivar, (Pulaski County) Waynesville, (Putnam County) Unionville, (Ralls County) New London, (Randolph County) Huntsville, (Ray County) Richmond, (Reynolds County) Centerville, (Ripley County) Doniphan, (St. Charles County) St. Charles, (St. Clair County) Osceola, (St. Francois County) Farmington, (St. Louis County) Clayton, (St. Louis County) St. Louis, (Ste. Genevieve County) Ste. Genevieve, (Saline County) Marshall, (Schuyler County) Lancaster, (Scotland County) Memphis, (Scott County) Benton, (Shannon County) Eminence, (Shelby County) Shelbyville, (Stoddard County) Bloomfield, (Stone County) Galena, (Sullivan County) Milan, (Taney County) Forsyth, (Texas County) Houston, (Vernon County) Nevada, (Warren County) Warrenton, (Washington County) Potosi, (Wayne County) Greenville, (Webster County) Marshfield, (Worth County) Grant City, and (Wright County) Hartville.

For further information see:

- Hehir, Donald. *Missouri Family Histories and Genealogies, A Bibliography*. Bowie, MD: Heritage Books, 1996.
- Hodges, Nadine, and Audrey L. Woodruff. *Missouri Pioneers: County and Genealogical Records*. 30 vols. Independence, MO: Woodruff, 1967–76.

Montana Records of births and deaths are maintained by the Montana Department of Public Health and Human Services, Division of Vital Records, while the marriage and divorce records are maintained by the cities where the events took place. Geographically, this is the fourth largest state in the Union; it achieved statehood in 1889 as the 41st state

to do so. French trappers probably came into the Montana area as early as the 1740s. At the time it was occupied by a number of Indian tribes. Those who lived on the plains were the Arapaho, Assiniboin, Atsina, Blackfeet, Cheyenne, and Crow. The mountains to the west were the home for the Bannock, Kalispel, Kutenai, Salish, and Shoshoni tribes.

Montana became a territory of the United States in 1864. The northwest part of the state was listed as part of the Oregon Territory from 1846 to 1853, the Washington Territory from 1853 to 1863, and the Idaho Territory from 1863 to 1864. The remainder of the state was counted as part of the Missouri Territory from 1812 to 1854, the Nebraska Territory from 1854 to 1861, and the Dakota Territory from 1861 to 1863. When the 1860 federal census was conducted, the eastern part of Montana was included with the unorganized part of the Nebraska Territory, while the western part was included in the Washington Territory. The 1870 and 1880 censuses were enumerated as the Montana Territory. All the federal census records for Montana can be found at the National Archives locations. A state census was apparently approved in the state legislature, but never taken. The 1870 and 1880 mortality schedules for this state can be found in the State Historical Society in Helena as well as in the National Archives.

The Work Projects Administration produced the *Guide to Public Vital Statistics Records in Montana* in 1941 and an *Inventory of the Vital Statistics Records of Churches and Religious Organizations in Montana* in 1942. Both books can be found in the Montana State Library in Helena as well as in some other libraries in the state and some genealogical libraries elsewhere. The Montana Department of Public Health and Human Services, Vital Records Division in Helena has the birth, marriage, death, immigration, naturalization, and military records for the state. It will issue certified copies of birth certificates that are acceptable for passport, Social Security, employment, and personal identification purposes for a small fee. However, it will issue certified copies of death certificates only to the next of kin or to persons with a legal right to the certificate. Other records of this sort are available from the State Archives in Helena and the various counties where the births and deaths took place. Divorce records starting in 1943 can be found at the district courts in the counties where each divorce was obtained, as can all probate matters, while guardianship records are located in the county probate courts.

All records of land transactions rest with the county clerk and recorder. The state makes no distinction between actions in equity and actions in law, both of which are under the jurisdiction of the district courts.

Researchers seeking information from county records can locate them at the following county seats: (Beaverhead County) Dillon, (Big Horn County) Hardin, (Blaine County) Chinook, (Broadwater County) Townsend, (Carbon County) Red Lodge, (Carter County) Ekalaka, (Cascade County) Great Falls, (Chouteau County) Fort Benton, (Custer County) Miles City, (Daniels County) Scobey, (Dawson County) Glendive, (Deer Lodge County) Anaconda, (Fallon County) Baker, (Fergus County) Lewistown, (Flathead County) Kalispell, (Gallatin County) Bozeman, (Garfield County) Jordan, (Glacier County) Cut Bank, (Golden Valley County) Ryegate, (Granite County) Philipsburg, (Hill County) Havre, (Jefferson County) Boulder, (Judith Basin County) Stanford, (Lake County) Polson, (Lewis and Clark County) Helena, (Liberty County) Chester, and (Lincoln County) Libby.

Also at (Madison County) Virginia City, (McCone County) Circle, (Meagher County) White Sulphur Springs, (Mineral County) Superior, (Missoula County) Missoula, (Musselshell County) Roundup, (Park County) Livingston, (Petroleum County) Winnett, (Phillips County) Malta, (Pondera County) Conrad, (Powder River County) Broadus, (Powell County) Deer Lodge, (Prairie County) Terry, (Ravalli County) Hamilton, (Richland County) Sidney, (Roosevelt County) Wolf Point, (Rosebud County) Forsyth, (Sanders County) Thompson Falls, (Sheridan County) Plentywood, (Silver Bow County) Butte, (Stillwater County) Columbus, (Sweet Grass County) Big Timber, (Teton County) Choteau, (Toole County) Shelby, (Treasure County) Hysham, (Valley County) Glasgow, (Wheatland County) Harlowton, (Wibaux County) Wibaux, and (Yellowstone County) Billings.

FOR FURTHER INFORMATION SEE:
• Nicklas, Laurie. *The Montana Locator, A Directory of Public Records for Locating People Dead or Alive.* Modesto, CA: The author, 1999.
• Parpart, Pauline K., and Donald E. Spritzer, comps. *Montana Data Index: A Reference Guide to Historical and Genealogical Resources.* Missoula, MT: Montana Library Association, 1992.

Moravian Records can be located in archives at Bethlehem, Pennsylvania, which is the American headquarters of this Protestant denomination, and at Winston-Salem, North Carolina. The Moravians trace their history back to 1457 after the death of the religious reformer John Huss in Bohemia. At first they called themselves *Unitas Fratrum* (Unity of Brethren), but now refer to themselves as Moravian Brethren or Herrnhuters after the estate in Saxony where they were formally organized in 1727. They stress the sole authority of the Bible and simplicity of worship, and they place much emphasis on fellowship and missionary work. Their ministry is composed of bishops, elders, and deacons. Moravian church music, especially singing, is known and enjoyed worldwide.

The Moravians suffered much persecution during the Thirty Years' War (1618–1648). Many members immigrated to America in 1735, settling first in North Carolina and then in Pennsylvania. The American, German, and British branches of the Unity of Brethren are under the overall jurisdiction of a general synod that meets every 10 years.

The Moravian Archives in Bethlehem is the repository for records of the Northern Province churches and houses more than a million pages of handwritten documents, many in 18th century German script. There are also many English-language documents, over 20,000 printed volumes and thousands of pamphlets, paintings, prints, maps, and photographs, as well as selected personal papers. Many of these materials contain information of genealogical interest to those seeking family history information concerning Moravian ancestors.

The archives in Winston-Salem houses the records of the Southern Province churches and their members. Most of these church diaries and other documents have been translated and published in a 12-volume series, *Records of the Moravians in North Carolina*. Each of these volumes is indexed for family names. This set can also be found in the North Carolina State Library at Raleigh, the library at Duke University in Durham, North Carolina, and in some local public libraries elsewhere in North Carolina.

Mormon Records in the field of genealogy are particularly numerous because of the church's religious belief that family relationships are eternal and not limited to earthly existence. Because of this, the members of this Church of Jesus Christ of Latter-day Saints hold that persons who did not know of the Mormon religion in life may indeed accept it after death, and that living persons can be baptized into the religion on behalf of the deceased. Ceremonies are held within the church in which a living Mormon acts as a representative of the dead person and is baptized for that person.

Accordingly, Mormon church members have an obligation to search out the records of their ancestors and carefully prove the connections from one generation to another. Thus the tracing of family lines as far back into history as possible opens up the prospect of bringing all the members of a single pedigree line into the faith of the Church of Jesus Christ of Latter-day Saints.

This religion was founded by Joseph Smith and his associates on April 6, 1830, after Smith, the son of a New England farmer, allegedly received a series of divine revelations. According to Smith's account, God the father and Jesus Christ appeared to him in a vision and advised him not to join any existing church but to prepare for an important task that would be revealed to him in due time. Three years later an angel named Moroni appeared in another vision and told him about a collection of golden plates on which the

history of early peoples of the Western Hemisphere were engraved in an ancient language. Smith claimed to have found these plates on a hill near Palmyra, New York, in 1827 and to have translated them. His translation is called the *Book of Mormon*.

In the early years the church grew rapidly. Mormon communities were established at Kirtland, Ohio; Independence, Missouri; and Nauvoo, Illinois. However, mobs attacked the Mormons in several of their settlements, and Smith himself was killed by a mob in Illinois. Mob violence eventually forced the majority of Mormons to migrate to the Territory of Utah, where they applied for admission to the Union as the state of Deseret. Several other churches accept the teachings in the *Book of Mormon*, but are not associated with the Church of Jesus Christ of Latter-Day Saints. The largest of these is the Reorganized Church of Jesus Christ of Latter-Day Saints, which has its headquarters in Independence, Missouri.

Mormons regard the organization of their church as divinely inspired. They have no professional clergy, but all members in good standing may participate in church government through several church organizations. A 38-man body, called the General Authorities, heads the church. Worthy male members of the church may enter the priesthood, which is given the church's authority to perform religious ceremonies and to act in God's name. The church now claims a membership of four million in the United States, most of whom live in the Western states, and perhaps slightly more in various other countries throughout the world. The church headquarters is in Salt Lake City, Utah.

Because of their interest in genealogical pedigrees, the Mormons have provided valuable resources to both Mormons and non–Mormons alike. These resources include the largest genealogical library in the world, the Family History Library in Salt Lake City, as well as many Family History Center libraries attached to their places of worship throughout the world.

The Mormons have been pioneers in utilizing the Internet to allow persons to search their library's database of over one billion birth, marriage, and death records. Their computer program, FamilySearch, runs on personal computers using CD-ROM technology and includes a number of databases, indexes, and catalogs that are useful to genealogists. These CD-ROM disks are updated regularly and are available from the Utah library or through any of the Family History Centers.

One section of the FamilySearch database is called the Ancestral File. The records from this section can also be found on the Internet, and include information on more than 15 million persons listed by name, year of birth, state or country, and a parent's or spouse's name. A researcher using the Ancestral File can enter the name of any person and, if that person's family name is in the database, retrieve the names of all persons by that same family name who are also in the database. Because of the rights of privacy, birthdates for living persons are never displayed in the Ancestral File.

Other sections of these CD-ROM disks include the International Genealogical Index, the Personal Ancestral File program, Social Security Death Index, Family History Library Catalog, and several other databases.

Mormon computer programmers have also designed two genealogical programs for use on personal computers: Personal Ancestral File and Legacy/Family Tree. These programs use both the PAF and GEDCOM methods for entering genealogical data, which have become the standards in various computer programs designed by others for genealogists. The Mormons also maintain several Websites devoted to genealogy, the best known of which are the Ancestry Archive and My-Trees. They can be accessed in English or Spanish. Furthermore, they provide a number of interactive e-mail forums that computer users can subscribe to at no cost. *See also* **Family History Centers; Family History Library; Genealogical Mailing Lists and Newsgroups; International Genealogical Index; Social Security Records.**

Mortality Schedules are probably one of the most overlooked resources available to genealogists. They were taken as part of the census enumerations for the years 1850, 1860,

1870, 1880, and 1885. The federal government's Census Act of 1850 mandated the taking of these mortality censuses. They were also scheduled for 1890 and 1900, but unfortunately the 1890 and 1900 mortality schedules no longer exist. The 1885 mortality schedule was an interdecennial census taken in 1885 only by Colorado, Florida, Nebraska, and the territories of South Dakota and New Mexico.

The enumerators were told to inquire about all persons who had died in the 12 months immediately preceding the taking of the census enumeration. The mortality records provide the names, ages, sex, months of death, places of birth, cause of death, and occupations for those who died. They also list the deceased's color, whether free or slave, marital status, place of birth (state, territory, or country), attending physician, and number of days ill. The parents' birthplaces were added to the list of questions in 1870, and in 1880 were added the place where the fatal disease was contracted and the number of years the deceased had been a resident of the area.

Although these records document less than a tenth of the deaths that occurred for the period, they provide an historically significant snapshot of the state of health during that time. Today we consider heart disease and cancer as the major threats to modern life, but dysentery, smallpox, cholera, and consumption were the illnesses that most afflicted our ancestors. If a family member is known to have lived at a certain place during a certain year and yet cannot be found in an expected census record, a check of the mortality schedules for that state may provide a record of that member's death. Once found, this can be the clue needed to locate an obituary, mortuary record, church death record, cemetery location, probate record, or land transfer record. Additionally, the cause of death shown on the mortality schedule may provide an indication of some genetic disease that may be useful to those making a record of a family's genetic history.

In 1934 the federal government offered copies of the mortality manuscripts to their respective states. They can now be found in the state archives for Alabama, Delaware, Maine, Mississippi, New York, Rhode Island,

and West Virginia, and in the state libraries of California, Connecticut, Indiana, Maryland, New Hampshire, Oregon, and Vermont, as well as in the library at the University of Arkansas. A typescript of the North Dakota mortality schedule is at the Idaho State Historical Society. The original schedules for the other states that declined or did not respond to the government's offer were given to the Daughters of the American Revolution library in Washington, DC. The complete set of mortality schedules can also be found at the National Archives in Washington, D.C., and at its regional centers. The decennial records are indexed from 1850 to 1880. For the 1885 one, only South Dakota has been indexed.

Mortgage Records are much like deeds in their form, although they are conditional transfers of legal titles for the purpose of securing a debt or a promise to repay money borrowed. They are not as useful to genealogical researchers as are most deeds, yet they do sometimes contain valuable clues regarding individuals' wealth and the location of their property.

One particularly valuable use of mortgage records is in locating the names of slaves in the Southern states. Such mortgage records document part (and sometimes all) of the people owned by certain slave masters during those masters' lifetimes. Often these mort-

gage records are the only source for the identities of various slaves who were later emancipated by the Civil War. Such slave mortgages name persons and identify family kinships. The growth of slave families can sometimes be followed in these records if the same slaves were repeatedly mortgaged. The deed books from Upson County, Georgia, from 1825 to 1865, record the names of 1,862 slaves.

Georgia, until 1827, had no law requiring mortgages to be recorded or specifications as to where they were to be recorded. Up to that date they may be found in the record books of any court of record, including the inferior courts, the courts of ordinary, or the superior courts. After December 1827, the legislature required all current mortgages to be recorded in the superior courts just as the real estate deeds were. Typically, the superior court clerks did not keep separate books for the real estate deeds, chattel deeds, and mortgages. All these records are usually found together in the superior court's deed record books, along with many other types of legal documents.

Mortuary Records *see* **Coroner and Mortician Records**

Mug Books *see* **Family Histories**

Muslim Genealogy *see* **Islamic Genealogy**

N

Name Abbreviations are often found among the genealogical archives, and most of them follow the forms of other abbreviations, although there are sometimes exceptions. Here are a few of the common abbreviation forms:

Aaron — Aar^n
Abraham — Abra^m
Andrew — Andr^w, And^w
Arthur — Art^r, Arth^r
Barbara — Barb^a
Benjamin — Benj^a, Benjn, Benj:
Charles— Chas, Char^s

Christopher — X^r, Xopher, Xofer
Daniel — Danl
David — Dav^d
Ebenezer — Eben^r
Elizabeth — Eliz^a
Franklin — Frankl^n, Frank^n, Frank:
Frederick — Fred^{ck}, Fredr^k
George — Geo: G^o
Gilbert — Gilb^t, Gil^{rt}
Hannah — Hanah
James— Ja^s, Jas:
Jeremiah — Jer^a, Jerem^a, Jer:
Jonathan — Jonath^n, Jon^n, Jon:

John — Jno, Jno:
Joseph — Jos, Jos:
Leonard — Leon^d
Margaret — Marg^t
Nathan — Nath^n
Nathaniel — Nathl, Nathan^l
Patrick — Patr^k
Richard — Rich^d, Rich:
Robert — Robt, Rob:
Samuel — Saml, Sam:
Stephen — Steph^n
Thomas— Thos, Tho:
Vincent — Vinc^t, Vinc^{nt}
Virginia — Virg^a, Virg:
William — Willm, W^m, Will:
Zachariah — Zach^a; Zachar^a, Zach:

Almost every given name of any length may be abbreviated, as are even surnames sometimes. Most of these abbreviations can be deciphered relatively easily. One can usually look through an entire document and find the name written out completely at some other location. The task of identifying a person if only a nickname is provided is usually much more difficult than deciphering an abbreviated form.

Name Changes are legally provided for in every state; the circumstances for changing one's name and the courts that have jurisdiction over such matters vary from state to state. In most cases a person will request a name change when a divorce or an adoption has just taken place.

The regular courts with divorce jurisdiction are usually the ones that oversee name changes. Some court clerks record these changes in separately indexed volumes, and others list them with the regular court orders or judgments. In any case, it is best for the researcher to make a list of any pedigree surname entries that may appear promising in the indexes and then later to check the case files referred to for the essential information. *See also* **Genealogy for Beginners.**

Names, Meaning of, is a subject of fascination to many genealogists. It is not known, of course, when people first began using names to designate themselves and their families, but the practice is certainly quite old and prob-

ably extends far back into prehistory. Names often carry information about one's genealogical roots, such as family names and clan names, which are, of course, inherited. Given names, what Westerners call first names, are generally bestowed after the birth of a child. Most of the common given names that are used in the West come from Hebrew, Greek, or Latin words, and also from the Teutonic languages. Most names in the Muslim world come from Arabic, although there is some borrowing from the Persian and Turkish languages. Names in India are most often derived from Sanskrit, the ancient Indo-European language of that country.

Sometimes in Great Britain and the United States one finds that a surname has been turned into a given name. Examples of this are Lincoln, Percy, and Sydney. Many leading figures in the United States, including Jefferson Davis, Washington Irving, Hamilton Fish, and Franklin Delano Roosevelt had such names. In Roman Catholic families, ever since the Council of Trent (1545–1563) it has been a common practice for parents to give each child the name of a saint. This is not difficult, since many of the ordinary Christian names have been borne by one or more saints.

Some of the common first names and their origins and meaning are as follows: Alexander (from Greek) meaning "helper of mankind"; Amy (from French) meaning "beloved"; Andrew (from Greek) meaning "manly"; Barbara (from Greek) meaning "stranger"; Brian (from Celtic) meaning "strong"; Charles (from Teutonic) meaning "man"; Darlene (from Anglo-Saxon) meaning "darling"; Deborah (from Hebrew) meaning "bee"; Frank (from Teutonic) meaning "free"; Helen (from Greek) meaning "light"; Jean (from Hebrew) meaning "gift of God"; Lois (from Greek) meaning "desirable"; Mary (from Hebrew) meaning "bitter"; Thomas (from Aramaic) meaning "twin"; and William (from Teutonic) meaning "helmet." Most public libraries have dictionaries of names and their meaning.

Extremely popular among the first names used by Muslims are various forms of the name Muhammad and those of his descendants, such as Omar, Ali, and Fatima. Military leaders in the Muslim community are also honored by parents naming their children after these heroes with such names as Tariq and Amir. Some Muslim names taken from the Koran, such as Ibrahim and Mariam, have their English Biblical equivalents in Abraham and Mary.

In the Hindu tradition most children are given three names, one of which usually is taken from the name of a Hindu god or goddess. These are names such as Krishna, Ajit, Shiva, and Indra for males, and Lakshimi and Sita for females. When Sanskrit vocabulary words are used for names, these may be Gita, which means "song," and Anand, which means "happiness."

Traditional African names may reflect circumstances at the time of a birth, such as Mwanajuma, which means "Friday" in one tribal dialect, Esi, which means "Sunday," and Weksa, which means "harvest time." The people of Africa are divided into over a thousand different ethnic groups and several hundreds of languages, and some of these groups now practice the religions of Islam and Christianity and have taken over the same naming practices that are common among persons of these religious groups. *See also* **Surnames.**

Naming Patterns are often carried on from generation to generation. Even quite unusual names may be passed on, which often provides a genealogist with circumstantial evidence for family connections. A child may often be given the name of one of his or her grandparents, or a boy might be given the name of one of his father's or mother's brothers, and a girl the name of one of her parents' sisters. It is said that American families and their British Isles cousins have had a tendency to name eldest sons for paternal grandfathers, second sons for maternal grandfathers, and later sons for their father and uncles. Popular heroes, presidents, friends, and prominent local citizens are also sometimes honored with namesakes.

It is not uncommon for the genealogist to find more than one child in the same family unit with the same given name. Usually this happens after the first child with that name has died and the family has decided to preserve the name by giving it to one of the later children. A Holmes family in Texas, for example, had three sons, all of whom died young: Alvie, Lester Leo, and Alvie Leo. Two had been named after an uncle in the same county who was named Alvie. However, in the case of the musical Bach family, Johann Christian Bach had a brother named Johann Christopher Friedrich Bach. These were two of many the surviving sons of the famous Johann Sebastian Bach.

Often census and other records identify a person only by a given name and the middle initial. Through studying middle names in a cluster of siblings and cousins, the researcher may find clues as to their relationships. Some families are also found to have used surnames as middle names. Such middle names may or may not prove to be derived from some ancestor.

National Archives and Records Administration in Washington, D.C., is the official repository for noncurrent, permanently valuable records that have been produced by the federal government since 1774, including national census records; records of all the wars and military engagements in which the United States has participated; almost two million county, state, and other maps; bounty land records; records of Native Americans, lists of ship passengers, and many other valuable records.

The National Archives has published a 304-page *Guide to Genealogical Research at the National Archives* that is available from the U.S. Government Printing Office (GPO). Other useful GPO publications include *Records and Policies of the Post Office Department Relating to Place Names* (1975), and *List of Selected Maps of States and Territories* (1971).

There are also branches of the National Archives that contain records relating to their specific areas as well as microfilm copies of many of the records in Washington, such as the census records. These branches all have reading rooms where the films and other records can be viewed. The branches are located in Anchorage, Alaska; Atlanta, Georgia; Boston, Massachusetts; Chicago, Illinois; Denver, Colorado; Fort Worth, Texas; Kansas City, Missouri; Laguna Niguel, California; New York City; Pittsfield, Massachusetts; Philadelphia, Pennsylvania; San Bruno, California; and Seattle, Washington.

Native American Records can be one of the most challenging areas of genealogical research. Although Native Americans occupied the land that became the United States for many centuries before any Europeans arrived, their written history is comparatively short. Before the 19th century, genealogical data about Native Americans was almost never recorded. The censuses of Southeastern Indians prior to their forced removal into Oklahoma in the 1830s are among the first records to list any information about Indian heads of households. There may also be church records at one or another of the Franciscan missions in the Southwest for the few Indian families that converted to Christianity.

The constant conflict between Native Americans and whites from the earliest settlement at Jamestown, Virginia, in 1607 to the massacre at Wounded Knee, South Dakota, in 1890 has left a record of three and a half centuries of mistreatment and injustice directed against most of the Indian tribes. Thus the gathering of genealogical data and statistics about Native Americans has only recently become an area of historical concern.

Finding the particular tribe to which an individual Indian belonged is the initial task necessary in doing Native American research. This is essential to further work because the vast majority of existing Native American records are grouped by tribe, clan, or nation. In some cases records may even be in the Mexican rather than U.S. repositories, because Mexico controlled portions of California, Arizona, New Mexico, and Texas with their large Indian populations until the end of the Mexican War in 1848. The Archives of the Big Bend at Sul Ross University in Alpine, Texas, have some of the Catholic Church records of baptisms and marriages of Indians at the churches that were once located in the Mexican part of what was annexed by the United States.

One difficulty in researching Native American records is the fact that kinship terms have varying meanings among the tribal groups. For example, the term "father" does not always indicate the natural parent. Some tribes were organized matriarchally and not patriarchally so that the lines of descent and property rights were passed through the mother's line. The researcher before beginning to work on Native American records might wisely consult one of the dictionaries or handbooks about native peoples in North America that can be found in most good libraries. One of the best of these is *The Harvard Encyclopedia of American Ethnic Groups* (Belknap Pr. of Harvard University, 1980), which treats Native Americans, among many other groups. Another resource that can be found in the best genealogical libraries and that probably will be of great help to those beginning research in this field is E. Kay Kirkham's two-volume *Our Native Americans and Their Records of Genealogical Value* (Logan, UT: Everton, 1980).

Between 1830 and 1850 the U.S. government followed a policy of removing Indians from areas east of the Mississippi River and forceably settling them on reservations west of that river. There are two important sets of records from this period at the National Archives in Washington, D.C.: an 1832 census of the Creek Nation and an 1835 census of the Cherokee Nation. These censuses were taken before these tribes were uprooted and sent west. However, these records do vary in usefulness. Some show the number of persons by age group and sex in each family, but others give only the names of the heads of families.

The 1870 federal population census was technically the first to designate Indians in the "color" column with an "I." Prior to that, enumerators were instructed to record only White ("W"), Black ("B"), or Mulatto ("M") persons in the 1850 and 1860 censuses, although one may find some exceptions in these censuses where an "I" is recorded. In 1880, besides the regular federal census, there were special enumerations of Indians who lived near military installations in the state of Washington, the Dakota territories, and California, but these schedules are incomplete.

From 1885 to 1940, Indian censuses were conducted by the agents on each federal reservation. On some reservations these censuses were taken every year, but on others none were taken at all. Likewise, the information collected varies. These censuses can be found among the National Archives files. There is also a card index for the 1898 to 1906 censuses of five tribes (Cherokee, Chickasaw, Choctaw, Creek, and Seminole) that was taken to verify their rights to tribal status. This index is available to researchers at the National Archives Southwest Region office in Fort Worth, Texas.

At the regional National Archives branches one can find the records of the Bureau of Indian Affairs for the relevant areas during the years between 1850 and 1952. These records usually include the birth, marriage, and death data for each tribe, as well as the educational records and tribal censuses. The Bureau of Indian Affairs in Washington, D.C., can provide information as to which Indian agency was responsible for each tribal group and where those agencies were located.

Besides the census rolls, which are arranged alphabetically by the names of the Indian agencies, the National Archives has the four-volume *Special Census of Indians Not Taxed* that was produced in 1880 for various tribes in North and South Dakota, Washington, and California. There are also valuable records called annuity rolls for the years between 1850 and 1887, which indicate the annual payment of money or goods to the heads of Indian families in a number of different tribes. Occasionally members of the various families are listed here by sex and age. Furthermore, beginning in the 1870s there are various school censuses of Indian children that list the students, their ages, where they were born, and the names of their parents.

Another source of Native American genealogical data is the Allotment Registers at the National Archives. Beginning in 1887, the federal government, by terms of the General Allotment Act, began to convey tracts of land to the Indians who were able to prove that they could supervise their own affairs. The registers were compiled between 1905 and 1930. In the Allotment Registers a researcher will find the Indian and English names of the allotted persons as well as their ages and birthdates, and the names, ages, and relationships of the other members of the family. Indians frequently used several different names during their lifetimes and frequently also an English name in their contacts with federal officials, complicating any research into Native American genealogy.

After 1910, Indians could prepare and file wills. These, too, can be found at the National Archives, along with the supporting papers giving names, tribal connections, dates of death, names of spouses, and other relevant information about various Indian families.

Ever since the earliest contact between the Indians and the white settlers, these contacts occasionally resulted in intermarriages. Unfortunately for genealogists, most of these marriages occurred on the fringes of settled areas and so were only common law actions performed according to Indian customs. Thus no official record would have been made of any of them. Even when a wife or husband of such a mixed marriage did get recorded in the county registers, the fact that one was a Native American is not always part of the record.

Occasionally one may find Indians labeled as such in the early census records, but without such labeling one might never know they were Indians. For example, in the 1840 census of Attala County, Mississippi, there are a number of Indian families identified in the columns for free persons of color. The heads of household, however, mostly have English names— Fisher Durant, John Smith, Charles Westly, Doctor Jack, George, and Washington. Only a few have obvious Indian names— Comotohana and Chunkchoo. In other censuses, Indians with only one name were often listed in the columns as though the word "Indian" was their surname.

It is well known that many African-Americans intermarried with Native Americans. Less widely known is that fact that many Native Americans also owned African slaves and fathered children with African slave women. Some of these Indian slave owners are found in the 1860 census rolls with the abbreviation "Ind" after their names— Eagle, James Johnson, John Glass, Rachel Rider, and Pigeon Halfbreed. In addition there were smaller numbers of "Free People of Color" who lived with many of the Indian tribes, married persons from those tribes, and whose descendants now claim ancestry from the Oklahoma Black Indian people. It is claimed that more than 20,000 African-Americans were adopted into the Cherokee, Choctaw, Chickasaw, Creek, and Seminole Nations before the end of the 19th century.

Naturalization and Citizenship Records

can usually be located in the courts of various counties, in regional archives that serve several counties within a state, and in county or state archives. Naturalization is the first step toward citizenship, and a certificate of citizenship indicates that the process has been successfully completed. These records, though highly useful, are often neglected as a source of information because they are difficult to locate.

During the colonial period in American history, each of the colonies set up its own process for granting citizenship to foreigners within the colony. English subjects required no naturalization process because people from England were not considered to be foreigners. Then, after the founding of the United States, Congress devised a three-step procedure to achieve citizenship that began with the filing of a Declaration of Intention ("First Papers") soon after an immigrant's arrival. This would be followed, after a required waiting period of usually about five years, by the filing of a Petition for Naturalization ("Final Papers"). Once the court granted this petition, the immigrant would receive his or her Citizenship Certificate.

In 1941 Congress dropped the first step. Now the filing of a naturalization petition was followed by the court's granting of citizenship, usually two to seven years later depending on the current law. Any court of record (federal, state, or county) had the authority to accept and approve or reject the naturaliza-

tion document, and each court kept its own records of the proceedings. The continual tinkering with laws governing naturalization has resulted in some confusion as to the process, where the records are, and what they might contain. There was no centralized depository for these records until 1906, when the Bureau of Immigration and Naturalization was established. Since then, duplicate copies of these records have been deposited with the bureau, although the originals remain in the courts. The bureau also established, for the first time, standard forms for the naturalization records. When located, these records can yield important information and sometimes even photographs.

Between 1855 and 1922, wives and children became citizens when the husband or father did. A woman became a citizen automatically if she married a native-born or naturalized citizen. However, after 1922 women had to file their own papers.

Naturalization records may be in various court volumes that may be labeled as declarations of intent, civil court minutes, oaths of allegiance, certificates of naturalization, or naturalization minutes. When one knows the location of the court where a particular naturalization document may be filed, one's search time can be considerably shortened. The naturalization document and the Citizenship Certificate do not have to be filed in the same court, which makes the search for such records more difficult. In any case, the naturalization document will normally provide much more detail than the certificate, such as the town and country of origin and birthdate of the immigrant, as well as the names or his or her parents.

Although duplicate naturalization records since 1906 are on file at the Bureau of Immigration and Naturalization Service, it can take a long time to receive a response from the bureau to any request. Researchers should use this source only as a last resort. The bureau does have an index to all the 1906 to 1956 naturalizations, but the index is not open to the public. The National Archives in Washington, D.C., has naturalizations from most of the federal courts, but only a few that were created in state or local courts, in this case ones that were donated by the courts to the National Archives. Some of the records of naturalizations have been published, such as the *Index of Naturalizations, Ashtabula County, Ohio, 1875–1906*, that was published by the Ashtabula County Genealogical Society.

Some comprehensive indexes to the pre-1906 naturalization records were prepared by the Work Projects Administration in the 1930s. This is true of the early naturalization records for New York City, Maine, Massachusetts, New Hampshire, and Rhode Island. The one for New York City is at the Federal Records Center in Bayonne, New Jersey, and the others are at the National Archives in Washington, D.C. The indexes are Soundexed for easy use.

For persons naturalized from 1749 through 1810 in New Jersey, the New Jersey State Library, Archives and History Division in Trenton has the records. In Massachusetts the naturalizations from 1885 to 1931 are on file at the Massachusetts State Archives in Boston. Also for New Jersey there is a Work Projects Administration *Guide to Naturalization Records* that was published in 1941.

Sometimes citizenship applications were not completed, but the papers might still have been filed. One can also look in the census records, court records, passport application records, voting registers, homestead records, and military records for proof of citizenship. *See also* **Immigrants; Immigration Records; Soundex System.**

Naval Records *see* Military Records

Nebraska Records are perhaps most readily found at the Nebraska Historical Society in Lincoln, which maintains a large collection of library, archival, and photographic materials that may be used in compiling family histories. The region this state occupies was peopled in the east by the Missouri, Omaha, Oto, and Ponca Indian tribes when the first white explorers arrived in the early 1700s. The Indians lived peacefully by farming and hunting along the rivers. In the western area, the Indian tribes were the Arapaho, Cheyenne, Comanche, and Sioux, wandering tribes that built no villages and did not cultivate the soil. In order to keep their hunting grounds,

these western tribes fought the white settlers ferociously.

The Louisiana Purchase in 1803 included what would later be designated as the Nebraska Territory, and in 1819 the U.S. Army established Fort Atkinson on the Missouri River about 16 miles north of present-day Omaha. Soon thereafter thousands of pioneers began to travel on the Oregon Trail through Nebraska toward the rich farmlands of Oregon and Washington. Congress created the Nebraska Territory in 1854, which included parts of Colorado, Montana, Wyoming, and North and South Dakota. The territory was then reduced to the present state size in 1861 with the creation of Colorado and Dakota Territories, and Nebraska became the 37th state in 1867.

The first federal census enumeration of Nebraska took place in 1860 when it was still a territory, and federal enumerations have been conducted there every 10 years since. These census listings can be seen at the various National Archives locations. Local censuses of 15 counties in eastern Nebraska were held in 1854 and 1856. The records are available at the Nebraska Historical Society library, which also contains the state archives. There was a census of Otoe and Cuming counties in 1865, and one for Stanton and Butler counties in 1869. In 1885 Nebraska took advantage of a federal option to receive partial payment for the taking of a statewide census. These records can be located in the National Archives in Washington, D.C., and at the Nebraska State Archives in Lincoln. The Nebraska mortality schedules for 1860 to 1880 are at the Historical Society.

The Historical Society has, besides the state and national census records, microfilm copies of the 1890 federal census of Civil War veterans and widows; naturalization records from the courts of Nebraska; various military records; Nebraska county plat books and atlases for various dates; more than 30,000 microfilm rolls of Nebraska newspapers; early birth, marriage, divorce, and death records that cannot be found at the State Vital Records Office; various probate records, and state and local government records. The Historical Society publishes a *Guide to Genealogical*

Research at the Nebraska State Historical Society that is free to visitors.

The State Vital Records Office in Lincoln has birth and death records since 1904 and marriage and divorce records since 1909. Copies of these records can be obtained for a small fee. Divorces in Nebraska are granted by the district courts in each county, but none has been preserved before that date. Guardianship records are kept in the county courts, as are the probate records. There is no distinction between equity and law actions in Nebraska; both are under the jurisdiction of the county district courts. Land records that have been administered by the courts are maintained by the county recorders.

The helpful *Guide to Public Vital Statistics Records in Nebraska* was compiled by the Work Projects Administration in 1941, and can be found in the Nebraska State Library and in the University of Nebraska Library, both of which are in Lincoln, as well as in some larger genealogical libraries in other states.

Researchers seeking information from county records can locate them at the following county seats: (Adams County) Hastings, (Antelope County) Neligh, (Arthur County) Arthur, (Banner County) Harrisburg, (Blaine County) Brewster, (Boone County) Albion Box, (Butte County) Alliance, (Boyd County) Butte, (Brown County) Ainsworth, (Buffalo County) Kearney, (Burt County) Tekamah, (Butler County) David City, (Cass County) Plattsmouth, (Cedar County) Hartington, (Chase County) Imperial, (Cherry County) Valentine, (Cheyenne County) Sidney, (Clay County) Clay Center, (Colfax County) Schuyler, (Cuming County) West Point, (Custer County) Broken Bow, (Dakota County) Dakota City, (Dawes County) Chadron, (Dawson County) Lexington, (Deuel County) Chappell, (Dixon County) Ponca, (Dodge County) Fremont, (Douglas County) Omaha, (Dundy County) Benkelman, (Fillmore County) Geneva, (Franklin County) Franklin, (Frontier County) Stockville, (Furnas County) Beaver City, (Gage County) Beatrice, (Garden County) Oshkosh, (Garfield County) Burwell, (Gosper County) Elwood, (Grant County) Hyannis, and (Greeley County) Greeley.

Also at (Hall County) Grand Island, (Hamilton County) Aurora, (Harlan County) Alma, (Hayes County) Hayes Center, (Hitchcock County) Trenton, (Holt County) O'Neill, (Hooker County) Mullen, (Howard County) St. Paul, (Jefferson County) Fairbury, (Johnson County) Tecumseh, (Kearney County) Minden, (Keith County) Ogallala, (Keya Paha County) Springview, (Kimball County) Kimball, (Knox County) Center, (Lancaster County) Lincoln, (Lincoln County) North Platte, (Logan County) Stapleton, (Loup County) Taylor, (Madison County) Madison, (McPherson County) Tryon, (Merrick County) Central City, (Morrill County) Bridgeport, (Nance County) Fullerton, (Nemaha County) Auburn, (Nuckolls County) Nelson, (Otoe County) Nebraska City, (Pawnee County) Pawnee City, (Perkins County) Grant, (Phelps County) Holdrege, (Pierce County) Pierce, (Platte County) Columbus, (Polk County) Osceola, (Red Willow County) McCook, (Richardson County) Falls City, (Rock County) Bassett, (Saline County) Wilber, (Sarpy County) Papillion, (Saunders County) Wahoo, (Scotts Bluff County) Gering, (Seward County) Seward, (Sheridan County) Rushville, (Sherman County) Loup City, (Sioux County) Harrison, (Stanton County) Stanton, (Thayer County) Hebron, (Thomas County) Thedford, (Thurston County) Pender, (Valley County) Ord, (Washington County) Blair, (Wayne County) Wayne, (Webster County) Red Cloud, (Wheeler County) Bartlett, and (York County) York.

FOR FURTHER INFORMATION SEE:
- *Nebraska, A Guide to Genealogical Research.* Lincoln, NE: Nebraska State Genealogical Society, 1984.
- *Source of Genealogical Help in Nebraska.* Burbank, CA: Southern California Genealogical Society, [n.d.].

Netherlands *see* **Dutch Genealogy**

Nevada Records begin with the end of the Mexican War in 1848, when the United States acquired the Nevada region from Mexico. Nevada was then part of a territory that included California, Utah, and parts of four other states. It achieved statehood in 1864 as the 36th state.

The first census of Nevada was conducted by the state from 1861 to 1863. This varies from county to county because the instructions given to the census takers were not clear. Some of the county records list only the male heads of household, others give only the statistics, while still others list all the family members. An index for the counties of Story and Ormsbee is located in the Nevada State Archives at Carson City. The state legislature authorized other censuses, but only one more was taken, in 1875. This census is indexed and can be found at the Nevada Historical Society as well as at the University of Nevada in Reno. The federal census of Nevada has been taken at 10-year intervals since 1870, and federal territorial enumerations in 1850 and 1860 were included with the Utah Territory census. All such federal census records can be seen at the National Archives locations throughout the country. The 1860 to 1880 mortality schedules can be found at the Nevada State Historical Society in Reno.

The Nevada State Archives was created in 1965, and furnish birth and death records since 1911. Earlier records of births and deaths remain with the county recorders in each county. Marriage and divorce records since 1968 can be obtained from the Vital Records Office in Carson City, which has an index of the marriages since 1968. Copies of such records are available for a small fee. These records are also available from the county recorders in each county where the marriage license or divorce decree was issued. Guardianship records and probate records can be found in the district courts. In Nevada there are eight judicial districts. Legal matters relating to land are filed in the counties where the actions took place.

The helpful *Guide to Public Vital Statistics Records in Nevada* (Work Projects Administration, 1941), can be found at the Nevada Historical Society and at the University of Nevada in Reno, as well as at some genealogical libraries in other states.

Researchers seeking information from county records can locate them at the following county seats: (Carson City County) Car-

son City, (Churchill County) Fallon, (Clark County) Las Vegas, (Douglas County) Minden, (Elko County) Elko, (Esmeralda County) Goldfield, (Eureka County) Eureka, (Humboldt County) Winnemucca, (Lander County) Battle Mountain, (Lincoln County) Pioche, (Lyon County) Yerington, (Mineral County) Hawthorne, (Nye County) Tonopah, (Pershing County) Lovelock, (Storey County) Virginia City, (Washoe County) Reno, and (White Pine County) Ely.

FOR FURTHER INFORMATION SEE:
- Greene, Diane E. *Nevada Guide to Genealogical Records.* Baltimore, MD: Clearfield Co., 2000.
- Lee, Joyce C. *Genealogical Prospecting in Nevada: A Guide to Nevada Directories.* Carson City, NV: Nevada State Library, 1984.

New Brunswick Records are located in the Provincial Archives on the campus of New Brunswick University and at the Vital Statistics Office, both of which are in Fredericton. This area of Canada was first explored by the French in 1534 and it soon became a center for fur trade with the tribes that belonged to the Algonkian Indian family of nations. The French called the region Acadia. In 1755, during the last of the French and Indian Wars, the British captured the region and expelled most of the French settlers. Then in 1783, after the American Revolution, some 14,000 persons from the United States arrived. They were Loyalists who had supported England during the revolution. Most of them settled in the lower St. John River Valley, where they established the city of Fredericton. New Brunswick became a province of Canada in 1784.

The Provincial Archives of New Brunswick holds many documents and records bearing upon the history of New Brunswick. Most are for the period from 1784 to the present, though there are some relating to the earlier exploration period. One section contains a list of soldiers who fought as Loyalists in the American Revolution. There is also a database of New Brunswick cemeteries; maps indicate where the cemeteries are. The archives contains copies of birth records from

1888 to 1907, with some going back to 1810, copies of death records from 1888 to 1951, and copies of marriage records from 1888 to 1951 with some going back to 1810. There are also census records that were taken before New Brunswick became a Canadian province. These censuses, which enumerated every person in New Brunswick, were taken in 1851, 1861, and 1871.

The government registration of births, marriages, and deaths in New Brunswick began in January 1888. This agency preserves all the records of births that have occurred within the last 95 years, and all records of the marriages and deaths that have occurred within the last 50 years. Copies of these records may be obtained from the Vital Statistics Office of the Department of Health and Wellness. Older records of this sort can be found at the Provincial Archives.

Persons seeking information relating to adoptions in New Brunswick are allowed to activate a search for their birth parents or siblings through the government's post-adoption program operated by the Vital Statistics Office. The program was recently expanded to allow birth mothers and fathers, as well as brothers and sisters, to activate a search for their adult children or siblings. As a general rule in Canada, prior to the early to mid–1900s when provincial authorities became involved in adoptions, children were usually placed with family, friends, or neighbors without the involvement of government authorities or official documentation.

New Brunswick land, divorce, and probate records are kept in county record offices located in the 15 county seats. These are: (Albert County) Hopewell Cape, (Carleton County) Woodstock, (Charlotte County) St. Andrews, (Gloucester County) Bathurst, (Kent County) Richibucto, (Kings County) Hampton, (Madawaska County) Edmundston, (Northumberland County) Newcastle, (Queens County) Gagetown, (Restigouche County), Dalhousie, (Saint John County) Saint John, (Sunbury County) Burton, (Victoria County) Andover, (Westmorland County) Dorchester, and (York County) Fredericton. *See also* **Census, Canadian.**

New England Historic-Genealogical Society (NEHGS) was established in 1845 in Boston, Massachusetts, the first such genealogical society in the United States. Since January 1847 its members have published a quarterly magazine that is available in most genealogical libraries, the *New England Historical and Genealogical Register*. The group's purpose, as stated in its mission statement, is to advance genealogical scholarship and develop the capabilities of both new and experienced researchers of family history by collecting, preserving, interpreting, and communicating reliable genealogical data with an emphasis on families and communities connected to New England.

The NEHGS claims a membership of over 20,000 throughout the world. In the city of Boston, it maintains a bookstore called Family Treasures that carries a wide collection of genealogical publications, including individual genealogies, how-to books, local histories, computer software, CD-ROM genealogical disks, and more. The store also features hundreds of used books, including many rare, out-of-print, and first-edition genealogies. The society also maintains a large genealogical library of some 200,000 volumes and a manuscript collection of more than a million items. Members can avail themselves of the organization's circulating library, and take part in numerous educational programs, conferences, and tours both in the United States and abroad.

The New England Historic-Genealogical Society services a Website, NewEnglandAncestors.org, and sends out a biweekly e-mail newsletter for members who use the computer extensively. Finally, it publishes another magazine for members, *New England Ancestors*, a 64-page bimonthly with popular features and columns designed to advance genealogical research.

New Hampshire Records include town warrants, tax records, deeds, wills, court and church records, letters and diaries, and newspapers and broadsides. Two branches of the Algonkian Indian family of nations lived in New Hampshire before the first white men arrived. In the early 1620s groups of settlers from England, who were led by David Thomson and Edward Hilton, began settlements here. The region was named New Hampshire by another settler, John Mason. In 1641 the Massachusetts Colony gained control of New Hampshire, but it then became a separate royal colony in 1680. The residents broke away from Great Britain in 1776, becoming the first colony to form a government wholly independent from Great Britain. New Hampshire became the ninth state of the Union when it ratified the U.S. Constitution on June 21, 1788.

This state was included in the first federal census of 1790, and federal censuses have been taken there every 10 years since. The records can be found at the National Archives in Washington, D.C., as well as at all the various National Archives branches. The state itself has never undertaken a census on its own. The mortality schedules from 1850 to 1880 can be found at the New Hampshire State Library at Concord.

Many of the early town records of New Hampshire were microfilmed and indexed in the 1930s, and are now available on microfilm at the State Library. These town records generally begin with the founding of the town, and may contain records of births, marriages, burials, cemeteries, appointments, estrays (records of stray animals), freemen's oaths (men becoming eligible to vote), land records, mortgages, name changes, care of the poor, school records, surveys, tax lists, town meeting minutes, voter registrations, and "warning outs" (of town). The original records can be found in the various town clerks' offices or at the New Hampshire Historical Society in Concord.

In looking through town records, one can occasionally find constable's records and early school records. The towns were required to establish schools under provincial and early state laws, but many did so only half-heartedly or not at all. Some of the town records also include references to debates over compliance with the school laws, and, although rare, records kept by schoolmasters. The town records are also likely to include tax records that can serve as an indication of the comparative worth of the property owners in the community. Used in conjunction with wills,

deeds, and inventories, the tax records provide insight into the economy of families and communities.

Until 1883 less than half of the population was listed in the state's vital records. Moreover, those early records often gave almost no information about parents and their birthplaces. But after 1901 the New Hampshire records of births, deaths, marriages and divorce decrees are reasonably complete and give much more genealogical information. The principal record keeper on the local level in the state is the town clerk, and the earliest records are called proprietor's records.

Copies of birth, death, and marriage records starting from 1883 can be obtained for a small fee from the Vital Records Office in Concord. Copies of earlier records are available from the town clerks where each of these events occurred. Divorce records since 1808 are available from the clerks of the superior courts in the various counties where the divorces were granted. All the probate records of wills that were processed in New Hampshire between 1735 and 1771 have been published. The transcripts of these early records are available at the archives of the New Hampshire Historical Society. Guardianship records are in the county probate courts.

The New Hampshire Historical Society is a major depository for private papers, with the diaries indexed by name and letters indexed by subject. The society also has a large collection of broadsides, newspapers, books, and pamphlets. Broadsides are announcements printed on one side and intended to be posted. State and local governments often used them to announce new laws, up-coming elections, meetings, and celebrations. Because they were posted, they had the potential of reaching a large number of people. The Historical Society furthermore has records of the New Hampshire Militia, including membership and muster rolls as well as lists of uniforms and equipment. Other militia records can be found in the State Archives, also located in Concord.

Deeds and probate records for the period from 1623 to 1771 have been indexed and can be found at the State Archives or on microfilm at the New Hampshire Historical

Society. All the records relating to land transactions have been kept at the county level. Since county boundaries have changed over the years, researchers must first determine in what county a particular town was located at any date in question.

Two important collections of town maps are preserved in the State Archives. One set includes maps drawn between the mid–18th and the mid–19th centuries to establish town boundaries. The others were drawn by legislative direction and submitted to the secretary of state between 1802 and 1806. These maps were used to compile an 1816 map of New Hampshire. Both sets must be interpreted with care because they bear differing relations to actual ownership. The State Archives has printed a useful *Guide to the State Archives.* Two 1942 Work Projects Administration guides can be found in the State Library as well as in some other libraries in New Hampshire and in a few genealogical libraries elsewhere. These are the *Guide to Public Vital Statistics Records in New Hampshire,* and *Guide to Church Vital Statistics in New Hampshire, Preliminary Edition.*

In the colonial period, New Hampshire religion was dominated by Congregationalism, the faith of the colony's Puritan founders. Virtually every New Hampshire town had at least one organized Congregational parish, its minister supported by public tax monies. Present in far fewer numbers were Quakers, Anglicans, and Presbyterians. The Quakers organized a modest network of meetings in the Piscataqua and Connecticut Valleys. The Anglicans were concentrated in Portsmouth and other centers of royal power, while the Presbyterians were concentrated in the Scotch-Irish settlements in the Londonderry areas. Methodism did not arrive in New Hampshire until 1790, but John Wesley's movement grew steadily in the state thereafter. The largest dissenting community, however, was the Separate-Baptists, pioneered in New Hampshire during the Revolution by the itinerancy of Chaplain Hezekiah Smith of Haverhill.

The membership lists of each congregation were kept by the pastor. In the case of the Congregational lists, there was often a distinction between two levels of membership: "full covenant" and "halfway." The former members had made a public testimony of their religious experience and were admitted by the vote of members. The latter agreed only to abide by the doctrinal teachings and moral discipline of the church, but made no personal profession of faith. Whenever a parish built a new meetinghouse or repaired an old one, funds were raised either by assessment or by rental of pews. The votes of the parish on significant matters ranged from salary and support arrangements for the ministers to the discipline of rebellious members. The matter of ministerial support was especially sensitive since salary settlements affected tax rates and often became the occasion for schismatic and dissenting citizens to press their political claim for religious toleration.

Researchers seeking information from county records can locate them at the following county seats: (Belknap County) Laconia, (Carroll County) Ossipee, (Cheshire County) Keene, (Coos County) Lancaster, (Grafton County) Woodsville, (Hillsboro County) Manchester and Nashua, (Merrimack County) Concord, (Rockingham County) Exeter, (Strafford County) Dover, and (Sullivan County) Newport.

FOR FURTHER INFORMATION SEE:
* Copeley, William. *New Hampshire Family Records.* 2 vols. Bowie, MD: Heritage Books, 1994.
* Crandall, Ralph J., ed. *Genealogical Research in New England.* Baltimore, MD: Genealogical Publishing Co., 1984.

New Jersey Records are found in most libraries and historical societies in the state, and copies of the various state censuses can be found in the New York Public Library as well as in the New Jersey State Library and adjoining New Jersey Archives in Trenton. The first settlers in New Jersey were the Dutch and the Swedes. The Dutch founded an outpost in Pavonia (now part of Jersey City) about 1630, but Indian uprisings soon destroyed it. The Dutch then built the fortified town of Bergen (also now part of Jersey City) and forced the Swedes out, in 1655, so that they could have sole rights to the fur trade. English armies pushed the Dutch out and thus won control of the area in 1664.

During much of the colonial period, New Jersey was divided into two sections—West Jersey and East Jersey—each with its own capital, one at Perth Amboy and the other at Burlington. New Jersey's location between New York City and Philadelphia made it a major battleground during the American Revolution. At the end of this war New Jersey, with its capital now at Trenton, became the third state of the Union after its leaders ratified the U.S. Constitution on December 18, 1787.

Federal censuses have been taken in New Jersey every 10 years since 1830, and state censuses were taken in 1855, 1865, 1885, 1905, and 1915, with a partial state census in 1875. The federal censuses can be found in all the National Archives locations. The state census records are in the New Jersey State Library and Archives in Trenton, and at the New York Public Library. The 1875 partial census only covered Essex and Sussex counties. The mortality schedules for 1860 though 1880 can also be found in the New Jersey State Library and Archives.

The State Library maintains a collection of published sources, including printed genealogies, maps, church records, local histories, city directories, legislative reports, legal digests, and periodicals. The New Jersey Archives is the official repository for all the area's colonial and state government records. Its collections include manuscripts and microfilms of pre–1900 county and town records.

Copies of the records of births, deaths, and marriages can be obtained from the New Jersey State Vital Records Office in Trenton for a small fee. For marriage records between 1848 and 1864, see the New Jersey Historical Society in Newark. The state's divorce records are held in the district courts of each county, though the earliest ones can be found at the New Jersey Archives. Guardianship records are in the county surrogate's court of each county's probate division. All New Jersey wills proved before 1901 have been filed in the State Library, and those since 1901 are in the adjoining New Jersey Archives. The will abstracts covering 1670 to 1817 have been pub-

lished and completely indexed. The 13 volumes of these abstracts can be found in the State Library as well as in other libraries in New Jersey and New York.

Historically there were two separate courts in New Jersey, law and chancery, but these functions are now combined and under the jurisdiction of the superior courts in each county. All land record actions before 1800 are in the State Library. Later actions of this sort are in the county register offices, and where these do not exist, in the county clerk's office.

Three helpful books about the New Jersey records were published by the Work Projects Administration in 1941 and 1942: the *Guide to Naturalization Records in New Jersey*, and the two-volume *Guide to Vital Statistics Records in New Jersey*. Volume one covers the public archives; volume two covers the church archives. These guides can be found in some New Jersey libraries and in some genealogical libraries elsewhere.

Other sources of genealogical information in New Jersey include the extensive collection of books, pamphlets, manuscripts, maps, card files, vertical files, census microfilms, indexed genealogy manuscript collections, and many other records in the New Jersey Historical Society Library. Included in this collection are over 10,000 folders of Bible records, tombstone inscriptions, and family data, and over 60 genealogical charts. The Rutgers University Archibald Stevens Alexander Library in New Brunswick has an emigrant register file, a collection of about 30 binders compiled by the Genealogical Society of New Jersey that pertain to New Jersey families who migrated to other parts of the country. The Newark Public Library in Newark and the Gloucester County Historical Society Library in Woodbury have significant genealogical collections.

Researchers seeking information from county records can locate them at the following county seats: (Atlantic County) Mays Landing, (Bergen County) Hackensack, (Burlington County) Mount Holly, (Camden County) Camden, (Cape May County) Cape May Courthouse, (Cumberland County) Bridgeton, (Essex County) Newark, (Gloucester County) Woodbury, (Hudson County) Jersey City, (Hunterdon County) Flemington, (Mercer County) Trenton, (Middlesex County) New Brunswick, (Monmouth County) Freehold, (Morris County) Morristown, (Ocean County) Toms River, (Passaic County) Paterson, (Salem County) Salem, (Somerset County) Somerville, (Sussex County) Newton, (Union County) Elizabeth, and (Warren County) Belvidere.

FOR FURTHER INFORMATION SEE:
- Lee, Francis Bazley. *Genealogical and Memorial History of the State of New Jersey.* 4 vols. New York: Lewis Historical Publishing, 1910.
- New Jersey State Archives. *Guide to Family History Sources in the New Jersey State Archives.* Trenton, NJ: New Jersey State Archives, [n.d.]

New Mexico Records concerning the original Spanish residents and the people living there today can be found in the Albuquerque Public Library, the New Mexico Archives in Santa Fe, the New Mexico Vital Records Office in Santa Fe, and the New Mexico Genealogical Society in Albuquerque. This state, which for a long time had been a province of Mexico, was ceded to the United States in 1848 following the Mexican War. It then became the Territory of New Mexico in 1850, which included Arizona and part of Colorado, and in 1912 it was designated as the 47th state.

Some genealogists of New Mexico's colonial period (1598–1821) have focused on the people who settled and resided in the province during this Spanish period. To find such information they have used unpublished and published primary sources, such as wills, legal documents, church records, military service records, personal memoirs, diaries, correspondence, newspapers, and family collections. Examples of these materials may be found in the state archives and at the Archives of the Archdiocese of Santa Fe. Other archival collections of such sources exist at the Bancroft Library of the University of California in Berkeley, the Huntington Library and Art Gallery in San Marino, California, and the Juárez Archives at the University of Texas at El Paso. The Arizona State Museum of the University of Arizona in Tucson also has compilations of names and family histories that aid genealogists studying this Spanish colonial period.

Censuses after New Mexico became a U.S. territory were taken every 10 years starting in 1850. The first census of New Mexico as a state was conducted in 1920. There were some early Spanish and Mexican censuses that can be found at the Albuquerque Public Library. None of them are complete, but they were taken in 1750, 1790, 1823, 1830, and 1845. Two books published by the New Mexico Genealogical Society describe these early censuses. The books can be consulted at the Albuquerque Public Library. There was also an 1885 territorial census taken by New Mexico representatives on the basis of a federal promise for partial reimbursement of costs. This census can be found at the National Archives in Washington, D. C., as can all the federal census listings of New Mexico. The 1850, 1860, and 1870 mortality schedules for New Mexico are in the State Historical Society at Santa Fe.

In 1917 New Mexico was the only state without a state health department, and thus without a vital records or health statistics component. The Spanish influenza epidemic that hit New Mexico in 1918 and World War I combined to make the need for such bureaucratic units apparent. Thus in 1919 a state board of health was created in Santa Fe; its first unit was a department of vital records. Since 1920 all New Mexico birth and death records have been collected and maintained there. The births and deaths that occurred before 1919 were recorded by various institutions, including some counties and churches. Access to the vital records since 1920 is restricted and will only be issued to immediate family members or others demonstrating a "tangible legal interest." All the birth records are closed for one hundred years from the date of birth, and death records are closed for 50 years from the date of death. Marriage records are maintained by the county clerks in each of the New Mexico counties where the licenses are issued. Divorce records are with the district court clerks in the jurisdiction where each divorce was granted. Additionally, many early marriage records can be found at the state archives in Santa Fe. Guardianship records are located in either the district courts or the county probate courts, which is where wills and other probate matters are also located. Legal matters relating to land transfers will be found in the county clerks' offices.

The helpful *Guide to Public Vital Statistics Records in New Mexico* (Work Projects Administration, 1942) can be found in the Albuquerque Public Library and in some other libraries in New Mexico, as well as in some genealogical libraries in other states. Catholic Church records are particularly rich in vital record information. Some have been abstracted and published by the New Mexico Genealogical Society, and some may be found in the Archives of the Archdiocese of Santa Fe. However, if one is searching for a particular Catholic individual and is unable to obtain vital record information through the state or genealogical society sources, one should search for sacramental information (baptisms, marriages, and burials) through parish records of Catholic churches in New Mexico.

Numerous cemetery records for New Mexico have also been published by the New Mexico Genealogical Society. This is an ongoing project conducted by the society members. Another source for genealogical materials relating to New Mexico are in the collections of Spanish documents at the Zimmerman Library of the University of New Mexico in Albuquerque.

Researchers seeking information from county records can locate them at the following county seats: (Bernalillo County) Albuquerque, (Catron County) Reserve, (Chaves County) Roswell, (Cibola County) Grants, (Colfax County) Raton, (Curry County) Clovis, (De Baca County) Fort Sumner, (Dona Ana County) Las Cruces, (Eddy County) Carlsbad, (Grant County) Silver City, (Guadalupe County) Santa Rosa, (Harding County) Mosquero, (Hidalgo County) Lordsburg, (Lea County) Lovington, (Lincoln County) Carrizozo, (Los Alamos County) Los Alamos, (Luna County) Deming, (McKinley County) Gallup, (Mora County) Mora, (Otero County) Alamogordo, (Quay County) Tucumcari,

(Rio Arriba County) Tierra Amarilla, (Roosevelt County) Portales, (San Juan County) Aztec, (San Miguel County) Las Vegas, (Sandoval County) Bernalillo, (Santa Fe County) Santa Fe, (Sierra County) Truth or Consequences, (Socorro County) Socorro, (Taos County) Taos, (Torrance County) Estancia, (Union County) Clayton, and (Valencia County) Los Lunas.

FOR FURTHER INFORMATION SEE:
- Esterly, Robert E. *Genealogical Resources in New Mexico.* Albuquerque, NM: New Mexico Genealogical Society, 1997.
- *Sources of Genealogical Help in New Mexico.* Burbank, CA: Southern California Genealogical Society, [n.d.]

New York Records in abundance are located at the New York Public Library and the New York State Library in Albany. Before the first white settlers arrived in this area, two of the largest and most powerful Indian groups in North America lived here. One group consisted of the Deleware, Mohican, Montank, Munsee, and Wappinger tribes of the Algonkian family of Indian nations. The other was the Iroquois, or Five Nations, consisting of the Cayuga, Mohawk, Oneida, Onondaga, and Seneca tribes. In 1609 Henry Hudson, an Englishman employed by the Dutch, sailed up what is now called the Hudson River in search of a northwest passage to the Orient. Soon afterward the Dutch established a number of trading posts and prosperous settlements along the Hudson River Valley, and in 1625 they established the settlement called New Amsterdam that eventually grew into the city of New York. But by 1664 they had surrendered New Amsterdam to England.

Representatives from New York approved the Declaration of Independence in 1776, and the former English colony became the 11th state to join the Union on July 26, 1788. The first federal census was conducted here in 1790. It consisted of the enumerations of Westchester County and Suffolk County. This and the other federal census records for New York can be seen at the various National Archives locations. State censuses were conducted in 1825, 1835, 1845, 1855, 1865, 1875, 1892, 1905, 1915, and 1925, but did not cover all counties. The records can be found in the New York State Library, and some can be found in the New York Public Library. The state census of 1855 is particularly useful because it gives the county of birth and length of residence in the then-current location for the listed individuals. The New York Genealogical and Biographical Society in New York City also has copies of the censuses for 1825 to 1875, and copies of those for individual counties can also be found in the various county clerks' offices. The New York state mortality records are at the State Library.

The records of births, marriages, and deaths that have occurred since 1881 in New York State, outside of New York City, are filed at the Vital Records Office in Albany. The birth records are available for a small fee if they have been on file for at least 75 years. Death and marriage records are available if they have been on file for at least 50 years. For Albany, Buffalo, and Yonkers, the state office only has the records beginning in 1914. Earlier vital records for these cities can be found in the city clerk's office for each city. For records of births that occurred in the five boroughs of New York City (Manhattan, Kings, Queens, the Bronx, and Staten Island), one must visit the New York City Department of Health and Mental Hygiene.

Also on file at the state Vital Records Office are the divorce records for all the state since 1963. These and earlier divorce records can also be found in the offices of the various county courts. There are two types of divorce records, one a divorce decree and the other a divorce certificate. The first is a document prepared by the court that sets forth the terms and conditions of the divorce. It is signed by a judge and filed with the county clerk of the county where the decree was issued. All divorces granted before 1963 are of this type. The divorce certificate is filed with the New York State Department of Health for all divorces granted on or after January 1, 1963. The document contains basic information about the husband and wife, and the date and place where the marriage ended. Copies of the divorce certificates are only available to the husband, wife, or persons with a New York State court order.

Guardianship records are filed in the county surrogates' courts, as are the records of will probates. The state Vital Records Section operates an adoption information registry designed to help adoptees obtain available non-identifying information about their birth parents. It also enables the reunion of registered adoptees with their birth parents and biological siblings. The records of all land transactions are filed with the various county clerks except for those in the counties of Manhattan, Kings, Queens, and the Bronx. There they are in the custody of the Register of the City of New York.

The immigration records for the Port of New York from 1820 to 1846, from 1897 to 1942, and from 1902 to 1943 can be found at the National Archives in Washington, D.C. The ones from 1897 to 1942 can also be accessed through the Ellis Island Website. Three helpful guides to New York resources were published by the Work Projects Administration in 1942: the *Guide to Public Vital Statistics Records in New York State (Inclusive of New York City)*, the *Guide to Vital Statistics Records in Churches in New York State (Exclusive of New York City)*, and the *Guide to Vital Statistics Records in the City of New York Churches*. They can all be found in the New York Public Library, as well as at the State Library and in some other public libraries and genealogical libraries in New York and some other states. *See also* **Ellis Island Records.**

The New York Public Library's Irma and Paul Milstein Division of United States History, Local History, and Genealogy contains one of the largest genealogical and local history collections available to the public in this country, and, as such, it is one of the most heavily used divisions in the library. It has indexes to births, 1888–1982, to deaths, 1888–1982, and to marriages, 1869–1937. It has hundreds of genealogical periodicals, numerous city and telephone directories from many parts of the United States and Canada, various handbooks and guides, family histories, and some of the census records for New York, New Jersey, Connecticut, and Puerto Rico, as well as various New York County censuses.

The library provides an 18-volume catalog, the *Dictionary Catalog of the Local His-*

tory & Genealogy Division, arranged by author, subject, and sometimes title. Also available here is a copy of *An Introduction to Genealogy at the State Library* that can also be found at the Albany site.

Researchers seeking information from county records can locate them at the following county seats: (Albany County) Albany, (Allegany County) Belmont, (Bronx County) Bronx, (Broome County) Binghamton, (Cattaraugus County) Little Valley, (Cayuga County) Auburn, (Chautauqua County) Mayville, (Chemung County) Elmira, (Chenango County) Norwich, (Clinton County) Plattsburgh, (Columbia County) Hudson, (Cortland County) Cortland, (Delaware County) Delhi, (Dutchess County) Poughkeepsie, (Erie County) Buffalo, (Essex County) Elizabethtown, (Franklin County) Malone, (Fulton County) Johnstown, (Genesee County) Batavia, (Greene County) Catskill, (Hamilton County) Lake Pleasant, (Herkimer County) Herkimer, (Jefferson County) Watertown, (Kings County) Brooklyn, (Lewis County) Lowville, and (Livingston County) Geneseo.

Also at (Madison County) Wampsville, (Monroe County) Rochester, (Montgomery County) Fonda, (Nassau County) Mineola, (New York County) New York, (Niagara County) Lockport, (Oneida County) Utica, (Onondaga County) Syracuse, (Ontario County) Canandaigua, (Orange County) Goshen, (Orleans County) Albion, (Oswego County) Oswego, (Otsego County) Cooperstown, (Putnam County) Carmel, (Queens County) Jamaica, (Rensselaer County) Troy, (Richmond County) St. George, (Rockland County) New City, (St. Lawrence County) Canton, (Saratoga County) Ballston Spa, (Schenectady County) Schenectady, (Schoharie County) Schoharie, (Schuyler County) Watkins Glen, (Seneca County) Waterloo, (Steuben County) Bath, (Suffolk County) Riverhead, (Sullivan County) Monticello, (Tioga County) Owego, (Tompkins County) Ithaca, (Ulster County) Kingston, (Warren County) Lake George, (Washington County) Hudson Falls, (Wayne County) Lyons, (Westchester County) White Plains, (Wyoming County) Warsaw, and (Yates County) Penn Yan.

For further information see:
- Burke, Kate. *Searching in New York: A Reference Guide to Public and Private Records.* Costa Mesa, CA: ISC Publications, 1987.
- Clint, Florence. *New York Area Key: A Guide to the Genealogical Records of the State of New York.* Elizabeth, CO: Keyline Publishers, 1979.

New Zealand Genealogy covers the indigenous Maori population as well as the European settlers who began to arrive in 1814. The area was first explored by Captain James Cook of the British navy in 1769. There was a series of wars that were fought between the English settlers and the Maori between 1845 and 1872. They ended when the Maori leader, Te Kooti, was forced to retreat to a remote area of the North Island. Britain granted New Zealand its own a constitution in 1852, and many of the libraries and museums in the main cities of New Zealand today have good resources for New Zealand history and sometimes for genealogy.

The registration of births and deaths of settlers in New Zealand began in 1848 and the registration of marriages in 1854. Prior to those dates, such records were recorded in the church parish registers. The registration of Maori births and deaths became compulsory in 1913, but a great many of the Maori births, deaths, and marriages were never registered as the law required. Beginning in 1955 the separate marriage laws and recording system for the Maoris and the settlers were amalgamated, as they were for birth and death registrations in 1962.

The registration act of 1848 required that each settler birth contain the child's name and sex, the parents' names, the occupation of the father, and the maiden name of the mother. After 1875 these records included the date and place of marriage for the parents and the age and birthplace of each parent. Then in 1912 the listing added the age and sex of all living siblings and the number and sex of any children of the birth child's parents who had died. For death records, the 1848 act required the listing of the name, age, sex, occupation, date of death, and cause of death. By 1875 the names of the parents of the deceased, the father's occupation, the mother's maiden name, the place of birth of the deceased, and the number of years that the deceased lived in New Zealand were added. If the deceased was married, the place of marriage, age at marriage, name of the spouse, sex and ages of any surviving children, and place and date of burial were also included. In 1912, the age of the surviving spouse was also included.

For marriages, the act of 1854 only required the date and place of marriage, names and ages of the couple, and occupation of the bridegroom. An act passed in 1880 added the birthplaces of each party, their residences, the names of all four parents, the occupations of the fathers, and the mothers' maiden names.

The vital statistics for the Maoris applied to all persons of half or more Maori ancestry for births and deaths during the years of 1913 to 1961, and 1911 to 1954 for all marriages. The birth records contained the first name and sex of the child, name and place of birth, full names of the parents, and tribe and degree of Maori ancestry for each parent. The death records gave the full name and residence of the deceased, the date and place of death, cause of death, the tribe to which he or she belonged, name of husband or wife, sex and age, number and sex of all living children, names of parents and their places of residence, and the degree of Maori ancestry. The marriage records were similar to those for the European settlers with the exception that only the parents' names were required. After 1955 the records for both groups were combined and the information listed was the same.

The vital records of New Zealand are not open to searches except by authorized members of the official registry staff. For a fee they will provide researchers with information from the birth, death, and marriage records, although some of the particulars may be omitted. For most purposes a genealogist does not need the actual certificate, so the information provided will probably be adequate.

The New Zealand Archives Act of 1957 established a national archives center in Wellington to preserve the public archives of this country. This is where government records of permanent value are deposited,

and a great deal of research is done by scholars, students, and others at this place. No items stored there can be destroyed without the approval of the chief archivist. The New Zealand National Archives publishes an annual summary of any new accessions to its holdings. The genealogist will also find useful records at the National Library in Wellington.

Newfoundland and Labrador Records can be found in the Provincial Archives at St. John's. By the late 1500s, English, French, Spanish, and Portuguese fishermen had established small settlements on the shores of Newfoundland. The area was then occupied mostly by Beothuk Indians. The English fishermen worked and settled mainly along the southern part of the east coast, while the French fleets controlled the north and south coasts. The ships of all these nations often anchored in the same harbor. In 1583 Sir Humphrey Gilbert arrived and claimed the whole region for England. This resulted in intensified conflicts with the French, and in 1662 French soldiers established a garrison at Placentia that grew into a fortified colony that threatened English authority in Newfoundland. The English and the French attacked each other's ships and settlements until 1713, when they signed the Treaty of Utrecht, which gave Britain the whole island. Britain obtained all of Canada by the Treaty of Paris in 1763, and the British government then placed the Labrador coast under the authority of Newfoundland's royal governor.

Meanwhile, during the late 1700s, Micmak Indians invaded Newfoundland from what is now Nova Scotia and fought against the Beothuks, wiping them out by 1829. The Micmaks settled around St. Georges Bay and along Newfoundland's southern coast. In Labrador, the Naskapi and Montagnais Indian tribes have lived for as long as anyone knows.

Censuses of Newfoundland for 1921, 1935, and 1945 have asked the following question of each person enumerated: "Are you a Micmac Indian?" Responses have not always been given, but in many cases a reply of "yes" or "no" was recorded. The 1935 census sometimes indicates aboriginal status under the heading of nationality, and the 1945 census indicates it under the heading of racial origin. The census records are available at the Provincial Archives. Two earlier censuses taken in 1691 and 1693 enumerated all persons living there at the time; one in 1704 listed only the heads of families.

Records of births, marriages, and deaths are available from the Vital Statistics Division of the Newfoundland Department of Health at St. John's. These vital statistics consist mainly of transcripts of the baptism and marriage records of various churches throughout Newfoundland and Labrador. Civil registration did not begin here until 1891. At that time all clergy were required to register with the government every baptism, marriage, and burial conducted within their jurisdictions. In the early 1940s the government became disturbed over the fact that the original parish registers held by some churches were in fragile condition and that the records of a few other churches had already been lost through fire. Thus the government asked the churches to transcribe their pre–1891 records and deposit the transcriptions with the Vital Statistics Division. They offered to pay the churches 10 cents a name as compensation. The burial records were not requested, although a few churches did submit a number of these. Divorces cannot be granted in the province. Residents can only obtain them by an act of the Canadian Parliament.

The collection of transcriptions is not complete, since many clergy and churches, particularly the Roman Catholic ones, did not respond to the request of the Vital Statistics Division. The collection is, in fact, predominately Protestant, having mostly records of the Church of England/Anglican, Congregational, Methodist, Presbyterian, and Reformed Episcopal Churches. Some churches did not copy their earliest registers.

The clergy of early parishes in Newfoundland and Labrador often were responsible for large geographical areas that included numerous communities. The boundaries of some of these parishes changed considerably through the years, and as more clergy became available to serve the people, parishes were

subdivided to include fewer places. In many cases a name is noted under a parish that was a considerable distance from the actual place of residence, because visiting clergy sometimes performed baptisms and marriages and then took the records back to their own parishes. People may also have visited or worked seasonally in other areas of Newfoundland and Labrador. When married there, the record would have been recorded there and not at their home parishes.

Copies cannot be made of any baptism, marriage, or burial records, but the Vital Statistics Division will issue certificates for those from 1892 to the present. The earlier records are indexed and on microfilm. They can be viewed at the Provincial Archives. Approximately 200 parishes within Newfoundland and Labrador are represented in this collection. The Provincial Archives has several publications that should help the researcher seeking information about the parish registers. They include the *Survey of Anglican, Roman Catholic and United Church Parishes in Newfoundland and Labrador*; *Finding Aid for the Registers of Vital Statistics Collection*; and *Alphabetical List of Pastoral Charges and Communities Served, United Church Conference Archives*.

The Newfoundland and Labrador Genealogical Society in St. John's provides access to a number of historical databases and an information service for genealogical researchers. It publishes a quarterly journal, *The Newfoundland Ancestor*. Its library includes collections of genealogical reference books, family histories, cemetery transcripts, genealogical periodicals, town directories, and censuses. *See also* **Census, Canadian.**

Newsgroups *see* **Genealogical Mailing Lists and Newsgroups**

Newspaper Sources are valuable for the information they may provide for genealogists. They often contain vital records such as the births, marriages, and deaths of persons who lived in a community. Newspaper items also reflect the day-to-day events surrounding those individuals found on a family tree, and the environment in which they lived. Although some newspapers still exist from the

18th century, for the most part they have become a tool to be used in 19th and 20th century research. A surprising number of newspapers have been indexed in recent years, and though not every name is included, the most useful ones for genealogical purposes can often be found.

Many newspapers maintain their own archives of past issues. If one is fortunate, one may find that the local newspaper offices have preserved copies of the other newspapers in that same area. A local library or state archive may also have microfilm copies of the particular newspapers one is seeking, and these are often available to researchers through the interlibrary loan. Newspaper abstracts often appear in genealogical periodicals and some have been published in book form.

The researcher should not limit an examination to just one newspaper, but should probably check all the ones published in the area where an event took place. It can also be rewarding to read multiple issues of a given paper in order to glean other tidbits about ancestors and their communities. Consider not only the paper's coverage of news and opinion but its cultural pages, advertisements, and public announcements. Often only a funeral notice will appear. However, if the individual was a prominent citizen, politician, religious leader, or early settler, a news story will usually provide more details about an individual's life.

If the newspapers being researched are weekly ones, as are most of those published in small towns, one should check at least three or four weeks following an event such as a death. Occasionally the notice will not be printed until a significant amount of time has passed. News items with social events will sometimes tell who attended a funeral, or who visited in the weeks prior to a death. In small town newspapers, a photo of the deceased may accompany an obituary. A wedding account may contain a photo of the bride or both bride and groom, and silver and golden wedding anniversary announcements may contain a photo of the couple and a list of their children.

Because locating local newspapers of the past can be difficult, it is wise for the researcher to consult the published county histories to learn the names of the newspapers for that area. Several reference books list the published newspapers, including Winifred Gregory's *American Newspapers 1821–1936; A Union List of Files Available in the United States and Canada,* and the *Ayer Directory of Publications.* These can be found in most of the larger libraries. If one finds that the particular town where an event took place did not have a local newspaper, one can check nearby towns or counties for their newspapers, since these papers likely served that area. Newspapers should be searched page by page because they do not have indexes as many genealogy books do. Rural newspapers typically include gossip columns arranged by townships. One can save some time by skimming through the particular township column that relates to the home area of the individual being sought.

Nicaragua *see* **Central American Genealogy**

North Carolina Records, including family histories, census records, abstracts of county and state records, bibliographies, and general books on genealogy can be found in the North Carolina State Library at Raleigh. Before the first white explorers arrived, about 35,000 Indians belonging to some 30 tribes lived here. They included the Cherokees, who lived in the western mountains; the Hatteras, who lived along the coast; and the Catawba, Chowanoc, and Tuscarora, who lived on the coastal plain and the Piedmont. In 1629, King Charles I of England gave all the land from Albemarle Sound in the north to the St. John's River on the south to eight of his favorite nobles and directed that the area should be called Carolina. The word comes from the word Carolus, the Latin form of Charles. When Carolina was divided in two, in 1712, the southern part was called South Carolina, and the northern, or older settlement, North Carolina.

Following the American Revolution, North Carolina became the 12th state to ratify the U.S. Constitution, in 1789. The first federal census, in 1790, included an enumeration of this state. It is available at the National Records Administration in Washington,

D.C., as well as at its various branches. An earlier, incomplete census of the area taken between 1785 and 1787 can be found in the North Carolina State Archives in Raleigh. The 1850 to 1880 mortality schedules can also be found in the State Archives.

Birth records since 1913 and death records since 1930 are located at the North Carolina Vital Records center in Raleigh. Copies can be obtained for a small fee. The death records from 1913 to 1955 can be found at the State Archives. Marriage records after 1868 should be available from the register of deeds in each county where a marriage took place, and those since 1962 can also be obtained from the Vital Records Center. Divorce records since 1958 are available from the clerk of superior court in the county where the divorce was granted. This is also where any guardianship records are filed.

Wills and other probate matters can be researched in the offices of the county clerks of the superior courts. However, wills enacted prior to 1760 were kept on a colony-wide basis and some were recorded by the secretary of the province. Such files as exist can be found in the North Carolina State Archives. There are also some military records and naturalization records on file at the archives. Land records are on file with the county register of deeds. In North Carolina there is no distinction between equity and law cases. Both are recorded in either the county district courts or the county superior courts.

The North Carolina State Library in Raleigh, which shares the same building as the State Archives, maintains an extensive collection of published materials for genealogical research, including family histories; census records and indexes; abstracts of county, state, and federal records; bibliographies; indexes, and general reference books on genealogy. The emphasis is on North Carolina, but the library also has extensive materials on the colonial and post-colonial periods, as well as the areas from which North Carolinians came and to which they migrated.

A helpful book (Work Projects Administration, 1942) is the *Guide to Vital Statistics Records in North Carolina*. It can be found in the State Library as well as in the University of North Carolina Library at Chapel Hill, the library at Duke University in Durham, and in some of the larger genealogical libraries in other states.

Researchers seeking information from county records can locate them at the following county seats: (Alamance County) Graham, (Alexander County) Taylorsville, (Alleghany County) Sparta, (Anson County) Wadesboro, (Ashe County) Jefferson, (Avery County) Newland, (Beaufort County) Washington, (Bertie County) Windsor, (Bladen County) Elizabethtown, (Brunswick County) Bolivia, (Buncombe County) Asheville, (Burke County) Morganton, (Cabarrus County) Concord, (Caldwell County) Lenoir, (Camden County) Camden, (Carteret County) Beaufort, (Caswell County) Yanceyville, (Catawba County) Newton, (Chatham County) Pittsboro, (Cherokee County) Murphy, (Chowan County) Edenton, (Clay County) Hayesville, (Cleveland County) Shelby, (Columbus County) Whiteville, (Craven County) New Bern, (Cumberland County) Fayetteville, (Currituck County) Currituck, (Dare County) Manteo, (Davidson County) Lexington, (Davie County) Mocksville, (Duplin County) Kenansville, (Durham County) Durham, (Edgecombe County) Tarboro, (Forsyth County) Winston-Salem, (Franklin County) Louisburg, (Gaston County) Gastonia, (Gates County) Gatesville, (Graham County) Robbinsville, (Granville County) Oxford, (Greene County) Snow Hill, and (Guilford County) Greensboro.

Also at (Halifax County) Halifax, (Harnett County) Lillington, (Haywood County) Waynesville, (Henderson County) Hendersonville, (Hertford County) Winton, (Hoke County) Raeford, (Hyde County) Swanquarter, (Iredell County) Statesville, (Jackson County) Sylva, (Johnston County) Smithfield, (Jones County) Trenton, (Lee County) Sanford, (Lenoir County) Kinston, (Lincoln County) Lincolnton, (Macon County) Franklin, (Madison County) Marshall, (Martin County) Williamston, (McDowell County) Marion, (Mecklenburg County) Charlotte, (Mitchell County) Bakersville, (Montgomery County) Troy, (Moore County) Carthage,

(Nash County) Nashville, (New Hanover County) Wilmington, (Northampton County) Jackson, (Onslow County) Jacksonville, (Orange County) Hillsborough, (Pamlico County) Bayboro, (Pasquotank County) Elizabeth City, (Pender County) Burgaw, (Perquimans County) Hertford, (Person County) Roxboro, (Pitt County) Greenville, (Polk County) Columbus, (Randolph County) Asheboro, (Richmond County) Rockingham, (Robeson County) Lumberton, (Rockingham County) Wentworth, (Rowan County) Salisbury, (Rutherford County) Rutherfordton, (Sampson County) Clinton, (Scotland County) Laurinburg, (Stanly County) Albemarle, (Stokes County) Danbury, (Surry County) Dobson, (Swain County) Bryson City, (Transylvania County) Brevard, (Tyrell County) Columbia, (Union County) Monroe, (Vance County) Henderson, (Wake County) Raleigh, (Warren County) Warrenton, (Washington County) Plymouth, (Watauga County) Boone, (Wayne County) Goldsboro, (Wilkes County) Wilkesboro, (Wilson County) Wilson, (Yadkin County) Yadkinville, and (Yancey County) Burnsville.

FOR FURTHER INFORMATION SEE:
- Draughon, Wallace R. *North Carolina Genealogical Reference: A Research Guide for All Genealogists, Both Amateur and Professional.* Durham, NC: Smith Publications, 1966.
- Hehir, Donald M. *Carolina Families: A Bibliography of Books about North and South Carolina Families.* Bowie, MD: Heritage Books, 1994.

North Dakota Records can be found at the North Dakota State Historical Society and North Dakota State Library, both of which are in Bismarck, as well as at the library of North Dakota State University in Fargo. When the first white explorers arrived in the North Dakota region they found several different Indian tribes living there, including the Dakota, or Lakota, nation that was sometimes called the Sioux by those who feared them. Other tribes were the Cheyenne, Mandan, Arikara, Assiniboin, and Hidatsa. The Chippewa, or Ojibway, came into the northern Red River Valley around 1800.

The first explorers were French Canadians, and the area was part of the land claimed by the French in 1762. They used North Dakota as a place in which to trade furs with the Indians. The United States obtained North Dakota as part of the Louisiana Purchase of 1803, and President Thomas Jefferson then sent an expedition led by Lewis and Clark to explore the northern parts of the Louisiana Territory and blaze a trail to the Pacific Ocean. Lewis and Clark reached central North Dakota in October, 1804. They built Fort Mandan on the east bank of the Missouri River, across from the present-day town of Stanton. The U.S. Congress designated North Dakota as part of the Dakota Territory in 1861, including both Dakotas, most of Wyoming, and Montana. The area was opened to homesteading in 1863. In 1864 Wyoming and Montana were taken from the Dakota Territory to form the Montana Territory, and in 1889 the two Dakotas were separated with North Dakota becoming the 39th state of the Union.

The first federal census of what was soon to be designated the Dakota Territory was conducted in 1860, although 10 years earlier what is now Pembina County in the western part of North Dakota had been enumerated as part of the Minnesota Territory records. Both of these census enumerations can be found at the National Archives in Washington, D.C., and its branches, as can all the other federal censuses for North Dakota. There were also censuses produced by the state itself that are now located in the library of the North Dakota State Historical Society. These include an 1857 census of Pembina County, and an 1885 census that was partially paid for by the federal government. The 1885 census gives the names, ages, occupations, and birthplaces for all family members, as well as the mortality schedules for Civil War veterans. However, there are a few counties missing from this 1885 listing. Furthermore, state censuses prepared in 1915 and 1925 give the names and ages of all family members. The mortality schedules for 1860 to 1880 can also be found at the North Dakota State Historical Society.

North Dakota birth, marriage, and death records are maintained by the Division of Vital

Records in Bismarck, which will supply copies for a small fee. Divorce records since 1949 can be located in the superior courts of each county, and guardianship records can be located in the county courts. Wills are also probated in the county courts. There is no distinction between equity and law actions in North Dakota. The county and district courts in all the counties have jurisdiction over such legal actions. Records for land transactions are maintained by the county registers of deeds.

Two helpful guides to North Dakota genealogical records were produced by the Work Projects Administration: the *Guide to Public Vital Statistics Records of North Dakota* (1941), and the *Guide to Church Vital Statistics Records in North Dakota* (1942). Both volumes can be found at the North Dakota State Library and at the North Dakota State University Library, as well as in some genealogical libraries in other states.

Researchers seeking information from county records can locate them at the following county seats: (Adams County) Hettinger, (Barnes County) Valley City, (Benson County) Minnewaukan, (Billings County) Medora, (Bottineau County) Bottineau, (Bowman County) Bowman, (Burke County) Bowbells, (Burleigh County) Bismarck, (Cass County) Fargo, (Cavalier County) Langdon, (Dickey County) Ellendale, (Divide County) Crosby, (Dunn County) Manning, (Eddy County) New Rockford, (Emmons County) Linton, (Foster County) Carrington, (Golden Valley County) Beach, (Grand Forks County) Grand Forks, (Grant County) Carson, (Griggs County) Cooperstown, (Hettinger County) Mott, (Kidder County) Steele, (La Moure County) La Moure, (Logan County) Napoleon, (McHenry County) Towner, (McIntosh County) Ashley, (McKenzie County) Watford City, (McLean County) Washburn, (Mercer County) Stanton, (Morton County) Mandan, (Mountrail County) Stanley, (Nelson County) Lakota, (Oliver County) Center, (Pembina County) Cavalier, (Pierce County) Rugby, (Ramsey County) Devils Lake, (Ransom County) Lisbon, (Renville County) Mohall, (Richland County) Wahpeton, (Rolette County) Rolla, (Sargent County)

Forman, (Sheridan County) McClusky, (Sioux County) Fort Yates, (Slope County) Amidon, (Stark County) Dickinson, (Steele County) Finley, (Stutsman County) Jamestown, (Towner County) Cando, (Traill County) Hillsboro, (Walsh County) Grafton, (Ward County) Minot, (Wells County) Fessenden, and (Williams County) Williston.

FOR FURTHER INFORMATION SEE:
- Aberle, George P. *Pioneers and Their Sons: One Hundred Sixty-Five Family Histories.* Bismarck, ND: Tumbleweed Press, 1980.
- Vexler, Robert I. *Chronology and Documentary Handbook of the State of North Dakota.* Dobbs Ferry, NY: Oceana Publications, 1978.

Northwest Territories Records can best be found at the Prince of Wales Northern Heritage Centre in Yellowknife. This vast region covers about a third of Canada and stretches from the northern boundaries of the Canadian provinces to within 500 miles of the North Pole. The region is the homeland of about 11,400 Canadian Eskimos and about 7,200 northern Indians. The capital is Yellowknife.

Vital statistics information for the Northwest Territories from 1925 to the present can be found at Vital Statistics Department of Health and Social Services in Inuvik. It includes birth, marriage, and death records. Land grant information is recorded with the Land Registration District in Yellowknife.

The Prince of Wales Northern Heritage Centre contains some 6,000 books, numerous photographs, various maps, sound recordings, videotapes, and film reels. Its records cover the years of 1845 to 1990, with the predominant amount of material encompassing the years from 1930 to 1980. The center's primary task is to ensure that a fair, accurate, and complete record of government activity is identified, acquired, preserved, and made accessible. The holdings document the history of the Northwest Territories, including among other things the oral tradition and history of the first Indian nations, the constitutional development and activities of the government in the Northwest Territories, the fur trade, aviation industry, and the development of the Northwest Territories mining industry. *See also* **Census, Canadian.**

Norwegian Genealogy includes church and civil registrations of births, marriages, and deaths, as well as emigration and census records. The church records particularly hold essential information about baptisms, marriages, and deaths, as well as confirmation dates and the movements of persons in and out of the various parishes.

The first mention of such parish registers in Norway was in 1668 when priests were requested to maintain these registers. This record-keeping did not become law until 1685. However, there are some much earlier parish registers. The oldest Norwegian parish register is from the Andebu parish beginning in 1623. The second oldest is from the Bragernes parish and dates from 1634. Despite the law, most priests in Norway did not start maintaining their parish registers until the end of the century, or later. Today there are only 127 Norwegian parishes that have such registers starting before 1700. Furthermore, fires and other calamities have resulted in the loss of numerous parish registers over the past three hundred years.

Reading parish registers where everything is written with unfamiliar letters in a foreign language can be somewhat daunting. But in many cases this is unnecessary because others have compiled the results into *bygdebøks*, or local history books. A *bygdebøk* is a valuable resource for any genealogist tracing Norwegian ancestry. Most *bygdebøker* (the Norwegian plural form of the word) can be characterized by being either thematic in scope and limited to one community, which can be more than one parish; covering every family who lived in a community during a certain period; or a history narrated chronologically and in a descriptive way. Most of the *bygdebøker* do have many pictures of individuals and farms.

The volumes that cover the farm history of a community go back as far as sources exist, and are arranged so that each chapter covers one main farm. For the genealogist these farm histories probably give the best information. Norwegian libraries have directories with every *bygdebøk* that has been published. The texts of such books are, of course, in Norwegian, but some *bygdebøker* include English summaries and explanations of special Norwegian words.

The frequent loss of parish registers due to fire led to a royal decree in 1812 that each parish should maintain a duplicate copy. The decree of 1812 also stated that one of these duplicates should never be kept under the same roof as the other. Finally, the decree required that the original parish register should be compared with the duplicate twice a year to ensure accuracy. The requirement only lasted from 1812 until 1820, but many sextons continued to maintain duplicate records until they had filled out all the blank pages in the book that they were currently using in 1820.

Norwegian parish registers do, unfortunately, contain errors, and so cross-checking the information can be an important part of using them. In some cases when a parish register is cross-checked with probate records one may find that there are a number of heirs whose baptisms were never entered in the parish registers. In addition, there may be persons who should have been heirs but are not found in the probate records. This indicates that they probably died without the priest having placed the dates of their funerals in the register.

For several hundred years Norwegian law required membership in the Lutheran State Church, and even after the repeal of that law in the 1800s, only a small minority of Norwegians declared themselves to be dissenters or non–Lutherans. Legal protection of religious freedom was not introduced until 1845, so Jews were not legally permitted into the country until 1851 when the Norwegian constitution was amended. Jews had, however, lived in Norway for at least three hundred years before this, and dissenters started to be recognized in the early to mid–1800s. The dissenter law of 1845 provided that Christians who were no longer members of the State Church could be married in a civil ceremony conducted by a rural or city magistrate. Non-Christians' right to be married in such a civil ceremony was not recognized until 1863, and it was not until 1891 that congregations of all faiths were given the right to conduct their own legally recognized marriage ceremonies. Although parish priests were asked to record the birth, marriage, and death records of dissenters in their parish books, few did so.

Civil registration of births was instituted after 1915, but even now marriages and deaths are still recorded by the clergy, as are baptisms. Both these records and those of the parish registers are under the supervision of the Central Bureau of Statistics in Oslo. Due to privacy laws, Norwegian parish registers cannot be released until 60 years after the last entry was made in the register.

A head-tax listing conducted between 1664 and 1666 contained the names of all men and boys over the age of 12 living in rural districts. It includes the farm names, names and ages of the owners, and the names and ages of all persons living in cottages on the farms. A 1701 military census included only the males in the rural districts who were over one year of age. The first census in Norway was conducted in 1769. Another was held in 1801 and every 10th year thereafter during most of the 19th century, and certainly from 1890. The National Archives in Oslo holds these census papers. Beginning in 1865, each individual's place of birth is given. Wills, when proved, are kept in the records of the various probate courts. The oldest of them date from 1660 and are preserved, together with local government records, in the regional state archives in Oslo, Hamar, Bergen, and Trondheim.

Emigration records were preserved for several Norwegian cities: Ålesund, Bergen, Olso, Kristiansand, Kristiansund, and Trondheim. These records list the names of the individuals, their ages, occupations, places of birth, and the dates and ships on which they sailed. They are also found in the regional state archives listed above.

One other location for many genealogical records in Norway is the Norwegian National Library in Oslo. This library has a good collection of local history books.

Nova Scotia Records begin with the Acadians, who once lived in the area that comprises present-day New Brunswick, Nova Scotia, and Prince Edward Island. In 1603, King Henry IV gave the land including Nova Scotia to a French explorer, Pierre du Guast, Sieur de Monts. The French called the region Acadia. Then in 1710, a combined force of troops from England and New England captured the fort at Port Royal from the French and renamed it Annapolis Royal. England did little to settle the area, and the French-speaking Acadians were the majority until about 1750. The English then began to deport the Acadians in 1755. Many fled to what is now New Brunswick. In 1758 the Cape Breton and Prince Edward Island areas fell to Britain; their French settlers were deported to France. In 1763 France ceded most of its maritime lands to England, and the area became known as Nova Scotia. Because of this great dispersion, the Acadian records are only complete for the early years of settlement. There are some good church registers from the late 1600s to 1755. Registers exist for Port Royal only for the earliest years.

The records can be found in the Nova Scotia Archives and Records Management Office in Halifax, which also has the records of various censuses that were conducted between 1671 and 1703. These include one for Acadia in 1671 that lists the names, ages, and places of origin for those living in the French settlement, as well as the censuses of 1686, 1693, and 1698 that list the Acadian names, ages, and number of animals each family owned. The census for Ile Royal in 1752 lists names, ages, and places of origin, while that for Halifax in 1753 lists only the heads of households. The one produced in 1770 includes the heads of households for many of the counties in Nova Scotia, which by then was under British control.

The Nova Scotia Archives has published an *Inventory of Manuscripts in the Public Archives of Nova Scotia* that describes its large collection of published and local family histories, cemetery records, census records (through 1881), church records, city directories, immigration lists, Loyalist listings, marriage records, periodicals, probate records, and vital records found in newspapers. The archives also has a listing of Anglican Church of Canada parish records for Nova Scotia, a list of the names of those required to pay a poll tax between 1791 and 1793, and a list of the approximately 2,000 persons killed in the disaster of December 1917 when a French munitions ship exploded in Halifax harbor.

Birth, marriage, and death records in this province begin in 1864, go to 1876, and then resume after 1909. They are maintained by the Register General of the Department of Health in Halifax. Between 1876 and 1909 there are only marriage records.

The records of land, probate, and civil actions such as divorces are located in the county seats of Nova Scotia's 18 counties. These are: (Annapolis County) Annapolis Royal, (Antigonish County) Antigonish, (Cape Breton County) Sydney, (Colchester County) Truro, (Cumberland County) Amherst, (Digby County) Digby, (Guysborough County) Guysborough, (Halifax County) Halifax, (Hants County) Windsor, (Inverness County) Port Hood, (Kings County) Kentville, (Lunenburg County) Lunenburg, (Pictou County) Pictou, (Queens County) Liverpool, (Richmond County) Arichat, (Shelbourne County) Shelbourne, (Victoria County) Baddeck, and (Yarmouth County) Yarmouth. *See also* **Census, Canadian.**

O

Obituaries are the death notices that are printed in daily and weekly newspapers. They provide information about deceased persons and their immediate relatives that cannot be found in cemeteries, census listings, or Social Security records. The information obituaries include about other family members may list the names of spouses and grandchildren that will not be found elsewhere.

Obituaries are generally published within a day or two of an individual's death, although this is not always the case. Large newspapers, such as *The New York Times,* publish regular indexes to the subjects covered in their pages, and the obituaries will usually be listed in alphabetical order under "deaths." Many of the larger newspapers also prepare information about famous people for obituaries far in advance of their deaths so that information is on hand for the preparation of an obituary when the event occurs. Newspaper workers sometimes refer to these files as the "ghoul pool." Because there has been plenty of time for the preparation of such an entry, the printed material is likely to be quite accurate.

The information for obituaries of lesser-known individuals is usually developed from the death certificates that are filed at funeral homes. Such information is provided to the funeral homes by family members or others who may not be certain as to the exact places or dates of a deceased's birth, or the names of his or her parents. For that reason it is always wise for the genealogist to check such information from the published obituaries against whatever other records can be found. *See also* **Coroner and Mortician Records.**

Occupations are sometimes found in census records, pedigree listings, and county directories. For the most part the names for these occupations are readily recognizable. However, names of occupations of persons living more than 200 years ago may seem quite strange. Here is a list of some of the less recognizable ones.

Accipitrary —falconer
Accomptant — accountant
Amanuensis — secretary or stenographer
Apiarian — beekeeper
Apronman — mechanic
Archiator — physician
Artificer — highly respected skilled craftsman
Banker — dug trenches and ditches
Barker — tanner
Bauer —farmer
Baxter — baker
Bedman — sexton

Bever — beverage maker
Boniface — keeper of an inn
Boothman — corn merchant
Brightsmith — metal worker
Burye Man — grave digger
Cafender — carpenter
Cambist — banker
Carnifex — butcher.
Castor — hat maker
Chapman — merchant.
Conner — inspector or tester
Costermonger — fruit seller
Couranteer — journalist
Crocker — potter
Curretter — broker
Depater — precious metal refiner
Dexter — dyer
Dog Leech — veterinarian
Drayman — cart driver
Earer — plowman
Eggler — egg or poultry dealer
Exchequer — revenue collector
Exciseman — excise tax collector
Faber — artisan or workman
Farandman — traveling merchant
Farrier — horse shoer or blacksmith
Feller — woodcutter
Feroner — ironmonger
Fever — blacksmith
Flauner — confectioner
Forger — blacksmith, worker at a forge
Friseur — hair dresser
Fruiterer — fruit seller
Gabeler — tax collector
Gangsman — foreman
Gater — watchman
Gatward — goat keeper
Ginour — engineer
Graffer — notary or scrivener
Greave — bailiff, foreman, sheriff
Gynour — engineer
Hodsman — mason's assistant
Hoghead — railroad engineer or train driver
Horse Leech — veterinarian, farrier
Hosteller — innkeeper
Infirmarian — in charge of an infirmary
Jerquer — custom house officer who searched ships
Jouster — fish monger
Joyner — skilled carpenter
Kedger — fisherman

Laster — shoe maker
Lattener — brass worker
Lehrer — teacher
Limner — draughtsman or artist
Litterman — groom (of horses)
Malemaker — maker of "males" or traveling bags
Malster — brewer, maker or seller of malts
Mercer — cloth seller
Molitor — miller
Noterer — notary
Ordinary Keeper — innkeeper
Peruker — wigmaker
Piner — laborer
Pistor — baker
Ponderator — inspector of weights and measures
Prediger — preacher
Quiller — operator of a machine that wound yarn onto spools
Redsmith — goldsmith
Reeve — church warden
Rodman — surveyor's assistant
Sandesman — ambassador or messenger
Sawyer — saws timber to boards
Scrivener — clerk, notary
Shrieve — sheriff
Slater — roofer
Sortor — tailor
Spicer — grocer or dealer in spices
Tabler — boarding house operator
Tinctor — dyer
Tippler — kept an ale house
Tonsor — Latin for barber
Trampler — lawyer
Upholder — upholsterer and also a seller of secondhand goods
Verderer — official in charge of the royal forest
Verrier — glazier
Wabster — weaver
Warder — in charge of prisoners
Way-Maker — employed to make roads
Whacker — horse or oxen team driver
Woodbreaker — one who made wooden water casks
Xylographer — maker of wooden blocks used in printing
Yatman — gate keeper
Zincographer — etcher of patterns on zinc plates for printing

Ohio Records can be found at the Ohio State Historical Society and at the State Library of Ohio, both of which are in Columbus, as well as at several other libraries and genealogical libraries around the state. Records of births, deaths, marriages, and divorces are stored at the Vital Statistics Office in Columbus.

When the first white settlers arrived here, they found several Indian tribes occupying the Ohio region. They included the Delaware, Miami, Shawnee, and Wyandot tribes. In 1747 the Ohio Company of Virginia was organized to colonize the Ohio River Valley. It was not until 1788, however, that the first permanent white settlement was established at what is now the town of Marietta. Ohio became a territory in 1799 and the 17th state of the Union in 1803.

A census was conducted in 1803 in preparation for statehood; the enumeration is preserved at the State Historical Society. The first federal census of Ohio was taken in 1820, and there have never been any state-authorized censuses. The records of the many federal censuses, taken every 10 years, can be found at all the various National Archives locations. The 1850, 1860, and 1880 Ohio mortality schedules are also housed at the State Historical Society

Records of births since 1908, marriages and divorces since 1949, and deaths since 1905 are at the Vital Statistics Office. Copies can be obtained for a small fee. For any of the births, marriages, and deaths that occurred earlier than these dates, the researcher should contact the probate courts in the counties where the events took place. For divorce records, one should contact the particular district court in the county where the divorce was processed. Guardianship records can be located in the various county probate courts, as can the processing of wills. Land matters rest with the various county recorders, and the courts of common pleas in the counties have jurisdiction over all equity and law cases.

Other good sources for genealogical information in Ohio are the Ohio Genealogical Society in Mansfield, the Ohio University Library in Athens, and the Oberlin College Library in Oberlin.

Researchers seeking information from county records can locate them at the following county seats: (Adams County) West Union, (Allen County) Lima, (Ashland County) Ashland, (Ashtabula County) Jefferson, (Athens County) Athens, (Auglaize County) Wapakoneta, (Belmont County) St. Clairsville, (Brown County) Georgetown, (Butler County) Hamilton, (Carroll County) Carrollton, (Champaign County) Urbana, (Clark County) Springfield, (Clermont County) Batavia, (Clinton County) Wilmington, (Columbiana County) Lisbon, (Coshocton County) Coshocton, (Crawford County) Bucyrus, (Cuyahoga County) Cleveland, (Darke County) Greenville, (Defiance County) Defiance, (Delaware County) Delaware, (Erie County) Sandusky, (Fairfield County) Lancaster, (Fayette County) Washington Court House, (Franklin County) Columbus, (Fulton County) Wauseon, (Gallia County) Gallipolis, (Geauga County) Chardon, (Greene County) Xenia, (Guernsey County) Cambridge, (Hamilton County) Cincinnati, (Hancock County) Findlay, (Hardin County) Kenton, (Harrison County) Cadiz, (Henry County) Napoleon, (Highland County) Hillsboro, (Hocking County) Logan, (Holmes County) Millersburg, and (Huron County) Norwalk.

Also at (Jackson County) Jackson, (Jefferson County) Steubenville, (Knox County) Mount Vernon, (Lake County) Painesville, (Lawrence County) Ironton, (Licking County) Newark, (Logan County) Bellefontaine, (Lorain County) Elyria, (Lucas County) Toledo, (Madison County) London, (Mahoning County) Youngstown, (Marion County) Marion, (Medina County) Medina, (Meigs County) Pomeroy, (Mercer County) Celina, (Miami County) Troy, (Monroe County) Woodsfield, (Montgomery County) Dayton, (Morgan County) McConnelsville, (Morrow County) Mount Gilead, (Muskingum County) Zanesville, (Noble County) Caldwell, (Ottawa County) Port Clinton, (Paulding County) Paulding, (Perry County) New Lexington, (Pickaway County) Circleville, (Pike County) Waverly, (Portage County) Ravenna, (Preble County) Eaton, (Putnam County) Ottawa, (Richland County) Mansfield, (Ross County) Chillicothe, (Sandusky

County) Fremont, (Scioto County) Portsmouth, (Seneca County) Tiffin, (Shelby County) Sidney, (Stark County) Canton, (Summit County) Akron, (Trumbull County) Warren, (Tuscarawas County) New Philadelphia, (Union County) Marysville, (Van Wert County) Van Wert, (Vinton County) McArthur, (Warren County) Lebanon, (Washington County) Marietta, (Wayne County) Wooster, (Williams County) Bryan, (Wood County) Bowling Green, and (Wyandot County) Upper Sandusky.

FOR FURTHER INFORMATION SEE:
• Bell, Carol Willsey. *Ohio Genealogical Guide.* Youngstown, OH: Bell Books, 1995.
• Heisey, John W. *Ohio Genealogical Research Guide.* Indianapolis, IN: Heritage House, 1987.

Oklahoma Records of births, marriages, deaths, immigration, naturalization, and military matters are located at the Vital Records Offices in either Oklahoma City or Tulsa, although some of these records are not open to public inspection. The United States gained the land in this area in 1803 as part of the Louisiana Purchase. It was a region through which many bands of Indians roamed in their pursuit of buffalo that grazed on the grasslands. Congress, in 1819, designated Oklahoma as part of the Arkansas Territory. Because the area was largely unoccupied by settlers, the federal government began prodding Indian tribes in the southwestern United States to move into the area. Then, in order to prepare the area for the Indian migration, the U.S. Army built Fort Towson and Fort Gibson within what later became the state of Oklahoma. The five major tribes that still occupied land in the eastern states—the Cherokee, Chickasaw, Choctaw, Creek, and Seminole—were forced under military command to move west and reestablish their communities in Oklahoma. By treaty the government then guaranteed that the Indians would be able to maintain their nations there "as long as grass shall grow and rivers run."

At first the Indians prospered. They cleared the land, built schools, and operated farms and ranches. But the Civil War (1861–1865) destroyed the prosperity and protection the Indians had enjoyed. Many of them were urged by supporters of the South to join the Confederacy, and many of them did. One Cherokee, Stand Watie, even became a Confederate brigadier general. At the war's end, Congress forced the five tribes to give up part of their land because they had supported the South. The land that was taken away from them soon filled with white settlers.

In 1889 the federal authorities declared almost 1,900,000 acres in central Oklahoma open for settlement and a wild race took place on April 22 as settlers rushed across the border to occupy fertile tracts of land. About 50,000 people had moved into Oklahoma by that evening. In a single day Guthrie and Oklahoma City became cities of more than 10,000 persons each. The next year Congress established the Territory of Oklahoma and set up Guthrie as its capital. In 1907 Oklahoma entered the Union as the 46th state, and in 1910 the state capital was moved from Guthrie to Oklahoma City.

The first territorial census of Oklahoma was conducted in 1890; the records are at the Oklahoma Historical Society in Oklahoma City. This census, which has been indexed and includes family members, does not contain any enumeration of those living in the Indian Territory. The federal census in 1860, when Oklahoma was part of the Arkansas Territory, includes the Oklahoma area as "Indian lands west of Arkansas." This census is in the National Archives in Washington, D.C. Another territorial census taken in 1900 included an enumeration of the Indian Territory along with the rest of the Oklahoma Territory. It also is at the National Archives in Washington, D.C. The first federal census of Oklahoma as a state took place in 1910. As with other federal census records of the states, the ones for Oklahoma can now be found at all the various National Archives locations.

Oklahoma began recording birth and death records in 1908, but it was not mandatory that these records be filed until 1917. Because birth and death records were not required in the past years as they are today, the filing process for many years prior to 1940 is somewhat sketchy. It is the responsibility for hospitals, attendants at birth, or funeral directors to file the birth or death certificate in a timely manner, but birth records are not open for public inspection. A birth certificate may be applied for by the person involved, an immediate next of kin, or an authorized agent who provides a statement indicating that they are working in the best interest of the registrant. Any individual may obtain a death certificate upon presenting a written application, proper information, and identification. Marriage and divorce records are available from the clerks of the county courthouses where the events took place. To obtain probate, land, guardianship, or civil and criminal court records, one should also contact the court clerk in the county in which the event occurred.

In 1941 the Work Projects Administration published a book that may be useful to researchers, the *Guide to Public Vital Statistics Records in Oklahoma*. It can be found at the Historical Society, the University of Tulsa McFarlin Library, and the State Genealogical Society in Oklahoma City, as well as in some other libraries in Oklahoma and a few larger genealogical libraries in other states.

Researchers seeking information from county records can locate them at the following county seats: (Adair County) Stilwell, (Alfalfa County) Cherokee, (Atoka County) Atoka, (Beaver County) Beaver, (Beckham County) Sayre, (Blaine County) Watonga, (Bryan County) Durant, (Caddo County) Anadarko, (Canadian County) El Reno, (Carter County) Ardmore, (Cherokee County) Tahlequah, (Choctaw County) Hugo, (Cimarron County) Boise City, (Cleveland County) Norman, (Coal County) Coalgate, (Comanche County) Lawton, (Cotton County) Walters, (Craig County) Vinita, (Creek County) Sapulpa, (Custer County) Arapaho, (Delaware County) Jay, (Dewey County) Taloga, (Ellis County) Arnett, (Garfield County) Enid, (Garvin County) Pauls Valley, (Grady County) Chickasha, (Grant County) Medford, (Greer County) Mangum, (Harmon County) Hollis, (Harper County) Buffalo, (Haskell County) Stigler, and (Hughes County) Holdenville.

Also at (Jackson County) Altus, (Jefferson County) Waurika, (Johnston County)

Tishomingo, (Kay County) Newkirk, (Kingfisher County) Kingfisher, (Kiowa County) Hobart, (Latimer County) Wilburton, (Le Flore County) Poteau, (Lincoln County) Chandler, (Logan County) Guthrie, (Love County) Marietta, (Major County) Fairview, (Marshall County) Madill, (Mayes County) Pryor, (McClain County) Purcell, (McCurtain County) Idabel, (McIntosh County) Eufaula, (Murray County) Sulphur, (Muskogee County) Muskogee, (Noble County) Perry, (Nowata County) Nowata, (Okfuskee County) Okemah, (Oklahoma County) Oklahoma City, (Okmulgee County) Okmulgee, (Osage County) Pawhuska, (Ottawa County) Miami, (Pawnee County) Pawnee, (Payne County) Stillwater, (Pittsburg County) McAlester, (Pontotoc County) Ada, (Potawatomie County) Shawnee, (Pushmataha County) Antlers, (Roger Mills County) Cheyenne, (Rogers County) Claremore, (Seminole County) Wewoka, (Sequoyah County) Sallisaw, (Stephens County) Duncan, (Texas County) Guymon, (Tillman County) Frederick, (Tulsa County) Tulsa, (Wagoner County) Wagoner, (Washington County) Bartlesville, (Washita County) Cordell, (Woods County) Alva, and (Woodward County) Woodward.

For further information see:
- Blessing, Patrick J. *Oklahoma: Records and Archives*. Tulsa, OK: University of Tulsa Publications, 1978.
- Federation of Oklahoma Genealogical Societies. *Directory of Oklahoma Sources*. Oklahoma City, OK: Federation of Oklahoma Genealogical Societies, 1993.

Online Library Catalogs are among the many marvels of the computer world and its connections to the Internet. Even though much genealogical research still requires the physical presence of a researcher in a library, accessing various electronic card catalogs can take much of the drudgery out of any search for family records. The use of the Internet speeds up the searching process and also opens up the possibility of accessing the card catalogs of various libraries all over the country and even in distant parts of the world.

Most modern libraries maintain online

catalogs of their holdings, and have many terminals distributed throughout the building so that one doesn't have to look up the subject, author, or title in a card catalog on one floor and then run to another floor to find the referenced material. But more than this, most of the leading libraries allow access to their online catalogs on the Internet, so that people can consult them from their home computers. For example, one can search through the four-million-book catalog of the Library of Congress by accessing its Website, www.loc.gov/catalog, or one can access the U.S. National Archives and Records Administration at www.nara.gov. The British Library also has an online catalog that anyone can access at http://www.blpc.bl.uk.

The Berkeley Digital Library at SunSite, hosted by the University of Queensland Library, provides an index to almost 2,000 Web pages and the online catalogs from more than 70 libraries in the U.S. and around the world. If a library has a Website, the name of the library will be hyperlinked by the SunSite system to that library's Website. Another Web-based reference source, the Internet Public Library (http://www.ipl.org/), has a broad and rich collection of resources, including reference materials, exhibits, magazines and serials, newspapers, online texts, and Web searching. This site does not have an online catalog, per se, but performs a function similar to that of a library catalog in organizing, classifying, and describing many of the information resources available on the World Wide Web.

Ontario Records in abundance can be found at the Ontario Provincial Archives in Toronto. In 1763, at the end of the French and Indian War, the Ontario region became a British possession. At that time there were only a few scattered French settlements near what are now Kingston, Niagara Falls, and Windsor. Little further settlement took place until 1784 when, during the American Revolution, many persons loyal to England began arriving from the United States. About 6,000 of these Loyalists had settled in Ontario by 1785. The British government gave them food, clothing, and land. In 1791 the Ontario region was designated as a province with the name Upper Canada, and in 1867, when the British North America Act created the Dominion of Canada, the province was renamed Ontario.

Historically, Canada has been the destination for millions of immigrants from around the world seeking a better life in North America. There have been frequent periods of migration between the United States and Canada, creating an interesting research problem for any genealogist. Passage to Canada was often less expensive than traveling to ports in the United States, so immigrants frequently traveled over the oceans to Canada and then on to the United States by land. Economic and social pressures have also played important roles in migration patterns. More than 12,000 records kept at the National Archives of Canada in Ottawa relate to immigrants arriving in Canada. This database can be helpful for researchers in the United States who are seeking Canadian ancestors.

The three primary collections of genealogical interest at the Archives of Ontario, however, are the vital statistics (birth, marriage, and death records), court records, and land registrations. The archives also preserves a copy of the Ontario Census on microfilm that it obtained from the National Archives of Canada, in addition to other federal microfilm rolls of provincial interest.

Birth, marriage, and death records, and indexes for those that exist, are from the Records of the Office of the Registrar General of Ontario. They cover births from 1869 to 1905, marriages from 1801 to 1920, and deaths from 1869 to 1930. All of these records are publicly available on microfilm. The most recent transfers of records, since 1906 for births, since 1921 for marriages, and since 1931 for deaths, are still closed, waiting to be microfilmed. For information on births after 1906, marriages after 1921, and deaths after 1931, or for any certificates, contact the office of the Registrar General in Thunder Bay.

Birth records at the Archives of Ontario include fathers' names and occupations, mothers' maiden names, the signatures and residences of the informants (usually relatives), the names of the persons assisting with the births, and the places and dates of birth.

The information in the marriage records varies widely, but usually contains the names of the bride, groom, and clergy, as well as the location and date. The records after 1869 also give ages, place of residence and birth, and information about the fathers, mothers, witnesses, and clergy. The death records give the age, sex, religious affiliation, birth place, date registered, and cause of death. After 1907, the place of burial and the names of parents are also usually included.

The Archives of Ontario has a guide to provincial vital statistics records, *Researching Birth, Death and Marriage Records in Ontario.* The archives also has a series of non-civil vital records that include those of cemetery transcriptions collected by the Ontario Genealogical Society in Toronto, miscellaneous church records, and various municipal censuses, school lists, and residency registers. Most of the church records are from the church archives of each denomination.

Wills and estate files probated in Ontario more than 20 years ago are likely to be found on microfilm in the collection of archives estate files. The wills list wives, children, and possibly grandchildren and other relatives who were alive when the will was made. The wills themselves were filed with the Court of Probate and the surrogate courts in the various counties where the actions took place. The archives has two surname indexes for the estate records filed before 1859, but not for the later ones. If a researcher knows the county in which a will was probated, it may be best to find the original record there rather than at the Archives of Ontario. However, the archives can be of great help in locating particular county records. Probate application books from 1859 to 1982, alphabetically arranged by the deceased's name and giving the courthouse where an application was made, are among the microfilm reels preserved at the Archives.

Starting in 1867 only the federal Parliament could grant a divorce in Ontario. Couples had to have a private members' bill requesting that their divorces be passed, usually without debate, through the legislature. But in 1927, the Supreme Court of Ontario was given the power to annul marriages and, in 1931, its jurisdiction was expanded to include granting divorces, alimony, and child custody. The Archives of Ontario has the surviving divorce files for the years 1927 to 1978. For divorce files after 1978, a researcher must contact the local courthouse where a divorce was filed.

Under Ontario's Adoption Act, passed in 1921, guardianships were granted through the surrogate courts. These actions are recorded in the registers, and later for some counties in separate guardianship books. For such adoption files, one must contact the Adoption Information Unit of the Ministry of Community and Social Services in Toronto.

Ontario land records fall into two categories: the early Crown Land records (property owned by the Crown) and later private property registrations (property owned by persons or corporations). The Archives of Ontario has an index to the homesteaders and first owners of Crown Land by surname and township. A series of microfilm reels shows the details of these Crown Land records. These original land grants can give an ancestor's location within the province and the date when the ancestor was living there. The archives has a microfilmed index to the patents that were issued on these lands once the administrative fees had been paid and the settler's duties completed. Copies of the original patents can be obtained from the Ministry of Natural Resources, Land and Natural Heritage Branch, in Peterborough.

The land records at the Ontario Archives also include the military land grants issued from 1901 to 1922, various township papers, private property records, and maps and survey records. Other types of records at the Ontario Archives include British military and naval records, United Empire Loyalist lists, immigration lists, records of Indian affairs, school records, a collection of newspaper files, local histories, city directories, voter lists, historical society journals, and genealogical publications.

The Ontario Archives do not maintain published genealogies, but they are available in the Canadiana Collection at the North York Central Library.

Ontario has both counties in the south and districts in the north, but the two are functionally the same. Researchers seeking information from any of their record offices can locate them in the following county and district seats: (Algoma District) Sault Ste. Marie, (Brant County) Brantford, (Bruce County) Walkerton, (Carleton County) Ottawa, (Cochrane District) Cochrane, (Dufferin County) Orangeville, (Dundas County) served by Cornwall in Stormont County, (Durham County) served by Coburg in Northumberland County, (Elgin County) St. Thomas, (Essex County) Windsor, (Frontenac County) Kingston, (Glengary County) served by Cornwall in Stormont County, (Grenville County) served by Brockville in Leeds County, (Grey County) Owen Sound, (Haldimand County) Cayuga, (Haliburton County) Minden, (Halton County) Milton, (Hastings County) Bellville, (Huron County) Goderich, (Kenora County) Kenora, (Kent County) Chatham, (Lambton County) Sernia, (Lanark County) Perth, (Leeds County) Brockville, (Lennox and Addington County) Napanee, and (Lincoln County) St. Catherines.

Also at (Manitoulin District) Gore Bay, (Middlesex County) London, (Muskoka County), Bracebridge, (Nipissing District) North Bay, (Norfolk County) Simcoe, (Northumberland County) Cobourg, (Ontario County) Whitby, (Oxford County) Woodstock, (Parry Sound District) Parry Sound, (Peel County) Brampton, (Perth County) Stratford, (Peterborough County) Peterborough, (Prescott County) L'Original, (Prince Edward County) Picton, (Rainy River District) Fort Frances, (Renfrew County) Pembroke, (Russell County) served by L'Original in Prescott County, (Simcoe County) Barrie, (Stormont County) Cornwall, (Sudbury District) Sudbury, (Temiskaming District) Haileybury, (Thunder Bay District) Port Arthur, (Victoria County) Lindsay, (Waterloo County) Kitchener, (Welland County) Welland, (Wellington County) Guelph (Wentworth County) Hamilton, and (York County) Toronto.

Oregon Records of particular use to genealogists can be found in the Oregon State Ar-

chives as well as at the Oregon State Library, both of which are in Salem. The area was occupied by many Indian tribes when the first white person touched land here in the 1500s. The Chinook Indians lived along the lower Columbia River, while the Clackama, Multnomah, and Tellamook tribes were living in the northwest part of the region. Other tribes in Oregon included the Bannock, Cayuse, Klamath, Modoc, Paiute, Umatilla, and Nez Percé. Meriweather Lewis and William Clark reached the mouth of the Columbia River in 1805 when they were exploring for a Northwest Passage on behalf of the U.S. government. In 1811 John Jacob Astor set up a fur trading post at Astoria, and in 1834 Methodist missionaries established the first permanent settlement in the Willamette Valley. Nine years later about a thousand persons migrated to Oregon from the East over what was to become known as the Oregon Trail.

Congress designated Oregon as a territory in 1848 with Oregon City as the capital. The capital was later moved to Salem. As a territory, Oregon included what are now the states of Washington and Idaho, as well as parts of British Columbia, Montana, and Wyoming. In 1859 Oregon was reduced to its present size when it joined the Union as the 33rd state. A census of the Oregon Territory was conducted in 1850, and from 1860 on Oregon was enumerated in the decennial national censuses. These records can be seen at the various National Archives locations. Several territorial and state censuses are now stored in the Oregon Archives. These censuses include ones for various counties taken between 1842 and 1846 and between 1850 and 1859; one taken of all males over 21 years of age in 1849; an 1865 census of Benton, Columbia, Marion, and Umatilla counties; an 1870 and 1875 census of Umatilla County; an 1885 census of Linn and Umatilla counties; an 1895 census of Linn, Morrow, Multnomah, and Marion counties; and a 1905 census of Baker, Lane, Linn, and Marion counties. The Oregon Historical Society in Portland has indexes to many of these. The mortality schedules for Oregon from 1850 to 1880 are in the State Archives.

The helpful *Guide to Public Vital Statis-*

tics Records in Oregon (Work Projects Administration, 1942) can be seen in a number of
Oregon libraries including the State Library,
as well as in several of the larger genealogical libraries elsewhere.

Records of births, marriages, divorces,
and deaths can be obtained from the Oregon
Vital Records Office in Portland. The birth
records (including indexes to them) have a
hundred-year access restriction, and the death
certificates have a 50-year access restriction.
Birth and death records begin in 1903, marriage records in 1906, and divorce records in
1925.

Divorce records can also be found at the
county circuit courts, as can guardianship and
probate records. There is no distinction between law and equity actions in Oregon.
Both are under the jurisdiction of the circuit
courts. Land records rest with the county
clerks, except for Linn, Marion, and Umatilla
counties, where they are handled by the county
recorder; Lane and Washington counties,
where they are handled by the director of
records and elections; Hood River County,
where they are handled by the department of
records and assessment; and Multnomah
County, where they are under the jurisdiction
of the department of records and elections,
recording division.

Naturalization records in Oregon are
found either at the Oregon State Archives or
among the files of the county clerk or trial
court administrator for the county where the
documents were processed. Naturalization
information may also be found in county
court journals, county court case files, circuit
court case files, probate records, and miscellaneous records. Extensive research may be
necessary in order to locate naturalization
records that have been interfiled within these
record series.

The Oregon State Archives has prepared
aids on the census, land, military, naturalization, probate matters, and vital records that
are useful sources for doing family research.
They are available at the archives or on the
archives Website. Specific adoption information in the archives may appear in state agency
or county court records, but this information
is restricted from public view and requires

written authorization from a "court of competent jurisdiction."

Both the Oregon State University Library
in Corvallis and the University of Oregon Library in Eugene have genealogical records
that the researcher may find of value in locating information about persons in this state,
but the State Library has the largest collection of such materials.

Researchers seeking information from
county records can locate them at the follow-
ing county seats: (Baker County) Baker, (Ben-
ton County) Corvallis, (Clackamas County)
Oregon City, (Clatsop County) Astoria, (Co-
lumbia County) Saint Helens, (Coos County)
Coquille, (Crook County) Prineville, (Curry
County) Gold Beach, (Deschutes County)
Bend, (Douglas County) Roseburg, (Gilliam
County) Condon, (Grant County) Canyon
City, (Harney County) Burns, (Hood River
County) Hood River, (Jackson County) Med-
ford, (Jefferson County) Madras, (Josephine
County) Grants Pass, (Klamath County)
Klamath Falls, (Lake County) Lakeview,
(Lane County) Eugene, (Lincoln County)
Newport, (Linn County) Albany, (Malheur
County) Vale, (Marion County) Salem, (Mor-
row County) Heppner, (Multnomah County)
Portland, (Polk County) Dallas, (Sherman
County) Moro, (Tillamook County) Tilla-
mook, (Umatilla County) Pendleton, (Union
County) La Grande, (Wallowa County) En-
terprise, (Wasco County) The Dalles, (Wash-
ington County) Hillsboro, (Wheeler County)
Fossil, and (Yamhill County) McMinnville.

FOR FURTHER INFORMATION SEE:
- Cogswell, Philip. *Capitol Names: Individu-
  als Woven into Oregon's History.* Portland,
  OR: Oregon Historical Society, 1977.
- Lenzen, Connie. *Guide to Genealogical
  Sources.* Portland, OR: Genealogical Forum
  of Oregon, 1994.

Orphan Train System was a program initiated in 1853 by Charles Loring Brace and
his New York Children's Aid Society. The aim
was to relieve some of the burden of the many
homeless children living in New York City
and some of the other cities on the East Coast.
At the time many immigrant children found
their parents unable to care for them, and in

desperation turned to the streets to sell newspapers, beg for food, or steal to get by. It is estimated that in 1854 there were some 34,000 homeless children in New York City alone.

There were not enough orphanages to hold all the homeless children, and many orphanages gave the children less than adequate care. Brace's idea was to send as many children as possible west by train to find homes with farm families. As he once wrote, "In every American community, especially in a western one, there are many spare places at the table of life. There is no harassing struggle for existence. They have enough for themselves and the stranger too." The New York Children's Aid Society set up a system in which train cars were filled with orphan children, supervised by two adult agents, and sent westward to stop at farming towns along the way. The society sent notices to Midwest towns announcing the time and date the orphans would be arriving, and as the train made its stops the children would be paraded in front of the crowd of onlookers.

Some of the families that took in one or more of these children wanted another farm hand. Others genuinely wanted to give a child a home. The train left a small part of its cargo at each stop until finally all the children found homes. The first such "orphan train" went to Dowagiac, Michigan, in 1854; the last one pulled into Trenton, Missouri in 1929.

Thus for 75 years these orphan trains moved from the East to locations in the Midwest and West. Estimates put the number of children relocated at 150,000 to 400,000. Some 94 percent of the placements were for English, Irish, and German immigrant children; the number of Italian and Jewish children who found homes was only about one percent.

Brace's group wasn't the only one sending homeless children to the rural Midwest. The Catholic Charities of New York also got into the act, perhaps because it saw Catholic children being placed in Protestant homes. In 1869 the Sisters of Mercy was sending its own "mercy trains" west. While following Brace's lead, the Catholic trains differed in that they found homes for the children before the trains left New York. Local parish priests served as the screening committee. They would announce the trains from the pulpit and those who wanted a child signed up, specifying whether they wanted a boy or a girl.

In many cases the orphan train experiment was successful, in others the right match of foster parent and orphan didn't happen. There were instances of abuse and neglect, forced labor and not enough food. Many children ended up as servants and work hands on family farms. In many cases, siblings were separated from each other and consequently, from the only family they knew. The Orphan Train Heritage Society of America, located in Springdale, Arkansas, operates as a clearing house for information, genealogical and otherwise, about these orphan train riders.

Orphans' Records *see* **Adoption Records; Guardianship Records**

Orthodox Church Records are located in each of the individual churches of the various branches of this religion. The Orthodox religion, also called the Eastern Orthodox religion, is the primary Christian church in Greece, Russia, Eastern Europe, and Western Asia. It consists of several independent and self-governing churches, as well as some that are not self-governing. Four of the self-governing churches hold places of special honor for historical reasons. These are the churches of Constantinople (in Turkey), Alexandria (in Egypt), Antioch (Damascus, Syria), and Jerusalem. Other major self-governing churches, in order of size, are those of Russia, Romania, Serbia, Greece, Bulgaria, Georgia (in Russia), Cyprus, Czechoslovakia, Poland, Albania, and Sinai (in Egypt).

The Eastern Orthodox Churches in North America are not fully self-governing because they were established by missionaries and settlers from other countries where self-governing Orthodox churches predominate. These American branches include the Albanian Orthodox Diocese of America, the American Carpatho-Russian Orthodox Diocese, the Antiochan Orthodox Christian Archdiocese of North America, the Bulgarian Eastern Orthodox Church, the Byelorussian Autocephalic Orthodox Church, the Greek Orthodox Archdiocese of North and South

America, and the Holy Cross Romania Orthodox Church.

There are archives that may contain some
genealogical information at the Albanian Orthodox Diocese in Jamaica Plain, Massachusetts; the Antiochan Orthodox Christian
Archdiocese in Englewood, New Jersey; the
Byzantine Catholic Seminary Library in
Pittsburgh, Pennsylvania; the Greek Orthodox Archdiocese in New York City; and the
Orthodox Church in America Headquarters
in Syosset, New York.

P

PAF *see* **Computer Programs for Genealogy**

Panama *see* **Central American Genealogy**

Paraguayan Genealogy records can be
found in the National Archives and the adjoining National Library in Asunción. The
state of Paraguay derives its name from the
river Paraguay (Parrot River), a tributary of
the Parana. Almost in the center of South
America, this river covers 406,752 square
kilometers. During the disastrous War of the
Triple Alliance (1865–70), Paraguay lost two-
thirds of all its adult males and much of its
territory. The country stagnated economi-
cally for the next half century. Then, during
the Chaco War of 1932–35, large, economi-
cally important areas were seized from Bolivia.

Civil registration in Paraguay was started
in 1880 but it did not become fully functional
until 1898 and 1899. The records that are
maintained under this civil registration include births, marriages, deaths, adoptions,
and recognitions of legitimacy. Copies of all
the civil registration records are maintained
in the National Archives where they are indexed according to the surnames and the localities from which they came. The original
records remain in the local jurisdictions. Unfortunately, many of the civil registration
records in the National Archives were destroyed during the war with Bolivia. There is
also an index at the National Archives to a series of wills that extend over the period from
1537 to 1846.

Parish records in Paraguay have been
poorly preserved, and some have been destroyed for various reasons. The colonial
records have nearly all disappeared. Cemetery inscriptions, however, are an important
tool for genealogical research in Paraguay.
Many are still quite readable. They are particularly useful because they give a record of
the names and dates for most of the men who
died in the wars of the country.

Besides the large number of Roman
Catholic churches in Paraguay, there are a
number of German Mennonite communities,
the oldest one being Fernheim. The German
Mennonites came from Canada, Russia, and
Poland, and first established their communities in the area of Puerto Casado. There are
about 10,000 Mennonites in Paraguay. Each
of the Mennonite communities maintains its
own records.

Passenger Lists for vessels arriving in the
United States can sometimes be one of the
richest sources of genealogical information.
They were compiled by captains or masters
of vessels, collectors of customs, and immigration officials at the ports of entry to comply with federal laws. The records of the lists
that are available at the National Archives in
Washington, D.C., some of its branches, and
some genealogical libraries, consist of customs
lists, transcripts and abstracts of customs
passenger lists, immigration passenger lists,
and indexes to those lists. The federal government did not begin keeping any records
of passenger arrivals until 1819, yet many
pre–1820 passenger lists were maintained by
state or local authorities, and have been published in a multitude of works that can be
found in various genealogical libraries.

One of the most complete listings is P.

William Filby's multivolume work, *Passenger and Immigration Lists Index: A Guide to Published Arrival Records of About 500,000 Passengers Who Came to the United States and Canada in the 17th, 18th, and 19th Centuries* (Gale Research, Detroit). This index was first published in 1981 as a master index of about 500,000 immigrants from 300 published sources. Updated annually, the index in 2001 contained approximately 3,530,000 individuals who arrived in United States and Canadian ports. Because it is indexed by name and is searchable by keywords, this resource is a must for all persons looking for passenger list information. For each individual listed, one will find the name and age of an immigrant, the place where more information about that person can be found, the year and place of immigration, and the names of family members with whom they traveled. All the major genealogical libraries subscribe to this index, although they may not have all the cumulated supplements. Several books, such as Peter Wilson Coldham's *The Complete Book of Emigrants in Bondage, 1614–1775* (Baltimore: Genealogical Publishing Co., 1992), deal exclusively with the arrivals of indentured servants and convicts.

Although the National Archives has passenger lists for at least 37 different ports, many of these lists include only a few ships and cover only a few years. For example, the passenger lists from Panama City, Florida, cover only the years 1927 to 1939. Three small Florida ports have lists for only one day. Virtually all modern immigrants arrived at one of seven different ports, whose records are available on microfilm (more than 11,000 rolls) at the National Archives. These are:

Baltimore —1891–1957 and 1897–1952
Boston —1891–1943, 1902–1906, 1906–1920, and 1899–1940
New Orleans—1903–1945 and 1900–1952
New York —1897–1948, 1897–1902, and 1902–1948
Philadelphia —1883–1945 and 1883–1948
San Francisco—1893–1953, 1954–1957, and 1893–1934
Seattle —1890–1957 and 1949–1954

Other ports, with significant passenger lists on microfilm include Key West, FL; Providence, RI; Galveston, TX; and Portland, ME.

In some cases, these passenger lists are also available in the cities where the ships arrived, along with some nonfederal lists not available elsewhere. The National Archives has indexes that have been compiled for many of these passenger lists. These indexes are all on microfilm; some have been Soundexed. The Soundex files were prepared by the Work Projects Administration on cards for each individual immigrant, not each family, which greatly increases the chances of locating a particular immigrant and then that immigrant's family members when the researcher suspects they may have arrived together. To protect the privacy of immigrants still living, the Immigration and Naturalization Service has placed a restriction against public viewing of any of the lists for those who have arrived during the last 50 years.

By far the largest number of immigrants came though the port of New York and Ellis Island. There is an *Index to Passenger Lists of Vessels Arriving at New York* for the periods 1820 to 1843 and 1897 to 1902, but there is none for the New York arrivals between 1847 and 1896. The records for 1902 to 1943 have been microfilmed, but not yet indexed. Unless an exact date of arrival for any particular immigrant can be determined, even with the index it may take many hours of searching to find the precise listing among the chronological lists of ship arrivals.

Generally the passenger records compiled following the passage of immigration laws are more useful than those produced earlier. The immigrants were asked questions as to what relatives they had in America, their addresses, and their relationships, as well as whether they had been in the United States previously. Later lists include physical descriptions of the immigrants and the names and addresses of their nearest relatives in their home countries.

To find an immigrant on a passenger list, one must have enough information from other sources, such as the birthdate and town of origin, as well as the original name of the immigrant. One also should remember that ship company officials and immigration officials recorded names as they heard them said, and thus often misspelled the names they heard, particularly when these names were pronounced with strange foreign accents. Many immigrants were also illiterate, and wouldn't have known how to spell their names even if asked to do so. *See also* **Ellis Island Records; Immigration Records; Soundex System.**

Passport Applications from 1789 forward are recorded on film at the National Archives in Washington, D.C., and at some of its branches. The Archives also has the information that was recorded on the passports that were issued between 1789 and 1905. Although passports were not required until World War I (and during a brief period in the Civil War), many individuals obtained them for extra protection. This was particularly true for male immigrants who wanted to visit the countries of their origin and were afraid they might be conscripted into military service when they journeyed there.

Early passport applications contain relatively little information, but from 1906 to 1925 each application includes the name of the applicant and date and place of birth; name, date, and place of birth of spouse or children; residence and occupation at the time of application; immediate travel plans; physical description; and a photograph. The Washington National Records Center in Suitland, Maryland, has the records of those issued between 1906 and 1925. These records have been microfilmed and can be found in some of the National Archives branch centers. Records of the U.S. Visa Office from 1910 to 1940 are open to the public and are located at the National Archives II Center in College Park, Maryland. They are arranged chronologically in 10-year groups. Indexes help the researcher find the names of particular individuals.

Pedigree Charts, or ancestor tables, are basic tools for any genealogical research. They are diagrams that are popularly called family trees because all the members and ancestors of a family are connected to one another by branches originating from a single progeni-

tor (earliest member of the line). The earliest known pedigree charts are those called "stemma" that are found on the atrium walls of Roman patrician homes. These genealogical exhibits consisted of small shrines, each containing a painted mask to represent a deceased member of the family. Seneca (4 B.C.?– 65 A.D.) and Pliny the Elder (A.D. 23–79) have written that these niches were connected to one another by lines indicating the degrees of affinity among the various ancestors. Sometimes a stemma was just a chart painted on the wall in which the names of the ancestors were connected by similar lines.

Pedigree charts are designed to show only the connections of ancestry and not all the information known about any individuals. Thus what is included for each entry listed on a pedigree chart is no more than the ancestor's name, date and place of baptism, date and place of marriage, and date and place of death or burial. Most pedigree charts have no more than the names with birth and death dates. All other information can be recorded on supplemental family group record sheets, handwritten notes, or computer generated documents. Large and complex pedigree charts may be quite impressive, but at the same time difficult to prepare and update. It is much easier to work with small sections of a chart that can be easily updated, later inserting these sections into a larger tree when it is convenient to do so.

There is no standard way to design a pedigree chart. Some are relatively simple; others are quite complicated, using codes and symbols that are difficult for anyone but the person who created the chart to interpret. Some show several family groups as well as lines of descent. Others show every family that has contributed to a single individual's ancestry, but as lines are added these charts soon become too large to handle. Most, however, show only the descent through the male lines, the lines that follow the family surname. Yet some other pedigree charts may be designed to show the descent through the various female lines. Whatever the case, any family researcher will soon find there are always gaps in the pedigree chart that must be filled in by further research.

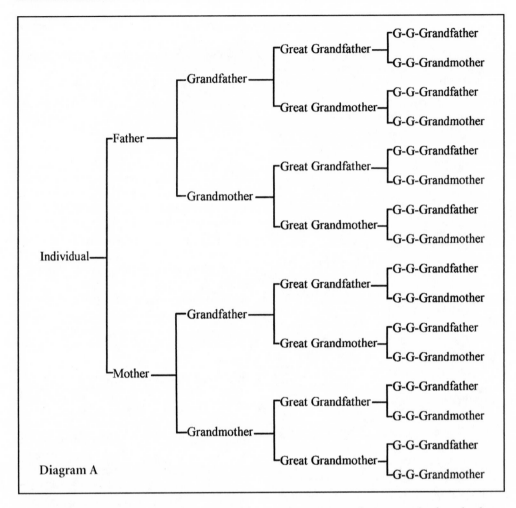

Diagram A

Probably the most common form of pedigree charts is as shown in Diagram A.

This type of chart is known as a total descent chart. When it extends back five generations, as the diagram does, it is called a *seize quartiers* by those using the terms of heraldry. If it goes back one more generation to include 32 great-great-great-grandparents, it is known as a *trente-deux quartiers*. This kind of pedigree chart only includes the direct ancestors, not any brothers, sisters, or other relatives.

The same information can be contained in a pedigree chart designed in the form of concentric circles, with the progenitor in the center and each subsequent generation forming a larger circle around the progenitor. This method tends to exaggerate the missing gaps in one's record. If the parents of any of the earlier ancestors have yet to be found, a large section of one of the circles will remain annoyingly empty. A variation on the concentric circle chart is the radial chart in which a series of small circles containing people's names are connected to the progenitor circle by lines radiating from it, with the outermost circles being those relatives who are still living or who have lived most recently.

To include brothers and sisters, the chart must be designed in a drop down manner, as shown in Diagram B.

Here the = sign is used for the word "married," and each child of the marriage is listed at the end of a descending line under the horizontal line below the progenitor and his wife, with the children by age listed from left to right. Twins can be shown by the further division of a single descending line (as

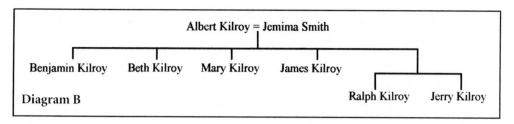

Diagram B

shown for Ralph and Jerry below). The children's wives can be listed with the = sign, and their children can be listed below these names in the same way that their parents' were. If anyone on the chart was married twice or three times, each spouse can be listed with further = signs to the right and left of the descendant's name. Illegitimate children can be shown by dotted or broken descending lines.

In drawing such a drop down chart, one needs to be sure that all members of the same generation appear in the same horizontal level across the page. One should never allow a line that shows someone else's descent to cross other lines of descent because this only causes confusion.

One other type of drop down chart looks like this:

Albert Kilroy (1802 – 1876)
└Jemima Smith (1803 – 1862)
  ──Benjamin Kilroy (1828 – 1884)
    └Diana Jones (1827 – 1894)
      ──Wanda Kilroy (1850 – 1870)
      ── Albert Kilroy (1851 – 1889)
      ── Samuel Kilroy (1852 – 1853)
      └─ Maggie Kilroy (1857 – 1892)
  ── Beth Kilroy (1830 – 1865)
  ── Mary Kilroy (1831 – 1845)
  ── James Kilroy (1835 – 1893)
    └Mary Smith (1836 – 1894)
      └─Joseph (1860 – 1904)
  ── Ralph Kilroy (1836 – 1852)
  └─ Jerry Kilroy (1837 – 1867)

Diagram C

It is much the same as the previous drop down chart except that the horizontal lines have now become vertical ones and vise versa. The entry for each child is indented from the

parents' entry to indicate that the child is of a different generation.

The information for which there is no room on a pedigree chart can be listed on another type of chart known as the family group record. For each pair of ancestors on a pedigree chart, one needs to have a separate family group sheet. These sheets should contain such information as the relationship to the preparer; date prepared; names, date of birth, and place of birth of both the husband and wife; the same for all the children; the father and mother of both the husband and wife and their places and cause of death; and other information about the initial husband and wife, such as the name of their church, occupations, etc. Some of the information on different family group records will be the same because siblings will have the same parents. Each person will be listed on at least two family group records, one of them as a child of two parents and one of them as a parent to other children. In the long run, these separate sheets, though seemingly redundant, will avoid much confusion.

Many genealogists design these family group record sheets for themselves so that each sheet has enough spaces to contain the desired information, but there are blank family group record sheets published and sold by various genealogical organizations, as well as a variety of different kinds of blank pedigree charts. Some of these can be purchased at genealogical libraries, or they can be ordered by mail from Everton Publishers, PO Box 368, Logan, Utah 84323. Some pedigree charts can also be downloaded from various websites, such as www.ancestry.com, www.heritagequest.com, www.misbach.org/pdfcharts/, and others.

Although a well-designed pedigree chart will provide a readily recognized graphic image of one's family tree, when that tree becomes too large to fit on a single page it must be turned into a text document that can hold the hundreds of related names that may eventually be uncovered through genealogical research. At this point all the names must be numbered in order to keep the record manageable and clear. Only by giving each name a separate number can the records of 10 or more different Williams and an equal number of different Janes be kept from causing total confusion.

Different genealogists have designed various numbering systems for this purpose. One of the first was that used by the Spanish genealogist, Jerome de Sosa, in 1676 and popularized by Stephan Kekule von Stradonitz in his 1896 *Ahnentafel Atlas*. (The word "ahnentafel" comes from German, where "ahnen" means ancestor and "tafel" means table or list.) This numbering process is now known as the Ahnentafel System, or sometimes as the Sosa-Stradonitz System. It is a method of numbering that begins with the most recent individual on a pedigree chart and then numbers the ancestors backwards so that the largest number is eventually given to the progenitor. Thus the number 1 is assigned to the subject of the list, numbers 2 and 3 to his or her father and mother, numbers 4 through 7 to the grandparents of number 1, numbers 8 to 15 to the great-grandparents, etc.

This numbering backwards to reach an original ancestor may work adequately for an individual's own records, but it is not very useful for others who are more likely to be interested in the many family lines that spread out from the progenitor. For these the ahnentafel process must be turned upside down so that the first number is given to the original ancestor.

A half dozen numbering systems in common use today do just this. They can be found in all the published books on particular family lines and in the family listings printed in various genealogical magazines. One of these is the Register System, developed by the New England Historic Genealogical Society. Another is the Modified Register System used by the National Genealogical Society. Both start with the progenitor as

Arabic number 1 and list the children with Roman numerals i, ii, iii, iv. In the Register System, wherever there is more information for an individual than just the birthdate, an Arabic numeral is also assigned, as follows:

> 1. Albert Kilroy
>   Children: surname KILROY
> 2. i   Benjamin
>   ii.   Beth
>   iii.   Mary
> 3. iv.   James
>   v.   Ralph
>   vi.   Jerry
>
> 2. Benjamin Kilroy
>   Children: surname KILROY
>   i.   Wanda
>   ii   Albert
>   iii.   Samuel
>   iv.   Maggie
>
> 3. James Kilroy
>   Children: surname KILROY
>   i.   Joseph

For the Modified Register System, the listing is much the same except that each child is given both an Arabic number and a Roman numeral, with the Arabic numbers continuing sequentially throughout the whole records. A "+" is put before any Arabic number where the name that holds further data is repeated later, as follows:

> 1. Albert Kilroy
>   Children: surname KILROY
> +2. i   Benjamin
> 3. ii.   Beth
> 4. iii.   Mary
> 5. iv.   James
> 6. v.   Ralph
> 7. vi.   Jerry
>
> 2. Benjamin Kilroy
>   Children: surname KILROY
> 8. i.   Wanda
> 9. ii   Albert
> 10. iii.   Samuel
> 11. iv.   Maggie

Then there is the Henry System named after Reginald Buchanan Henry, who used it in his *Genealogies of the Families of the Presidents*, published in 1935. In this system, the progenitor is given number 1; his first child is given the number 11, and his next child, the number 12. The eldest child of number 11 will be numbered 111 and the next child 112, etc. When anyone in the line of descent has more than nine children, the 10th one will be given the letter X, the 11th will be given A, the 12th will be given B, and the 13th will be given C.

The Henry System has been modified in at least two ways by other genealogists. One way places the numbers assigned to more than nine children in parentheses. Thus the 10th child of number 111 will be 111(10) and the next one 111(11). Another uses hyphens to distinguish the children above number nine: 1118, 1119, 1-1-1-10, 1-1-1-11.

There is also the d'Aboville System, which is similar to the Henry System except that each digit is separated by a period. Thus the numbers become 1.1.1.8, 1.1.1.9, 1.1.1.10, and 1.1.1.11. The resulting descendant list has a much more uniform look with this system than those using parentheses and mixtures of Roman and Arabic numbers and letters of the alphabet. A variation of the d'Aboville System uses a hyphen in place of the periods: 1-1-1-8, 1-1-1-9, 1-1-1-10, 1-1-1-11.

Another method of recording the numbers, one that is used in works such as *Burke's Peerage*, employs a series of Arabic and Roman numerals along with alphabet letters and parentheses, for example:

Albert Kilroy
1. Benjamin
  (i) Wanda
  (ii) Albert
    (a) Mary
    (b) Albert, Jr.
  (iii) Samuel
  (iv) Maggie
2. Beth
3. Mary

A system popular in South Africa is the de Villiers/Pama System originally used by Christopher de Villiers in his *Genealogies of Old Cape Families*, published in the 1890s, and further developed by Dr. Cor Pama. Here the progenitor is given the letter "a" and the children the letter "b" and the grandchildren the letter "c" as follows:

a Albert Kilroy
  b1 Benjamin Kilroy
    c1 Wanda Kilroy
    c2 Albert Kilroy
    c3 Samuel Kilroy
    c4 Maggie Kilroy
  b2 Beth Kilroy
  b3 Mary Kilroy
  b4 James Kilroy
    c1 Joseph Kilroy
  b5 Ralph Kilroy
  b6 Jerry Kilroy

There are, of course, other possibilities, but they may be of interest only to a mathematician. The systems listed above are the most commonly used, and every genealogist eventually settles on the numbering system most suitable to his or her own taste.

When one uses a computer-generated genealogical program, the program will assign code numbers to each entry in a manner that only the person who designed the program may understand. The program will also automatically link parents to children and husbands to wives. The computer user doesn't have to worry about getting the names in order because the program does this. Yet, as the number of computer entries grows into the thousands, the computer's memory will be taxed and the program will likely become infuriatingly slow. In any case, if one wishes to prepare a book or an article for publication, then it will be necessary to ignore the computer print-out and to insert numbers manually according to one of the established numbering systems.

Penmanship *see* **Handwriting Errors**

Pennsylvania Records can be found in abundance at the Historical Society of Pennsylvania in Philadelphia and at the Pennsylvania State Library in Harrisburg. The first settlement in this area was set up by the Swedes in 1643, near what is now Philadelphia. Prior to that Pennsylvania was occupied by various Algonkian and Iroquoian Indian tribes. In 1655, Dutch troops led by Peter Stuyvesant came into Pennsylvania and captured the Swedish settlement. They held the region until

1664 when English troops arrived and drove out the Dutch. Then, in 1681, King Charles II of England gave the region to William Penn in payment for debts to Penn's father. Penn was a Quaker and promoted the concept of freedom of religion for all persons living in the region.

From the late 1600s to the middle 1700s, the English colonists fought several wars against the French colonists and their Indian allies. One of the most brutal battles of this French and Indian War took place in 1754 in western Pennsylvania. This war ended with a British victory in 1763. The First Continental Congress met in Philadelphia on September 5, 1774, and voted to stop all trade with Great Britain. In 1776 the Continental Congress adopted the Declaration of Independence in the Pennsylvania State House, now Philadelphia's Independence Hall. Pennsylvania was one of the original 13 states, and the second one to join the Union, in 1787.

The first census of Pennsylvania was the national one enumerated in 1790. (There have never been any separate state censuses taken.) This and the other federal censuses taken in Pennsylvania can be seen at the various National Archives locations. The mortality records of 1850 to 1880 can be found in the State Library. Records of births, deaths, marriages, and divorces can be found at the Pennsylvania Vital Records Office in New Castle. Copies can be obtained for a small fee. There is also an adoption registry at the Vital Records Office where adoptees born in Pennsylvania can obtain information relating to the medical history of their parents at the time they were placed for adoption. Divorce records since 1946 are found in the various counties' courts of common pleas. Wills and guardianship records also rest in the counties, the wills with the county register of wills, and guardianship matters with the county orphans' court.

Records relating to land matters are in the files of each county and can be obtained from the county recorder of deeds. In Pennsylvania a distinction is maintained between equity and law actions, but the courts of common pleas have jurisdiction over both. Immigration records for those landing by ship at the port of Philadelphia between 1883 and 1945 are available at the National Archives in Washington, D.C., and at some of its branches in other states.

The State Library has a well-developed index of local histories, family histories, periodicals, and many compilations of cemetery, church, and Bible records. Other sources of genealogical information in Pennsylvania include the Genealogical Society of Pennsylvania at Philadelphia, the Chester County Historical Society at West Chester, the Carnegie Library of Pittsburgh, and the Pennsylvania State Archives at Harrisburg.

Researchers seeking information from county records can locate them at the following county seats: (Adams County) Gettysburg, (Allegheny County) Pittsburgh, (Armstrong County) Kittanning, (Beaver County) Beaver, (Bedford County) Bedford, (Berks County) Reading, (Blair County) Hollidaysburg, (Bradford County) Towanda, (Bucks County) Doylestown, (Butler County) Butler, (Cambria County) Ebensburg, (Cameron County) Emporium, (Carbon County) Jim Thorpe, (Centre County) Bellefonte, (Chester County) West Chester, (Clarion County) Clarion, (Clearfield County) Clearfield, (Clinton County) Lock Haven, (Columbia County) Bloomsburg, (Crawford County) Meadville, (Cumberland County) Carlisle, (Dauphin County) Harrisburg, (Delaware County) Media, (Elk County) Ridgway, (Erie County) Erie, (Fayette County) Uniontown, (Forest County) Tionesta, (Franklin County) Chambersburg, and (Fulton County) McConnellsburg.

Also at (Greene County) Waynesburg, (Huntingdon County) Huntingdon, (Indiana County) Indiana, (Jefferson County) Brookville, (Juniata County) Mifflintown, (Lackawanna County) Scranton, (Lancaster County) Lancaster, (Lawrence County) New Castle, (Lebanon County) Lebanon, (Lehigh County) Allentown, (Luzerne County) Wilkes-Barre, (Lycoming County) Williamsport, (McKean County) Smethport, (Mercer County) Mercer, (Mifflin County) Lewistown, (Monroe County) Stroudsburg, (Montgomery County) Norristown, (Montour County) Danville, (Northampton County)

Easton, (Northumberland County) Sunbury, (Perry County) New Bloomfield, (Philadelphia County) Philadelphia, (Pike County) Milford, (Potter County) Coudersport, (Schuylkill County) Pottsville, (Snyder County) Middleburg, (Somerset County) Somerset, (Sullivan County) Laporte, (Susquehanna County) Montrose, (Tioga County) Wellsboro, (Union County) Lewisburg, (Venango County) Franklin, (Warren County) Warren, (Washington County) Washington, (Wayne County) Honesdale, (Westmoreland County) Greensburg, (Wyoming County) Tunkhannock, and (York County) York.

FOR FURTHER INFORMATION SEE:

• Clint, Florence. *Pennsylvania Area Key: A Guide to the Genealogical Records of the State of Pennsylvania; Including Maps, Histories, Charts and Other Helpful Materials.* Denver, CO: Area Keys, 1976.
• Egle, William Henry. *Pennsylvania Genealogies, Chiefly Scotch-Irish and German.* Baltimore, MD: Genealogical Publishing, 1969.

Pension Claims for those who served in the Civil War, Spanish-American War, Philippine Insurrection, Boxer Rebellion, and for a few others who served in the regular Army, Navy, and Marines are on file at the National Archives in Washington, D.C., as well at some of its branches in various states. These files are indexed by the surnames and then by state from which each soldier served. The applications for such pensions often contain supporting evidence that is valuable to genealogists. Unfortunately the Civil War applications filed prior to 1800 were burned in a War Department fire in November 1800.

Until 1818, all applications for Revolutionary War pensions had to be from needy and disabled (invalid) veterans or the indigent heirs of deceased veterans. However, in 1818, Congress authorized pensions to be based on service without disability as a requirement; need was still a prerequisite. Then, between 1828 and 1832, Congress liberalized this program so that need was no longer a consideration. Five acts, passed between 1862 and 1907, provided pensions for all who had served in the Union Army.

In the years following the Civil War a number of states also granted Confederate army pensions to veterans. Because these Confederate pensions were not federal pensions, their records are not at the National Archives. The Confederate pensions were granted by the states to the veterans who resided in those states at the times of their pension applications. Thus a soldier who served from Louisiana, but who lived later in Texas, would file his petition in Texas. Some states have published indexes to their Confederate pensions, which can be found in the state archives or state historical societies of the states that granted the pensions.

Pentecostal Records of any individual members of the many Pentecostal churches can be located only at the particular churches to which they belonged. There are more than three dozen different Pentecostal groups in the United States alone, most of them in the South and in impoverished urban areas. The largest is the Assemblies of God, which claims more than 8,600 churches with a membership of more than 1,100,000. Another group is the Fire Baptized Holiness Church, with some 40 churches and less than 1,000 members. The Pentecostal movement dates from 1906, when members of the congregation of the Azusa Street Mission in Los Angeles, California, experienced a "baptism in the Spirit." Since the end of World War II, Pentecostalism has spread rapidly in areas of South America and Africa.

Pentecostal churches base their faith on certain religious experiences recorded in the New Testament. They teach that each Christian should seek to be "filled with the Holy Spirit," and the "proof" of this may come when the person speaks in tongues, i.e., speaks in a "language" that is unrecognizable. Pentecostals also believe that they can receive other supernatural gifts, such as the ability to prophesy and to heal by the laying on of hands. Apart from these shared beliefs, Pentecostal denominations do not usually resemble one another, and many of the churches they establish are short lived storefront congregations.

In the 1950s, faith healing, represented

most prominently by the television evangelist Oral Roberts, was at its peak among Pentecostalists. After that, prosperity through faith became a dominant theme. It was not until 1994 that the various Pentecostal churches in America voted to end their practice of racial segregation by creating a national multiracial association. Within the Roman Catholic Church there is a movement somewhat similar to that of the Pentecostals, which is termed the charismatic renewal movement. *See also* **Assemblies of God Records.**

Periodicals *see* **Genealogical Periodicals**

Personal Ancestral File *see* **Computer Programs for Genealogy**

Peruvian Genealogy gets strong support from the Peruvian Genealogical Society, the Instituto Peruano de Investigaciones Genealógicas, in Lima. It publishes a widely read genealogical magazine. Although Peru declared independence from Spain in 1821, it was not until 1826 that the Spanish forces were finally defeated. Modern Peru is divided into 24 departments, 141 provinces, and 1,321 municipalities. Most of the records from the colonial period have been lost through fire, humidity, and earthquakes. What remains can be found in the National Archives of Peru and National Library of Peru, both of which are located in Lima.

An attempt to establish civil registration in 1852 was soon disbanded. It was not reestablished across the country until 1936. Yet there were earlier periods when birth, marriage, and death statistics were collected in different areas of Peru. Information gathered included records of naturalization, adoption, and the legitimacy of children. The old city municipality in Lima has records of deaths for the city from 1857 to 1867, and births and marriages of Peruvians born outside of Peru between 1886 and 1911.

Some of the oldest birth and other vital records can be found in the parish registers of the various Catholic churches throughout Peru. The ones in Lima go back to 1538, as do some in other parishes throughout the country. Those for Lima have been microfilmed and can be viewed at the National Archives.

There were censuses taken in Peru in the years 1535, 1569, 1791, 1836, 1850, 1862, 1876, 1940, 1961, and 1972. Most of these records have been destroyed, and the majority were only of a statistical nature and therefore of little use to genealogists. None of them is available to the researcher. There is, however, a census of burials in Peruvian cemeteries, starting from 1825, that is stored in the archbishop's archive in Lima, the Archive de la Beneficencia. This may be helpful in establishing birth and death dates.

Starting in 1825 it was forbidden to bury corpses in any of the churches or churchyards. Consequently, from that year many public and private cemeteries have been established. Prior to that many graves were located in catacombs below the churches. It is estimated that between 50,000 and 70,000 bodies are buried in such catacombs.

As in other countries, wills and other notarial records can be found in the various notarial archives in the cities and towns of Peru. These public registries (registros públicos) also contain all the transactions that involve the buying and selling of land.

The National Archives holds a printed index that lists the notarial records for the cities of Lima and Callao starting in 1559. It also has an index of the wills, codicils, and other documents for the city of Lima. There are records of property descriptions and locations; records relating to water rights, labor disputes and like matters that give names and biographical information about the participants; records dealing with civil and criminal disputes between Indians and Spaniards; and residency records for royal officials during the colonial period. The National Library has a collection of wills that were processed between 1561 and 1876, records relating to land sales between 1528 and 1900, and many other records that a genealogist may find useful.

Those working on Peruvian genealogy will probably find it helpful to consult the many-volumed *Encyclopedia Heraldica y Genealogica: Hispano-Americana*, a copy of which is at the National Library. It gives the histories of a number of Peruvian families, as well as those in Spain and other Latin American countries.

Photographs can be one of the most fascinating aspects of family history research. Starting in the late 19th century, it became possible for people to have their photographs taken relatively cheaply at a photographer's studio, and many families employed photographers to record important events such as weddings. By the end of World War I it became common for persons to own their own cameras; today these have been replaced in part by equally low-cost digital cameras. Thus many people have large collections of photographs of their family, friends, travels, and special events.

Photographs pass between generations in a variety of ways, and one may be surprised at the number of old photographs that relatives still keep in boxes, trunks, and photograph albums. These photos can provide a wealth of useful information to any recorder of family history, assuming that someone has taken the time to include identifying information with the photos.

Although the first permanent photograph with a camera was taken by Joseph Niépce in 1826 in France, Louis Daguerre, another Frenchman, is generally credited with producing the first useable photographic method in 1839. This was the daguerreotype process that utilized a copper plate, the image being developed by mercury vapor. Until the late 1850s, daguerreotype photographs were the only kind made by photographers in America. Then, from about 1855 into the 1860s, photographers began to record their images on glass plates known as ambrotypes. They then turned to ferrotypes, or tintypes, in which a plate of iron was used to hold the image. Such tintypes were more durable and less expensive than were the ambrotypes. These tintypes continued to be used in photography until the early 1900s.

Paper coated with salt and silver nitrate was perfected by the British scientist William H. F. Talbot in 1841, but this process was not widely used at the time because the daguerreotype process produced a much clearer picture. In 1888, George Eastman, an American, revolutionized photography by developing and marketing the Kodak camera that held a roll of film rather than glass or iron plates. The film consisted of light-sensitive gelatin that was coated onto a paper backing. In developing such pictures, Eastman's company transferred the gelatin onto a glass plate. From this prints could be made. But the process of transferring the emulsion was difficult and required too much skill for amateur photographers.

In 1889, Eastman substituted a celluloid base for the paper, and printing photographs became much easier because the gelatin emulsion did not have to be removed from the base. By 1900, card-mounted prints were being superseded by durable paper photographs produced by amateur photographers on home cameras. These, of course, are the ones that are found in many household collections today.

Faded and irreplaceable photographs can be preserved for a long time by storing them in a dark, acid-free environment. This will slow the deterioration process, but nothing can stop it altogether. However, there are methods of restoration that may be used to reprint images. The original fragile photo can be scanned and then restored digitally, a process best left to the professional. When completed, the image can be converted to a film negative and printed. Photographs today can also be converted into digital images to be saved on computer disks so that they can be seen on computer screens. As such, they will be preserved as pixels that may not deteriorate over time.

Paintings as well as photographs of relatives can sometimes be located, particularly if the subjects were affluent enough to pay itinerant portrait painters to produce them or famous enough to have institutions finance the rendering of such portraits. In most cases a family will still preserve these images, and sometimes they may be found in various portrait museums.

Physicians' Records *see* **Medical Records**

Polish Records *see* **Eastern European Genealogy**

Portuguese Genealogy can provide much material that is helpful in the preparation of family histories, although it is not easy to obtain the data without visiting the country. In many instances the parish registers go back to at least 1570, although quite a few were lost in the Lisbon earthquake of 1755. Some have been deposited in the National Archives of Portugal in Lisbon, others are in the district archives, and still others remain in the individual parishes. Civil registration did not begin until 1878, and these records are under the supervision of local officials. A few civil registrations started as early as 1832. These have been stored by the Inspector Superior of Libraries and Archives (Direccâo-General do Registo e Notariodo do Ministerio da Justiça) in Lisbon.

For questions regarding births, marriages, filial descent, prenuptial contracts, deaths, emancipation, and the care and guardianship of minors, one should also contact the Director Superior of Libraries and Archives in Lisbon. The records themselves are located in the offices of the civil registrars (Conservatoria de Registro Civil) in each of the towns where these events occurred. Wills, when they are public, are processed by individual notaries and remain in their files after the testator's death. Some are preserved in the central archives (Arquivo dos Registos Paroquiais) in Lisbon, and some are also preserved in the archives of the various districts.

The national archives (Arquivo Nacional da Tôrre do Tombo) in Lisbon has a collection of materials relating to genealogy, including files of early parish registers, wills, and a series of armorial bearings. The main source of records on Portuguese heraldry, however, is located at the Instituto Portugues de Heraldica in Lisbon.

Presbyterian Records can be found in local churches and at two historical archives, one in Pennsylvania and the other in North Carolina. This Protestant church was founded by John Knox, the leader of the Protestant Reformation in Scotland. From 1560 until his death in 1572, Knox was Scotland's most powerful political and religious leader. The term presbyter is a New Testament word for elder. Presbyterian congregations are governed by boards, called sessions or consistories, which are composed of the minister and a number of elected lay elders.

The first Presbyterian congregation in the United States was established on Long Island in 1640. Today there are several separate denominations of Presbyterians in North America, including the United Presbyterian Church in the U.S.A, which is the largest Presbyterian denomination in America; the Presbyterian Church in the United States, which was formed by a group of Southern churches that broke away from the United Presbyterian Church; the Orthodox Presbyterian Church; the Unofficial Presbyterian Church in America, and a number of independent Presbyterian churches. In Canada, the former Presbyterian Church is now part of the United Church of Canada that was formed in 1925 by the merger of a number of different Canadian Protestant denominations.

The Presbyterian Historical Society, headquartered in Philadelphia, maintains the national archives of the Presbyterian Church (U.S.A.) and supervises a regional center in Montreat, North Carolina. This society serves the church's national agencies, middle governing bodies, and local congregations, as well as scholars and the general public. The Philadelphia center documents the "northern stream" predecessor denominations and their work, congregations, and middle governing bodies in 36 states, and the work of the current denomination's national agencies. The North Carolina center documents the "southern stream" predecessor denominations and congregations and middle governing bodies in the presbyteries of 14 southern states: Texas, Oklahoma, Arkansas, Louisiana, Mississippi, Alabama, Florida, Georgia, South Carolina, North Carolina, Tennessee, Kentucky, West Virginia, and Virginia.

Both centers have copies of Alfred Nevin's *Encyclopedia of the Presbyterian Church in the United States of America: Including the Northern and Southern Assemblies*, published in 1884 in Philadelphia. This encyclopedia can also be found in a number of genealogical libraries. There are some Presbyterian congregation records at the Thomason Library at Clinton, South Carolina, on the campus of Presbyterian College. These genealogical records relate to individuals associated with the Presbyterian College and to Presbyterian ministers who served in South Carolina.

Information regarding births, marriages, and deaths of ordinary members of Presbyterian churches can best be found by consulting the records preserved at the churches where the persons were members, if such locations are known. The historical center records tend to concentrate on the development of the movement in the United States, inter-church decisions, and biographical material about some of the leaders of this movement.

In Canada, the Presbyterian Church Archives in Toronto hold many original church records for various Canadian Presbyterian congregations, as does the Canadian National Archives at Ottawa. Yet, following the merger of the Presbyterians into the United Church of Canada, all the later records have become part of the United Church Archives in Toronto. The types of Presbyterian records that are at the National Archives include births and baptisms, marriages, and deaths and burials; communion rolls and registers; minutes of the Presbyterian Church sessions, or the governing meetings; and the histories of various Presbyterian congregations in Canada.

Prince Edward Island Records can be found at the Provincial Archives, the Prince Edward Island University library, and the Prince Edward Island Genealogical Society, all of which are in Charlottetown. Prince Edward Island is the smallest, yet most thickly populated, of all Canada's provinces. French colonists began to settle the area as early as 1720 and set up communities near present-day Charlottetown and Georgetown. At the time it was occupied by Indians of the Micmac tribe. In 1758 British troops took possession of Prince Edward Island during the French and Indian War. They changed its name to St. John's Island and made it a part of Nova Scotia. Then, in 1769, it became a separate British colony. Its name was changed to Prince Edward Island in 1799. The island entered the Dominion of Canada in 1873 as the seventh province.

Prince Edward Island began recording

births in 1840 and marriages in 1886, but it was not until 1906 that it became mandatory for all births and deaths to be collected by the government. The province began to register stillbirths in 1920 when it officially joined the federal system of reporting vital statistics. The year 1930 saw the beginning of adoption registration in the province, while the registration of divorces did not take place until 1946. The adoption records are restricted because of the confidentiality of the information in them. Application for access to these records must be made through Adoption Services of the Department of Health and Social Services Agency in Charlottetown. To request birth, marriage, or death certificates, genealogists must contact the Vital Statistics Division in Montague. However, most of these records are also considered to be confidential.

Wills are filed with the supreme court at Charlottetown. A child not named in the will of his parents has no legal recourse. Probate records later than 1920 are held at the Estates Division of the Sir Louis Henry Davies Law Courts in Charlottetown. There are just three counties on Prince Edward Island, but the record offices in the county seats for these counties hold all the land records. These county seats are: (Prince County) Summerside, (Queens County) Charlottetown, and (Kings County) Georgetown.

The Provincial Archives has a large collection of genealogical materials, including government records, correspondence files, journals, newspapers, photographs, maps, sound recordings, and the provincial census records for 1841 and 1881, which list only the heads of families. It has a card index composed of family names with entries compiled from census records, extant passenger lists, marriage registers, selected newspapers, *Meacham's Atlas*, funeral home registers, cemetery transcripts and other sources. There are baptism records prior to 1886 taken from various church records across the island. There are also death records prior to 1906 and marriage register books from 1832 to 1923, as well as records of marriage licenses from 1787 to 1919 and marriage bond records from 1849 to 1902.

The newspapers in the archives include most of the issues of Prince Edward Island newspapers on microfilm. The archives also has land records and maps prior to 1900 that may be helpful in pinpointing the localities where persons lived at the time, and there is a series of early rent books, kept by proprietors or their agents. The archives has microfilmed a large number of church records from parishes across Prince Edward Island. A few of these from Acadian parishes and those of St. Paul's Anglican Church in Charlottetown predate 1800, but the majority date from 1830 on. They include records of the Church of Scotland, St. John's Presbyterian Church in Belfast, and St. Peter's Anglican Church in Charlottetown.

The archives has an extensive collection of records from the various courts in Prince Edward Island dating from the 1790s to the 1950s. The wills and administrations from 1807 to 1920 may be useful in documenting land transfers, may also contain family names and spell out family relationships. The archives also has supreme court and chancery court records from 1787 to 1958, including minute books and case papers.

Similar but less extensive collections of genealogical records can be found at the Robertson Library of the University of Prince Edward Island, as well as at the offices of the Prince Edward Island Genealogical Society. *See also* **Census, Canadian.**

Prison Records are likely to be examined only occasionally in the family research process, but they do sometimes contain useful historical and genealogical information. These records can be difficult to locate, often difficult to read when they are handwritten and faded, and probably should always be used in conjunction with court records, newspaper accounts, coroners' records, and other sources of information.

The first prison in the United States was the Walnut Street Jail in Philadelphia, established in 1790. It was designed after the workhouses in Europe, particularly the one in London. Other early American prisons included one at Auburn, New York, founded in 1825, and the Eastern State Penitentiary at Cherry Hill in Philadelphia, founded in 1829.

As is true today, the early prisons were operated by federal, state, local, and military authorities. A listing of all the correctional facilities that are still in use can be found in the *Directory: Juvenile and Adult Correctional Departments, Institutions, Agencies and Paroling Authorities*, published by the American Correctional Association of Laurel, Maryland.

Prison records include admission and discharge books, biographical registers, hospital record books, registers of prisoners, death warrants, clemency files, and lists of executions. If one knows the place of imprisonment, one can write directly to that prison or to the department of corrections in that state to request a copy of the particular record that is desired. If one does not know the place of imprisonment, a great deal of detective work may be required to locate it. Modern prison records—those within the past 72 years—fall under the jurisdiction of privacy laws and will not be released, but family members can obtain the records of deceased convicts by contacting the prison or correctional institution directly.

Privacy Act of 1974 was passed by the U.S. Congress in an effort to balance the government's need for information about individuals with the right of those individuals to be protected against an unwarranted invasion of their privacy by the federal agencies' collection and disclosure of such personal information. It extended the Freedom of Information Act of 1966.

The Privacy Act was passed because Congress was concerned with the potential abuses resulting from the government's increasing use of computers to store and retrieve personal data by means of universal identifiers, such as Social Security numbers. It was also passed at a time when Congress was actively investigating some of the federal abuses stemming from the Watergate scandal. Its purpose was to establish a code of "fair information practices," requiring federal agencies to comply with statutory norms in the collection, maintenance, and dissemination of records. The act restricts the disclosure of personally identifiable federal records to parties other than those involved, while granting individuals increased rights of access to the ones maintained on themselves. It also gives individuals the right to seek the amendment of the records maintained on themselves if it can be proved that these records are not accurate, relevant, timely, or complete.

Under certain circumstances an individual may be entitled to receive more information under the Privacy Act than under the Freedom of Information Act. Under the Freedom of Information Act anyone can request access to any agency record. Privacy Act requests are more limited and can be made only by U.S. citizens or aliens lawfully admitted for permanent U.S. residence, by those who are seeking information about themselves, or for information in a system of records maintained under their names or other personal identifiers. According to the Justice Department, even if a request does not mention the Privacy Act, the department automatically treats such requests as being made under both the Freedom of Information Act and the Privacy Act whenever it is appropriate to do so. In this way, requesters receive the maximum amount of information available to them under the law. *See also* **Freedom of Information Act.**

Probate Records are court records that deal with the distribution of a person's estate. These records consist of wills, inventories, and estate settlements. As such, they often contain information of great value to the genealogist. Wills can enumerate the possessions that individuals and families thought to be of significance and value. Along with inventories, they may indicate how such wealth was held. Every individual named in a will and every relationship stated therein increases the value of these documents to the family researcher.

Each state has, and in colonial days each colony had, its own laws of probate. Most of the early wills left property to a male heir, though sometimes even these early wills contained a spouse's name and children's names. Throughout history many persons have died

without leaving any property of value and hence no record of probate, but roughly half of the residents of the United States have either left wills or have been mentioned in them. The majority of wills have been left by men of property, though some men and women of humble means have also left them.

If a person dies leaving a valid will, the legal term used for this situation is that the person died testate. If there is no will, that person is said to have died intestate. The records for both these situations comprise a valuable genealogical resource. Statutory probate law in the United States is a product of state legislation rather than federal legislation, so the laws relating to wills and estate settlements differ somewhat from state to state.

The action to prove and admit a will is initiated by a relative, and sometimes a creditor, after the death of the individual who made the will. Notice is given by the clerk of the court that the will is to be processed on some particular day and that anyone contesting it can appear at that time. The court then requires proof through the testimony of witnesses that the will was indeed signed by the deceased. If the court then approves the probate, the will is transcribed by a clerk into a will book where it is assigned a page number and indexed under the name of the deceased.

In searching for these probate records, the genealogist needs to know the exact place of residence of the deceased at the time of his or her death because that is where the record will be found. Often a person may live in a particular locality for most of his or her life, but apparently leave no records to be found at a time one might expect that person to have died. In this case, it is likely that the person moved to another place in old age, perhaps to live with offspring. The probate record would have been made and recorded in that new jurisdiction.

Historically, under common law, a married woman was considered to be incompetent to make a will involving real estate, even when she had the consent of her husband. She could, however, prepare a will of personal property if she had her husband's consent. Widows and unmarried women were not restricted in this way and could do as they pleased about making wills. In more recent years, legislation has been adopted to give married women the same probate rights as their husbands.

When a man died intestate, the widow by law received at least a third of household goods and real estate until her death or remarriage. The remainder of the property would be divided among the children. If, for various reasons, a court decided that an estate should not be divided, it would be given to the eldest male child on the condition that siblings would be paid for their shares. *See also* **Wills.**

Professional Genealogists are usually persons who have been officially recognized by the Board for Certification of Genealogists (BCG). They are specialists who conduct family history research for others, librarians with expertise in archival records of genealogical interest, and teachers certified to conduct courses in pedigree maintenance and development.

The certification of professional genealogists began in 1964 when libraries and other archival institutions began to recognize that there was a need to formulate high standards for genealogical research and to register competent persons qualified for this type of work. The BCG was established to meet this demand, and the board of trustees that was named to oversee the organization includes distinguished genealogists, historians, and archivists from all parts of the United States.

The BCG is authorized to approve applications for certification, to determine if the applicants are qualified to do research by an examination of their works, to issue certificates of approval to those who qualify, and to maintain lists of genealogists and record searchers available to libraries, societies, and private institutions. Those whom the BCG approves are entitled to place the initials "C.G." (certified genealogist) after their names. Anyone wishing certification is advised to contact the BCG in Washington, D.C., to obtain instructions as to how to proceed. The BCG will provide an application form and details as to the qualifications required to meet its standards for approval.

A certified genealogist is considered to be proficient in all areas of genealogical research and a person experienced in the compilation of well-crafted family histories. There are also five other certification categories awarded by the BCG: the certified genealogical records specialist (CGRS), the certified American Indian lineage specialist (CAILS), the certified American lineage specialist (CALA), the certified genealogical instructor (CGI), and the certified genealogical lecturer (CGL). *See also* **Genealogical Courses; Genealogy as a Profession.**

Professional Societies *see* **Societies and Fraternal Organizations**

Public Domain Lands were the original landed estates of all the American people. This property at one time covered three-fourths of the continental area of the United States, including all Alaska — a total of one billion, eight hundred million acres. Portions of this land were first awarded by the Continental Congress early in the American Revolution to private and noncommissioned officers for their service in the Continental Army. Later such bounty lands were also awarded to soldiers for their service in the War of 1812, the Indian wars, and the Mexican War. Scrip was issued to the veterans that could be exchanged for titles at any public land office.

Under the Ordinance of 1785, all federal lands were to be surveyed into vertical strips called ranges, each six miles wide, and horizontal strips of townships, each six miles wide. The first such public-domain surveys (1785–88) were in Ohio and the land surveyed was open to purchase for cash or with bounty land warrants. The land office was located at first in the Treasury Department in New York, a long way from Ohio. But in 1800, President John Adams signed a new public land law that moved the land office to the area where land was being distributed.

When each of the public domain states (Alabama, Alaska, Arizona, Arkansas, California, Colorado, Florida, Idaho, Illinois, Indiana, Iowa, Kansas, Louisiana, Michigan, Minnesota, Mississippi, Missouri, Montana, Nebraska, Nevada, New Mexico, North

Dakota, Ohio, Oklahoma, Oregon, South Dakota, Utah, Washington, Wisconsin, and Wyoming) was admitted to the Union, it received grants of public lands that it could use or dispose of for public purposes. There were school grants, road grants, canal grants, river grants, railroad grants, swamp grants, desert grants, internal improvement grants, and in 1862, a grant to all states to provide funds for agricultural colleges.

In 1862, a Five Year Homestead Act permitted each settler to obtain as much as 160 acres of public lands, at an average price of $1.25 per acre, on which to construct a house and begin cultivation. The settlers then received titles to the land only after they resided there for five years. The time was reduced to three years by the Homestead Act of 1912. Later bills provided for larger homesteads, up to 320 acres and 640 acres for stock raising.

Two sets of tract books were kept for these public domain lands, one in the individual land offices and one in Washington, D.C., and now located at the National Archives regional branches that serve the state in question. The local records from the individual land offices are often found at state land offices, historical societies, or state archives. The individual case file for each land entry is the source of potentially valuable information for genealogists. *See also* **Homestead Act.**

Public Health Records are maintained by the many departments of public health in each city throughout the United States, many of which were first established in the 1860s. As early as 1904, some 60 cities in America required the registration of all tubercular patients by the various public health departments. Four years later 84 cities had such registration laws, requiring physicians and other health care providers to report the names and addresses of all those found to have tuberculosis. Where such records still exist, they are in the files of these city public health centers.

Tuberculosis is not the only disease over which public health departments have been concerned. In more recent years they have kept records on a wide variety of diseases that have the potential of growing into epidemics. In order to find out if any public health records exist for the time period in which a particular ancestor may have been affected by such an epidemic, one should contact the department of public health in the city where that person lived at the time. *See also* **Medical Records.**

Public Welfare Records are seldom examined by family researchers, partly because they are scattered through various state and national repositories so that specific records may be difficult to locate. But they do contain information about such matters as applications for aid to minor children, the elderly, and the indigent; almshouse and poorhouse records; and public burials. Thus they can sometimes be useful, particularly if such information can be found nowhere else.

The Social Security Act of 1935 has provided a legal basis for most of the welfare programs in the United States, both social insurance and public insurance. National, state, and local public-assistance programs now pay out more than $40 billion annually. In Canada the primary public welfare programs are the Canadian pension plan, unemployment insurance, family and youth allowances, and medical and hospital insurance.

Public welfare records can be found in state public welfare offices, in state vital statistics offices, in state historical society archives, in some university libraries, and in the offices of state planning boards. The researcher should contact the information services of any state in which such records are being sought in order to learn where the particular records may be stored.

Puerto Rican Genealogy begins about 1600 with a few parish listings of deaths that can be found at the ecclesiastical archive in San Juan. But it was not until 1885, when the Spanish civil registration law was applied to Puerto Rico, that vital records were maintained in any organized way. After the Spanish-American War in 1898, Puerto Rico became a protectorate of the United States. Civil registration of all marriages, whether religious or civil, became a requirement in 1900. In 1918 it was made mandatory that all marriages be conducted by civil authorities, whether an accompanying religious ceremony took place or not.

Vital statistics regarding births, marriages, and deaths since 1931 have been filed with the Department of Health's Demographic Registry in San Juan. Earlier records of this sort, dating from 1885, can be located in the record offices of the particular municipalities. Copies of these records, filling some 5,000 volumes, are held at the Historic Archive in the city of Bayamón. A 224-page listing of these records is available at the San Juan Demographic Registry. The files relating to divorces are maintained in the superior courts where the divorces were granted.

Other sources for birth, death, and marriage occurrences can be found in church records and in cemeteries, as well as in newspapers, military records, family Bibles, letters, and other family documents. Existing parish registers are either in the hands of local parish priests or at the Archbishop's Archive in San Juan. The baptism records at the Archbishop's Archive go back to 1672, marriage records to 1653, and death records to 1600.

The National Archives in San Juan is a center for genealogical and historical information. The notarial records here are of particular interest because there is an alphabetical card index to the names of Puerto Rican individuals found at various institutions in Spain. This information is constantly being updated and includes the sources for the information about each of the names.

There are Puerto Rican census records for 1900, 1910 and 1920 in the National Archives in Washington, D.C., as well as military records for Puerto Ricans who were drafted into the U.S. Army and fought in both World War I and World War II. The National Archives also has some immigration records for Puerto Ricans who moved to the United States.

Hunter College in New York City has an extensive collection of Puerto Rican migration records in its archives, El Centro de Estudios Puertorriqueños, which includes files relating to Puerto Ricans who resided in New York City between 1930 and 1959, complete with picture identifications. *See also* **Immigration Records.**

Q

Quaker Records, or the records of the Religious Society of Friends, are considerably more consistent in nature than those of most other religious denominations. Unfortunately, there is no central location for these records. Some are deposited in library archives, some in bank vaults, some in bureau drawers, but most are in the hands of the members of more than one hundred Quaker meeting places across the country.

Quakers have been known throughout history for their humanitarian activities, their opposition to war, their leadership in prison reform and the humane treatment of mental patients, and their campaigns to remove barriers of racial inequality. The Friends Church

was organized a little over three hundred years ago (1647) by George Fox of England, a weaver's son. From the beginning, the Quakers emphasized inward spiritual experiences rather than specific creeds. The term Quaker was originally applied to this group as an insult, after Fox said to an English judge that he should "tremble at the Word of the Lord."

Within a few short years after Fox began preaching to groups in England thousands of persons throughout that country had embraced his message. Many were persecuted as dissenters for their beliefs. In 1671, Fox and 12 others came to America and trekked up and down the Atlantic Seaboard preaching to the colonists. Later, one of these Quakers,

John Archdale, became the governor of the Carolinas. One-half of the representatives of the Carolinas legislature at that time were members of the Friends.

A renewed outbreak of persecution of Quakers in England led 17 of them to purchase the colony of East Jersey in America so that it could serve as a refuge where Friends could practice their faith without interference. Robert Barclay, a brilliant young Scottish Quaker theologian, served as governor of that colony for a time. In 1681 William Penn, a Quaker, was granted the land of Pennsylvania by the King of England so that he might start a colony in America. Penn met with the Indians under the great elm at Shackamason, the ancient meeting place of the tribes, and made friends with them. He purchased land from the Indians at a fair price and concluded a treaty with them that was agreeable to all. He also designed a government dedicated to religious freedom, to equality, and to peace, and he laid out Philadelphia as the first planned city in the New World. Pennsylvania thus became Penn's "Holy Experiment."

By 1691, at the time of Fox's death, there were some 40,000 Quakers in England and America, many of whom were then living in Virginia, Rhode Island, Massachusetts, Maryland, New Jersey, and Pennsylvania. They had organized Quaker meetings in all the colonies except Connecticut and South Carolina. By 1884 there were 971 Quaker ministers in the United States, of whom 371 were women.

The loose organizational structure of the Religious Society of Friends has always given a great deal of liberty to their meetings, and has resulted in a variety of worship and spiritual patterns in different parts of America, Europe, and other places in the world. Throughout the years there have also been several splits among the members of the movement. For example, Elias Hicks, in 1828, led his followers out of the main body of Quakers because of differences over whether Jesus was a Divine Being or not. They formed a separate Hicksite group. The Hicksites established their own meetings and were soon "disowned" by the orthodox members. However, the Hicksites later founded Swarthmore College in Pennsylvania. Another break-off took place in 1845 in Rhode Island by followers of John Wilbur. This group became known as Wilburites.

George Fox had admonished the Quakers to keep vital records and to make wills. He also directed that records be kept in every meeting of the births of the children of members and the burials of the dead. The members of the Religious Society of Friends have been faithful in doing this, and thus their records have been preserved, particularly those of the English Quakers who were not permitted to be listed in the parish registers of the Church of England.

Quaker business meetings are guided by a clerk, who after a period of silent waiting, states a particular issue and listens to the other members' suggestions. No votes are taken, but the consideration process continues until even opposing minorities are satisfied that their position has had a hearing and that it has been considered. The primary records kept by the various meetings include, besides births and deaths, the marriages, certificates of removal, and disownments. Among the most useful to genealogists are the certificates of removal, which give the member's name and occupation, the name of the meeting of which the member is in good standing, and other statements about the individual made by other members of the meeting. When a member is received into a new meeting, the former residence is made a part of the record. A disownment is the record of a termination of membership from the Society. A Friends marriage record or certificate will be signed by all those present, and thus also has unusual value for a genealogist.

In using Quaker records one needs to realize that the Friends always use numbers in referring to months and days of the week, as it has been their practice not to recognize the names of the Pagan gods for which most months are commonly named. Thus the number 2-7-2001 will be used in their records instead of February 7, 2001.

The late William Wade Hinshaw of Washington, D.C., published six volumes devoted to Quaker records, the *Encyclopedia of American Quaker Genealogy*, which covers the records of meetings in North Carolina, Pennsylvania, New Jersey, Ohio, Virginia, and some in New York City and Long Island. These books and other records can be found in the libraries of several Quaker colleges, such as Swarthmore College in Pennsylvania, Earlham College in Indiana, and Guilford College in North Carolina.

The Friends Collection at Earlham College is one of the four or five largest collections of Quaker records in the world, with more than 12,000 books and nearly as many pamphlets, some going back to the 17th century when the Society of Friends was founded. These works are supplemented with an extensive collection of Quaker genealogical materials, such as personal diaries and letters. In Canada, the Quaker archives are located at Pickering College in Ontario.

Quebec Records of births, marriages, and deaths have been registered by the clergy, both Catholic and Protestant, since the early 17th century. It was not until 1926 that there was any registration of births and deaths for those who did not belong to a church. When the first French explorers arrived in what is now the Province of Quebec in 1534, Eskimos and several Indian tribes were living there. By 1608 Samuel de Champlain of France had established a permanent settlement named Quebec City, and the region was soon ruled by France. However, the British captured Quebec City in 1759, during the French and Indian War. After that, England controlled the mostly–French-speaking area. The British North American Act of 1867 created the Dominion of Canada and formed the Province of Quebec. The act recognized French, in addition to English, as one of Quebec's two official languages.

The earliest records in Quebec were often more diligently written down (and today are more easily accessible) than later ones because record keeping when the region was under French control was somewhat more thorough than it became after the British took over. None of the French or British records was combined with others and maintained in one central jurisdiction until 1994, when all the post–1899 records were moved into govern-

ment facilities in Quebec City and Montreal. These records are now closed to researchers.

At the same time, the government took the responsibility for the registration of births and deaths out of the hands of the churches, and church records of such events now have no legal weight. However, church records of marriages are still legal documents. Most, but not all of the pre–1880 Protestant civil registers and the pre–1900 Catholic civil registers for Quebec are now available on microfilm and can be consulted at the nine regional archives (Archives Nationale du Québec) and at the libraries of various Quebec historical societies. These regional archives are located in the cities or towns of Quebec, Montreal, Rimouski, Sherbrooke, Chicoutimi, Hull, Trois-Rivieres, Rouyn, and Sept-Îles.

Researchers wishing to locate a birth, marriage, or death record in Quebec must know the religion of the person, the date of the event, and the community where the person lived in order to find the appropriate microfilm roll, and they must know the exact date of a birth, marriage, or death in order for the archives to issue a certificate relating to any of those events.

In 1903 an act was passed requiring that marriage records be sent to the parishes where the groom and bride were baptized. Thus for the late 19th century, baptism records of the groom or bride will probably also include a copy of a form showing when, where, and to whom he or she was married. It was not until the 1960s that any civil marriage, that is a marriage outside of the church, could be conducted, and prior to the reform of the Canadian divorce laws in 1968, it took a bill of Parliament to receive a divorce in Quebec. The divorce records are now only open to the people involved.

An interesting type of record one will only find within the registers of the Catholic Church is that of the rehabilitation of marriages. Since the Catholic Church only recognized marriages performed in a Catholic Church as being legitimate, all other marriages—those in a Protestant Church or by a justice of the peace — had to be rehabilitated in a special service in order to be recognized by the Catholic Church.

Because illegitimacy carries a stigma, some Protestant families simply didn't bother to baptize illegitimate children. But the Catholic faith puts a high premium on baptism, so its priests are allowed to baptize illegitimate children as "Inconnu(e)," which literally means unknown. In Montreal there are many volumes of the records of "Inconnu" children. Many of these children were baptized simply as Marie Inconnue or Joseph Inconnu. Sometimes one can identify the families of these children through the census records if the family reported the child to the census taker.

Another unusual entry type that one may find on occasion in both Protestant and Catholic church records is the notation that someone was buried by a coroner's warrant. This means that the person in question died under circumstances where foul play was a possibility, and a coroner was called in to ascertain cause of death so further legal steps could be taken, if necessary.

Recently a huge database has been made available to computer users having access to the Internet for researching people born in Quebec before 1800. Known as the Programme de recherche en démographie historique (PRDH), it was developed by the University of Montreal. The PRDH database contains approximately 690,000 baptismal, marriage, and burial records that were obtained from 153 parishes, missions, and institutions. It also includes a list of Acadians who settled in Quebec. The file for each individual gives the date and place of birth, marriage(s), and death, as well as family and conjugal ties with other individuals. Accessing the PRDH Web-site permits the researcher to find a limited amount of information about any individual in the database, but enough to determine whether an individual is listed therein. For further information the researcher must subscribe so that he or she can obtain the complete record and navigate between the different components of the database.

Parish records of wills, deeds, orphan records, and other notarial records can often be found at the district courts in Quebec. The cities and towns where the district courts are located are as follows: (Abitibi District) Amos, (Arthabaska District) Arthabaska, (Beauce District) St-Joseph de Beauce, (Beauharnois District) Valleyfield, (Bedford District) Sweetsburg, (Bonaventure District) New Carlisle, (Chicoutimi District) Chicoutimi, (Drummond District) Drummondville, (Gaspe District) Pierce, (Hauterive District) Baie Comeau, (Hull District) Hull, (Iberville District) St-Jean, (Joliette District) Joliette, (Kamouraska District) Riviere-de-Loup, (Labelle District) Mont-Laurier, (Magantic District) Thetford Mines, (Montmagny District) Montmagny, (Montreal District) Montreal, (Nicolet District) Nicolet, (Pontiac District) Campbell's Bay, (Quebec District) Quebec City, (Richelieu District) Sorel (Rimouski District) Rimouski, (Roberval District) Roberval, (Rouyn-Noranda District) Rouyn, (Saguenay District) Sherbrooke, (St-Hyacinthe District) St-Hyacinthe, (St-Maurice District) Shawinigan, (Temiscamingue District) Ville-Marie, (Terebone District) St-Jerome, and (Trois-Rivieres District) Trois-Rivieres. *See also* **Census, Canadian.**

R

Railroad Retirement Records start in 1937 when the Railroad Retirement Board was established. All railroad employees were covered by the Railroad Retirement Act and were eligible to receive pensions from this board, much as other workers have been eligible for Social Security when they retire. Because ear-lier railroad workers' records are scattered throughout various archives and repositories, and many have been lost or destroyed, the Railroad Retirement Board's records may be the only viable place to gather information about any man or woman who was a railroader.

After the passage of the Railroad Retirement Act, provisions were made to assign a separate block of numbers (700–729) for the first three digits of any Social Security number given to an employee of the nation's railroads. In some cases a person may have worked for both the railroad and for other industries, and have been given two different numbers—one for participation in Social Security and one for railroad retirement. These persons may have even collected multiple benefits under the two programs.

The railroad retirement records are maintained in Chicago, Illinois, and the board there is helpful in providing information about railroad employees for a small fee, if one can provide an employee's name, position, the railroad worked for, and where and when the worker was employed. However, the board will not release information on persons who are still living without their written consent. Since the records are kept under each employee's unique Social Security number, this is probably the best way to request information. You can often find the number on the person's death certificate. In some cases, it is possible to locate a railroad retirement record by using only the full name, address, and birth and death dates of the person. However, this is not possible with relatively common surnames unless the number is included.

Around the peak of the railroad industry in the early 1920s, as many as 2.25 million people worked for the various railroad companies. The individual railroad retirement records include: applications for participation in railroad retirement, statements of railroad service, applications for employee annuities, certificates of termination of service, and notices of deaths and statements of compensation.

During the late 1960s, the Railroad Retirement Board approved a policy of allowing for the destruction of records that were older than 30 years from the date that the last payment was made to a claimant or to a claimant's beneficiary. Genealogists, however, strenuously objected to this policy, so it was put on hold. Some of the records, however, were destroyed, and no attempt to microfilm them was undertaken prior to that destruction.

If a person was not working for a railroad after 1936, his or her name will not be found in these records, but there are some sources of information that can be consulted for data about earlier workers. They include the *Biographical Directory of Railway Officials of America* that was issued periodically during the 19th century. Copies for 1885, 1906, 1913, and 1922 can be found at the California State Railroad Museum Library in Sacramento. This library also has some 50 drawers containing employment cards for those working for the Southern Pacific Railroad that date back to 1903.

Real Estate Records *see* **Tax and Real Estate Records**

Reformed Church Records can be found in the Archives for the Reformed Church in New Brunswick, New Jersey, as well as in the library of the Holland Society in New York and some other New York and New Jersey libraries. They can also be found at the various churches and colleges that have been established by this denomination. The Reformed Church in America is an offspring of the Dutch Reformed Church in the Netherlands. The first such congregation was organized on Manhattan Island in 1628 by Dutch and Walloon colonists, and it received a charter from the English king in 1696. The doctrines of the church are based on the teachings of John Calvin.

Although the first congregation, named the Reformed Dutch Church of New Amsterdam, was established in 1628, its records of baptisms and marriages don't start until 1639, and the books containing these records end in 1801. The second such church was established in Flatbush in 1654 and its records extend, with some gaps, from 1677 to 1872. The third was set up in Brooklyn in 1660 with records extending from 1660 to 1710. As the Dutch moved into New Jersey, they soon established the Bergen Reformed Dutch Church in what is now Jersey City. Churches also were soon started in upper New York State, such as the Albany Reformed Dutch Church.

As with any denomination, dissent soon erupted among these early churches. The most serious disagreement was one over whether the Dutch minister should be ordained in Amsterdam or in America. The "Coetus" party desired separation from the authority of Amsterdam, and said that the minister should be ordained in America. The opposing party, called the "Conferentie," wanted ministers only ordained in Amsterdam. By 1755 both the towns of Hackensack and Schraalenburgh had two congregations because of this disagreement. By 1822, those who wanted to adhere to the strict Dutch doctrines and rituals were forming what were called "True Reformed Dutch" churches.

A number of the Reformed Dutch Church records have been published and can be found in the New Brunswick Archives, the library of the Holland Society, and the New Jersey State Library in Trenton. Record books can also be found in the individual churches. To locate the birth, marriage, or death dates for a specific individual, one must know where that person settled. Then one can consult the church records of any Reformed Church in that vicinity. The early records of these churches are frequently the only records that can be found of such events before vital statistics were recorded by the various states where the churches are located.

A certain pattern was followed in entering the Reformed Church records, whether they are in Dutch or since have been translated into English. The date of baptism (sometimes the date of birth also) is recorded first, then the name of the child, the names of the parents, and finally the names of the witnesses. In the original Dutch, the following words are used: "kinder" for child, "ouders" for parents, "geboren" for born, "gedopt" for baptized, and "getuygen" for witnesses.

The Dutch colonists followed a certain practice when naming their children. The first children were named after the grandparents, usually the first son after the paternal grandfather, the second after the maternal grandfather, the first daughter after the maternal grandmother, and the second daughter after the paternal grandmother. After this, other children were usually named for their aunts and uncles. Knowing this practice can be a great aid in looking at the Reformed Church records. Also of great value are the

names of the witnesses, because they would include members of the family, usually brothers and sisters of the parents, or else the grandparents themselves, if the child were being named after them. These naming practices continued until about 1800, but with more conservative families, a little bit longer. The Dutch records also usually give the wife's maiden name in the baptismal and marriage records, which is useful.

The Reformed Church founded Hope College in Holland, Michigan; Central College in Pella, Iowa; and Northwestern College in Orange City, Iowa. These institutions all have libraries where church records can also be found.

Regional Histories *see* **County Histories.**

Relationships are commonly recognized when one uses terms such as father, mother, grandfather, great grandmother, aunt, or uncle. However, the relationships between cousins can be more complex. The children of two siblings are first cousins to each other, while the children of two first cousins are second cousins to each other. Determining who might be a seventh cousin once removed and who might be a sixth cousin once removed may require consulting a relationship chart. These charts can be found in some books on genealogy as well as on Websites.

The designations "junior" and "senior" usually refer to a father and son with the same first name, but this is not always the case in the genealogical records. Sometimes these terms were used to refer to two different persons of the same name who lived in the same locality, and often they were used for an uncle and nephew rather than for a father and son.

In the older documents, such as 17th-century wills, the term "cousin" is frequently applied to any relative who was not a brother or sister. Thus a person composing a will might refer to his grandchild as a cousin, or he might apply the same term to an uncle, aunt, nephew, or niece. "Son-in-law" and "daughter-in-law" were frequently used to refer to stepchildren rather than to the husband or wife of a child, and "son" and "daughter" were often used in the way we now use such in-law terms.

Furthermore, the use of "brother" at that time might refer to a genetic brother, but it also might be a reference to a stepbrother, brother-in-law, or even a brother in the church. The same is true of the use of "sister." The terms "mother" and "father" might mean mother-in-law or father-in-law, or they could refer to a stepparent acquired through the remarriage of a parent.

In colonial records the terms "Mrs." or "Mistress" (frequently abbreviated to "Mrs." in wills) was used to designate social distinction. Thus these terms might even refer to an unmarried girl of 17 who was a member of a family that had considerable wealth and standing in the community. In some early documents Mrs. was used to refer to a widow rather than a wife. "Goodman" and "goodwife" were titles for those who were respected by other members of the community but who were persons who didn't yet merit the titles "Mr." and "Mrs."

Research Methods involve the systematic collecting and analysis of related materials. As such, they play an important part in genealogy as well as many other fields of interest. The research methods used in genealogy are not unlike those used in all the sciences and in industry. The discovery of previously unknown facts through genealogical research, as well as the discovery of such facts in science, often leads to a revision of the accepted ideas in the light of these new facts. In other words, the finding of new names in a census or new family lines in a county history can lead to a complete reconstruction of a previously accepted family tree.

Like a scientist following basic research methods, the experienced genealogist begins with an idea or theory about the subject, in this case the history of a particular family obtained from stories passed down over generations to the descendants or a written account compiled by someone else who has been interested in that specific family line. Genealogists refer to this step as the "preliminary survey." It is, of course, wise to start with such data for there is no need to waste time going over the same areas of knowledge that others have already mined.

If what had been previously done was carefully researched, this will make the task much easier for the genealogist, who can resume research where the previous work stopped. But if the previous work seems fraught with holes, the place of beginning may be quite different. In either case, a genealogist's continuing work will be influenced somewhat by what was already done. In genealogical research, just as in scientific research, each new step is planned and chosen from the results of the previous step.

Once the preliminary study is completed, the genealogist can begin to collect further information that relates to the family name that he or she might be researching. The data will come from lists of vital statistics, a series of government documents, books, or a number of other published sources. The researcher may also gather information from members of the family or artifacts that once belonged to that family in order to find whatever can be located about individuals with that particular family name. Whatever is found may confirm the assumptions that the genealogist had at the start of the research project, but more likely these findings will lead to a new analysis of the data and a revision of the previous assumptions.

Thus the research process comprises a cycle in which the gathering of relevant data leads to an analysis of the data and a new understanding of the pedigree record, which in turn gives direction to the accumulation of more data that may once again result in a revision of the pedigree record. Each turn assures a more exact and truer account of the family tree.

An essential ingredient in research is taking notes. Those genealogists who demonstrate the best abilities in doing research are also those who keep the best notes and records, and organize them in a way that permits easy access. It is important at all times to know what has been done, why it was done, and the results that came from it. One's notes should make it possible for anyone to check quickly the completeness and accuracy of each record. No one should ever have to redo the research because the sources have been forgotten or because no one is sure anymore that it was done correctly in the first place. Undocumented "facts" in the end have no weight of authority.

The notes that are taken should be as complete as possible, but no more so than the project demands. They should be written clearly enough so that they don't have to be recopied. That is a waste of effort. Every time something is recopied there is a chance for error. Furthermore, all notes should include the date when each search was conducted and the condition of the records that were searched. Finally, one should never throw away any research notes. The very ones that are thrown away or lost will inevitably be the ones most needed in the future.

A well organized list of the sources that were examined will prevent any duplication of effort. This "research index" should include the name of the author, compiler, or editor for each book that has been consulted, as well as the title and edition, publisher, place and date of publication, and the page number(s) where applicable. The research index should also list both the books in which information was found and those that proved useless so that neither will be needed again when looking for particular data. Of course, if one is doing research for another project, it is be possible that these books might be consulted again. Many genealogists find it helpful to keep a separate research index for each library that they use and for each separate research project.

As soon as it appears that all the information one is seeking has been found, that is time to stop looking further and evaluate the findings in depth. Without such a proper analysis there can be no sense of direction and one can become lost in the mechanics of note taking. Complete and finished records should now be compiled from the data collected. All the notes should be examined to be sure that there are no loose ends. It is highly likely that at this point some of the sheets that hold notes will suggest places where more research should be done. Thus the completion of the finished records will point out the direction in which research should continue.

In the end, although this is not really part of the research process, the genealogist needs to make the results of his or her findings available to others. This can be done by publication in a genealogical magazine, in book form, or on the Internet. If one has spent a great deal of time in collecting the material, which is likely, why not let others use it and at the same time save them the arduous task of having to repeat the process?

All the above observations notwithstanding, roadblocks in research eventually face every genealogist. They occur, for example, when information is seemingly impossible to locate about the parents of a particular person, or when a young soldier killed in the Civil War was too young at the time of the 10-year census to have his name listed in the records. The soldier might even have had a wife and child, but never owned any land to leave a trail in county record books. The only way to deal with such seemingly impassable roadblocks is to look in another direction to solve the problem.

Perhaps these persons had brothers or sisters for which information can be found that will be helpful in establishing facts about them. Perhaps another library or archive will provide clues or a series of more comprehensive documents that include their names. Perhaps there are living descendants who have family Bibles or other memorabilia that contain information about the persons being sought. Thus the search needs to be broadened in order to locate any meaningful data.

Sometimes a roadblock occurs because there is a gap in the records of some particular time or place owing to intentional destruction or damage by fire or other causes. Perhaps an individual entry was never added to the records or the name was copied incorrectly into an index. One then needs to seek alternate sources that may provide similar information. Again the solution comes from casting a wider net.

Or there are blocks that loom up because the genealogist has not gathered enough of the right sort of information or because the information found is inaccurate. Here the data needs to be rechecked and the searcher needs to expand his or her vision of the geographical area and time frame for the search.

Holding tenaciously to misinformation can easily prevent progress in locating the right connections needed to expand one's pedigree chart.

At the same time, blocks may occur when the scale of the search becomes too large, i.e., when a researcher is trying to cover too many years, too large a geographical area, too common a surname, or a combination of all these factors. Here it is best to narrow the search to a single person or a small group of persons. One can always expand the search again when a particular segment of it is fully comprehended.

A formidable block may arise when one's research turns up several equally plausible solutions or equally likely names in the records that have been researched. Here one must trace backwards and forwards from each of the possible solutions, eliminating one after another until the correct one is established. This may mean going over the original research and sources once more. It may mean gathering as much knowledge as possible about the siblings or other close relations in order to eliminate extra lines. It may mean that one will have to spend many hours in a number of libraries and on the Internet just to get the wrong names or solutions out of the way.

Finally, as the searching process takes one into other cultures, a researcher may be blocked by language difficulties and unreadable forms of handwriting. Here the only solution may be to consult language experts and other genealogists who are somewhat familiar with the records being examined. Most librarians are willing to assist researchers in finding helpful sources to overcome such research problems.

Rhode Island Records can be located at the Rhode Island Archives and the Rhode Island Historical Society, both of which are in Providence. When the first Europeans arrived in this area, it was populated by five tribes of the Algonkian Indian family — the Narraganset, Niantic, Nipmuck, Pequot, and Wampanoag. The first permanent Rhode Island settlement of whites was that of colonists led by Roger Williams in 1636. He named his colony Providence. In 1638 William Coddington, John Clarke, Anne Hutchinson, and others left Massachusetts in search of religious freedom and founded the settlement of Pocasset on Aquidneck Island. The name was changed to Portsmouth when Coddington and Clarke departed to move south and establish Newport in 1639. England granted Rhode Island a charter in 1644. In 1774 Rhode Island prohibited the importation of slaves, and in 1776 the residents declared their independence from England. Rhode Island became the 13th state when it ratified the U.S. Constitution in 1790.

There have been a number of independent state censuses conducted by Rhode Island. The ones that are stored in the Rhode Island Archives are those of 1865, 1875, 1885, 1915, 1925, and 1935. The Rhode Island Historical Society has a copy of the 1865 census. A census taken in 1774 was published in book form in 1858 by E. E. Brownell of Baltimore; it was titled *Census of the Inhabitants of the Colony of Rhode Island and Providence Plantations, 1774, taken by order of the General Assembly*. This book can be found at the Historical Society as well as in a number of Rhode Island libraries and several genealogical libraries elsewhere. The first national census enumeration in Rhode Island was in 1790, the year it became a state. This and the later federal census listings can be seen at the various National Archives locations. The census mortality schedules for 1850 to 1880 can be found at the Rhode Island State Library in Providence.

The vital records of Rhode Island from 1636 to 1850 have been published in 21 volumes as *The Arnold Collection of Vital Records*. These books can be viewed in most of the larger genealogical libraries and are available at the State Library and at the State Historical Society. For more recent records of births, marriages, and deaths, one should contact the Rhode Island Vital Records office in Providence. Copies can be obtained for a small fee. Divorce records since 1962 are maintained in the family courts of Rhode Island's five counties, while guardianship records lie with the probate courts in the towns where they were processed. The same is true of the all wills that have been probated.

Two useful books published by the Work Projects Administration are *Summary of Legislation Concerning Vital Statistics in Rhode Island* (1937), and *Guide to Public Vital Statistics Records: Births, Marriages, Deaths in the State of Rhode Island and Providence Plantations* (1941). These volumes can be seen at the State Library, the State Historical Society, the John Hay Library at Brown University, as well as in some genealogical libraries in other states. The John Hay Library also has other genealogical records of interest in its collection.

Land records in Rhode Island are recorded with the various town and city clerks, with the exception of those for the city of Providence, which are in the office of its recorder of deeds. The state courts make no distinction between equity and law actions. The immigration records for ships arriving at the Port of Providence between 1911 and 1943 can be found at the National Archives in Washington, D.C.

Researchers seeking divorce information from the family courts in the five counties can locate them at the following county seats: (Bristol County) Bristol, (Kent County) East Greenwich, (Newport County) Newport, (Providence County) Providence, and (Washington County) West Kingston.

FOR FURTHER INFORMATION SEE:
- Austin, John Osborne. *The Genealogical Dictionary of Rhode Island: Comprising Three Generations of Settlers Who Came Before 1690 (with Many Families Carried to the Fourth Generation)*. Baltimore, MD: Genealogical Publishing Co., 1978.
- Savage, James. *A Genealogical Dictionary of the First Settlers of New England*. 4 vols. Baltimore, MD: Genealogical Publishing Co., 1965.

Roman Catholic Records, in many instances, predate the keeping of vital records by civil authorities. In most cases the Roman Catholic Church has as good records of births, marriages, and deaths among their membership as any other religious organization. By church law these records have been carefully maintained, and in most cases have been well preserved. However, most of the records are still located in the parishes where they were recorded, and church law stipulates that they may be searched only by the parish priests. In some places the records have been centralized in archives maintained by the diocese, but these are relatively rare. Until relatively recently most of the Roman Catholic records were recorded in Latin, although sometimes they are written in the native language of the local priest, who might be German, Polish, Hungarian, or Irish. There are few indexes, so that the records can be difficult to locate even if a researcher knows the exact parish where they are kept.

The oldest family documented in the records of the Catholic Church in America is the Solana family of St. Augustine, Florida. According to the marriage record there, Vicente Solana and Maria Viscente were married at the Cathedral of St. Augustine on July 4, 1594. Some descendants of this family still live today in that ancient city. There are also old records from the many missions that early Catholic priests established in what is now Alabama, Arizona, California, Colorado, Florida, Georgia, Louisiana, Mississippi, Missouri, New Mexico, Texas, and Utah. Various Spanish, French, Native American, and African-American pedigrees have been traced back through these records. The earliest records for some of these missions were destroyed in Native American uprisings. For example, in Utah, where over 14,000 Native Americans had been baptized by 1617, 34,000 by 1626, and 86,000 by 1630, the knowledge of these missions has mostly been lost to history because the destruction was so complete when the Utes rose up, killed many of the priests, razed the missions, and stopped up all the mines in which they had been forced to work.

The main information given in the parish baptism records are the dates, names of both parents (often including the mother's maiden name), the names of two sponsors, and the address of the parents. Illegitimate births are also faithfully recorded. The marriage records include the date of marriage, church in which the ceremony took place, the names of both parties (including the bride's maiden name), and the names of two witnesses. The address of the couple's parents is usually given, though not always. Death or burial records contain the date and place of burial, as well as the age of the deceased. These records are usually not maintained as well as are the birth and marriage records.

In order to access the vast collection of parish records, it is essential to determine at which parish a specific individual worshipped. One way this can be done is to obtain the name of the place where a person lived from some other source. Newspaper obituaries or death notices may provide such information. A city directory may give an exact home address, or it may be found in the federal census listings. Parishes in the Catholic community are based on geographical divisions, and most church members who live within the parish area will be related to the particular parish church there. However, there are also parishes based on ethnicity, so that if the person was German, he or she probably attended a German parish even though the closest Catholic Church might have been Irish or Italian. For Catholic cemeteries that serve those from a number of different parishes, the cemetery records will usually list the specific parishes for each interred person.

Other records of use to genealogical and historical researchers are found in the parish history or anniversary book. The content of these documents varies greatly, but most parishes have published them to commemorate a fiftieth or one hundredth anniversary. They may include parish membership lists and group photographs, as well as a general history of the church, school, and priests of the parish. These books can be found at the church itself, at a local library, or in historical society archives. One excellent collection of them is at the Theodore M. Hesburgh Library at Notre Dame, Indiana. This collection contains printed parish histories and newspaper accounts of more than 1,300 Catholic parishes.

Parish censuses, records of contributors, and church society membership lists can also be found among parish records. It is wise to remember that the Catholic Church has operated schools, hospitals, and orphanages for centuries. All these institutions have created records regarding the people they served. Yet most of these records are confidential and not open to public inspection.

Another mainstay of the Catholic Church has been the existence of religious orders. Throughout history many Catholics have chosen the life of a priest, nun, or religious brother, and each religious order has kept records of its members. Such files often include photographs and a complete record of the individual's service to the church.

Romanian Records *see* **Eastern European Genealogy**

Rome, Ancient *see* **Ancient Greek and Roman Genealogy**

Russian Genealogy has never been an easy area in which to do research, and only in the past decade have Russian genealogists begun to openly admit their interest in the subject and to organize genealogical interest groups. Wars, revolutions, and ignorance have also destroyed a significant part of written records.

It was not until 1722 that the Russians instituted any kind of system for keeping vital statistics. This was part of the various westernizing changes ordered by Czar Peter the Great. The new system required that the established Orthodox clergy maintain records relating to births, marriages, and burials within their parishes. Other smaller denominations, such as the Roman Catholics, Lutherans, Muslims, and Jews, were also required to keep such records of their congregations. Copies of some of these records have been stored in the state and regional archives.

There are also records for the men who registered for universal military service, which was enforced from 1874 to 1918. These draftee lists include the names, dates, places of birth, and fathers' names. All males 21 years of age were required to go to the local military office in October of each year to register. Approximately a third of these men were drafted for six to nine years of active service. These records are also located in state and regional archives.

After the Communists came to power

in 1918, laws were enforced to register births, marriages, and deaths as part of the civil code. The records were maintained by town and city offices under the supervision of the Ministry of Internal Affairs because the authority of the Orthodox Church had been curtailed. Birth records compiled after 1918 contain the first and family name of each child, as well as the names, ages, addresses, and occupations of the parents. The marriage entries contain the same data that were listed on each individual's identity papers, as well as any change of names that might have taken place, information about previous divorces, and any record of having been adopted if that was the case. Death records only list the names and ages of the individuals.

The Russian archives can be useful only if one has definite information to pinpoint the search, such as exact names, dates, and locations. If an ancestor served in a military regiment, one will need to know the year of his or her service. Street addresses and village names are needed in order to find church records. Though offices and factories may keep personnel files in their archives almost indefinitely, one must have the exact date of a person's departure from a job in order to locate employment information. Such records usually contain a mandatory handwritten autobiography and filled-in detailed questionnaire forms. The files of dismissed office and factory personnel are archived in alphabetical order. Without exact names, locations,

and dates no Russian archive is going to be of much help.

The regional archives only keep records dating back to about 1790, but earlier information can be found in state archives located in Moscow and St. Petersburg. The researcher should be aware of the fact that few people in Russia, including archive officials, speak or understand foreign languages, so all communication must be done in Russian. Russian archives also tend to charge foreigners 10 times or more than what they charge Russian citizens for any searches. And one needs to be prepared to wait. It takes the average Russian archivist from one to five months to answer any genealogy request, even after a payment has been made.

Besides the regional and town archives in Russia, genealogical records can be found at the state historical archives in both St. Petersburg and Moscow, as well as at the state military historical archive in Moscow and the state naval archive in St. Petersburg. Furthermore, there are some genealogical records, particularly for Jewish families, at the Russian State Library in St. Petersuburg.

After the Russian revolution of 1918, many upper-class Russians fled to other countries. These emigrés have endeavored to preserve the records of their families. The Union de la Noblesse Russe in Paris, France, maintains a collection of such records and has published several books about them.

S

Salvation Army Records of births, marriages, and deaths are maintained at the various Salvation Army Corps locations where the members have been assigned, although the officials at these locations may be somewhat reluctant to provide such information to genealogists. This Protestant service organization was established in England in 1865 by William Booth, a former Methodist minister. Its members, both men and women,

wear military-type uniforms and have a semimilitary system of leadership. They provide food, shelter, and clothing for the needy, and maintain hospitals for unwed mothers, lowcost lodging quarters, industrial homes where people can work to rebuild their characters, and nurseries for babies of working mothers.

The members who are full-time workers are designated as officers and are given military-like ranks according to their dedication and years of service. Those called soldiers do not usually work full-time for the Salvation Army, but belong to a local corps. They may be commissioned in such capacities as band members, songsters, local officers, young people's workers.

Some Salvation Army officers' career cards (summary of appointments and promotions) have survived, but most, especially those from the early years, have not. Many of the records were lost when the International Headquarters in London was destroyed by bombs during the Second World War. Officers' appointments and promotions may be listed in the organization's magazine, *The War Cry*, or in *The Officer* magazine. Brief announcements, reports or tributes are also usually included in these Salvation Army periodicals when officers marry, retire, or die.

Some of the corps locations have produced histories that list such details, but it can take a long time to search through these unindexed volumes if a date for a marriage or a death is not known. At the Salvation Army Heritage Centre in London there is a library in which the registrar general's records of births, marriages, and deaths are maintained. The organization was brought to the United States in 1880, and now has over 9,000 centers and approximately 385,000 members there. In all there are over 26,000 Salvation Army officers in the United States and elsewhere. The U.S. headquarters is in New York City.

Saskatchewan Records of births, marriages and deaths, the earliest from 1878, are at the Vital Statistics Office in Regina, although only those collected after 1919 are complete. The region that comprises this province was first explored in 1690, after King Charles II of England granted rights to engage in fur trading there to the Hudson's Bay Company of London. At that time the area was occupied by three Indian groups—the Chippewyan, Assiniboine, and Plains Cree. French-Canadian fur traders established several trading posts in Saskatchewan in the 1740s, and in 1774 Cumberland House became the first permanent settlement. Saskatchewan was made a province of Canada in 1905.

Although the vital records are located in Regina, to gain access to them one must submit a written application to the director showing a relationship to the person whose record is desired. If the person in question is still living, the researcher must also obtain the subject's consent. Divorce records can be found at the Court of the Queen's Bench in Regina.

Copies of the census records for Saskatchewan are stored at the National Archives sites in both Regina and Saskatoon, at the library of the Saskatchewan Genealogical Society in Regina, and at some other libraries in the province. There are name indexes for the 1881 and 1891 census records, but in order to search the 1901 records one must know the name of the community where a person lived at the time.

The Saskatchewan Archives, located at the two different sites, was established under legislation in 1945 as a joint university-government agency. The archives maintains the official records of the government of Saskatchewan as well as documentary material from the local government and those private sources "having a bearing on the history of Saskatchewan." This wide-ranging mandate has allowed the Saskatchewan Archives to build up one of the most comprehensive archival collections in Canada. The two sites for the archives are on the campuses of the University of Saskatchewan and the University of Regina.

Some of the archives collections include records relating to Indian treaties, surrenders, and agreements; documents pertaining to the French and British colonial periods; selected records from the archives of the Catholic Church in the province; and the homestead records for the province. The original files for the homestead records are at the Saskatoon location, and a microfilm copy is at the Regina location. The homestead records provide limited information about each homesteader, such as age, date of entry and patent right, the number of members of his family, and often, but not always, his place of birth, former place of residence, and previous occupation. In looking for other land records, one needs to go to the individual district land registration offices at North Battleford, Humboldt, Moose Jaw, Prince Albert, Regina, Saskatoon, Swift Current, and Yorkton.

The Saskatchewan Archives also has records of the people who entered Saskatchewan from across the United States border at the 10 official points of entry for the period of 1908–1924. These records were kept mostly for people traveling by train and not for those who entered by road or on foot. Those listed from 1919 to 1924 are in alphabetical order.

Another good source for genealogical records in Saskatchewan is the Saskatchewan Genealogical Society, which claims to have the largest genealogical lending library in Canada. Its collection consists of 1,153 microfilms; 34,457 microfiche records; and 19,500 books, periodicals, and maps from throughout the world. The society members are engaged in compiling cemetery records for the province as an ongoing project.

The Saskatoon Public Library has an index to the obituaries that have appeared in the *Saskatoon Star Phoenix*, while the Regina Public Library has an index to the obituaries that appeared between 1935 and 1943 in the *Regina Leader-Post*. Local history books are also available at these two libraries. Many Saskatchewan communities have published such local histories, and they can be useful in genealogical research. These books not only provide a history of the community, but they often list people in the community as well as organizations and the activities over the years.

City directories listing residents can be found at the Regina Public Library, Saskatoon Public Library, University of Saskatchewan Library, and the University of Regina Library. Many of these are old directories, such as *Henderson's Directory for Western Canada* (1885–1908), the *McPhillips Saskatchewan Directory* for 1888 that lists farmers and businesses in the Prince Albert and Battleford areas, and *Wrigley's Saskatchewan Directory* of 1921 and 1922 that lists cities, towns, villages, hamlets, and settlements along with their major businesses and the people employed by these businesses. *See also* **Census, Canadian.**

School Records, if these still exist, include school census records taken at the local or county level and records kept by individual schools, such as attendance and grade records, faculty and alumni lists, and school yearbooks. They can sometimes be helpful in determining individual ages and parentage, as well as residences and citizenship when such information is provided on the record.

School census records will provide the names and ages of all the school children in a district at a particular time. If such records cannot be found in a school's district office, they can sometimes be found in local or state archives and historical societies. Enrollment and transcript records maintained by schools can be much more informative than the census records, but because of privacy laws, many schools and universities refuse to release them. When they do so, the process can be involved and require authorization from living relatives.

Lists of former students and alumni that are kept in the schools are more readily available. Some of these for colleges and universities have been published and can be found in genealogical and historical societies. School yearbooks, alumni directories and other alumni publications, catalogs, and college and high school newspapers may be stored in school libraries or within special collections in college and local libraries. The largest collection of yearbooks is the 2,500-volume collection available through Yearbook Archives in Merrick, New York. This collection, however, is mainly devoted to yearbooks of celebrities. The schools may also have alumni records that include addresses.

Nationally affiliated organizations, such as sororities, fraternities, honor societies, and service organizations may maintain histories of the chapters on a particular campus, and they can give the researcher addresses for the national offices of these organizations that may have preserved records of the chapters. Local schools may also be willing to provide information on former students, particularly if the family has lived in the community for an extended time. There may even be literature on school reunions that have been held that include existing addresses for graduates.

Science and Genealogy have been related in a number of ways, some of which have been useful to society and others that have been destructive. Probably the first use that scientists made of genealogy was in designing biological diagrams to show the evolutionary development of plants and animals. Pallas, a German naturalist and student of Linnaeus in the 17th century, in a communication to another scientist, included a tree diagram depicting the degrees of morphological affinity that he perceived among various animals. His diagram was clearly taken from the family trees that genealogists were making popular at that time. Chronological charts of this sort were used by historians to describe family connections as early as A.D. 1100. A manuscript prepared at that time illustrates the royal pedigree line of the French Carolingian kings by a series of circles that contain the names of the heads of families. The circles are connected by lines to indicate descent. Another chart from this period shows a Saxon line composed in the same general way.

Zoologists and botanists found such trees to be useful in depicting the connections among various animals and among various plant types. Such biological trees can still be found in almost any elementary biology text, and many museums have giant "family tree" paintings that illustrate animals and humans evolving over hundreds of thousands of years from early life forms.

Today there is far more interest in genealogy among medical people because of the recognition that hereditary diseases pass from one generation to another along family lines. Among these hereditary tendencies are a number of medical conditions such as heart disease, diabetes, blindness, and deafness. Even cancer is beginning to surprise us with the extent of its genetic links.

It is estimated that over 15 million Americans suffer from inherited diseases, and one-third of all childhood hospitalizations, almost half of all infant deaths, and an even larger number of miscarriages are hereditary in nature, as are many cases of mental retardation. In fact, it is believed that there are almost 5,000 hereditary illnesses, some of them extremely rare. Facial characteristics, even facial expressions, may continue for generations in a family, and the study of these expressions through photographs can give the genealogist a clue as to family relationships.

The work that geneticists are now doing in the field of DNA analysis is revolutionary. It is not only being used by police departments to convict criminals and by defense attorneys to free innocent people, but to demonstrate the genetic links among people and the evolution of species as a result of small changes in the structure of the DNA molecule. Where no family records exist, it is theoretically possible to establish genealogical connectivity through the study of an individual's DNA. Using a 12-marker test, family relationships can be determined over a period in excess of a few thousand years.

The field of eugenics is particularly dependent on genealogy for much of its data, and no genealogist can remain blind to the part that heredity plays in human destiny. As everyone knows, in the breeding of dogs and horses, careful pedigree records are always kept so that the breeds can be improved over time. Of course no such records are ever kept in regard to human mating, so the human strains that sometimes lead to mental defects have sometimes continued through several generations.

Certainly the studies that have been conducted by eugenicists are of high potential value. They aim at the betterment of social conditions for future generations by raising human efficiency and preventing the reproduction of the unfit whenever the family pedigree indicates that most of the progeny are almost certain to be genetically defective.

However, eugenics often has been used in destructive rather than constructive ways. The sudden interest in genealogy in Hitler's Third Reich is only one of the more recent examples of the way in which eugenics has been used in destructive ways, and as an excuse to murder large numbers of people, which has given rise to the term genocide. In South Africa, before the post-apartheid government was established, interest in genealogy was promoted by those of Dutch descent in an effort to prove though eugenics that their apartheid policy was justified and that an all-white descent made them superior to all the other South Africans.

Scottish Genealogy has a long and distinguished record that begins with the histories of the various clans of Scotland. Many of these records are based on oral tradition, and some extend back to the year one thousand. Scotland was united in the ninth century by Kenneth MacAlpin, and Scotland and England have had the same monarchs since 1603 and the same parliament since 1707. However, there are elements of Scottish law and administration that are somewhat different from those found in England.

The parish registers in Scotland did not record baptisms, marriages, and deaths before the year 1700. The records from more than 900 such parishes are located in the Scotland New Register House at Edinburgh. These records vary greatly from one parish to another in quality and legibility. Nevertheless, these old parish registers constitute the main source of information on people living in Scotland prior to the mid–19th century. The parish birth records usually include the mother's maiden name as well as the names of the godparents, who were most often relatives or close friends. The marriage records are generally the proclamations of marriage rather than records of the marriage itself. Prior to 1690 the keeping of registers was frustrated by the struggles between Presbyterians and Episcopalians over dominance in the established church. Eventually the Presbyterians prevailed and established the Scottish Church.

As for other church records, the Methodists, Quakers, Congregationalists, and Catholics were considered to be non-conformists and their records were held by the local congregations. Some of these records have since been placed in the Scottish Record Office. A 1560 act of the Scottish Parliament banned the celebration of the Catholic mass in any Scottish Church, and Catholics in Scotland were persecuted from the 16th through the 17th centuries. Catholic support for the 1745 rebellion, led by Bonnie Prince Charlie against the King of England, resulted in all Catholics being declared outlaws. Many of the Quaker records are still at the various Friends Meeting Houses in Edinburgh, Glasgow, and Aberdeen.

Scotland has required the civil registration of births, marriages, and deaths since 1855. These records can also be found at the New Register House. Birth records from 1929 and death records from 1974 give the mother's maiden name, while the death records starting in 1868 include age at the time of death, and from 1969 include the date of birth. Other records held in either of the two Scottish Record Offices in Edinburgh, the New Register House or the Old Register House, include children adopted since 1930; divorce records since 1984; deaths of Scottish servicemen in the Boer War and World War I and II; army records of births, marriages, and deaths of Scottish personnel on military bases; births and deaths of Scottish personnel on vessels at sea, and deaths of Scots on registered British aircraft.

The census records for Scotland, which are public records, can also be found at one of the two Scottish Record Offices. These census records are opened to the public 70 years after they were compiled. As for the records of probate that are in these archives, until 1868 Scottish law required that most of the property of a deceased man should be given to his eldest son or, if there was no son, to any of his daughters equally. The remainder could then be given to the surviving spouse. After 1868, the law allowed the property to be bequeathed according to the wishes of the deceased as stated in his will. Until the 16th century all such testaments were handled by church courts; after that they were assigned to secular commissary courts.

The Scottish Record Offices have some manuscripts that detail Scottish family pedigrees. The ones for the Lowland Scots are more extensive than those for the Highlanders partly because in Lowland Scotland surnames were used much earlier than they were in the Highlands. Until a little over 200 years ago the Highlanders and their clans were regarded by the Scottish clans of the Lowlands with much the same distaste that the Colonial Americans viewed the Native American Indian tribes.

A hearth tax was levied in Scotland from 1691 to 1695, just as it was in England, and poll taxes were levied from 1693 to 1699. The surviving lists of these tax records can be found at the Scottish Record Offices. There were also taxes assessed for servants and apprenticeships, some records of which are there. The Record Offices also hold the land records of Crown grants, such as Crown charters, Great Seal charters, and Privy Seal charters. These records fill about 50,000 volumes and they are indexed, but conducting a search through them can be time consuming. Other court records in Scotland are difficult to use because of the number of courts and the lack of indexes.

Records of regiments, soldiers, and sailors since 1707 can be found both at the Public Record Office in London and at the Scottish Record Offices. Most of the records for business enterprises in Scotland are held by the registrar of companies in Edinburgh, though a list of the registered companies can be found at the Scottish Record Offices. Scotland had many guilds in the early days, including the Edinburgh Company of Merchants founded in 1505 and the guilds of bakers, tailors, and weavers in Dundee, all of which were incorporated in 1575.

The National Library of Scotland in Edinburgh has a large collection of Scottish newspapers, including copies of the *Edinburgh Evening Courant*, founded in 1718; the *Glasgow Journal* and *Aberdeen Journal*, both founded in 1748; the *Edinburgh Weekly Chronicle*, the *Edinburgh Star*, and the *Edinburgh News*, founded in 1808; and the *Evening Post*, founded in 1827. All provide obituaries and other information concerning people in Scotland. Many of the newspapers have been indexed. The National Library, as well as the Scottish Record Offices, have the surviving electoral registers compiled since 1832.

Since medieval times, the use of coats of arms has been supervised by the Lord Lyon King of Arms, now located at the New Register House in Edinburgh. Scottish arms are only granted to each particular man and not to his heirs. Thus the younger sons of a grantee are not permitted to use their father's arms, and must apply to the Lord Lyon for a grant to use suitably differentiated versions of those arms. Books containing the arms that have been registered up to 1973 can be found at the New Register House, the National Library, or at the offices of the Heraldry Society in Edinburgh.

Finally, the Scots Ancestry Research Society in Edinburgh and the Genealogical Society, also in Edinburgh, can provide helpful resources for the genealogist. Those seeking information in Glasgow should visit the Mitchell Library where the city archives are located. *See also* **Census, British.**

Search Engines *see* **Computer Search Engines**

Seventh-Day Adventist Records *see* **Adventist Records**

Ship Arrivals *see* **Passenger Lists**

Social Security Records provide birth and death dates that can sometimes be obtained in no other way. The records can be acquired from the Social Security Administration in Baltimore, Maryland. The Social Security system was established in 1935 to provide a pension plan for all working people in the United States. Within the first two years, approximately 30 million Americans had applied for Social Security. There was another rush to enter the system when Medicare was enacted in 1965.

Beginning in 1967, the Department of Defense began using Social Security numbers in place of military service numbers, and since 1972 Social Security numbers have been awarded to legally admitted aliens upon their entry to the U.S. Parents, since 1989, have been permitted to automatically obtain a Social Security number for any newborn infant when the birth is registered in a state. Social Security numbers were initially assigned at local post offices, then at Social Security field offices, but since 1972 all the cards have been issued from the central Baltimore office. The first three digits of a Social Security number indicate the state of issuance.

Because it was charged with providing Social Security benefits for all eligible citizens, the Social Security Administration has kept careful track of millions of Americans. When-ever persons died, this was reported to the agency, which now has death records cover-ing more than 62 million people who have lived in the United States and possessed a So-cial Security number.

While the Social Security records of liv-ing persons are protected by the rights of pri-vacy, the records of deceased persons, known as the United States Social Security Death Index, are readily available to genealogists. This is by far the largest database of death in-formation on 20th century Americans. The records can be obtained from either the agency itself or from several Websites such as RootsWeb; Ancestry, Inc.; FamilyTreeMaker; Lineages, Inc.; and SierraHome. A CD-ROM version can be purchased from the Family History Library in Utah. Getting this same kind of information directly from the Social Security Administration takes more effort than getting it from Websites, but the records the agency supplies are more complete. Often genealogists find the name of a person for whom they are seeking Social Security in-formation on one of the Websites, and then send to Baltimore for the complete record that includes such information as the person's full name, birthdate and place, death date and place, sometimes the parents' names, the spouse's name, and employment information, as well as the Social Security number. The number is sometimes needed to obtain other types of information from state records offices. Nearly all the persons in this Death Index database died after 1961, though there are a few records for persons who died as early as 1937. *See also* **Railroad Retirement Records.**

Societies and Fraternal Organizations

possess large quantities of genealogical ma-terial in their archives. Because there are so many associations of this type, there are myriads of sources for such information, in-cluding membership records with the names of each member and the date and place where he or she joined. Often such membership lists also give the date and place of birth, place of residence, names of wives and parents, names of children, education, business, reli-gion, and other affiliations, as well as a per-sonal description and even a photograph. Some of the patriotic societies also maintain records of each member's descent from the ancestor(s) in whose memory the society was established. Thus the DAR library keeps members' descent records from ancestors who fought in the American Revolution.

The *Encyclopedia of Associations* that can be found in most libraries provides a comprehensive list of the thousands of soci-eties and interest associations in America. The size of this compilation is truly her-culean, and its systematic arrangement can be helpful for finding the addresses of the na-tional headquarters of most business, trade, and special interest associations. Special at-tention should be given to those organiza-tions in the appropriate field that publish yearbooks, membership directories, rosters, and newsletters. (Newsletters often include obituaries of their long-time associates.)

Organizations that are civic or social in-clude groups such as chambers of commerce, Lion's Clubs, Rotary International, and the YMCA. They are usually open to anyone who might wish to join. Those that are strictly fraternal include the Masons, Shriners, Odd Fellows, Knights of Columbus, Elks, and Moose. Most of these are secret lodges, with passwords, ceremonies, and initiation rights. To obtain information from any of these groups, a researcher must contact the local chapter, since that is where any records are most likely maintained. In rare cases, such records may have been given to organization libraries, archives, or museums on the local or state level.

The Masons' fraternal organization has existed in America for more than 200 years, and some of its records go back into the 18th century. Masonic records deal with member-ship, not biographical data, though some-times they include a number of death dates. Access to such records depends on the will-ingness of the individual lodge or state grand lodge to release them. Some of the fraternal organizations, such as the International Order of Odd Fellows, maintain their own ceme-teries where there will be grave markers with birth and death dates.

Local histories, newspapers, obituary

notices, tombstones, and family histories can aid one in finding out to which organization a particular ancestor might have belonged. Notices of fraternal and civic organization meetings, special functions, and the elections of officers have always been regular news items of some community newspapers. Yet locating the desired organization is just the first step. Next one must persuade its officers to allow access to their records or to be willing to look up information on a researcher's behalf, and many of the fraternal organizations are hesitant to do so.

The membership records of professional societies, such as the American Chemical Society, American Society of Mechanical Engineers, and so on, are readily available to genealogical researchers. One only needs to write to the national headquarters of such organizations with the approximate date of a person's membership for them to locate the information. The same is true of university clubs and college alumni associations. These groups, of course, require all members to be college graduates or to have some college education, so their records will yield the educational background of each person under investigation.

Greek letter fraternities and sororities also provide good records. The records of the Phi Beta Kappa society go back to the year 1776 and lists of its members appear in books that can be found in many genealogical libraries. Because fraternities are careful to follow "legacies," that is, the children of members, so as to consider them for membership, these organizations all maintain good membership lists. The oldest of the college fraternities still in existence is the Kappa Alpha Society, the first chapter of which was started in 1825 at Union College, New York.

Lists of both active and inactive fraternities can be found in *Baird's Manual of American College Fraternities*, available at most of the larger libraries. All the colleges and universities where these fraternities have chapters are indicated in this book. To obtain the records of extinct chapters one should contact the National Interfraternity Conference, whose address can be found in *Baird's Manual*. The secretary of this organization may

be able to advise the researcher as to the location of such records, or if not, may be able to refer the researcher to a member who knows their whereabouts. In any case, the listing in *Baird's* should indicate the location of any surviving chapters of the desired fraternity, and consulting yearbooks of the colleges where it was represented may provide the names of members who could be consulted.

The number and type of patriotic and heritage organizations formed around military service and events abound. Some of these are the American Legion, Amvets, Catholic War Veterans, Disabled American Veterans, Jewish War Veterans of the U.S.A., Military Order of the Loyal Legion of the United States, Military Order of the Purple Heart, Sons of Confederate Veterans, Sons of Union Veterans of the Civil War, Veterans of the Vietnam War, Veterans of Foreign Wars, and Vietnam Veterans of America. A number of these groups hold regular reunions and have documented them in their publications. For example, in 1898, the Association of Survivors, Regular Brigade (an association of Civil War veterans) published the proceedings of four annual reunions it held from September 1894 through September 1897. Among the historical sketches of association members was a listing of members who had died since the last published roster, indicating the company and regiment to which the individual belonged. *See also* **Daughters of the American Revolution Records; Ethnic Heritage; Family Reunions; Historical Societies; Lineage Societies.**

Societies, Genealogical *see* **Genealogical Societies**

Societies, Historical *see* **Historical Societies**

Societies, Lineage *see* **Lineage Societies**

Society of the Cincinnati is an organization composed of the descendants of the commissioned officers in the Continental Army or Navy and commissioned officers of the French army or navy who served in the Revolutionary War. It was founded by some of these officers in 1783, and was the first patriotic society to be established in the United States. It was organized at Fishkill, New York. George Washington served as this society's first president from 1783 until his death in 1799.

Branches of this society were later established in the 13 original states and in France. Its name commemorates Lucius Quinctius Cincinnatus, a legendary Roman hero of the fifth century B.C. Cincinnatus was twice called to lead Roman armies in defense of the republic, and each time he refused rewards for his services, preferring to return to his farm as a simple republican citizen. The society's motto, *Omnia relinquit servare rempublicam*, means "He gave up everything to serve the republic." The insignia of the society was designed in 1784 by Major Pierre Charles L'Enfant, who designed the layout for the city of Washington.

Today the society continues as a not-for-profit organization that supports educational, cultural, and literary activities that promote the ideals of liberty and constitutional government. Its headquarters is in Washington, D.C., and its library has some genealogical materials of interest regarding those who served in the American Revolution.

Sons of the American Revolution (SAR) is a national heritage society open to anyone who can establish his or her ancestry extending back to someone who fought in the American Revolution. The SAR was organized in 1889, and today maintains an historical and genealogical library that contains over 50,000 items, including a collection of 1,200 books and 750 journal articles devoted exclusively to the life of George Washington; 8,000 family history books on microfiche, half of which are out of print, and 8,000 reels of federal census records. The library is located in Louisville, Kentucky. It is open to anyone, and members can use it free of charge. Others must pay a nominal fee for each day's use.

Sororities *see* **Societies and Fraternal Organizations**

Soundex System was devised during the 1930s under the auspices of the Works Progress Administration (WPA). Its purpose was to record and alphabetize the names and other pertinent data for all persons enumerated in the censuses of 1880 and later. The surnames and other information were transcribed by WPA workers onto cards that were then were alphabetically arranged so that all names sounding alike, regardless of spelling differences or errors, could be identified and coded by each state.

In the Soundex system, three-digit numbers were assigned to follow the initial letters of each surname. The initial letters themselves were never numbered. Thus, for example, if the surname was Kuhne, the index card would be alphabetized in the "K" segment of the index and would be followed by its three-digit number, in this case K–500. Although the system appears at first to be complex, it is simple, and overcomes problems that sometimes surface when different census enumerators have spelled the same surname in different ways (Kuhne, Kune, Koone, etc.).

Before searching for a particular name of any individual recorded on the census rolls that have been Soundexed, one must determine the code number assigned to the surname. The code numbers used are as follows:

1 = b, p, f, v
2 = c, s, k, g, j, q, x, z
3 = d, t
4 = l
5 = m, n
6 = r

The letters a, e, i, o, u, y, w, and h are not coded. A surname yielding no code numbers, such as Lee, will be coded as L–000, and a surname yielding two code numbers, such as Ebell, will have one zero added and be coded as E–140. A name yielding three or more code numbers will be coded with the first letter and then the three first digits in the name. Thus Ebelson will be coded as E–142 (not E–1425).

Where two key letters or equivalents appear together, or one key letter immediately follows or precedes an equivalent, the two are coded as one letter by a single number.

Three examples of this are the name Kelley (K–400), Lloyd (L–300), and Buerck (B–620). If several surnames have the same code, the WPA cards for them will be arranged alphabetically by the given names. Thus all the Johnstones will follow all the Jinkats. Prefixes to surnames such as "D," "de," "Di," "dela," "du," "le," "van," or "Von" were sometimes disregarded in the coding process. For example, the name Van Lind was coded as L–530, with the only letters coded being n and d.

The following names in Soundex code are typical examples of the coding system.

Allricht — A–462 (letters coded: l, r, c)
Eberhard — E–166 (letters coded: b, r, r)
Engebrethson — E–521 (letters coded: n, g, b)
Helmbach — H–512 (letters coded: m, b, c)
Hildebrand — H–431 (letters coded: l, d, b)
Kavanagh — K–152 (letters coded: v, n, g)
McGee — M–200 (letters coded: c)
Zitzmeinn — Z–325 (letters coded: t, z. m)

Three areas in which variations in coding may differ from the above system were those for Asian names, American Indian names, and the names of religious nuns. Phonetically spelled Asian and American Indian names were sometimes coded as if they were one continuous name. For example, the Indian name Shinka-Wa-Sa might have been coded as either "Shinka" (S–520) or "Sa" (S–000). The names of nuns were coded as if "Sister" was the surname, i.e., S–236. Anyone looking for the names of nuns should be aware of the fact that within the S–236 area the names are not necessarily in alphabetical order, although all the sisters were grouped together and all the Scudder names (also coded as S–236) were listed as a group in front of them.

The 1880 census was provided with Soundex coding only for households that had children up to 10 years of age. The 1900 census Soundex coding includes all households, and the 1910 census Soundex coding includes all households only for the states of Alabama, Arkansas, California, Florida, Georgia, Illinois, Kansas, Kentucky, Louisiana, Michigan, Mississippi, Missouri, North Carolina, Ohio, Oklahoma, Pennsylvania, South Carolina, Tennessee, Texas, Virginia, and West Vir-

ginia. The 1920 census Soundex coding again includes all households for all the states.

The WPA was disbanded before the workers were able to complete much of the Soundex coding for the 1930 census, so the only states completed were the Southeastern ones: Alabama, Arizona, Florida, Georgia, Louisiana, Mississippi, North Carolina, South Carolina, Tennessee, and Virginia. A few counties in Kentucky and West Virginia were also done. To locate census entries for the other states, researchers must obtain an exact address for the individual they are seeking on the census rolls, which, of course, is far more difficult than finding a name in an alphabetized list.

Despite the apparent complexity of the Soundex numbering system, it has made searching through the census records easier for any genealogist. But if calculating Soundex numbers seems to be too complex, some Websites will do this work for researchers.

In addition to the Soundex numbering system, the enumerators used a series of codes in making notations on the cards they transcribed. These codes mostly relate to relationships of household residents to the head of household. The abbreviations are as follows:

A — aunt
AdD — adopted daughter
AdS — adopted son
At — attendant
B — brother
BL — brother-in-law
Bo — border
C — cousin
D — daughter
DL — daughter-in-law
F — father
FB — foster brother
FF — foster father
FL — foster-in-law
FM — foster mother
FSi — foster sister
GA — great aunt
GD — granddaughter
GF — grandfather
GGF — great-grandfather
GGGF — great-great-grandfather

GGGM — great-great-grandmother
GGM — great-grandmother
GM — grandmother
Gni — Grandniece
GS — grandson
GU — great-uncle
Hh — hired hand
I — inmate
L — lodger
M — mother
ML — mother-in-law
N — nephew
Ni — niece
NR — not recorded
Nu — nurse
OF — officer
P — patient
Pa — partner
Pr — prisoner
Pri — principal
Pu — pupil
R — roomer
S — son
SB — stepbrother
SBL — stepbrother-in-law
Se — servant
SF — stepfather
SFL — stepfather-in-law
Si — sister
SiL — sister-in-law
SL — son-in-law
SM — stepmother
SML — stepmother-in-law
SS — stepson
Ssi — stepsister
SsiL — stepsister-in-law
SSL — stepson-in-law
Su — superintendent
U — uncle
W — wife
WA — warden

Also regarding citizenship status:

A — alien
NA — naturalized
PA — first papers filed

South African Records *see* **African Genealogy**

South American Genealogy *see* **Argentine Genealogy; Bolivian Genealogy; Brazilian Genealogy; Chilean Genealogy; Columbian Genealogy; Ecuadorian Genealogy; Paraguayan Genealogy; Peruvian Genealogy; Uruguayan Genealogy; Venezuelan Genealogy**

South Carolina Records include state censuses, vital records, and many other types of documents such as those relating to the Confederacy during the Civil War. Before any white settlers came to this area in the mid–1600s, more than 30 Indian tribes lived here, including the Catawba, who belonged to the Siouan Indian language family; the Cherokee, who belonged to the Iroquoian language family; and the Yamasee, who belonged to the Muskhogean language family. The first permanent white settlement was set up by English settlers at Albemarle Point in 1670. In 1719 South Carolina became a separate royal province of England, but during the 1760s, Great Britain passed a series of laws that caused great unrest among the colonists. South Carolina joined the American Revolution in 1776 and soon became the scene of many important battles. One of these, the Battle of Kings Mountain, was a turning point in the Revolution. South Carolina became the eighth state of the Union in 1788. At the start of the Civil War, in 1860, South Carolina seceded from the Union. It was readmitted in 1868.

The first of the 10-year national censuses for South Carolina took place in 1790, and this as well as the later ones can be seen at the various National Archives locations. There have been a number of state censuses. One in 1829 covered the Fairfield and Laurens districts; one in 1839 covered the Kershaw and Chesterfield districts; another in 1869 covered all the counties except Clarendon, Oconee, and Spartenburg; and the one in 1875 covered the counties of Clarendon, Newberry, and Marlboro, as well as producing partial returns for Abbeville, Beaufort, Fairfield, Lancaster, and Sumner counties. These census reports can be seen at the South Carolina Department of Archives and History in Columbia. The state mortality schedules for 1850 to 1880 can also be seen there.

Records of births and deaths since 1915

are available from the South Carolina Vital Records Office in Columbia, as are marriage records since 1950 and divorce records since 1962. Copies can be obtained for a small fee from the Vital Records Office. Earlier marriage records can be obtained from the probate offices in the counties where the marriage licenses were issued. This is also true for wills probated before 1915, although those before 1875 were all probated in Charleston. Divorce records from 1949 should be available from the county clerks in the counties where the petitions were filed. Divorce was not legal in South Carolina until 1949. Births and deaths for the city of Charleston between 1877 and 1821 are on file at the Charleston County Health Department. The Florence County Health Department has those for the city of Florence between 1895 and 1914, while the Newberry County Health Department has them for the city of Newberry for the late 1800s. The guardianship records for the state are located in the district courts of each county.

There are two ports in South Carolina where immigrants arrived, Charleston and Georgetown. The immigration passenger records from 1906 to 1945 from Charleston and from 1923 to 1939 for Georgetown are stored at the National Archives in Washington, D.C.

Land records in the state are with the clerks of the county courts, with the exception of those filed prior to 1785, which were all recorded at Charleston. There is no distinction between equity and law actions in South Carolina. The county courts and the courts of common pleas have concurrent jurisdiction.

The South Carolina Department of Archives and History in Columbia has some materials relating to the genealogy of residents of the state, as does the South Carolina State Library in Columbia and the State Historical Society in Charleston. Another good collection of family history and genealogical materials can be found at the Laurens County Library in Laurens. This collection includes a death certificate index on microfiche for the years 1915 to 1944; county will and estate records, as well as land records, on microfilm

for 1785 to 1900; a state newspaper collection; maps, family histories, and church records; and military records from the Civil War through World War II. One other source of genealogical materials is the library at the University of South Carolina in Columbia.

Researchers seeking information from county records can locate them at the following county seats: (Abbeville County) Abbeville, (Aiken County) Aiken, (Allendale County) Allendale, (Anderson County) Anderson, (Bamberg County) Bamberg, (Barnwell County) Barnwell, (Beaufort County) Beaufort, (Berkeley County) Moncks Corner, (Calhoun County) St. Matthews, (Charleston County) Charleston, (Cherokee County) Gaffney, (Chester County) Chester, (Chesterfield County) Chesterfield, (Clarendon County) Manning, (Colleton County) Walterboro, (Darlington County) Darlington, (Dillon County) Dillon, (Dorchester County) St. George, (Edgefield County) Edgefield, (Fairfield County) Winnsboro, (Florence County) Florence, (Georgetown County) Georgetown, (Greenville County) Greenville, (Greenwood County) Greenwood, (Hampton County) Hampton, (Horry County) Conway, (Jasper County) Ridgeland, (Kershaw County) Camden, (Lancaster County) Lancaster, (Laurens County) Laurens, (Lee County) Bishopville, (Lexington County) Lexington, (Marion County) Marion, (Marlboro County) Bennettsville, (McCormick County) McCormick, (Newberry County) Newberry, (Oconee County) Walhalla, (Orangeburg County) Orangeburg, (Pickens County) Pickens, (Richland County) Columbia, (Saluda County) Saluda, (Spartanburg County) Spartanburg, (Sumter County) Sumter, (Union County) Union, (Williamsburg County) Kingstree, and (York County) York.

FOR FURTHER INFORMATION SEE:
- Cote, Richard N. *Local and Family History in South Carolina: A Bibliography*. Easley, SC: Southern Historical Press, 1981.
- Hendrix, Ge Lee Corley. *Research in South Carolina*. Arlington, VA: National Genealogical Society, 1992.

South Dakota Records of births, marriages, and deaths are maintained in duplicate by the county courts and the South Dakota State Vital Records Office. The United States acquired South Dakota from France through the Louisiana Purchase in 1803. Meriweather Lewis and William Clark then passed through the area in 1804 on their expedition to and from the Pacific Ocean. The first settlement in South Dakota was not established until 1817, near what is now Fort Pierre. Congress created the Dakota Territory in 1861, and designated South Dakota as the 40th state in 1889.

A territorial census was conducted in 1860 that included the western part in the Nebraska Territory and the eastern part in the Dakota Territory. The state conducted its own censuses in 1885, 1905, 1915, 1925, 1935, and 1945, which complement the national census of this state that was taken in 1890 and every 10 years since. Unfortunately, most of the 1890 census was destroyed in a fire, and only the records for Jefferson Township in Union County remain. The national census records are at the various National Archives locations. The state censuses all include Beadle, Brule, Prat (now Jones), Presbo (now Lyman), Campbell, and Charles Mix counties. The 1885 census also includes Edmunds, Fall River, Faulk, Hand, Hanson, Hutchinson, Hyde, Lake, Lincoln, Marshall, McPherson, Moody, Roberts, Sanborn, Spink, Stanley, and Turner counties. The state census records are at the South Dakota Historical Society and State Archives in Pierre. The mortality schedules for 1860 to 1880 can also be found at the State Historical Society.

South Dakota began requiring the registration of births and deaths in 1906, but the registration was sporadic for several years. A number of pre–1906 birth records were filed later. All the records were stored with the clerks of the county courts and duplicate copies were sent to the Vital Records Office of the State Department of Health in Pierre. To obtain a copy from the Vital Records Office, one must provide the date of birth, place of birth, father's name, and mother's name, including her maiden name, with a small fee. Duplicate copies of the marriage and divorce records were also sent to the Vital Records Office, although it is best to obtain copies of these records from the clerks in the counties where the events took place. Guardianship records are filed with the clerks of the county district courts.

The *Guide to Public Vital Statistics Records in South Dakota* (Work Projects Administration, 1942) will help any researcher searching for South Dakota records. It is available at the State Library in Pierre, as well as in some other libraries in South Dakota and in some genealogical libraries elsewhere. South Dakota land records are on file in offices of the county recorders of deeds, and both equity and law cases in this state are under the jurisdiction of the county courts.

Researchers seeking information from county records can locate them at the following county seats: (Aurora County) Plankinton, (Beadle County) Huron, (Bennett County) Martin, (Bon Homme County) Tyndall, (Brookings County) Brookings, (Brown County) Aberdeen, (Brule County) Chamberlain, (Buffalo County) Gannvalley, (Butte County) Belle Fourche, (Campbell County) Mound City, (Charles Mix County) Lake Andes, (Clark County) Clark, (Clay County) Vermillion, (Codington County) Watertown, (Corson County) McIntosh, (Custer County) Custer, (Davison County) Mitchell, (Day County) Webster, (Deuel County) Clear Lake, (Dewey County) Timber Lake, (Douglas County) Armour, (Edmunds County) Ipswich, (Fall River County) Hot Springs, (Faulk County) Faulkton, (Grant County) Milbank, (Gregory County) Burke, (Haakon County) Philip, (Hamlin County) Hayti, (Hand County) Miller, (Hanson County) Alexandria, (Harding County) Buffalo, (Hughes County) Pierre, (Hutchinson County) Olivet, and (Hyde County) Highmore.

Also at (Jackson County) Kadoka, (Jerauld County) Wessington Springs, (Jones County) Murdo, (Kingsbury County) De Smet, (Lake County) Madison, (Lawrence County) Deadwood, (Lincoln County) Canton, (Lyman County) Kennebec, (Marshall County) Britton, (McCook County) Salem, (McPherson County) Leola, (Meade County) Sturgis, (Mellette County) White River, (Miner County) Howard, (Minnehaha

County) Sioux Falls, (Moody County) Flandreau, (Pennington County) Rapid City, (Perkins County) Bison, (Potter County) Gettysburg, (Roberts County) Sisseton, (Sanborn County) Woonsocket, (Shannon County) Hot Springs, (Spink County) Redfield, (Stanley County) Fort Pierre, (Sully County) Onida, (Todd County) Winner, (Tripp County) Winner, (Turner County) Parker, (Union County) Elk Point, (Walworth County) Selby, (Yankton County) Yankton, and (Ziebach County) Dupree.

FOR FURTHER INFORMATION SEE:
- Alexander, Ruth A., et al., comps. *South Dakota: Changing, Changeless, 1899–1989.* Rapid City, SD: South Dakota Library Association, 1985.
- Wagner, Sally Roesch. *Daughters of Dakota.* 6 vols. Aberdeen, SD: South Dakota Daughters of Dakota, 1989.

Spanish Genealogy is filled with many rich resources. The Catholic parishes in Spain, which were charged with recording baptisms, marriages, and burials by Cardinal Cisneros in 1570, are the oldest in Europe. Some 1,636 of the 19,000 Spanish parishes have registers that contain such information from earlier than 1570. The oldest one is that of the parish of Verda in the diocese of Salsona, begun in 1394. *The Guidebook of the Spanish Church*, which comprises 14 volumes, lists all the parishes in Spain as well as their dioceses and dates when the earliest registers were kept. These volumes can be found at the National Library of Spain in Madrid as well as in other large libraries in Spain, some genealogical libraries in the United States, and probably at most Spanish consuls' offices. In seeking access to any parish register or other information from a local priest, the proper way to address the individual is as The Revdo Sr Sura Párocco.

Civil registrations of births, marriages, and deaths began in Spain in 1870 under the auspices of the justices of municipalities, of districts, and of the peace. The various municipalities today still maintain these records in their archives.

Wills made in the presence of notaries had to satisfy the Justice of First Instance before they could be entered into the registries of the district. Those that have been proved during the last 25 years are kept in the offices of the various notaries, but after 25 years they will be sent to the archives of the notaries in charge of probate matters, in the capitals of the provinces: Albacete, Palma de Mallorca, Barcelona, Burgos, Caceres, La Coruna, Granada, Madrid, Pamplona, Oviedo, Las Palmas de Gran Canaria, Seville, Valencia, and Valladolid y Zaragoza.

Spanish surnames contain both the father's surname and the mother's surname in that order, sometimes separated by the word "y" (and). This can be valuable in genealogical research, since knowing the full surname automatically gives one the surnames for both parents. Often, civil and church records will include both surnames of the grandparents, which naturally provides the researcher with the surnames of the great-grandparents as well. If José López marries María Famosa, their son will be named Juan López Famosa. And if the son, Juan, in turn marries Isabel Fernández García, the son of Juan and Isabel could be named Pedro López Fernández, Pedro López y Fernández, Pedro López Famosa y Fernández, or Pedro López Famosa y Fernández García — the last two forms preserving the "Famosa" surname for future generations.

In Hispanic cultures, wives retain their maiden names when they marry. They can legally add their husbands' surname(s) after their own, preceded by the word "de" (of, i.e., spouse of). Thus, in the preceding example, Isabel Fernández could sign her name as Isabel Fernández de López, or as Isabel Fernández García de López Famosa. If her husband has died, she may use the words "viuda de" (widow of) instead of the "de."

It was common in the past for individuals to be baptized with a string of middle names, usually honoring ancestors, godparents, or benefactors. In religious families one of the middle names would often correspond to the name of the saint whose feast day corresponded to the individual's birthday. This practice may provide the genealogist with a clue as to an individual's birthday. The saints' feast days can be found by referring to a

Catholic Church calendar. In the past it was illegal in most Hispanic counties to change one's name. In order to do so required an act of the legislature. Thus it was a rare occurrence.

The National Library of Spain has an extensive catalog of genealogical documents and manuscripts. The General Military Archives in Segovia also has records on some 850,000 individuals who served in the military from the 17th through the 19th centuries, as well as beyond. These records contain the surnames, Christian names, ranks, branch of service, and other information. The Historical National Archives of Madrid holds documents relating to the four great orders of chivalry — Santiago, Alcántara, Caltrava, and Montesa. These orders began during the middle ages in the struggle against the Moors. Most of the noble Spanish families can trace their ancestry back to a member who was in one of these orders. The Archivo de La Corona de Aragon in Barcelona has some of the oldest legal, royal, and ecclesiastical records in Europe, many dating back to the 11th century.

The International Institute of Genealogy and Heraldry and Federation of Similar Corporations (Instituto Internacional de Genealogiá y Heraldica, y Federación di corporaciones Afines) is a useful institution in Madrid that can aid researchers in Spanish family research. The institute receives government support and produces many publications, all in Spanish, about its work.

In most of the Spanish libraries, and in some of the larger libraries in South America and the United States, one can also find the *Encyclopedia Heraldica y Genealogica: Hispano-Americana*, compiled by Albert and Garciá Caraffa. It is composed of scores of volumes and gives the arms and histories of a multitude of families in Spain and Latin America.

Spelling Variations in genealogical records may occur for a variety of reasons. Often they happen because the writer makes a mistake in transcribing some record, just as the writer might put down an inaccurate date. If the record was produced more than a hun-

dred years ago, it is possible that the one who wrote the word(s) didn't know the correct spelling form. At that time a large percentage of the population couldn't read, and fewer still could write much more than their own names. Most people who did write did not concern themselves particularly with standard spellings. They wrote words just the way those words sounded.

Spelling variations also occur when the words are properly written in different ways by persons of two different cultures. For example, it is correct to write "colour" in England, but not in the United States where the correct form is "color." Or the American word is "center," while the British word is "centre," and the American word is "optimization," while the British word is "optimisation."

None of these variations are much of a problem when the modern reader can decipher the intent of the written words, but spelling variations can be daunting when found in names (particularly surnames) and locations. The following caution appears in the 1879 work, *History of Fulton County, Illinois*: "Proper names, too, are so varied that without a personal acquaintance with each individual, it is often impossible to spell them correctly. Even members of the same family sometimes spell their names differently, such as Philips, Phillips, Philipps, and Phillipps. And as for dates, when given verbally, they are sometimes as different as the people giving them."

The above points out the common fallacy in assuming that if a name is not spelled a certain way, then it cannot belong to the same family. More often than not the names found in the records that are spelled differently — even in census records — turn out to be members of the same family. In using the indexes found in genealogy books or county record books it is always wise to be aware of possible different spellings.

Here is a list of a few spelling variations that have been found in names, both given ones and surnames:

Austin, Auston, Austyn, Austynn, Austynne, Austen, Austenn, Austenne, Austinne

Bailey, Bailee, Bailea, Bailie, Baylee, Baylea, Bayleigh, , Baeleigh, Baelea, Bailee

Caroline, Carolyn, Carolynn, Carolynne, Carolin, Carolinn, Carolinne

Dina, Deena Deenah, Deana, Deanah, Deana

Eleanor, Elinor, Elinore, Elanor, Elanore

Felicia, Feleesha, Feleasha, Feleacia, Feleecia, Felisha

Gwendolyn, Gwyndolyn, Gwendolen, Gwendolynn, Gwendolenn, Gwendalyn

Hayden, Haydn, Haydyn, Naydin, Hayden, Haydon, Haydun

Isabel, Isabell, Isabelle, Isobel, Isobell, Isobelle

Jacob, Jakob, Jacub, Jakub, Jaycob, Jaykob, Jaycub, Jaykub

Kelley, Kelly, Kellie, Keli, Keleigh, Kelleigh, Kellea

Lucas, Loukas, Lucus, Lukus

Michael, Micheal, Mikael, Mykal, Mychal

Nocholas, Nicolas, Nikolas, Nickolas, Nikoles, Nicoles, Nickoles, Niclas, Niklas

Owen, Owenn, Owyn, Owynn

Peyton, Payton, Peighton, Paytin, Peytin, Paytun, Peytun, Peytan, Paytan

Reilly, Riley, Rilee, Rylee, Rylea, Rylea, Ryley, Ryleigh

Susannah, Susanna, Suzannah, Suzana

Tina, Teena, Teenah, Teana, Teanah

Victor, Fiktor, Victor

Wallace, Wallis, Wallice

Zoe, Zoey, Zoee, Zoie

See also **Handwriting Errors.**

State Archives contain thousands of documents generated by various agencies and departments of the state government. In some states they will be found in a state library, in others in a state historical society library, and in still others in a facility specifically named the state archives. Whatever the case, these institutions are much the same in the collections of documents they house.

At such state archives the researcher will find, besides state documents, maps of the state, newspapers published in various cities of the state, private papers and business papers produced by prominent citizens, as well as samples of correspondence by many of these same persons. There are also likely to be local and county histories, state censuses, appellate court records, county directories, some church records, lists of cemetery inscriptions, genealogical periodicals, and other data of particular value to any genealogist.

State archives in the Eastern states are likely to have collections of colonial and Revolutionary War records in their files, while those in the South may have pension applications and other records from the time of these states' participation in the Confederacy. Each of the state archives has its own indexing and finding methods to help researchers locate the information that they have stored.

Surname Dictionaries *see* **Biographical Dictionaries**

Surnames did not come into general use in Europe until sometime between the 11th and 15th centuries, but they were first used in China as early as 2852 B.C. when Emperor Fushi decreed their requirement for all families. Today the Chinese commonly have three names, with the surname placed first, followed by a generation name and then the given name. During Biblical times in the Near East people were often referred to by their given names and the locality in which they resided, such as "Jesus of Nazareth," but the locality name did not constitute a surname. By the time of the Roman emperors some people were using three names, although one was sufficient for most. The name Gaius Julius Caesar is a case in point. Some Romans even added a fourth name to commemorate some illustrious action or remarkable event. By the fall of the Roman Empire, the process was becoming quite confused, and the use of single names again became the common practice.

Surnames did not become customary in Europe until about the 13th century, and then they were used only for wealthy and noble families. At first these names were not hereditary, but merely described relatives of one person. Thus the son of Robert Johnson might be known as Henry Robertson, or Henry, son of Robert. In his 1586 book, *Remaines of a Greater Worke Concerning Britaine*, William Camden wrote:

About the yeare of our Lord 1000 ... surnames began to be taken up in France, and in England about the time of the Conquest, or else a very little before, under King Edward the Confessor, who was all Frenchified ... but the French and wee termed them Surnames, not because they are the names of the sire, or the father, but because they are super added to Christian names as the Spanish called them Renombres, as Renames.

Although hereditary surnames had become common in England by the early 1300s, they were not even universal as late as 1465. During the reign of Edward V (1470–1483), a law was passed requiring the Irish to take on surnames in order to make them easier to control: "They shall take unto them a Surname, either of some Town, or some Color, as Black or Brown, or some Art or Science, as Smyth or Carpenter, or some Office, as Cooke or Butler." Other ethnic groups that adopted hereditary surnames comparatively late include the Dutch, Norse, and Welsh, some refusing to do so until the 17th century. Only in the past two centuries have middle names become commonplace.

As populations grew, the need to identify individuals by surnames became a necessity. Though surnames were once little more than convenient labels to distinguish one James or Robert from another, they have since become charged with a greater significance. They have become badges of honor and symbols of the continuity of a family line, intimately associated with its achievements and prestige. A surname has become the "good name" to be proud of and to protect as one's most treasured possession.

Most English surnames are derived from the names of places or occupations, and a few from some peculiar trait or nickname. Atwood, for example, is derived from Atte Wood, that is, from the fact that a person lived at, or by, a wood. Thus John Atte Wood became distinguished from John Atte Lea (now Atleigh, or more simply Lee), or John who lived by the meadow. Atwell was a dweller near a well; Bywater was one living beside a lake or stream; Beecher or Beechman resided near a grove of beech trees, and Kirkman lived near a church. Surnames derived from occupations include: Chandler from candle

maker, Thatcher from a roof thatcher, and Sherman from the occupation of a shear man. The multitude of persons named Smith probably derives from the fact that every hamlet in England needed at least one smith to work with metals.

There are surnames derived from the father's given name, such as Johnson and Admason; those derived from the mother's given name (Catling and Marguerite); from physical descriptions (Black, Short, and Long); from social status (Bachelor and Knight); from one's character (Stern and Gentle); from animals (Lamb and Fox); and those derived from the weather (Winter and Spring). If a surname ends in land, ton, ville, ham, don, burg, berry, field, fort, caster, chester, thorpe, veld, stead, stad, grad or any similar place-specific suffix, one can probably find its origin in a place name of the countryside.

The suffix "kin" was used in surnames as a diminutive. Thus Tomkin referred to little Thomas, Wilkin to little William, and Perkin to little Peter. The Irish "O" in names such as O'Brien, meant the grandson of Brien, and the Scottish use of "Mac" or "Mc" meant son of. Fitz, as used in England, often indicated illegitimacy, so Fitzroy meant the illegitimate son of the King (from the French, Fils de Roi).

For each of these surnames there seem to be a multitude of spellings and pronunciations. One needs to remember that when surnames were first adopted, most people in Europe were illiterate and had to rely on priests, officials, and clerks to record them. Frequently such recorders put down the words as they heard them, sometimes with accents that sounded strange to their ears and sometimes because of their own peculiar modes of spelling. Immigrants entering the United States over the years presented the officials at entry ports with the same problem. Thus the name Bauch was recorded by an official as Baugh; the name Micsza, as McShea; and the German names Schwarz and Zimmerman became their English equivalents of Black and Carpenter. In many cases these changes in a surname occurred so long ago that no one is anymore aware of the original spelling or pronunciation. To the genealogist, the evolution of most surnames has become an interesting subject. One can find a number of books on shelves of medium and large libraries that give long lists of surnames and their origins.

It is probable that there is a greater variety of surnames in the United States and Canada than anywhere else in the world because so many have entered these two countries from almost every region on this planet. Thus, while the majority of North American surnames are of Western European origin, many come from Southern and Eastern Europe, the Middle East, and parts of Asia. Some immigrants, shortly after they disembarked, changed their names into something that seemed more "North American" so as to leave their past behind them, while others translated their "foreign sounding" names into English equivalents. *See also* **Name Abbreviations; Name Changes; Names, Meaning of; Naming Patterns.**

Swedish Genealogy is relatively easy to research because the public records have been efficiently maintained throughout the centuries and one can find many sources to assist one in the research. One of these, *Finding Your Forefathers*, is a booklet issued by the Royal Ministry for Foreign Affairs through its Press and Information Service.

For more than 300 years the clergy of the Swedish Lutheran Church have been charged with the duty of keeping parish records of births, marriages, and deaths. The order was issued in 1686. One can occasionally find church records of these events that were recorded even before that date. Besides the vital statistics, one may find communion records and entries regarding the movements of individuals and families in and out of the various parishes. Each parish conducted censuses of the residents within their parish boundaries. These censuses are known as household examination rolls; the parish officials listed all the residents and their knowledge of the scriptures and reading ability. These household examination rolls also give the names, including the maiden names of the women, occupations, birthdates and places of birth, marriage dates, former places

of residency, legitimacy of children, and dates of death when such has occurred. The records are the most complete for the years between 1800 and 1895.

Starting in 1946, it has been the practice for the record of each individual to be sent from the home parish to whatever parish that individual moves. In other words, the record follows the individual from parish to parish throughout his or her life. If the person dies or emigrates, the record then goes to the Central Bureau of Statistics in Stockholm.

The regional archives, located in Uppsala, Vadstena, Lund, Göteborg, and Härnösand hold the church records that are more than one hundred years old, as well as the records from the county administrative boards and lower courts. Here one will find probate records that have been kept from about 1725, although some date to as early as 1660. They contain, besides the names of the deceased, inventories of their property and the relationships of persons named in the wills of the deceased. The Swedish National Archive in Stockholm also has some genealogical materials of interest, although this is primarily a depository for papers of the central government.

One other set of records that are useful to genealogists are the emigration records that can be found at the Swedish Emigrant Institute in Växsjö. The major ports of departure from Sweden for emigrés were Göteborg, Malmö, and Stockholm. The Swenson Center, located at Augustana College in Rock Island, Illinois, is an archives and research institute for the study of Swedish immigration to North America. Its library and archival holdings are extensive, including materials from all sectors of the Swedish immigrant community in the United States and Canada. It contains many of the Swedish parish records on microfiche.

Swiss Genealogy records are stored in 20 cantons and six half-cantons. There is no central registry. As a country Switzerland had its beginnings in 1291 when three Swiss cantons— Uri, Schwyz, and Nidevalden — signed the Perpetual Covenant setting up the Swiss Confederation. It was not until 1848, however, that Switzerland, now 22 cantons, adopted a constitution that established federal power over the confederation. The researcher needs to remember that four languages are in use in Switzerland — German, spoken by most people, French, Italian, and Romasch, the tongue of a small minority. Thus records can be found in all of these languages.

Before 1848 the civil registry of births, marriages, and deaths was in the hands of each of the cantons, though the Catholic and Protestant Churches actually carried out this responsibility until 1876. It was only then that the civil authorities took over the duty, and the church records for 1834 to 1875 were given to the registrar's office in each of the cantons. Thus parish registers exist for Protestants from about 1525 and for Catholics from about 1580. During the 17th and 18th centuries, most of Switzerland predominantly belonged to one of these two major Christian religions. Most of the "mixed" cantons were not established until late in the 19th century.

Baptism records (Taufbücher) give the dates and places of baptism as well as the babies' names and those of their parents. Marriage records (Ehebücher) name the couples and the date and place of marriage. Not until after 1700 are the names of the fathers and sometimes the mothers of the bride and groom given. Death records are basically burial records (Beerdigungen — Sépultures — Sepolture) that name the deceased, the date, and often the name of a spouse and sometimes even the names of parents and deceased children.

The present civil registry system was established for all of Switzerland in 1876, but some of the cantons began such a system much earlier. Geneva began it in 1798; Vaud in 1821; Neuchâtel in 1825; Baselland in 1827; Solothurn, Fribourg, Glarus, and Schaffhausen in 1849; Valais in 1853; Ticino in 1855; and Sankt Gallen in 1867. The birth records give the name, date and place of birth, as well as the parents' names, occupations, and place of residence. The marriage records give the groom's and bride's names, ages, places of residence and occupations; date and place of

marriage; parents' names, places of residence and occupations; witnesses' names. Death records give the name, age, sometimes the birthplace, date and place of death, name of the surviving spouse, informant's name and place of residence, and sometimes the names of parents and one child or several children.

Access to the civil registration records is restricted to the canton officials, though they will sometimes open them to private persons and they are usually willing to provide an abstract of any desired register. In most cantons the archives will have copies of all the church records still in existence on microfilm. Some of the actual parish registers can be found in the state archives at Neuchâtel and Solothurn. Copies of the civil records, or family certificates (Familienschein), are usually available only to Swiss citizens, and since 1998, only to direct descendants. Thus researchers are advised to have proof of such a relationship when making a request for such a family certificate from a cantonal civil registration office.

Many libraries in Switzerland, such as the Swiss National Library in Bern, have the three-volume *Familiennamenbuch (Swiss Surname Book)* which lists the family names of all citizens from 1600 to 1962 in alphabetical order. The names are listed by the counties and villages where the families are found. This book is helpful in locating particular families for the first time so that they can later be found in the Swiss parish and civil records. Families that became extinct before 1962 will not be found in the *Swiss Surname Book*. The notes at the beginning of each volume are written in French, German, and Italian.

Census listings of families living in particular parish areas are found in the Haushaltungsregisters, which provide the names and places of birth of family members, as well as their ages, parents, grandparents, brothers, and sisters. These documents are available from 1764 for the city of Bern, 1798 for the city of Geneva, and from 1811 to 1850 at 15-year intervals in some cantons. After 1850 censuses were held at 10-year intervals throughout Switzerland. The census records are stored in the state archives at Neuchâtel and Solothurn as well as in various other city archives throughout the country.

The city archives and city libraries have various genealogical records for Swiss families from the 15th to the 19th centuries. These records include pedigrees, descendant charts, and family chronicles of old and prominent families. A bibliography of them has been compiled by Mario von Moos. It can be found in most Swiss libraries, and an American edition (*Bibliography of Swiss Genealogies*, Picton Pr., 1993) is available.

The city archives also preserve records of the apprentices and freemen belonging to guilds from the 16th to the 19th centuries, as well as military records of the cantons from the 15th to the 18th centuries, and those of the federal army from 1848 to the present. These records give the names and residences of the soldiers, and the age and rank for the later ones. There are also lists of landholders and renters, court records, and the records of notaries. The latter records are generally in the offices of the notaries, though the municipal archives are likely to have indexes of the testaments that will give a partial account of the contents.

A Swiss society for heraldry, the Schweizerische Heraldische Gesellschaft, maintains pedigrees of Swiss families that go back several centuries. The society promotes the display of coats of arms that can be found at the entrance to many houses and in the glass windows of many churches. The Dom church in Bern is particularly endowed with rich examples of heraldic glass.

Finally the researcher would be wise to visit the Swiss Federal Archives and the Library of the Genealogical Society of Switzerland, both in Bern. Each has a great deal of information of use to genealogists, and the Genealogical Society can be most helpful to family researchers looking for records in Switzerland.

Symbols can occasionally be found in genealogical records, particularly secondary ones, where the transcribers have adopted shorthand methods to record the information. Symbols are also often used in heraldry designs.

Some of the more common ones are:

*	–	Born
(*)	–	Born illegitimate
X	–	Baptized or christened
ᴑ	–	Baptized or christened
ᴖ	–	Baptized or christened
O	–	Betrothed
OO	–	Married
O/O	–	Divorced
O-O	–	Common-law marriage
†	–	Died
⪫	–	Died
□	–	Buried
▭	–	Buried
† †	–	No further issue
(†)	–	No further issue

There are also alphabetical symbols that are used, such as:

d.s.p.— died without issue
d.s.p.l.— died without legitimate issue
d.s.p.m.s.— died without surviving male issue
d.s.p.s— died without surviving issue
d.unm — died unmarried
d.v.m.— died in the lifetime of his mother
d.v.p.— died in the lifetime of his father
Inst — present month
Liber — book or volume
Nepos— grandson
Nunc or Nun — an oral will, written by a witness
Ob — he/she died
Rel. or Relict — widow or widower
Res. or Residue — widow or widower
Sic — exact copy as written
Testes— witnesses
Ult — late
Ux or vs— wife
Viz — namely

Pictorial symbols are mostly found in the designs on tombstones and also occasionally in designs used in heraldry. These include:

Anchor — mariner
Axe, steel knife, and cleaver — butcher
Bowl (for bleeding) and a razor — barber
Chalice — sacraments
Cherub — innocence

Crown — glory of life after death
Dog — good master
Dove — peace and eternal life
Hammer and anvil — smith
Harp — praise to the God
Hearts (two) — marriage
Horns — wisdom, rebirth
Lamb — innocence
Lily — innocence, purity
Lion — courage
Rake and spade — gardener
Rose (full bloom) — prime of life

Scales — merchant
Shuttle and stretchers — weaver
Stalk of corn — farmer
Sun — renewed life
Swords crossed — high military rank
Thistles — Scottish descent
Tree trunk — short life
Trumpeters — harbingers of the Resurrection
Urn — immortality, remembrance
Wedge and level — maso
Weeping willow — grief
Wheat — divine harvest

T

Tartans *see* **Clan Tartans**

Tax and Real Estate Records can provide a sort of census of the residents in any town, in that all taxpayers and their property are listed in such records. Because the federal census is taken only once every 10 years, tax lists can serve as intermediate records to locate people in a particular town and to indicate when they may have moved away, or at least stopped paying taxes. Such records usually indicate how much land these individuals owned at a particular time and the value and size of their home plots, their business locations, or their farms. The lists can also indicate a family's standing in a community and perhaps its interests.

There are different kinds of tax records. Those imposed on real property show the amount of land owned by an individual and its value. They also document the acquisition or divestiture of land. Those imposed on personal property can often be of more value to the genealogist because they include the names of the various persons well established in a community who may own no land, as well as those who do. In the past, particularly in the Southern states, there were also poll taxes and taxes on all free white males in a community.

In using tax records to find genealogical data it is best to examine them in combina-

tion with other records such as deeds, marriage records, and probate matters. Used in conjunction with the information from this other data, tax records can provide much additional information about the people involved. When using tax records one should follow such records from the first appearance of the person's name in the listings to the point at which the name disappears from the rolls to obtain a clear record of the individual's economic activity in the community during the full time.

The National Archives in Washington, D.C., has lists for the first direct tax that was placed on real property and slaves by the various states in 1798, including record lists for Connecticut, Delaware, the District of Columbia, Maine, Maryland, Massachusetts, New Hampshire, Pennsylvania, Rhode Island, Tennessee, and Vermont. There are also lists of the assessments by the Internal Revenue Service during the Civil War levied on various businesses to pay for the war effort. Carriages, yachts, gold and silver plate, and billiard tables were among the items taxed. These records do not give any genealogical information, but do provide an idea of the economic status of those who are listed.

Real estate records may be useful. One can find valuable information in the deeds that were negotiated for the sale of land because they indicate the places of residence for both the sellers and the buyers. When a purchaser buys a piece of property before he or she moves into a county, the deed will list the buyer's place of immediate origin. If a seller puts property up for sale after moving away, the deed will indicate to what place he or she will have moved. Knowing these facts can be of great help in further genealogical research.

Most deeds and other land records are well indexed, both by the names of the buyers and by the names of the sellers. The indexes are usually in separate volumes, but sometimes they are combined. However, if there is more than one buyer or seller, the indexes will list just the first one named on the document. One should remember that in many states there are a number of other land indexes in addition to those for the buyers and sellers. To cover the land records completely, many genealogists check all such indexes.

TCP/IP *see* **Computer Genealogy Files**

Teaching Genealogy *see* **Genealogy as a Profession**

Techniques in Genealogical Research *see* **Research Methods**

Telephone Directories are sometimes among the most valuable resources for a family history researcher. Just as city directories can be used to locate family members, telephone directories will provide exact home addresses. When examined from year to year, they can indicate the movement of a family from one address to another. The two types of directories do not necessarily duplicate one another; a comparison between the two may reveal discrepancies that can provide new information, corroborate evidence already known, or contradict other evidence. Furthermore, a person or family arriving in a location after the cut-off date for the completion of a city directory may be included in the more frequently published telephone directory but not in the city directory. Using the two together can fine-tune the arrival date of a family in an area and in evaluating other evidence.

Telephone companies began to print directories shortly after the first telephones came into use, primarily because such volumes could demonstrate the value of their service to customers. The directories also produced additional revenue in the form of advertising by business subscribers, but such books were never intended for long-term use; they were intended to be replaced annually. Telephone directories are therefore printed on relatively low grade paper, much as newspapers are. The acid content in this paper will cause deterioration over time so that the pages of older telephone directories yellow with the years and become brittle. As such, they are somewhat less durable than most city directories.

As "ephemeral materials," telephone directories are difficult to preserve and store. Librarians faced with the problem of limited shelf space frequently dispose of the old telephone directories because they are probably not used as much as the other types of directories. However, those of any year may be valuable resources for research in genealogy, so such destruction is indeed a tragedy from the genealogist's perspective. It is often necessary to visit many different libraries to find telephone directories for a city during desired years.

Since the government's recent release of the 1930 census records, telephone directories have become essential tools for locating the people in these records. Only a small portion of the 1930 census was ever indexed by the Soundex method so that persons cannot be located through an alphabetized listing of surnames. The researcher must first find the exact address where an individual lived in 1930 in order to find that person in the census. This requires locating the individual first in a telephone directory. *See also* **City Directories.**

Tennessee Records can be found at the Tennessee State Library and Archives in Nashville, as well as at the Vital Records Office, also in Nashville. The first whites to come into this area in 1540 were a party of Spanish explorers, under the leadership of Hernando de Soto. They raided Indian villages in the valley of the Tennessee and then moved westward, going all the way to the Mississippi River. The Indian tribes living in Tennessee at the time were Cherokee and Chickasaw peoples. No other European explorers returned to the region until 1673, when an English troop led by James Needham and Gabriel Arthur explored the Tennessee River Valley. That same year the French Canadians Louis Joliet and Father Jacques Marquette also explored the region. By 1683 France had surrendered all the lands east of the Mississippi, which included what is now the state of Tennessee, to Great Britain. Following the American Revolution, Tennessee adopted a constitution in preparation for statehood in 1796, and that same year joined the Union as the 16th state. The Chickasaw Indians sold all their land in Tennessee to the U.S. government in 1818, and in 1838 the Cherokees were forced out of the state.

The first available section of Tennessee among the national 10-year census listings is that for Rutherford County in 1810. The other parts of the census for this state no longer exist. Some of the counties in the 1820 census are also missing. However, these parts and the later full-state census enumerations can be found at the National Archives and its various branches. There have never been any separate censuses conducted by the state of Tennessee alone. The mortality schedules from 1850 to 1880 can also be found at the National Archives.

Copies of Tennessee vital records, such as birth and death certificates and marriage licenses, can be obtained from the state's Vital Records Office for a small fee. It also has copies of divorce decrees since 1945. These divorce records and earlier ones can also be obtained from the circuit court in any county where a divorce was adjudicated. Wills and other probate matters can be found in the county courts in all the counties except Davidson, Dyer, Hamilton, and Shelby. The wills for Davidson and Shelby counties are in the county probate courts; for Dyer County, they are in the common law court; and for Hamilton County they are in the chancery court. Guardianship matters can be found in both the county courts and the county chancery courts.

Land records in Tennessee are stored with the various county registers of deeds. Equity and law cases are handled in this state by two separate courts in every county, with the equity matters in the chancery courts and actions at law in the circuit courts.

The Work Projects Administration produced the useful *Guide to Public Vital Statistics in Tennessee* (1941), and *Guide to Church Vital Statistics in Tennessee* (1942). Both volumes can be found in the Tennessee State Library and Archives, as well as in some of the other larger libraries in Tennessee and in a few genealogical libraries elsewhere.

The State Library and Archives maintains a large collection of records relating to the history and other events in the state, including copies of some of the earliest county records as well as copies of such records for which the originals have been lost in courthouse fires and other disasters. The archives also has military records for those from Tennessee who served in the War of 1812, the Civil War, and World Wars I and II. There are indexes to the death records in Tennessee from 1908 to 1912 and a partial index to those from 1914 to 1925. The State Library also has microfilm copies of Tennessee newspapers and an index to newspaper obituaries. Furthermore, the State Library has records of the Cherokee Indians, volumes of local history, biographies of prominent persons in the state, and various city directories. The University of Tennessee at Knoxville also has an extensive collection of books and other data of interest to genealogists.

Researchers seeking information from county records can locate them at the following county seats: (Anderson County) Clinton, (Bedford County) Shelbyville, (Benton County) Camden, (Bledsoe County) Pikeville, (Blount County) Maryville, (Bradley County) Cleveland, (Campbell County) Jacksboro, (Cannon County) Woodbury, (Carroll County) Huntingdon, (Carter County) Elizabethton, (Cheatham County) Ashland City, (Chester County) Henderson, (Claiborne County) Tazewell, (Clay County) Celina, (Cocke County) Newport, (Coffee County) Manchester, (Crockett County) Alamo, (Cumberland County) Crossville, (Davidson

County) Nashville, (De Kalb County) Smith-ville, (Decatur County) Decaturville, (Dick-son County) Charlotte, (Dyer County) Dyersburg, (Fayette County) Somerville, (Fentress County) Jamestown, (Franklin County) Winchester, (Gibson County) Trenton, (Giles County) Pulaski, (Grainger County) Rutledge, (Greene County) Greeneville, (Grundy County) Altamont, (Hamblen County) Morristown, (Hamilton County) Chattanooga, (Hancock County) Sneedville, (Hardeman County) Bolivar, (Hardin County) Savannah, (Hawkins County) Rogersville, (Haywood County) Brownsville, (Henderson County) Lexington, (Henry County) Paris, (Hickman County) Centerville, (Houston County) Erin, and (Humphreys County) Waverly.

Also at (Jackson County) Gainesboro, (Jefferson County) Dandridge, (Johnson County) Mountain City, (Knox County) Knoxville, (Lake County) Tiptonville, (Lauderdale County) Ripley, (Lawrence County) Lawrenceburg, (Lewis County) Hohenwald, (Lincoln County) Fayetteville, (Loudon County) Loudon, (Macon County) Lafayette, (Madison County) Jackson, (Marion County) Jasper, (Marshall County) Lewisburg, (Maury County) Columbia, (McMinn County) Athens, (McNairy County) Selmer, (Meigs County) Decatur, (Monroe County) Madisonville, (Montgomery County) Clarksville, (Moore County) Lynchburg, (Morgan County) Wartburg, (Obion County) Union City, (Overton County) Livingston, (Perry County) Linden, (Pickett County) Byrdstown, (Polk County) Benton, (Putnam County) Cookeville, (Rhea County) Dayton, (Roane County) Kingston, (Robertson County) Springfield, (Rutherford County) Murfreesboro, (Scott County) Huntsville, (Sequatchie County) Dunlap, (Sevier County) Sevierville, (Shelby County) Memphis, (Smith County) Carthage, (Stewart County) Dover, (Sullivan County) Blountville, (Sumner County) Gallatin, (Tipton County) Covington, (Trousdale County) Hartsville, (Unicoi County) Erwin, (Union County) Maynardville, (Van Buren County) Spencer, (Warren County) McMinnville, (Washington County) Jonesboro, (Wayne County) Waynesboro, (Weakley County) Dresden, (White County) Sparta, (Williamson County) Franklin, and (Wilson County) Lebanon.

FOR FURTHER INFORMATION SEE:
- Bamman, Gale Williams. *Research in Tennessee*. Arlington, VA: National Genealogical Society, 1993.
- Fulcher, Richard Carlton. *Guide to County Records and Genealogical Resources in Tennessee*. Baltimore, MD: Genealogical Publishing Co., 1987.

Territorial Papers, though not available for all states, can be one of the best sources for lists of the early inhabitants in particular areas in the United States. They contain letters that deal with many issues, postal schedules, militia muster rolls, appointments, petitions to Congress, voter lists, jury lists, some maps, and more.

Such territorial papers can be found in many large public libraries, as well as in university and research libraries. The territories include those of Alabama, Arkansas, Florida, Illinois, Indiana, Iowa, Louisiana, Michigan, Mississippi, Missouri, Ohio, Oregon, Minnesota, Tennessee, Vermont, and Wisconsin. The U.S. Government Printing Office has published a listing of the *Territorial Papers of the United States* for the years between 1934 and 1975.

A microfilm collection of the *Territorial Papers of the United States Senate* at the National Archives in Washington, D.C. covers various years from 1789 through 1873. These are: Alabama and Arkansas (1818–1836); Arizona and the Dakotas (1857–1873); Colorado and Nevada (1860–1868); Florida (1806–1845); Idaho, Montana, and Wyoming (1863–1871); Indiana (1792–1830); Kansas and Nebraska (1853–1867); Louisiana-Missouri (1804–1822); Louisiana (Territory of Orleans, 1803–1815); Michigan (1803–1847); Minnesota (1847–1868); Mississippi (1799–1818); New Mexico (1840–1854); Ohio (Territory Northwest of the Ohio River, 1789–1808); Oregon (1824–1871); Tennessee (Territory South of the Ohio River, 1789–1808); Utah and Washington (1849–1868); and Wisconsin (1834–1849).

In some states, such as Utah, territorial

papers have been produced by state executives. The ones stored at the Utah State Library in Salt Lake City contain the proceedings of Utah's legislative assembly and the actions of the governor from 1850 through 1896.

Texas Records can be found in abundance at the Texas State Library in Austin as well as in a number of university and city libraries around the state. Parts of Texas were explored by Spanish expeditions in the early 1500s, and Spanish missionaries built two missions there in 1682, near present-day El Paso. In 1718 the Spaniards built a fort on the site of present-day San Antonio. By 1821 Texas had become a part of the new empire of Mexico, but Texas declared independence from Mexico in 1836, and joined the Union in 1845 as the 28th state.

The first time Texas was enumerated among the states during the 10-year U.S. censuses was in 1850. The census records for that year and the following enumerations can be seen at any of the National Archives centers. There have never been any Texas state censuses, although some Mexican censuses included the cities of San Antonio, Nacogdoches, and Austin. These censuses have been printed in several issues of the *National Genealogical Society Quarterly*, as well as in book form. The Texas mortality schedules from 1850 to 1880 can be found in the Texas State Library.

The records of births since 1926, marriages since 1967, divorces since 1968, and deaths since 1964 can be found at the Texas Vital Records Office in Austin. Copies can be obtained for a small fee. Earlier records of this sort must be located at the district courts in the counties where such events occurred. Wills in Texas are generally probated in the county courts, but in some of the larger counties probate courts handle them. Guardianship matters are also handled by the county courts, or the probate courts in the larger counties. There is no distinction between equity and law cases in Texas. Both are under the jurisdiction of the county courts and the district courts. Records of land transactions can be obtained from the various county clerks.

The *Guide to Public Vital Statistics Records in Texas* (Work Projects Administration, 1941) has some useful information for genealogists. Copies can be found at the Texas State Library and in some other libraries in Texas and some of the larger genealogical libraries elsewhere.

The Texas State Library has a series of indexes to Texas births, deaths, marriages, and divorces even though it does not have the certificates themselves. It also has an index to the Confederate pension applications, an index to the Texas adjutant general's service records from 1836 to 1935, a list of county tax rolls from the early years through the 1970s, many Texas city directories and telephone books, a collection of Texas newspapers, the 1867 voters' registration lists, and an index of the Texas convict ledgers.

Other libraries in Texas that have valuable collections of genealogical records and books for research include the Dallas Public Library, the Fort Worth Public Library, the Houston Public Library, the San Antonio Public Library, the University of Texas Libraries at Austin and San Antonio, and the Rice University Fondren Library at Houston.

Researchers seeking information from county records can locate them at the following county seats: (Anderson County) Palestine, (Andrews County) Andrews, (Angelina County) Lufkin, (Aransas County) Rockport, (Archer County) Archer City, (Armstrong County) Claude, (Atascosa County) Jourdanton, (Austin County) Bellville, (Bailey County) Muleshoe, (Bandera County) Bandera, (Bastrop County) Bastrop, (Baylor County) Seymour, (Bee County) Beeville, (Bell County) Belton, (Bexar County) San Antonio, (Blanco County) Johnson City, (Borden County) Gail, (Bosque County) Meridian, (Bowie County) Boston, (Brazoria County) Angleton, (Brazos County) Bryan, (Brewster County) Alpine, (Briscoe County) Silverton, (Brooks County) Falfurrias, (Brown County) Brownwood, (Burleson County) Caldwell, (Burnet County) Burnet, (Caldwell County) Lockhart, (Calhoun County) Port Lavaca, (Callahan County) Baird, (Cameron County) Brownsville, (Camp County) Pittsburg, (Carson County) Panhandle, (Cass

County) Linden, (Castro County) Dimmitt, (Chambers County) Anahuac, (Cherokee County) Rusk, (Childress County) Childress, (Clay County) Henrietta, (Cochran County) Morton, (Coke County) Robert Lee, (Coleman County) Coleman, (Collin County) McKinney, (Collingsworth County) Wellington, (Colorado County) Columbus, (Comal County) New Braunfels, (Comanche County) Comanche, (Concho County) Paint Rock, (Cooke County) Gainesville, (Coryell County) Gatesville, (Cottle County) Paducah, (Crane County) Crane, (Crockett County) Ozona, (Crosby County) Crosbyton, and (Culberson County) Van Horn.

Also at (Dallam County) Dalhart, (Dallas County) Dallas, (Dawson County) Lamesa, (De Witt County) Cuero, (Deaf Smith County) Hereford, (Delta County) Cooper, (Denton County) Denton, (Dickens County) Dickens, (Dimmit County) Carrizo Springs, (Donley County) Clarendon, (Duval County) San Diego, (Eastland County) Eastland, (Ector County) Odessa, (Edwards County) Rocksprings, (El Paso County) El Paso, (Ellis County) Waxahachie, (Erath County) Stephenville, (Falls County) Marlin, (Fannin County) Bonham, (Fayette County) La Grange, (Fisher County) Roby, (Floyd County) Floydada, (Foard County) Crowell, (Fort Bend County) Richmond, (Franklin County) Mt. Vernon, (Freestone County) Fairfield, (Frio County) Pearsall, (Gaines County) Seminole, (Galveston County) Galveston, (Garza County) Post, (Gillespie County) Fredericksburg, (Glasscock County) Garden City, (Goliad County) Goliad, (Gonzales County) Gonzales, (Gray County) Pampa, (Grayson County) Sherman, (Gregg County) Longview, (Grimes County) Anderson, (Guadalupe County) Seguin, (Hale County) Plainview, (Hall County) Memphis, (Hamilton County) Hamilton, (Hansford County) Spearman, (Hardeman County) Quanah, (Hardin County) Kountze, (Harris County) Houston, (Harrison County) Marshall, (Hartley County) Channing, (Haskell County) Haskell, (Hays County) San Marcos, (Hemphill County) Canadian, (Henderson County) Athens, (Hidalgo County) Edinburg, (Hill County) Hillsboro, (Hockley

County) Levelland, (Hood County) Granbury, (Hopkins County) Sulphur Springs, (Houston County) Crockett, (Howard County) Big Spring, (Hudspeth County) Sierra Blanca, (Hunt County) Greenville, and (Hutchinson County) Stinnett.

Furthermore they can be found at (Irion County) Mertzon, (Jack County) Jacksboro, (Jackson County) Edna, (Jasper County) Jasper, (Jeff Davis County) Fort Davis, (Jefferson County) Beaumont, (Jim Hogg County) Hebbronville, (Jim Wells County) Alice, (Johnson County) Cleburne, (Jones County) Anson, (Karnes County) Karnes City, (Kaufman County) Kaufman, (Kendall County) Boerne, (Kenedy County) Sarita, (Kent County) Jayton, (Kerr County) Kerrville, (Kimble County) Junction, (King County) Guthrie, (Kinney County) Brackettville, (Kleberg County) Kingsville, (Knox County) Benjamin, (La Salle County) Cotulla, (Lamar County) Paris, (Lamb County) Littlefield, (Lampasas County) Lampasas, (Lavaca County) Hallettsville, (Lee County) Giddings, (Leon County) Centerville, (Liberty County) Liberty, (Limestone County) Groesbeck, (Lipscomb County) Lipscomb, (Live Oak County) George West, (Llano County) Llano, (Loving County) Mentone, (Lubbock County) Lubbock, (Lynn County) Tahoka, (Madison County) Madisonville, (Marion County) Jefferson, (Martin County) Stanton, (Mason County) Mason, (Matagorda County) Bay City, (Maverick County) Eagle Pass, (McCulloch County) Brady, (McLennan County) Waco, (McMullen County) Tilden, (Medina County) Hondo, (Menard County) Menard, (Midland County) Midland, (Milam County) Cameron, (Mills County) Goldthwaite, (Mitchell County) Colorado City, (Montague County) Montague, (Montgomery County) Conroe, (Moore County) Dumas, (Morris County) Daingerfield, (Motley County) Matador, (Nacogdoches County) Nacogdoches, (Navarro County) Corsicana, (Newton County) Newton, (Nolan County) Sweetwater, and (Nueces County) Corpus Christi.

And also at (Ochiltree County) Perryton, (Oldham County) Vega, (Orange County) Orange, (Palo Pinto County) Palo Pinto,

(Panola County) Carthage, (Parker County) Weatherford, (Parmer County) Farwell, (Pecos County) Fort Stockton, (Polk County) Livingston, (Potter County) Amarillo, (Presidio County) Marfa, (Rains County) Emory, (Randall County) Canyon, (Reagan County) Big Lake, (Real County) Leakey, (Red River County) Clarksville, (Reeves County) Pecos, (Refugio County) Refugio, (Roberts County) Miami, (Robertson County) Franklin, (Rockwall County) Rockwall, (Runnels County) Ballinger, (Rusk County) Henderson, (Sabine County) Hemphill, (San Augustine County) San Augustine, (San Jacinto County) Coldspring, (San Patricio County) Sinton, (San Saba County) San Saba, (Schleicher County) Eldorado, (Scurry County) Snyder, (Shackelford County) Albany, (Shelby County) Center, (Sherman County) Stratford, (Smith County) Tyler, (Somervell County) Glen Rose, (Starr County) Rio Grande City, (Stephens County) Breckenridge, (Sterling County) Sterling City, (Stonewall County) Aspermont, (Sutton County) Sonora, (Swisher County) Tulia, (Tarrant County) Fort Worth, (Taylor County) Abilene, (Terrell County) Sanderson, (Terry County) Brownfield, (Throckmorton County) Throckmorton, (Titus County) Mount Pleasant, (Tom Green County) San Angelo, (Travis County) Austin, (Trinity County) Groveton, (Tyler County) Woodville, (Upshur County) Gilmer, (Upton County) Rankin, (Uvalde County) Uvalde, (Val Verde County) Del Rio, (Van Zandt County) Canton, (Victoria County) Victoria, (Walker County) Huntsville, (Waller County) Hempstead, (Ward County) Monahans, (Washington County) Brenham, (Webb County) Laredo, (Wharton County) Wharton, (Wheeler County) Wheeler, (Wichita County) Wichita Falls, (Wilbarger County) Vernon, (Willacy County) Raymondville, (Williamson County) Georgetown, (Wilson County) Floresville, (Winkler County) Kermit, (Wise County) Decatur, (Wood County) Quitman, (Yoakum County) Plains, (Young County) Graham, (Zapata County) Zapata, and (Zavala County) Crystal City.

FOR FURTHER INFORMATION SEE:
- Bookstruck, Llowy DeWitt. *Research in Texas.* Arlington, VA: National Genealogical Society, 1992.
- Corbin, John. *Catalog of Genealogical Materials in Texas Libraries.* Austin, TX: Texas State Library and Historical Commission, 1965.

Text Formats *see* **Genealogical Text Formats for Computers**

Tiny Tafels *see* **Genealogical Text Formats for Computers**

Title, Land *see* **Land Records**

Titles of Respect that are generally used today are such terms as Mr., Mrs., Miss, and Ms., as well as designations for those who have achieved a particular educational level or distinction, such as BA, MFA (Master of Fine Arts), Ph.D., MD, or Dr. There are also some titles that indicate particular places in society and that are placed after a person's name, such as CEO (chief executive officer), Mgr. (manager) and Sgt. or Lt. (ranks in the army).

Some titles that appear in early genealogical records that may not be familiar to the average researcher. For example, the terms Mr. and Mrs. were only used for members of the upper classes in early colonial times in America, as they were then used in England, and the terms goodman and goodwife, sometimes shortened to goody, referred to the head and mistress of a household and not to the moral quality of the person being designated.

The title Esquire (Esqr) was used at first only for persons who had the right to bear arms, and anyone with the word "Esquire" at the end of his name was slightly under a knight in social standing. During the same period a person designated as a Gentleman (Gentl^n) would have been a step lower than the one designated as Esquire. But these terms have since become somewhat loose and now, when found, are mainly used for persons of some influence in a community. In the United States, in the old South, planters were given the title Colonel, though this had nothing to do with any military rank. It merely indicated their position in society.

Many other titles that could be cited, but most of their meanings are obvious and present no problem to the genealogist. The value of titles, when found in the records, is that they often provide an additional means by which to distinguish different individuals who use the same given name.

Town Histories *see* **County Histories**

U

Union Veterans and Widows are listed in a special 1890 census that is available at the National Archives in Washington, D.C., as well as at the various National Archives sites around the nation. The listing includes the names of the veterans and/or their widows, the military units in which they served, the local residences for those veterans or widows including their street addresses, and a notation about any war injuries or disabilities. Although not complete, the listing does fill 118 rolls of microfilm. It is organized by states and then alphabetically by counties. Occasionally a Confederate soldier is included in these records, as are most of the Southerners who joined the Union side when the Union armies passed through their local areas. Some black soldiers are identified as members of the United States Colored Troops.

Another listing of those who received pensions for their Civil War service was prepared in 1883 at the direction of the U.S. Congress. This list, "Pensioners on the Roll as of January 1, 1883," primarily includes the Union veterans from the Civil War, but also lists the survivors then living of the War of 1812. These records have the names, locations, certificates or pension file numbers, monthly amounts received, effective dates of the pensions, and reasons for the benefits. *See also* **Pension Claims.**

Unions, Labor *see* **Labor Union Records**

Unitarian and Universalist Records can be found in the archives of the individual churches and at the archives of the Unitarian-Universalist Association in Boston. This Protestant denomination developed out of protests against the prevailing doctrine of the Trinity as held by orthodox Christians. In the early 1800s Hosea Ballou started the Universalist movement in the United States and at about the same time William Ellery Channing established Unitarianism in this country, though advocates of Unitarianism had existed in Europe as early as the 1500s. Both denominations in the United States were centered in New England; the two groups joined together in 1961. They designated Boston as the place for their headquarters.

Over the years this movement has spread to urban areas across the United States and Canada, and there are a few affiliated groups in Europe and Asia. The association's member churches are local, self-governing congregations and fellowships. Records of the history and leaders of this movement can be found at the archives of the Unitarian-Universalist Association in Boston. The archives also has some records of births, marriages, and deaths from individual churches, although not many. These are best located at the various churches where such events took place. There is also archival material at the Meadville Theological School Library in Chicago.

United Church of Christ Records are primarily located at individual churches, although there is a major collection of church documents in the denomination's Boston library, as well as some records in a few university libraries elsewhere. These may include records of baptisms, marriages, burials, lists of communicants, and records of dismissals from the church. This Protestant denomination was officially formed in 1961 when the Congregational Christian Churches and the Evangelical and Reformed Church merged and declared a constitution in force. The Congregational movement traces back to Robert Browne in England, who argued as early as 1582 that the Church of England was too corrupt to be supported by true Christians. He urged that they separate from it and form their own autonomous churches. In the United States Congregationalism dates from 1620, the year that the Pilgrims landed at Plymouth Rock.

The Congregational form of church government is one in which each individual congregation is fully self-governing. Its essential principles, as understood by the New England churches, were codified in "A Platform of Church Discipline" (1648), commonly called the Cambridge Platform, and some of the early theorists of congregationalism were dissenting clergymen such as William Ames, John Cotton, and Thomas Hooker.

The major collection of Congregational records, most of them from New England, is at the Congregational Library in Boston. Here there are approximately 900 separate archival and manuscript collections from the United Church of Christ tradition throughout the world. These collections include local church records, records of ministerial associations and conferences, records of missionary organizations, and records of church women's societies. The library and its archives are particularly useful for documenting three different periods of Congregational history: early Congregational history; the Evangelical revival in early 19th-century Massachusetts; and the formation of the United Church of Christ.

Uruguayan Genealogy records are maintained in the National Archives (Archivo General de la Nación) in Motevideo, established in 1926 from the collection of materials that had been held in the Archivo y Museo Historico National and from various ministries and archives that had records of national interest. South American patriots drove the Spanish colonialists out of Montevideo in 1814. In 1816 Brazil occupied the territory, calling it "Banda Oriental," and incorporated

it into its own national territory in 1821. The Uruguayans proclaimed their independence in 1825, and were recognized as independent following a short war with Brazil in 1828.

Civil registration was instituted in 1879 with the records kept in duplicate, one copy being kept locally and the other going to the Dirección General del Registro Civil in Montevideo. There they are indexed by the year, department, section, and surname.

The parish records in Uruguay provide valuable information for the genealogist and are relatively well preserved. However, there are less than 50 parishes in Uruguay that have any parish records dating before 1900. There is no central location for the records and they have to be located at each of the parish churches. The state began to designate official cemeteries in 1879. The cemetery records located at the sites may provide valuable information for family historians regarding birth and death dates.

Land records from 1900 to the present are stored in the archive of the Oficiana de Catastro in Montevideo. Those before 1900 are in the National Archives. The National Archives also has the census records for Montevideo, La Rosa, Achucarro, Soriano, Cenelones, Minas, San José, Maldonado, Paysandú, Cerro Largo, Tacuarembo, Solto, Durazno, and Villa de la Florida that were conducted in various years from 1726 to 1855.

USENET *see* **Genealogical Mailing Lists and Newsgroups**

Uses of Genealogy for purposes other than the creation of family trees and family histories can be found in the fields of law, historical research, medicine, and genetics. One of the most practical of these is the use of genealogy in a law court when such records are produced to prove a will at times that knowledge of descent must be shown to resolve a family dispute over property left by the deceased.

Historians working in fields that have nothing to do with genealogy often consult published genealogical records to add family history elements to their narratives. At the same time medical doctors have, with considerable success, examined genealogical records to find the origins and nature of unusual hereditary diseases that are sometimes found to recur among families. Geneticists are now sometimes using genealogical data to confirm some of the discoveries that they are making in the process of unraveling the genetic code. *See also* **Science and Genealogy.**

U.S. Geological Survey *see* **Maps**

Utah Records are found in abundance at the Family History Library in Salt Lake City and at the headquarters of the Utah Genealogical Association, also in Salt Lake City. Members of the Church of Jesus Christ of Latter-day Saints, or Mormons, were the first permanent white settlers in Utah. They were led there by Brigham Young during a journey to the West to escape the persecution this religious group had experienced at their several settlements in Ohio, Illinois, and Missouri. The Mormons reached the Great Salt Lake region of Utah in 1847. Although Utah had been claimed by Mexico some years earlier, the United States took over the area in 1848. Congress then designated the area as the Utah Territory in 1850. In 1896 Utah became the 45th state of the Union.

The first national census to include residents of Utah was the 1850 census of the Utah Territory, which then encompassed almost all of Nevada, the western part of Colorado, and the southern section of Wyoming. This and the subsequent national censuses of the state of Utah can be found at the various National Archives centers. A state census taken in 1856 can be found in the Family History Library. The mortality schedules for 1850 to 1880 are at the National Archives.

Copies of birth and death records since 1905 can be obtained from the Office of Vital Records and Health Statistics in Salt Lake City for a small fee. Such records from 1890 to 1904 in Salt Lake City or in Ogden can be provided by the two cities' boards of health, while those that occurred elsewhere in the state during this period can be found in the various county clerks' offices. The state Vital Records Office has only the marriage records since 1978. Earlier ones can be obtained from the county clerks in the counties where the marriage licenses were issued, and all divorce records since 1958 must be obtained from the county clerks where the divorces were granted. The Utah State Archives Research Center in Salt Lake City will provide copies of Utah death certificates that are more than 50 years old, starting in 1904. It also has microfilm copies of most of the birth and death records for the counties of Utah from 1898 to 1905. Wills in Utah are probated by the district courts in each county, as are the guardianship rulings.

The records of land transactions in Utah are held by the various county recorders. Utah distinguishes between equity and law matters, though they can be administered in the same action and are both under the jurisdiction of the county district courts.

The *Guide to the Public Vital Statistics Records in Utah* (Work Projects Administration, 1941) may be helpful in the search for various records in this state. The book can be found at the Family History Library, as well as at some of the larger genealogical libraries in other states. Other places that can provide information about Utah genealogy are the Utah Historical Society and the Utah State Library, both of which are in Salt Lake City.

Researchers seeking information from county records can locate them at the following county seats: (Beaver County) Beaver, (Box Elder County) Brigham City, (Cache County) Logan, (Carbon County) Price, (Daggett County) Manila, (Davis County) Farmington, (Duchesne County) Duchesne, (Emery County) Castle Dale, (Garfield County) Panguitch, (Grand County) Moab, (Iron County) Parowan, (Juab County) Nephi, (Kane County) Kanab, (Millard County) Fillmore, (Morgan County) Morgan, (Piute County) Junction, (Rich County) Randolph, (Salt Lake County) Salt Lake City, (San Juan County) Monticello, (Sanpete County) Manti, (Sevier County) Richfield, (Summit County) Coalville, (Tooele County) Tooele, (Uintah County) Vernal, (Utah County) Provo, (Wasatch County) Heber City, (Washington County) St. George, (Wayne County) Loa, and (Weber County) Ogden.

FOR FURTHER INFORMATION SEE:
• *Directory of Special Information Resources in Utah, 1982.* Salt Lake City, UT: Utah Library Association, 1987.

• Jaussi, Laureen, and Gloria Chaston. *Genealogical Records of Utah.* Salt Lake City, UT: Deseret Book Co., 1974.

V

Venezuelan Genealogy records include the birth, marriage, and death statistics that are recorded in the civil registration process, many ecclesiastical records of the Catholic Church, and many records of notaries that are held in the various federal district offices. The coast of Venezuela was discovered by Christopher Columbus during his third voyage in 1498. Its name, meaning "Little Venice," was given it by reason of the fact that Alonso de Ojeda, who first explored the coast, in 1499, found a small aboriginal village built on piles in one of the gulfs to the west. Venezuela later was one of the three countries that emerged from the collapse of Gran Colombia in 1830 (the others being Colombia and Ecuador). The country is now composed of 20 federal states and a federal district at Caracas, which is the seat of the national government.

Venezuela is somewhat more advanced than most other Latin-American countries in conducting censuses, and national ones have been held in 1873, 1881, 1891, 1920, 1926, 1936, 1941, 1950, 1960, and 1971. None of the records from these is open to researchers at this time.

Venezuela's civil registration began in 1873, and the books of births, marriages, and deaths are kept in duplicate. One copy is held in the various towns and cities where these events took place, and the other is maintained at the Oficina Principal de Registro of the particular federal district that has jurisdiction.

Parish registers kept by the churches have been lost in many cases in Venezuela. However, the diocese of Mérida had done much to preserve the records from the parishes within its jurisdiction, and the archbishopric

of Caracas has a good archive of the records there. The archbishopric has even published a general catalog of its holdings, which include marriage records from 1617 to 1948, wills from 1595 to 1879, and church censuses from 1623 to 1869.

Both the National Archives (Archivo General de la Nacion) and the National Library (Edificio Nueva Sede Foro Liberator) have good collections of materials that may be useful to genealogists, including marriage records and court litigations, historical records from the colonial era, documents of the Venezuelan struggle for independence, and a wide variety of governmental papers. The library has biographical and genealogical documents that are probably of some interest to any family historian dealing with matters in the Republic of Venezuela.

Vermont Records can be found at the library of the Vermont Historical Society in Montpelier, said to have the largest collection of genealogical materials in the state, as well as at the Vermont State Archives and Vermont State Library, both of which are also in Montpelier. Vermont was chiefly an Indian hunting ground before the first white men came. The Algonkian family of Indian tribes claimed the region until bands of Iroquois drove them out in the 1500s. The Algonkians returned during the early 1600s and, with the help of French troops from Canada, defeated the Iroquois. England gained control of Vermont in 1763 and held it as part of New York, but by 1775 the people there were in revolt against the British troops. They declared Vermont to be an independent republic in 1777, and in 1791 Vermont became the 14th state to join the Union.

Vermont residents were enumerated in the first national census of 1890 and from then on in each of the 10-year national censuses. These records can be found at the various National Archives centers. No state censuses are known to have been taken in Vermont, but an early listing of heads of families living in the part of New York that is now Vermont was conducted in 1771. This has been published as the *Vermont 1771 Census*, and can be found at the Vermont Historical Society library. The mortality schedules for this state, from 1850 to 1880, are located at the State Library.

Copies of the records of births, marriages, and deaths since 1955 and divorces since 1968 can be obtained from the Vermont Vital Records office in Burlington for a small fee, or from the town clerks where these events occurred. Earlier records, those from 1764 to 1954, are available from the Vermont Public Records office in Montpelier or, again, from the various town clerks. The public records office also has a wide variety of public records including those involving land, probate, and naturalization matters. The records of wills that have been probated remain with the district courts in each county, though a copy of each will is also recorded in the town clerk's office where the will was originally entered. Guardianship records are in the county probate courts.

There is an index to the vital records of Vermont from the earliest days up to 1870 in the secretary of state's office in Montpelier, as well as an index to the vital records from 1871 to 1908. An index to Vermont cemetery inscriptions from various cemeteries throughout the state can be found at the Historical Society library. This library also has a series of published histories of some of the Vermont churches— Congregational, Baptist, Methodist and Roman Catholic. Some volumes, such as the *History of the Baptists in Vermont*, provide a list of the founding dates for all of the Baptist congregations in Vermont as well as lists of prominent members. The *Inventory of the Town, Village and City Archives of Vermont* includes a directory of churches in Vermont, and an inventory of Protestant Episcopal churches in the diocese of Montpelier.

Land deeds in Vermont have generally been filed with the town clerks, although some have been stored at the county level. The town clerks also have records of deeds recorded in the 1780s but drawn up in the 1760 to 1780 period when Vermont was part of Cumberland and Gloucester counties of New York. There is a strict separation between law and equity cases in the Vermont courts. The equity cases are under the jurisdiction of the chancery courts and the law actions are under the control of the district and county courts.

The State Library has microfilm copies of more than 20 early Vermont newspapers as well as an extensive collection of indexed periodicals. One other library with a good collection of newspapers, as well as family histories and other genealogical data, is the Ilsley Library at Middlebury.

Researchers seeking information from county records can locate them at the following county seats: (Addison County) Middlebury, (Bennington County) Bennington and Manchester, (Caledonia County) St. Johnsbury, (Chittenden County) Burlington, (Essex County) Guildhall, (Franklin County) St. Albans, (Grand Isle County) North Hero, (Lamoille County) Hyde Park, (Orange County) Chelsea, (Orleans County) Newport, (Rutland County) Rutland, (Washington County) Montpelier, (Windham County) Newfane, and (Windsor County) Woodstock.

FOR FURTHER INFORMATION SEE:
- Carleton, Hiram. *Genealogical and Family History of the State of Vermont*. 2 vols. New York: Lewis Publishing Co., 1903.
- Eichholz, Alice. *Collecting Vermont Ancestors*. Montpelier, VT: New Trails, 1986.

Veterans' Records *see* **Military Records**

Virginia Records can be found in the Virginia State Library Archives and at the Virginia State Historical Society, both in Richmond, as well as in various university collections such as those at the University of Virginia in Charlottesville. The first Europeans to settle in Virginia were a group of Spanish Jesuits who established a mission there in 1570, but within a few months the settlement had been destroyed by the Indians whom they were intending to serve. Queen Elizabeth I of England gave Sir Walter Raleigh permission to establish a colony in Virginia in 1584, but his attempt also failed, in this case because the colonists did not have enough supplies. The next attempt at settlement was successful. In 1606, King James I of England chartered the Virginia Company of London to establish the colony of Jamestown. Yet in 1624 the king revoked the Virginia Company's charter and made Virginia a royal colony. The colonists declared their independence from England in 1776 and adopted their own constitution. Virginia became the 10th state of the Union in 1788, and George Washington, a Virginian, became the first president of the United States.

Until 1792 Virginia included what is now the state of Kentucky, and until 1863 it also included what is now West Virginia. The first of the 10-year national censuses of Virginia was that of 1810. The enumerations of all these Virginia censuses can be seen at the various National Archives centers. There has never been a separate state census. The 1850 and 1880 mortality schedules are stored in the Virginia State Library, while the 1860 mortality schedule is in the Duke University Library in Durham, North Carolina.

The Virginia Office of Vital Records in Richmond has the birth and death certificates that have been listed in this state, as well as the marriage licenses and divorce decrees. Genealogists can obtain copies of death, marriage and divorce records for a small fee, if they are more than 50 years older than the date of the event. Copies of birth records must be older than one hundred years. To obtain more recent records of this sort, one must be the next of kin. Copies can also be obtained from the various county clerks in the counties where such events took place. The Virginia State Library Archives in Richmond has copies of the surviving birth and death records for the period 1853 to 1896, and marriage records prior to 1936. It also has Bible, church, census, land, military, and tax records, as well as some lists of passenger arrivals at the ports of Boston and New York.

Wills are probated in Virginia in the county circuit courts, except in incorporated cities that have their own corporation courts. The cities of Richmond, Norfolk, and Roanoke have city chancery courts. Guardianship records can be found in the county courts of equity. Virginia distinguishes between law and equity matters, though both are administered by the same courts. Research in the Virginia counties can be complicated because of idiosyncrasies in the state's court system and because some old Virginia counties have been absorbed by the independent cities. The researcher working in this area would be well advised to consult *A Hornbook of Virginia History* (Virginia State Library, 1965). One can also find good genealogical information at the James Madison University Library in Harrisonburg.

Researchers seeking information from county records can locate them at the following county seats: (Accomack County) Accomac, (Albemarle County) Charlottesville, (Alleghany County) Covington, (Amelia County) Amelia Court House, (Amherst County) Amherst, (Appomattox County) Appomattox, (Arlington County) Arlington, (Augusta County) Staunton, (Bath County) Warm Springs, (Bedford County) Bedford, (Bland County) Bland, (Botetourt County) Fincastle, (Brunswick County) Lawrenceville, (Buchanan County) Grundy, (Buckingham County) Buckingham, (Campbell County) Rustburg, (Caroline County) Bowling Green, (Carroll County) Hillsville, (Charles City County) Charles City, (Charlotte County) Charlotte Court House, (Chesterfield County) Chesterfield, (Clarke County) Berryville, (Craig County) New Castle, (Culpeper County) Culpeper, (Cumberland County) Cumberland, (Dickenson County) Clintwood, (Dinwiddie County) Dinwiddie, (Essex County) Tappahannock, (Fairfax County) Fairfax, (Fauquier County) Warrenton, (Floyd County) Floyd, (Fluvanna County) Palmyra, (Franklin County) Rocky Mount, (Frederick County) Winchester, (Giles County) Pearisburg, (Gloucester County) Gloucester, (Goochland County) Goochland, (Grayson County) Independence, (Greene County) Stanardsville, (Greensville County) Emporia, (Halifax County) Halifax, (Hanover

County) Hanover, (Henrico County) Richmond, (Henry County) Martinsville, (Highland County) Monterey, (Isle of Wight County) Isle of Wight, (James City County) Williamsburg, (King and Queen County) King and Queen Court House, (King George County) King George, and (King William County) King William.

Also at (Lancaster County) Lancaster, (Lee County) Jonesville, (Loudoun County) Leesburg, (Louisa County) Louisa, (Lunenburg County) Lunenburg, (Madison County) Madison, (Mathews County) Mathews, (Mecklenburg County) Boydton, (Middlesex County) Saluda, (Montgomery County) Christiansburg, (Nansemond County) Suffolk, (Nelson County) Lovingston, (New Kent County) New Kent, (Northampton County) Eastville, (Northumberland County) Heathsville, (Nottoway County) Nottoway, (Orange County) Orange, (Page County) Luray, (Patrick County) Stuart, (Pittsylvania County) Chatham, (Powhatan County) Powhatan, (Prince Edward County) Farmville, (Prince George County) Prince George, (Prince William County) Manassas, (Pulaski County) Pulaski, (Rappahannock County) Washington, (Richmond County) Warsaw, (Roanoke County) Salem, (Rockbridge County) Lexington, (Rockingham County) Harrisonburg, (Russell County) Lebanon, (Scott County) Gate City, (Shenandoah County) Woodstock, (Smyth County) Marion, (Southampton County) Courtland, (Spotsylvania County) Spotsylvania, (Stafford County) Stafford, (Surry County) Surry, (Sussex County) Sussex, (Tazewell County) Tazewell, (Warren County) Front Royal, (Washington County) Abingdon, (Westmoreland County) Montross, (Wise County) Wise, (Wythe County) Wytheville, and (York County) Yorktown.

FOR FURTHER INFORMATION SEE:
- Clay, Robert Young. *Virginia Genealogical Resources.* Detroit, MI: Detroit Society of Genealogical Research, 1980.
- Grundset, Eric. *Research in Virginia.* Arlington, VA: National Genealogical Society, 1998.

Vital Records are perhaps the most important statistics with which one can build a family tree. These are, in a sense, the central life events: births, marriages, and deaths. Thus they are prime sources of genealogical information. Every state has an office charged with the responsibility for preserving these records and dispersing copies of them to either the public in general or to authorized persons. Some state offices restrict access to such records by anyone other than family members, and these offices usually don't have records for the years before the states established them. In such cases the records must be sought elsewhere, and searching for them may take some effort. They may be scattered in county courthouses and health departments, in church archives, and in local historical society libraries.

In colonial times, most of the vital statistics were recorded by individual churches. The colony of Virginia passed the first law in the New World that required the collection of vital statistics records. In 1632 the Grand Assembly of Virginia told the ministers or wardens from all the churches to appear in court on the first day of June to show records of their christenings, marriages, and burials for the preceding year. In 1639, the general court of the Massachusetts Bay Colony ordered all the town clerks in that colony to list the actual births and deaths instead of the christenings and burials. This Massachusetts act placed the burden for keeping such records on the civil authorities rather than the church officials. Shortly afterward, Connecticut and some of the other New England colonies did likewise.

In 1644 the Massachusetts colony decided to penalize all those who failed to report such vital events, and in 1692 the legislature required the payment of a registration fee of three pence for each birth, marriage, or death that was reported. This fee allowed for the provision by town clerks of certificates attesting to these events. Fines were also assessed on those who failed to report the happenings.

In other countries the requirement for recording vital statistics moved somewhat slower. By 1883 only a tenth of the world's population lived in areas that had any regular registration of births, marriages, and deaths. The countries that did so included Austria, Bavaria, Belgium, Denmark, England, Finland, France, Norway, Prussia, Saxony, Sweden, and Wales. In most of these countries the registration was done at first by the churches. England and Wales did not begin the systematic registration of vital records until 1837.

The vital records in the United States are not kept on a national level, as they are in Britain and many other European countries. Instead they are largely the responsibility of the individual states. Thus each state has developed its own system of registration, and each state makes its own laws as to how and when such records may be made public.

Perhaps the most important person to influence the way that vital statistics are kept in the United States was Lemuel Shattuck of Massachusetts. He lobbied for a statute in Massachusetts based on England's Registration Act of 1836, which had established a central government registry office with the responsibility to record all births, marriages, and deaths. A similar act was passed by the Massachusetts legislature in 1842 and amended to strengthen it in 1844. This was the first legislation in America to require the establishment of a central filing office and to provide standard forms for recording of the vital records. Shattuck founded the American Statistical Association as a pressure group to work as well for such legislation in other states. *See also* **Birth Records; Death Records; Marriage Records.**

Voting Lists can be helpful in tracking individuals because they usually include names, addresses, telephone numbers, party affiliations, and dates of birth. Some of them also may have the date of a voter's first registration, citizenship data, physical description, and his or her Social Security number. Such records are usually located in county offices, though they may have been transferred to state archives. Accessibility to such registers depends upon the laws of each state, although in most cases the intent is to have them open to public inspection. Some states will even release voter registration information over the telephone; others require a request in writing or a personal visit.

Prior to 1906, each state has its own residence requirements for the eligibility of aliens to vote. In the 1880s, some 18 states only required that aliens file a declaration of intention to become citizens in order to have voting privileges. But by 1905, this number had been reduced to nine: the states of Arkansas, Indiana, Kansas, Michigan, Missouri, Nebraska, Oregon, Texas, and Wisconsin. Then, after 1906, proof of citizenship was required in every state before any immigrant could vote.

Most states did not allow women to vote until the Nineteenth Amendment to the Constitution was passed in 1920, and American Indians did not gain voting rights in all the states until 1948. Furthermore, several Southern states tried to deprive African-Americans of their voting rights through a series of state laws that were later declared unconstitutional by the Supreme Court. One of these laws required that voters pay a poll tax, the cost of which kept most blacks and poor whites from registering. Another was the requirement that all voters must pass a literacy test in order to have the right to vote. Congress and the Supreme Court banished such tests in 1970. Today only those adults who suffer severe mental illness or retardation, or those who have been convicted of certain crimes are denied the right to vote. Voting records are usually kept for only five years, though some counties will have voting records that go back much earlier.

W

Wales *see* **Welsh Genealogy**

Washington State Records can be found in the Washington State Archives and Washington State Library in Olympia, as well as in various public libraries such as the one in

Seattle. Many Indians lived in the Washington area before the first whites arrived. They included the Cayuse, Colville, Nez Perce, Okanogan, Spokane, and Yakima tribes east of the Cascade mountains, and the Chinook, Clallum, Clatsop, Nisqually, Nooksak, and Puyallup tribes west of the Cascades. The Lewis and Clark expedition reached the Washington area in 1805 and a British-Canadian fur trading post was established near present-day Spokane in 1810. A treaty between the United States and Great Britain set Washington's northern boundary at the 49th parallel in 1846. By 1853 Congress had designated the Washington Territory, and by 1889 Washington had become the 42nd state.

The 1860 national census of the Washington Territory, which included the present state of Washington and what later became the Idaho Territory and small parts of Montana and Wyoming, can be found at the various National Archives centers, as can the 1870 territorial census and the subsequent Washington state censuses that were taken every 10 years. A series of state censuses was conducted almost every year, from 1856 to 1892, each time in different counties. These state censuses are preserved at the Washington State Archives. The auditor census rolls that were compiled by the county assessors for these census records from 1871 to 1892 are in the State Library as well as in the Seattle Public Library. An 1849 Oregon territorial census includes what is now Washington state; it can be found at both the Oregon State Archives in Salem and the Oregon Historical Society in Portland. The mortality schedules from 1860 to 1880 are at the Washington State Library.

Birth and death records since 1907, and marriage and divorce records since 1968, can be obtained from the Department of Health Center for Vital Records in Olympia for a small fee. Earlier records of these events can be obtained from the county auditors in the counties where the births and deaths took place or where the marriage licenses were issued. The earlier divorce records are obtainable from the clerks of the counties where each divorce was granted. For copies of any will, one needs to go to the particular county court that was involved in adjudicating the matter, and for guardianship records one must consult the various county superior courts. Matters relating to land transfers and other land records are handled by the various county auditors. There is no formal distinction between equity and law matters in Washington state.

The Work Projects Administration published the *Guide to the Public Vital Statistics Records in Washington* (1941), and the *Guide to Church Vital Statistics Records in Washington: Preliminary Edition* (1942). Copies can be found at the Washington State Library and at the Washington Historical Society in Tacoma, as well as in some of the larger genealogical libraries in other states.

The Washington State Library has a relatively small genealogy collection that deals only with persons in Washington. It does, however, have microfilm copies of Washington newspapers from nearly all time periods, and the staff is currently cooperating with the State Archives in indexing the census data that has been collected in Washington. It also has an index of Washington deaths from 1907 to 1995 on microfilm, a good collection of city directories, and a name and subject index for persons who have lived in the state.

The Washington State Genealogical Society in Olympia has a collection of cemetery records, church records, newspapers, military records, immigration and naturalization records, and family records that have been found in letters and Bibles. The Seattle Public Library has an extensive collection of books and documents that may be useful to genealogists, as does the Tacoma Public Library.

Researchers seeking information from county records can locate them at the following county seats: (Adams County) Ritzville, (Asotin County) Asotin, (Benton County) Prosser, (Chelan County) Wenatchee, (Clallam County) Port Angeles, (Clark County) Vancouver, (Columbia County) Dayton, (Cowlitz County) Kelso, (Douglas County) Waterville, (Ferry County) Republic, (Franklin County) Pasco, (Garfield County) Pomeroy, (Grant County) Ephrata, (Grays Harbor

County) Montesano, (Island County) Coupeville, (Jefferson County) Port Townsend, (King County) Seattle, (Kitsap County) Port Orchard, (Kittitas County) Ellensburg, (Klickitat County) Goldendale, (Lewis County) Chehalis, (Lincoln County) Davenport, (Mason County) Shelton, (Okanogan County) Okanogan, (Pacific County) South Bend, (Pend Oreille County) Newport, (Pierce County) Tacoma, (San Juan County) Friday Harbor, (Skagit County) Mount Vernon, (Skamania County) Stevenson, (Snohomish County) Everett, (Spokane County) Spokane, (Stevens County) Colville, (Thurston County) Olympia, (Wahkiakum County) Cathlamet, (Walla Walla County) Walla Walla, (Whatcom County) Bellingham, (Whitman County) Colfax, (Yakima County) Yakima.

FOR FURTHER INFORMATION SEE:
- *Genealogical Resources in Washington State: A Guide to Genealogical Records Held at Repositories, Government Agencies and Archives.* Olympia, WA: Washington Division of Archives and Records Management, 1983.
- Tacoma-Pierce County Genealogical Society. *Bibliography of Washington State Historical Society Library.* 3 vols. Tacoma, WA: The Society, [n.d.]

Websites *see* **Genealogical Websites; World Wide Web**

Welfare Records *see* **Public Welfare Records**

Welsh Genealogy prior to 1536, when Wales and England came under the same administration, is only an oral tradition that affixes a family heritage to one or more of the Roman-British intermarriages of the fifth century A.D. For example, Magnus Maximus, the governor of Roman Wales, has been hailed as an ancestor to several Welsh princes, even though this Roman ruler ended in disgrace after his soldiers were defeated when they tried to install him as emperor of Rome in A.D. 385.

Because Wales has been linked to England for so long, many Welsh records and family papers can be found in libraries in both Wales and England. Many of the most interesting among these Welsh records are at the National Library of Wales in Aberystwyth. The researcher in Welsh genealogy should also look for other records in the Kew Public Record Office and in the London Public Record Office.

Beginning in September 1538, it was incumbent upon every parish in Wales to keep a register of baptisms, marriages, and burials. Some of these registers still survive from the 16th century, but for most parishes they only exist from the 17th or 18th centuries. These registers frequently give the names, dates, places, ages, parents, and relationships of those listed. The National Library of Wales has registers for over four hundred of the parishes, and others can be found in the appropriate county record offices.

Civil registration of births, marriages and deaths began in 1837, but because there was no penalty for any failure to register until 1875, there are probably many omissions. These records were sent quarterly to the Welsh area record offices in Clwyd, Dyfed, Glamorgan, Gwent, Gwyneed, and Powys where indexes of them were compiled. These indexes can be seen at the National Library. The events were recorded separately and not by family name, so each entry has to be located in the quarterly alphabetical indexes of births, marriages, or deaths. The birth certificates give the date and place of birth, the name and occupation of the father, the name and maiden name of the mother, and the name and address of the registration informant. The marriage certificates give the names and ages of the contracting parties, their marital status and addresses, the names and occupations of their fathers, the date and place of the marriage, and the names of witnesses. The death certificates record the name, age, date, place, occupation, and cause of death of the deceased.

For the most part the records of nonconformist denominations have not been kept as consistently as those of the established church. The Welsh Calvinistic Methodists (later the Presbyterian Church of Wales), the Congregationalists, and the Countess of Huntingdon's Connection were especially popular nonconformist groups. The surviving registers of some 1,350 Welsh nonconformist chapels (estimates suggest there were more than 5,500) can be found at the Public Record Office in London, though microfilm copies of these registers are located at some of the county record offices. The records of Welsh Quakers are at the London Public Records Office or at Friends House in London.

The wills and other probate records of Wales, proved before 1858, were handled in the court of the archdeacon, bishop, or archbishop who had jurisdiction over the place where a deceased died or held property. Those wills were generally filed among the records of the court, though a register copy was also made. Many of these documents survive among family archives in the various record offices, as well as at the National Library of Wales and the Public Records Office in London. Copies of most of the wills administered after 1858 can be found at the National Library.

The National Library also has copies of the weekly newspapers founded in Swansea in 1804 and Carmarthen in 1810, as well as copies of many other Welsh newspapers. This library is one of the six in the British Isles that has the privilege of receiving a copy of every book published in Britain. A large number of valuable genealogical manuscripts have also been donated to the National Library by various individuals. Furthermore, it has a collection of electoral registers, town and county directories, land deeds, and military records.

School records in Wales survive from the mid–19th century in the various county record offices. They include admission registers for the pupils, giving their names and the addresses of their parents. Some teachers' log books provide more information about individual pupils. Most of the county record offices also have the maps that were produced in response to the Tithe Commutation Act of 1836 requiring all land owners to pay tithes based on the value of their land. These maps, many of them photocopies, are accompanied by lists of the apportionments. Copies of them can also be found at the National Li-

brary and at the London Public Record Office. The apportionment lists give the names of landowners, names of those occupying the land, the names and descriptions of the property, the quantity of land and state of cultivation, and the amount of rent-charge payable in lieu of tithes.

The National Library and the libraries of the University of Wales at Bangor, the University of Wales at Lampeter, and the University of Wales at Swansea have collections of family and estate records, some of which date from the 13th century, as well as records of local businesses and industries, political parties, and trade unions in Wales. Other useful genealogical manuscripts can be found at the British Museum Library in London.

The researcher who works in the field of Welsh genealogy needs to have some knowledge of the Welsh language, and particularly of Welsh surnames. In many cases one will find writing in both English and Welsh in the same document. Thus a Welsh/English dictionary will be useful.

Hereditary surnames did not come into general use in Wales until the 16th and 17th centuries. Before this, the Welsh used the patronymic system in which a son was given his father's name with the addition of a word meaning son of (mab, map, ab, or ap). Thus one will find records for Dafydd ap Gwilym, Hywel ab Owain, and Thomas ab William, all of which indicate these were the sons of Gwilym, Owain, and William. Furthermore, the names Dafydd and Gwilym may be recorded at a different point in the same document by their English forms, David and William. Add to this the fact that there are hundreds of persons named David or William living in the same counties of Wales at much the same time and one soon realizes that tracing family lines in Wales can be confusing. One also has to be alert to variant spellings. For example, the name Gruffud eventually became Gruffydd, then Griffith, and finally the surname Griffiths. *See also* **Census, British.**

West Virginia Records can be found at the West Virginia State Archives and History

Library in Charleston and at the Marshall University Library in Huntington. White settlers began to arrive in this area about 1727 when it was mostly used by Indians as their hunting grounds. The tribes included the Cherokee, Conoy, Delaware, Shawnee, and Susquehanna. None of them, however, claimed the rugged area as a permanent home. The Indians often attacked the white settlers because they were rapidly taking over these hunting grounds, and although King George III refused to let the colonists take land west of the Alleghenies until treaties could be negotiated with the Indians, the Scotch-Irish, Germans, and Dutch ignored this order. From the first, Virginia and West Virginia were combined as the Virginia Colony. Yet by the beginning of the American Revolution people in the western area were sending petitions to Congress asking for a separate government, and at the start of the Civil War in 1861, the counties of western Virginia refused to secede from the Union with the rest of Virginia. They thus formed the state of West Virginia in 1863, the 35th state to join the Union.

Until the 1870 national census, West Virginia residents were enumerated with those of Virginia; their census records from 1810 through 1860 can be found among the Virginia census records at the various National Archives centers. There have never been any separate state censuses taken in West Virginia. The mortality schedules for 1860, 1870, and 1880 can be found at the West Virginia State Archives and History Library in Charleston.

The West Virginia Vital Registration Office in Charleston has birth and death records since 1917, marriage records since 1921, and divorce records since 1968. Copies may be obtained for a small fee. A fire in 1921 destroyed many of these records. Earlier birth, marriage, and death records can be obtained from the clerks of the various county courts where these events occurred, while earlier divorce records can be obtained from the county clerks of the circuit court, chancery side. Wills that have been probated are in the county courts, while the guardianship records are in the chancery sections of the county circuit courts. Land transactions can be found in the county courts. There is no distinction between law and equity matters in West Virginia. Both are under the jurisdiction of the district courts.

The Work Projects Administration published the *Inventory of Public Vital Statistics Records in West Virginia: Births, Deaths, and Marriages* (1941), and the *Guide to Church Vital Statistics Records in West Virginia* (1942). These books can be found in the State Archives and History Library, as well as in some of the larger genealogical libraries in other states. The State Archives and History Library has guides on research in adoptions, civil war records, revolutionary war records, and state government records. It also has various manuscripts, microforms, photographs, naturalization records, maps, state government records, and county court records on microfilm.

The Marshall University Library in Huntington has a good collection of genealogy and local history materials in its special collections department on the third floor. The library also publishes a guide to researching genealogy in its collections, and the staff is helpful in locating the materials listed in this guide. Another library that should not be overlooked for genealogical materials is the West Virginia University Library in Morgantown.

Researchers seeking information from county records can locate them at the following county seats: (Barbour County) Philippi, (Berkeley County) Martinsburg, (Boone County) Madison, (Braxton County) Sutton, (Brooke County) Wellsburg, (Cabell County) Huntington, (Calhoun County) Grantsville, (Clay County) Clay, (Doddridge County) West Union, (Fayette County) Fayetteville, (Gilmer County) Glenville, (Grant County) Petersburg, (Greenbrier County) Lewisburg, (Hampshire County) Romney, (Hancock County) New Cumberland, (Hardy County) Moorfield, (Harrison County) Clarksburg, (Jackson County) Ripley, (Jefferson County) Charles Town, (Kanawha County) Charleston, (Lewis County) Weston, (Lincoln County) Hamlin, (Logan County) Logan, (Marion County) Fairmont, (Marshall County) Moundsville, (Mason County) Point

Pleasant, (McDowell County) Welch, (Mercer County) Princeton, (Mineral County) Keyser, (Mingo County) Williamson, (Monongalia County) Morgantown, (Monroe County) Union, (Morgan County) Berkeley Springs, (Nicholas County) Summersville, (Ohio County) Wheeling, (Pendleton County) Franklin, (Pleasants County) St. Marys, (Pocahontas County) Marlinton, (Preston County) Kingwood, (Putnam County) Winfield, (Raleigh County) Beckley, (Randolph County) Elkins, (Ritchie County) Harrisville, (Roane County) Spencer, (Summers County) Hinton, (Taylor County) Grafton, (Tucker County) Parsons, (Tyler County) Middlebourne, (Upshur County) Buckhannon, (Wayne County) Wayne, (Webster County) Webster Springs, (Wetzel County) New Martinsville, (Wirt County) Elizabeth, (Wood County) Parkersburg, and (Wyoming County) Pineville.

FOR FURTHER INFORMATION SEE:
- McGinnis, Carol. *West Virginia Genealogy: Sources and Resources.* Baltimore, MD: Genealogical Publishing Co., 1988.
- Stewart, Robert Armistead. *Index to Printed Virginia Genealogies.* Baltimore, MD: Genealogical Publishing Co., 1970.

Who's Who guides, found in most libraries, can be of some help in genealogical research, particularly if one is looking for information about persons who distinguished themselves in some particular field. There are volumes such as *Who's Who in Science, Who's Who in Law, Who's Who in Medicine,* and *Who's Who in Government.* Each contains a series of short biographies arranged alphabetically about leading people in the fields the book covers. There are also books about who's who in baseball, who's who in cricket, among African-Americans, who's who in the theater, poetry, music, and who's who in the theater or the movies. Some *Who's Who* titles are devoted to persons in more restricted fields, such as the American Rose Society, the World Council of Churches, American high school students, and Canadian films and television. For the most part all such books can be found in the same section of the library, so it is relatively

easy to examine the titles of all those owned by any particular library.

Some of these guides, such as *Who's Who in America,* are updated every year; others, like *Who Was Who in America,* are less often revised. For all major nations there are also who's who volumes that give the biographies of their various leaders in many fields. Sometimes the biographical material contained in who's who entries may differ from that found in other sources and may even be incorrect. This is because the persons listed have usually prepared, or at least approved, their own entries, so the material tends to be biased in their favor. The companies that publish such volumes are careful not to offend those who are listed, in the hope that they will purchase a copy of the book that contains an entry about them. *See also* **Biographical Dictionaries.**

Wills always are open to public inspection once they have been filed and the person for whom each was written has died. This accessibility enables potential heirs to satisfy themselves that all they might have been entitled to receive in any will has indeed been given to them. Wills are important to genealogists because they usually contain many family references. Although the probate laws may vary from state to state, one can usually find a copy of any will in the particular county courthouse that dealt with it. Since these wills and administrations are usually indexed alphabetically by surnames for the year in which they were processed, it is relatively easy to look them up.

Historically wills have been used since pre–Christian times. Several ancient wills are listed in the records of the time. Sir William M. R. Petrie, the Egyptologist, found a will dated to 2550 B.C. among some papyrus records he excavated some years ago. There are also several wills mentioned in Greek manuscripts, and the Biblical book of Genesis mentions the will of Jacob. Many English wills exist from the time of the Norman Conquest of 1066, written on sheets of parchment.

Most wills in the United States are filed in the county courts where they were probated in conjunction with the testator's place of residence. Most wills are indexed by the name of the deceased. In a few counties, however, there may also be reverse indexes in which names listed are those of the beneficiaries. If this is the case, no researcher should overlook these reverse indexes after an examination of the testator's index.

One needs to learn to discriminate among different kinds of wills. Some have been written with great care and clearly indicate which children are to receive what portions of an estate. Others, particularly some of the older ones, were carelessly composed or hastily drawn up, probably when the testator was dying. In such cases one should not assume that all the children or other heirs were named. Usually, when a person died intestate, the court would order the distribution of property to all the children. But in cases where the court deems that certain of the children had already received their share during the lifetime of the deceased, the filed distribution may not name all the surviving children.

Some of the indexes of wills have been published in books that can be found in genealogical libraries. A case in point is Clayton Torrence's *Virginia Wills and Administrations 1632–1800*, that was published in Baltimore in 1965. It is an index to the early estates in Virginia. Similar indexes have been published for wills in New York State and a number of other states. *See also* **Probate Records.**

Wisconsin Records of genealogical interest can be found at the Wisconsin Historical Society in Madison and at the University of Wisconsin libraries in both Madison and Milwaukee. When the first European explorers arrived in this area, in the early 1600s, Winnebago, Dakota, and Menominee Indians lived there. Many other tribes moved into Wisconsin in the later 1600s, most of them having been driven from their eastern homelands by white settlers. England gained the Wisconsin region from the French in 1763 under the terms of the Treaty of Paris, and in 1783 it became a part of the United States. Congress created the Wisconsin Territory in

1836, and in 1848 Wisconsin became the 30th state of the Union.

Wisconsin was part of the Indiana Territory from 1800 to 1809, part of the Illinois Territory from 1809 to 1818, and part of the Michigan Territory from 1818 to 1836. When it became the Wisconsin Territory, its boundaries extended all the way to the Missouri River and included what later became the Minnesota Territory and a large part of the Dakota Territory. When the first of the 10-year national censuses was taken in Wisconsin, in 1820, the area was included as part of the Michigan Territory records. The same was true for the 1830 census. These national records can be found at the various National Archives centers.

A series of Wisconsin state censuses has been taken for 1836, 1838, 1842, 1846, 1847, 1855, 1865, 1875, 1885, 1895, and 1905. These records can all be found at the Wisconsin Historical Society. Only fragments remain for the 1865 census. Those for Milwaukee County in 1846 and 1847 have been indexed. The University of Wisconsin in Milwaukee has the 1865 records for Ozaukee and Sheboygan counties. The Wisconsin mortality schedules for 1850 to 1880 can be found at the Wisconsin Historical Society.

Birth, death, and marriage certificates for Wisconsin residents since 1907 are located at the Vital Records Office in Madison, where copies can be obtained for a small fee. Those that are dated earlier can be found at the Wisconsin Historical Society, which claims to have one of the largest genealogical collections in the country, including more than 100,000 Wisconsin obituaries and biographical sketches. It also has records of immigration, naturalization, military lists, cemeteries, family histories, local histories, Wisconsin churches, files of Wisconsin newspapers, and a large number of maps. Significant genealogical records can also be found at the Wisconsin State Library in Madison and the library of the University of Wisconsin at Madison.

Three useful Work Projects Administration guides can be found at the Wisconsin Historical Society, and at some other libraries in Wisconsin and in some of the larger genealogical libraries elsewhere. These are the *Guide to Public Vital Statistics Records in Wisconsin* (1941), *Guide to Church Vital Statistics Records in Wisconsin* (1942), and *An Outline of Vital Statistics Laws of Wisconsin* (1941).

Wills and other probate matters in Wisconsin are handled by the county courts, as are divorce matters and guardianships. Copies of divorce records since 1907 can also be found at the Vital Records Office. Records of land transactions are registered with the various county recorders of deeds. There is no distinction between law and equity actions in Wisconsin, and the circuit courts have jurisdiction over all such matters.

Researchers seeking information from county records can locate them at the following county seats: (Adams County) Friendship, (Ashland County) Ashland, (Barron County) Barron, (Bayfield County) Washburn, (Brown County) Green, (Buffalo County) Alma, (Burnett County) Grantsburg, (Calumet County) Chilton, (Chippewa County) Chippewa Falls, (Clark County) Neillsville, (Columbia County) Portage, (Crawford County) Prairie du Chien, (Dane County) Madison, (Dodge County) Juneau, (Door County) Sturgeon Bay, (Douglas County) Superior, (Dunn County) Menomonee, (Eau Claire County) Eau Claire, (Florence County) Florence, (Fond du Lac County) Fond du Lac, (Forest County) Crandon, (Grant County) Lancaster, (Green County) Monroe, (Green Lake County) Green Lake, (Iowa County) Dodgeville, (Iron County) Hurley, (Jackson County) Black River Falls, (Jefferson County) Jefferson, (Juneau County) Mauston, (Kenosha County) Kenosha, (Kewaunee County) Kewaunee, (La Crosse County) La Crosse, (Lafayette County) Darlington, (Langlade County) Antigo, and (Lincoln County) Merrill.

Also at (Manitowoc County) Manitowoc, (Marathon County) Wausau, (Marinette County) Marinette, (Marquette County) Montello, (Menominee County) Keshena, (Milwaukee County) Milwaukee, (Monroe County) Sparta, (Oconto County) Oconto, (Oneida County) Rhinelander, (Outagamie County) Appleton, (Ozaukee County) Port Washington, (Pepin County) Durand, (Pierce County) Ellsworth, (Polk County) Balsam Lake, (Portage County) Stevens Point, (Price County) Phillips, (Racine County) Racine, (Richland County) Richland, (Rock County) Janesville, (Rusk County) Ladysmith, (St. Croix County) Hudson, (Sauk County) Baraboo, (Sawyer County) Hayward, (Shawano County) Shawano, (Sheboygan County) Sheboygan, (Taylor County) Medford, (Trempealeau County) Whitehall, (Vernon County) Viroqua, (Vilas County) Eagle River, (Walworth County) Elkhorn, (Washburn County) Shell Lake, (Washington County) West Bend, (Waukesha County) Waukesha, (Waupaca County) Waupaca, (Waushara County) Wautoma, (Winnebago County) Oshkosh, and (Wood County) Wisconsin Rapids.

FOR FURTHER INFORMATION SEE:
- Danky, James P. *Genealogical Research: An Introduction to the Resources of the State Historical Society of Wisconsin.* Madison, WI: State Historical Society of Wisconsin, 1986.
- Herrick, Linda M. *Wisconsin Genealogical Research Origins.* Janesville, WI: n.p., 1996.

Women, Finding Records of, can be somewhat of a challenge. The task is made difficult because laws and social practices in the past relegated most women to a nearly non-existent status. Married women were considered to be the "property" of their husbands and they had almost no legal rights. They did not buy or sell property, pay taxes, vote, serve in the military, or even leave wills. When women do show up in the records, often their full names are missing and they are listed simply as "wife of" or "daughter of" a male family member. The process in finding such female ancestors is further complicated by multiple marriages and name changes.

The problem has even been compounded by some family historians who have concentrated on male ancestors simply because they carried the family surname from generation to generation. These genealogists left little room in their books or other documents for the women who played an equally important part in the history of such families.

In researching female ancestors, one not only needs to use the records common to all ancestors (censuses, wills, probates, land deeds, passenger lists, naturalization records, church records, etc.), but one also needs to find records that exclusively or primarily concerned women. Fortunately, a wealth of women's social history has been published recently that can be read, studied, and used to fill in some of the missing gaps in a family history. Several hundred books are published each year that focus specifically on the lives of women both in the past and today.

More than 50 current and historical women's magazines and newspapers have published biographical material about women. The titles of some of them are familiar, but the older ones are not so well known, though copies can be found in some libraries. They include *Ladies' Companion* (1840–44), *Woman's Journal* (1870–1916), *Church Woman* (1943–49), *Lucifer: The Light Bearer* (1897–1901), *Eugenesia* (Mexico, 1943–45), and *Black Sash* (South Africa, 1956–72). Early women's liberation periodicals, such as *Shrew*, *Rat*, and *Velvet Fist*, can also be found in a few libraries.

There is, of course, a vast amount of unpublished material about the lives of women. Many libraries, courthouses, universities, and historical societies have collections of unpublished letters, diaries, manuscripts, and other documents. Some of these collections can now be accessed on the Internet, or if the actual documents are not there, then there may be indexes to them and information as to how they may be accessed. The researcher should remember that often women's letters and diaries may be stored in state archives or historical society libraries other than in the state where the women lived.

Following the American Revolution, hundreds of women went to school and became teachers, and after the Civil War, many more thousands of them joined this profession. They taught in elementary schools, boarding schools, normal schools, women's seminaries (many founded in the 1800s), colleges, and even some universities. Records from these schools, if still in existence, may provide a wealth of genealogical information about such teachers. Often a local historical society can be of help in locating the records

of the schools that may have closed. Many states did not allow married women to teach, and so most of these schoolteachers during the 19th century were female, young, and single.

Another source of material about women can be found in the records of women's clubs, lineage and patriotic societies, and school sororities. Very useful genealogical data can sometimes be found in the archives of these organizations. Records are also maintained by the Girl Scouts and Camp Fire Girls; unions, such as the International Ladies Garment Workers; sisterhoods, such as the Eastern Star; women's colleges, such as Barnard and Smith; the American Association of University Women (AAUW); the National Board of the YWCA, and the Planned Parenthood Federation of America.

Midwives' journals are still another source of genealogical data, although this is not an area in which most researchers would probably explore. In the 19th century midwives were far more common than pediatricians and gynecologists. Many of them kept journals, and large numbers of them were in practice. Hospital records may also contain useful information about women that cannot be found elsewhere, as can public welfare records.

Though legislation allowing women to vote was not passed until 1920, some states had permitted them to vote in the mid–1800s. The state and national petitions calling for women's suffrage, stored in some libraries, contain lists of names that can be linked to various family trees, as do the voter registration lists.

For further information see:
- Carmack, Sharon DeBartolo. *A Genealogist's Guide to Discovering Your Female Ancestors: Special Strategies for Uncovering Hard-to-Find Information About Your Female Lineage.* Cincinnati: Betterway Books, 1998.
- Schaefer, Christina K. *The Hidden Half of the Family: A Sourcebook for Women's Genealogy.* Baltimore: Genealogical Publishing Co., 1999.

See also **Medical Records; Public Welfare Records.**

Word Abbreviations are found throughout genealogical records. The practice of abbreviating is most commonly used in the earliest English and American records, probably as a carry-over from the practice of abbreviating the Latin texts that were once used in all official documents. In most cases the abbreviations are recognizable, but the same word can often be abbreviated in several ways. Here are some typical examples:

about —ca. (*circa*)
according — accotd^g
account or accompt — acco^t, acc^t
acre or acres— a.
administration — admin^{ion}, admon., admon:
administrator — admin^r
aforesaid — afors^d, fors^d, afors:, afsd.
aged — ae, aet
also known as— a.k.a.
and —&
and so forth —&c, etc.
baptized — bp.
born — b.
birthplace — b.p., b.pl.
captain —capt^n, capt:
cemetery —cem.
church —chh
christened —chr.
daughter — dau, dau^r
deceased — dec^d
deed book — D.B.
died — d.
died without issue — d.s.p (*decessit sine prole*)
died young — d.y.
ditto— do, d^o
Esquire — Esq;, Esqr, Esq.
executor — exec^r, ex^r, ex^{or}, exor:
executrix — exec^x, ex^x, ex^{ix}
Gentleman — Gentl^n. Gent:, Gent.
gravestone — g.s.
honorable — hon^{ble}. hon:
improvement — improvem^t, improv^t
inventory — invent^y, inv:
Junior — Junr, J^r, Jun:
Minister of the Gospel — M.G.
mother of — m/o
namely — viz, viz: vizt (videlicet)
near — nr.
no date — n.d.
paid — p^d

pair — p^r
per — p^r
personal — person^l, p'son^l
probate — prob^t
received — rec^d, recv^d
receipt — rec^t
record — rec^d
register — reg^r, regist^r
said — s^d
Senior — Senr, S^r, Sen:
son of — s/o
testament — testam^t, testa:
the — ye, y^e

As one can see, most of these abbreviations have been formed by merely shortening the word, but some have been formed by inserting an apostrophe to produce a contraction (p'son^l).

If one has difficulty interpreting a particular abbreviation, examine the context of the writing and look further in the text for other examples that may give a clue. In preparing a genealogy, try not to use abbreviations. But if you do use them, be sure to use the same form of abbreviation in every case. *See also* **Name Abbreviations.**

Work Projects Administration *see* **WPA Records**

Works Progress Administration *see* **WPA Records**

World Wide Web, usually designated by its initials as WWW, or "the Web," is an array of resources that can be accessed by computers linked to the Internet. These resources are organized by a hypertext system that allows the computer user to move easily from one resource to another, even though they may be stored on a variety of different computers. With the aid of computer programs known as browsers, the user can access pages of text, pictures of all sorts, music or other sounds, and other types of information that appear on the computer screen when a user points to links on the screen that bring forward the desired objects.

The Web was developed in 1989 by Timothy Berners-Lee, a British computer scientist, for the purpose of sharing information among scientists working in the field of high-energy physics at the CERN research facility near Geneva, Switzerland. Within a short time of its development, universities and businesses were availing themselves of the ability of the Web to transfer large amounts of information among their departments and from one institution to another. Not long afterward many ordinary computer users were accessing the Web to communicate with other users all over the world. The further development of the Web has been guided by the WWW Consortium based at Massachusetts Institute of Technology.

The hypertext system used on the Internet allows a reader to jump at will to related sites and from any point on the screen rather than having to read a text from beginning to end before moving on, as one usually does when reading a book. Hypertext was the brain child of Ted Nelson, an early computer visionary. According to Nelson, "the ultimate hypertext goal is the global accumulation of knowledge.... It should be a universal publishing system where every interested person has direct access to humanity's accumulated knowledge — in effect, the ultimate publishing system where each person is both contributor and user."

Databases now exist on the Internet that index and provide the texts of thousands of medical journals published annually throughout the world. Others catalogue the minute details of archaeological investigations at hundreds of sites. Still others store a multiple number of maps, charts, and satellite and aerial photographs. There is even a database managed by the University of California that includes all the known Greek texts up to A.D. 600. The amount of information on the Internet is now in fact so large and comprehensive that no human being or even a group of human beings could hope to read through it within an average lifetime. The Web has given those with personal computers the potential to access much more information than exists in the average local library.

Although the Internet is a fantastic tool for finding information, one needs to remember not to take everything found there as documented truth; anything that seems the least bit doubtful should be verified. This is particularly important in the case of the dates and places one finds in Web pages of material related to genealogy. One can usually verify this information by emailing those who posted the pages to ask for their sources.

Besides the World Wide Websites hosted by state vital records offices, the local information links hosted by genealogy associations, and the catalog indexes hosted by college and public libraries, one may find many family trees posted at various Websites. It is not difficult to publish such trees online. Making such a family tree available for others to view can be a great way to get in touch with those who may be researching the same family name, and doing so can be most helpful to other genealogists, but such Websites need to be updated frequently, whenever new information is collected. Unfortunately, many old and outdated pages are often found as one surfs the World Wide Web.

WPA Records were compiled by the Works Progress Administration (WPA), which was renamed the Work Projects Administration in 1939. This was one of the programs created during the depths of the Great Depression of the 1930s to relieve unemployment. It was part of President Franklin D. Roosevelt's New Deal, and it was established under the authority of the Emergency Relief Appropriation Act of 1935. The WPA was designed as a nation-wide program of "small useful projects" to provide employment for needy, but employable workers. About 85 percent of the funds spent on the various WPA programs went directly into wages and salaries.

Of all the New Deal programs, the Works Progress Administration is the most famous because it affected so many people's lives. During its existence it employed more than 8.5 million persons who worked for an average salary of $41.57 a month. The WPA employees built 651,087 miles of highways, and repaired or improved 124,031 bridges, 125,110 public buildings, 8,192 public parks, and 853 airport landing fields. They also engaged in slum clearance, reforestation, and rural rehabilitation. The program furthermore supported tens of thousands of artists by funding the creation of 2,566 murals and 17,744 pieces of sculpture that decorate public buildings nationwide. The art, theater, music, and writing programs that were sponsored by the WPA eventually resulted in the creation of the present-day National Foundation for the Arts and National Endowment for the Humanities.

Under the leadership of Harry Hopkins, an enthusiastic ex–social worker who had come from modest means, the WPA eventually allocated more than $11 million in employment relief before it was canceled in 1943. The work relief program was more expensive than direct relief payments would have been, but it was worth the added cost, Hopkins observed. "Give a man a dole, and you save his body but destroy his spirit. Give him a job and you save both body and spirit."

The Federal Writers' Project, which was one of the programs sponsored by the WPA, prepared state and regional guide books, organized and compiled the records of archives, indexed newspapers, and conducted useful sociological and historical investigations. In all, the Federal Writers Project employed 6,686 writers at its peak in April 1936, and engaged in active projects in every one of the then 48 states and the District of Columbia. It had produced some 800 titles by October 1941, and printed some 3.5 million copies. It is best-known for its American Guide Series that produced comprehensive guidebooks for every state, as well as Alaska, Guam, Puerto Rico, and Washington, D.C. To this day, the American Guide Series constitutes the most comprehensive encyclopedia of Americana ever published; several of the volumes have been reissued recently, some in updated form.

The Federal Writers Historical Records Survey resulted in the publication of a series of guides to the vital statistics records found in the county courthouses and church archives of 39 states. For some states several volumes contained both civil and church-related records that genealogists will find of value. The various books can be found in state and county libraries, as well as in some of the larger genealogical libraries.

A caveat regarding the use of these WPA records: The information they contain was current at the time (the early 1940s), but is now often dated. This in no way detracts from the basic value of these works or from the monumental task completed by the WPA archivists of the Depression years.

Wyoming Records are mainly found in the Wyoming State Archives and Library in Cheyenne. Indian hunters lived in the Wyoming area at least 11,000 years ago. When the first white settlers arrived there in the early 1800s they found Arapaho, Bannock, Blackfeet, Cheyenne, Crow, Flathead, Nez Percé, Shoshoni, Sioux, and Ute families throughout the area. A thriving fur trade with the Indians was soon established, and Fort Bridger was erected. The Union Pacific Railroad entered Wyoming in 1867, and Congress designated the Wyoming Territory in 1869. In 1890 Wyoming became the 44th state.

The 1850 national census included the residents of Wyoming with the enumeration of Utah, and the 1860 census included them as part of the Nebraska Territory. Then in the 1870 and 1880 censuses they were listed in the Wyoming Territory. These censuses can all be seen at the various National Archives sites. The only state census that has been taken was one in 1869 that can be found in the Wyoming Archives. It included the names of all the family members. Mortality schedules of 1870 and 1880 are stored at the State Law Library in Cheyenne.

The Wyoming Vital Records Services office in Cheyenne has records of births and deaths since 1909 and marriage and divorce records since 1941. It will provide birth certificates to the specific individual named if he or she is over 18 years of age, to either parent of the one named on the certificate, to a lawyer representing the named individual, or to a legal guardian for a small fee. Death certificates may be obtained by immediate family members or by lawyers representing them. Marriage and divorce records may be obtained by either party or by a lawyer acting on their behalf. For earlier marriage and divorce records one should contact the county clerks in the counties where the events took place. That is where one will also find probated wills, guardianship records, and land records for the counties of Wyoming. There is no distinction between law and equity matters in the district courts.

Death, marriage, and divorce records over 50 years old can also be found at the State Archives and Library. These records may be obtained by anyone providing enough information to locate the record in question. The library also has copies of the census records from 1870 to 1920, newspapers on microfilm (not indexed), heritage books, city directories from 1884 to the present, family history books, and photo collections. The Laramie County Library, also in Cheyenne, has county record books, census indexes, and a number of published genealogies. The researcher will also find considerable genealogical information at the University of Wyoming Heritage Center in Laramie.

The Work Projects Administration issued *Guide to Public Vital Statistics Records in Wyoming* (1941) and *Guide to Vital Statistics Records in Wyoming: Church Archives* (1942). Both volumes are available at the State Library, Laramie County Library, and in some other libraries in Wyoming, as well as in some genealogical libraries elsewhere.

Researchers seeking information from county records can locate them at the following county seats: (Albany County) Laramie, (Big Horn County) Basin Springs, (Campbell County) Gillette, (Carbon County) Rawlings, (Converse County) Douglas, (Fremont County) Lander, (Goshen County) Torrington, (Hot Springs County) Thermopolis, (Johnson County) Buffalo, (Laramie County) Cheyenne, (Lincoln County) Kemmerer, (Natrona County) Casper, (Niobrara County) Lusk, (Park County) Cody, (Platte County) Wheatland, (Sheridan County) Sheridan, (Sublette County) Pinedale, (Sweetwater County) Green River, (Teton County) Jackson, (Uinta County) Evanston, (Washakie County) Worland, and (Weston County) Newcastle.

FOR FURTHER INFORMATION SEE:
- Donahue, Jim, ed. *Guide to the County Archives of Wyoming.* Cheyenne, WY: Wyoming State Archives, 1991.
- Spiros, Joyce V. H. *Genealogical Guide to Wyoming.* Gallup, NM: Verlene Publisher, 1982.

Y

Yugoslavian Records *see* **Eastern European Genealogy**

Yukon Records are located at the Yukon Archives at Whitehorse, which is next to Yukon College. This archive is responsible for acquiring, preserving, and making available documentary sources related to Yukon history, cultures, and development. A British fur trader, Robert Campbell, was the first white person to explore the Yukon region on behalf of the Hudson's Bay Company. He set up a trading post there, but it was looted and burned a short time later by Chilkat Indians. In 1896 gold was discovered there on a tributary of the Klondike River, resulting in a large influx of miners during the Klondike Gold Rush of 1897 and 1898. By 1898 there were an estimated 35,000 persons living in the Yukon Territory. Within a few years, most of the surface gold had been exhausted and the miners drifted away. The town of Whitehorse eventually had railroad service, and became the distributing point for the entire territory. Whitehorse was designated as the capital of the Yukon Territory of Canada in 1951.

The Yukon Archives maintains a library of over 21,000 volumes for reference in its reading room. It also offers a periodic lecture series, film showings, displays, radio broadcasts, and newspaper articles on selected topics in Yukon history. Those who live in the

Yukon are encouraged to deposit business and society records, family papers, diaries, photographs, church and school records, political papers, and other memorabilia in the archives for permanent preservation. Documents from the archives' central registry date back to 1896 and pertain to a wide range of subjects, including education, elections, wildlife, transportation, legislation, and land. Among the territorial records are territorial and Gold Commissioner's Court records, and estate files of the public administrator.

The archives has the records of various Yukon organizations, associations, and businesses. These include the papers of the White Pass and Yukon Route, 1899–1960, documenting river, rail and land operations; correspondence and dredging records of the Yukon Gold Company, 1907–1920; records of the Whitehorse Chapter of the Arctic Brotherhood, 1901–1903; Yukon Order of Pioneer records, 1886–1980; Anglican Church Diocese of Yukon records, 1898–1988; Whitehorse Chamber of Commerce records, 1945–1981; Yukon Sourdough Rendezvous files, 1963–1978; Yukon Teachers Association records, 1955–1969; Imperial Order Daughters of the Empire records, 1903–1979; Whitehorse Drama Club files, 1946–1972; Whitehorse Copper records, 1964–1979; Arctic Winter Games records, 1970–1988; and Taylor and Drury Mayo Branch records, 1919–1960.

The newspaper collection consists of over 50 different journals, including the *Dawson News*, 1899–1953; *Klondike Nugget*, 1898–1903; *Yukon Sun*, 1899–1904; *Whitehorse Star*, 1901 to date, and other early Yukon newspapers in their original form and on microfilm. Birth, marriage, and death records for the Yukon can be found at the Vital Statistics Office in Whitehorse. *See also* **Census, Canadian.**

Z

Zip and Unzip Files *see* **Computer Genealogy Files**

ADDRESS LIST

This list is arranged under four major headings — United States, Canada, United Kingdom and Ireland, Other Countries — and subarranged alphabetically, by states, provinces and countries.

United States

ALABAMA

Alabama Center for Health Statistics
P.O. Box 5625
Montgomery, AL 36103

American College of Heraldry
Drawer CG, University of Alabama
Tuscaloosa, AL 35486

Alabama Department of Archives and History
624 Washington Avenue
Montgomery, AL 36130

Samford University Library
800 Lakeshore Drive
Birmingham, AL 35229

ALASKA

Alaska Bureau of Vital Statistics
P.O. Box 110675
Juneau, AK 99811

Alaska State Archives and Records Management
141 Willoughby Avenue
Juneau, AK 99801

Alaska State Library
P.O. Box 110571
Juneau, AK 99811

National Archives Pacific Alaska Region
(Anchorage)
254 West Third Avenue
Anchorage, AK 99501

ARIZONA

Arizona Department of Library, Archives, and
Public Records
State Capitol, Suite 442, 1700 West Washington
Phoenix, AZ 85007

Arizona Historical Society Research Library
949 E. 2nd Street
Tucson, AZ 85719

Arizona State Museum
1013 East University Blvd.
Tucson, AZ 85721

Charles Trumbull Heyden Library
Arizona State University
Tempe, AZ 85287

University of Arizona Library
1510 East University
Tucson, AZ 85721

ARKANSAS

Arkansas History Commission and State
Archives
One Capitol Mall
Little Rock, AR 72201

Arkansas State Library
One Capitol Mall
Little Rock, AR 72201

Division of Vital Records, Arkansas Department
of Health
4815 West Markham Street
Little Rock, AR 72201

Orphan Train Heritage Society
614 East Emma Ave. #115
Springdale, AR 72764

CALIFORNIA

Bancroft Library
University of California
Berkeley, CA 94720

California Department of Health Services
601 North 7th Street
Sacramento, CA 94234

California Genealogical Society
300 Brannan Street, Suite 409
San Francisco, CA 94107

California State Archives
1020 "O" Street
Sacramento, CA 95814

California State Library
Library and Courts Building 1, 814 Capital Mall
Sacramento, CA 95814

California State Railroad Museum Library
111 I Street
Sacramento, CA 95814

Huntington Library and Art Gallery
1151 Oxford Road
San Marino, CA 91108

National Archives Pacific Region (Laguna Niguel)
24000 Avila Road
Laguna Niguel, CA 92677

National Archives Pacific Region (San Bruno)
1000 Commodore Drive
San Bruno, CA 94066

Office of Vital Records
901 Commerce Street, P.O. Box 730241
Sacramento, CA 94244

COLORADO

Colorado State Archives
1313 Sherman Street, Room 1B–20
Denver, CO 80203

Denver Public Library
10 West 14th Avenue Parkway
Denver, CO 80204

National Archives Rocky Mountain Region
(Denver)
Denver Federal Center, Building 48
Denver, CO 80225

CONNECTICUT

Connecticut Department of Public Health, Vital
Records Section
150 Washington Street
Hartford, CT 06106

Connecticut Historical Society
1 Elizabeth Street
Hartford, CT 06105

Connecticut State Library
231 Capitol Avenue
Hartford, CT 06106

DELAWARE

Bureau of Vital Statistics, Division of Public
Health
P.O. Box 637
Dover, DE 19903

Delaware Genealogical Society
505 Market Street Mall
Wilmington, DE 19801

Delaware Public Archives
Hall of Records
Dover, DE 19901

Historical Society of Delaware
505 Market Street Mall
Wilmington, DE 19801

DISTRICT OF COLUMBIA

Board for Certification of Genealogists
1307 New Hampshire Avenue, N.W.
Washington, DC 20036

Bureau of Indian Affairs
1951 Constitution Avenue NW
Washington, DC 20245

Bureau of Medicine and Surgery
2300 E Street NW
Washington, DC 20372

Commandant of the U.S. Coast Guard
Washington, DC 20590

DAR Library
1776 D Street, N.W.
Washington, DC 20006

Immigration and Naturalization Service
425 I Street NW
Washington, DC 20536

Local History and Genealogy Reading Room
Library of Congress
Jefferson Building LJ G20
Washington, DC 20540

National Archives and Records Administration
8th and Pennsylvania Ave. NW
Washington, DC 20408

Society of the Cincinnati
2118 Massachusetts Ave. NW
Washington, D.C., 20008

U.S. Government Printing Office
732 N. Capitol Street, NW
Washington, D.C. 20401

U.S. Holocaust Memorial Museum
100 Raoul Wallenberg Place, SW
Washington, D.C. 20024

FLORIDA

Florida State Archives, R. A. Gray Building
500 South Bronough Street
Tallahassee, FL 32399

Florida State Historical Society
1320 Highland Avenue
Melbourne, FL 32935

Florida State Library, R. A. Gray Building
500 South Bronough Street
Tallahassee, FL 32399

GEORGIA

Confederate Pension and Record Department
401 State Capitol
Atlanta, GA 30334

Georgia Historical Society
501 Whitaker Street
Savannah, GA 31401

Georgia State Genealogical Society
P.O. Box 54575
Atlanta, GA 30308

Georgia State Library
156 Trinity Avenue, S.W.
Atlanta, GA 30303

Georgia Vital Records Service
47 Trinity Avenue SW
Atlanta, GA 30334

National Archives Southeast Region (Atlanta)
1557 St. Joseph Avenue
East Point GA 30344

HAWAII

Hawaiian Historical Society
560 Kawaiahao Street
Honolulu, HI 96813

Hawaiian State Archives, Department of
    Accounting and General Services
Kekauluohi Building, Iolani Palace Grounds
Honolulu, HI 96813

University of Hawaii Library at Manoa
2550 The Mall
Honolulu, HI 96822

Vital Records Section of the State Department
    of Health
1250 Punchbowl Street
Honolulu, HI 96813

IDAHO

Bureau of Vital Statistics, State House
450 West State Street
Boise, ID 83720

Idaho State Library
325 West State Street
Boise, ID 83702

ILLINOIS

Augustana College
639 38th Street
Rock Island, IL 61201

Booth Library
Eastern Illinois University
600 Lincoln Ave.
Charleston, IL 61920

Brethren Historical Library and Archives
1451 Dundee Avenue
Elgin, IL 60120

Evangelical Lutheran Church of America Archives
8765 West Higgins Road
Chicago, IL 60631

Founders Memorial Library
Northern Illinois University
DeKalb, IL 60155

Illinois Department of Public Health, Division of
    Vital Records
605 West Jefferson Street
Springfield, IL 62761.

Illinois State Archives
Margaret Cross Norton Building, Capitol
    Complex
Springfield, IL 62756

Illinois State Genealogical Society
P.O. Box 10195
Springfield, IL 62791

Illinois State Library
300 South Second Street
Springfield, IL 62701

Meadville Theological School of Lombard
  College Library
5701 S. Woodlawn Ave.
Chicago, IL 60637

Milner Library
Illinois State University
Normal, IL 61790

Morris Library
Southern Illinois University
Carbondale, IL 62901

National Archives Great Lakes Region (Chicago)
7358 South Pulaski Road
Chicago, IL 60629

Newberry Library
80 West Walton Street
Chicago, IL 60610

North Park University
3225 West Foster Avenue
Chicago, IL 60625

Ronald Williams Library
Northeastern Illinois University
5500 N. St. Louis Ave.
Chicago, IL 60625

University of Illinois Library
One University Plaza
Springfield, IL 62703

U.S. Railroad Retirement Board, Office of
  Public Affairs
844 N. Rush Street
Chicago, IL 60611

Western Illinois University Library
University Circle
Macomb. IL 61455

INDIANA

Allen County Public Library
900 Webster Street
Fort Wayne, IN 46802

Earlham College Library
801 National Road West
Richmond, IN 47374

Harold and Wilma Good Library
Goshen College
1700 S. Main Street
Goshen, IN 46526

Indiana Genealogical Society
P.O. Box 10507
Fort Wayne, IN 46852

Indiana Historical Society
Indiana State Library and Historical Building
315 West Ohio Street
Indianapolis, IN 46202

Indiana State Archives
State Library Building
140 North Senate Avenue
Indianapolis, IN 46204

Indiana State Library
140 North Senate Avenue
Indianapolis, IN 46204

Indiana Vital Records
State Department of Health
2 North Meridian Street
Indianapolis, IN 46204

Theodore M. Hesburgh Library
University of Notre Dame
Notre Dame, IN 46556

United Brethren Historical Center
2303 College Ave.
Huntington, IN 46750

IOWA

Central College
812 University Street
Pella, IA 50219

Iowa Genealogical Society
P. O. Box 7735
Des Moines, IA 50322

Iowa Vital Records
Iowa Department of Public Health
321 E. 12th
Des Moines, IA 50319

Ramaker Library
Northwestern College
101 7th Street SW
Orange City, IA 51041

KANSAS

Kansas Office of Vital Statistics
1000 SW Jackson Street
Topeka, KS 66612

Kansas State Historical Society
6425 W. Sixth Avenue
Topeka, KS 66615

Kansas State Library
State Capitol Building
Topeka, KS 66612

Mennonite Library and Archives
Bethel College
300 East 27th Street
North Newton, KS 67117

Spencer Research Library
University of Kansas
Lawrence, KS 66045

KENTUCKY

Ancestral Trails Historical Society
P.O Box 463
Vine Grove, KY 40200

Kentucky Department for Libraries and Archives
300 Coffee Tree Road
Frankfort, KY 40602

Kentucky Genealogical Society
P.O Box 153
Frankfort, KY 40602

Kentucky Historical Society
Old State Capitol Annex, P.O. Box 1792
Frankfort, KY 40602

Kentucky Office of Vital Statistics
275 East Main Street
Frankfort, KY 40601

Margaret I. King Library
University of Kentucky
Lexington, KY 40506

Sons of the American Revolution Library
1000 South Fourth Street
Louisville, KY 40203

LOUISIANA

Louisiana Department of Health and Hospitals
1210 Capitol Access Road
Baton Rouge, LA 70821

Louisiana Division
New Orleans Public Library
219 Loyola Avenue
New Orleans, LA 70112

Louisiana State Archives
Essen Lane, P.O. Box 94125
Baton Rouge, LA 70804

Louisiana State Library
760 North Third Street, P.O. Box 131
Baton Rouge, LA 70821

MAINE

Maine Division of Archives Services
84 State House Station
Augusta, ME 04333

Maine Historical Society
485 Congress Street
Portland, Maine 04101

Maine State Library
84 State House Station
Augusta, ME 04333

Maine Vital Records Office
Department of Human Services
221 State Street
Augusta, ME 04333

MARYLAND

Baltimore Court of Common Pleas
100 North Holiday Street
Baltimore, MD 21202

Division of Vital Records
Department of Health and Mental Hygiene
6550 Reistertown Avenue, P.O. Box 68760
Baltimore, MD 21215

Maryland Hall of Records
350 Rowe Blvd.
Annapolis, MD 21401

Maryland State Archives
350 Rowe Boulevard
Annapolis, MD 21401

Maryland State Library
400 Cathedral Street
Baltimore, MD 21201

National Archives II Center
8601 Adelphi Road
College Park, MD 20740

Office of Central Records Operations
Social Security Administration
FOIA Workgroup, P.O. Box 17772
300 North Greene Street
Baltimore, MD 21290

Washington National Records Center
4205 Suitland Road
Suitland, MD 20746

MASSACHUSETTS

Albania Orthodox Diocese of America
54 Burroughs Street
Jamaica Plain, MA 02130

American Jewish Historical Society
2 Thornton Road
Waltham, MA 02154

Association for Gravestone Studies
278 Main Street, Suite 207
Greenfield, MA 01301

Boston Public Library
Copley Square
Boston, MA 02117

Church History, A221
First Church of Christ Scientist
175 Huntington Ave.
Boston, MA 02115

Congregational Library
14 Beacon Street
Boston, MA 01018

Massachusetts Offi\ce of the State Quartermaster
44 Salisbury Street
Worcester, MA 01609

Massachusetts State Archives
220 Morrissey Boulevard
Boston, MA 02125

Massachusetts State Library
648 Beacon Street
Boston MA 02215

Massachusetts State Vital Records Office
150 Mount Vernon Street
Dorchester, MA 02125

National Archives Northeast Region (Boston)
380 Trapelo Road
Waltham, MA 02154

National Archives Northeast Region (Pittsfield)
100 Dan Fox Drive
Pittsfield, MA 01201

New England Historic-Genealogical Society
101 Newbury Street
Boston, MA 02116

Plymouth County Commissioners Office in
  Plymouth
11 Lincoln Street
Plymouth, MA 02360

Registry of Vital Records and Statistics
470 Atlantic Avenue
Boston, MA 02210

Unitarian-Univeralist Association Archives
23 Beacon Street
Boston, MA 02108

MICHIGAN

Adventist Heritage Center
James White Library
Berrien Springs, MI 49104

Bentley Historical Library
University of Michigan
1150 Beal Avenue
Ann Arbor, MI 48109

Detroit Health Department
1151 Taylor
Detroit, MI 48202

Detroit Public Library
5201 Woodward Avenue
Detroit, MI 48202

Hope College
265 College Avenue
Holland, MI 49423

James White Library
Andrews University
Berrien Springs, MI 49104

Library of Michigan
717 West Allegan Street
P.O. Box 30007
Lansing, MI 48909

Michigan Historical Center
Michigan Department of State
717 West Allegan Street
Lansing, MI 48918

Michigan State Vital Records Office
3423 North Martin Luther King Blvd.
P.O. Box 30195
Lansing, MI 48909

Purdy-Kresge Library
Wayne State University
Detroit, MI 48202

Walter P. Reuther Library
5401 Cass Ave.
Detroit, MI 48202

MINNESOTA

Minnesota Genealogical Society
5768 Olson Memorial Highway
Golden Valley, MN 55422

Minnesota Historical Society
345 Kellogg Boulevard West
St Paul, MN 55102

Minnesota State Library
Capitol Square Building
550 Cedar Street
St. Paul, MN 55101

Office of the State Register
Minnesota Department of Health
717 Delaware Street SE, P.O. Box 9441
Minneapolis, MN 55440

Wilson Library
University of Minnesota
309 19th Avenue South
Minneapolis, MN 55455

MISSISSIPPI

Mississippi Department of Archives and History
P.O. Box 571
Jackson, MS 39205

Mississippi Historical and Genealogical
  Association
618 Avalon Road
Jackson, MS 39206

Mississippi State Library
1221 Ellis Avenue
P. O. Box 10700
Jackson, MS 39289

Mississippi Vital Records
State Department of Health
571 Stadium Dr., P.O. Box 1700
Jackson, MS 39215

MISSOURI

Flower Pentecostal Heritage Center
1445 North Boonville Avenue
Springfield, MO 65802

Lutheran Church — Missouri Synod
1333 South Kirkwood Road
St. Louis, MO 63122

Military Records
National Personnel Records Center
9700 Page Avenue
St. Louis, MO 63132

Missouri Bureau of Vital Records
930 Wildwood
P.O. Box 570
Jefferson City, MO 65102

Missouri State Archives
600 West Main Street, P.O. Box 778
Jefferson City, MO 65102

Missouri State Historical Society
University of Missouri
23 Ellis Library
Columbia, MO 65201

Missouri State Historical Society
225 South Skinner
St. Louis, MO 63112

National Archives Central Plains Region
  (Kansas City)
2312 East Bannister Road
Kansas City, MO 64131

University of Missouri-Columbia
Columbia, MO 65211

MONTANA

Montana Historical Society
225 North Roberts
Helena, MT 59601

Montana State Archives
Records Management Bureau
P. O. Box 202801
Helena, MT 59620

Montana State Library
1515 East 6th Avenue
P. O. Box 201800
Helena, MT 59620

Vital Records Division
Montana Department of Public Health and
  Human Services
P.O. Box 4210
111 North Sanders
Helena, MT 59604

NEBRASKA

Nebraska Historical Society
1500 R Street
Lincoln, NE 68501

Nebraska State Library
The Atrium
1200 North Street
Lincoln, NE 68508

Nebraska Vital Records Office
301 Centennial Mall South
Lincoln, NE 68509

University of Nebraska at Lincoln
South Love Library
Lincoln, NE 68588

NEVADA

Getchell Library
University of Nevada at Reno
Reno, NV 89557

Nevada Historical Society
700 Twin Lakes Drive
Las Vegas, NV 89107

Nevada State Archives and Records Management
100 N. Stewart Street
Carson City, NV 89701

Nevada Vital Records Office
Division of Health — Vital Statistics
505 East King Street
Carson City, NV 89710

NEW HAMPSHIRE

New Hampshire Division of Records
  Management and Archives
71 South Fruit Street
Concord, NH 03301

New Hampshire Historical Society
30 Park Street
Concord, NH 03301

New Hampshire State Library
20 Park Street
Concord, NH 03301

New Hampshire State Vital Records Office
6 Hazen Drive
Concord, NH 03301

NEW JERSEY

Antiochan Orthodox Christian Archdiocese of
  North America
358 Mountain Road
Englewood, NJ 07631

Archibald Stevens Alexander Library
Rutgers University
169 College Avenue
New Brunswick, NJ 08903

Archives for the Reformed Church in America
21 Seminary Place
New Brunswick, NJ 08901

Federal Records Center
GSA Military Ocean Terminal Building 22
Bayonne, NJ 07002

Gloucester County Historical Society Library
17 Hunter Street
Woodbury, NJ 08096

New Jersey Historical Society
52 Park Place
Newark, NJ 07102

New Jersey State Library and Archives
185 West State Street
Trenton, NJ 08625

New Jersey State Vital Records Office
Department of State Building
225 West State Street
Trenton, NJ 08625

Newark Public Library
5 Washington Street
Newark, NJ 07101

New Mexico

Albuquerque Public Library
423 Central Ave. NE
Albuquerque, NM 87125

Archdiocese of Santa Fe
223 Cathedral Place
Santa Fe, NM 87501

New Mexico Genealogical Society
P.O. Box 8283
Albuquerque, NM 87198

New Mexico State Archives
404 Montezuma
Santa Fe, NM 87503

New Mexico State Historical Society
P.O. Box 4638
Santa Fe, NM 87501

New Mexico Vital Records Office
1105 South Saint Francis Drive
Santa Fe, NM 87502

Zimmerman Library
University of New Mexico
Albuquerque, NM 87131

New York

Albany City Clerk
Room 202, City Hall
Albany, NY 12207

Buffalo City Clerk
Room 1308
65 Niagara Square
Buffalo, NY 14202

Cornell University Library
201 Olin Library
Cornell University
Ithaca, NY 14853

Ellis Island Immigration Museum
New York, NY 10004

Episcopal Records Administration Center
815 Second Ave.
New York, NY 10017

Greek Orthodox Archdiocese
10 East 79th Street
New York, NY 10021

Holland Society of New York
122 East 58th Street
New York, NY 10022

Jacqueline Grennan Wexler Library
Hunter College
695 Park Avenue
New York, NY 10021

Leo Baeck Institute
129 East 73rd Street
New York, NY 10021

National Archives Northeast Region (New York)
201 Varick Street
New York, NY 10014

New York City Department of Health and
  Mental Hygiene
253 Broadway
New York, NY 10007

New York City Register
31 Chambers Street
New York, NY 10007

New York Genealogical and Biographical Society
122 East 58th Street
New York, NY 10022

New York Public Library
5th Avenue and 42nd Street
New York, NY 10018

New York State Archives
New York Department of Education Cultural
  Education Center
Albany, NY 12230

New York State Library
Empire State Plaza
Cultural Education Center
Albany, NY 12230

New York State Vital Records Office
Empire State Plaza
Albany, NY 12237

Orthodox Church in America
6850 Northern Boulevard
Syosset, NY 11791

Salvation Army Headquarters
120 West 14th Street
New York, NY 10011

Samuel Colgate Historical Library
1100 South Goodman Street
Rochester, NY 14620

World Federation of Hungarian Jews
136 East 39th Street
New York, NY 10016

Yearbook Archives
38 Range Drive
Merrick, NY 11566

YIVO Institute for Jewish Research
Suite 1100
555 West 57th Street
New York, NY 10019

Yonkers City Clerk
Room 107, City Hall
Yonkers, NY 10701

NORTH CAROLINA

Duke University Library
P. O. Box 90185
Durham, NC 27708

Hege Library
Guilford College Library
5800 West Friendly Ave.
Greensboro, NC 27410

Moravian Archives
Box L, Davis Center
Salem College
Winston-Salem, N.C. 27108

North Carolina Presbyterian Historical Society
P.O. Box 849
Montreat, NC 28757

North Carolina State Archives and State Library
109 East Jones Street
Raleigh, NC 27601

NORTH DAKOTA

North Dakota Division of Vital Records
600 East Boulevard Avenue
Bismarck, ND 58505

North Dakota State Historical Society
612 East Boulevard Avenue
Bismarck, ND 58505

North Dakota State Library
604 East Boulevard Avenue
Bismarck, ND 58505

North Dakota State University Libraries
1201 Albrecht Boulevard
Fargo, ND 58105

OHIO

Oberlin College Library
Mudd Center
Oberlin, OH 44074

Ohio Genealogical Society
34 Sturgis Avenue
Mansfield, OH 44906

Ohio Historical Society
1982 Velma Ave.
Columbus, OH 43211

Ohio State Library
65 South Front Street
Columbus, OH 43215

Ohio University Library
Park Place
Athens, OH 45701

Ohio Vital Statistics
P.O. Box 15098
Columbus, OH 43215

OKLAHOMA

McFarlin Library
University of Tulsa
2933 East 6th Street
Tulsa, OK 74104

Oklahoma Genealogical Society
P.O. Box 12986
Oklahoma City, OK 73157

Oklahoma Historical Society
2100 North Lincoln Boulevard
Oklahoma City, OK 73105

Vital Records Service
Oklahoma State Department Of Health
1000 Northeast 10th
Oklahoma City, OK 73117

Vital Records Service
Tulsa Office
108 N. Greenwood Street
Tulsa, OK 74120

OREGON

Oregon Historical Society
260 12th Street SE
Portland, OR 97301

Oregon State Archives
800 Summer Street, NE
Salem, OR 97310

Oregon State Library
250 Winter Street, NE
Salem, OR 97310

Oregon State University Archives
94 Kerr Administration Building
Corvallis, OR 97331

Oregon State Vital Records Office
800 NE Oregon Street
Portland, OR 97293

University of Oregon Library
1299 University of Oregon
Eugene, OR 97403

PENNSYLVANIA

American Baptist Archives Center
P.O. Box 85
Valley Forge, PA 19482

Byzantine Catholic Seminary Library
3605 Perrysville Avenue
Pittsburgh, PA 15214

Carnegie Library of Pittsburgh
4400 Forbes Avenue
Pittsburgh, PA 15213

Chester County Historical Society
225 N. High Street
West Chester, PA 19380

Friends Historical Library
Swarthmore College
500 College Avenue
Swarthmore, PA 19081

Genealogical Society of Pennsylvania
1305 Locust Street
Philadelphia, PA 19107

Grand Army of the Republic Museum and Library
4278 Griscom Street
Philadelphia, PA 19124

Lutheran Historical Society
61 Seminary Ridge
Gettysburg, PA 17325

Magill Library
Haverford College
370 Lancaster Ave.
Haverford, PA 19041

Moravian Archives
41 W. Locust Street
Bethlehem, PA 18018

National Archives Mid-Atlantic Region
(Philadelphia)
Ninth and Market Streets
Philadelphia, PA 19107

Pennsylvania Historical Society
1300 Locust Street
Philadelphia, PA 19107

Pennsylvania State Archives
P.O. Box 1026
Harrisburg, PA 17108

Pennsylvania State Library
Commonwealth and Walnut Streets
Harrisburg, PA 17105

Pennsylvania Vital Records Office
101 South Mercer Street
New Castle, PA 16103

Philadelphia Presbyterian Historical Society
425 Lombard Street
Philadelphia, PA 19147

RHODE ISLAND

John Hay Library
Brown University
20 Prospect Street
Providence, RI 02912

Rhode Island Archives
337 Westminster Street
Providence, RI 02903

Rhode Island Historical Society
121 Hope Street
Providence, RI 02906

Rhode Island State Library
300 Richmond Street
Providence, RI 02903

Rhode Island Vital Records Office
Rhode Island Dept of Health
3 Capitol Hill
Providence, RI 02908

SOUTH CAROLINA

Charleston County Health Department
334 Calhoun Street
Charleston, SC 29401

Florence County Health Department
1705 West Evans Street
Florence, SC 29501

Laurens County Library
1017 West Main Street
Laurens, SC 29360

Newberry County Health Department
1308 Hunt Street
Newberry, SC 29108

South Carolina Department of Archives and
History
8301 Parklane Road
Columbia, SC 29223

South Carolina Historical Society
100 Meeting Street
Charleston, SC 29401

South Carolina State Archives
1430 Senate Street
Columbia, SC 29211

South Carolina State Library
1500 Senate Street
Columbia, SC 29211

South Carolina State Vital Records Office
2600 Bull Street
Columbia, SC 29201

Thomason Library of the Presbyterian College
211 E. Maple Street
Clinton, SC 29325

University of South Carolina Library
1322 Greene Street
Columbia, SC 29208

SOUTH DAKOTA

Heritage Hall Museum and Archives
748 S. Main Street
Freeman, SD 57029

South Dakota Historical Society and State
Archives
900 Governors Drive
Pierre, SD 57501

South Dakota State Library
800 Governors Drive
Pierre, SD 57501

South Dakota Vital Records
Department of Health
600 E. Capitol
Pierre, SD 57501

TENNESSEE

American Association of State and Local History
1717 Church Street
Nashville, TN 37203

Disciples of Christ Historical Society Library
1101 19th Avenue, South
Nashville, TN 37212

John C. Hodges Library
University of Tennessee
1015 Volunteer Boulevard
Knoxville, TN 37996

Southern Baptist Historical Library and Archives
901 Commerce Street
Nashville, TN 37203

Tennessee State Library and Archives
403 7th Avenue North
Nashville, TN 37243

Tennessee State Vital Records Office, Central
Services Building
421 5th Avenue North
Nashville, TN 37247

TEXAS

Brite Divinity School Library
Texas Christian University
PO Box 32904
Fort Worth, TX 76219

Dallas Memorial Center for Holocaust Studies
7900 Northaven Road
Dallas, TX 75230

Dallas Public Library
1515 Young Street
Dallas, TX 75201

Episcopal Seminary of the Southwest
606 Rathervue Place
Austin, TX 78768

Fondren Library
Rice University
6100 South Main Street
Houston, TX 77251

Fort Worth Public Library
300 Taylor Street
Fort Worth, TX 76102

Houston Public Library
500 McKinney
Houston, TX 77002

Juárez Archives at the University of Texas
500 West University Ave.
El Paso, TX 79968

National Archives Southwest Region
501 West Felix Street
Building 1, Dock 1
P.O. Box 62165
Fort Worth, TX 76115

San Antonio Public Library
600 Soledad Street
San Antonio, TX 78205

Sul Ross University
PO Box 1495
Alpine, TX 79832

Texas State Library
Lorenzo de Zavala Building
1201 Brazos
Austin, TX 78701

Texas Vital Records Office
P. O. Box 12040
Austin, TX 78711

University of Texas at Austin
P.O. Box P
Austin, TX 78713

University of Texas at San Antonio Library
6900 North Loop 1604 West
San Antonio, TX 78249

University of Texas Pan American Library
1201 West University Drive
Edinburg, TX 78541

UTAH

Genealogical Society of Utah
35 North West Temple Street
Salt Lake City, UT 84150

Office of Vital Records and Health Statistics
Utah Department of Health
288 North 1460 West
Salt Lake City, UT 84114

Utah Family History Library
35 North West Temple Street
Salt Lake City, UT 84150

Utah Genealogical Association
P.O. Box 1144
Salt Lake City, UT 84110

Utah Historical Society
300 Rio Grande
Salt Lake City, UT 84110

Utah State Archives
State Capitol
Archives Building
Salt Lake City, UT 84114

Utah State Library
2150 South 300 West
Salt Lake City, UT 84115

VERMONT

Baley Howe Library
University of Vermont
Burlington, VT 05405

Ilsley Public Library
75 Main Street
Middlebury, VT 05753

Vermont Historical Society
109 State Street
Montpelier, VT 05609

Vermont Public Records Office
133 State Street
Montpelier, VT 05602

Vermont Secretary of State's Office
26 Terrace Street
Montpelier, VT 05609

Vermont State Archives
26 Terrace Street
Montpelier, VT 05609

Vermont Vital Records Office
108 Cherry Street
Burlington, VT 05402

VIRGINIA

Alderman Library
University of Virginia
Charlottesville, VA 22903

Alexander Mack-Memorial Library
East College Street
Bridgewater, VA 22812

Bureau of Land Management
7450 Boston Blvd.
Springfield, VA 22153

Carrier Library
James Madison University
Harrisonburg, VA 22807

National Genealogical Society
4527 17th Street N.
Arlington, VA 22207

U.S. Geological Survey
523 National Center
Renton, VA 20192

Virginia Historical Society
428 North Boulevard
Richmond, VA 23221

Virginia Office of Vital Records
P.O. Box 1000
Richmond, VA 23218

Virginia State Library
800 East Broad Street
Richmond, VA 23219

WASHINGTON

Center for Vital Records
Department of Health
P.O. Box 9709
Olympia, WA 98507

Mortvedt Library
Pacific Lutheran University
1010 122nd Street South
Tacoma, WA 98447

National Archives
Pacific Alaska Region
6125 San Point Way N.E.
Seattle, WA 95115

Seattle Public Library
1000 Fourth Avenue
Seattle, WA 98104

Tacoma Public Library
1102 Tacoma Avenue, South
Tacoma, WA 94802

Washington State Archives
P.O. Box 40220
Olympia, WA 98504

Washington State Genealogical Society
P.O. Box 1422
Olympia, WA 98507

Washington State Historical Society
315 North Stadium Way
Tacoma, WA 98403

Washington State Library
415 15th Avenue S.W
Olympia, WA 98504

WEST VIRGINIA

James E. Morrow Library
Marshall University
Huntington, WV 25755

West Virginia State Archives and History Library
1900 Kanawha Boulevard, East
Charleston, WV 25305

West Virginia University Library
1549 University Avenue
Morgantown, WV 26506

West Virginia Vital Registration Office
350 Capitol Street
Charleston, WV 25301

WISCONSIN

Milwaukee Urban Archives
University of Wisconsin at Milwaukee
P. O. Box 604
Milwaukee, WI 53201

University of Wisconsin Memorial Library
728 State Street
Madison, WI 53706

Wisconsin State Historical Society
816 State Street
Madison, WI 53706

Wisconsin State Library
125 South Webster Street
Madison, WI 53707

Wisconsin Vital Records
1 West Wilson Street
Madison, WI 53701

WYOMING

Laramie County Library
2800 Central Avenue
Cheyenne, WY 82001

University of Wyoming Heritage Center
P.O. Box 3624
Laramie, WY 82071

Wyoming State Archives and Library
2301 Central Ave.
Cheyenne, WY 82002

Wyoming State Law Library
2310 Capitol Avenue
Cheyenne, WY 82002

Wyoming Vital Records Services
Hathaway Building
Cheyenne, WY 82002

Canada

ALBERTA

Alberta Genealogical Society
#116, 10440 108th Ave.
Edmonton, Alberta T5H 3Z9
Canada

Alberta Provincial Archives
12845 102nd Ave.
Edmonton, Alberta T5N 0M6
Canada

Alberta Synod of the Presbyterian Church
2112 35th Avenue NW
Edmonton, Alberta
Canada

Anglican Church of Canada Diocese in Edmonton
St. Peter's Anglican Church
11035 127th Street
Edmonton, Alberta T5M 0T3
Canada

Edmonton Branch of the Alberta Genealogical
Society
10440 108th Avenue, Room 116
Edmonton, Alberta T5H 3Z9
Canada

Edmonton Library
7 Sir Winston Churchill Square
Edmonton, Alberta T5J 2V4
Canada

Lutheran Church, Alberta Synod
7100 Ada Boulevard
Edmonton, Alberta, T5B 4E4
Canada

BRITISH COLUMBIA

Archives Association of British Columbia
P.O. Box 78530, University Post Office
Vancouver, BC V6T 1Z4
Canada

British Columbia Archives
655 Belleville Street
Victoria, BC V8V 1X4
Canada

British Columbia Vital Statistics Agency
818 Fort Street
Victoria, BC V8W 1H8
Canada

Vancouver City Archives
1150 Chestnut Street
Vancouver, BC V6J 3J9
Canada

Vancouver Provincial Supreme Court
800 Smithe
Vancouver BC V62 2E1
Canada

Vancouver Public Library Central Branch
350 West Georgia Street
Vancouver, BC V6B 6B1
Canada

Victoria City Archives
#1 Centennial Square
Victoria, BC V8W 1P6
Canada

MANITOBA

Archives of Manitoba
200 Vaughan Street
Winnipeg, Manitoba R3C 1T5
Canada

Hudson's Bay Company Archives
200 Vaughan Street
Winnipeg, Manitoba R3C 1T5
Canada

Mennonite Heritage Centre
600 Shaftesbury Blvd.,Winnipeg
Manitoba R3P 0M4
Canada

NEW BRUNSWICK

New Brunswick Provincial Archives
Bonar Law — Bennett Building
23 Dineen Drive, U.N.B. Campus
Fredericton, New Brunswick E3B 5H1
Canada

Vital Statistics Office of the Department of
Health and Wellness
Suite 203, 435 King Street
Fredericton, New Brunswick E3B 5H1
Canada

NEWFOUNDLAND

Newfoundland and Labrador Genealogical Society
354 Water St.
St. John's, Newfoundland A1C 1C4
Canada

Provincial Archives of Newfoundland and Labrador
Colonial Building, Military Road
St. John's, Newfoundland A1C 2C9
Canada

Vital Statistics Division of the Newfoundland
Department of Health
P.O. Box 8700
St. John's, Newfoundland A1B 4J6
Canada

NORTHWEST TERRITORIES

Prince of Wales Northern Heritage Centre in
Yellowknife
P.O. Box 1320
Northwest Territories X1A 2L9
Canada

Registrar of Titles, Land Registration District
Yellowknife
Northwest Territories X0E 1H0
Canada

Vital Statistics Department of Health and Social
Services
Government of the Northwest Territories
Inuvik, Northwest Territories X0E 0T0
Canada

NOVA SCOTIA

Nova Scotia Archives and Records Management
6016 University Avenue, Halifax
Nova Scotia B3H 1W4
Canada

Registrar General, Department of Public Health
1723 Hollis Street
Halifax, Nova Scotia B3J 2M9
Canada

ONTARIO

Anglican General Synod Archives
600 Jarvis Street
Toronto, ONT M4Y 2J6
Canada

McMaster Divinity College
Hamilton, ONT L8S 4K1
Canada

Ministry of Natural Resources, Crown Patent
  Register
300 Water Street
Peterborough, ONT K9J 8M5
Canada

National Archives of Canada, Genealogy Unit
395 Wellington Street
Ottawa, ONT K1A 0N3
Canada

North York Central Library
5120 Yonge Street
North York, ONT M2N 5N7
Canada

Office of the Registrar General
Box 4600
Thunder Bay, ONT P7B 6L8
Canada

Ontario Adoption Information Unit of the
  Ministry of Community and Social Services
2 Bloor Street West
Toronto, ONT M7A 1E9
Canada

Ontario Archives
77 Grenville Street
Toronto, ONT M5S 1B3
Canada

Ontario Genealogical Society
40 Orchard View Blvd. Suite 102
Toronto, ONT M4R 1B9
Canada

Pickering College Library
16945 Bayview Ave.
Pickering, ONT L3Y 4X2
Canada

Presbyterian Church Archives
50 Wynford Drive
Toronto, ONT M3C 1J7
Canada

Statistics Canada
R. H. Coats Building, 17th Floor
Ottawa K1A 0T6
Canada

United Church of Canada, Victoria University
  Archives
73 Queen's Park Crescent, East
Toronto, ONT M5S 1K7
Canada

PRINCE EDWARD ISLAND

Prince Edward Island Adoption Services
16 Garfield Street
Charlottetown, PEI C1A 7N8
Canada

Prince Edward Island Genealogical Society
P.O. Box 2744
Charlottetown, PEI C1A 8C4
Canada

Prince Edward Island Provincial Archives
Hon. George Coles Building, Richmond Street
Charlottetown, PEI C1A 7M4
Canada

Prince Edward Island Vital Statistics
35 Douses Road
Montague, PEI C0A 1R0
Canada

Robertson Library
The University of Prince Edward Island
550 University Avenue
Charlottetown, PEI C1A 4P3
Canada

Sir Louis Henry Davies Law Courts Estates Division
42 Water Street
Charlottetown, PEI C1A 8C1
Canada

QUEBEC

Quebec Abitibi-Témiscamingue et Nord
    Regional Archive
27 Rue du Terminus Ouest
Rouyn-Noranda, Quebec J9X 2P3
Canada

Quebec Bas-Saint-Laurent et Gaspésie-Îles-de-
    la-Madeleine Regional Archive
337, Rue Moreault
Rimouski, Quebec G5L 1P4
Canada

Quebec Côte-Nord Regional Archive
700 Boulevard Laure
Sept-Îles, Quebec G4R 1Y1
Canada

Quebec Estrie Regional Archive
740 Rue Galt Ouest
Sherbrooke, Quebec J1H 1Z3
Canada

Quebec Mauricie et Centre Regional Archive
225 Rue des Forges
Trois-Rivières Quebec G9A 2G7
Canada

Quebec Montreal Regional Archive
535 Avenue Viger Est
Montreal, Quebec H2L 2P3
Canada

Quebec Outaouais Regional Archive
170 Rue de l'Hôtel-de-Ville
Hull, Quebec J8X 4C2
Canada

Quebec Regional Archive, Pavillon Louis-
    Jacques-Casault, Cité Universitaire
C.P. 10450 Sainte-Foy
Quebec, Quebec G1V 4N1
Canada

Quebec Saguenay-Lac-Saint-Jean Regional Archive
930 Rue Jacques-Cartier Est, 1 Etage
Chicoutimi, Quebec G7H 2A9
Canada

SASKATCHEWAN

Regina Public Library
2311 12th Ave.
Regina, Saskatchewan S4P 3Z5
Canada

Saskatchewan Archives Board, Murray Building
University of Saskatchewan, 3 Campus Drive
Saskatoon, Saskatchewan S7N 5A4
Canada

Saskatchewan Archives Board
University of Regina
3303 Hillsdale Street
Regina, Saskatchewan S4S 0A2
Canada

Saskatchewan Court of the Queen's Bench
2425 Victoria Ave
Regina, Saskatchewan S4P 3V7
Canada

Saskatchewan Genealogical Society
1870 Lorne Street
Regina, Saskatchewan S4P 2L9
Canada

Saskatchewan Vital Statistics
1942 Hamilton Street
Regina, Saskatchewan S4P 3V7
Canada

Saskatoon Public Library
23rd Street East
Saskatoon, Saskatchewan S7K 0J6
Canada

YUKON TERRITORY

Yukon Archives
P.O. Box 6053
Whitehorse, Yukon Y1A 5L7
Canada

Yukon Vital Statistics Office
204 Lambert Street, 4th Floor
Whitehorse, Yukon Y1A 3T2
Canada

United Kingdom and Ireland

ENGLAND

Angus Library of Regents' Park College
Pusey Street,
Oxford OX1 2LB
UK

British Association of Cemeteries in South Asia
761/2 Chartfield Avenue, Putney
London SW15 6HQ
UK

British Library
Colindale Avenue
London NW9 5HE
UK

British Museum
Great Russell Street
London WC1B 3DG
UK

Catholic Record Society
114 Mount Street
London W1X 6AX
UK

College of Arms
Queen Victoria Street
London EC4V 4BT
UK

Family Records Center
1 Middleton Street
London EC1R 1UW
UK

Friends House
Easton Road
London NW1 2BJ
UK

General Register Office at St. Catherine's House
10 Kingsway
London WC2B 6TP
UK

Guildhall Library
Aldermanbury
London EC2P 2EJ
UK

Huguenot Society of London
University College, Gower Street
London WC1E 6BT
UK

Jewish Historical Society of England
33 Seymour Place
London W1H 5AP
UK

Kew Public Records Office
Ruskin Avenue, Kew
Richmond, Surrey TW9 4DU
UK

London Metropolitan Archives
40 Northampton Road
London EC1R 0HB
UK

London Office for National Statistics
1 Drummond Gate
London SW1V 2QQ
UK

London Public Records Office
40 Northampton Road
London EC1R 0HB
UK

Principal Probate Registry of Somerset House Strand
London WC2R 0RN
UK

Salvation Army International Heritage Centre
101 Queen Victoria Street
London EC4P 4EP
UK

Society of Genealogists in London
14 Charterhouse Buildings, Goswell Road
London EC1M 7BA
UK

Strict and Particular Baptist Headquarters
Dunstable Baptist Chapel
St. Mary's Gate
Dunstable LU6 3SW
UK

Westminster Archives
10 St. Ann's Street
London SW1P 2DE
UK

SCOTLAND

General Register Office, New Register House
Charlotte Square
Edinburgh, Scotland EH1 3YT
UK

General Register Office, Old Register House
Princes Street
Edinburgh, Scotland EH1 3YY
UK

Glasgow City Archives
Mitchell Library, North Street
Glasgow, Scotland G3 7DN
UK

National Library of Scotland
George IV Bridge
Edinburgh, Scotland EH1 1EW
UK

Registrar of Companies
Companies House
37 Castle Terrace
Edinburgh, Scotland EH1 2EB
UK

Scots Ancestry Research Society
8 York Road
Edinburgh, Scotland EH5 3EH
UK

Scottish Genealogy Society
15 Victoria Terrace
Edinburgh, Scotland EH1 2JL
UK

Scottish Heraldry Society
25 Craigentinny Crescent
Edinburgh, Scotland EH7 6QA
UK

WALES

The Baptist Union
Ty Ilston, 94 Heol Mansel
Swansea, Wales SA1 5TZ
UK

National Library of Wales
Aberystwyth
Ceredigion, Wales SY23 3BU
UK

University of Wales at Bangor
Bangor
Gwynedd, Wales LL57 2UW
UK

University of Wales at Lampeter
Lampeter
Ceredigion, Wales SA48 7ED
UK

University of Wales at Swansea
Singleton Park
Swansea, Wales SA2 8PP
UK

IRELAND

Association of Professional Genealogists of
    Ireland
30 Harlech Crescent, Clonskeagh
Dublin 14
Ireland

Charlemont House
Parnell Square
Dublin 1
Ireland

Friends Historical Library
Swanbrook House, Morehampton Road
Dublin 4
Ireland

Ireland Public Record Office
Bishop Street
Dublin 8
Ireland

Irish Jewish Museum
3–4 Walworth Road, South Circular Road
Dublin 8
Ireland

National Archives of Ireland
Bishop Street
Dublin 8
Ireland

National Library of Ireland
Kildare Street
Dublin 2
Ireland

Registrar General, Joyce House
8–11 Lombard Street East
Dublin 2
Ireland

Republic of Ireland Heraldic Archives at Dublin
  Castle
2 Kildare Street
Dublin 2
Ireland

Trinity College Library
College Street
Dublin 2
Ireland

NORTHERN IRELAND

Association of Ulster Genealogists and Record
  Agents
Glen Cottage, Glenmarchan Road
Belfast, Northern Ireland BT4 2NZ
UK

Baptist Union
19 Ballinderry Road, Lisburn
Belfast, Northern Ireland BT28 2SA
UK

Friends Meeting House in Lisburn
Railway Street
County Antrim, Northern Ireland BY28 1EP
UK

Genealogical Society in Belfast
12 College Square East
Belfast, Northern Ireland BT1 6DD
UK

National Archives of Northern Ireland
66 Balmoral Avenue
Belfast, Northern Ireland BT9 6NY
UK

Northern Ireland Registrar General
Oxford House, 49–55 Chichester Srteet
Belfast, Northern Ireland BT1 4HL
UK

Presbyterian Historical Society in Belfast
Room 218 Church House, Fisherwick Place
Belfast, Northern Ireland BT1 6DW
UK

Public Record Office of Northern Ireland
Balmoral Avenue
Belfast, Northern Ireland BT9 6NY
UK

Other Countries

ARGENTINA

Archivo de Actuaciones
Av. 13 No. 770, 1900 La Plata
Buenos Aires
Argentina

Archivo General de la Nación (National Archives)
Av. Leandro N. Alem 246
1003 Buenos Aires
Argentina

Archivo General de Tribunales
Av. 80 Leandro N. Alem 246
1003 Buenos Aires
Argentina

Instituto Argentino de Ciencias Genealogicas
Balcarce 1064
1064 Buenos Aires
Argentina

National Library of Argentina (Biblioteca
  Nacional)
Mexico 564
1097 Buenos Aires
Argentina

AUSTRALIA

Australian Capitol Territory Archives
G.P.O. Box 158
Canberra, ACT 2601
Australia

Canberra National Archives
P.O. Box 7425
Canberra, ACT 2610
Australia

Church of England Historical Society
G.P.O. Box 2902
Sydney, New South Wales 2001
Australia

La Trobe University Library
Bundora
Melbourne, Victoria 3083
Australia

Mitchell Library
Macquarie Street
Sydney, New South Wales 2000
Australia

National Library of Australia
Canberra, ACT 2600
Australia

New South Wales Archival Authority
Level 3, 66 Harrington Street
Sydney, New South Wales 2000
Australia

New South Wales State Archives
2 Globe Street, The Rocks
Sydney, New South Wales 2000
Australia

New South Wales Supreme Court
Level 5, Law Courts Building
Queen's Square
Sydney, New South Wales 2000
Australia

Norfolk Island Mitchell Library
Macquarie Street
Sydney, New South Wales 2000
Australia

Northern Territory Archives Service
Old Law Faculty Building
Northern Territory University, Kahlin Avenue
Darwin, NT 0801
Australia

Queensland State Archives
435 Compton Road
Runcorn, Queensland 4113
Australia

State Archives of Western Australia
Culture Centre, James Street
Perth, Western Australia 6000
Australia

State Library of New South Wales
Macquarie Street
Sydney, New South Wales 2000
Australia

Swan River Battye Library
Library Building, Perth Cultural Centre
Perth, Western Australia 6000
Australia

Tasmania Archives Office
77 Murray Street
Hobart, Tasmania 7000
Australia

Victoria State Archives
Level 2, Casseldon Place
2 Lonsdale Street
Melbourne, Victoria 3000
Australia

Western Australia Records Office
Alexander Library Building, Perth Cultural
    Centre
Perth, Western Australia 6000
Australia

AUSTRIA

Archives of Austria (Statistisches Zentralamt)
1–1030 Wein, Nottendorfergasser 2/
A-1000 Wein Minoritenplatz 1 Vienna
Austria

Austrian National Library
Josefsplatz 1, Postfach 308
A–1015 Vienna
Austria

Jewish Record Center
Israelitische Kultusgemeinde Wien,
    Matrikelamt
Seitenstettengasse 4
A–100, Vienna
Austria

BELGIUM

Le Conseil Héraldique
Parc du Cinquantenaire 10
B-1040, Brussels
Belgium

National State Archives
Ruisbroe,straat 2–10
B–1000 Brussels
Belgium

Royal Library
4 Blvd. de l'Empereur
1000 Brussels
Belgium

BOLIVIA

Archivo del Cabildo Eclesiástico (Diocesan
    Archives)
Basilica de la Vega
La Paz
Bolivia

Archivo Nacional de Bolivia (National Archives
    of Bolivia)
Calle España 25, Casilla 338
Sucre
Bolivia

Archivo y Bibloteca Nacional
Casilla 793
Sucre
Bolivia

Biblioteca Nacional de Bolivia (National Library
of Bolivia)
Calle España 25, Casilla 338
Sucre
Bolivia

General Archive of Civil Rregistration
Calle Fernando Gualhulla 725
La Paz
Bolivia

Instituto Boliviano de Genealogía
Casilla del Correo 335
La Paz
Bolivia

BRAZIL

Colégio Basileiro de Genealogia
Avenida Augusto Severo 8, CEP 20021–000 Lapa
Rio de Janeiro, RJ
Brazil

National Archives of Brazil (Arquivo Nacional)
R. Azeredo Coutinho, 77. Centro, CEP
20.230–170
Rio de Janeiro, RJ
Brazil

National Museum of History
Praça Merechal Âncora, near to Praça XV,
20.021–200
Rio de Janeiro, RJ
Brazil

BULGARIA

Bulgarian Ministry of Justice
1 Slavoamsla Street
1040 Sofia
Bulgaria

Bulgarian National Library
88 Vassil Leviski Blvd.
1504 Sofia
Bulgaria

CHILE

Archivo Nacional (National Archives)
Miraflores #50
Santiago
Chile

Biblioteca Nacional, (National Library)
Av. Bernardo O'Higgins 651
Santiago
Chile

Biblioteca y Archivo Histórico de la
Inmigración Alemaná
(Museum of German Immigration)
Av. Vitacura 5875
Santiago
Chile

Central Office of Civil Registration
Huérfanos 1570
Santiago
Chile

Instituto Chileno de Investigaciones Genealógicas
Calle Londres 65, 3er piso
Santiago
Chile

CHINA

Shanghai Library
1555 Huai Hai Zhong Lu
Shanghai 200031
China

COLOMBIA

Biblioteca Nacional de Colombia (National
Library)
Calle 24, 5–60
Apartado 27600, Bogotá
Colombia

COSTA RICA

Archivo de la Curia Eclesiastica
Apartado 497
1000 San Jose
Costa Rica

National Archives of Costa Rica
Calle 7, Av 4
San José
Costa Rica

CUBA

Archivo National de Cuba
Compostela y San Isidro
Havana 1
Cuba

CZECHOSLOVAKIA

Státní ústrední archiv (Czech National
Archives)
Archivni 6, 149 00
Prague 4
Czech Republic

DENMARK

Copenhagen University
Universitatsparken 5
DK 2100 Copenhagen
Denmark

Danish State Archives
Rigsdagsgarden, 9
DK 1218 Copenhagen
Denmark

National Library of Denmark
P.O. Box 2149
1016 Copenhagen K
Denmark

ECUADOR

Archivo Nacional de Historia (National Archives)
Avenida 6 de Diciembre 332
Apartado 67, Quito
Ecuador

Biblioteca Nacional (National Library)
García Moreno y Sucre
Apartado 163, Quito
Ecuador

EGYPT

Greater Cairo Library
15 Mohamed Mazhaar Street, Zamalck
Cairo
Egypt

EL SALVADOR

El Salvador National Archives (Archivo General
  de la Nación)
Palacio Nacional, Costado Sur Poniente Planta
  Baja
Calle Rubén Dario y, Avenida Cuscatlán
San Salvador
El Salvador

Ministerio del Interior
Alameda Juan Pablo, 2 Distrito Comercial
Central Edificio B–3, Central de Gobierno
San Salvador
El Salvador

ESTONIA

Estonian Biographical Center
Tiigi 1051
51003 Tartu
Estonia

Estonian Historical Archives
J. Liivi 4
50409 Tartu
Estonia

National Library of Estonia (Esti
  Rahvusraamatukogu)
Tònismägi 2
EE0100 Tallinn
Estonia

FINLAND

Finnish Central Archives
P.O. Box 258
00171 Helsinki
Finland

Helsinki University Library
P.O. Box 15
FIN–00014 Helsinki
Finland

FRANCE

Bureau Genealogique, Union de la Noblesse Russe
10 Square de Chattilon
75014 Paris
France

French Military Archives
Château de Vincennes, Avenue de Paris
94300 Vincennes
France

French National Archives
60, rue des Francs-Bourgeois
75141 Paris
France

Genealogical Library in Paris (Bibliothèque
  Généalogique)
231, rue Vendóme
69003 Lyon
France

Heraldry Society of France (Conseil Français
  d'héraldique)
108, Bd De La Corniche
22700 Perros-Guirec
France

Library of French Protestantism
54, rue des Saints-Pères
75007 Paris
France

Public Library of Information in Paris
  (Bibliothèque Publique d'information)
Centre Pompidou, 19, rue Beaubourg
75197 Paris
France

GERMANY

Deutsches Adelsarchiv
Schwanalee 21
35037 Marburg
Germany

Geheimes Staatsarchiv
Preussischer Kulturbestiz
Archivstrasse 12-14
D–14195 Berlin
Germany

German Genealogical Society
Biebricher Allee 168
D–65203 Wiesbaden
Germany

National Library of Germany
Adickesallee 1
69322 Frankfurt am Main
Germany

GREECE

Civil Registration Division of the Ministry of
  the Interior
27 Stadiou Str. and 2 Draganatsiou Str.
101 83 Athens
Greece

Greek First Court of Instance, Ministry of Justice
P.O. Box M60
Athens
Greece

Greek Orthodox Archdiocese
Agies Filotheis 21
10556 Athens
Greece

National Library of Greece
32 Panepistimiou Avenue
106 79 Athens
Greece

GUATEMALA

Guatemala National Archives (Archivo General
  de Centro América)
4 Avda 7–16, Zona 1
Guatemala City
Guatemala

HONDURAS

Honduras National Archives
6a Avda Salvador Mendiela
Tegucigalpa
Honduras

Tegucigalpa City Museum
Vila Roy Building, Bario Buenos Bario
Tegucigalpa
Honduras

HUNGARY

Budapest City Archives
Városházu 9–11
H12052 Budapest
Hungary

Hadtortenelmi leveltar (Archives of Military
  History)
Kapisztrán tér 2–4
1014 Budapest
Hungary

Hungarian National Archives
Bécsi Kapu tér 2–4
1014 Budapest
Hungary

Hungarian National Library
Buda Royal Palace Wing F
H–1827 Budapest
Hungary

National Széchényi Library (Budapest National
  Library)
Palice of the Buda Castle
Budapest
Hungary

ICELAND

Icelandic National Archives
Langavegur 162
Rejkjavik
Iceland

National and University Library of Iceland
Arngrimsgata 3, IS
107 Rejkjavik
Iceland

Statistical Bureau of Iceland
Borgartuni 21a
150 Rejkjavik
Iceland

ISRAEL

Central Archives for the History of the Jewish
  People
Hebrew University Campus Sprinzak Building
Jerusalem 91010
Israel

Yad Vashem Museum
P.O.B. 3477
Jerusalem 91034
Israel

ITALY

Archivio Notrale, Ispettatore Generale
Corso Tinnascimento, 40 Palazzo della Sapienza
00186 Rome
Italy

Collegio Araldico
Via Santa Maria dell'Anima 16
00186 Rome
Italy

Instituto Centrale de Statistica
Via Balbo 16
00184 Rome
Italy

Italian National Archives, Archivio Centrale
  della Stato
Via Gaeta 8A
00185, Rome
Italy

Library of Parma
Palazzo della Pilotta, I–43100
Parma
Italy

Vatican Library
Biblioteca Apostolica Vaticana, Cortile del
  Belvedere
00120 Citt'a del Vaticano

JAPAN

Civil Affairs Bureau of the Ministry of Justice
Central Government Office Complex
Tokyo
Japan

Japanese National Archives
3–2 Kitanomaru Koen, Chiyoda-ku
Tokyo 102-0091
Japan

KOREA

Korean National Library
San 60–1, Panpo-Dong, Seacho-Gu
Seoul
Korea

LATVIA

Latvian National Library
14 K. Barona
Riga LV–1423
Latvia

LITHUANIA

Lithuanian Historical Archives
Gerosios Vilties 10
Vilnius 2009
Lithuania

National Library of Lithuania
Gedimino pr. 51
Vilnius 2600
Lithuania

MEXICO

Archivo General de la Nación
Palacio Naçional
Mexico City 1
Mexico

NETHERLANDS

Centraal Bureau voor Genealogie (CBG)
Prins Willem-Alexanderhof 24
The Hague
The Netherlands

Dutch Central Registry of Wills (Central
  Testamenten Register)
Kalvermarkt 53, Postbus 20300
2500 EH The Hague
The Netherlands

Rijksarchief Archives
Prins Willem-Alexanderhof 20
The Hague
The Netherlands

NEW ZEALAND

New Zealand National Archives
10 Mulgrave Street, Thorndon
Wellington
New Zealand

New Zealand National Library
P.O. Box 1467
Wellington
New Zealand

New Zealand Register-General for Births,
  Deaths, and Marriages
P.O Box 8023, Lambton Quay
Wellington
New Zealand

NICARAGUA

Nicaraguan National Archives
Del Cine Cabrera 2 1/2 c. al lago
Managua
Nicaragua

NORWAY

Norwegian Central Bureau of Statistics
Kongens Gate 6
N0033 Oslo
Norway

Norwegian National Archives
Folke Bernadottes vei 21, Postboks 4013 Ullevål
  Hageby
N–0806 Oslo
Norway

Norwegian National Library
Postboks 2674 Solli
N–0203 Oslo
Norway

PANAMA

Panama National Archives (Archivo National)
Apdo 6618
Panama City
Panama

PARAGUAY

Archivo Nacional (National Archives)
Mariscal Estigarriba 95
Asunción
Paraguay

PERU

Archive de la Beneficencia (Archbishop's Archive)
Plaza de Armas s/n, Apartado 1512
Lima
Perú

Archivo General de la Nacion (National Archives)
Palacio de Justica, Apartado 3124
Lima 100
Perú

Biblioteca Nacional del Perú (National Library
of Peru)
Avenida Abancay, Apartado 2335
Lima
Perú

Instituto Peruano de Investigaciones
Genealógicas
Avenida Pezet 1005, Apt. 601, San Isidro
Lima 27
Perú

POLAND

Central Archives
Archiwum Glowne Akt Dawanych w Warszawie
ul, Dluga 7
00–263 Warsaw
Poland

Polish National Library
Niepodleglosci 213
02–086 Warsaw
Poland

PORTUGAL

Arquivo dos Registos Paroquiais (Central Archives)
Rua dos Prazeres 41-r/c
Lisbon 2
Portugal

Arquivo Nacional da Tôrre do Tombo (National
Archives)
Alameda do Universidade, P–1649–010
Lisbon
Portugal

Direccâo-General do Registo e Notariodo do
Ministerio da Justiça
(Director Superior of Lbraries and Archives)
av. 5 de Outubro, 202 1064–803
Lisbon
Portugal

Instituto Portugues de Heraldica
Largo do Carmo
Lisbon 2
Portugal

PUERTO RICO

Archivo Arquidiocesano (Ecclesiastical Archive)
de San Juan
Apartado 9021967
San Juan
Puerto Rico 00901

Archivo General de Puerto Rico (National
Archives)
Avenida Ponce de Leon 500, Puerta de Tierra
San Juan
Puerto Rico 00905

Department of Health, Demographic Registry
P.O. Box 11854, Fernandez Juncos Station
San Juan
Puerto Rico 00910

ROMANIA

Romanian National Library
Str. Ion Ghica 4, sector 3
79708 Bucharest
Romania

RUSSIA

Central Historical Archive of Moscow
Profsoyuznaya, 80
117393 Moscow
Russia

Central State Archive of Moscow Region
Azovskaya, 17
113149 Moscow
Russia

Central State Archive of St. Petersburg
Varfolomeyevskaya, 15
193171 St. Petersburg
Russia

Russian State Historical Archive
Angliyskaya Embankment, 4
190000 St. Petersburg
Russia

Russian State Library in St. Petersburg
18, Sadovaya
191069 St. Petersburg
Russia

Russian State Military Historical Archive
2 Baumanskaya, 3
107864 Moscow
Russia

Russian State Naval Archive
Millionnaya, 36
191065 St. Petersburg
Russia

South Africa

Genealogical Institute of South Africa
115 Banghoek Road
Stellenbosch
South Africa

National Archives of South Africa
24 Hamilton Street, Arcadia
Pretoria 0001
South Africa

South Africa Department of the Interior
24 Hamilton Street, Arcadia
Pretoria 0001
South Africa

Spain

Archivo de La Corona de Aragon
2 Barcelona
Spain

Cronistas de Armas, Ministry of Justice
28000 Madrid
Spain

General Military Archives
Plaza Reina Victoria Eugenia
40071 Segovia
Spain

Historical National Archives
Concepcion Contel Calle Serrano 115
28006 Madrid
Spain

Instituto Internacional de Genealogiá y Heraldica
y Federación di corporaciones Afines
   (International Institute of Genealogy and
   Heraldry)
Apartado de Corres 12
28079 Madrid
Spain

National Library of Spain
Paseo de Recoletos 20-22
28071 Madrid
Spain

Sweden

National Archive in Stockholm (Riksarkivet)
Box 12541
0229 Stockholm
Sweden

Statistica Centralbyran
(Central Bureau of Statistics)
Karlavagen 100
10250 Stockholm
Sweden

Swedish Emigrant Institute and Museum
P. O. Box 201
351 04 Växsjö
Sweden

Switzerland

Library of the Genealogical Society of
   Switzerland (SGFF)
c/o Schweiz. Landesbibliothek, Hallwylstr. 15
CH-3003 Bern
Switzerland

Schweizerische Hearldische Gesellschaft
Bibliotheque Cantonale et Universtaire,
   Postfach
CH-Fribourg
Switzerland

Swiss Federal Archives
Archivstrasse 24
CH-3003 Bern
Switzerland

Swiss National Library
HallwylstraBe 15
CH-3003 Bern
Switzerland

Swiss Society of Heraldry (Schweizerische
   Heraldische Gesellschaft)
Zwinglistrasse 28
St. Gall
Switzerland

Uruguay

Archivo General de la Nación
1474 Convencion
Montevideo
Uruguay

Dirección General del Registro Civil
Ministerio de Educacion y Cultura
Av. Uraguay 933
Montevideo
Uruguay

Oficiana de Catastro
Avda. Rondeau No 1437
Montevideo
Uruguay

VENEZEULA

Archdiocese of Caracas
22–24 Buleval Panteon Nacional
1030 Caracas
Venezeula

Archivo General de la Nacion
(National Archives)
Santa Capilla a Carmelitas, Anemida Urdaneta
1010 Caraca
Venezeula

Edificio Nueva Sede Foro Liberator
(National Library)
Final Avenida Panteón
Caracas
Venezuela

BIBLIOGRAPHY

Aberle, George P. *Pioneers and Their Sons: One Hundred Sixty-Five Family Histories.* Bismarck, ND: Tumbleweed Press, 1980.

Adams, Marilyn. *Georgia Local and Family History Sources in Print.* Clarkston, GA: Heritage Research, 1982.

Alexander, Ruth A., et al., comps. *South Dakota: Changing, Changeless, 1899-1989.* Rapid City: South Dakota Library Association, 1985.

Anderson, Alloa Caviness. *Genealogy in Michigan: What, When, Where.* Ann Arbor, MI: A. Anderson, P. Bender, 1978.

Austin, John Osborne. *The Genealogical Dictionary of Rhode Island.* Baltimore: Genealogical Publishing Co., 1978.

Bamman, Gale Williams. *Research in Tennessee.* Arlington, VA: National Genealogical Society, 1993.

Banfield, Marilyn Davis. *Researching in Alabama: A Genealogical Guide.* Easley, SC: Southern Historical Press, 1987.

Beatty, John D. *Research in Indiana.* Arlington, VA: National Genealogical Society, 1992.

Beckstead, Gayle, and Mary Lou Kozub. *Searching in Illinois.* Costa Mesa, CA: ISC Publications, 1984.

Bell, Carol Willsey. *Ohio Genealogical Guide.* Youngstown, OH: Bell Books, 1995.

Bentley, Elizabeth Petty. *County Courthouse Book.* Baltimore: Genealogical Publishing Company, 1995.

_____. *The Genealogist's Address Book.* Baltimore: Genealogical Publishing Company, 1991.

Blessing, Patrick J. *Oklahoma: Records and Archives.* Tulsa: University of Tulsa Publications, 1978.

Bodziony, Gill Dodd. *Genealogy and Local History: A Bibliography.* State Library, Tallahassee, FL, 1978.

Boling, Yvette G. *A Guide to Printed Sources for Genealogical and Historical Research in the Louisiana Parishes.* Jefferson, LA: Self-published, 1985.

Bookstruck, Llowy DeWitt. *Research in Texas.* Arlington, VA: National Genealogical Society, 1992.

Boudreau, Dennis M. *Beginning Franco American Genealogy.* Pawtucket, RI: American French Genealogical Society, 1986.

Bradbury, Connie Malcolm, and David Albert Hales. *Alaska Sources, a Guide to Historical Records and Information Resources.* North Salt Lake City: Heritage Quest, 2001.

Burke, Kate. *Searching in New York: A Reference Guide to Public and Private Records.* Costa Mesa, CA: ISC Publications, 1987.

Burrage, Henry Sweetser. *Genealogical and Family History of the State of Maine,* 4 vols. New York City: Lewis Historical Publishing Company, 1909.

Byers, Paula K., ed. *African American Genealogical Sourcebook.* Detroit: Gale Research, 1995.

_____. *Native American Genealogical Sourcebook.* Detroit: Gale Research, 1995.

Carlberg, Nancy Ellen. *Beginning Norwegian Research.* Anaheim, CA: Carlberg Press, 1991.

Carleton, Hiram. *Genealogical and Family History of the State of Vermont,* 2 vols. New York City: Lewis Publishing Co., 1903.

Carmack, Saron DeBartolo. *Discovering Your Immigrant & Ethnic Ancestors.* Cincinnati: Betterway Books, 2000.

Carr, Peter E. *Guide to Cuban Genealogical Research: Records and Sources.* Chicago: Adams Press, 1991.

Carty, Mickey Dimon. *Searching in Indiana: A Reference Guide to Public and Private Records.* Costa Mesa, CA: ISC Publications, 1985.

Central Massachusetts Genealogical Society. *A Guide to Genealogical and Historical Holdings of Massachusetts Libraries.* Westminster: The Society, 1997.

Chambers World Gazetteer: A–Z of Geographical Information. New York: Columbia University Press, 1988.

Choquette, Margarita, et al. *The Beginners Guide to Finnish Genealogical Research.* Bountiful, UT: Thomsen's Genealogical Center, 1985.

Chorzempa, Rosemary A. *Polish Roots.* Baltimore: Genealogical Publishing Co., 1993.

Clark, Georgia H., and R. Bruce Parham, comps. *Arkansas County and Local Histories: A Bibliography.* Self-published: Fayetteville, AR, 1976.

Clay, Robert Young. *Virginia Genealogical Resources.* Detroit: Detroit Society of Genealogical Research, 1980.

Clifford, Karen. *Genealogy, The Internet and Your Genealogy Computer Program.* Baltimore: Genealogical Publishing Company, 2001.

Clint, Florence R. *Colorado Area Key: A Comprehensive Study of Genealogical Records Sources of CO, Including Maps and a Brief General History.* Fountain Valley, CA: Edin Press, 1968.

_____. *New York Area Key: A Guide to the Genealogical Records of the State of New York.* Elizabeth, CO: Keyline Publishers, 1979.

_____. *Pennsylvania Area Key: A Guide to the Genealogical Records of the State of Pennsylvania; Including Maps, Histories, Charts and Other Helpful Materials.* Denver: Area Keys, 1976.

Cogswell, Philip. *Capitol Names: Individuals Woven into Oregon's History.* Portland: Oregon Historical Society, 1977.

Coldham, Peter Wilson. *The Complete Book of Emigrants in Bondage, 1614–1775.* Baltimore: Genealogical Publishing Company, 1992.

Colletta, John Philip. *Finding Italian Roots: The Complete Guide for Americans.* Baltimore: Genealogical Publishing Co. 1996.

Colorado Families: A Territorial Heritage. Denver: Colorado Genealogical Society, 1981.

Conrad, Agnes C. *Genealogical Sources in Hawaii.* Honolulu: Hawaii Library Association, 1987.

Copeley, William. *New Hampshire Family Records, Vol. I and II.* Bowie, MD: Heritage Books, 1994.

Corbin, John. *Catalog of Genealogical Materials in Texas Libraries.* Austin: Texas State Library and Historical Commission, 1965.

Cote, Richard N. *Local and Family History in South Carolina: A Bibliography.* Easley, SC: Southern Historical Press, 1981.

Cox, Mrs. Edgar L., and Thomas W. Westerfield. *Kentucky Family Records,* 19 vols. Owensburg: West Kentucky Family Research Association, 1970–95.

Crandall, Ralph J., ed. *Genealogical Research in New England.* Baltimore: Genealogical Publishing Co., 1984.

Croom, Emily. *Genealogist Companion and Sourcebook.* Cincinnati: Betterway Books, 1994.

Crowe, Elizabeth Powell. *Genealogy Online.* New York: McGraw-Hill, 2000.

Danky, James P. *Genealogical Research: An Introduction to the Resources of the State Historical Society of Wisconsin.* Madison: State Historical Society of Wisconsin, 1986.

Davis, Robert Scott, Jr. *A Researcher's Library of Georgia History.* Greenville, SC: Southern Historical Press, 1991.

DeBartolo, Sharon Carmack. *A Genealogist's Guide to Discovering Your Female Ancestors.* Cincinnati: Betterway Books, 1998.

Delaware Genealogical Research Guide. Wilmington: Delaware Genealogical Society, 1989.

Delaware Public Archives Commission. *Delaware Archives,* 3 vols. Wilmington: James and Walls, 1875.

Dictionary of Louisiana Biography, 2 vols. New Orleans: Louisiana Historical Association, 1988.

Directory of Special Information Resources in Utah, 1982. Salt Lake City: Utah Library Association, 1987.

Doane, Gilbert H., and James B. Bell. *Searching for Your Ancestors.* Minneapolis: University of Minnesota Press, 1908.

Donahue, Jim, ed. *Guide to the County Archives of Wyoming.* Cheyenne: Wyoming State Archives, 1991.

Draughon, Wallace R. *North Carolina Genealogical Reference: A Research Guide for All Genealogists, Both Amateur and Professional.* Durham, NC: Smith Publications, 1966.

Eales, Anne Bruner, and Robert M. Kvasnicka. *Genealogical Researching in the National Archives of the United States,* 3rd edition. Washington, DC: National Archives, 2000.

Egle, William Henry. *Pennsylvania Genealogies, Chiefly Scotch-Irish and German.* Baltimore: Genealogical Publishing, 1969.

Eichholz, Alice. *Collecting Vermont Ancestors.* Montpelier, VT: New Trails, 1986.

Elliott, Wendy L. *Research in Alabama.* Bountiful, UT: American Genealogical Lending Library, 1987.

Esterly, Robert E. *Genealogical Resources in New*

Mexico. Albuquerque: New Mexico Genealogical Society, 1997.

Falley, Margaret Dickson. *Irish and Scotch-Irish Ancestral Research: A Guide to the Genealogical Records, Methods and Sources in Ireland.* Baltimore: Genealogical Publishing Company, 1981.

Federation of Oklahoma Genealogical Societies. *Directory of Oklahoma Sources.* Oklahoma City: Federation of Oklahoma Genealogical Societies, 1993.

Filby, F. William. *A Bibliography of American County Histories.* Baltimore: Genealogical Publishing Company, 1985.

_____. *Passenger and Immigration Lists Index.* Detroit: Gale Research, 1981.

Fowler, Ila Earle. *Kentucky Pioneers and Their Descendants.* Baltimore: Genealogical Publishing Co., 1967.

Frost, John Eldridge. *Maine Genealogy: A Bibliographical Guide.* Portland: Maine Historical Society, 1985.

Fulcher, Richard Carlton. *Guide to County Records and Genealogical Resources in Tennessee.* Baltimore: Genealogical Publishing Co., 1987.

Genealogical and Historical Atlas of the United States of America. Logan, UT: Everton, 1976.

Genealogical Resources in Washington State. Olympia: Washington Division of Archives and Records Management, 1983.

Giles, Barbara S. *Connecticut Genealogical Resources: Including Selected Bibliographies.* Seattle: Ficke Genealogical Foundation, 1991.

Gooldy, Pat, and Ray Gooldy. *Manual for Illinois Genealogical Research.* Indianapolis: Ye Olde Genealogie Shoppe, 1994.

Greene, Diane E. *Nevada Guide to Genealogical Records.* Baltimore: Clearfield Co., 2000.

Greenwood, Val D. *The Researcher's Guide to American Genealogy.* Baltimore: Genealogical Publishing Company, 1973.

Greer, George. *Early Virginia Immigrants, 1623–1666.* Baltimore: Genealogical Publishing Company, 1912.

Grundset, Eric. *Research in Virginia.* Arlington, VA: National Genealogical Society, 1998.

Guide to Genealogical Research in the National Archives. Washington, DC: The National Archives and Records Service, 1983.

Handybook for Genealogists: United States of America. Draper, UT: Everton Publishers, 2002.

Harris, Katherine, comp. *Guide to Manuscripts.* Iowa City: State Historical Society of Iowa, 1973.

Heber, Mark D. *Ancestral Trails: The Complete Guide to British Genealogy and Family History.* Baltimore: Genealogical Publishing Company, 1997.

Hehir, Donald M. *Carolina Families: A Bibliography of Books about North and South Carolina Families.* Bowie, MD: Heritage Books, 1994.

_____. *Missouri Family Histories and Genealogies, A Bibliography.* Bowie, MD: Heritage Books, 1996.

Heisey, John W. *Maryland Genealogical Library Guide.* Morgantown, PA: Masthof Press, 1998.

_____. *Ohio Genealogical Research Guide.* Indianapolis: Heritage House, 1987.

Henderson, Thomas W., and Ronald E. Tomlin, comps. *Guide to Official Records in the Mississippi Department of Archives and History.* Jackson: Mississippi Department of Archives and History, 1975.

Hendrix, Ge Lee Corley. *Research in South Carolina.* Arlington, VA: National Genealogical Society, 1992.

Herbert, Mirana C., and Barbara McNeil. *Biography and Genealogy Master Index.* Detroit: Gale Research Company, 1980– (ongoing).

Herrick, Linda M. *Wisconsin Genealogical Research Origins.* Janesville, WI, 1996.

Historical and Biographical Record of the Territory of Arizona. Chicago: McFarland and Poole, 1896.

Hodges, Nadine, and Audrey L. Woodruff. *Missouri Pioneers: County and Genealogical Records,* 30 vols. Independence, MO: Woodruff, 1967–76.

Idaho Genealogical Society. *Footprints Through Idaho,* 3 vols. Boise: Idaho Genealogical Society, 1989.

Irvine, Sherry. *Your Scottish Ancestry: A Guide for North Americans.* Salt Lake City: Ancestry, Inc., 1997.

Jacobus, Donald Lines. *Genealogy as Pastime and Profession.* Baltimore: Genealogical Publishing Company, 1996.

Jaussi, Laureen, and Gloria Chaston. *Genealogical Records of Utah.* Salt Lake City: Deseret Book Co., 1974.

Johansson, Carl-Erik. *Cradled in Sweden.* Draper, UT: Everton Publishers, 1995.

_____. *Tracing Your Icelandic Family Tree.* Winnipeg, Manitoba: Wheatfield Press, 1975.

Kemp, Thomas J. *Connecticut Researcher's Handbook.* Detroit: Gale Research, 1981.

_____. *International Vital Records Handbook.* Baltimore: Genealogical Publishing Company.

_____. *Virtual Roots: A Guide to Genealogy and Local History on the World Wide Web.* Wilmington, DE: Scholarly Resources Inc., 1997.

Kirkeby, Lucille L. *Holdings of Genealogical Value in Minnesota's County Museums.* Brainard, MN: L. Kirkeby, 1986.

Kirkham, E. Kay. *Our Native Americans and Their*

Records of Genealogical Value, 2 vols. Logan, UT: Everton, 1980.

Koken, Paul, and Theodore N. Constant and S. G. Canoutas. *History of the Greeks in the Americas, 1453-1938.* Ann Arbor, MI: Proctor Publications, 1995.

Lee, Francis Bazley. *Genealogical and Memorial History of the State of New Jersey*, 4 vols. New York City: Lewis Historical Publishing, 1910.

Lee, Joyce C. *Genealogical Prospecting in Nevada: A Guide to Nevada Directories.* Carson City: Nevada State Library, 1984.

Lenzen, Connie. *Guide to Genealogical Sources.* Portland: Genealogical Forum of Oregon, 1994.

Lind, Marilyn. *Continuing Your Genealogical Research in Minnesota.* Cloquet, MN: Linden Tree, 1986.

Liscomb, Anne S., and Kathleen S. Hutchinson. *Tracing Your Mississippi Ancestors.* Jackson: University Press of Mississippi, 1994.

Low, Jennie W. Chooey. *China Connection: Finding Ancestral Roots for Chinese in America.* San Francisco: JWC Low Co., 1994.

Luster, Arlene D. C. *A Directory of Libraries and Information Sources in Hawaii and the Pacific Islands.* Honolulu: Hawaii Library Association, 1972.

Magocsi, Paul R. *The Russian Americans.* Broomall, PA: Chelsea House, 1989.

Marshall, George W. *The Genealogist's Guide to Printed Pedigrees.* London: G. Bell & Sons, last updated 1912.

Maryland Genealogies. Baltimore: Genealogical Publishing Co., Inc., 1997.

Matthews, Harry Bradshaw. *African American Genealogical Research: How to Trace Your Family History.* Baldwin, NY: Matthews Heritage Services, 1992.

McGinnis, Carol. *Michigan Genealogy Sources and Resources.* Baltimore: Genealogical Publishing Company, 1987.

_____. *West Virginia Genealogy: Sources and Resources.* Baltimore: Genealogical Publishing Company, 1988.

Meyerink, Kory. *Printed Sources: A Guide to Published Genealogical Records.* Salt Lake City: Ancestry, 1998.

Miller, Okga K. *Genealogical Research for Czech and Slovak Americans.* Detroit: Gale Research, 1978.

Milner, Paul, and Linda Jones. *A Genealogist's Guide to Discovering Your English Ancestors.* Cincinnati: Betterway Books, 2000.

Mitchell, Brian. *Pocket Guide to Irish Genealogy.* Baltimore: Genealogical Publishing Co., 1991.

Montalto, Nicholas V. *The International Institute Movement: A Guide to Records of Immigrant Society Agencies in the United States.* Minneapolis: Immigration Research Center, 1978.

Moody, Suzanne, and Joel Wurl. *The Immigration History Research Center: A Guide to Collections.* Westport, CT: Greenwood Press, 1991.

Neagles, James C. *The Library of Congress: A Guide to Genealogical and Historic Research.* Salt Lake City: Ancestry, 1990.

Nebraska, A Guide to Genealogical Research. Lincoln: Nebraska State Genealogical Society, 1984.

New Jersey State Archives. *Guide to Family History Sources in the New Jersey State Archives.* Trenton: New Jersey State Archives, [n.d.].

Nicklas, Laurie. *The California Locator: A Directory of Public Records for Locating People Dead or Alive in California.* Modesto, CA: Self-published, 1994.

_____. *The Montana Locator, A Directory of Public Records for Locating People Dead or Alive.* Modesto, CA: Self-published, 1999.

Pap, Leo. *The Portuguese-Americans.* New York: Twayne Publishers, 1981.

Parpart, Pauline K., and Donald E. Spritzer, comps. *Montana Data Index: A Reference Guide to Historical and Genealogical Resources.* Missoula: Montana Library Association, 1992.

Peterson, Becki. *Iowa County Records Manual.* Iowa City: State Historical Society of Iowa, 1987.

Peterson, Clarence S. *Consolidated Bibliography of County Histories in Fifty States in 1961.* Baltimore: Genealogical Publishing Company, 1963.

Pine, L. G. *The Genealogist's Encyclopedia.* New York: Weybright and Talley, 1969.

Platt, Lyman D. *Hispanic Surnames and Family History.* Baltimore: Genealogical Publishing Company, 1996.

Pompey, Sherman L. *Genealogical Records of California.* Fresno, CA: Sherman L. Pompey, 1968.

Rider, Fremont J., ed. *The American Genealogical-Biographical Index*, 181 volumes. Middletown, CT: Godfrey Memorial Library, 1942–1952, and 1952–present.

Robb, H. Amanda, and Andrew Chesler. *Encyclopedia of American Family Names.* New York: Harper Collins Publishers, 1995.

Rooney, Doris Dockstader, et al. *Kansas Genealogical Society Six-Generation Ancestor Tables.* Dodge City: Kansas Genealogical Society, 1976.

Rose, Christine, and Kay Ingalls. *Complete Idiot's Guide to Genealogy.* Fort Smith, AR: Alpha Books, 1997.

Rottenberg, Dan. *Finding Our Fathers: A Guidebook in Jewish Genealogy.* Baltimore: Genealogical Publishing Company, 1986.

Rowlands, John, ed. *Welsh Family History: A*

Guide to Research. Baltimore: Genealogical Publishing Company, 1999.

Runk, J.M. *Biographical and Genealogical History of the State of Delaware.* Chambersburg, PA: Self-published, 1899.

Ryskamp, George R. *Finding Your Hispanic Roots.* Baltimore: Genealogical Publishing Company, 1997.

_____, and Peggy Ryskamp. *A Student's Guide to Mexican American History.* Phoenix: Oryx Publishers, 1996.

Savage, James. *A Genealogical Dictionary of the First Settlers of New England,* 4 vols. Baltimore: Genealogical Publishing Company, 1965.

Schaefer, Christina K. *The Hidden Half of the Family: A Sourcebook for Women's Genealogy.* Baltimore: Genealogical Publishing Company, 1999.

Schlyter, Danial. *Czechoslovakia: A Handbook of Czechoslovak Genealogical Research.* Buffalo Grove, IL: Genun, 1985.

Schweitzer, George K. *Massachusetts Genealogical Research.* Knoxville: George K. Schweitzer, 1990.

Senekovic, Dagmar. *Handy Guide to Austrian Genealogical Records.* Draper, UT: Everton Publishers, 1979.

Skordas, Gust. *The Early Settlers of Maryland: An Index to the Names of Immigrants Compiled from Records of Land Patents, 1633-1680.* Baltimore: Genealogical Publishing Company, 1968.

Smith, Clifford Neal. *Encyclopedia of German-American Genealogical Research.* New York: R. R. Bowker, 1976.

Smith, Patricia D. *Kansas Biographical Index: Statewide and Regional Histories.* Garden City, KS: Patricia D. Smith, 1994.

Sources of Genealogical Help in Idaho. Burbank: Southern California Genealogical Society, [n.d.].

Sources of Genealogical Help in Nebraska. Burbank: Southern California Genealogical Society, [n.d.].

Sources of Genealogical Help in New Mexico. Burbank: Southern California Genealogical Society, [n.d.].

Spiros, Joyce V. H. *Genealogical Guide to Arizona and Nevada.* Gallup, NM: Verlene Publishing, 1983.

Spiros, Joyce V. H. *Genealogical Guide to Wyoming.* Gallup, NM: Verlene Publisher, 1982.

Stewart, Robert Armistead. *Index to Printed Virginia Genealogies.* Baltimore: Genealogical Publishing Company, 1970.

Streets, David H. *Slave Genealogy: A Research Guide with Case Studies.* Bowie, MD: Heritage Books, 1986.

Suess, Jared H. *Handy Guide to Hungarian Genealogical Research.* Draper, UT: Everton Publishers, 1980.

Szucs, Loretto Dennis, and Sandra Hargreaves Luebking. *The Source: A Guidebook of American Genealogy.* Salt Lake City: Ancestry, 1997.

Tacoma-Pierce County Genealogical Society. *Bibliography of Washington State Historical Society Library,* 3 vols. Tacoma, WA: The Society, [n.d.].

Taylor, Anne Wood. *Florida Pioneers and Their Descendants.* Tallahassee: Florida State Genealogical Society, 1992.

The Biography and Genealogy Master Index. Detroit: Gale Research, 1975.

Thomsen, Finn A. *Beginners Guide to Danish Research.* Bountiful, UT: Thomsen's Genealogical Center, 1984.

Ulibarri, George S. *Documenting Alaskan History: Guide to Federal Archives Relating to Alaska.* Fairbanks: University of Alaska Press, 1982.

U.S. Government Printing Office. *A Citizen's Guide on Using the Freedom of Information Act and the Privacy Act to Request Government Records.* [n.d.]

Vexler, Robert I. *Chronology and Documentary Handbook of the State of North Dakota.* Dobbs Ferry, NY: Oceana Publications, 1978.

Wagner, Sally Roesch. *Daughters of Dakota,* 6 vols. Aberdeen: South Dakota Daughters of Dakota, 1989.

Wagoner, Claudia. *Arkansas Researchers' Handbook.* Fayetteville, AR: Research Plus, 1986.

Wellauer, Maralyn A. *Tracing Your Swiss Roots.* Milwaukee: Self-published, 1979.

Yamaguchi, Yoji. *A Student's Guide to Japanese American Genealogy.* Phoenix, AZ: Oryx Press, 1996.

Zubatsky, David S., and Irwin M. Berent's. *Sourcebook for Jewish Genealogies and Family Histories.* Bergen, NJ: Avotaynu, 1996.

INDEX

323